Wayne Federman and Marshall Terrill
In collaboration with Jackie Maravich

PETE MARAVICH

THE AUTHORIZED BIOGRAPHY OF PISTOL PETE

FOCUS
ON THE FAMILY

A Focus on the Family Resource Published
by Tyndale House Publishers, Inc.
FocusOnTheFamily.com

A Focus on the Family book published by
Tyndale House Publishers, Inc., Carol Stream, Illinois 60188

Focus on the Family and the accompanying logo and design are trademarks of Focus
on the Family, Colorado Springs, CO 80995.

TYNDALE and Tyndale's quill logo are registered trademarks of Tyndale House
Publishers, Inc.

Revised and reprinted from the book titled *Maravich* by Wayne Federman and Marshall
Terrill.

All Scripture quotations, unless otherwise indicated, are taken from the *Holy Bible,
New International Version*®. NIV®. Copyright © 1973, 1978, 1984 by International Bible
Society. Used by permission of Zondervan Publishing House. All rights reserved.

Scripture quotations marked (KJV) are taken from the *King James Version*.

Editors: Larry Weeden and Brandy Bruce
Cover design by Joseph Sapulich
Cover photo courtesy www.thesportgallery.com

Library of Congress Cataloging-in-Publication Data
Federman, Wayne.
  Pete Maravich / by Wayne Federman and Marshall Terrill ; in collaboration with Jackie
Maravich.
    p. cm.
  Originally published: Wilmington, Del. : Sport Classic Books, c2006.
  ISBN-13: 978-1-58997-535-4
  ISBN-10: 1-58997-535-9
  1. Maravich, Pete, 1947-1988. 2. Basketball players—United States—Biography. I. Terrill,
Marshall. II. Title.
  GV884.M3F43 2008
  796.323092—dc22
  [B]

                                                        2008016579

Printed in the United States of America
1 2 3 4 5 6 7 8 9 / 13 12 11 10 09 08

For
Peter, Jackie, Jaeson, and Joshua

Pistol Pete

Contents

PART 5: APPENDIX

Foreword

Pete Maravich may have had as big an impact on the game of basketball as any player in modern history. If a chronicle of his unprecedented athletic achievements is what you're looking for, you'll certainly find it within the pages of this book: more than 40 NCAA records (many of which still stand today); an average of 44 points per game at LSU and 24 points per game over his 10 years in the NBA; five *Sports Illustrated* covers; and an illustrious collection of awards, records, milestones, and landmarks too numerous to list.

Even today, two decades after his death, the name "Pistol Pete" inspires awe, respect, and admiration from those both inside and outside the world of sports. He was an icon in the days before salary caps, ESPN, and one-and-done college careers. He was the real deal.

Nevertheless, the awards, records, and recognition were not what ultimately defined Pete Maravich. By his own admission, he reached a point in his life where he realized that fame and fortune were ultimately meaningless in the eternal scheme of things. As he would later say, "Money will buy you anything but happiness. It'll pay your fare to every place but heaven." And so, on a rainy night in 1982, he asked Jesus Christ to fill his life and his heart. For the remainder of his days on earth, which ended in 1988, "Pistol Pete's" passion was not basketball or any other earthly pursuit, but his love for God and his desire to share it with others.

And that is where he and I crossed paths for the first time. I did not know Pete well, but we did begin to develop a friendship when, in 1987, I invited him to share his story on our *Focus on the Family* radio program. On January 5, 1988, the day the broadcast was to be recorded, I had the audacity to invite Pistol Pete to join me and several of my colleagues for an early morning pick-up basketball game at a local church gym. Early morning games of this sort had been a tri-weekly tradition among us for years.

The sports legend was very gracious to accept our invitation and to endeavor not to embarrass the rest of us too severely while we lumbered around the court as only over-the-hill guys can.

I quickly learned that Pete had been suffering from unidentified pain in his right shoulder for many months. If it had been in his left, physicians would have suspected it was his heart. The problem was incorrectly diagnosed as "neuralgia." Aside from playing in the NBA Legends game, he had not been on the basketball court in more than a year. Nevertheless, we had a good time that morning.

Pete moved at about one-third his normal speed, and the rest of us huffed and puffed to keep up. We played for about 45 minutes and then took a break to get a drink. Pete and I stayed on the court and talked while waiting for the other players to come back. He spoke of his desire to play more recreational basketball after his struggles with shoulder pain were over.

"How do you feel today?" I asked.

"I feel great," he said.

Those were Pete's last words. I turned to walk away and, for some reason, looked back in time to see him go down. His face and body hit the boards hard. Still, I thought he was teasing. Pete had a great sense of humor, and I assumed that he was playing off his final comment about feeling good.

I hurried over to where he lay, still expecting to see him get up laughing. But then I saw that he was having a seizure. I held his tongue to keep his air passage open and called for the other guys to come help me. The seizure lasted about 20 seconds, and then Pete stopped breathing. We started CPR immediately but were never able to get another heartbeat or breath.

Pete died in my arms.

Several of us accompanied the ambulance to the hospital, where we prayerfully watched the emergency room staff try to revive him for another 45 minutes. But it was no use.

An autopsy revealed a few days later that Pete suffered from a congenital heart malformation and never knew it. That was why his shoulder had been hurting. How he was able to perform such incredible exploits on the basketball court for so many years is a medical mystery. He was destined to drop dead at a fairly young age, and only God knows why it happened during the brief moment when his path crossed mine.

In the world of sports, it's not about how you start; it's about how you finish. If you're a coach, no one will remember your early victories if your team loses the big game at the end of the season. At the same time, legends are made by those who overcome losses and disappointments early to emerge victorious when the championship trophy is up for grabs. Those are the "dream teams" that people remember.

Pistol Pete's life was like that. Without a doubt, his massive, record-smashing contributions to the game of basketball are worthy of the accolades he has received. But his accomplishments and his trophies did not give him satisfaction. Pete found lasting peace and contentment in the saving grace of God, and I believe he would want to be remembered first and foremost as a passionate follower of Jesus Christ. It's not about how you start; it's about how you finish.

During our basketball game on the morning Pete died, he was wearing a T-shirt that read, "Looking unto Jesus," which is a reference to Hebrews 12:2. That says it all, doesn't it? You'll read a lot about basketball and trophies and fame in this book, and there's no denying the remarkable achievements of one of America's truly great basketball players. However, in the end, I believe the simple message contained on that T-shirt tells you all you need to know about Pete Maravich.

JAMES C. DOBSON, PH.D.
Founder and Chairman of Focus on the Family

Prologue

"He was unstoppable. It's as if they had melted down all 12 Harlem Globetrotters and then filled up this skinny 6-6 white frame with everything they had."
—RALPH WILEY, SPORTSWRITER

"Pete had a strange, strange upbringing. Hoops were put so much beyond where they deserved to be. See, basketball is a thing to be used. Or it'll use you."
—AL MCGUIRE, HALL OF FAME BASKETBALL COACH

On August 18, 1970, Pete Maravich was in the Catskill Mountains, a region in upstate New York whose many resorts had long been regarded as a tough proving ground for up-and-coming entertainers. He was scheduled to present a basketball show at Kutshers Country Club.

By the late summer of 1970, "Pistol Pete" was already a legend. With his signature gray socks flopping around his ankles and his shaggy hair flying in the breeze, he had dazzled the sports world with jaw-dropping displays of basketball wizardry while a student at Louisiana State University. Over 83 varsity games he scored 3,667 points—an average of 44.2 points each game.

Although he had yet to play in an NBA game, several months earlier he had signed a historic contract with the Atlanta Hawks and inked endorsement deals with manufacturers of basketballs, sneakers, and hair products.

He was at Kutshers to participate in the Stokes Memorial All-Star Game, an annual fund-raiser to benefit Maurice Stokes, the 1956 NBA Rookie of the Year with the Cincinnati Royals who had been badly injured during a game in 1958. The Stokes matchup typically featured a mix of NBA veterans and promising newcomers like Maravich and fellow rookie Dave Cowens.

Maravich had agreed to perform his crowd-pleasing basketball clinic before the game tipped off. Joining him for this exhibition was Marques Haynes, the dribbling sensation who had spent seven seasons with the barnstorming Harlem Globetrotters. The future and the past met on the court that hot August afternoon.

Several hundred onlookers were mesmerized as Pete ran through his amazing repertoire of shooting, dribbling, and passing drills. As the demonstration neared its conclusion, journalist Jim O'Brien noticed that a young boy had walked over to Pete's father, Press, to ask a question.

"How long," the youngster asked, "did it take Pete to learn to do that?"

"All his life," Press answered.

"Oh," said the boy as he walked away. "I don't have that much time."

Part 1

Early Days

Pete Maravich in high school

1

Birth of a
Legend

"To tell my life story is to tell my father's story, the two are so interwoven."
—PETE MARAVICH

"Farewell, then, Age of Iron; all hail, King Steel."
—ANDREW CARNEGIE

On August 22, 1875, outside Pittsburgh, Pennsylvania, Scottish immigrant Andrew Carnegie began producing steel utilizing a new invention called the Bessemer Converter. The converter revolutionized the industry by blasting air through the super-heated liquid metal and removing impurities, thus spawning the era of low-cost steel production. The ubiquitous metal provided the super-structure for the greatest industrialized economy on earth and the demand for it grew exponentially. To satisfy America's voracious appetite for steel, manufacturers like Carnegie needed a large pool of strong, hard-working laborers.

It was the promise of steady employment that lured Pete Maravich's paternal grandparents, Vajo and Sarah (Radulovich), to western Pennsylvania. They left Dreznica, Lika (later Yugoslavia) and became part of a huge Serbian migration to the United States at the close of the nineteenth century.

The Serbs quickly gained a reputation as tough, hard laborers who would accept backbreaking jobs in the copper, gold, coal, and steel industries. It was dangerous work with minimal government safeguards or union protection. Vajo Maravich found steady employment as a locomotive engineer for a mill and started a family. Although Vajo and Sarah could barely speak English, they rented a small house on Sarah Street on the south side of Pittsburgh and had 10 children. They were living the immigrants' dream in a new world full of opportunities, but their life was about to take a tragic turn.

One evening in 1917, while working the midnight shift, Vajo was killed in a train accident in Clairton, Pennsylvania. More misery struck Sarah and her children in the fall of 1918 when the worldwide flu epidemic spread to the United States. It was the most lethal epidemic in human history, killing an estimated 30 million worldwide and 195,000 Americans in October alone—the deadliest month in U.S. history. By the time the killer flu ran its course more than 550,000 Americans had died, including nine of Sarah's children. The only surviving child was a robust boy named Peter who, by most accounts, had turned three on August 29, 1918.

Somehow Sarah found the strength to overcome her staggering tragedy. She married another steel worker named George Kosanovich, and bore him two children, Sam and Mark. In the early 1920s, the family of five moved 20 miles northwest to Aliquippa, Pennsylvania, one of 13 "River Bottom Communities."

Andrew Carnegie's old plants (by then renamed U.S. Steel) weren't the only gainful employers in Western Pennsylvania. A slew of manufacturers set up shop along the rural river towns. Basketball historian Ralph Ferrante, who grew up not far away in Ellwood City, remembered the steel mill towns of Pennsylvania as tough, brutal communities whose landscapes reflected the blue-collar lifestyle.

"It was an old, awful, dirty town with smoke stacks dominating the skyline and polluting the air," Ferrante said. "There were mills in every town along the Ohio River: Aliquippa, Ambridge, Beaver Falls, Monaca, New Brighton, Rochester, and Ellwood City. We called them 'dirty little towns.' It wasn't meant to be derogatory, but they were dirty because of the mills, which were going 24 hours a day, seven days a week."

Peter Maravich was raised in this dank, loud, toxic community. The family settled at 418 Hopewell Avenue in the northern part of Aliquippa known as Logstown Section—Plan 2. His stepfather worked for the huge Jones and Laughlin (J&L) steel company. Dr. Steve Zernich, who knew the family and played basketball with Peter, recalled the Aliquippa community was segregated by ethnicity, race, and employment status.

"Aliquippa was mostly ethnics," Zernich explained. "J&L built homes in various plans from 1 to 12. Serbian, Croatian, and some Slavs lived in Logstown—Plan 2. West Aliquippa was Italian. Plan 11 was blacks. Plan 6 was where the bosses lived. It was the type of town where everyone had their own section."

Peter was a quick-witted, energetic, and industrious youngster. "He always had to be doing something," recalled his stepbrother Sam Kosanovich. One of his first jobs was hawking street copies of the *Pittsburgh Press*, a job that led to his nickname. "As a kid he used to walk down the street and scream, '*Pittsburgh Press! Pittsburgh Press!*' So we called him 'Press,'" recalled Kosanovich. The nickname suited him fine—for Press thought Peter was a "sissy" name.

It was music, not sports, that was emphasized in the Kosanovich home. Press's stepfather and cousins spent many evenings eating, drinking wine, and singing old Serbian folk songs. Press was coerced into taking banjo, violin, and even harp lessons, but it was basketball, a sport still in its infancy, that captured his imagination.

Press and his friends played on the street for hours. They didn't have a ball, so they improvised, placing a rock in a tin can, wrapping the can in newspapers, and then winding it all with electrical tape. They shot the "ball" into a bottomless apple basket nailed to a light pole.

The boys played into the night—coping with inclement weather and a local cop named Officer Istock, who tried to enforce a 9 P.M. curfew. It took a religious intervention to eventually improve the boys' hoop environment. Reverend Ernest Anderson of the Woodlawn Mission, a local Protestant church, offered Press and his friends a deal: He'd welcome them into the church's new state-of-the-art gym (wood floor, wooden backboards, nets, and leather basketballs) if they'd attend Bible study three times a week. The basketball-hungry kids readily agreed.

"Only after we learned our Bible lessons did we head for the basketball court," Press recalled in a 1971 piece he wrote for *Coaches Digest*. "There in the church I learned a thrilling, invigorating game. We managed to get in five days of play weekly—after we'd convinced the Reverend Mr. Anderson that we'd been attentive scholars."

The young hoopsters, led by Press, played whenever they could and named themselves the "Daniel Boys"—after the biblical figure.

The reverend's arrangement mirrored the origins of the game. Basketball's originator, James Naismith, was a divinity doctorate that loved athletics. In his youth he excelled in boxing, gymnastics, soccer, and rugby. While working at a Young Men's Christian Association (YMCA) training school in Springfield, Massachusetts, he invented "Basket Ball." Dr. Naismith believed that clean, hard, and square athletic competition was a conduit to spiritual righteousness. He referred to the union as "muscular Christianity," and he believed his new game would help spread the message.

It wouldn't be the last time that Christianity, basketball, and the Maraviches intersected.

"Basketball, more so than football, was a real Americanization sport for

Press Maravich," said Phil Hart, editor of *Serb World U.S.A.* Press would spend the next seven decades contemplating the complexities and possibilities of the game. In Pittsburgh, he would sometimes attend games played by the professional barnstorming teams of the day. He was mesmerized by the sport's beauty, synchronization, and physicality. His idols were Nat Holman, Henry "Dutch" Dehnert, and Joe Lapchick. All played for the Original Celtics, a team that was then based in New York City.

Press blossomed at the high-school level under the guidance of long-time Aliquippa High coach and former pro player, Nate Lippe. Maravich mastered the fundamentals and developed a quick-release set shot. He'd dribble down the court, stop on a dime, and fire up two-handed, flat-footed set shots that frequently found their mark. At a solid six-feet, 185 pounds, Press became a high school sports hero. A fleet-footed forward, he once scored 28 points on his own at a time when most teams struggled to score that many in an entire game. Press was voted team captain his junior and senior years (1935 and 1936) and was selected All-Section for three straight seasons.

Away from school, Press worked as a pipe threader on the graveyard shift at the mill. For three years the teenager juggled school, work, and basketball by depriving himself of sleep. He received a Vocational Prep degree upon graduation in spring of 1936. Soon basketball provided him an opportunity to return to the same company where his father had been employed. He went to work at J&L's Blooming Mill and competed in the company's basketball league. His team won the 1936 league championship. Thanks to his prowess on the court, J&L rewarded him with a higher paying job as an inspector.

But Press had his heart set on attending college, a rare aspiration in an era when only 19 percent of Americans even completed high school. He believed basketball could provide a scholarship and a passport out of the hard, dreary life of a steel town.

"Press was a visionary," said Dr. Michael Zernich, who also lived in Aliquippa. "There were those of us who had the option of getting out and there were those who were stuck. One of the fellows who played on my high school team fell off of a platform and into a vat of molten steel. There was no one looking over the steel mill saying this is unsafe. Basketball became Press's ticket out."

Press was offered partial basketball scholarships from Duke, Duquesne, and Long Island universities. Unfortunately the Kosanovich family could not afford to pay the difference. Then Press caught a lucky break. One of his high school rivals, Mike Winne of Ambridge, suggested he visit Davis & Elkins

College in Elkins, West Virginia, about 150 miles south of Pittsburgh. Bud Shelton, the school's new basketball coach, took an instant liking to Press and offered him a full scholarship, a rarity in 1937. Before heading off to college, Press again led his Blooming Mill team, composed of Doc Dzurko, Richard Thomas, Nick Wukas, Bill Philipovich, and Pete Suder, to the championship of the J&L League.

Press thrived at college. The handsome, fast-talking, tobacco-chewing Serb immediately ingratiated himself with the faculty and student body. He loved the academic atmosphere and quickly taught himself shorthand and typing—skills that came in handy as a student and then later, as a basketball coach. As a scholarship athlete Press was also required to play football—which he did reluctantly. But it was in basketball, as the team's starting left guard, where he made a name for himself. He arrived just as the NCAA updated its rules, eliminating a jump ball after every basket. The game was speeding up and Press blossomed as a result.

A January 3, 1941, *New York Times* article described a showdown at the Brooklyn School of Pharmacy gymnasium, where the undefeated (9-0) Long Island University, coached by the legendary Clair Bee, beat Davis & Elkins 54-42:

> *Only the sensational shooting of Peter Maravich kept Davis & Elkins in the game. He was high scorer with 27 points, tallying his team's first ten baskets and the only foul shot in the second period.*

Press's scholarship did not cover all his expenses. He still had to pay for books, clothes, and food on the weekends. The small town of Elkins, nestled at the foot of the Appalachian Mountains, offered plenty in terms of natural beauty but, with the depression in its eighth year, provided little in terms of jobs. Press earned extra cash by helping families start their coal furnaces in the morning. He charged 25 cents. On weekends he put his scholarship in jeopardy and covertly played semi-pro basketball for the Clarksburg Pure Oilers, using the alias "Peter Munell." For $10 a game, Press competed against the barnstorming teams of the day like the Harlem Globetrotters, Original Celtics, Detroit Eagles, and Rochester Royals.

Press amassed 1,326 points in four seasons at D&E, a school scoring record that stood for nine years. He was twice voted "best looking man on campus," as well as student-body president and captain of the basketball team. He was also twice named to the All-West Virginia Conference team, and inducted into the Davis & Elkins Hall of Fame in 1978.

Press graduated in the spring of 1941 with a bachelor of arts in Business Administration and a bachelor of science in Physical Education. He returned to Aliquippa to find work, but despite holding two college degrees, he could only find work as a pipe threader. So he enlisted in the Navy and, while waiting to be called up, continued to play for the Clarksburg Pure Oilers. There Press developed a close friendship with his teammate Jules Rivlin, a creative, flamboyant player who shared his passion for the game.

Rivlin had also played college ball in West Virginia, at Marshall University under visionary coach Cam Henderson, who helped pioneer the fast-break offense. Henderson believed every offensive possession was an opportunity for a team to push the ball up court with its players filling specific, numbered "lanes." In the center lane was the team's best ball handler and passer, a player who could survey the floor and exploit the easiest scoring opportunity. On the Marshall University team that man was Jules Rivlin.

"I went right down the middle," Rivlin explained in 2000. "I went down to the foul line and stopped and I learned to stop on a dime. Sometimes I would look one way, pass the other. I first threw the ball behind my back in 1937. My college coach, may he rest in peace, wouldn't let anybody do that except me."

Rivlin and Maravich became fast friends, playing ball and experimenting with offensive schemes, creative ball handling, and deceptive passing. The Oilers home games, promoted by local sportswriter Wade Pepper, were played in Clarksburg and Fairmont, West Virginia.

In the third week of the season, in a game against the Detroit Eagles, Press scorched the defending world champions for 30 points. The Eagles' head coach was Henry "Dutch" Dehnert, Press's boyhood idol from the Original Celtics. Dehnert liked what he saw in Maravich and offered him a position with the Eagles. Press agreed and played 75 games in 1941–42 for Detroit before his call-up telegram arrived from the War Department.

After donning a Navy uniform his training took him to various locations around the country: Anacostia Naval Air Station in Washington, D.C., New Orleans, Louisiana (where he mastered Morse Code), and finally Pensacola, Florida. Lieutenant Maravich was commissioned an Ensign and received his "wings" in September 1942.

After a short stay at the North Island Naval Air Station in San Diego, Press was shipped to the Pacific. While receiving some final training in Hawaii, Press was named player-coach of the Kaneohe Klippers basketball team and, under his guidance, they won the 1943 Service Basketball Championship for the city of Honolulu.

Press served with the legendary "Black Cat" Squadron (VP-12) that received its nickname because their planes (Catalina PBY-5A) were painted black. In a sense the Black Cats were a low-tech stealth unit. They flew primarily at night using stars for navigation. Their missions included reconnaissance, air sea rescue, dive-bombing, mine laying, and torpedo attacks. The squadron was originally based at Henderson Field on Guadalcanal, but moved closer to Japan as the Pacific campaign progressed.

Wes Hicks, a crew member in Press's squadron, recalled a particularly dangerous rescue in July 1943.

"We landed in heavy seas to pick up a fighter pilot who had ditched his aircraft," said Hicks. "Then, with the fighter pilot still aboard, we picked up Marine Colonel Linscott off the beach from our Bougainvillea invasion. Picking up Colonel Linscott was no easy trick. He had gone in with the initial wave and we were ordered to pick him back up from a small boat just offshore two days later. To accomplish this, we had to land under fire from Japanese shore batteries and we were fighting heavy seas. But we got the Colonel aboard safely and out of there."

After completing his combat duty, Press became a flight instructor in Pensacola and dreamed of one day becoming a commercial airline pilot. He was weighing a job offer from the U.S. government (instructing pilots in China) when Paul Birch, coach of the Youngstown Bears of the professional National Basketball League, invited Press to join his team. Press said "no thank you" to Uncle Sam and "yes" to Coach Birch. Armed with a colorful new vocabulary, compliments of the Navy, Press joined the Bears almost a third of the way into its 1945-46 season and played 31 games, averaging 5.6 points a contest.

In the spring of 1946, just outside Aliquippa, Press noticed a beautiful young woman working as a taxi dispatcher. As he approached her, she asked, "What's with all the stitches? You a boxer?"

Press explained that he was, in fact, a professional basketball player. The two had an immediate connection. Her name was Helen Montini. She was also Serbian, the daughter of a steel worker, and had attended Aliquippa High where she was a popular cheerleader. Press asked her out just minutes into their conversation, and several evenings later they went to Bill Green's Night Club in Pleasant Hills, a suburb of Pittsburgh.

"It was really the biggest and best nightspot in all of Pittsburgh and the South Hills," recalled Harold Wiegel, Jr., who grew up near the famed club off Old Clairton Road and Route 51. "That was the place to go if you really wanted to impress someone."

As Press performed a dip at the end of their first dance, he said, "We should be married."

Helen replied, "You're crazy. Married?"

"That's right," he said.

As the night grew Press learned that Helen, just 22, was already a widow. Her husband, Elvidio Montini, was killed during the Battle of the Bulge, one of almost 19,000 American deaths in the terrible clash on the German/Belgian border. Elvidio and Helen had one son, Ronnie. Neither Helen's previous marriage nor her three-year-old boy dissuaded Press, and soon afterward, they decided to tie the knot.

In June 1946, Press and Helen recited their vows at the St. Elijah Serbian Orthodox Church in Aliquippa in front of almost 500 guests, an eclectic mix of family, Serbs, locals, Navy men, and college and pro basketball players. The newlyweds honeymooned in Chicago. It was there that Press revealed his dream of becoming a commercial airline pilot and earning a comfortable, stable living for the young couple.

Helen was staggered. Traumatized by her first husband's death and her father's abandonment, she shuddered at the thought of possibly losing another man. She pleaded with Press to select another, less risky, profession. Press was at a loss for words.

"Okay, what do you suggest I do to support us?" Press asked.

"Every story you've ever told me concerns coaching basketball," Helen replied. "How about that? What about basketball?"

"For you, I'll go into coaching," Press replied.

In the fall of 1946, Press began his final season as a basketball player. Once again, his coach was Paul Birch, only this time their team was the Pittsburgh Ironmen of the brand new Basketball Association of America—a league that eventually became the National Basketball Association (NBA). On the road he roomed with the squad's best player, Coulby Gunther. In those days pro basketball was a low-scoring game in which shooting accuracy was anemic by modern standards. Gunther, for instance, led the Ironmen with 14.1 points per game and was the league's fourth most accurate shooter at only 33.6 percent. Maravich played in 51 games and averaged 4.5 points for the Ironmen. Earlier in the season he learned that Helen was pregnant. She was due in June.

On June 22, 1947, Press sped home after a Serbian League basketball game, helped Helen into the family car, and raced to the delivery room at Sewickley Valley Hospital. With a chaw of Mail Pouch tobacco in the corner of his mouth, Press made the 10-mile trek in record time.

"Doc, I want a son," Press told obstetrician H. B. Jones upon arrival. "If it's a boy, I'll pay you. If it's a girl, you pay me."

Jones agreed to the terms. Moments later, the doctor emerged from the delivery room and said to the new father, "You pay."

Peering through the pane glass of the maternity ward, Press saw his son for the first time and marveled, "Look at those hands! Look at those feet! The kid's got it I tell you," Press said to anyone within earshot.

The proud parents named their son Peter Press Maravich.

Years later, Press told a reporter, "As an infant, he already had instinctive ability. You could see it in the way he reacted to things around him. The toys in his crib, the things he played around the house. To tell you the truth, I think he was born with a basketball in his genes."

Gunther, Press's Ironmen teammate, recalled a visit to the Maravich home. "His dad already had a small basketball in the baby's hands," Gunther recalled. "And informed me that Pete would not only be a great one, but have a great hook shot—which was my specialty."

That fall, Press, with family in tow, embarked on his coaching career. Helen, like many post-WWII brides, was content being a homemaker, taking care of her two sons. The Maravich family hopped from school to school as Press worked his way up the coaching ladder. His first stop was West Virginia, where in 1947-48 he was an assistant coach and director of intramural sports at his alma mater, Davis & Elkins. From there he took an assistant coaching position in basketball (and football) under Lee Patton at the University of West Virginia, where he also earned a master's degree in Recreation and Health Education.

Press was carving out his own American success story. Although his parents had minimal education and barely spoke English, their son had earned a graduate degree. His thesis, *Basketball Scouting* (co-authored by James Steel), was the first book published on the "science" of evaluating talent. Press had come a long way from the soot-filled immigrant towns of western Pennsylvania.

In 1949 Press earned his first head-coaching assignment at West Virginia Wesleyan. A year later he returned to Davis & Elkins for a two-year head coaching stint. He arrived to discover his old team was still playing in a local high school gym.

"I went to the president, and he told me they only had $35 in the athletic kitty," Maravich later said. "I got some of the boys together, and we went out and got a tractor and sawed down some trees."

Next, Maravich contacted a local reporter and a photographer.

"Ground Cleared for Gymnasium" read the following day's paper.

The industrious coach made good on his promise to build a new gym. He rounded up retired carpenters to help build what would become Press's most enduring legacy in West Virginia. The 1,500-seat gym was erected without construction permits from the city of Elkins or approval from Davis & Elkins' governing board. It was completed within a year and still stands to this day.

In general, Press's days at Davis & Elkins were frustrating. He never received his promised bonus money and was stretched thin by multiple duties as athletic director, assistant football coach, and typing and shorthand teacher. Yet he tallied a respectable 37-21 record before returning to suburban Pittsburgh in 1952 after receiving a more lucrative offer from Baldwin High School. Two years later, his life came full circle when he accepted the coaching job at his old school, Aliquippa High.

The Maraviches rented a house in a section of Aliquippa known as Sheffield Terrace. There, Press began another project—a calculated plan to steep his youngest boy in the game of basketball. When Pete was two, Press gave him a basketball for Christmas. Surprisingly, the boy didn't care much for it, preferring to play with an old trumpet.

"Pete was as enthusiastic about basketball as going to the dentist," Press once quipped to a reporter. Eventually Press tried a more subtle approach. He would enthusiastically shoot baskets each night after dinner as young Pete watched intently. Finally he coaxed his son to join him.

"Pete, where's your basketball?" Press asked. "Come over here and take a shot."

Pete missed the first set shot, not even hitting the net. Press looked for an expression on his son's face and detected a hint of anger. Pete chased down the bouncing ball and attempted another shot. Again he missed. Another shot—another miss. But he never gave up trying.

"When he got mad and kept shooting," smiled Press, "I had him hooked." It was the first step in molding a prodigy.

Pete Maravich's basketball apprenticeship coincided with the start of his formal education at New Sheffield Elementary School, a five-minute walk from his home. Ron Juth, a sophomore on Press's varsity team when Pete was just a first grader, noticed the young boy's attachment to the game. "Pete always had a basketball in his hands," Juth said. "While he was only seven years old, I could see that he was already special."

In the winter of 1955, Press helped launch a local Biddy Basketball League. The Biddy program, intended for boys from first to fifth grade, used a smaller ball, a shortened free-throw line, and eight-foot baskets. Regular-season games were held in the New Sheffield school gymnasium.

The league met on Saturdays during winter and drew kids from the five elementary schools in the Aliquippa area. Several special players got their start in the program: George Zatezalo, Rich Lupcho, and Paul Milanovich went on to all play NCAA Division I college basketball. Press Maravich helped out by running drills with the kids before the games.

Almost 50 years later, Michael Keller, a fellow Biddy leaguer, still recalled the detailed instructions Press barked out in the winter of 1955. "Rear pivot. Front pivot. Bend those knees. Pivot on the ball of your foot. Chest pass. Thumbs must be centered over the ball. Step forward with your right leg. Keep your elbows in, rotate your arms out, and snap your wrist as you release with an extended follow through. Again."

Press not only espoused forward-thinking concepts, but also introduced gadgets to improve skills, recalled Paul Milanovich. "He had special glasses for kids that he would put on you so you couldn't look down. He had the bottoms darkened out so that you couldn't see the basketball when you were dribbling. And he would stand in front of you blowing the whistle and point left and right and back and forward, and he just grilled you for, it seemed like, forever. Press always felt you had to have the foundation before you put the roof on."

Michael Keller remembered eight-year-old Pete as not only fundamentally sound but also quite advanced.

"Pete was one of the better players in that league, which is amazing considering the gap in physical maturity between an eight-year-old and a 12-year-old," Keller said. "He could dribble exceptionally well with both hands. He would come down the court so fast, and then pull up with a dramatic quick stop. I remember those big feet in white basketball shoes [Converse All Stars]."

Pete made a big impression, but he didn't cut a very imposing figure. He was short and scrawny for his age, but Press made sure to develop Pete's confidence while hoping his body would someday catch up.

"I knew I had to get Pete to master the fundamentals," Press told a reporter. "But fundamentals can be dull. I learned to watch his face. That was the indicator. For instance, if he was practicing the chest pass, I'd wait until that bored look started creeping onto his face. Then I'd make him switch to, say, a one-handed pass. I'd watch him again. When he started looking bored, I'd say let's try something different. So we'd go to a behind-the-back pass. It excited Pete, kept his interest, and he practiced it as hard and long as anything else."

Pete's first basketball uniform was green and gold and bore the letters of team sponsor, Duich Amoco, a local gas station.

Observers described young Pete's demeanor as hyper, wide-eyed, and wired up. Keller remembered an incident in which their Biddy coach, Tom Diaddigo, called a timeout in the fourth quarter of a game to give instructions to Pete.

"Tom was telling Pete something," recalled Keller. "I really don't know what he told Pete, but Pete snapped back. I am pretty sure he swore. I know it was disrespectful. Tom then said something back to Pete, who got really scared. If I had to guess, I would say that Tom told Pete that he was going to talk to Press."

According to Keller, Pete panicked and pushed open the gym doors and ran into the school's darkened hallway. Diaddigo instructed his team to find "that smart-mouth kid" and bring him back to the gym. A search party of parents and players fanned out and eventually discovered Pete trembling in the closet of a second-story classroom.

"Pete was brought back into the gym and sat down on the bench, where he stayed while the game was finally completed," Keller said.

The playoffs and finals of the Biddy league were moved from the New Sheffield gym to a larger venue at Aliquippa High. For Richard Lewis, who played with Pete on the Duich Amoco team, the high school's showers were a luxury. He lived in a home with only a bathtub. In the finals, with Press helping out, Duich Amoco beat C & L Supermarket. Pete had his first championship.

Lewis often visited the Maravich home and, on the surface, it seemed quite normal. Mrs. Maravich would mix up a batch of Kool-Aid as Richard, Ronnie, and Pete (who already hated to lose) played hoops in the driveway. But Press created a dynamic that was disconcerting. "I remember feeling really sorry for Ronnie, since it was so apparent—even to someone my age— that Pete was his dad's favorite," recalled Lewis. "Not that he went easy on Pete. Not at all. He was lucky that he had in Pete a boy who had as much desire to excel as Press had to push him mercilessly. When it was time for me to go home to dinner, they would still be going at it hot and heavy."

In just a year, the constant drilling made a huge difference in Pete's game, noted Michael Keller.

"He was very sure of himself," said Keller. "When we got back together in the winter of 1956, Pete was nine. We were doing a simple layup drill. Pete was immediately in front of me, awaiting the pass from the rebounder, when he turned around and said, 'Mike, this is getting boring. Watch what I'm going to do.' He received this pass, drove in, jumped up, spun around 360 degrees, and laid the ball right in. I do know one thing: nine-year-old kids didn't shoot like that in 1956."

Press had his plate full with the Aliquippa High School team. He sent out letters to the parents of his players instructing them on everything from bed times, conditioning, specific diet, and meal times ("Have mother make this three hours before game time"). He organized a team field trip to New York's Madison Square Garden to watch a double header. In the first game the Harlem Globetrotters squared off against their perennial patsies, the Washington Generals, while the second game featured the Knicks, coached by Joe Lapchick, against a traveling team of college all-stars. It was a formidable squad that included future professional players like Louisiana State's Bob Pettit, Furman's Frank Selvy, Kentucky's Frank Ramsey, Maryland's Gene Shue, and Iona's Richie Guerin.

Press used specific conditioning drills, according to future NFL Hall of Famer Mike Ditka, who played for Press on the Aliquippa varsity. "He used to run us up and down the steps and all around the gymnasium. He put that steely look on you and you knew he meant business. He made you aware of what was important and he demanded that you do it that way."

"He was very precise in everything he did," added longtime friend Joe Pukach, who played under Press at Davis & Elkins and was one of his assistants at Aliquippa High. "And you practiced that way for him. He was so perfect in everything he did, and the way he presented it to you."

Even though he never liked playing for Paul Birch, Press seemed to emulate his former, super-intense coach. Keller remembered a stinging loss (71-49) to rival Midland that had Press's blood boiling.

"Press was so upset at his team that after the game his players got off the bus at Aliquippa High School and he marched them into the gym and conducted a two-hour practice until about midnight," Keller recalled.

To keep his emotions in check, Press developed a peculiar habit of chewing on towels during games.

Press's first Aliquippa High team (1954-55) rang up a respectable record of 11-11, and improved to 15-7 in his second year. By the end of that season it was clear he was ready for a new challenge. He caught wind of a head coaching position at Clemson College in South Carolina and sent out a resume. Clemson was a member of the burgeoning Atlantic Coast Conference (ACC) and Press was extremely eager to coach there, as were over a hundred other applicants. Press drove to South Carolina to personally make his case to Clemson's athletic director Frank Howard.

"Why should I hire you, Yank?" Howard asked.

Press, no slouch in the self-confidence department, told Howard he was simply the best man for the job. They never broached the topic of compensation.

Two months later, when he was offered the position, Press was stunned to learn he had to accept a $2,000 annual cut in pay—a fact that didn't appeal to Helen. Press accepted Clemson's offer of $96 per week.

Western Pennsylvania was, and remains, the breeding ground for scores of superb football players, including Johnny Unitas, Tony Dorsett, Mike Ditka, Joe Montana, Larry Brown, Dan Marino, Ty Law, and Joe Namath. Even the local NFL franchise, the Steelers, is named after the product and industry that drew many immigrants to the region. Those hard, loud, soot-filled communities also produced Press Maravich—a creative basketball visionary who hoped to transfer his dream of hardwood brilliance into his child.

One day, not long before the Maraviches left Pittsburgh for South Carolina, Press took Pete aside, "You've seen me do my summer camps, and teach kids how to play basketball, right? I want you to know, your mother and I can't afford to send you to college. But with my teaching and many hours of practice, you could possibly earn a scholarship that would pay for your education. And you know what? If you really become good, you might even play pro basketball like I did, and they'll pay you for doing it!"

Then came the kicker.

"And then you might play in the world championship game, and if you win that game, they'll give you a big diamond ring . . . and on that day, they'll say Peter Press Maravich is one of the best 12 players in the world."

A basketball scholarship, a professional career, and a world championship ring became young Pete's three obsessions as the Maravich family migrated south. He was just nine years old.

2

Happy Days

"I loved my childhood. If I could go back and live again from 5 to 14, you could have the rest of my life."

—PETE MARAVICH

"One thing about Pete, he has always wanted to win at any cost. We used to play HORSE or 21. I had a behind-the-back shot that I used when I was in trouble. He'd scream that it was unfair. And when I was about to shoot, he'd stick out his tongue, make funny faces, jump up and down. Anything to win. He's like Adolf Hitler in that respect."

—PRESS MARAVICH

Pete Maravich was a scrawny fourth grader when his family moved to Clemson, South Carolina in the summer of 1956.

"At the time, Clemson was a lot like Mayberry," recalled David Senn, a longtime resident. "Small and very quaint."

Clemson, a rural town of approximately 2,000 people, didn't even warrant a stoplight in the early 1950s, but locals fought to have one installed after too many drivers sped dangerously through town on Highway 123. The businesses on College Avenue were of the mom-and-pop variety. In addition to the post office and a municipal building, local merchants included the L. C. Martin Drug Company, Judge Keller's General Merchandise, Sinclair Gasoline, Harper's 5 & 10, Sloan's Men's Store, Evans Grocery, Clemson Pool Hall, Clemson Theater, and Dan's, a hamburger joint owned by Dan Gentry, an active booster of Clemson athletics.

"The hamburgers at Dan's were not like today—you know, the frozen premade patties," recalled Clemson resident Bob Bruner. "At Dan's, you could reach in the frozen storage area and grab a fistful of meat. Dan had this white plastic chef hat and one of these tank top undershirts." The special included hamburger steak, French fries, onion rings, biscuits, and all-you-can-drink iced tea for 99 cents. It was a meal young Pete Maravich feasted on many times.

Clemson's economy was largely supported by the college or the nearby textile mills. Press's $5,000 annual salary fell approximately $900 short of the national median income. It was enough, however, for a down payment on a modest home nestled in a 50-acre subdivision called Woodland Heights. The house, about two miles from town at 402 Highland Drive, was where young Pete came of age.

Pete was a peculiar kid in this new land. He took his basketball with him everywhere and wasn't shy about boasting that he was the coach's son. He often walked alone, bouncing his ball for the entire two-mile trek into town. Pete made sure to use his left hand as often as his right. His father, Press, had repeatedly demonstrated dribbling fundamentals: eyes up, wrist snap, and finger pad control. To gain an even better feel for the ball, Pete taught himself to dribble on the railroad tracks along the Seneca River.

One day, while perusing the goods at L. C. Martin Drug Store, he was spinning the ball on his right forefinger. A local kid bet him that he couldn't keep the ball spinning for an hour. Pete accepted the $5 wager and soon a crowd gathered at the soda fountain. After approximately 15 minutes, the nail on Pete's index finger started to bleed and his arm began to tire. Without missing a beat, Pete switched the ball to his middle finger. As the minutes passed, he moved the spinning ball from finger to finger on his right hand, and then to each finger on his left hand. As the hour approached, Pete spun the ball on his knuckles and thumbs as a growing crowd cheered him on. He collected his $5 and added an early chapter to his legend.

In Clemson, the local Young Men's Christian Association (YMCA) occupied a three-story brick building that housed a swimming pool, two rooms with pool tables, dorm rooms, a barbershop, and an undersized gymnasium that measured a narrow 30 feet across. "If you stepped out of bounds, you were likely to hit the wall," recalled Tommy Senn, who played there in his youth. It was in this claustrophobic gym that Pete laid the foundation of his adult life.

Eight hours a day during the summer and four during the school year, Pete slavishly practiced every aspect of the game, most days by himself. "I'd never seen anybody so obsessed with basketball," said friend Kent Lawrence. "I remember waiting with Pete for the YMCA to open on Saturday mornings and I'd play until the afternoon. Of course, that was just a warmup session for Pete." On Sundays, the Y was closed, but that didn't prevent Pete from climbing through a basement window to log several more hours of practice.

As Pete mastered the basic fundamentals—passing, dribbling, and shooting—Press challenged his son with a more advanced series of drills that later became known as "Homework Basketball." Primarily geared toward ball handling, the drills were designed to ease the monotony of practice while increasing strength, quickness, hand-eye coordination, and confidence. They had intriguing names such as the ricochet, crab catch, pendulum, around the world, pretzel, space clap, draw, see-saw, punching bag, and the flap jack. Every day Pete would run through his expanding checklist, methodically perfecting each drill until it became second nature.

"I never met anyone more dedicated to the sport," recalled legendary college basketball coach Lefty Driesell. "Pete used to go off by himself and throw hundreds of passes off the wall—between his legs, behind his back, off his head. Then he would go to the center court circle and work on dribbling. Every possible dribble you could imagine. He would be doing it in 100-degree heat."

Pete also developed his shooting touch with series of stimulating drills. Again, first he mastered the basics: set shot, basic overhand layup, underhand layup, reverse layup, crossover layup, hook shot, and, as he got older and stronger, a jump shot. To alleviate the boredom and boost his confidence Pete would mix and match different skill sets. He could spin the ball on a finger, toss it up, and then bounce it into the basket off his head. Or, if he chose, send it in off his fist or shoulder. Pete learned to throw in shots behind his back and by bouncing the ball off the floor. His young mind conjured all manner of spectacular shots, passes, and dribbles, and he perfected them over many hours, days, and months on the YMCA court.

Press stoked his son's imagination with a mental technique called "conceptualization" or "image shooting." "Imagine a little man who plays basketball all the time," Press instructed. "When you shoot, so does the little man. When you shoot the ball, so does the little man. Except the little man never misses."

Father and son made a perfect team. Press wanted to create the world's most innovative basketball player and Pete was a highly motivated student. "I didn't look up to college players or professionals," Pete told Glen Hibdon of *Tulsa World* in 1987. "All I had was my dad. I wanted to make my mother and father proud."

"He was just a small kid, kind of shy, and not real talkative," recalled another longtime Clemson resident, Betty Higby, who was two years older than Pete. "We'd shoot hoops and play one another. A lot of times when his friends were out riding bikes and swimming, he would be in alone in the gym playing basketball. I was one of the few girls at the time who liked basketball and oftentimes it was just me and Pete."

Unlike his older brother Ronnie, who was broad and athletic, Pete was undersized, a real concern for him, recalled classmate Jane Cobb Wolfe. "He was small for his age, but he had these huge feet," Wolfe said. "He was so concerned about being tall. I remember telling him, 'Pete, don't worry. You've got to grow into those feet of yours.' Others were growing much faster than him."

Pete was so desperate to be taller that he began hanging from the doorframe after dinner every night.

In addition to the YMCA gym, Pete, as the son of the new head coach at Clemson, had access to the college's basketball facility, Fike Fieldhouse (also known as the "Little Gym.") Before and after varsity practice and during breaks, Pete honed his skills. When Pete grew weary of working with his dad, Press's assistant coach Bobby Roberts took over the lessons. Roberts was amazed by the frail kid's talent level and dedication. "He was so skinny and weak looking that he had to start the ball from the floor on his long shots. It looked like a major struggle on every shot," Roberts said. "For all four years I was an assistant at Clemson, Pete was in the gym. He got out of school at 3:00 and he was in the gym by 3:15."

Later on, as his confidence swelled, Pete began challenging the Clemson basketball players to games of HORSE and Around-the-World. His repertoire included off-balance, behind-the-back, corkscrew, reverse, and bounce shots he'd mastered during his many practice hours at the YMCA. One of Pete's opponents was Clemson basketball star Donnie Mahaffey. "Pete was just a little squirt," Mahaffey told the *Atlanta Journal and Constitution*. "But even then he had all these shots. He beat me playing HORSE and the next day it was all over campus."

Playing HORSE with the Clemson players was a real thrill, Pete recalled, and quite profitable. "I used to win my movie money from those guys," Pete said. "At the time, admission to the Clemson Theater was just a quarter."

The air-conditioned movie house offered sanctuary for Pete on oppressively hot and humid Carolina summer days. He, of course, brought along his basketball so he could practice his dribbling as he watched the feature from his aisle seat. In order to develop both hands equally, he would move to the opposite aisle halfway through the movie.

"I remember one time Pete said, 'Hey, let's go to the flick,' which is what we called the movies," recalled friend David Senn. "I told him I didn't have enough money and he said he'd pay my way. When you went to the movies, you didn't sit next to Pete—the basketball did. I always sat a seat away from Pete because when the movie started, he began dribbling that basketball until someone told him to stop. I wasn't going to tell him to stop because he paid my way, so he could do whatever he wanted."

Clemson resident Carolyn Lindsay said she and her husband, Slack, often went to the movies back then. They always knew when Pete was in attendance. "We could always hear that ball thumping throughout the feature," Lindsay said.

When Pete turned 11, he got a bicycle and taught himself to dribble while pedaling the two miles into town. If that wasn't an odd enough sight, Press dreamed up an even more outrageous visual. One morning father and son were in the car when Press made a rather odd request. "He drove out on the highway. He looked around and there were no cars coming," recalled Pete. "He said, 'Now put yourself out of the passenger side of the car. I'm going to drive at various speeds, and I want to see if you can control the basketball.'"

Pete was taken aback. "Dad, are you nuts? What's happened to you?"

Press snapped, "No, I'm not nuts. You do as I say!"

With Press driving at five miles per hour, Pete hung his arm out the window and began dribbling the basketball. When Pete showed he could control the ball, Press accelerated to 10 mph, then 15 mph, until finally topping out just below 20.

Neighbor Dag Wilson called it a scene he'd never forget. "I'd see Press drive Pete around and around the block and Pete would be in the back seat, on the right-hand side, hanging out of the car and dribbling the ball," said Wilson. "Then he'd switch over to his left hand and Press would drive him around the block a couple of more times. People would say, 'There go those Maraviches again.' People thought they were nuts."

Whatever the townies thought, Pete understood the drill helped develop a better feel for the ball and build confidence.

The family home was also the site for some creative practice sessions. To improve his ball handling under difficult circumstances, Pete blindfolded himself and dribbled throughout the house after carefully memorizing the placement of furniture and the sounds of the ball on different surfaces. He also developed a low, super-speedy dribble, performed while seated cross-legged on the floor. He called that his "television dribble."

Bill Hensley, the former North Carolina State University sports information director, witnessed several impromptu, living-room exhibitions by

Maravich and later described them to *Four Corners* author Joe Menzer. "We would go to Press's house and watch Pete put on a show," Hensley said. "He would put on gloves and a blindfold and dribble the ball behind him, between his legs, off the wall. Press would make him wear gloves and dribble with either hand. He made him wear the gloves so Pete wouldn't feel the ball, so Pete would have a better touch handling it once he took the gloves off."

Press's attempts to motivate his young son were relentless. As he tucked Pete in at night, he told the boy he had just six functions in life—"You think, you pray, you sleep, you dream, you walk, you play basketball. That's all I want you to do."

Pete needed little convincing and started to sleep with his basketball. He would lie on his back, staring at the ceiling, and methodically practice his shooting release. "Fingertip control, backspin, follow-through . . . fingertip control, backspin, follow-through . . ." he whispered, until sleep ended the exercise.

One night a ferocious thunderstorm awoke him. Pete walked to the window and studied the large raindrops pelting the ground and muddying the basketball court. After several minutes, he crawled out the bedroom window and onto the waterlogged court. As sheets of rain poured over him and lightning streaked the sky, Pete broke into a dead run, bouncing the ball between his legs and behind his back. "After several minutes, I stopped dribbling and lifted the ball toward the sky watching the rain cleanse the mud from it," Pete wrote in his autobiography years later. "A huge smile curled across my lips, for I knew if I could dribble the ball under these conditions, I would easily dribble around a man on a court."

Neighbor Howard Bagwell confirmed that extreme conditions never kept young Pete from practicing. "I can still hear that ball bouncing in the carport. It didn't matter what the weather was, even if it was snowing. Pete would be out there with an overcoat and gloves shooting basketball."

When he wasn't perfecting his skills, Pete became a student of basketball strategy. He was a fixture in Clemson's field house and accompanied Press on several scouting trips. Pete studied his father's coaching moves and began to identify plays and patterns, even offering advice on certain offensive schemes. On game nights, little Pete could often be seen peering from behind the Clemson team bench.

His father was rapidly developing a fine reputation as a coach in the competitive Atlantic Coast Conference, despite some major obstacles. During those early years, football ruled the roost. "Back then in the old South, you weren't a man unless you played football," said South Carolina resident Kent Lawrence, who attended high school with Pete.

"Duke and the University of North Carolina got all the top recruits at the time," explained Tommy Risher, a walk-on at Clemson in the early 1960s. "You couldn't get anybody to come to Clemson. It was a country town and basketball is a city sport. Had Clemson been in another basketball conference, they would have done fine." Also, in the pre-Civil Rights era in the Deep South recruiting black players was not an option. "It just wasn't the trend down here," said Bob Bradley, sports information director at the time. "We didn't have our first black football player until 1970."

Press once described his Clemson squad as "no speed, no height, no bench, no stamina." He used his Pennsylvania contacts to recruit players from his home state despite protests from Frank Howard, Clemson's athletic director and head football coach. Howard urged Maravich to recruit southern boys in order to boost local pride and please the board of trustees. But Press ignored the request and, in 1956-57, assembled a crack freshman squad that included four Pennsylvanians and a West Virginian. Their record was 17-1. His varsity squad didn't fare as well—stumbling to a 7-17 record in an inaugural season in which Press engaged in lots of nervous towel chewing on the bench.

Press regularly invited opposing coaches to his home for dinner and late night bull sessions.

"My coach was Bones McKinney. He and Press were good friends," remembered Billy Packer, who at the time played for Wake Forest and eventually achieved fame as a television commentator. "It was just a different era—coaches were competitors but close friends." Duke's Vic Bubas, UNC's Frank McGuire, Maryland's Bud Milliken, Virginia's Bill McCann, and N.C. State's Everett Case were also part of this coaching fraternity. Many of them joined McKinney at the Maravich home where they would talk basketball philosophy well into the night. Young Pete made sure to quietly listen in on the conversation.

The Maravich family became quite popular around town. Press, always quick with a joke, an anecdote, or a fascinating fact, was particularly well liked. Neighbors Bob and Louise Bradley grew very fond of the Maravich family and recalled inviting them to dinner one evening. "We cooked two chickens. Usually we didn't cook but one, but they had those two boys [Pete and Ronnie] and so we figured it would take two fryers for everybody," remembered Bob Bradley. "The funny thing is, there was one piece of chicken left on the platter when they went home. But Louise and I later found out, when they went on a picnic together, that they normally cooked four chickens. We figured the night they spent at our house, Press and Helen must have been kicking those kids to keep them from grabbing up that last piece of chicken. Pete might have been skinny all his life, but we learned fast that boy could eat."

Local residents recalled Press as fast-talking and gregarious, while his wife, Helen, seemed shy, polite, and a bit nervous.

"Helen was just an exceptionally nice person. Very quiet, very nice, very pleasant," recalled Don Carver, who played under Press and later coached Pete for two years at Daniel High School. "I would describe her as a mother who supported her family. If Pete needed to go to practice, she'd take him. Probably one of the nicest mothers I have ever met."

Bob Bradley also enjoyed Helen's polite demeanor but, on occasion, observed a darker side of her personality. "She'd yell at Press and yell that dinner was ready. She could never say it in a calm tone. 'Sit down and have a seat!' she'd yell at them."

That was the same impression she made on Jimmy Lever, one of Ronnie's classmates. "She had a temper and there were fights all the time," Lever said. "Ronnie and I would just take off and get out of there whenever one would break out."

Another close neighbor, Howard Bagwell, also recalled family fights. "They'd argue up there and fight. You could hear them hollering and screaming up the block. Press one time locked the door and wouldn't let anybody in. It was almost comical. Very emotional family. In a way, I was like Pete's second father. He'd stay more at our house than he stayed at his own."

Bagwell recalled that Pete was quiet and well behaved except in the heat of competition. The two would play croquet, Ping-Pong, and even board games. "You had to keep playing him until he won because he hated to lose so much," Bagwell said. "Even something as simple as losing in a game of Monopoly or checkers would draw out the worst in Pete, who, when losing, would *accidentally* kick the board."

Pete took his obsession with basketball into the classroom, occasionally to his detriment. Susan Lindsay Bishop recalled a serious moment in fourth grade when the students were required to stand and reveal their vocational dreams.

"I remember Peter said he was going to become a professional basketball player and the other boys hooted him out of the room," Bishop said. "They just bedeviled him because he was such a small guy for his age."

Linda Price Durham, a classmate of Pete's at Calhoun-Clemson Elementary School, remembered that he constantly sketched basketballs on the outside of his notebook. "He just doodled when the teacher was talking," Durham said. "His head seemed elsewhere."

Lola Hawkins, Pete's math teacher, often caught him shooting air baskets in class. "He had a good mind but did average schoolwork. He didn't have that much time to study," recalled Hawkins. "Pete would sometimes say that he would be on the court until nine o'clock at night. Then some mornings he would be up at 6 A.M. and playing basketball." Hawkins spoke to Pete's dad during a parent-teacher conference but found Press aligned with his son. "He said that he wanted his boy to make it in basketball. I remember telling him, 'Well, he's got to get out of school first.' He said, 'Don't worry about that. I'll see to it that he gets into college and gets to be a basketball star.' Press really wasn't interested in Pete doing a whole lot of schoolwork."

In the fall of 1959, Pete, then a 12-year-old in seventh grade at Calhoun-Clemson Elementary School, beat out boys several years his senior to make the Daniel High School junior varsity basketball team. Although he was clearly talented for his age, varsity coach Howard Bagwell was reluctant to let him practice with the older boys. "Pete was a very skinny, frail kid. I mean he was a little bitty guy. I was really afraid to play him with the varsity," Bagwell said.

During an early season junior varsity game, Pete experienced a life-changing moment. There were only about 90 spectators in Daniel's gym as Pete Maravich dribbled down court, leading a fast break. It was an easy three-on-one scoring opportunity. But he noticed that the legs of the defender were backpedaling in a rhythmic pattern, like the shutter gate of a movie projector. That gave him an idea. After a few more steps, Pete whipped a behind-the-back bounce pass *through the defender's legs*. The ball landed softly in the hands of a streaking teammate, who made an easy layup. The small crowd gasped and then leapt to its feet, whooping with delight. Thirty seconds later the awestruck spectators were still applauding. The electric rush of the moment was imprinted on the psyche of the 12-year-old. "The crowd, I want to tell you, they went berserk. I couldn't believe it," Pete told reporters years later. "I think, right then, showtime was born in Pete Maravich."

Several role models inspired Pete's on-court showmanship. There was his father Press, Marshall coach Jules Rivlin, Clemson players Larry "Choppy" Patterson and George Krajeck, and Daniel High's own hot-shot Dickie Senn.

Senn's younger brother, David, said Dickie learned his flashy moves playing in Washington, D.C.'s city game. "In 1956, my father was working on his

Ph.D. at the University of Maryland," explained David Senn. "We lived in Silver Spring [adjacent to D.C.], where Dickie played a lot of basketball. When we came back in 1958, he was the first in this area to throw a behind-the-back and no-look pass."

Clemson resident Billy Harper also bolsters the claim that Dickie Senn (nicknamed "Tricky Dick") influenced Pete. "When Dickie came back from Washington, D.C., playing that style of ball, Pete just emulated everything Dickie did."

It's impossible to quantify the extent to which any one player or coach influenced Pete, but ultimately it was Pete's methodical self instruction combined with his inspired creativity that produced his immense catalog of skills. "My dad worked with him a lot," recalled his brother Ronnie in 2000. "But he did a lot of that stuff on his own. Behind-the-back and through-the-legs. That was Pete."

Years later sportswriter Dave Kindred added his own perspective. "You can't watch Maravich film and say, 'I'm going to do that.' To do what Maravich did with the basketball is a gift from God."

Pete received equal billing with his older brother Ronnie in a January 6, 1960, *Anderson Independent* article entitled, "Father's Prospects":

> *The words "basketball" and "Maravich" are synonymous here. Tuesday night Ronnie Maravich, a junior, broke the Daniel High School single-game scoring record with 37 points as Daniel whipped Pickens, 91-48. In the Bee team game, Pete Maravich, a seventh grader and the Bee team's leading scorer, scored 14 points in leading his team to a 44-21 win over Pickens' Bee Team. Both are sons of Clemson College basketball coach Press Maravich.*

At times, Pete felt overwhelmed by the attention and pressure from his father. Once, while logging his normal eight-hour practice session at the YMCA gym on a 100-degree day, Pete began to question his obsessive training. He stopped dribbling the ball and fell to the floor in tears. "Other kids are out swimming and playing," he said to himself. "Why am I here? Why do I have this desire? Why am I killing myself?"

Shortly before the school year, Pete had a nightmare that deeply shook him. "All I know is one night I jumped out of my window with a basketball under my arm," Pete told a reporter, years after the incident. "I ran as fast as I could into the woods, which must have been a couple of miles away. And I slept there, holding the basketball in my arms. It was really weird."

Through the tears and nightmares Pete continued his regimen and incredibly, the following year in eighth grade, he earned a spot on the varsity team. At the time, Daniel High fielded athletic teams composed of students in grades 9 through 12. Pete, who still attended Calhoun-Clemson Elementary on College Avenue, was the lone exception.

"Daniel had a rule that if anyone was athletic enough to play on the team, they could," said Pete Carlisle, who replaced coach Howard Bagwell in the fall of 1960. "Pete was an eighth grader but he tried out for the high-school team and made it. His legs and arms were so small, but he was a total delight for me. He was so talented, and yet so small and fragile."

That meant Pete and his brother Ronnie were teammates. Ronnie, 6-4 and 190 pounds, was Daniel's star forward and team captain. The Lions, led by Ronnie and Dickie Senn, were coming off a great 19-3 season and a conference championship.

Ronnie was a complex young man. He was a James Dean-era rebel complete with leather jacket and a short fuse. He liked to drink, smoke, and chase girls. He ran afoul of the law from time to time, once for stealing an Edsel and another time for setting off M-80s in the girls' restroom. However, he was also a gifted natural athlete who won all-state honors in both football (he played linebacker and tight end) and basketball. Ronnie detested schoolwork and skipped out so often that the football coach had to call in a few favors just to keep him on the roster.

"Ronnie certainly didn't have Pete's dedication to basketball, but Pete didn't have Ronnie's social skills," observed Walter Cox, a 1960 Daniel High graduate who played varsity basketball with the elder brother. "Ronnie was quite popular with the ladies and was the most rebellious out of all of us."

Although Ronnie was the big man on campus, he didn't receive as much attention at home. Clemson player Larry Seitz recalled Ronnie's relationship with Press was very complicated. "I don't think Ronnie was treated by Press the same way he treated Pete. He didn't show a lot of affection for Press even though I know he cared for him," Seitz said. "I remember one time Press was hung in effigy and he wanted to find out who did it. . . . [Ronnie] felt more for his dad than he let on."

Dag Wilson, an assistant coach that season, noted that Ronnie never gave his little brother preferential treatment. "He used to beat Pete around in practice, knock him around and I saw him make Pete cry. I saw tears in his eyes. Ronnie really treated him badly."

While Pete's varsity teammates were growing into manhood, Pete was still physically and emotionally very much a boy. "We called him 'hairless' for obvious reasons," said teammate Walter Cox. Pete was so self-conscious he refused to shower with the team and would leave the gym wearing his uniform under his street clothes.

In his first regular-season game, eighth grader Pete Maravich, wearing No. 3, created something of a stir when he trotted out for warmups. He was 5-2, barely 90 pounds, with a large head, wide eyes, a buzz cut, and a malnourished appearance. A stream of catcalls rained from the bleachers. "When everybody saw this little runt come into the game, they all laughed," remembered Jim Howard, son of Clemson athletic director Frank Howard.

Pete began his varsity career on the bench. That starting lineup was Jim Sutherland, Charles Stuart, Jim Lever, Dickie Senn, and Ronnie. When Pete finally came off the bench, well into the game, his teammates refused to pass him the ball. Afterward, he went home, headed straight for his bedroom, and sobbed uncontrollably.

"Pete had a rough time his first year," Press told a reporter years later. "He was conscious of his size and the way the other fellows were treating him. We used to have long talks at night, especially when a practice or a game was particularly trying. I've always believed that while physical condition plays a great role in basketball, a player's emotional make up is of equal or greater importance. You need a good emotional attitude—the confidence in yourself and in your ability to bounce back."

In his second game, Pete's teammates continued to ignore him. But with the score tied late in the game, Daniel held the ball, and with the seconds ticking down, Pete was the only player open. The ball swung out to him and he lobbed a one-handed push shot from the hip. The ball arched into the air, hit the front of the rim, bounced off the backboard, and settled into the net. The 20-foot heave was Pete's first varsity basket and won the game for Daniel.

It also garnered Pete some much-needed respect. His teammates eventually grew to appreciate his quirky ball handling and sharpshooting. They incorporated the young trickster into the offense and, late in the season, coach Pete Carlisle placed him on the starting five, much to the dismay of 5-9, 160-pound senior Charles Stuart. "I started at the first of the season and he beat me out at some point," Stuart said in 2004. "I still tell people that I once started in front of Pete Maravich, one of the greatest players of all time. However, I forget to tell them that I was a senior when he was in eighth grade."

The Maravich brothers' relationship was strengthened over the season. "Ronnie was not thrilled that Peter, in eighth grade, was on his senior year team," said Susan Lindsay Bishop. "In one game, I remember Peter was knocked to the floor and didn't get up for a few moments. Ronnie went over and gently picked him up. It was memorable to those of us who knew the dynamics of the pair."

Howard Bagwell, who had moved from Daniel to Anderson High School that year, recalled a particularly physical game. "Pete was doing everything on the court," Bagwell said. "He was dribbling behind his back and doing all that stuff and making monkeys out of all the Anderson players. One of them finally had enough and just hit him, knocked him up into the stands. Now Ronnie and Pete used to fuss all the time at each other. But Ronnie was mean as a snake if anyone ever messed with Pete. The next thing you know we had a free-for-all. Ronnie just knocked the devil out of the guy who hit Pete."

Ronnie suspected the opposing teams' roughhousing of Pete was a clever way of getting a two-for-one expulsion. "They used to send in the hatchet man to knock him [Pete] down so they could get me mad and go after him, and the referee would kick me out too," said Ronnie, who led the state that season in technical fouls. In one game, Ronnie went into the crowd and decked a rowdy fan who threw ice at Pete.

Pete later realized that Ronnie's big-brother interventions improved their relationship. "I knew it was strange for him to have his little brother on his team, especially when he could only think of me as the little pest who bugged him at home," Pete penned in his memoir. "But our brotherhood grew stronger as teammates."

The Maravich bond grew even stronger in the spring when they teamed up for the Southern Textile Basketball Tournament. The tourney, which began back in 1921, was composed of teams sponsored by the local mills. "It was a better class of basketball than the high schools because the league would allow you to pick the best players in the area," according to Clemson resident Dubby Robinson, who participated in many tournaments. "In high school ball, if you looked at somebody the wrong way, they'd call a foul. In textile ball, they let you play."

Over the years, the annual March tournament featured several talented cagers. In addition to Maravich, future professionals like Billy Cunningham, Doug Moe, Mickey Davis, Tree Rollins, and Larry Nance displayed their early basketball chops in the 4,000-seat Greenville Memorial Auditorium. "Teams from all around the South came to play in the Greenville Memorial Auditorium, which I thought was the biggest place in the world at the time," said Jim Sutherland, who played alongside Pete and Ronnie Maravich on the Cannon Mill team from Central, South Carolina.

The Cannon team, coached by Daniel High's Pete Carlisle, easily ran the table at the tournament. It edged Slater Mill, 75-72, in the Class C title game on March 11, 1961. Ronnie led the team with 32 while Pete chipped in 18 points and collected his first, post–Biddy ball, championship trophy.

Surprisingly, when baseball season arrived, Pete showed an interest in playing the national pastime. He rummaged through a closet at home, found an old catcher's mitt and ball, and coaxed his father to hit him some flies. Press, who believed a true champion had to be myopic in his quest for excellence, was cool to his son's new diversion. As Pete readied himself for the first fly ball, Press gripped the bat and swung with all of his force while muttering under his breath, "I hope he doesn't choose baseball over basketball." The ball shot high into the sky and Pete lost sight of it in the sun's glare. It came down on the center of his forehead, sending him to the ground.

Press raced to his son and discovered a knot the size of a small egg on Pete's forehead, including a fresh imprint of the baseball's stitches. "I got hit by a baseball once," Press fibbed to his child. "Knocked me out of commission for a week."

"Really?" Pete asked, fighting back the tears.

"That's right. Put me in the hospital. That's why I stuck with basketball."

In the fall, Pete tried his hand at football. When Press caught wind of the situation he persuaded the high school football coach to let Pete take a few snaps at quarterback. The defense tattooed the undersized passer with vicious tackles and late hits, and Pete soon turned in his shoulder pads.

Pete also discovered he was a natural at both bowling and pocket billiards. His brother Ronnie had a reputation as a bit of a pool shark and introduced the game to Pete who, by age 13, had become quite proficient playing at the YMCA. One day, in search of new competition and excitement, Pete took his cue to the Clemson Pool Hall. "It was a place where all the sharks came in and scammed the students," recalled Frank Cox.

The hall had just a handful of tables and a few pinball machines, but was teeming with action. "Lots of gambling going on there with pinball and pool," said David Senn. Pete's 25-cent weekly allowance was often his ante into the popular nine-ball matches. The player who knocked in the ninth and final ball would take the quarter and young Pete often left the hall with several dollars in quarters.

In September of 1961, Pete entered the ninth grade at D. W. Daniel High School. His fervent dream of a growth spurt was partially answered that year as he sprouted to 5-8, although he was still scrawny at 120 pounds. He also began to gain confidence socially, attending football games and weekend parties at various homes. "A group of us, which consisted of 15 boys and 15 girls, would usually meet at 7:30 P.M. on Friday nights," recalled Crossie McDowell Cox. "We didn't drink or cut out the lights, but we'd dance. It was healthy and wonderful and Pete was definitely a part of it all."

Cox remembered Pete as shy, sweet, and quiet. The group often listened and danced to Chicago radio station WLS or played the latest hit 45s. Early Motown singers such as Marvin Gaye and Smokey Robinson and the Miracles never failed to get them on the dance floor (Pete eventually mastered the Shag). And slower numbers by Andy Williams and Johnny Mathis could be counted on to mellow the mood.

One evening in early 1962, Pete's innocence was tested by what he later described as a life-altering experience. "I had my first taste of alcohol. I had a beer at 14 years of age on the steps of a Methodist Church in Clemson," Pete recalled in a 1985 speech. "And I liked it. I liked it a lot. For all you young people tonight, let me tell you this: Don't ever take that first drink, don't ever take that first drink and don't ever take that first drug, because it will never be your last."

Friend Kent Lawrence recalled a time at Daniel High when he and Pete got into trouble for bursting a water pipe in biology class. "These water pipes came up out of the floor about 18 to 24 inches and had a cap on the top. We had a contest to see who could balance themselves the longest on top with one foot. I went first, and after a minute or so, I fell off. Pete gets on and is on there for a while, and then slips off. Well, the pipe broke and water shot straight up out of the pipe and knocked out a ceiling tile and sprayed us. So we quietly slipped back into the classroom but 15 minutes later the water started to flood the classroom. Practically flooded the entire wing of the school. It wasn't hard to find out who the culprits were since we were the only two soaking wet."

The mischievous teens received after-school detention and their parents paid for the repairs.

As the 1961-62 basketball season approached, Pete was hoping to lead Daniel High to a successful campaign. Pete and Jim Sutherland were the only returning starters on the varsity squad (Ronnie Maravich was off to Georgia Southern University on a football scholarship). "It was a very tough situation to be in because I knew we weren't going to have a very good team," recalled Don Carver, the new head basketball coach.

"Pete would wait for me every evening after JV football practice, which must have been around 6:00 to 6:30 P.M.," said Carver. "We'd play the best out of 11 goals. He could not shoot a jump shot because he wasn't strong enough, so he would bring up a one-handed push shot from off his hip. You'd think, *Well, I've got him now because I can block his shot.* Once you went out on Pete, he was gone, already around you because he was so fast. He could handle the ball and drive very well. Left hand or right hand. And if you didn't cover him, he'd shoot on you. He would win one night. I would win one night. Keep in mind, I was 6-4 and weighed 220 pounds. And I wasn't going to give him anything because I wanted him to get better."

Teammate Kent Lawrence recalled that Maravich, as a freshman, was already a big drawing card. "I remember going to away games and watching people stand in line to buy tickets, and it was all because of Pete. Almost every game we played when Pete was in high school was a sellout."

Maravich gave the fans an eyeful one Friday night in December 1961. Jerry McLeese, sports editor of the *Anderson Independent*, reported the fireworks:

> To look at the box score on the Daniel High basketball game, you would hardly recognize that Ronnie Maravich has graduated. Ronnie was the leading scorer for the Lions last year. Friday night Pistol Pete Maravich, brother of Ronnie Maravich, popped in 33 points against Pendleton.

McLeese's reference to the famous "Pistol Pete" nickname was actually a rare occurrence during Maravich's high school days. The catchy moniker originated because Pete's shooting motion back then—firing the ball up from his right hip—resembled a gunfighter pulling a six-shooter from his holster.

Daniel ended the season a disappointing 9-9 but Pete anticipated a more successful sophomore season. However his plans were on hold because his father was fielding a new coaching offer, from another state.

Press Maravich's tenure at Clemson was, judged strictly by the numbers, a study in mediocrity. During his six seasons the Tigers logged a 66-134 record.

To his credit, Press managed to keep his sense of humor as the losses piled up. Early on, after a crushing road loss, his image was hung in effigy. He looked at the doll and quipped, "I'm glad to see somebody around here that interested in basketball."

To most observers, Coach Maravich's Achilles' heel was his failure to recruit blue-chip players. Jerry West, a sensation at East Bank High in West Virginia in the late 1950s, was pursued unsuccessfully by Press. That's what made Clemson's run in the 1962 ACC Tournament so remarkable. Postseason usually meant one-and-out for the hapless Clemson Tigers. But play-ing with just sophomores and juniors, and utilizing a creative zone defense that Press named "Junto" (joined united together), Clemson upset both N.C. State and Duke. They eventually lost in the tournament final to an excellent Wake Forest team. (Wake, led by Len Chappell and Billy Packer, advanced to the Final Four of that year's NCAA Tournament.) It remains the only time Clemson has ever played in an ACC conference final.

Clemson's postseason run caught the eye of legendary N.C. State coach Everett Case. "Case once told me, 'If a team beats you one time, you go out there and hire the coach,'" recalled Lou Pucillo, who played under Case from 1955 to 1959. "Well, that was Press Maravich."

During the summer of 1962, while earning some extra money coaching in a Puerto Rican professional league, Press received the first of many phone calls from N.C. State. He was offered the top *assistant coaching* position at N.C. State with a guarantee that, upon Case's mandatory retirement in 1965, Mar-avich would inherit the program.

Case also set his sights on young Pete. When State had come to play at Clemson, Press always invited Case to his home after the game, win or lose. On several occasions, Pete was marched into the living room for a dribbling exhibition. Case hoped Press would bring his remarkable son to play at State.

Press faced a tough decision. Moving from head coach to assistant coach wasn't exactly a promotion. On the other hand, N.C. State was among the region's premier basketball programs. The deciding factor turned out to be money. Press asked Clemson athletic director Frank Howard for a raise, but was shot down.

"Some people thought I was nuts," Press told a reporter. "Here I was a head coach at an Atlantic Coast Conference school, and the basketball pro-gram was just getting to the point where I always wanted it. But I was earn-ing $5,000 and it just wasn't enough. When North Carolina State offered me $8,500 to be an assistant to Everett Case, I couldn't pass it up."

Because the negotiations lasted late into the summer, Pete had already registered at Daniel for his sophomore year.

Press Maravich began his N.C. State coaching career living alone at the YMCA in Raleigh, North Carolina, while Pete and his mom stayed on in Clemson.

Pete's attentions were somewhat divided in tenth grade as he joined both the track team (he ran the mile) and Latin club at Daniel High. But hoops still dominated his agenda.

Pete now had a reputation as a dangerous scorer and he began to receive a lot of attention from opponents and spectators. Don Carver recalled an intense battle in front of 1,800 rabid fans at Anderson High School. The game was tied with a minute to go, and Pete was readying to take two foul shots. "Someone in the crowd threw an ice ball at Pete and missed his eye by two inches. I jumped up and went down to the Anderson coach and told him in so many words that if another object was thrown at any one of my players, I would hold him personally responsible. The Anderson coach then got on the sound system and told everyone to calm down. Pete went back to the foul line and sank both of his foul shots. Pete scored 21 points that night and we won the game. His basketball career would have changed if that ice ball had hit him in the eye."

In a game against Seneca High School, Billy Harper, Pete's friend from the summer leagues, recalled receiving orders to rough him up. "I was a year older than Pete in high school and he scored something like 35 points against us one night. And I was the guy who covered him," Harper said. "Well, the next time we played, my coach, Dave Nelson, pulled me aside and said, 'I don't care what you have to do, but don't let that kid score no 35 points again.' Even though Pete and I were friends, I ran him into a brick wall. It caused a riot. But that's how we played. Intense."

After compiling a solid 17-3 record, Daniel faced a tough matchup against Greer High in the Western AA Tournament. The teams had met twice that season, with Greer handing Daniel its first loss (breaking a 10-game winning streak) on January 11. Daniel won the rematch, 81-77, on February 2 behind Pete's 26 points and Jim Sutherland's season-high 37. Greer, however, took the "rubber" match in the tournament.

"It was a hurtful loss," explained Sutherland. "Our problem was that we lacked good players. Pete and I did all the scoring, but we really needed one more good player. We didn't quite have it."

Maravich and several other Daniel players received a consolation of sorts when they again romped through the 1963 Southern Textile Tournament. Coached by Don Carver, the Cannon Mill team defeated Greer Mill, 78-72, for Pete's second Class C championship in three years. Sutherland led the way with 24 points while Pete added 17.

Jack Federline, a freshman at Clemson who played on the championship Cannon Mill team, recalled seeing something special in Maravich. "He threw lots of passes that other people would not have attempted," Federline recalled in 1999. "There was a fast break where he went down the middle, and I filled out the lane. He faked it toward me and went the other way, then faked it to the other guy, then whipped it around his back. It hit me in the head. I never saw it coming."

As Helen and Pete prepared to join Press in North Carolina, Pete took a final trip with his friends in the summer of 1963. Every summer the teens rented a cottage on Ocean Drive in Myrtle Beach, South Carolina. "The trips would be chaperoned by adults and the boys stayed upstairs while the girls stayed downstairs. One of my favorite memories of Pete is dancing with a lampshade on his head to the song, "It's My Party." Pete really cut loose and his real personality came out," recalled friend Jane Cobb Wolfe. "The last time I saw him was in Myrtle Beach the summer he left. It was very emotional. I remember he was wearing this big straw hat but it was a very sad occasion. The other thing I recall about Pete was that he had this thing about cleanliness—he was kind of a nut about being clean. The girls cooked and the boys cleaned the dishes, and Pete made sure the dishes were done properly."

It was also where Pete said good-bye to his most serious crush, Susan Lindsay. Over Christmas the two had attended a Teen Canteen dance at the Episcopal church. After a few false starts, Pete finally asked her to slow dance. During the number, he presented her with a bracelet that was picked out by Helen.

"Here's something that my mom got for you," Pete said shyly.

"I think it's the mom part I remember the most," Lindsay (now Bishop) said almost 40 years later. "Just how shy and innocent Pete was."

Frank Cox remembered a farewell party for Pete that took place at the YMCA. "It was a pretty sober occasion. There were a few tears on everyone's part," Cox recalled. "Pete had an engaging smile and a real dependency on people. I think from a family standpoint, the Maraviches were ready to go, but Pete wasn't."

For the Maravich clan, the seven years in quaint Clemson provided significant transformations.

Pete, the skinny, awkward kid who became consumed with every aspect of basketball, was becoming, in his words, a "basketball android."

Press advanced on two tracks. First, he forged a reputation as an intelligent, innovative college coach, handpicked to lead one of the nations' premiere programs. Secondly, he continued to mold his youngest son into the most skilled basketball magician the world would ever see.

Ronnie, the carefree rebel and all-state athlete, dropped out of Georgia Southern University, switched gears, and chose the most rigid and disciplined of all professions: the United States Marine Corps.

And Helen Maravich began to feel more and more isolated from the sports world in which her family was immersed.

Pete Maravich continued to cherish the memories of those seven years in South Carolina. In 1987, when he was developing a movie based on his life, he set the narrative in Clemson. For he believed that it was there, living in the house on Highland Drive, that he had been truly happy.

3

Tobacco Road

"Pete, more than anybody I've ever known in the sport of basketball—and I'm going to make a fairly astounding statement—was a team player. He could score 35 points, but if he lost, he was really down. He could score 15 points and if we won, he'd really be happy. He just absolutely hated to lose."
    —OLIN BROADWAY, BROUGHTON HIGH COACH, PETE'S JUNIOR YEAR

"Pete was everything a coach would want in a basketball player. If you had a computer and put in the data for a basketball player, it would come out as Pete Maravich."
    —ED MCLEAN, BROUGHTON HIGH COACH, PETE'S SENIOR YEAR

Press Maravich's basketball odyssey in some ways paralleled America's economic journey from the smoke-filled days of the industrial revolution to the heady frontier of high tech. When Press first discovered hoops in the 1920s, his hometown in western Pennsylvania was often covered with a layer of crunchy soot spewed from local smokestacks. Forty years later, when he brought his family to Raleigh he discovered a region evolving from a 19th century-style, agricultural and textile economy into a white-collar community dotted with state-of-the-art technology firms.

To nurture this emerging sector, forward-thinking leaders from business, government, and academia created the Research Triangle Park back in 1959. To this day the 7,000-acre park, surrounded by thick pine forests, is home to cutting-edge telecommunication, biotechnology, environmental health science, micro-fabrication, and super-computing research and development firms.

The Research *Triangle* is so named because it lies between the three campuses of Duke University in Durham, North Carolina State University in Raleigh, and the University of North Carolina in Chapel Hill. In time those universities, along with Wake Forest in Winston Salem, developed into college basketball powerhouses and came to be known as the "Big Four."

This move to prominence was due, in no small part, to the success of N.C. State coach Everett Case. Case was cut from the same cloth as Press Maravich. They were World War II Navy veterans, held master's degrees, and were passionate about basketball. Affectionately known as "The Old Gray Fox," thanks to his "crazy like a fox" reputation and thinning gray hair, Case compiled a comically lopsided record of 726-57 as an Indiana high school coach. When he came to N.C. State in 1946, he introduced a high-octane brand of basketball that spawned a rabid fan base.

For fans of State basketball it wasn't just Case's potent offense and swarming defense that delighted the patrons. They were also charmed by the many never-before-seen "theatrical" elements he appropriated from Indiana. He dimmed the lights during player introductions and cut down the nets after tournament wins. He brought in a pep band, an organist, and an applause meter. Most famously, Case initiated a Christmas tournament called the Dixie Classic that exploited the rivalry of the "Big Four" and showcased the nation's top college basketball teams.

Case's "show" played to sell-out crowds in the ultimate theater— Reynolds Coliseum. Built in 1949, the 12,900-seat "shoe-box" was the perfect arena to accommodate the region's growing appetite for hoops. Reynolds came to symbolize big-time southern basketball and was eventually regarded as the Madison Square Garden of the South.

Helen and Pete finally joined Press in Raleigh in the summer of 1963, and the family settled into a brand new, three-bedroom home at 508 North Glen Drive, a 10-minute drive from the university.

Pete enrolled in summer school at Raleigh's Needham-Broughton High School (hereby referred to as Broughton). There he met Mike Jordan (not to be confused with future basketball legend Michael Jordan). "We were two people who didn't know anyone else, so naturally, we gravitated toward each other," Jordan said. "We both ended up in the same American history class. He was a happy-go-lucky kid. Not real extroverted until he got to know you."

The two quickly discovered a common interest in basketball and spent quite a bit of time at the YMCA on Hillsborough Street. Constructed in 1960, the Raleigh YMCA was quite a bit larger than the Clemson version. Press purchased his son a membership ($60) and the boys began exploring the facilities. Pete made an immediate impression on his new friend when he took to the court. "He could do some things I had never seen anybody do before. I had never seen anyone dribble the ball behind their back and pass it between their legs," recalled Jordan. When Pete wasn't involved in pick-up games or shooting competitions, he would run through his ball handling drills alone on the handball courts.

Under the auspices of Jack Thomas, the Y sponsored youth and adult basketball leagues. Thomas remembered Press on the curb outside the build-ing pressuring him to allow 15-year-old Pete into the adult league. "Press twisted my arm verbally and said that Pete would dominate the youth league and wouldn't learn anything from it," recalled Thomas. "I got to thinking, and told him I'd do it on one condition—if I saw Pete was over his head in com-petition, I would reserve the right to put him in the youth league. Press said, 'Good enough,' and we shook hands."

In Pete's first outing with the adult team, he poured in 40 points for the Comets. When he added 91 points over the following two games, there was no more talk of youth leagues.

Pete's summer league play also caught the eye of former Wake Forest star, and then Broughton High School coach, Olin Broadway. "It was obvious that Pete had plenty of skills," recalled Broadway. "But he also had that very rare court moxie. He could sense where other players were."

Pete befriended the coach's little brother Jimmy (who also competed in the summer league) and they would spend up to 10 hours a day at the YMCA. One late afternoon Pete asked his friend to rebound while he practiced free throws. "After making 178 straight, he finally missed," recalled Broadway.

November 1, 1963, marked the first practice for the Broughton varsity, and transfer student Pete Maravich found himself in a battle for a starting job. The roster boasted a tightly knit unit of four seniors who had played together the previous two seasons. Before Pete's arrival, the projected starting lineup was Jimmy Broadway and Doug Bridges as forwards, Billy Trot and Ed Parker in the backcourt, and junior Dickie Smith at center. Coach Broadway was sold on Pete's skills but wondered about his stamina.

"You have to remember, Pete was not that strong as a high schooler," recalled teammate Mike Pedneau. "He wasn't a marathoner, that's for sure."

Before the season began, Paul Phillips of the *Raleigh Times* interviewed Pete. "He was extremely introspective and shy," Phillips recalled. "You had to practically pull words out of him sometimes. He just wanted to play; he didn't want to talk about it."

When the season commenced on December 3, Pete had won a spot in the starting lineup from bespectacled senior guard, Ed Parker. Broughton provided different jersey numbers for their home (white) and road (purple) uniforms. Pete chose No. 20 for home games and, in honor of his brother Ronnie, No. 23 on the road.

The team was expected to make a serious run at the state championship. No one was surprised when the squad blew through the early part of the season, losing only one conference game to Durham. Pete was now six feet tall and a reed-thin 140 pounds but, thanks to years of coordination drills, he managed to avoid the "clumsy stage" many teenagers experience. His ability to set up his teammates belied his years.

"Pete Maravich had every talent that Bob Cousy ever had, and that's saying a lot. I know that's what I was thinking at the time," said Coach Broadway, who used to scrimmage against Cousy (a perennial NBA All-Star) in summer camps. "It was that same kind of court savvy . . . knowing where everybody was on the court. How did he know? I don't know, but us mere mortals don't have that same kind of court sense."

Pete's skills were also refined on the court at Reynolds Coliseum. During Christmas break that season he caught the eye of one of N.C. State's assistant coaches, Lou Pucillo. "The first time I ever saw Pete play was in a pick-up game. It was the fall of 1963. It must have been around exam time because everything was closed, but the players' locker room was open. For whatever reasons, we only had nine players. Pete must have been just 14 or 15 years old [16, actually] at the time. Press said, 'Take off your shoes.' He was just in his socks at Reynolds Coliseum practicing. Both Case and myself were astonished when this kid, against a good varsity basketball team, was dribbling around the corner and made four straight shots into the basket. Case called timeout and yelled, 'Somebody needs to go out there and guard that little weasel!'"

N.C. State's freshman coach Les Robinson also recalled Pete's pick-up games at Reynolds. "I'm going to say it was December 21 or 22, and it was our last scrimmage before the holidays. One morning, we played from 10 A.M. till about 1 or 2 P.M. Just three-on-three, including Pete Maravich. Now keep in mind, three or four of these guys were starters on the N.C. State team who won the ACC Tournament that year and beat Duke, the number one team in the country. So these were good players. That day, he made mincemeat of a whole bunch of college players. When Pete left, Pete Coker, a player, said to me, 'Les, that's the greatest performance I have ever seen in this place.' Just an unbelievable day."

N.C. State guard Tom Mattocks guarded Pete in those scrimmages. "Sometimes Pete played in his socks, sometimes in shoes. We about split the games we played," the 6-2 Mattocks recalled. "I never blocked a shot of his. The thing that really impressed me about him was his confidence. Here was this high school kid playing against a starting college ballplayer and he's shooting hook shots. I never had the nerve to take a hook shot in my life, and he's popping them in from both sides . . . and hitting them.

"Then I watched him shooting all by himself one day. He was taking all kinds of crazy shots, behind his back, over his head, hooks from all over. I guess he practiced them so much that he knew he could make them when it counted. But I'll admit that while I thought he'd be a big star, I never thought he'd be averaging over 40 points a game some day."

As 1964 began, the Broughton Caps were on a roll and Maravich led the way with a 19-point scoring average. The well-balanced squad was anchored by the senior co-captains Doug Bridges and Jimmy Broadway. Together with Dickie Smith, Billy Trot, Steve Horney, and Pete, they were referred to as the "Sizzling Six." The *News and Observer* anointed the team the school's "Best Ever."

Broughton assumed first place in the conference by soundly defeating Durham (avenging their earlier loss), 75-62 on February 14, 1964. The team finished the regular season at 13-3 and began preparations for the conference playoffs and state tournament. The coaching staff adopted the slogan: "Go for Broke."

After an opening round bye, Broughton faced the formidable Wilmington Wildcats in the conference semifinals, on February 29. Coached by the North Carolina high school legend, Leon Brogden, Wilmington owned several state championships. Pete began the game ice cold. "I remember counting at least 20 times before he hit his first shot," said Broughton student Patrick Hannon. Despite Pete's horrendous shooting, the Caps stayed close and forced overtime. Maravich redeemed himself with a clutch basket with 1:36 remaining, but Wilmington tied it up again. In the second overtime period, Pete hit back-to-back field goals to give the Caps a 55-53 lead and then sealed the victory with four consecutive foul shots. Pete scored all eight of Broughton's points in the second overtime as the Caps advanced with a 59-55 victory.

"That's what I call confidence," said Paul Phillips of the *Raleigh Times*. "Most kids would have been so uptight after missing 19 shots they wouldn't have even tried a layup."

Broughton had a slightly easier time beating Fayetteville, with its 6-11 center Rusty Clark, in the final game of the Eastern 4-A Conference Tournament. Because the Caps held the lead throughout the game Fayetteville was forced to foul. Pete hit 11 of his game-high 29 points from the free-throw line, including four straight points on two one-and-one opportunities in the last minute of the game. With the 63-60 victory, Broughton won the

Eastern conference title for the first time in nine years. The next day the "Go For Broke" team was back in the gym preparing for the state finals at the Greensboro Coliseum.

On Thursday evening, March 6, 1964, Broughton took on Winston-Salem's Reynolds High. It was a game Maravich would never forget. Broughton held a 60-54 lead with 3:38 remaining when Reynolds went on a 6-0 run to tie the contest, 60-60. Pete's 15-footer glanced off the rim as time expired.

The teams were again knotted, 62-62, near the end of overtime. With the clock winding down, Broughton's Jimmy Broadway launched a 22-foot shot that dramatically swished through just as the buzzer sounded. "We grabbed him, carried him around the court and we were crazy," Pete recalled 16 years later in an interview with Leigh Montville of the *Boston Globe*. "But there were two officials. One from our conference and one from their conference. The one from our conference said he didn't know if it beat the buzzer. The one from their conference immediately said it didn't."

Broadway's heroic heave was waved off and the game continued into a second overtime. With 26 seconds remaining and Reynolds leading 64-62, Broadway was fouled while taking a shot. He made the first free throw but his second attempt rimmed out, and Broughton's season was over. The final score: 64-63.

It was a devastating, heartbreaking loss for the "Sizzling Six." "Boy, that's one of those days you repress in your brain," Billy Trot said more than 40 years later.

"The kid who made the shot [Jimmy Broadway] actually went berserk in the locker room. Broke everything. Had to be strapped down," Pete recalled.

And as for Pete? "I cried for two weeks."

The 1963-64 Broughton Caps were one of the best teams Pete ever played for. The plucky squad went 19-4 and was a perfect 12-0 at home. Two of its four losses were by a single point. Pete was the leading scorer with 19.3 points per game.

But the sting of the season-ending defeat was especially difficult to endure.

"I should have celebrated the Caps 19-4 record, but all I could think of were the stupid mistakes I had made to contribute to the defeat that we had lost our chance at the title," Pete wrote in his autobiography. "For months after the season, I was haunted by the championship slipping from our hands." Of all the skills that Press drove his son to acquire, the ability to shrug off a loss was not on the list.

Later in the spring, Pete tried his hand at tennis along with basketball teammates Billy Trot and Ed Parker. Unfortunately Pete lacked rudimentary tennis skills, one observer described his technique as punching at the ball. Nor did Pete seem to grasp the etiquette of the "gentleman's game." "There was one day he was practicing," recalled Ed Watkins, underclassman at Broughton, "and there was a questionable call. It was right on the line. Pete said, '. . . if you ever call another one like that, I'll whip your [expletive].'"

On the home front the Maravich family got a surprise when Ronnie's girlfriend, Romona, gave birth to a baby girl. The local paper reported that Press and Helen gushed over the new arrival like typical grandparents. But when the young parents expressed an interest in giving up the child for adoption, Press and Helen stepped in and agreed to raise the child as their own. At age 15, Pete Maravich had a new baby sister, Diana Marie. Over the summer Pete attended a number of basketball camps and participated again in the YMCA tournament adult league—this time for the Vagabonds. He was joined by two Broughton teammates, Steve Horney and Citadel-bound Doug Bridges. The trio led the team to the championship, with Pete scoring 43, 44, and 34 points in the final three games.

Once established as a star athlete, Pete's social confidence and status soared at Broughton High. Making friends became a breeze and he was no longer painfully awkward around girls (one of his favorites was local beauty Vada Palma). He joined both the French and Monogram clubs, volunteered for the school newspaper (Hi-Times) and the yearbook (Latipac—Capital spelled backward), and was also a homeroom officer. Pete was often spotted in a Broughton hallway attempting to improve his vertical leap by jumping and tapping a specific spot on a sign.

However, when it came to academics, Maravich was not motivated. "Pete wasn't a bad student, but he didn't apply himself real well," his friend, and English classmate, Mike Jordan recalled. "He was not a scholar."

Patrick Hannon, who shared an algebra class with Pete, agreed. "I sat beside him and he was never prepared. He always wanted me to give him the answers," said Hannon. "I think he received Ds or Fs and barely got out of high school." Teammate Billy Trot thought Pete's concentration might have been the underlying problem. "Pete was not dumb, he was actually a very bright guy," Trot observed. "He couldn't sit still. Somebody today would diagnose him and give him Ritalin. He just could not sit still in the classroom."

Friend and teammate Mike Pedneau socialized with Pete, often visiting Captain's pool hall. "Pete's hand-eye coordination with a pool cue and his understanding of angles and bounce was phenomenal," said Pedneau.

Pedneau was also there for Pete's first taste of whiskey. The two drove to the ABC store in downtown Raleigh and picked up a half pint. Then they drove around the city listening to rock 'n' roll, stopping for some Char-Grill burgers on Hillsborough Street, and talking nonstop about girls and basketball. "I reckon we were 16 or 17 years old. Pete's body didn't metabolize alcohol well at all and he couldn't handle it," Pedneau recalled. "He never drank to excess in high school that I knew of and didn't drink much after that."

When Pete returned home, with bloodshot eyes and reeking of alcohol, it didn't go unnoticed by Press.

"You're drunk!" Press roared. "Get in here."

As Pete approached, Press took a swing at him, but missed. Pete darted to his room, followed by Helen, who arrived in time to calm down Press.

Pete knew too well of his father's use of physical punishment. "My dad used to put the belt to me and Ronnie all the time," Pete explained to George White of the *Houston Chronicle*. "Boy it was unbelievable. He'd put that old razor strap to us."

Pete awoke the next morning at 5:00, determined to return to his father's good graces. He mowed the lawn, raked the leaves, and washed the car. But Press was not mollified. "You're grounded for six weekends. And if you leave this place, I'll shoot you!" Press barked.

Just two other players returned for Pete's senior season at Broughton, Dickie Smith and Joe Maughan. Ed McLean, a recent graduate of Western Carolina University, replaced Olin Broadway as the team's head coach.

"Olin Broadway was a great, great coach. A good disciplinarian. He didn't let Pete do what he wanted to do his junior year. I remember one day all Pete did was run laps while the rest of the team practiced because Pete did not listen to him," recalled Maughan. "When he was a senior, he was more of an individual because the team relied on his scoring. Pete's full arsenal was on display that season. McLean was convinced that Pete was a once-in-a-lifetime player."

It helped that Pete's unlikely dream of a growth spurt was actually realized. As a senior he stood just shy of 6-4 and was still growing (his father was 6 feet tall and his mother was 5-7). The extra height gave his game a new dimension. He could now back down smaller players and throw in soft hooks or bank shots. Little Pete Maravich, who once struggled to heave shots from his hip, was now a slashing, long-legged, jump-shooting teenager. And his new coach gave him the green light. "There was no question in my mind he was destined for greatness. You just drew up on paper what you'd like your guard to be and it was Pete," said McLean, who made Maravich the team captain.

Right before Christmas the team traveled to Charlotte and played two non-conference teams on consecutive nights. On December 22, Pete popped in 38 points in a 70-68 win over the East Mecklenburg Eagles. *Charlotte News* reporter Emil Parker described Pete as "a slender burr-head with more moves than an octopus."

The following night Pete went on a scoring tear, hitting, according to the *Charlotte News*, "every conceivable shot." He scored 43 points including 18 of the final 20. But despite his scoring, Broughton lost 89-77 to the Garinger Wildcats. Afterward one of the Garinger players sagely predicted Maravich's future. "Guess we'll be seeing that boy on television."

The Broughton team was just 3-3, but tales of Pete's scoring exploits began to spread throughout the state and beyond.

"The senior at Raleigh's Broughton High stands 6-3 1/2, moves with the grace and precision of works in a Swiss watch, and is averaging 33.8 points for his first six games," wrote Bob Myers in a biographical piece for the *Charlotte News*. "Pete is hitting 60 percent from the floor and 80 from the foul line . . . Maravich has more moves than a hula girl."

In yet another newspaper feature, George Kolb of the *Raleigh News and Observer* explored the unique relationship between Pete and his dad. "Basketball is always being spoken between this father-son, player-coach tandem," wrote Kolb. But buried deep in the narrative was an ominous quote. "Mother just sits back and sort of listens when she manages to see us both at one time," Pete told Kolb.

Helen Maravich was slipping further away from the outside world. With her hands full caring for the new baby, she was rarely seen at games or social events. Friends noticed she began drinking heavily and even hallucinating conversations with long-dead relatives. It was the start of a long, steep decline. "When they moved from Clemson, I'll bet you two-thirds of the boxes in their home were left unpacked," recalled N.C. State sports information director Frank Weedon. "Helen was going through some depression and just never got around to it."

As 1965 commenced, Pete continued his scoring exhibitions and everywhere Broughton played, fans filled the gym to watch the young phenom. The local papers did not refer to Pete as the "Pistol" during his two seasons at Broughton High. "String bean," "octopus," and "flash" were just a few of the creative descriptions of the young hot-shot.

As Pete's legend grew, opposing teams zeroed in on him. "I gave each of my starters a picture of Pete to carry in their wallets. I wanted them ready to stop him. And if we could, I knew we'd win," recalled Paul Williamson, athletic director at Durham High School. "Well, along comes game time and before our game, Pete struts over to our bench and says to me he's going to run us to death. And he did it, too. Although we won the game, Pete still scored 38 points. They still talk about it here in Durham."

N.C. State guard Eddie Biedenbach recalled sitting at the press table with some reporters when Pete connected on a remarkable streak of sensational shots. "Pete hit five shots in a row from the corner," Biedenbach said. "His sixth shot was where he was leaning back parallel with the baseline and shot the ball over the backboard and hit nothing but net. I pounded the table so hard it knocked all of the writers' Cokes over."

On January 8, 1965, Broughton hosted Enloe High School. Enloe had a scoring machine of its own in 6-6 sophomore Randy Denton, a future star at Duke University and later with the Carolina Cougars of the American Basketball Association (ABA). Enloe won a squeaker, 63-61, using a box-and-one defense to hold Pete to 20 points—12 below his scoring average.

Broughton exacted a measure of revenge on February 2, when 1,500 fans jammed into the Enloe High School gym. Maravich went on a tear, making 18 of 28 shots from the floor and 11 of 12 from the foul line as his career-high 47 points propelled Broughton to an exciting 81-73 victory. At the end of the game, Pete's teammates carried him off the floor on their shoulders.

"Besides his phenomenal point-making," reported Grady Elmore in the *Raleigh News and Observer*, "Maravich excelled also as a ball hawk, making numerous pass interceptions and steals." Pete's 47-point record stood at Broughton from February 1965 until December 2000 when Shavlik Randolph, grandson of N.C. State hoops legend Ronnie Shavlik, bucketed 50 points.

Despite Pete's individual efforts, Broughton finished the regular season with a disappointing 8-12 record. In the postseason tournament the Caps were fifth-seeded in the Eastern 4-A conference and drew a first-round matchup against a formidable Wilmington team.

In the first half, Pete tore the transverse arch in his right foot and went down in a heap. Assistant coach Don Leggett and head coach Ed McLean recommended he sit out the rest of the game but Pete played on. He racked up 42 points and although the rest of his team combined for a paltry 17, it was enough for a 59-56 Broughton victory.

By the tipoff of the next evening game, Pete's foot had swollen significantly. He had the trainer wrap his foot and place it in a shoe several sizes larger than his regular size 12. "Pete was dragging one foot behind the other and it was obvious that it was killing him," McLean recalled. "It was one of the gutsiest performances I have ever seen." Pete modified his game to compensate for his injury and went old-school. He reverted to a two-handed set-shooter, popping in long-range bombs as he dragged around his aching foot in the oversized shoe. Pete hit for 45 points but it wasn't enough as Fayetteville eliminated Broughton, 76–61.

Pete's senior year at Broughton, unfortunately, became a template for his career. He was usually the best player on a weak team, and the blame for losses fell squarely on his shoulders.

In 23 games as a senior, Pete averaged 32.5 points (shooting 55 percent). Playing four eight-minute quarters, he was scoring a point-a-minute. His two-year average at Broughton was 25.6. "There is no question in my mind he's the greatest high school player I have ever seen," said his coach, Ed McLean. "I learned more from Pete about basketball than he ever learned from me."

Due largely to the efforts of sports editor Paul Phillips of the *Raleigh Times*, Pete's exploits came to the attention of editors at *Parade* magazine. Every year since 1957, *Parade* has named five high school All-Americans. The list over the years has included such future NBA stars as Magic Johnson, Shaquille O'Neal, Michael Jordan, Jerry Lucas, Kobe Bryant, Kevin Garnett, LeBron James, Moses Malone, Wesley Unseld, Allen Iverson, and Isiah Thomas.

In 1964–65, *Parade* selected the following first team: Richard Braucher, Sim Hill, Don Ross, Lew Alcindor, and Pete Maravich. The magazine wrote of Broughton High's basketball magician:

Son of North Carolina Coach Press Maravich. Fabulous shooter. Lowest point production for one game: 18. Went over 40 three times. Led the team in assists, in addition to scoring.

Pete wasn't the only Maravich to have a stellar year. In early December 1964, after a loss to Wake Forest, N.C. State head coach Everett Case told his two assistants, Press Maravich and Charlie Bryant, that he had coached his last game. "Fellas, I just can't take this any longer," Case whispered. The next morning he made it official. "Basketball has been left in good hands at State," Case told the media. "There's no one more dedicated to basketball than Press Maravich. He'll do a fine job."

Not long after, Case was diagnosed with cancer.

Press hadn't been a head coach for over two seasons. "It's different, mighty different. Even the towel doesn't taste the same," he quipped.

He installed a motion offense, running guards off double screens. The players responded by reeling off 11 consecutive wins before losing to Duke and then UNC, coached by Dean Smith and his assistant, Larry Brown.

Bill Ballenger of the *Charlotte News* called N.C. State, "the motliest gang of backyard athletes."

"[Coach Maravich] had a guard who was offered only one scholarship [Larry Worsley], a pot-bellied bald Korean War veteran [Larry Lakins] at center, an Ivy League transfer [Pete Coker] with lungs so undersized he could play only ten minutes at a time between rests, and a thieving guard named 'Wild Horse' [Eddie Biedenbach] who couldn't shoot," wrote Ballenger.

Besides the motion offense, Press stressed a swarming, suffocating zone-press defense. By the end of the season, State had the top-rated defense in the conference.

"He had this team playing so well offensively and, particularly, defensively," recalled Case's assistant Lou Pucillo. "They were so precise. I can attest that when Press was the head coach at N.C. State for two years, he was absolutely brilliant."

On March 6, 1965, that brilliance was on display in the finals of the ACC Tournament when State squared off against Duke. The Wolfpack had disposed of Virginia and Maryland in the first two rounds. On paper the contest seemed a bit unfair. Duke, loaded with future pro players and ranked No. 8 in the nation, led the ACC in scoring, margin of victory, field-goal percentage, and rebounding.

In front of a frenzied crowd at Reynolds Coliseum, N.C. State's 6-5 junior Larry Worsley had the night of his life. Worsley came off the bench and scored a career-high 30 points as he made 14 of his 19 shots from the field (he averaged just 5.2 points per game throughout the regular season). With 2:37 remaining, Eddie Biedenbach scored a crucial basket, and was fouled. Press was so excited he ran onto the court and kissed the sophomore guard on the cheek. After the emotional coach retreated to the bench, Biedenbach stepped to the line and calmly converted the free throw, giving State an 83-78 lead. The Blue Devils were unable to close the gap, and N.C. State had a thrilling 91–85 upset.

State's Cinderella season ended on March 12, when it was trounced in the second round of the NCAA Tournament by Princeton, led by future Hall of Famer Bill Bradley, the College Player of the Year. The Wolfpack found some redemption in a consolation game, downing the Jack Ramsay coached St. Joseph Hawks, 103-81. In the final UPI poll, N.C. State was ranked No. 12. For Press Maravich, this rag-tag group of overachievers would always be his favorite team.

N.C. State's success in 1965 changed Press's life. He was suddenly in great demand as a lecturer, clinic instructor, and guest columnist for sports magazines.

But, while Press's future looked bright, Pete's lackluster academic performance cast a cloud over his prospects. He longed to enroll at N.C. State and play for his dad but his SAT score was below the newly enacted ACC minimum of 800.

"The day [Saturday, March 6, 1965] we were playing Duke and upset them in the ACC Tournament was the same day Pete had to take the college boards," remembered State player Eddie Biedenbach. "I think that was his fourth time. At the pregame meal, he walked in. I said, 'Pete, how did you do on the exam?' He said, 'I couldn't concentrate. This is a big game.' He lived and died for his dad's teams. He was more concerned about the game than his board test. Let me say this—Pete was smart. He did not apply himself. It bothered me because I wanted Pete and Press to stay at N.C. State." Ultimately, Press decided to postpone Pete's freshman year in college, opting, instead, for a year of preparatory school. He hoped an extra year of seasoning would help Pete mature physically and improve his SAT scores.

Pete received his high school diploma from Broughton in a ceremony at the Raleigh Memorial Coliseum. Two months later, on August 3, 1965, in the state's 16th annual East-West All-Star basketball game, Pete provided a final jaw-dropping performance that North Carolinians still talk about to this day.

Leon Brock, head coach at Stedman High School, was selected to coach the East squad. "Of course, Pete was one of my first choices," Brock said. "He could do things with the basketball that were unbelievable. I mean he could make that basketball talk." Brock's team practiced for the better part of four days at the old Greensboro High School gym. On the first day, Brock told Pete he would not try to change over four days what Pete had learned in the previous four years. The practice sessions focused primarily on the fast break. "I felt there was enough offensive power I wouldn't have to worry about working on defense," Brock said.

Pete joined what was, perhaps, the most dominant front line of his career, anchored by Fayetteville's 6-11 Rusty Clark and New Bern's 6-9 Bill Bunting. Both had already signed to play for Dean Smith at the University of North Carolina.

Coach Brock was a nervous wreck the week of the game, despite having what looked on paper like a stacked team. "Pete at that time was the greatest basketball player in high school I'd ever seen," Brock said. "I had never coached another player of that talent before."

Maravich and Clark, whose teams had battled each other six times over a two-year period (3-3), were finally teammates. "Pete was a good friend, but he was a bit on the wild side," Clark recalled. One night the two ventured into a Greensboro pub called the Ivy Room and Pete got hustled by a local pool shark. "We weren't drinking or anything but Pete lived a little on the fast track for me."

The game in the Greensboro Coliseum set an attendance record, with many there to see the *Parade* All-American. To the crowd's delight, Pete, wearing No. 1, performed some fancy dribbling during warmups. However, when the game began, his shooting touch was missing. Nothing would drop. Ball after ball fell short or rimmed out and soon the crowd voiced their displeasure. "Even though Pete missed the first nine shots, I wasn't about to take him out of the game," Brock said. "He was the one who brought those fans to the game, despite the fact they were really booing him."

Pete hit on five of his next nine attempts and had 12 points at the half as the heavily favored East led by just two points, 40-38. The coach, the crowd, and Pete's teammates were not too happy with his play. "He wasn't going inside to myself or Bill Bunting and I told him, 'Pass it to us on the inside,' because it was a much higher percentage shot than his 25-footers," recalled Clark.

Maravich took Clark's advice, feeding the post for three easy baskets in the opening minutes of the third quarter. The rest of the second half was all Pete. "A man playing among boys," is how Walt Riddle in the *Greensboro Record* saw it.

The West's coach Ray Whitley shuttled in several fresh players—Dale Stubbs, Jim Gilliam, Frank Webster, Bob Albright—to try and slow Pete down, but none were up to the task.

"You can explain the whole story in just two words—Pete Maravich," gushed A. J. Carr in the *Greensboro Daily News*. "[He] dribbled behind his back, hit every shot imaginable, some unimaginable, and flipped Bob Cousy passes to his towering teammates." One of Pete's incredible baskets was a hook shot launched from deep in the left corner.

When Pete left the game with 50 seconds remaining, the crowd leapt to its feet and showered him in applause. He scored 30 second-half points which gave him 42 (17-36, 8-8) for the game—a scoring record that stands to this day, surviving challenges from the likes of Bob McAdoo, Bobby Jones, David Thompson, John Lucas, Phil Ford, and hundreds of North Carolina high school phenoms. Brock said years later, "That will go down as the all-time best basketball team the East has ever fielded." The 110-79 victory was also the most lopsided in the event's history.

"All-American Pete Maravich, scorching the nets to mere ashes . . . lived up to all expectations in leading an East assault on virtually every scoring record," reported Tom Northington in the *Greensboro Daily News*. "The slender backcourt flash left his detractors guarding only thin air."

Unfortunately, many gifted high-school basketball players were not invited to the game that year. One of them was Lawrence Dunn, who attended the all-black Berry O'Kelly School. He and Pete were the county's high scorers but, in 1965, North Carolina did not permit interracial competition.

Dunn recalled the two crossed paths at an awards banquet held at the Raleigh Sports Club. "Pete got basketball Player of the Year. I got *independent* basketball player that year" recalled Dunn. After the ceremony, Pete rushed to Greensboro to prep for the All-Star Game while Dunn remained behind. "That hurt me as much as anything in my life. Pete went to the game and I went to a dance they were having at my school. People asked why I wasn't playing. That hurt."

"I wasn't a personal friend of Pete. We more were like rivals," Dunn said. "He knew who I was and I certainly knew who he was. Pete is somebody that got a lot of notoriety. I accepted that. I never said I was better than him. I know that he loved basketball better than anything. But I'll always wonder what was out there. That's why I really hated that I couldn't play in that East-West All-Star Game. I just always would like to know how I would have done." (Herm Gilliam, a future NBA teammate of Pete's, was also excluded.)

In 1966, one year too late for Lawrence Dunn, the contest was finally opened to every player in the state. Dunn continued his basketball life in North Carolina and years later, ironically, coached the East squad in the annual All-Star Game.

In just two seasons in Raleigh, Pete became a legend throughout North Carolina and, with an assist from *Parade* magazine, gained his first taste of national exposure. Meanwhile, Press's risky gamble to accept an assistant coaching position had paid handsome dividends. He'd led an underdog Wolfpack team to the NCAA Tournament and been voted ACC Coach of the Year. He was unquestionably a rising star in the southern coaching fraternity.

The Press and Pete Maravich show was on a roll.

4

The Lost Year

"It is at Southwood College that Pete Maravich will play his basketball this winter."
—Earle Hellen, sports editor, *Greensboro Record*

"Pete would shoot anybody for money—foul shots, jumpers, HORSE. I saw him spin the ball on his finger, throw it up in the air, bounce it off his head, and bank it in. I wouldn't dare play HORSE against him."
—Dickie Walker, Southwood College teammate

The Basketball Hall of Fame, the official NBA and NCAA guides, and every book written about Maravich (including his own) claim that Pete attended Edwards Military Institute in Salemburg, North Carolina, during the 1965-66 academic year. That is a slight misrepresentation, one Pete and his father purposely never corrected. He did complete a season of preparatory school, but not at Edwards, which folded in the spring of 1965. Instead, he attended the newly created Southwood College, a military school—some say a poor man's Citadel—located on the grounds of the old Edwards Academy.

Pete had three priorities at Southwood College: improve his game, strengthen his physique, and raise his SAT scores.

Pete was unhappy about living away from home for the first time. Press assigned Les Robinson, then coach of N.C. State's freshman team, the task of driving him to Salemburg. The trip took about 80 minutes and Pete sulked most of the way, Robinson recalled in a 1999 interview.

"I don't want to go. I'm not going," whined Pete.

"You have to. There's no choice. You want to play at N.C. State next year?" Robinson asked.

"You don't have to live there," retorted Pete. "You get to go home to your nice home and a wife."

Upon arrival, Robinson and Maravich went to check out Pete's dorm room on the third floor. It was a dreary room with cement walls, two beds, two desks, and a closet. Robinson looked at the prep All-American and quietly said, "Look, you have to do this." Then Pete tied a rope to a leg of his bed and extended the rope out the window. Apparently his father instructed him to have an exit in case of a fire.

The routine at Southwood was strict and regimented. Reveille sounded at 6:30 A.M., followed by inspections, formations, and a synchronized march to breakfast. Students were required to wear gray military uniforms every weekday.

The upside was that the Southwood Red Rams basketball team was loaded with talented players from up and down the East Coast. Chris Speciale and Fred Kornblith hailed from New York; John Lange came from New Jersey; and Bob Porterfield Jr. (son of major league pitcher Bob Porterfield) was recruited from Florida. "We were all there for the same reason," said Dickie Walker, who had led the state of Virginia in scoring (32 points per game) at James Blair High. "To get a scholarship to a major college."

John Lange, who met Chris Speciale on the train ride from New York, first heard the Maravich name while on board. "I told a passenger in Virginia that we were going to Southwood College for basketball. He said, 'Oh you'll get to play with Maravich.' I had never heard the name but I'll never forget how that stranger described Pete to us: 'Two broomsticks in sneakers.'"

Pete's roommate was his backcourt partner in the East-West All-Star Game, Willie Taylor, from Kingston, North Carolina.

Leading this group was head coach E. V. "Pete" Meadows, a gregarious, portly gentleman who became extremely popular with the team. Meadows, an ex-Golden Gloves boxing champ, attempted to equalize players' minutes to give everyone a good opportunity to showcase for the swarms of college recruiters who descended on games and practices. He also shielded his team from the scouts and kept a detailed file of each player's recruitment letters.

Southwood's schedule was peppered with several levels of competition, ranging from other military academies to junior colleges to freshman squads from major colleges. In fact, the freshman teams from the "Big Four" (UNC, N.C. State, Duke, and Wake Forest) were all on Southwood's schedule.

Because their games weren't sanctioned, Southwood players began organized practices as soon as they arrived on campus. "We started basketball the day we got to school. There's no October 15 in prep school. None of that bull," recalled Dickie Walker.

Pete dazzled his teammates right away. "The first time I saw him play, I just knew that there was a lot more to come. There was a magic-type quality," Walker said. "We went to the gym and during a run we had a three-on-one.

I was in the right-hand lane and I was sure he was going to pass the ball to me. Then he put it behind his back so I thought he was going to pass it to the guy in the left lane. Then he continued and put the ball all around his body and it went back to me. Pete just had something special about him."

Pete was also connected. His dad was the current ACC "Coach of the Year," and with that came some privileges. Press provided the entire Southwood team with tickets for an NBA exhibition double header at Reynolds Coliseum. One game pitted the world-champion Boston Celtics against the Philadelphia 76ers: Bill Russell vs. Wilt Chamberlain. Pete, who religiously watched whenever NBA games were televised (ABC broadcast just a game of the week), was thrilled to see the legends in person. Afterward, the two stars conducted a clinic together.

Southwood's season began on November 16, with an easy victory over Louisburg Junior College, 127-83. Pete had an impressive 34 points and the game featured the debut of his floppy wool socks. Southwood players all wore two pairs: knee-highs topped by sweat socks. Some players used tape to hold up the sweats, but Pete just let them sag. That look was to become his trademark.

For years, legend had it that Pete stole the "floppy" socks from the equipment room at N.C. State after working out with some Wolfpack players. "No matter what anybody tells you, those were N.C. State practice socks," said Les Robinson, who was there at the time. "We wore them in practice. One of the side benefits was to prevent blisters. These gray socks were unlike anything I had seen before. They were like hunting socks. I don't know who came up with the idea—probably the equipment man. But we only wore them in practice. Next thing you know, Pete was wearing them in games."

But according to Pete's good friend Bob Sanford, the socks came from his dresser. Pete would stay at Sanford's apartment during the summer months and play basketball up to 10 hours a day at the Raleigh YMCA.

"I used to wear these white cotton socks with these gray wool socks over them," recalled Sanford. "You could only get them at Johnson-Lambe sporting goods here in Raleigh. As they would get old, they'd get flimsy and fall around to your ankles. As usual, Pete had nothing to wear when he stayed with me, so he borrowed a lot of my clothes. One night, he went into my drawer where there were six or seven pairs of the gray socks, two or three of which were worn out. He grabbed a pair of the old ones."

Years later, Pete seemed to corroborate Sanford's version. "I was going to play ball with my friend Bob Sanford, and I forgot my socks," he told an interviewer in Baton Rouge. "So I borrowed a pair of old, gray, thick work socks from him. They were a little bit large and fell over my shoes. I had always felt slow because of my big feet, but the floppy socks covered half my shoes and made my feet look smaller, and somehow, it made me feel faster. I know it's a psychological thing but I've been wearing them ever since."

Southwood won its next two games before driving to Louisburg for a two-day Thanksgiving tournament. Prior to the trip Coach Meadows treated the entire team to a home-cooked turkey dinner at his house.

In the first game of the tournament Southwood overwhelmed Virginia's Newport News Apprentice, 113-72, with Pete and Dickie Walker scoring 40 and 27 points respectively. In the final game, Maravich and Walker scored 41 and 37, as the Red Rams defeated Hargrave Military Academy of Virginia, 103-67.

The headline in the *Sampson Independent* read: "Hot-Handed Rams Sweep Thanksgiving Tournament—As Pistol Pete Pops 41."

The Rams were undefeated through November, averaging more than 100 points a game, but December promised a tougher schedule. On December 10, Southwood faced the Duke freshmen in Durham. Playing for the Blue Devils that evening was Claudius Claiborne, the first black player in the history of the ACC. It's a tradition at Duke's Indoor Arena (later renamed Cameron Arena) for fans to taunt the visiting squad. Pete received an extra level of derision because the Blue Devil fans knew his dad's hated Wolfpack team had vanquished Duke in the ACC Tournament the previous spring. "They were unmerciful," recalled teammate John Lange.

But, according to one Duke fan, Pete had an unusual reaction. "We started razzing him. Usually this would panic an opponent, especially a freshman," recalled Vince Staten in the *Kentucky Courier-Journal* in 1997. "But not this kid. He liked it. He gave us grins and winks. And he gave us the game of a lifetime. First time he crossed mid-court and launched what had to be a 40-footer. Swish. We really started razzing him. So the next time up the court he did the same thing. With the same result. Swish. He gave us a look but not an angry look. It said, 'Watch this.' Our freshman coach—you may have heard of him, Chuck Daly—double-teamed him from then on. Didn't matter. This kid could shoot over any two guys. Anywhere from 40 feet in, he was a threat. He was the definition of unstoppable. Once, near the end of the first half, he was trapped at mid-court. He flipped a pass behind his back through two defenders, to a man wide open under the goal. Our fans gave him a standing ovation. Whether his team won or ours did is lost in my memory. All I remember is an unbelievable night from the greatest high school basketball player I have ever seen."

Duke did prevail despite the 27 memorable points from Maravich. "He's [Pete's] finding our ball tougher than in high school," Pete Meadows told a local reporter. "I've had to get on to him about being an individualist, but he takes it pretty well." Afterward, the team sat in the bleachers and watched Duke's varsity defeat the defending national champion UCLA Bruins, 82–66.

Pete was especially excited about Southwood's next contest, a father-son showdown between the N.C. State freshmen and Southwood College. Although Press didn't coach the frosh team, the game still generated a lot of buzz. So many fans wanted to see the "Maravich vs. Maravich" duel that the game was moved to a larger venue in nearby Clinton. The proceeds from the game, sponsored by the local Lions Club, went to various organizations serving the blind.

On Wednesday, December 15, the teams faced off with Press watching from the stands. Pete scored 26 points and Walker added 21, as Southwood trounced N.C. State, 90–73.

Next up was a Christmas tournament hosted by Mount Olive College, the first edition of an annual tourney that would later be named the "Pickle Classic." On consecutive nights at Olive's Henderson Gymnasium, Southwood beat South Carolina Baptist and then Mount Olive. Pete scored 59 points over two nights and was selected tournament MVP. As 1965 came to a close, Southwood's record stood at an impressive 11-2.

Southwood continued its mostly winning ways into 1966, with two games in particular providing extra drama. The first was a rematch with the N.C. State freshman squad, this time on the Wolfpack's home court in Raleigh, the city of Pete's high school glory. Pete later said the showdown was the highlight of the entire season. Many fans from Broughton High School jammed the sold-out Reynolds Coliseum on February 5—and Pete gave them their money's worth. He chalked up 33 points (14-28, 5-6) as Southwood downed State 91-57. He topped off his performance with a crowd-pleasing dribbling exhibition when the game was out of reach in the second half.

"It was really something—our taking State that way," Pete remarked. "After they gave the game the big father-against-son buildup. It made winning that much more enjoyable." Later that evening, in the varsity game, Press enjoyed his part of the double header as N.C. State easily beat Clemson, 76-58.

Four days later, Southwood entertained Baptist College of Charleston (now Charleston Southern University). It was the third meeting between the schools and the teams had split the first two contests. Pete's former Clemson neighbor, Howard Bagwell, was Baptist's head coach. (Bagwell hardly recognized the 6-4 Maravich earlier in the season.)

When the two teams came out for warmups, the bleachers in the South-wood gym were empty. Suddenly the back door flew open and a mock funeral procession entered. The creative students solemnly carried in a casket, accompanied by a sign that read, BAPTIST. A stream of students followed and soon the gym was filled with super-charged fans pumped up in antici-pation of another memorable game from Maravich. Pete didn't disappoint.

When the final horn sounded his 22 field goals and six free throws added up to 50 points, the first but hardly the last time he reached the half-century mark. Southwood won, 104-83, and a local newspaper headline blared: "50? Maravich."

Pete, quite naturally, enjoyed his offensive outbursts but discovered his high scoring led to impossible expectations. "One day I scored 50 points, and the next day the newspapers had it in big headlines," Pete told a reporter years later. "They just didn't seem to think it was possible for a prep-school kid to score that much in one game. I think that kicked everything off. After that, folks got to be conscious of how many points I scored from game to game."

Southwood finished the year with a record of 20-5—impressive for a team that played only four home games. Meadows presented five different awards and Pete was named Most Outstanding Player. Dickie Walker was awarded Most Valuable Player.

Even with his season in the rear-view mirror, Pete continued to work on his game relentlessly. "Once the season was over you would have mandatory study until 9:00 or 9:30 then we'd go to that old gym and play basketball until midnight or 1:00. Pete would never get tired. It seemed he could run for-ever," said Walker. "Now, we were not supposed to go out after hours. The commandant, Lieutenant Colonel Church, used to come over and we thought he would kick us out. But he allowed it."

Daily life at Southwood seemed simple and innocent. Students could buy a cheeseburger from Mrs. Martin at the snack bar for 25 cents; milk was a dime, a ham and cheese sandwich cost 20 cents. The school celebrated Hal-loween, Thanksgiving, and threw an annual Christmas party with music pro-vided by The Dynamics. Clubs on campus included glee, camera, bridge, pep, and projectionists. The motto of Southwood College was "Light Dispels Darkness." But, as the following story suggests, it wasn't all light for Pete.

Darrel Campbell, who helped Pete write his autobiography, remembers a cryptic late night phone call from a stranger just days after Maravich's death in 1988.

"I just need to speak to you," said the stranger.

"About what?" Campbell asked.

"Well, I was a classmate of Pete's and I just wanted to tell somebody about the way I treated him."

"What do you mean?"

"Back at prep school we all heard stories about how Pete was this bas-ketball stud. The cock of the walk. But we picked on him. Real bad. He was scrawny—like a beanpole. I remember one day he was just walking across the commons and I pushed him to the ground. We were all really rough on him. And I always wanted to say to him that I was sorry. Now it's too late."

Other than a pool hall in Salemburg, there was not much beyond the Southwood campus to entice a student. Pete would occasionally take his cue skills into town to blow off a little steam and earn some pocket change.

Because Salemburg was dry, players would hitchhike to bars in Fay-etteville on weekends. "We never drank in Salemburg. Now Fayetteville, that was a whole different story," recalled Dickie Walker. "Fayetteville is almost all military and one night we were in a bar. Of course we've got lots of guys from our team 6-8 and bigger, and so Pete would kid with people. Well, some of the soldiers took it the wrong way and a fight breaks out. And I got Pete out of there. Always an adventure with him."

After basketball season ended, Pete spent as many weekends as possible in Raleigh. There, along with freshman N.C. State coach Les Robinson, he would scrimmage against visiting prospects hoping for a scholarship. "He didn't want to be at Southwood. If he could swing it, he was here," remem-bered Robinson. "He loved working out with recruits. Pete and I would play every recruit that came in. Usually, you brought them in two at a time, and we'd beat these guys 21-2, 21-5, 21-4. I'd then go back and tell Coach Mar-avich, 'This player won't be able to cut it here in the ACC.' Years later I real-ized that I was making an unfair comparison. My judgment was skewed because I was basing everything on if a guy could guard Pete. But . . . nobody could guard Pete. We knew Pete was good, but we didn't know how good."

One of the recruits Robinson misjudged was Chad Calabria. Calabria had a stellar collegiate career at the University of Iowa and was later drafted by the NBA's Phoenix Suns.

Once again, Pete wasn't the only Maravich making noise in North Car-olina. Press added to his growing national reputation by coaxing another remarkable season out of his N.C. State players. In 1966 the Wolfpack returned to the finals of the ACC Tournament but lost a squeaker to Duke, 71-66.

Over two seasons Press compiled a 40-12 record. His 13-game turn-around in 1964-65 is the largest of any ACC coach to date. His .833 ACC

Tournament winning percentage remains the highest in the history of the conference. Press came close to repeating as conference Coach of the Year in 1966, barely losing to Duke's Vic Bubas.

On March 15, Press signed Pete's longtime friend (and North Carolina high school Player of the Year) Nelson Isley to a scholarship. Nelson was tight with both Maraviches and, for many years, roomed with Pete at the Campbell College summer basketball camp. The boys seemed inseparable and planned to play college ball together. It seemed like the Isley/Maravich era at N.C. State was about to commence.

But Pete was still having trouble holding up his end of the bargain. He could not seem to reach the ACC's minimum SAT score of 800. "Pete was a bright kid, but he was never into his studies that much," observed Les Robinson. "I could really relate to him because I was the exact same way. He just lacked that discipline and he couldn't make that score."

On his last try, Pete fell just shy of the mark with a 780. That failure put Press in a bind because his own son, one of the nation's top college prospects, was now ineligible to play at N.C. State. West Virginia University, coached by Bucky Waters, became Pete's fallback choice, followed by the University of Pittsburgh, and then Georgia Tech.

Press desperately wanted to coach his son. And, after all his success at N.C. State, he felt he was seriously underpaid. He went to N.C. State's administration and asked that the university supplement his salary of $8,500 by paying for his rent, laundry, groceries, and other living expenses. The school firmly refused, so Press began to shop around for another job. The NBA's Baltimore Bullets offered him a head coaching position, as did Louisiana State University.

Jim Corbett, LSU's athletic director, saw a golden opportunity to land a two-for-one deal: father and son. He dreamed of establishing a basketball tradition in the football-crazed region. In fact, there were already plans afoot to build a new basketball arena on campus. When Corbett first spoke to Press on the telephone, he got a taste of the feisty Serb's sense of humor. Press later recounted the conversation for *Atlanta Journal* reporter Furman Bisher.

"This is Jim Corbett, the athletic director at LSU, and I'd like to talk to you about our basketball coaching job."

Press shot back, "Yeah, and this is Adolf Hitler, and war is [expletive] when you finish second."

The conversation improved to the point where Press, feeling confident, brazenly asked for the moon: a five-year contract at double his current salary. Surprisingly, Corbett agreed—with one condition—Pete had to play at LSU.

Before making a final decision, Press sought the advice of Everett Case, the man who spearheaded the growth of "Tobacco Road" basketball. From Case's perspective the LSU position presented a wonderful opportunity for Press to create in Louisiana what Case had wrought in the Carolinas.

Next, Press had to get Pete on board. Paul Milanovich, a family friend from Aliquippa, knew Pete had his heart set on attending West Virginia. "Pete was actually coming to Morgantown while Press was in Baton Rouge negotiating his contract," Milanovich said in 2000. "Press knew Pete was on his way to West Virginia. He called here [Aliquippa] to get someone to stop Pete at the Pittsburgh Airport before he got his connecting flight. Finally, Joe Pukach got a hold of him at the airport and brought him back to Aliquippa. Press flew straight into Pittsburgh and made Pete sign the letter of intent with LSU."

At first Pete thought his father was joking, and declined to sign. "If you don't sign this paper, don't ever come home again," Press coldly told his son. (He also bribed him with a new Volkswagen Beetle.) Although LSU wasn't on his radar, Pete signed the letter. With that pen stroke, Pete was a step closer to achieving the first part of his childhood dream—playing college basketball.

On April 30, 1966, Press Maravich called a press conference to announce his departure from N.C. State University. His timing couldn't have been worse. Everett Case, the "Old Gray Fox," the man who brought Press to State, succumbed to cancer the same day. It was an unfortunate coincidence that left many Wolfpack fans with a sour feeling.

The Maraviches never referred to Southwood College again and also began to pretend Pete was younger, listing his birth year as 1948, not the actual 1947.

After 10 years in the Carolinas, the family was headed further south, this time to the college town of Baton Rouge. It was here, in this sleepy backwater city, that Press Maravich would unleash one of the most spectacular players in basketball history: a 6-5, mop-topped beanpole with a mind-boggling array of skills who would annihilate every major college scoring record, leaving awestruck fans and astonished historians to wonder if the standards he set would ever be reached again. And best of all for Press Maravich, this scoring machine, this unstoppable force, this once-in-a-lifetime player was his own son.

Pete Maravich was coming to the bayou.

Part 2

Louisiana State

All–Time NCAA scoring champion, January 31, 1970.

5

Baby Bengal

"I know the coach I want. Press Maravich. And he brings his kid with him. This kid could become one of the greatest players in the country."
—JAMES J. CORBETT, LSU ATHLETIC DIRECTOR

"In high school, passes were chest or bounce passes and you were looking at the guy you threw it to. All of a sudden, these passes were coming from between his legs, behind his back, at full speed while being guarded. Playing with him was like something out of a dream."
—RANDY LAMONT, LSU TEAMMATE

Louisiana State University (and Agricultural and Mechanical College) is located on more than 2,000 acres of prime real estate in Baton Rouge. The gorgeous campus features ornate buildings, vast lawns, grand magnolias, and hundreds of massive oak trees. The Mississippi River flows by on its western border. With more than 30,000 students and 1,300 full-time professors, the school is the premier state university in Louisiana.

Originally named "The Seminary of Learning for the State of Louisiana," LSU opened its doors on January 2, 1860—a full 10 years before the game of football was invented and 31 years before Dr. James Naismith created the game of basketball. In what would turn out to be a cruel irony, its first superintendent was West Point graduate William Tecumseh Sherman. The same Sherman who, in 1864 as a Union general, ordered his soldiers to cut a 70-mile swath of destruction through Georgia in what came to be known as "Sherman's march to the sea."

Sherman's former college did not fare well during the war. The school was badly damaged by marauding Northern troops who torched its library and supplies. The campus, originally located in Pineville, eventually moved to the state capital of Baton Rouge. It was in this location that LSU flourished and rose to prominence in the antebellum South.

When the Maravich family arrived at LSU, in the early summer of 1966, football owned the hearts of local fans. The sport was an obsession, bordering on religion, for the 165,000 residents of Baton Rouge and thousands more around Louisiana. On Saturdays in the fall, when the team played at home, fans would flock to Baton Rouge from across the state, filling all 67,510 seats in Tiger Stadium.

From 1936 to 1966, LSU appeared in 13 postseason bowl games, captured two Southeastern Conference titles, and one national championship. Tiger Stadium, dubbed "Death Valley," was bedlam on game days as loud, rabid fans often made it impossible for opposing players to hear their quarterback. One time-honored ritual, guaranteed to rattle opponents, involved wheeling "Mike," the Bengal tiger mascot, around the sidelines in his cage. The routine often climaxed when Mike roared into a microphone dangling near his face.

It seemed every Louisiana resident knew the team's history, especially the exploits of the 1958 national championship team and their overachieving third-team defensive squad nicknamed the "Chinese Bandits." Or the thrilling 89-yard punt return by future Heisman Trophy winner, Billy Cannon, on Halloween night in 1959.

The unbridled enthusiasm for LSU football stood in stark contrast to the campus-wide apathy for its basketball program. But it hadn't always been that way. Varsity basketball began at LSU eight years into the new century and, by 1935, the Tigers had won a "mythical" national title. That squad was led by Malcolm "Sparky" Wade, a 5-9 guard from Jena, Louisiana, who averaged a team-high 12.7 points per game.

Seventeen years later, LSU basketball coach Harry Rabenhorst recruited an extraordinary local athlete named Bob Pettit. Standing 6-9 and playing center, Pettit became the school's first three-time All-SEC selection as well as a two-time All-American. He led the Tigers to a second-place SEC finish in 1952, conference titles in 1953 and 1954, and a trip to the NCAA Final Four in 1953. He averaged 27.4 points and 14.6 rebounds per game.

Pettit's graduation in 1954 was followed by an era of mediocrity. Even the hiring of legendary Indiana high school coach Jay McCreary didn't turn the team around. McCreary had compiled an amazing 134-32 record at Muncie Central High School, but it was one of his 32 losses that brought him the most attention. That setback came on March 20, 1954, when a small, rural school from Milan, Indiana, (total enrollment 150) upset McCreary's heavily favored team to win the state high school title. The Cinderella story of Milan's win over Muncie Central was retold in the 1986 motion picture *Hoosiers*.

LSU athletic director Jim Corbett often joked about his desire to be trampled to death after a major victory by the LSU basketball team. "Basketball was about the third or fourth rung on the ladder," recalled Wayne Tipton, who played for LSU in the mid-1960s. "The whole state bled football."

Then Corbett landed Press and Pete Maravich. In the 12 seasons before they arrived on campus, LSU's basketball record was 108-189.

In late May 1966, Press met Donald Ray Kennard, Pete's academic counselor. The two hit if off right away. "Press was one of the greatest, most entertaining guys I've ever met," recalled Kennard, who subsequently became a Louisiana state representative. "Press told me, 'Donald Ray is too long. From now on you're X-Ray.'"

Press explained his son's struggles in the classroom. "Press told me, 'X-Ray, you're in charge of his academics. Pete knows his basketball but you're going to have to ride herd over him. . . . He's coming down June 1st. I want you to get him a summer job. I don't want him sitting around doing nothing.'"

Kennard contacted Dick Kelly, a rabid LSU booster who frequently employed Tiger athletes in his drugstore, Professional Pharmacy, located just off campus. Kelly agreed to hire Pete as a stock boy.

Several days later, Kennard met 18-year-old Pete Maravich. Like many who encountered Pete in a non-basketball environment, Kennard found him extremely shy and reserved, almost painfully so. "Your hours are about 8 A.M. to 5 P.M.," Kennard explained to Pete. "Mr. Kelly is a big ol' football player. He's about 5-foot-10, weighs about 280 pounds, and he'll break you in two if you don't do what you're supposed to do." Throughout the conversation, Pete said little and avoided direct eye contact.

On his first day of work at the drugstore, Pete showed up at 7:45 A.M., with a basketball under his arm. Kelly placed the basketball on a shelf at the back of the store. Pete's duties as a stock boy included sweeping, making deliveries, unloading boxes, stocking shelves, and removing items like baby formula when they had passed their expiration dates. Pete was allowed one 15-minute break mid-morning, an hour for lunch, and a 15-minute break in the afternoon.

At about 9:45 A.M. on his first day, Pete was ready for his mid-morning break. He approached his boss, "Mr. Kelly, may I have my basketball?"

"Basketball?"

"Yes, sir. I just want to work on my fundamentals back here in the stock-room if that's all right?"

Kelly later told Kennard that what happened next was the "dangdest" thing he had ever seen. In the small stockroom, Pete began a "mesmerizing" workout of "spinning that ball on all five fingers, doing gyrations between his legs, behind his back, bouncing it off his head." Fifteen minutes later, Pete calmly put the ball back on the shelf and returned to work.

At noon Pete asked for the ball again. This time he went out into the sweltering June heat and dribbled around the cars in the parking lot for 30 minutes. Then he strolled over to the Salt and Pepper Restaurant for a sandwich. At 3:45 P.M.—during his final break—he started another round of drills, only this time in a corner of the drugstore. Pete's antics began drawing a small crowd. Kelly called Kennard that evening and gushed, "You did me a favor. This was great for business in the afternoon. This kid is unbelievable." Soon Pete was putting on daily basketball demonstrations in the aisles of Professional Pharmacy.

In the summer of 1966 Press Maravich began to impose his will on Baton Rouge. As he had done years earlier at Davis & Elkins, Press was determined to spread the gospel of basketball throughout the town. With infectious enthusiasm he conducted dozens of basketball clinics, formed a local pep band (the Court Jesters), taught a master's course on basketball, and even talked his way into writing a column—*Two Minutes of Basketball with Press Maravich*—for a local newspaper.

Press also produced a 30-minute film that featured Pete demonstrating his "Homework Basketball" drills, and screened it frequently in gyms and meeting halls. Copies of the legendary 16mm film eventually made their way to basketball camps from coast to coast and were used as a motivational tool well into the next decade. After seeing Pete's improvisational style in the film, Carl Stewart, the black coach of Baton Rouge's McKinley High School, reportedly blurted out, ". . . he's one of us."

However, the arrival of the Maraviches didn't exactly create a buzz among the local press corps. Many sports writers were turned off by Press's brash proclamations about the alleged phenomenal abilities of his son.

"Basketball was a joke at LSU after Pettit graduated. We used to call them 'The Toothless Tigers,'" recalled Peter Finney, then associate editor of the *New Orleans States-Item*. "When the Maraviches hit town, the most people would do was take a wait-and-see-attitude."

Bud Johnson, LSU's new sports information director, also needed convincing. "You hear about these supposed 'great' athletes scoring a tremendous amount of points. Pete came right out of prep school and he was about 6-foot-4 and only 165 pounds. I was very, very skeptical."

Eventually Press persuaded Johnson to attend one of his basketball classes. "It was in that class that I first saw Pete Maravich. He put on a display for his father's summer physical education class for teachers studying for a master's degree. Well, I had never seen anybody handle the ball like that except for maybe Cousy. He did things with the ball that I had never seen before."

But it wasn't just Pete's ball handling wizardry that sold Johnson. "Prior to him ever playing a game that season, he impressed me as someone who was a very dedicated offseason player. He was coming from North Carolina to Louisiana where it's hotter, more humid, and it lasts longer. Pete said to me once in the summer of 1966, 'I don't see anybody around town playing basketball.' I said, 'Pete, that's not something you do in 95-degree weather.' The very next day, I saw him in the middle of the day—high noon—on an outdoor concrete court, challenging the heat. He was trying to prove that he could do it, that the heat was not going to bother him."

In 1966, Broussard Hall, where scholarship athletes were housed, was undergoing a major expansion, which included a new wing for the football team. As September approached, all the newly remodeled rooms were issued to football players, so the basketball team was forced temporarily into Pleasant Hall, the university's hotel. It was there that Pete met his freshman roommate, Randy Lamont.

Lamont hailed from Apple River, Illinois. Like Pete, he didn't know a soul when he arrived on campus. "The first thing that Pete and I did together, like basketball players do, is to go find a court and play," Lamont recalled.

Lamont noticed Pete's demeanor changed when he stepped on the floor. "His easygoing manner disappeared," Lamont recalled. "His passes would hit you square in the chest and you'd go, 'Where did that come from?' It took quite a bit of time to adjust to his style. But I knew right then, it was going to be an interesting four years."

Brad Brian, a 5-11 guard (and co-captain of the LSU varsity), recalled his first encounter with Maravich. Pete was on the sidelines of the old armory gym, quietly spinning a ball on his finger, when he was invited to join a pickup game between some freshmen and varsity players.

"Who's that?" Brian quietly asked a teammate.

"That's Coach Maravich's son."

Brian and his teammates relished the idea of showing the "skinny toothpick" from Carolina a thing or two about Louisiana basketball. "We heard that [northerners were superior] many times from Illinois players, or Indiana players. But it never panned out, so we always kinda giggled about it." A game of five-on-five began and Brian got a glimpse of Maravich's bag of tricks.

"Pete came on the floor and just put on a clinic," recalled Brian. "He was so deceptively quick. He was hitting people in the back of the head and the stomach with his passes. He faked a behind-the-back pass and brought it all the way around and laid it up. Then he dribbled between his legs and I didn't realize what he had done until a few seconds later. I saw him do something new every single possession of the game."

After Maravich's team won easily, Brian rushed back to his dorm room and phoned his older brother. "Buy every season ticket you can get your hands on," Brian instructed him. "I've just seen the greatest basketball player in my life."

Pete was trying to balance three areas of his life at LSU. In descending order of importance they were: athletic, social, and academic.

His basketball life was on track. Pete understood the opportunity LSU afforded him. He thought if he could turn some heads over the next few years, the other two jewels in his dream—a pro contract and a championship ring—might become a reality.

Pete's social life got a boost when he decided to pledge to the South's oldest college fraternity, Sigma Alpha Epsilon (SAE). On campus, SAE was known for its extravagant, alcohol-drenched parties. Pete's friends noticed that a beer or two seemed to transform him from shy to gregarious. Frosh teammate Bryan Flanagan remembered, "Pete was an SAE and I was a Sigma Chi. Their fraternity drank a lot more than we did. Not that we didn't do our share, but those guys were a little wilder and Pete fit in well over there."

LSU freshmen were required to wear a purple and gold beanie and subject themselves to some gentle hazing rituals. One custom was particularly colorful. While attending the first home football game of the season, the frosh were forced to wear their pajamas and remain standing until the Tigers scored a touchdown.

With an enrollment of 10,719 men and just 5,735 women, the dating odds for underclassmen were extremely long. Plus the female students were required to keep "hours." The young women were due back in their dorms or sorority houses by 11 P.M. on weekdays and 1 A.M. on weekends.

The least important area of concern for Pete was, as usual, his education. At a meeting with his academic counselor, Donald Kennard, they decided Pete would major in business. Kennard ran through the requirements: English, business administration, physical science or astronomy, and math.

LSU had an extensive academic support system. Incoming student athletes were required to study in their rooms (with the door open) every Monday through Thursday evening from 7:30 to 9:30. Proctors walked the halls and if an athlete needed extra help with any subject, a team of tutors was standing by in the squad room. If, after their first semester, the student athlete achieved a 2.0 average or better, the mandatory study was no longer compulsory. Pete liked to listen to his collection of 45s while studying. Kennard noticed that the small record player usually had a thick stack of 45s piled on the changer, ready to drop on the turntable.

For the first month of basketball practice, the varsity and freshman teams shared the University High lab gym. On Saturday, October 15, 1966, Pete walked onto the undersized court and, with no warmup, launched a 25-foot jump shot. "Stopped, popped, and hit it," Bernbrock recalled. "Didn't even take his warmup pants off."

Then, to loosen up, Pete started shooting long-range "Dolph Schayes-style" set shots. Schayes, a scoring machine for the NBA's Syracuse Nationals, had perfected his two-handed push shot during a 16-year Hall of Fame career. Pete employed this "old-school" technique for shot attempts in the 30-45 foot range.

Team manager David Tate didn't think much of the shooting display. "The other manager [Dexter Bott] and I were sitting on the bleachers and he told me that Coach Maravich's son was supposed to be a pretty good ball player," Tate said. "And this one kid was shooting shots out at the half-court circle. We knew that guy wouldn't make the team because they shoot jump shots nowadays."

Also observing from the bleachers was John Hutchison, a former player and coach at Mississippi State. He had heard Press rave about Pete's talents and was dubious.

"This I gotta see," Hutchison mumbled to himself. As the scrimmage began, Pete provided a glimpse into basketball's future. "I was seeing things I'd never seen before," Hutchison recalled. "I couldn't believe it. I began to pay attention. But I wasn't totally sold on it because I was thinking of a game situation with the pressure on—if he could still do those things."

When the 90-minute practice session concluded, Hutchison introduced himself to Coach Maravich and, after a minute of small talk, bluntly asked, "Press, do you really think Pete could deliver a behind-the-back pass, full speed, in a game situation?"

Press responded with two words: "Watch this." He tore an $8^{1}/_{2}$ x 11 inch piece of paper from a notebook and taped it to a wall, roughly at mid-court. Then Press summoned Pete and whispered some instructions. Pete took a basketball to the far end of the floor and, when Press blew his whistle, dribbled up the court at full speed.

"Well, Pete came down at full stride, and right before he hit the half-court line, he passed the ball behind his back. And hit the piece of paper!" Hutchison said. "Then Pete repeated the drill but this time beginning his sprint from the opposite basket and using his left hand. He hit the paper every single time down the court, with either hand. I couldn't believe it. After the seventh attempt, I walked up to the piece of paper and saw the basketball imprint. That made a believer out of me right away."

Word of Pete's exploits began to travel around campus and soon scores of people were showing up just to watch *practice*. And what they saw during those fall months of 1966 was the beginning of a basketball renaissance at LSU.

Flanagan remembered those practices, especially trying to disrupt Pete in fast-break drills. "I knew he was fancy because I watched him in warmups," Flanagan said. "Once I thought he was going to go behind his back. So I faked his fake and intercepted a behind-the-back pass. I thought to myself, *I can play with this guy*. Then we turned around and did it all over again on the other end of the floor. I'm still on defense and Pete is at the point again. Well, this time he whipped the ball behind his back, but held it, and brought the ball back out again and in for a layup. My jaw and jockstrap just fell to the floor."

On November 23, just eight days before their opening games, the frosh and varsity squads were finally permitted to practice inside LSU's arena, the John M. Parker Agricultural Coliseum. Typically the arena was booked for horse shows in the fall and the rodeo in late February. LSU's basketball games were sandwiched between those two annual commitments.

Nicknamed both "The Cow Palace" and "The Ag Center," the dowdy arena opened in April 1938 and sat nearly 9,000. It was an all-purpose facility, hosting political rallies, graduation ceremonies, cattle auctions, livestock shows, and rodeos. The farm animals left behind a lingering odor and the ceiling often leaked. When a portable wooden basketball court was laid over the massive dirt floor, the building was transformed into a low-tech hoops arena. And Pete Maravich's exploits under its flimsy metal roof would become the stuff of legend.

"Pete loved the Cow Palace," recalled freshman trainer Billy Simmons. "He always commented that the floor was great for his legs because it was set on piers and beams rather than a concrete slab, making the floor soft."

As the opening game approached, frosh coach Greg Bernbrock decided to use a three-guard offense. Joining Pete in the backcourt were Jeff Tribbett, a six-footer from Lebanon, Indiana, who played on the same high school team as schoolboy legend Rick Mount, and Rich Hickman, a six-footer whom Press had recruited from Aliquippa, Pennsylvania.

The starting five was rounded out by Drew Corley, a 6-5, 195-pound forward from Carl Sandburg High in Illinois, and Pete's roommate, Randy Lamont, a 6-8, 220-pound center, also from Illinois.

"What we had was a good group of athletes, but more importantly, we had great team chemistry," said Bernbrock. "We had four players that filled in nicely around Pete and their skills were exactly what we were looking for. They gelled very well as a team." Not one of the starters hailed from Louisiana.

One week before the season started the freshman and varsity teams faced off in an exhibition game. Freshman backup guard Dan Richey remembered, "Those guys physically killed us, but Pete got 49 points. There wasn't much of a crowd, but the buzz was, 'Man, LSU has a star, and he's a freshman!'"

At 5:45 P.M. on Thursday, December 1, 1966, the Maravich era at LSU began. The Baby Bengals took on Southeastern Louisiana College and, amazingly, a near capacity crowd jammed the Ag Center.

Southeastern guard, Larry Bagley, was a Louisiana native who relished the idea of beating LSU. "Since Hammond [where Southeastern was located] is so close to Baton Rouge, some of the local players were mad at LSU for not recruiting them, so they looked at the game as a payback," said Bagley.

Then Bagley learned of his assignment in a classic "good-news, bad-news" scenario. "The coach [Glenn Bowman] never told our team who would start. So just before we went out, he would read off the starters. After reading four names he finally read my name—which was a very big relief," recalled Bagley. "But then, he said he wanted me to guard Pete Maravich."

Earlier that week Bagley had read about Pete's exploits in the *Morning Advocate*. "We had all read about him in the varsity vs. freshman game and knew there was a player named Maravich that could score a bunch," Bagley said.

He scanned the large crowd during warmups and noticed his parents at center court. Sitting next to them was John McKeithen, the governor of Louisiana. This was not your ordinary game.

"I still remember the LSU team coming out. And Pete wasn't dressed exactly like the other players. Floppy socks, those low cut Converse shoes, and a gold necklace," Bagley said. "Wearing jewelry was something that wasn't done then and, of course, now there are rules prohibiting that."

Maravich wore No. 24. A year later he would switch to No. 23, his brother's high school number (also worn in the 1930s by Tiger great Sparky Wade).

"I kept looking for a tremendous basketball player," recalled Southeastern

Louisiana's sports information director Larry Hymel. "Looking for some giant superstar. And then I saw him. Maravich. He was just a skinny kid. He sure didn't look much like a basketball player."

Also in the stands was Billy Abrams, an LSU freshman who had heard fantastic rumors about his classmate. As the game began, Billy had trouble squaring those pronouncements with the reality unfolding before him. Pete grabbed the opening tip, dribbled down the right side of the floor, and stopped near the corner. He pivoted, jumped, and fired up a 20-footer.

"It hit the side of the backboard and the ball careened out of bounds behind the basket," recalled Abrams. "And I just shook my head and said, 'Oh, great.' This is the guy everybody's telling me about? This is the all-star basketball player that's gonna score 50 a game?"

Soon after that embarrassing misfire, Pete and his teammates started to click. Before long the Baby Bengals were dominating and the crowd was gasping at the exploits of the skinny magician. "In one night I tried to turn all the basketball skeptics into disciples, exposing them to a basketball game elevated from the normal sluggish, controlled tempo to a wide-open, catch-us-if-you-can style," Maravich wrote in his autobiography.

Bagley, a 17-year-old trying to defend a basketball genius in front of a hostile crowd, his parents, and the governor, had little chance. "I was a 6-5, 180-pound guard/forward and I was the best defender on our team," Bagley said. "I had learned to anticipate plays by watching other players' eyes. So, when I guarded Pete, especially on the fast break, I watched his eyes. Pete was the only player I ever guarded that never looked where he passed. He would come down the court and look straight in my eyes and never take them off me. And then [he] would make an unbelievable, spectacular pass to a teammate. Of all the dribbling and shooting, that was the most remarkable thing about him to me."

As the game progressed, Billy Abrams grew increasingly astounded by Maravich's capabilities. "After that first shot, it was just amazing," Abrams said. "I can still remember walking out of the Ag Center just shaking my head. I couldn't believe what I'd just seen."

What Abrams was lucky enough to witness was a 119-70 LSU victory featuring a spectacular triple-double by Maravich. Pete racked up a mind-boggling 50 points, 14 rebounds, and 11 assists. He had a hand in 72 of LSU's 119 points. On defense, he held Bagley to 14 points. The Maravich era was off to a promising start.

Unfortunately the LSU varsity did not fare as well, losing a squeaker, 89-88, to the smaller Southeastern Louisiana squad. It looked as though the varsity would endure another season of mediocrity.

After their dazzling opener the Baby Bengals became a hot ticket and, by the third home game, were selling out. A block of seats in the Ag Center was reserved each game for LSU students. "There were a limited number of student seats and the games started at 5:45. I would start to leave the fraternity house and walk over there earlier and earlier to make sure they let me in. The student crowd would begin to build out in front sometime after 3:00. Then probably 5:15, they'd open the doors and you'd just flash your student ID and walk right in," remembered Billy Abrams.

While the varsity continued to struggle, Pete Maravich and the freshman team were unstoppable, winning consistently and thrilling huge crowds with high-octane basketball. Unfortunately for the varsity, these huge crowds were only interested in seeing Pete and his teammates. As soon as the freshman game ended, many fans filed out of the building.

"The freshman games were at 5:45 P.M. and the varsity games were at 8:00 P.M.," recalled Dan Richey. "As a student or fan, you couldn't give up the entire night, so you either had to make a choice between the freshman game with this superstar or go to the lackluster varsity game. After that first game, the choice was obvious."

Team manager David Tate used to sit on the bench and watch the varsity react as the fans spilled out after the frosh game. "The players were heartbroken," recalled Tate.

"It was demoralizing to get dressed during the games and watch the freshmen play to a packed house, and when we came out, there were only 2,500 people left in the stands," added varsity co-captain, Brad Brian.

The freshman team was clicking on the court and learning to read Pete. If he dipped his shoulder or looked away, it could signal a behind-the-back or over-the-shoulder pass. Jeff Tribbett was the designated point guard but virtually every offensive possession ran through Pete. The most effective set play was called "The Special," where Pete ran off two screens while the other guards crossed. Rich Hickman knew the team's golden rule, "Never relax when Pete Maravich had the ball. You had to expect anything at any time."

One of the Baby Bengals' early opponents was the Baton Rouge Hawks, an independent AAU team led by player/coach John Hutchison.

"I could play defense. I'm 6-1, could dunk, and obviously jump. I was a very, very physical player," recalled Hutchison. "Pete's speed down the floor was unbelievable because he had the greatest change of pace I had ever seen. That's what really throws people off. He could be cruising, then change his pace on the ball. If he went to the baseline and you tried to cut him off, well, he could pull a reverse dribble and then spin on you. You just didn't have a chance. That was Pete. He scored 66 points and no one had ever scored that many points against the Hawks before."

The freshman starting five was becoming a tight-knit group on and off the court. Many nights the team would cram into Pete's new tan Volkswagen Bug and head out on the town. They dined in local restaurants and frequented movie houses like the Paramount, Hart, Broadmoor, and the Gordon (actor Steve McQueen was a particular favorite of Maravich's). Sometimes after LSU football games, they would watch television or head back to the gym and play ball until two or three in the morning.

"We did the college scene," said Paul Milanovich, a freshman reserve. "The drinking age in Louisiana was 18 or 19 at that time and we went to the local watering holes. We did a dance, enjoyed ourselves as college boys, but we really never got into bad trouble. We were a mischievous group, and Pete sure had a mischievous streak in him."

But not all freshman players shared the bond that was developing between Pete and the other starters.

"I felt like I never fit in with those guys," said freshman teammate Bryan Flanagan. "They had things going on at Broussard Hall, the jock dorm, that I wasn't privy to. I was a walk-on, so I just had to suck it all up."

Flanagan also felt Pete could be mean-spirited.

"I remember one time practicing in the John Parker Coliseum," Flanagan said. "We were on a fast break and I took the ball. Pete was at mid-court and I crossed over and beat him because he wouldn't play defense. Well, he grabbed my arm and spun me one way and I lost the ball. And everybody kind of laughed. Coach Bernbrock thought I was dogging it and made me run the stairs. Pete just laughed, but he never told the coach that he grabbed my arm or that it was his fault. He just walked away. That was typical."

Meanwhile, Press Maravich was having problems with the varsity team. He was trying to squeeze out wins with a squad that had five returning lettermen from the 6-20 team of the previous season.

"There are no lofty expectations of the 1966-1967 Tiger basketball team," read that year's media guide. That was an understatement. By the third game, against Texas, Press was badly frustrated. He delivered a terse pregame "pep talk": "Okay you bunch of [expletive], keep it as close as you can tonight." A couple of players were so incensed they refused to play. But after an emergency team meeting, the "striking" players relented and took the court. LSU lost 114-78.

As the season progressed, Press began to shift his focus, concentrating more on the freshman team than his varsity squad. He delegated greater coaching responsibilities to his assistant, Jay McCreary, and eventually decided to combine the practices.

Freshman Dan Richey liked the new arrangement. "The first string varsity practiced against the first-team freshmen. Second team varsity scrimmaged the second-team freshmen. In other words, if you're playing up, which the freshmen were doing, they're only going to get better. And we did get better every week."

Pete's game also benefited. "We practiced with the freshmen a lot and it was my job to push Pete to the left, where he was weak," remembered then senior forward Wayne Tipton. "And eventually his left was better than anything we had going. It just took his game to another level."

For the varsity players who had to "play down," the scrimmages were of little value. "Our season was centered around beating the freshmen in practice. That's a heck of a way to look at it, but that was it," said Brad Brian. "Press was so focused on Pete that he really didn't coach the varsity as much. He didn't spend a whole lot of time with us seniors, so there were some bad feelings about that."

Making matters worse, Press publicly bragged that the freshman squad dominated the scrimmages. "I don't know if we lost more than twice to them," said Brian. "The stories Press used to tell the media that they beat us every day in practice were not true. That was even more demoralizing to us."

Also, many players perceived a regional bias in coach Maravich and McCreary. Both were considered "Yankees" who recruited almost exclusively north of the Mason-Dixon Line. "Press had an attitude if you weren't from the North, you couldn't play basketball. And he exemplified this on a daily basis by showing favoritism to the northern recruits," recalled freshman reserve Robbie Lowther, Jr.

The pressure of the new job was giving Press an ulcer. To relieve the stress he chewed tobacco, gnawed on towels, took tranquilizers, and gulped antacid tablets by the fistful.

The tense situation boiled over on December 30, when the varsity played in the Poinsettia Classic, a tournament held in Greenville, South Carolina. LSU's opening game had been a major disappointment for Press as they lost to Clemson, 92-82, spoiling his homecoming. The next night LSU endured a 19-point loss to Rice in the consolation game. It was the Tigers' seventh defeat in nine games. An enraged Press stormed into the locker room and accused his team of intentionally throwing the game.

" . . . we couldn't have thrown a game if we had to," said Brad Brian. "He supposedly had us investigated, but whether he did or not, I don't know. But that's the way he treated us."

As the varsity melted down, the freshmen got stronger. On January 7, the varsity was scheduled to appear on television as part of the SEC's *Game of the Week*. Because the broadcast began at 2 P.M., the game preceded the freshman team's. True to form, the varsity was easily beaten by the University of Florida, 87–70. After its victory, the Florida team sat courtside, curious to watch Maravich.

Against a local AAU team sponsored by Borden Milk, Pete put on another electrifying show. At one point, with the fans screaming, "Shoot Pete! Shoot Pete!" he drained three consecutive two-handed set shots from just inside mid-court. As each rainbow whistled through the net, the arena exploded.

"The Florida varsity players were coming up out of their chairs," recalled Billy Abrams. "It was astonishing. Jumping up, turning around, and slapping each other's hands. I was having more fun watching them watch Pete than I was watching Pete."

Pete finished with 40 points (17–30, 6–9, 11 rebounds, 18 assists) as the Baby Bengals chalked up another victory. Turned on by the crowd, Pete demonstrated his love for creative basketball, his determination to win, and his passion to entertain.

"Pete was an unconscious competent," explained Greg Bernbrock. "He may not have known exactly what he was going to do on the floor—and no book can tell you how to do it. But he did things instinctively. He was such a marvelously gifted athlete and so competitive. But it was the roar of the crowd that would bring him to the greatest heights as a player and a show-man time and time again."

Flushed with excitement, Pete drank a few beers after the contest. After all, it was Saturday night and he was fast becoming the most famous athlete on campus. As the evening wore on, he found himself in a drunken con-frontation with a football player. The jawing escalated to physical contact and the athletes had to be separated, but not before Pete twisted a knee.

The injury wasn't serious, but Press was furious. He knew Pete had trou-ble handling beer and decided to lay down the law to the entire team. He decreed that any future alcohol or curfew violation would result in expul-sion. "You're off the team," Press told the boys. "No questions asked."

Press then suspended his son for one game.

In that game Jeff Tribbett was given the green light to shoot as Pete watched from the bench in street clothes. Tribbett came up big, scoring 52 points in a 97-82 victory over Southern Mississippi. The Baby Bengals ran their record to 13-0.

After the suspension was lifted, Pete continued his prolific marksmanship scoring 50 points against Loyola, 57 against Auburn, and 53 at Mississippi State.

The residents of Hattiesburg, Mississippi, still talk about the day Pete came to play University of Southern Mississippi. On February 9, 1967, more than 8,000 fans packed the Reed Green Coliseum—unheard of for a fresh-man game. Southern Miss' Wendell Ladner, determined not to be embar-rassed in front of the home crowd, played aggressive, physical defense against Pete. Midway in the first half, he undercut Pete, flipping him in the air and head first onto the floor. Blood poured from Pete's forehead and he was rushed to the school's infirmary.

Doctors stopped the bleeding and stitched him up. With a bandage above his right eye and seven stitches across his brow, Pete returned for the second half. The accident seemed to motivate Pete, who put on a stunning shooting exhibition, firing in 31 second-half points to bring his game total to 42 (15-29,12-12, 11 rebounds, 4 assists) in a thrilling 94-86 LSU victory.

With the basketball season winding down, Press arranged a bonus matchup between the freshman teams of LSU and the University of Ten-nessee. Tennessee was also undefeated so the game served as an unofficial "SEC Freshman Championship." LSU had a 16-0 record and loads of confi-dence as it boarded the flight to Knoxville for the season's final contest.

The game didn't begin well for the Baby Bengals. "I remember it like it was yesterday. We got behind right away," said Dan Richey. "They had a bet-ter team than we did. Plus they were playing at home. We weren't even in the game for most of it."

Although Tennessee's 1-3-1 defense was giving Pete fits, LSU managed to close the gap to 75-73 with eight seconds remaining. They got the ball to Maravich, who split two defenders and stopped on a dime, causing Tennessee's center to tumble into him. "Pete created the foul because he thought two shots at the free-throw line was a better risk than a rushed Hail Mary shot," recalled LSU's Robbie Lowther.

Maravich was shooting 83.6 percent from the free-throw line. He ap-peared calm as the Tennessee crowd began screaming. Pete methodically bounced the ball a few times and swished it through. The score now stood 75-74. By the time the referee handed the ball to Pete for his second attempt, the noise was deafening. Once again, he eyed the front of the rim. A possible per-fect season rested on this one shot. "I'll never forget it," said Greg Bernbrock.

"He lofted it up. It went inside the cylinder twice, it went round and round, and somehow or another, it came back out. It would have given us the perfect season."

Actually, it would have forced the game into overtime. But it wasn't to be. The Volunteers successfully ran out the clock, handing LSU a stinging 75-74 defeat.

The loss, coupled with a weak shooting night, 31 points (12-36, 7-9, 6 rebounds, 6 assists), sent Pete into a deep funk. By the time Press made his way into the locker room to console his son, he was nowhere to be found. But Press had to put Pete's disappearance out of his mind as he prepared the varsity for its game (LSU lost, 87-60).

Later that evening, father and son met up at the Holiday Inn in Knoxville, approximately two miles from the Tennessee campus.

"What happened to you?" Press inquired.

"I left the field house by myself," Pete said, holding back the tears. "I walked back."

Press understood the feeling. About 30 years earlier, he had walked 12 miles home after Rochester defeated his Aliquippa High School team.

Later Pete remembered the devastation of that loss. "I felt like I had let the team down. I knew how badly they all wanted that undefeated season and I had messed it all up by blowing a foul shot. A foul shot! The easiest thing in the world to make and I missed the biggest one I ever had to shoot."

Crushing as it was, the loss did not diminish Maravich's monster season. He averaged 43.6 points, 10.4 rebounds, and 7.3 assists as the Baby Bengals finished 16-1. Press's LSU varsity, on the other hand, limped through a 3-23 campaign.

With the loss weighing heavily on Pete's mind, he and Jeff Tribbett drove to Ft. Lauderdale for spring break, where they enjoyed free room and board courtesy of Tribbett's aunt and uncle. It was Pete's first visit to Florida and he loved the beach. The two sunned by day and chased women by night. On a few afternoons, they strolled to the cement basketball courts at the south end of the beach to find some action.

It was a tricky place for visitors to play because hot sand, kicked up by ocean breezes, blew across the courts occasionally. Pete and Tribbett acclimated quickly and soon were hustling other vacationing college kids for easy money. They spent the cash in several of the bars that lined the Ft. Lauderdale strip.

Back at LSU, Pete spent the last few months of his freshman year relaxing. He played tennis and golf. Sometimes he and other varsity players like Wayne Tipton and Buddy Shirley traveled to Brad Brian's house in Baton

Rouge for raucous parties. But mostly he loved driving around with his buddies packed into his Volkswagen. Occasionally it was dinner (Pete's favorite: steak and eggs) or a movie that brought the crew together, but more often than not it was the siren call of the local bars.

LSU was an alcohol-free campus, and so no intoxicants were allowed within a mile of the school. The drinking age in Louisiana was 18 at the time, which meant thousands of LSU students were legally permitted to patronize the bars of Baton Rouge. Many drove their cars to the taverns and many drove back to campus intoxicated. Pete, in his little Beetle, was occasionally among that group.

As a result, Pete racked up a few DUIs his freshman year. Although school officials and local police attempted to hush it up, his drinking offenses became well known on campus. One judge required him to record radio commercials espousing the virtues of defensive driving.

"It was a situation with college guys going out and blowing off a lot of steam," recalled Tribbett. "College kids like to party and have a good time, that's part of the deal, right? From October to March, we didn't do anything. We had to be in shape for basketball. We weren't out at fraternity parties going crazy. Did he [Pete] get out of hand sometimes? Sure he did. Did other people get out of hand? Sure. Did I get out of hand? Yes. It's not something I'm proud of. But it happens."

Academically, Pete chose the path of least resistance. Unlike his father, Pete did the minimum amount of schoolwork and was always more motivated to play a pick-up game of hoops, catch a movie, or shoot pool rather than study. One of his frosh classes was Introduction to Horticulture 101. "He got a B-plus with no effort whatsoever," remembered instructor Earl Barrios. "A lot of athletes took my course. It was quite easy."

Things were a bit tougher in sociology. As finals approached, Pete needed help from teammate Dan Richey. Pete learned that Richey had compiled a comprehensive course review that would be a perfect study guide for the exam.

"Man, I'd like to have one of those," said Pete not so subtly.

"Pete, I need something for something," replied Richey.

"What do you want?"

"I've got this brother of mine at home. He's a good kid and I'd like for you to write him a letter and inspire him to be the best that he can be."

Richey recalled: "I never thought I'd see a letter from Pete, but . . . he wrote the letter for me and all I had to was drop it in the mail. My brother loved that letter so much that he had it tacked on his wall for years."

March 21, 1967

Dear Bob,
Since meeting you at one of our freshman basketball games, your brother Dan
has talked about you quite a lot. He has relayed to me your dedicated ambi-
tion to become a basketball player. I would just like to impress upon you a few
short points to remember while you are growing up in the greatest game in the
world today. Always remember Bob, that to become a great basketball player,
you must possess deep dedication to yourself. You should always strive to be
better, and never settle for second billing. To play basketball requires a tremen-
dous amount of practice and conditioning. At your ripe age, you should practice
a minimum of one hour a day. When you reach high school, you will begin to
compete against several top-notch players, but if you are willing to work while
you are young, you will have a big step on many of the players. All of these
points can be summed up in one three-letter word, and this word is "guts." If
you want to be great Bob, practice, practice, and practice. Well, I must get back
to my studies; I'll be looking forward to reading about you. Good luck and
shoot 'em down.
> *Your Pal,*
> *Pete Maravich*

Even though Pete miscounted the number of letters in the word "guts,"
he met his end of the bargain, got the study guide, and passed sociology.

Carol Percy, an LSU student, remembers taking English with Pete. "[Our
instructor] seemed thrilled to have the Pistol Pete in her class and it was very
clear her demeanor changed when addressing him," Percy said. "She did not
give As, which annoyed me as English was always one of my best subjects.
Back then, grades were posted by student ID number, without names, but in
A-B-C order. When final grades were posted there was only one "A" in the
class, and we all stood there figuring out it had to be Pete as it was midway
down the page. It was no secret that athletes at LSU were practically given
their grades."

On the home front, Press and Pete were dealing with a chronically troubled Helen. She was geographically isolated from her friends in Pennsylvania
and South Carolina, removed from the basketball world of Pete and Press, and
worried about Ronnie who was fighting in Vietnam. Adding to her stress load,
she was the prime caregiver for Diana, an active three-year-old. Her emotional
breakdown, which began in Raleigh, only worsened in Baton Rouge.

Her behavior at Pete's games grew more erratic and, by season's end,

Press had barred her from the Ag Center. Helen sought solace in a liquor bottle. "She kept saying to me, 'Joyce, I'm not the same person you knew back in Clemson,'" recalled family friend Joyce Bagwell.

Cindy Marshall remembers meeting Helen, a friend of her parents, during that time period. Helen greeted the Marshall family with hugs and smiles. But as the visit wore on, Helen's demeanor transformed dramatically. "I remember being struck by her beauty and the extreme sadness in her eyes," said Marshall. "Press arrived a few hours after we did, and the talk immediately turned to basketball. I remember my mother and Helen going into a separate room and shutting the door. The Helen in that room was completely different than the woman who greeted us. When we left later that day, my mother cried for the plight of her old friend."

The strain in the Maravich home was palpable. Press often came home in the evenings and found the house in shambles. Many days Helen was unable to function, on a few occasions she left recently purchased groceries in the car to spoil. On those days it was left to Press to cook, clean, do laundry, and watch over Diana. He also had a basketball program to run.

During the summer of 1967, his last in relative anonymity, Pete performed his basketball drills at various camps in Pennsylvania, New York, Maryland, and North Carolina. His stays at the camps ranged from an afternoon to a week or two.

Pete had distilled the "Homework Basketball" drills into an entertaining clinic. Belying his shy demeanor, Pete confidently ran through the eye-popping demonstration with military precision. He loved inspiring kids. Plus, it was a great way to earn extra spending money.

"Charlie Scott, Mike Maloy, Pete, myself, and a few players from the New York-New Jersey area were working at a basketball camp at Davidson College where Lefty Driesell coached," recalled basketball Hall of Famer Dave Cowens. "We were all staying in the same dorm and each guy would coach a team. What Pete would do was demonstrate and lecture for the kids because of his ability with the ball. They had pro coaches and players teach but Pete was the only college player giving a demonstration." Cowens and the other players got $35 a week while Pete was pulling down $100 *per demonstration*.

Pete was invited to perform his clinic in California for a Christian organization named Athletes in Action. Fred Crowell, the program's basketball coach, knew Press and asked if Pete would do a demonstration for a group of 40-50 high school kids. The idea appealed to Pete, mainly because it would give him a chance to visit sunny California.

The religious aspect of the job offer was no draw for Pete. Since the age of seven, he had only worshipped basketball. Required to attend church services with his parents when the family lived in Clemson, he had been bored by the Sunday ritual. "I would literally sit there and count ticks in my head, 'One, two, three,' and I would go up to a minute, and then count to an hour until I got out of there," said Pete. "I felt that if I were in church for an hour, somebody in Philadelphia, L.A., Boston, or New York was playing basketball. And when it came down to getting that scholarship, I would not get it.

"I was not raised in a Christian home. I was raised in a church home. When we moved down to Clemson, they really didn't have time to go, but they made sure that I did. But when I got into church, I never did hear anything. I never heard who Jesus Christ was when I was young because I didn't want to hear."

Pete and a friend from campus named Kenny piled into the Volkswagen and began the long drive to California. Along the way they discussed Vietnam, race riots, girls, and basketball while listening to the Rolling Stones and the Beatles, whose groundbreaking *Sgt. Pepper's* album had just been released. The trip took five days and, shortly after arriving in Arrowhead Springs, Pete began to regret his decision.

"We got on this campus, and I saw these people, and they were all sitting around playing music," Pete recalled. "And they were singing songs under trees, and they were holding hands in prayer under trees, and I was completely embarrassed. I didn't want any part of that. I told my friend, 'Hey, we gotta get out of here. I'm going to hurry up and do my clinic and get out of here. These people are nuts. What are they smoking?'"

The next day Pete got his trip to the beach, but it was with a group of people who were more interested in saving souls than romping in the surf. Bill Battle, an All-American football player at the University of Alabama, led the young missionaries onto the sand with a reluctant Pete bringing up the rear.

"I went with them to the California beaches, and he [Battle] goes right up to the worst looking group," Pete recalled. "Hair down to here, body covered in tattoos, smoking a joint, drinking. There were about four or five of them. Real mean looking, ugly, and they didn't smell very good. I stayed way in the background. He [Battle] went up to the meanest looking guy and said, 'You know, I'd really like to share something with you folks.' And he witnessed to them. Some left right away and said, 'Oh you Jesus freaks.' I turned my head. I didn't want any part of it."

By the third day, Pete still had not presented his clinic, and it appeared as if he might not get the opportunity. "For three days, I finally heard who Jesus Christ was. I heard how he had died for me. I heard that I wasn't a very good person. I always thought I was good. I mean I was a pretty good guy. I never really hurt anybody. Sure, I'd go out and get drunk. But I mostly hurt myself."

One afternoon, Bill Bright, leader of Campus Crusade for Christ, delivered a message to more than 1,000 people. At the end of his sermon, Bright invited all in the audience step forward and receive Christ. When Kenny began to rise, Pete was mortified.

"My friend got up. I said, 'What are you doing?' He said, 'Pete, I don't know what to tell you. I really don't know what to tell you. I've just received Christ into my life.' I said, 'Kenny, maybe it was something you ate.' And I grabbed him by the arm. I literally tried to steal away his salvation. I said, 'Don't go up there. You'll embarrass me.'"

As his friend walked forward, Maravich had his own spiritual conversation, "You're not going to get me, God. You're not going to get me. I'm going to be on a pro basketball team, be on a championship team, and make a million dollars. That's what I want in life. I reject you."

The car ride back to Louisiana was not nearly as fun. Pete was seething as Kenny read out loud from the Bible. After about the fifth verse, Pete lowered his mirrored sunglasses to indicate his disdain. When that didn't work he turned up the radio to drown out his now born-again friend. "As my friend quoted scriptures," said Pete, "I remembered the 124 assists I had on the year, wishing I would have had one more to win the Tennessee game."

Summer turned to fall and the 1967-68 season loomed on the horizon. The year would present a major challenge for Pete Maravich. All eyes would be watching to see if he could repeat his stunning freshman success against older and bigger varsity players. And, for the first time in his life, his father would officially be his head coach.

Press, of course, relished the prospect.

"Pete's freshman year was just a preview. Wait till you see him with the varsity," Press beamed. "It'll be something special. He can do more things with the ball—and without it—than any kid in the country. Cousy never saw such moves. Will he be this team's leading scorer? You bet your life he will, unless he breaks both legs. And if I know him, even that won't stop him. This kid lives for basketball. He'll play and he'll shoot just as often as he gets clear. No doubt about it. I'd have to be crazy not to let him shoot."

Press Maravich wasn't kidding.

6

Showtime

"This boy is near as the complete basketball player you'll see anywhere."
—ADOLPH RUPP, UNIVERSITY OF KENTUCKY COACH

"Marvelous Pete Maravich. Dribbling, shooting, passing, rebounding. He can go left or right with equal facility, he has every shot known to man, with both hands, but, amazingly, the strongest part of his game is his deft passing."
—CURRY KIRKPATRICK IN *SPORTS ILLUSTRATED*

A s the 1967–68 season approached, the nation's most prominent collegiate player was UCLA's giant center Lew Alcindor. The previous year, the 7-2 sophomore sensation and his UCLA teammates dominated college basketball, going undefeated on a relentless march to the NCAA championship. Most prognosticators felt the Bruins were a lock to repeat as champions in the second year of "King Lew's" reign. The NCAA did place a small obstacle in Alcindor's way, though, by initiating a new rule: "No player will be allowed to dunk a basketball in a game or in warmups."

In its Annual College Basketball Preview issue, *Sports Illustrated* spotlighted an unknown scoring sensation who "is a good bet to become the first sophomore to win the scoring title since Oscar Robertson accomplished that a decade ago." The magazine was referring to 5-9 Calvin Murphy, a quicksilver guard who averaged 48.9 points as a freshman at Niagara College in upstate New York.

A few sportswriters named Pete Maravich to their "preseason All America" teams but, for the most part, he was still largely unknown.

But deep in Louisiana, the word was out. Thousands of fans had witnessed Maravich tear through freshman squads and were eager to see if his flashy style would succeed against the nation's best college talent. Perhaps Pete could lead LSU to the same success it enjoyed during the halcyon days of Bob Pettit.

"I just want to play on a winner," Pete told reporter Paul Phillips. "There's a mighty long list of big scorers who didn't play on a winner. I don't want to get on that list."

One indicator of the fan's faith in Pete was season ticket sales: all 4,000 were sold, remarkable considering the team was coming off a 3-23 season. "Before Press Maravich came," recalled Bud Johnson, former LSU information director, "our season ticket sale was about 40. I used to make my wife go to the games so there would be one less empty seat."

For Pete, playing on the varsity meant finally being coached by the man who molded him.

"I wanted to play for my dad and I think he wanted to coach me," Pete said at the time. "We knew how tough it would be on both of us if we went to the same school, but a chance to revive basketball at a place like LSU seemed like an appealing challenge."

LSU's roster had no seniors as Press decided to build around Pete and his teammates from the freshman squad. Junior Ralph Jukkola was the single returning starter. "I hope our fans won't expect too much from the team this year," Press warned the press corps. "We're the youngest team in the Southeastern Conference and have the least depth."

The biggest challenge for Press and his assistant, Jay McCreary, would be overcoming the team's lack of height. Of the starting five, Randy Lamont at 6-8 and Pete at 6-5 were decent sized, but 6-3 Jukkola was small for a forward, and the guards, Rich Hickman and Jeff Tribbett, were undersized at six feet tall. Press hoped to compensate with a running, attacking offense led by his high-scoring son, and a smothering defense that pressured the ball from end to end.

On December 2, 1967, the moment of truth arrived. "This is what I have worked for all these years," Pete told Paul Phillips. "I just hope that people will realize that I am not a superman, that I am just another fish in the pond."

The malodorous Agricultural Center was filled to capacity for Pete's varsity debut, against the University of Tampa. In attendance were Louisiana Governor John McKeithen; the former governor, Jimmie Davis; jazz trumpeter Al Hirt; and actor James Drury, star of the NBC television series *The Virginian.*

When LSU ran onto the floor, Pete wore his old lucky No. 23 jersey. No longer stick-thin, he weighed nearly 180. Bunching down over his black, low-top Chuck Taylor sneakers were a pair of thick gray socks. The socks would become a permanent part of his uniform this season. Pete whipped the crowd into a frenzy during warmups with an entertaining mix of dribbling drills, fancy passes, and jaw-dropping shots from various angles and distances.

It was the birth of "Showtime," a term that described the electric atmosphere Pete generated whenever he performed his basketball wizardry. "It's supposed to be a no-no to talk about basketball as entertainment," Maravich told *SPORT* magazine. "That's bull. I believe you make your fans. You create them by giving them a show."

Pete's debut was stunning. He scored 48 points (20-50, 8-9, 16 rebounds, 4 assists) as LSU pulled away in the second half to beat Tampa, 97-81. Under Press's guidance, the 1967-68 LSU Tigers had their first win and a blueprint for the future: Get the ball to Pete.

Observing the pandemonium that evening was Bennie Lennox, a scout from the University of Texas. He was astonished at Pete's shooting range. "Maravich was hitting goals from a distance almost impossible to believe," said Lennox.

Across the nation fans picked up their Sunday newspapers and read AP and UPI accounts of the game. Pete's scoring total and catchy nickname jumped off the page: 48 points scored in the varsity debut of "Pistol Pete" Maravich. The fever that had inflicted Louisianans was beginning to spread.

LSU had little time to rest (or celebrate) as it flew to Austin the next day for a matchup with the University of Texas. Jeff Tribbett was Pete's roommate at LSU's Broussard Hall but Pete's road roommate was junior Rusty Bergman. Press liked the idea of an upper classman keeping an eye on his son.

Coach Maravich was looking to avenge a crushing 36-point loss to Texas one year earlier. Leon Black, Texas's new head coach, told the *Austin American*, "LSU had one of the five best freshman basketball teams in the country last year and I think it's significant that four sophomores will be starting against us."

Five thousand fans squeezed into tiny Gregory Gymnasium to cheer on the undefeated Longhorns. "Texas had the most obnoxious crowd," remembered Jukkola. "They would always stand up and sing "The Eyes of Texas are Upon You," before the national anthem. Then they threw ice at us on the bench. They were really hostile."

Coach Black decided to aggressively pressure Pete and gave the assignment to 6-3 guard John Matzinger. In less than five minutes Matzinger had picked up three personal fouls so 6-1 senior Billy Arnold took on the task of stopping Pete. Arnold was equally overmatched, and by game's end Pete had racked up 42 points (15-34, 12-16, 5 rebounds, 5 assists) in an 87-74 LSU romp.

Pete told an AP reporter afterward: "I'm only shooting 40 percent and that's not too good. I should be shooting over 50 percent. I'm in a slump." Press was more concerned that, for the second consecutive game, LSU had been out-rebounded.

The Pistol Pete express continued to roll as Maravich broke out of his "slump," scoring 51 points (22-43, 7-11, 9 rebounds, 4 assists), in a 90-56 blowout of Loyola of New Orleans. Now 3-0, LSU had already matched its win total from the previous year.

In mid-December LSU traveled north to participate in the Milwaukee Classic, a two-day tournament co-sponsored by the University of Wisconsin and Marquette University. Interest in the local teams, combined with Maravich's growing fan base, resulted in the Milwaukee Arena (capacity 11,138) selling out in advance for the first time in the tournament's seven-year history.

Opening against Wisconsin, the defending tournament champion, LSU struggled for over half the game. But with 8:30 left to play, the Tigers mounted a furious rally that cut a 13-point Wisconsin lead to one. "The charge was led by gangly Pete Maravich, certainly the most remarkable superstar the classic has yet seen," reported Terry Bledsoe in the *Milwaukee Journal*. "His long hair bouncing, his feet encased in socks that sagged and drooped like yesterday's spaghetti, Maravich shot 42 times. But he also displayed a marksmanship that defied both probability and gravity."

With 2:09 left, Pete fouled out when he drove the lane and plowed into a defender. Despite his 42 points, LSU had their first loss of the season, 96-94.

"With his touch, no late lead against Louisiana will ever be safe," said Al McGuire, then head coach of Marquette. "I know he's already had the build-up but take a long, long look. This boy will be a three-time All-American."

Wisconsin advanced to the final against Marquette, leaving LSU and Florida State in the consolation game. FSU was led by future Hall of Fame center Dave Cowens, who was gaining a reputation for his rugged, intimidating physical play. Years later he remembered the game as one of the wildest in his college career. "Pete was basically a one-man show out there. He didn't have a great supporting cast," recalled Cowens. "He would sometimes take a couple of steps past half court and let it fly. It was more like a street game. To score 230 points [both teams] in a college game is a lot of points. We just went up and down the court without a break. I recall pulling down 30 rebounds."

Actually, Cowens pulled down 31 boards as Florida State crushed LSU, 130-100, despite another 42-point night (17-41, 8-10, 5 rebounds, 9 assists) from Maravich. The tournament exposed LSU's greatest weakness—an inability to control the backboards. In its two losses, LSU was out-rebounded 140-91.

LSU, now 3-2, returned to Baton Rouge and geared up for a slate of Southeastern Conference games. The Tigers hosted Ole Miss, Mississippi State, Alabama, and Auburn. Each team entered the Ag Center with elaborate defensive schemes to stop the Pistol. None were effective as Pete seemingly scored at will, averaging 47.2 points over the four games, all LSU victories.

In the Mississippi State game, Pete's 58 points (22-40, 14-16, 8 rebounds, 3 assists) tied Bob Pettit's single-game SEC scoring mark. Incredibly, 40 of Maravich's points came in the second half. Veteran referee Lou Bello, who worked the contest, told Bruce Phillips of the *State-Times* afterward: "I have seen all of the great modern scorers. Groat, Heyman, Mullins of Duke; Rosenbluth, Cunningham, Lewis of UNC; Hemric, Long of Wake Forest; Dickey, Ranzino of N.C. State, Grady Wallace of South Carolina, Buzz Wilkinson of Virginia, Robertson of Cincinnati; Lucas of Ohio State; Bradley of Princeton. And in this, my 27th year of officiating, I have never seen a shooter and scorer with the range and accuracy of Pete Maravich."

Nine games into the season LSU stood 7-2, with a surprising 4-0 conference record. The SEC wins were significant because, at that time, only conference champions were invited to the (23 team) NCAA Tournament.

After just one month of varsity basketball, Pete was scoring more than 45 points per game. His average had never dipped below 41.6—the scoring mark set by Furman's Frank Selvy in 1954. Selvy's single-season record had withstood 13 years of challenges from some of the game's greatest players, including Oscar Robertson, Bill Bradley, and Rick Barry. Maravich was making a serious run at the record and, as the season wore on, the sports world began to take notice.

"He's as good as any basketball player I've ever seen," said Doug Moe, an All-American at North Carolina and a top scorer in the ABA. "Some people say he shoots too much but you've got to take into consideration the men he's playing with. I would definitely have to put him in a class with Oscar Robertson when Oscar was a sophomore."

Maravich's teammates were even surprised at his proficiency. "Even when Pete was averaging 43 as a freshman, I didn't realize he was going to be that good," said Tribbett. "I just didn't think anyone could score like that in the big time."

Of course, for Pete to score that many points he had to put up a lot of shots and soon a small chorus of critics began to harp on his rampant gunning. By January 1968, Press had grown weary of responding to this charge. "No, I don't think Pete shoots too much," Press grumbled to reporter Paul Atkinson of *The Sporting News*. "I wish he'd shoot a thousand times a game."

Pete responded to his critics by pointing to LSU's win-loss record. Pete had played 29 games for LSU and had lost three.

On January 5, 1968, the LSU Tigers boarded their DC-3 and headed for Jacksonville, Florida. Tagging along to chronicle the escalating mania surrounding the team were several beat reporters from Baton Rouge's two daily papers: the *Morning Advocate* and the *State-Times*. After landing, the group piled into three rental cars and drove to Gainesville to face the University of Florida.

The Gators had their own rising star, center Neal Walk, a rebounding machine with a 26-point scoring average. "I was a year ahead of Pete but he was already in magazines and newspapers," recalled Walk. In front of more than 6,800 screaming fans, Walk poured in 39 points and gathered 21 rebounds to lead Florida to a 97-90 victory. Gator guards Mike Leatherwood and Victor Vasquez combined to hold Pete to *just* 32 points (9-22, 14-17, 10 rebounds, 8 assists).

"I was very pleased with the defensive job our boys did on Maravich," said Gators coach Tommy Bartlett. "Any time you stop a man who is averaging over 45 points a game with 32, well I think it's a pretty good job." Again LSU lost the battle for rebounds, 53-37.

From Gainesville, the LSU entourage traveled to Athens to face the University of Georgia. Awaiting them in the Georgia Coliseum—a venue with a listed seating capacity of 10,512—were more than 13,000 rabid Bulldog fans. "That was the hottest ticket around," recalled Georgia's reserve guard Nick Gimpel. "Every fire law was broken when Maravich came to town."

Pete's fame was drawing fans from every quarter. "Come on, who didn't want to watch this guy play?" said Jeff Tribbett. "But at times it felt like Pistol Pete's traveling circus."

Gimpel still remembers the game with exacting detail. "When I first saw Maravich, I thought he was very stoppable. Coach Rosemond said to me, 'You've played against guys better than this guy—go get him!' I wasn't in the game but 30 seconds when Pete swished a shot from what surely would have been three-point land today. Then he took a hook shot from the foul line and made it. No one had ever done that to me before. It was embarrassing. He was far, far better than I had envisioned. As much as I wanted to cover and stop him, I was just amazed at what he could do."

Rosemond switched his defensive alignment and put 6-4, 200 pound Ray Jefferds on Pete. Herb White, a Georgia guard and future NBA player, recalled the matchup: "Ray Jefferds was one of the meanest, toughest guys I have ever met. He was a great defensive player and Pete was just making him look foolish out there. Right before half time, Pete pulled up just beyond the line at half court. He let go a two-handed set shot from about 35 feet that knocked out the bottom. When Jefferds came in the locker room—we had this big metal container that held all the Coca-Colas—he just picked that thing up and threw it all the way down to the other end against the wall. He was infuriated with what Pete was doing to him."

Although Jefferds was frustrated, Pete's point total at intermission was just 16. "We went in at half time and almost started to cheer that we had shut him down," Gimpel recalled. "Then he came back in the second half and socked it to us. He was the most exceptional basketball player I had ever seen."

With four seconds remaining in the game, and LSU clinging to a 77-76 lead, Pete was fouled and went to the line in a "one and one" situation, meaning he had to make the first shot in order to take the second. Rosemond called a timeout hoping to rattle Pete, a tactic known as "icing" the shooter.

In the huddle, Press turned to his boy. "We really need these points. Just relax and do what you have to do."

"Don't worry, Coach," Pete replied.

The exchange stuck with Press. "You know, that was the first time that skinny little runt ever called me 'Coach.'"

Pete calmly drained both free throws and clinched the victory, 79-76. He finished with 42 points (14-37, 14-17, 11 rebounds, 5 assists). Afterward Rosemond called Pete "the best offensive player in America. With his ability to do everything with a ball, he puts more pressure on the defense than most teams that have three or four great players."

After the game, Pete signed autographs for nearly two hours. He felt an obligation to every fan and would usually scribble, "Pistol Pete."

Beat reporters traveling with LSU witnessed a good deal more than basketball games. They also caught glimpses of the occasionally volatile relationship between coach and son. Press was complex. He could be vicious and callous one moment, gregarious and fun-loving the next. He had a habit of lacing every criticism (and often praise) with a colorful obscenity. His indifference, too, could be hurtful.

LSU player Rusty Bergman remembers: "Press used to say, 'When I quit talking to you, when I quit paying attention to you, that's when you're in trouble and I've given up on you.'" Press would use profanity as a sign of affection. "He didn't mean it in a vulgar way," Bergman explained. "Of course, when Press would get mad, he would turn into the ugliest human being I'd ever seen. He would scare you for sure."

Tribbett recalled his first meeting with the coach. "He got out a black-board and said, 'If this board represents all knowledge of basketball,' then he drew a basketball on the board. 'This is what I know.' Then he drew a tiny little dot and said, 'And this is how much you know.'"

Although Pete had a shy demeanor, he could also be moody, headstrong, and disrespectful—even during practice. "I was brought up with no back talk allowed to the coach," said Jukkola. "At first it shocked me. I was never in a program where you could yell at the coach." When father and son clashed, it was bizarre to witness. The two would ferociously scream obscenities at each other and then abruptly make up, laugh, and hug.

Press even whacked Pete on the head during a game after his son questioned a coaching decision. According to Pete, Press was drawing up a double screen, a play known as "Big John," when Pete expressed some doubt. Press stared at his son, then slapped him across the top of the head—in full view of the sold-out arena. "I'm the coach and don't you forget it," Press barked. *State-Times* reporter Sam King witnessed Press slap Pete hard across the face in practice as well.

LSU's next opponent was Tulane, located in New Orleans just 75 miles from Baton Rouge. The game had been sold out for three weeks. The Green Wave's new head coach, Tom Nissalke, had spent much of that time devising a strategy to stop Pete. "We charted Pete in the last 10 games and hoped to defend him successfully by making him go left," Nissalke told a reporter.

Throughout the game Tulane's coach yelled: "Make him go left! He can't go left!" But Press wasn't worried. "They forced Pete over to that side where he likes to shoot his bank shot," said Press. "It's one of his best shots; he just hasn't used it much before because he hasn't had to."

Maravich finished with 52 points (20-42, 12-15, 5 rebounds, 8 assists) as the Tigers notched another road victory and moved to 9-3 on the season. In the *Morning Advocate*, Frank Wilson wrote, "Pete Maravich amazed the 5,500 fans that jammed the Tulane Gymnasium Thursday night with a spectacular display of basketball showmanship, coupled with accurate shooting which earned him a standing ovation from the crowd when he finally left the game in the final minute."

Papa Press said through a smile, "Pete gave them a show, didn't he?"

The Tulane game was followed by a two-week study break for LSU, and during the interim, sportswriters around the country dashed off reams of copy about Maravich's early-season exploits.

A UPI story headlined "Pistol Pete and the Yankees Rock 'n' Roll":

Pistol Pete is, of course, Pete Maravich who pumped in 52 points as LSU topped Tulane Thursday night to boost its record to 9-3. The Yankees are his supporting cast who come mainly from north of the Mason-Dixon Line.

Almost like magic, basketball fans are pouring out of the hills and over-flowing gymnasiums. It used to be hard to get up a quorum for basketball at some Southeastern points; now, when Pistol Pete is in town, it's hard to find a seat.

Shortly thereafter *Time Magazine* hit the newsstand with its own gushing article entitled, "A Guy Named Pete":

Pete Maravich looks, as one sportswriter put it, "like a cross between a clarinet and a filter king." But basketball, at least in college, is a game for shooters not bruisers, and in that department Pete comes on like gunsmoke. He has pumped in an incredible 202 field goals and 136 free throws for 504 points and a 45-point average per game. No one in college or pro ball even comes close this year.

Some players are best close in; with driving layups, looping hook shots and little tap-ins. Others are long distance gunners. Maravich has the feathery touch and fluid coordination to do it all.

Not that Pete is a ball hog. He is enough of a team player to lead the squad in both assists and rebounds. But, as his father says, "He's got to put it up there for us to go anywhere. I'll kill him if he doesn't shoot."

The Sporting News ran a full-page feature by Paul Atkinson: "Showman Maravich: LSU's Soph Cage Flash."

Atkinson noted that Press was toying with an audacious plan to meet the growing demand for tickets. He proposed installation of a temporary floor over the football field in cavernous Tiger Stadium to increase capacity from 10,000 to 67,200. "The Globetrotters do it all the time," Press explained.

For the remainder of the season, WBRZ, the NBC affiliate in Baton Rouge, telecast replays of the Tigers' home games at 10:30 P.M. In town, Maravich's soaring popularity was influencing the look of many neighborhoods. "There's no question that Pete put up hoops in driveways all over Baton Rouge," said LSU's Bud Johnson. "Backboards were not a part of the predominant landscape."

The local Steinberg Sport Centers, which historically specialized in firearms, began selling basketballs, goals, and backboards. As the goals went up across the region, Louisiana started to resemble Indiana.

For decades, Baton Rouge merchants had relied on free-spending Tiger football fans to buff up their bottom lines. But now restaurants, motels, gas stations, and taverns bustled with unexpected winter business as the hoop squad drew huge crowds to the Ag Center. "Pete Maravich for President" buttons began selling at a brisk rate.

On Tuesday, January 23, 1968, on ABC, Pete watched the first-ever color telecast of the NBA All-Star Game. Starting that evening were his three basketball idols: Elgin Baylor, Oscar Robertson, and his favorite, Jerry West.

From Baylor he learned the "hesitation" shot. Most jump shots are released as the player reaches the pinnacle of his leap. But Baylor could seemingly hang in the air and release the ball while descending back to the floor. Although it was a difficult shot to master, it provided an effective way to avoid blocks and draw fouls.

From Robertson he learned the importance of seeing patterns unfold on the court. Press encouraged Pete to visualize "two, maybe three patterns ahead." Robertson was the complete ballplayer: a relentless scorer, a superb playmaker, and a tenacious rebounder.

From West, Pete appropriated his lightning-fast, stop-and-pop jumper. "If you watch Jerry West, he's got the quickest release of them all," Pete told the States-Item's Peter Finney. "Compared to him, I'm slow."

On January 24, the state of Louisiana opened up contracting bids for the job of building a new basketball facility at LSU. A blueprint for a new sports arena had been created years earlier by the architectural firm of Wilson and Coleman, but the project languished until Pete's stardom lit a fire under Governor McKeithen and the state legislature.

"The artist's rendering of the building was on our media guide for five years in a row. We kept trying to promise this building to new recruits," recalled Bud Johnson. "But it took one man to make it all happen—Pete Maravich—and he never got a chance to play in it." The center opened in 1971, the year after Pete left LSU.

When the season resumed after exams, LSU faced a Clemson team coached by Press's former assistant, Bobby Roberts. The matchup would provide Pete with a blast from the past. Clemson's star player was George "Butch" Zatezalo, who had battled Pete, as a child, back in the Biddy ball program. Zatezalo, a graduate of Aliquippa's Center High School, was the ACC's leading scorer, averaging 27 points per game. Pennsylvania papers dubbed the contest the "Aliquippa Showdown."

The two had a brief reunion prior to warmups and then Pete joined his teammates for LSU's entertaining pregame routine, a demonstration that left Zatezalo in awe.

In the first part, called the "Zip Zip," the Tigers formed a circle and performed several "Homework Basketball" ball handling drills. LSU's pep band, the Court Jesters, played "Sweet Georgia Brown" as the drills became faster and faster. The second part of the warmup, the "Globie," consisted of a simple layup line with Pete in the pivot. As players streaked to the basket, Pete hit them with passes fired from every point on the compass—between his legs, around his back, off his foot, off his elbow, and over his shoulder.

"Man, when that music starts I go crazy. I move that ball around my body so fast that sometimes even I don't know where it is. I mean I move!" Pete told reporter Furman Bisher.

"All basketball teams do layup lines, but with LSU, it was definitely somewhat of a show before the game," recalled LSU student Billy Abrams. "Like a cross between college basketball and the Harlem Globetrotters."

Prior to tipoff, Pete dribbled over to the sidelines to say a quick hello to Coach Roberts, who asked, "Pete, have you got a jump shot now?" The last time Roberts had seen Pete, he was flinging shots from his hip, pistol-style.

"Yeah, Coach. I got me a jump shot, and I'm going to show it to you when the game starts," Pete replied with a sly smile.

The game was one of the most bizarre in Pete's college career. The referees, Don Wedge and T. D. Norris, called a total of 48 fouls, awarding Clemson 37 free throws and LSU 29. Pete fouled out with more than 12 minutes remaining, causing LSU fans to bombard the court with food, drinks, and paper cups. Arena announcer Ace Higgins urged the angry crowd to stop its ugly display and, two technical fouls later, the fans finally calmed down.

LSU scored a convincing 104-81 win, but Wedge and Norris had to be escorted from the court by four Baton Rouge police officers. Zatezalo attempted to find Pete but as he turned the corner, he witnessed a livid Press Maravich cursing a blue streak at the referees. Between profanities Press made the point that the fans had paid to see the leading scorers from the SEC and ACC—who hailed from the same small town—duel it out on the court.

Zatezalo managed a mini-reunion with Pete and fellow Aliquippans Rich Lupcho, Rich Hickman, and Paul Milanovich. As the meeting wound down, Pete offered some advice, "There is nothing wrong with your game, except that you just don't shoot enough." Zatezalo laughed heartily as he walked to the team bus, thinking, *Here I am averaging over 20 points a game and he tells me I don't shoot enough.*

Carefully observing the Clemson game was Harry Lancaster, the senior assistant coach at the University of Kentucky. "The boy [Pete] is like no other I have ever seen," Lancaster said after the game. "The beauty of it all is that he can hurt you from the inside or the outside." Lancaster's scouting report noted that of the 14 shots Pete made against Clemson, seven were launched from beyond 20 feet.

At the time, Kentucky was the gold-standard in the SEC. The Wildcats simply dominated in men's basketball. Although other programs occasionally had conference-winning seasons, it was only a matter of time before Kentucky regained the top spot. This was largely due to the coaching and recruiting skills of their coach, Adolph Rupp, who led the Wildcats for 42 seasons. Rupp's teams captured four NCAA championships and one NIT title employing an up-tempo, "racehorse" style offense. Until Dean Smith passed him in the spring of 1997, Rupp had won more games than any coach in Division I history.

Kentucky visited Baton Rouge on Saturday, January 27. The powerhouse Wildcats were expected to win the conference with major contributions from three outstanding sophomores: Mike Casey, Mike Pratt, and Dan Issel.

"Pete always stepped it up another level against Kentucky," noted Tribbett, who witnessed Pete's intense preparation for game days. "We didn't start the mental preparation at 4 P.M. It doesn't work that way. It's a slow building process starting a couple of days before the game. I saw that rooming with Pete. Our classes ended where we could get to practice and were done by about 1:30 P.M. We'd go back, eat lunch, take a brief nap, lay down and think. Getting mentally prepared for the game was serious to us. We didn't go out there to lose. We were competitors."

Rupp wasn't planning on losing either. In addition to his assistant's scouting trip, Rupp studied game film of Pete—unusual behavior for the super-confident coach. Pat Riley, who played for Rupp from 1964 to 1967, recalled, "We never studied the opponents tape. It used to be a running joke that he [Rupp] would take the scouting report on us and give it to the opponent and say, 'Stop us.'"

With television cameras broadcasting the game throughout the South, Maravich came out firing, hitting several shots in a row. After several minutes, Rupp had seen enough and called timeout. "I said we wouldn't play him [Pete] any way but one-on-one. We tried and you saw what happened," explained Rupp afterward. "When I saw him get going at the beginning of this game, I told the boys to drop off the other LSU players and cover Maravich as much as they could."

When play resumed, Maravich faced a modified zone defense with at least two players guarding him at all times, forcing him to pass the ball or hoist up fiercely contested shots. Rupp's defensive tweak proved effective as Kentucky crushed the Tigers, 121–95.

"I just watched Maravich hit for 52 points against my boys. Now that's what I call shooting," Rupp said after the game.

While Pete appreciated Rupp's praise, the Kentucky loss was a cold splash of reality for LSU. Losing at home to the SEC's top team made the dream of a conference championship more remote.

Off the court both Maraviches were beginning to wear down from the constant exposure. "Pete's been subjected to so much media attention in the last weeks that he's mentally haggard," said Press.

In retrospect, LSU sports information director Bud Johnson feels he may have overbooked Pete. "My goal was to get publicity for the program so that the school could recruit better athletes. I possibly made a mistake in allowing the media to interview him during the season. We let anybody that wanted to talk to Pete talk to him. And I arranged that. We had TV crews showing up at practice, literally stopping practice. They would have not dared do that for LSU football. UCLA protected their players. Lew Alcindor was allowed to be interviewed only before or after the season."

The scrutiny was also starting to eat away at Press. When reporters questioned why Pete was shooting so much, Press interpreted the queries as criticism. His hair became grayer and the lines in his face grew deeper. He took tranquilizers to help him sleep, drank antacid to soothe his ulcers, gulped cups of coffee, and continued his tobacco chewing habit.

Every day scores of letters arrived at the basketball office, most of them adoring fan mail but occasionally Press would receive hurtful accusations about his coaching motives. A small faction charged that he was just "using" Pete and the LSU program to secure an NBA contract.

Two nights after the disappointing loss to Kentucky, LSU hosted Vanderbilt at the Ag Center. Wearing a uniform for Vandy that night was sophomore forward Perry Wallace, the first black basketball player in the SEC. Back in April 1966, during his first news conference as LSU's head coach, Press mused about recruiting black players. But he was rebuked several days later by the university president, Dr. John A. Hunter. "My coach was misquoted," Hunter told the media. Press had coached interracial teams in Pennsylvania, but his dream of integrating LSU basketball would have to wait a few years.

Vanderbilt was among the NCAA's top-scoring teams, and the pace was lightning quick as both teams launched more than 40 shots in the first half. At the half-time buzzer Maravich hit a fall-away jumper to give him 29 points and tie the score 53–53. But fatigue caught up with Maravich in the second half (he was playing with a 101-degree fever) and he committed four costly turnovers and missed 18 shots.

"It's pretty hard to say that a fellow who scores 54 points is having a bad night, but that's exactly what Pete Maravich had," reported *Morning Advocate* sports editor Bud Montet after LSU's 99-91 loss. "He was ill over the weekend and it showed up on the court. He lacked his usual sharp hand and many of his shots rimmed the basket and refused to drop."

The Tigers then flew to Kentucky for a rematch with the Wildcats. For LSU to have any chance of winning the SEC title it almost certainly had to beat Kentucky, the nation's ninth-ranked team. Pete had blistered Kentucky for 52 points in a loss in Baton Rouge and Wildcat fans wondered if he could repeat that performance in their building. Two days before the game, all 11,800 tickets were sold.

Kentucky fans, much like the fans at Madison Square Garden in New York, had a reputation for appreciating quality basketball, and Maravich was anxious to please. Early in the game, Pete led a three-on-one break against Kentucky's 6-9 Dan Issel. At the foul line Maravich whipped the ball behind his back and bounced a perfect strike between Issel's legs to a cutting LSU teammate who scored easily. Even Wildcat fans jumped to their feet and applauded the audacious maneuver.

"Pete was the best passer and ball handler that I have ever seen," recalled Issel, who later played 16 seasons for the Denver Nuggets. "He made phenomenal passes."

Despite some thrilling passing, Pete couldn't singlehandedly win the game. John McGill of the *Lexington Herald-Leader* wrote, "Pete Maravich did just about what he was supposed to do, scoring 44 points, but team balance prevailed."

The box score supported McGill's analysis as Kentucky out-shot (51 percent to 42 percent) and out-rebounded (53-44) the under-sized Tigers in a 109-96 win.

"Pete Maravich isn't a gunner or a showoff," Rupp explained afterward. "He's a standout—a determined youngster. That's the thing I like about him. He's going to set a lot of records before he's through."

Just days after the tough loss at Kentucky, the Tigers faced another formidable team when it squared off against Tennessee. The Volunteers, coached by Ray Mears, were defending SEC champions and were led by a future NBA center, seven-foot, 251-pound Tom Boerwinkle. Tennessee's style of play stood in stark contrast to LSU's. The Tigers preferred up-tempo, run-and-gun basketball; Tennessee featured a deliberate offense and a tenacious, smothering

defense anchored by its scrappy guards, Bill Justus and Bill Hann. A year earlier, Tennessee had the No. 1 defense in the nation, allowing a mere 54 points
per game. Coach Mears had a simple plan for LSU: "We did not want Pete to
get his hands on the ball. Ever."

Mears devised a zone defense nicknamed "Chinese" after LSU football's
famed Chinese Bandits. The clever scheme had two parts. When LSU had
possession in the backcourt, two Tennessee guards would swarm Pete to deny
him the ball. Then, as the ball came over the mid-court line, the Vols reverted
to a modified box-and-one zone. The point guard, usually Billy Hann, would
shadow Pete wherever he went while the other four players guarded areas of
the court. Should Pete get to the ball, a Vols player would abandon the zone
and, with Hann, trap Maravich.

The scheme worked as Maravich shot just 9 of 34 (.265) from the field,
the lowest shooting percentage of his college career, and tallied a mere 21
points as the Volunteers marched to an 87-67 win.

LSU hoped to reverse its losing ways against the Auburn Tigers in Alabama. Auburn was in the process of building a new auditorium and played
its home games in a converted airplane hanger called "The Sports Arena,"
better known as the "The Barn." The drafty building held less than 3,000 and
its front-row seats were just a few feet from the sidelines.

Right from the start, Pete was the target of unrelenting taunts. Robert
Farr, an Auburn student at the time, recalled Maravich's reaction. "When he
came out, the fans really got onto him about his long hair and baggy socks.
Every time he made a shot during warmups, people would sarcastically cheer.
Then, if he'd miss, they'd go 'Ohhhhh.' Well, Pete kind of picked up on what
they were doing, and he walked over to the goal and shot a layup. Of course
they went, 'Yeah!' Well, he stood under the goal and shot layups as fast as he
could. And he hit like 30 in a row. Pretty soon, he was getting a standing ovation. When he finished, he kind of tipped his hat, smiled and walked off."

But the baskets didn't come as easily in the game. Although he scored 25
straight points during a hot stretch in the second half (believed to be an unofficial NCAA record), Pete converted just 18 of 47 shots overall. His LSU
teammates were just as cold, making only nine shots, as LSU lost 74-69. But
one might not have divined that from the next day's newspaper headlines.

"Babe Ruth of College Basketball Buckets 49" topped Ted Meier's AP
story after the Auburn loss. "Pistol Pete Maravich draws fans to watch his fantastic shooting in much the same manner as the Sultan of Swat did baseball
fans when he was hitting home runs for the New York Yankees."

"Maravich Cracks Season Scoring Record in SEC" headlined Sam

King's story in the *State-Times*. The sub-headline, however, referred to a less positive story. "But Tigs Lose, 74-69." Pete later chose to add King's article to the appendix of his autobiography, *Heir to a Dream*. It was the only news story from his three years on the LSU varsity that he reprinted in his book.

The Auburn loss, LSU's fifth straight defeat, was a low point in the season. During the losing stretch Pete was credited with just nine assists. The option of passing seldom seemed to cross his mind and there were grumblings on the team and in the media. "While the hotshot Pistol is shooting away, his teammates are wasting away with nothing to do but watch his antics and double-figure scoring," charged one critic.

"It's only natural that everyone wanted to shoot a little more," said teammate Rich Hickman. "Sure, when we were losing, there was some griping. We all accepted the situation for what it was. But it was tough on recruits, tough on some players that just got there."

One such recruit was Steve Shumaker, a 6-7, 218-pound center from Burlington Junior College in Iowa. More than two dozen Division I schools attempted to recruit him, but repeated calls from Press Maravich, Bob Pettit, and the governor of Louisiana helped convince Shumaker to sign with LSU.

"Press called me more than the other coaches and ended up giving me a lot of [expletive] and I listened to it," Shumaker said. "I went down there, and it was all set up for the Maraviches to run the show. I never had the opportunity to go to war and win a spot on the roster. The starting five, all handpicked by Press, just threw the ball to Pete.

"I've played basketball all my life and it's a team game. It's not basketball when one guy shoots the ball 50 times a game and doesn't have to guard anybody. The bottom line was the Maraviches weren't playing team ball at LSU."

Shumaker developed personal animosity toward Press, and wasn't too keen on Pete, either. He believed Press demonstrated overt favoritism. Once, when he got into a physical confrontation with Pete during practice, Press punished just Shumaker.

Later he felt that Pete out-and-out lied to him. Apparently in December 1967, Shumaker and teammate Mark Bernbrock planned to drive to the New Orleans airport to catch flights home for the Christmas vacation. The night before, Pete asked to borrow Shumaker's car. At first Shumaker refused but relented when Pete promised to return it well before Shumaker's flight. The following morning Maravich and the car were nowhere to be found. Ralph Jukkola got his teammates to the airport on time, but Shumaker was livid. He seethed for the entire flight, knowing Pete had his car for the next two weeks.

"His word was no good," said Shumaker. "I know Pete was wonderful in a lot of people's eyes. But I guarantee you he was a spoiled little brat when I knew him. And that's because he had his daddy. What are you going to do when daddy is the coach?"

Rich Hickman could sympathize. "When recruits came in they were used to getting the two- and three-inch headlines in the local newspaper. But here Pete was going to get the publicity and he was going to get the glory. We all knew what our roles were."

After the Tigers split a pair of home games, beating Florida 93-92 in overtime and losing 78-73 to Georgia, LSU flew into Tuscaloosa to face the University of Alabama at the Memorial Coliseum, a brand new venue that featured a rubberized tartan floor. A crowd of 15,014 pushed through the turnstiles, setting an SEC attendance record.

"Back then 6,000 or 7,000 was good for us because Alabama wasn't a basketball school," said David Williams, who played at Alabama. "It was the first time that I know of that the Coliseum was full and it was Pete who packed it."

And it was a game Pete almost didn't play.

Near the end of the Georgia game, Pete hit the floor hard after a collision, deeply bruising his left hip bone. Pete absorbed a lot of body shots from opponents trying to disrupt his rhythm and usually he bounced right up. But this hip injury (a "pointer") kept him out of practice for a week.

Although hobbled, Pete began entertaining the crowd with his ever-expanding repertoire of shots. "During warmups, Maravich would stand on the foul line and bounce in free throws off the floor, a dozen or so in a row. Sometimes the crowds would get to counting when he would bounce them in. People would show up an hour before the game just to see him," recalled Williams.

Surprisingly a significant number of the 15,000 patrons ended up cheering for Pete. "It was obvious from the outset that fans were with Pete. They [Alabama fans] were as quick to 'oooh' and 'ahhh' his behind-the-back passing and between-the-legs dribbling as the most avid LSU fans," reported Mike Cook in the Baton Rouge *State-Times*. "As the game progressed, it became not a matter of who would win the game, but how many points Maravich would get."

With 15 seconds remaining, Pete had 57 points (at one point hitting eight straight baskets including two 35-foot set shots). Tribbett attempted a free throw that rimmed out, but Jukkola wrestled the rebound away from an Alabama player. "I had an easy path to the basket," Jukkola remembered. "But I stopped and passed the ball back out to Pete."

Pete took the pass at the half-court line, dribbled once, and let fly an awkward two-handed heave. The ball snapped through the net and the arena erupted. His 59th point set a SEC single-game scoring record. As hundreds of Alabama fans poured onto the floor to join the celebration, Pete's teammates hoisted him onto their shoulders.

In the locker room Pete made a point of personally thanking his teammates. "He always gave credit where credit was due," Jukkola said. "Pete was great for doing that sort of thing. Granted, I would have rather been the star on the team, but after you played with Pete, you knew why he was the star."

Jukkola, a junior, was enjoying a productive season alongside Pete. His shooting percentage rose from 41.5 to 67.9—easily the best in the conference. Columnist Dan Hardesty of the *State-Times* noted the jump in Jukkola's efficiency: "Nothing could more strikingly prove the value of Pete Maravich. Here is a player [Jukkola] who has improved his free-throw shooting two percentage points between his sophomore and junior seasons, but has improved his field-goal percentage an incredible 25 percentage points at the same time. Jukkola is getting good shots at the basket because Maravich has attracted a crowd elsewhere."

The Tigers' next stop was Starkville, Mississippi, described by Randy Lamont as "a barn in the middle of nowhere." An overflow crowd of approximately 6,000 looked on in Mississippi State's Maroon Gym as Pete popped in 34 points and delivered another amazing stunt.

"Pete had his man out on the left side of the key and faked like he was going to shoot, and the defender had his legs kind of wide," recalled LSU announcer John Ferguson. "Now—this is the truth—Pete bounced that . . . ball between the defender's legs and caught it behind him for a layup. I felt so sorry for the defender. But the truth of the matter is that it was a magnificent thing to see." LSU beat Mississippi State for the second time that year, 94-83, and improved to 13-9.

The Tigers' final home game was against cross-town rival Tulane on February 21. The largest crowd of the season poured into the Ag Center hoping to witness basketball history. Pete, with 984 points and a 44.7 average, was on the brink of scoring 1,000 points for the season. No sophomore in NCAA history had ever done that.

Maravich swished in his first shot, a 15-foot jumper from the right corner. With those two points he broke the sophomore scoring record set 10 years earlier by Oscar Robertson. (The "Big O" chalked up his 984 points over 28 games; Pete surpassed him 30 seconds into his 23rd game.) With Pete just shy of 1,000 points, the crowd wildly cheered each of his shot attempts.

Finally, with 8:31 remaining in the first half, Pete banked in a layup and it was done. The action was stopped, Pete was presented with the ball, and the Tiger faithful gave him a thunderous, two-minute standing ovation. LSU trailed Tulane by three points at that juncture but the ceremony seemed to loosen Pete up and he stroked in another 15 points by half time.

Pete wasn't the only Maravich showered in applause that Wednesday evening. At a special half-time ceremony, Press received an award from the Student Government Association for "bringing basketball back to LSU." The fans rocked the arena as they expressed appreciation for Press Maravich, whose long basketball journey had taken him from dingy high school gyms in western Pennsylvania to this adoring crowd in a converted rodeo arena in southern Louisiana.

Pete's hot hand continued in the second half and, despite being double and triple teamed, he finished with 55 points (21-47, 13-15, 5 rebounds, 0 assists) as LSU won, 99-92. The 14-9 Tigers were now assured a winning record for only the second time since 1954.

Pete had amassed 1,039 points with three games left to play. No sophomore had ever reached 1,000 points. No sophomore has reached it since.

With every basket, Pete established new NCAA and SEC scoring records, and when LSU played the University of Mississippi, he helped set another attendance mark.

The largest crowd to watch a basketball game in the history of the state—8,500—came to Rebel Coliseum on February 24 to see Ole Miss take on LSU. "I saw Pete three straight years at Ole Miss when I was there," recalled its legendary football star Archie Manning, father of current NFL quarterbacks Peyton and Eli. "And he was absolutely phenomenal each and every time I saw him play."

On that night Pete bucketed 40 points (13-26, 14-16, 4 rebounds, 8 assists) but the Tigers lost a squeaker, 87-85.

Five days later, Pete learned that he'd been named First Team All-American. At the time, several organizations employed a variety of sampling methods to determine the nation's five best college basketball players. United Press International polled 347 newspaper, television, and radio sports editors. The National Enterprise Association asked 12 current NBA coaches and their talent scouts. The U.S. Basketball Writers Association polled its members. Associated Press queried 322 sportswriters and broadcasters. *The Sporting News* asked NBA general managers. Plus various magazines, such as *Basketball Weekly*, compiled their own lists.

Because so many voters weighed in, it wasn't uncommon for the lists to differ. But in the spring of 1968, there was unanimity about four players: Elvin Hayes of Houston, Lew Alcindor of UCLA, Wesley Unseld of Louisville, and Pete Maravich of LSU. Then, depending on the media group, the fifth spot was filled by Larry Miller of North Carolina, Calvin Murphy of Niagara, Don May of Dayton, or Jo Jo White of Kansas.

UPI, AP, and the U.S. Basketball Writers also selected a single Player of the Year. Elvin Hayes was the easy winner. The 6-9 center, who grew up in Rayville, Louisiana, led the University of Houston to an undefeated regular season and was third in the nation in scoring (behind Maravich and Calvin Murphy) with 36 points per game.

AP published its vote tallies for the Player of the Year:

Elvin Hayes	222.5
Lew Alcindor	41.5
Pete Maravich	23
Larry Miller	6
Bob Lanier	6
Wesley Unseld	4

The accolades for Maravich kept coming. He landed on the cover of *Sports Illustrated*. The headline from the March 4, 1968 issue read: "LSU's Pistol Pete—The Hottest Shot."

Early in the season S.I. dispatched Curry Kirkpatrick, a young staff writer, to Baton Rouge to follow Maravich for a couple of weeks. Kirkpatrick, who had graduated from the University of North Carolina just three years earlier, composed a superb profile that was informative, entertaining, and laced with poetic imagery—"his moves of velvet and his shots of satin." Kirkpatrick seemed astounded by what he had witnessed. More than Pete's fluid dribbling, uncanny shooting, and deceptive passing—the young writer was struck by Pete's carefree demeanor.

"Curry Kirkpatrick probably wrote the definitive piece on Pete during his sophomore year," says Marty Mule, who wrote for the LSU school newspaper, *The Reveille*, and later covered the NBA's Jazz. "*Sports Illustrated* really put him on the map. Put him into the national consciousness of the country."

A perfect complement to Curry's insightful piece was photographer Rich Clarkson's iconic portrait of Maravich. In the photo Pete is wearing his purple and gold warmup jacket and his arms are wrapped around a basketball as his sad brown eyes stare at the camera.

Pete's brother, Ronnie, was completing his final combat tour in Vietnam when the issue reached Southeast Asia. "One of the guys in my platoon had mail call and here came a *Sports Illustrated* with Pete on the front," remembered Ronnie. "Well, now I know the kid's made it."

In addition to the All-American selections and the *Sports Illustrated* cover, Pete received another honor when he was invited, along with 32 other Division I players, to try out for the U.S. Olympic Basketball team scheduled to compete in the Summer Games in Mexico City. But first there were two road games to finish out his sophomore season.

On March 2, LSU faced defense-minded Tennessee in Knoxville and more than 13,600 fans packed the Stokley Athletic Center. Banners were draped over the balcony in the upper deck. One read: "JAM THE PISTOL."

In the first half, a determined Billy Hann shadowed Pete and held him to just nine points. In the second half, Bill Justus took over and continued to harass Pete. The collapsing "Chinese" defense was once again stifling. "We were triple teaming him in some instances," remembered center Tom Boerwinkle.

LSU lost 74–71 and Pete scored just 17 points. It was his lowest total of the year (and college career) and he was outscored by teammate Ralph Jukkola, who rang up 22.

Tennessee coach Ray Mears was later flabbergasted by some responses he got from local fans. "I got letters from people here in Knoxville saying, 'Hey, how come you didn't let Pistol Pete play? We came to see him play, and you didn't let him,'" remembered Mears. "Boy did that [tick me off!] I'm trying to win a ballgame and hold him down. They wanted to see him play and score."

The NCAA sent a film crew to Knoxville that evening to capture highlights of Maravich for its 1968 College All-American film. Turned out they picked the worst night of the season. Pete made just seven shots (five were featured in the film). The slow-motion clips demonstrated how he double-clutched, head faked, or expertly utilized the Elgin Baylor "hesitation shot" to free up his shooting hand against the swarming UT defense.

Two nights after the loss to Tennessee, LSU dropped its final game of the season to a well-balanced Vanderbilt squad. Playing before a packed house in Nashville, the Tigers took a quick 14-6 lead but, with the Commodores shooting 60 percent from the floor, Vanderbilt drubbed LSU, 115–86. But the game's story was still Maravich's stat line: 42 points (17-39, 8-11, 6 rebounds, 9 assists).

LSU finished the 1967-68 season with a 14-12 record, a remarkable turnaround from 3-23 the previous season. On March 5, the team's booster organization, the Tipoff Club, held its annual basketball banquet. Sparsely attended in previous years, this time a capacity crowd jammed the LSU Union Center for the speeches and trophy presentations.

Press was more than pleased with his team's success, his son's explosion to the top of the college basketball strata and, most of all, the renewed interest in basketball in a football-obsessed region. Attendance for LSU's 26 games surpassed 230,000 people, an astonishing number that included many people who had never attended a basketball game before. Pete and his amazingly unselfish teammates hoped to bring them back for more.

Press received a signed basketball from Pete. It was inscribed: "I present this ball to you Dad. With your guidance and nurturing you made this possible. 1,138 points."

"Playing for my father was a lot tougher on both of us than I ever imagined," Pete told the *States-Item*'s Peter Finney. If they were close before, their battle against a small chorus of critics deepened their bond.

Pete Maravich, in his first varsity season, averaged a historic 43.8 points per game, and became a modern sports icon. But his growing popularity brought a loss of privacy. Gone were the days of anonymity when he could hustle carnival booth operators for stuffed animals or win beer money in pickup games on a Ft. Lauderdale beach.

It seemed the whole country knew of the skinny basketball wizard with the floppy socks. He was basketball's first rock star. He was *Pistol Pete*.

7

Olympic Trials
(and Tribulations)

"I wasn't too happy about Pete trying out. I knew there would be some politics involved. But he felt it was a once in a lifetime chance."

—PRESS MARAVICH

"Hank Iba and the old, slow down, lethargic—pass the ball around 15 times—go to the big man type of basketball. Well, of course, Pistol Pete was up and down the floor. The flash, the flair. The coaches in the committees were not ready for that brand of basketball."

—CALVIN MURPHY, 1968 OLYMPIC HOPEFUL

The driving force behind America's involvement in Olympic basketball was Dr. Forrest "Phog" Allen, a protégé of Dr. James Naismith, the game's inventor. Allen, head coach at the University of Kansas, spent nearly a decade urging officials of the International Olympic Committee to add the "YMCA game" to the Olympics. On November 9, 1934, he realized his goal. Allen received a cablegram from the secretary of the Olympic Committee announcing that men's basketball would be a medal sport at the 1936 summer games in Berlin.

In August 1936, as war clouds gathered over Europe, the United States sent a 14-man team—seven from a team sponsored by Universal Pictures, six from the Globe Oilers (national AAU champs), and one collegian from the University of Washington—to Germany.

Twenty-two nations fielded teams and, fittingly, Dr. Naismith, then 75, was on hand to witness his sport make its Olympic debut. America was scheduled to play Spain in its first game but concern about an escalating civil war back home caused the Spaniards to forfeit and withdraw their delegation from Berlin. The U.S. squad then cruised through the competition, beating

Estonia (European Champs), the Philippines, Mexico, and Canada. The gold medal contest against the Canadians was played outdoors in a rain shower on a bed of muddy clay. The final score: 19-8.

After Berlin, the U.S. basketball team would go on to capture gold at each of the next five Olympics. Typically, the U.S. roster was a mixture of college players and corporate-sponsored amateur squads. For instance, the 1960 team included collegiate All-Americans Jerry West and Oscar Robertson, along with amateurs like Lester Lane of the Wichita Vickers, and Allen Kelley of the Peoria Caterpillars.

By 1968, though, the job of selecting the U.S. squad had become more difficult as the pool of potential Olympians had expanded. In addition to major college and amateur players, there were junior college, small college, and armed forces players to be considered.

Pete Maravich was one of 88 players to accept invitations to try out for the 1968 team. Many of the nation's top college players, however, chose not to attend. Elvin Hayes, Player of the Year at Houston, signed with the San Diego Rockets of the NBA and spent the summer barnstorming with his own Texas All-Stars. Wesley Unseld of Louisville and Don May of Dayton, citing fatigue, and Larry Miller of North Carolina, nursing an injury, were other notable absentees.

Although billed as the Summer Olympics, the 1968 games in Mexico City were actually scheduled for October 12-27, which was midway through the first semester of the U.S. academic year. This conflict was one reason why Lew Alcindor did not participate. "What everyone seems to forget is that I would have lost a whole quarter (of college classes) by going to the Olympics," Alcindor told the *New York Times*. "I would not have been able to graduate in June."

SEC Commissioner A. M. Coleman issued a statement stating the conference would allow Pete to remain eligible even if he missed a large chunk of the fall semester. "Everyone in the conference hopes he makes the team," Coleman told the *Morning Advocate*. "It would bring a lot of honor and publicity to our group."

But injuries, early signings, and scheduling conflicts were minor nuisances compared with a potential firestorm that faced Iba and the Olympic selection committee: a proposed Olympic boycott by America's black athletes.

In 1967, Harry Edwards, a part-time sociology instructor at San Jose State, was appalled by the segregation and discrimination endured by black student athletes. His complaints to school administrators were ignored so he called for a "disruption" of San Jose State's opening home football game against Texas-El Paso. Despite the objections of newly elected California

Governor Ronald Reagan, San Jose's President Robert D. Clarke cancelled the game. It was the first time a major college sporting event was cancelled due to a political protest on campus. Emboldened by his success, Edwards set his sights on the Summer Olympics and issued a statement in the fall of 1967:

> For years we have participated in the Olympic Games, carrying the U.S. on our backs with victories and race relations are worse than ever. Now they are shooting people in the streets. We're not trying to lose the Olympics for Americans. It's time for the Black people to stand up as men and women and refuse to be utilized as performing animals for a little extra dog food. You see, this may be our last opportunity to settle this mess short of violence.

The proposed boycott forced athletes (current and retired) to choose sides. Among those supporting the boycott were Lew Alcindor, the Harvard University crew team, decathlete Bill Toomey, hammer-thrower Hal Connolly, and his discus-throwing wife, Olga.

University of Kansas guard Jo Jo White said his loyalty was to the game and his country. "I make up my own mind and I've decided to play," countered White. "I don't care if I'm the only one. They can go ahead and boycott—I'm playing."

Other athletes, however, straddled the line.

"As far as I'm concerned, there is no boycott yet," University of North Carolina star Charlie Scott told *Sports Illustrated*. "If the boycott does come about and it's total, well, I'm not going to be the only Negro out there. I'll go along with them. But if it's scattered, my choice is to play."

Edwards added fuel to the controversy: "I don't think any black athletes will go to the Olympics. If they do, I don't think they'll come back. Some of them are going to have accidents. The black athlete who goes will be a traitor to his race and will be treated as such."

Eventually the proposed boycott collapsed when legendary athletes including Jesse Owens, Jackie Robinson, Willie Mays, and Joe Louis opposed the action.

The 45-man Olympic Basketball Committee divided the 88 candidates into eight 11-man squads; four teams representing the NCAA, and one each for the AAU, junior colleges, NAIA, and the armed forces. Practice and scrimmaging began in Indianapolis on March 23. Unfortunately, on the second day of workouts, Pete pulled his groin muscle.

On March 25, the four NCAA squads played their first public exhibition, a double header at the Kentucky Fairgrounds and Exposition Center in Louisville. Pete, wearing No. 5, was placed on the East team, joining Mike Casey of Kentucky as the only sophomores on the roster.

John Bach, the East's coach out of Fordham University, kept Maravich on the bench to start the game, shocking many in the crowd of 7,000. He started Casey and Rick Adelman at the guard positions. "I felt on the basis of what I had seen in practice, this was the best lineup," Bach told the *Louisville Courier Journal and Times*. "You have to ignore personalities and put the best team out there."

When Maravich finally entered the game, he drew louder cheers than hometown favorite Casey. His intricate ball handling, behind-the-back dribbling, and blind-side passes wowed the crowd and set up several easy scores for the East in its 83-74 win. Tennessee's Tom Boerwinkle led the team with 23 points and 18 rebounds while Pete, still tender from his injury, played less than half the game, took three shots and made one. His two points were more than 41 below his LSU average.

"We more or less stuck to our patterns and I think we came up with a pretty good team effort," Maravich told reporters afterward. "I'm not the coach."

The players returned to Indiana and several participated in the College All-Star Game sponsored by the National Association of Basketball Coaches. The contest, in its sixth year, was normally restricted to seniors, but because 1968 was an Olympic year, underclassmen were allowed to participate. The game, played under international rules, permitted dunking and utilized a shot clock.

On Saturday afternoon, March 30, 1968, more than 14,500 fans jammed the bleachers at Butler University's famed Hinkle Fieldhouse, setting a college All-Star attendance record.

Besides the Indiana debut of Pistol Pete, the contest also presented a compelling subplot with the participation of Rick Mount on the West squad (coached by Tex Winter). Mount, a former "Mr. Basketball," was the latest on a list of larger-than-life Indiana hoopsters that included John Wooden, Oscar Robertson, and Terry Dischinger. Like Maravich, Mount was a basketball junkie. He practiced hour after hour and, by eighth grade, enjoyed a stellar statewide reputation. Mount's weapon was a silky-smooth jump shot that was accurate from anywhere within 30 feet. His scoring exploits at Lebanon High were so noteworthy that he became the first high school athlete to grace the cover of *Sports Illustrated*. Mount opted to attend Purdue University and ended his sophomore season in 1968 with a 28.5 scoring average while shooting 44 percent from the field.

The Maravich vs. Mount showdown created so much interest that the game was nationally televised, a first for the state of Indiana.

Pete came out firing—connecting on his first six field-goal attempts. He also electrified the Hoosier fans with pinpoint passing and audacious ball handling. The game was close as the lead changed six times in the evenly matched duel. Pete's groin injury was still hampering him, though, and midway through the second half, he asked to be taken out of the game. Mount, meanwhile, lived up to his billing, hitting eight of his last nine shots before fouling out with 3:20 remaining. The West won, 95-88, and Mount led all scorers with 24 points.

Local sportswriters and broadcasters voted on the game's MVP. The tally was razor thin as Maravich edged out Mount by a single vote. Although Pete scored just 16 points (8-14), his 11 assists were the deciding factor. The Indiana faithful erupted in a sustained ovation when Pete was announced as the "Star of Stars."

"The basketball-conscious fans saw exactly what they came to see—a superlative, no-holds barred contest in which two of the nation's most prolific scorers met head-to-head," reported Ray Marquette in the *Indianapolis Star.*

As the Olympic hopefuls traveled to Albuquerque for the final leg of the trials, Pete hoped that his MVP selection at the All-Star Game—based more on playmaking than scoring—would impress the coaches. It was wishful thinking.

"The very first day of workouts [in New Mexico], we all knew Pete wouldn't make the team because of his style of play," recalled 6-3 Stu Lantz, a University of Nebraska standout. "He really didn't have any chance. But there was no question that he was probably the best player at camp."

Lantz had read about Maravich's scoring exploits but was dubious about his abilities. After all, thought Lantz, LSU's offense was designed by Pete's father to get him the ball. But after Lantz saw Maravich in action, he became an admirer. "Pete was truly amazing," said Lantz. "He opened up everybody's eyes. He could flat out play."

The Olympic Committee wasn't so sure. "We have as fine a group of shooters as I've seen in a long time, but in Olympic basketball the important things are the baseline and under the bucket," Iba explained.

On the morning of April 4, the headline of the *Albuquerque Journal* sport section read, "Dazzling Maravich Heads All-Star Game Tonight."

But intestinal flu struck the camp and Pete, along with a dozen others, was stricken. That evening, Maravich's renamed "Blue" squad faced the Junior College All-Stars, featuring 18-year-old Spencer Haywood, a 6-8, 225-pound power forward from Trinidad State in Colorado.

Haywood recalled that Pete and Bach seemed to clash, which was surprising considering the close relationship between Bach and Press Maravich. "Press and I were very good friends. He spent weekends at my house when he came east recruiting, when he was at Clemson," Bach recalled years later.

Once again, Pete began the game on the bench, this time behind Casey and Princeton's Joe Heiser. He made only a brief appearance, hit three shots (out of 12), and snared five rebounds in an embarrassing 88-70 loss.

The next day Pete, still smarting from the muscle pull and fighting the flu, mustered up all the energy he could to get out of bed. He was an hour late for practice and that may have been the last straw. Although he started the game, he logged only nine minutes, scoring six points, as his Blue squad won, 97-92. When the press inquired if he and Bach were feuding, Pete mumbled, "No comment," and bolted into the locker room.

The *Albuquerque Journal* headline blazed: "Pistol Pete Rides the Bench."

On April 6, before the last of his team's three exhibition contests, Pete decided to release some frustration. During the pregame warmups, the Pistol put on an impromptu Showtime clinic. He started off with behind-the-back layups, then shot a few half-court hook shots, and even bounced a couple in off the floor. And if that wasn't enough to rile the committee, Pete finished off the exhibition with a circus shot from his catalog of HORSE tricks. He spun the ball on his finger, threw it up in the air, and bounced it off his head into the cylinder.

"That last scrimmage game in Albuquerque, Pete was on a fast break, stopped and bounced the ball off the floor and into the basket, something I had seen him do in practice, but never in a game situation," recalled Steve Ellis, who traveled from Louisiana to watch the games. "He had fun that day. The pressure was off to make the team, and the real Maravich emerged."

The committee was unimpressed with both Maravich's petulant behavior and his offensive production. In three exhibitions, Pete shot a dismal 11-39 from the floor and scored only 24 points.

On April 7, the 12-member Olympic team was announced and, as expected, Maravich was not on the roster. Future pros Calvin Murphy, Tom Boerwinkle, Rick Mount, Dan Issel, Rick Adelman, Stu Lantz, and Otto Moore were also passed over.

"Mount displayed an unbelievable scoring talent, and Calvin Murphy had that dynamic little-man game that was so good," Bach recalled. "You could say at the top of the world was Maravich, who had the dribbling skills of Murphy and the shooting ability of Mount. I guess all three of them left there a little puzzled."

LSU teammate Jeff Tribbett recalled Maravich was more than puzzled—he was furious. "We talked about that whole thing when he got back. Hank Iba wanted a no-frills player. A role player. Pete was in the process of changing the game of basketball. Back then people would call you a 'hot dog' if you dribbled behind your back. All of a sudden, it's a new method of play and I don't think the coaches understood that at the time. You see it all the time in college now, but back then, it was never used," recalled Tribbett.

Bach said the reason Pete didn't make the team was neither his nor Iba's decision. "The ultimate choice rested in the hands of the Byzantine 45-man Olympic Committee. Iba, for all his strengths, absolutely believed in the committee furnishing the team to him. He would say, 'That's the American way' and 'Let the American process continue.' I know that the committee gave him the team they felt would play Henry Iba basketball," said Bach. "I don't remember my vote but to say I cut Pete is giving me far more power than I had."

Pete's rejection strained Bach's relationship with his old colleague, Press Maravich, "It took him a very long time to speak to me again."

In a 1984 interview, the rejection still bothered Pete. "The Olympics are a political event, not a sporting event. I knew what was going on. I was told not to go to the Olympic Trials because I was not wanted. It hurt me. I would have liked to have represented the United States."

In contrast to Pete's disappointment, was the joy of Spencer Haywood, an obscure junior college player who became the breakout star on the '68 squad. "A bad break for the Pistol, but another stroke of fortune for me," Haywood wrote in his 1992 autobiography. "Had Peter made the team, he would have been the hero and the star; I would have been a role player, instead of the guy who carried the team."

The 1968 Olympic squad, led by Haywood, Bill Hosket, Jo Jo White, Charlie Scott, and the Army's Mike Silliman, ran the table and continued the U.S.A. tradition of basketball gold.

Back in Louisiana, LSU's board of supervisors awarded Press Maravich a five-year contract extension and a salary increase. He celebrated his long-sought security by purchasing a new, dark blue Plymouth GTX. Two-and-a-half months later, Pete borrowed it for a special occasion. He drove the Plymouth to the airport to pick up Ronnie, who had just completed a seven-year hitch with the U.S. Marines.

Pete thought the stylish new car, rather than his Volkswagen Beetle, was a more appropriate transport for the returning veteran. The expensive vehicle was evidence of how much the Maravich family had achieved since Ronnie joined the Marines in 1962.

The brothers' raucous reunion lasted into the late hours. On the way home, Pete smashed the new GTX into a stalled car. Somehow he convinced Press that it was an innocent accident and that he should just be grateful that his boys were alive and uninjured.

Pete generally spent his summers working at basketball camps. Coaches and players like Ray Meyer, Bob Cousy, Charles "Lefty" Driesell, "Easy" Ed McCauley, and Dolph Schayes all ran their own camps, and Pete's "Homework Basketball" clinic was in great demand.

But for decades, one camp was a second home for Pete and his dad. The Campbell College Basketball School operated on the grounds of Campbell College, a small junior college in rural Buies Creek, North Carolina. In the early 1950s, the school constructed a beautiful, intimate gymnasium and named it after textile executive Howard Carter. In 1954, Campbell's head basketball coach Fred McCall teamed up with Wake Forest's Horace "Bones" McKinney and started a small basketball camp.

"When you're young, you want to start new things and see what happens," McCall told the *Fayetteville Observer*. About 125 kids attended the first year, each paying $25 for a week of instruction.

In 1956, when he took the head coaching position at Clemson, Press Maravich joined the Campbell staff, striking up a close friendship with McCall. That same year, nine-year-old Pete first attended as a camper. He also gained a close friend, Nelson Isley. Together they dreamed of playing college and pro ball together.

The camp had a magical aura and head coaches from rival programs happily joined the faculty at Campbell.

Even UCLA's legendary coach John Wooden signed on. "Wooden worked the camp for two weeks every summer," recalled former counselor Bob Burke. "He didn't just come in, talk to the kids for 45 minutes, and leave. He stayed here, stood in line in the cafeteria like the rest of us."

One camper remembered a Wooden lecture that began with precise instructions on the correct way to don socks and lace up sneakers (always "double knot"). Then Wooden flipped a basketball to 18-year-old Pete Maravich, who was standing at the top of the key. "Mr. Maravich will now demonstrate the one-handed jump shot." Pete methodically drained 20 consecutive shots. Wooden looked out and said, "That, gentleman, is the one-handed jump shot."

But Wooden's usual station was not in the Carter Gym feeding shooters.

"I worked with Coach Wooden there six years. He always took the defensive gym," remembered Pete's friend Nelson Isley. "We were so impressed with him because here he was coming in with all the national championships. You would think that he might be a figurehead. It was just the opposite. He was going to the little gym, the defensive gym, the one in the high school across the street."

Coach Wooden's bunkmate was Press Maravich. They were the unofficial ringleaders of the camp and a bit of an odd couple. "I just loved him. But we're different people, you know," Wooden admitted. "Press was one of the most profane coaches I've ever known. No one has ever heard me use a word of profanity. But that was just his way of talking. But after you got to know him, you understood, and it wouldn't bother you at all."

And when it came to basketball, Wooden was especially effusive in his praise of his friend. "I had tremendous respect for his knowledge of the game. Press Maravich knew as much about the game of basketball as any coach I've ever known."

Conversely, Wooden disapproved of what Press was doing with his son. "Originally Pete was in junior high school and Press was teaching him fancy things. Pete could do more things with a basketball, even then. But I kept telling Press, 'You know, you're going to ruin him.' 'Oh no,' Press would say. 'He's going to be the first million dollar pro player—you wait and see.' That was against my ideas of teaching. All these trick things with the ball. I didn't believe in that. But that was Press's ambition. He said, 'I'm going to make him a million dollars. He's going to be the first million-dollar pro basketball player.'"

Press even managed to lure Wooden into a possible NCAA violation. When Lew Alcindor joined the varsity roster for UCLA in 1966, Press offered a $5 wager that the Bruins would go undefeated over the next three seasons. Wooden accepted. Following UCLA's first national title, a win over the University of Louisville in March 1967, Press approached his friend. "I'm ready to collect $1.67 of that bet now," Press said. Wooden said the wager wasn't complete.

Press retorted, "Okay, so don't. I'll report you to the NCAA for betting against your own team."

Press's salty vocabulary and direct approach were sometimes shocking for the young campers. One former camper recalled an occasion when Press spoke to an audience of 30 teenage boys. A 13-year-old stood up and told Press that Pete was his idol, and he wanted to know how to emulate his son's success.

Press paused and asked his captive audience, "How many of you have girlfriends?" About half the kids raised their hands.

"How many of you go out with your girlfriends on Saturday night?" Again, about half said "yes."

"How many of you practice in the gym on Saturday nights?" Press continued. No hands went up.

"How many of your girlfriends are going to put you through college?" Again, no hands.

Press concluded his sermon, "Then you should be home [with] the basketball instead of [with] your girlfriends." There were no further questions.

At night, the counselors and some of the best campers would face off in competitive full-court games. Even when Pete was still at Daniel High, he would sometimes play in the counselor game. One summer Bob Cousy, who was finishing up his Hall of Fame career with the Boston Celtics, participated in the late-night action. Pete entered the game late and immediately threw a floor-length pass loaded with backspin that rotated off the floor into a teammate's hand. Then he fired in a deep set shot. Cousy grabbed the ball after it went through the net, put it under his arm, and said, "Timeout. Who . . . is that kid? Bones? Who . . . is that kid?" Press, watching from the bench, seemed to literally swell with pride.

The camp was also a place where Pete enjoyed placing bets. He wagered a Pepsi with Len Chappell, the All-American from Wake Forest University, that he could make 24 of 25 free throws and 20 would be clean swishes. Pete hit 25 straight with just two grazing the rim. He got his Pepsi. Pete challenged the college star again. "He was probably in the eighth or ninth grade," recalled Chappell. "He beat me in HORSE. And then, he bet me a milkshake that he'd outscore me in college. I was a good shooter. I averaged 30 points a game my senior year at Wake Forest." Years later, Chappell said, Pete collected on the milkshake bet.

One of the many youngsters that Pete inspired at camp was future NBA player M. L. Carr. "It was my sophomore year in high school, and that would have made it 1967. Pete was the main attraction, along with Coach Wooden," recalled Carr. "That year, Pete pulled me and a couple of other kids aside and worked with us on ball handling. He said to me, 'If you work on these ball handling drills, I can't guarantee you'll be a great player, but you'll be a better player than you were.' The feeling was unbelievable, that he would take the time to do that. At the time, I was not that coordinated. Pete was the best ball handler there was, so I went to work. I worked on them relentlessly and went from a six-point average a year in my sophomore year to a 22-point average. I really gained a passion for the game because of what Pete did for me. Even today, I have a picture of him in my office. My career probably wouldn't have happened if it wasn't for him."

But for many of the camp's alumni, it wasn't the drills, workstations, or scrimmages they most fondly recall; it was the late night bull sessions. "Bones is an ordained Baptist minister. And with Bones, Press, and John Wooden together, that was a crew," said Nelson Isley. "At night when the camp closed down and those three would be in a room, it got very, very crowded. Everybody tried to get into the door just to hear the stories. Then [Duke's] Vic Bubas started to come there. Bubas and the three of them, it was like, legends. You're talking about some war stories. We just sat there for hours and hours just listening to them. Just talking about basketball."

John Wooden, Press Maravich, Bobby Cremins, Lefty Driesell, Dolph Schayes, Bill Sharman, Bobby Roberts, Babe McCarthy, Terry Holland, Charlie Bryant, Eddie Biedenbach, Walt Serbiac, Vic Bubas, Bones McKinney—all passed on their knowledge and passion for the game during their summers at Campbell. In later years, Nate Archibald, Michael Jordan, James Worthy, Danny Ferry, Christian Laettner, and Bobby Hurley continued the tradition.

By contrast, many of today's basketball camps are corporate-owned venues where precocious teens showcase their talents to agents, scouts, and sneaker representatives. These mega-camps are a world apart from the tiny, humid gym at Campbell College where generations of boys (and eventually girls) developed a love of basketball. Fred McCall's quixotic creation is still in operation, the longest running basketball camp in the nation.

Ronnie Maravich accompanied Pete to a few summer clinics at the end of the summer. The trips gave them an opportunity to catch up and have a little fun. After one final demonstration at a camp in California, Pennsylvania, the brothers headed home. After a day of driving, they stopped for the night. Ronnie uncharacteristically decided to call it an early evening so Pete took a taxi to a run-down tavern. Pete recalled what happened next.

He slid into a booth and quickly downed two beers before a mysterious young woman appeared at his side and struck up a conversation.

"How are you, sweetie?" asked the young woman.

"I'm just fine."

"Do you mind if I sit here?"

"Suit yourself."

Not a minute passed before she had a drink in her hand. As she took her first sip, a huge man from the bar angrily approached the booth.

"What are you doing with my girl?"

"I'm not doing anything with her, sir," Pete said politely, speaking barely above a whisper. "I'm just sitting here, having a cold beer. I don't want any trouble."

The hostile stranger, who Pete estimated at 6-5 and 275 pounds, reached into the booth and pushed Pete hard. "I grew up knowing that you never back down from anybody, and I don't care what the odds were," Pete said in a 1985 speech. "I wasn't going to back down."

Pete pushed back and a stare down ensued. The bartender asked them to take it outside. Pete was not about to walk away.

He shot out of the booth and pushed through the crowd, hoping that once he got through the back door exit, he could lie in wait and hit the man with a surprise punch. "I was really going to get this guy when he came out," Pete said. "But he never came." Thinking his tormentor had been talked out of the confrontation, Pete headed toward a dimly lit telephone booth to call a taxi. But as he crossed the parking lot, the man exited the bar, screaming obscenities.

Pete turned and started walking toward the man. But he never saw the man's accomplice who slammed Pete in the back of the head with a black-jack. The blow knocked him to the ground and drew blood. Pete struggled to his feet, swinging wildly at his two assailants, but it was no contest. They beat him to the ground and pounded his head repeatedly with the blackjack.

With blood streaming down Pete's face, a woman emerged from the dark and knelt beside Pete. She smiled. Pete recognized her; it was the woman from the bar. As Pete lay there, she removed a .25 caliber pistol from her purse and put the barrel into Pete's mouth. Then she cocked the trigger.

"You're a dead man, 'Pistol Pete,'" she whispered. "How about that?"

Pete's reaction must have surprised her. He didn't beg or plead for his life. "I began thinking of all the junk in my life and how one pull of the trigger could make it all go away," he recalled. "I would suffer no more disappointments. I wouldn't have to try for the championship ring. I thought I would finally have peace if she would just pull the trigger."

Perhaps it was Pete's calmness that flustered the stranger. Or perhaps she never intended to commit murder. Whatever the reason, she withdrew the gun and disappeared into the night.

It took a few minutes before Pete could pull himself together and call Ronnie at the hotel. As he held the receiver to his bloody head, the police finally arrived. They assumed the bleeding Maravich was the instigator, so Pete was booked for disturbing the peace and spent the night in a county jail.

8

Pandemonium
in Sneakers

"Not since Gone with the Wind *has a show captivated the South like Pete Maravich did last season."*
 —SPORTS ILLUSTRATED COLLEGE BASKETBALL PREVIEW, 1968-69

"It's very simple. Pete has to shoot 40 times a game for us to win. He just has to."
 —JEFF TRIBBETT, PETE'S LSU TEAMMATE

By his junior year, Pete Maravich's favorite bar in Baton Rouge was Southdowns. The small establishment on Perkins Road was his refuge, a place to have a few beers, unwind, listen to the jukebox, and escape the pressures of his growing national fame.

"Pete once led the city in drinking longnecks," ex-LSU basketball player Tommy Hess recalled to *State-Times* reporter Joe Macaluso. "He was able to shut down Southdowns every night."

One September night in 1968, Pete was drinking at Southdowns when, in the mirror behind the bar, he caught the reflection of a beautiful young woman. Pete had never seen her before and he swirled on his bar stool for a better look. He was immediately mesmerized by her effervescent good looks. She seemed to radiate fun.

"I turned back on my stool and kept an eye on her in the mirror as the evening progressed," Pete wrote in his autobiography. "She was unaware that I was monitoring her every move. The physical attraction to the girl was amazing. I felt a burning desire within me unlike I had ever known. No one ever caught my eye as she did."

Pete did recognize Jack Moore, one of the guys in her group of friends. As soon as she left, Pete cornered Moore and demanded to know her name.

"Jackie Elliser," he replied.

"Can you get me a date with her?" Pete asked. Moore agreed to pass along the offer.

Jackie's response to the request was underwhelming, "Who is this Pete Maravich?"

"He's only the most recognized name in college basketball," Moore tried to explain. Jackie was unimpressed. Sports meant nothing to her. "I'd never even been to a basketball game," she recalled more than 30 years later. "I never watched it, I never even liked physical education in high school. I might have gone to a few football games, but I was never into basketball." Besides, her dating schedule was full and she shuddered at the thought of a blind date. Jackie sent the message back to Pete: no thank you.

But Moore kept trying and Jackie eventually allowed Moore to pass on her phone number. Pete called the very next day.

"I said, 'I don't know. I'll have to think about it,'" Jackie recalled. "He called back later that week. I said, 'Well, OK.'" They decided to attend LSU's opening home football game versus Texas A&M.

Jackie was the stunning product of an international marriage. Her father, Simon Elliser, was a 25-year-old interpreter with the Army Anti-Aircraft Battalion stationed in Normandy, France, during the final campaigns of World War II. During his tour he fell in love with a lovely 19-year-old interpreter for the French government named Huguette Garinot.

Simon began courting Huguette in 1944 and when his deployment concluded in February 1945, he proposed. Huguette accepted and the newly-weds moved to Baton Rouge where they raised two daughters, Jackie and Linda. "It took a lot of guts for my mother to leave all her family and her country to move to the United States, where she didn't know anyone," said Jackie.

Through the years the Elliser family always returned to Compiègne, France, each summer to visit the scenic countryside 40 miles north of Paris.

On September 21, 1968, Pete drove his Volkswagen to the Elliser house, about eight miles from campus. Simon answered the door and immediately recognized the star athlete. He ushered Pete inside, introduced Jackie's mom, and went in search of his daughter. He found her primping in front of her bedroom mirror. "What are you doing with that tall, skinny kid?" Simon joked.

Jackie, who stood 5-5, thought to herself, *Well, if he isn't my type, there are plenty of fish in the sea.* Then she entered the living room and 22-year-old Jackie Elliser met 21-year-old Pete Maravich.

"I thought he was a little goofy because of his complexion and his feet were so huge. I thought they were corrective walking shoes," Jackie recalled. "All he needed was the bar between them."

On their way to the football game, they stopped at a party and Pete had a few beers. It was already the second half before they arrived at the game.

"We got all the way to the top of stadium, and Pete said, 'Where are my tickets?'" Jackie recalled. They returned to the car and checked the floor, glove compartment, and dashboard. No tickets. Then Pete looked in his jacket pocket and found them. They had been with him all along.

The couple made it back to the stadium for the last quarter and witnessed the end of a tense game. With seconds remaining, and LSU leading 13-12, Texas A&M attempted a 60-yard field goal to win the game. It fell short and LSU won its season opener. Pete managed to awkwardly kiss his date as the game ended.

Afterward, Pete and Jackie parked at a nearby Catholic church where they talked and laughed for hours. As Pete leaned in for another kiss, a loud rapping on the passenger-side window interrupted his move. It was a priest from the church.

"Father, we were just talking . . ." a flustered Jackie explained.

"I'm not here for confession," said the priest. "I just need you to move your car."

Pete and Jackie's first date lasted nearly 12 hours, and ended with a promise to continue seeing each other. "We connected immediately," Jackie said. "That was it. It was meant to be."

However, when Pete invited Jackie to a Dionne Warwick concert a few days later, she declined, saying was under the weather. In reality, Jackie already had another date scheduled for that night. Her deception might have gone undetected except that her date brought her to Southdowns for a nightcap. Unfortunately, Pete strolled in a few minutes later.

"Pete came in the back door with another couple, so we took off for the front door," Jackie said.

But Pete glimpsed Jackie out of the corner of his eye. After a week of no communication, Jackie concluded that Pete was holding a grudge and decided to call him and try to explain. Not long after that conversation, Pete showed up on her doorstep holding a brown stuffed dog. He claimed it was a prize from a local fair.

"You say it's new, huh?" Jackie asked.

"Yeah," Pete said.

"So how did it get this Band-Aid on its butt?"

Pete sheepishly confessed to stealing the dog from his little sister's bedroom. The two resumed their courtship and, over the next few dates, a deep affection grew between them. Pete loved that Jackie was more taken with his quirky sense of humor than his basketball skills.

Soon the time came for Jackie to meet the Maraviches. She was petrified at first but Helen was welcoming and put her at ease. Press was another story.

"When I met Press, I thought he hated me because of the way he talked. The first time I met them, I went to their house, I brought my purse and some soft drinks," Jackie recalled. "When I left their house, I didn't know where my purse was. I was so nervous that I had placed my purse in the refrigerator with the drinks."

Jackie eventually charmed both parents and was welcomed into the family. Jackie, her father, Simon, and Diana were soon regulars at LSU basketball games, watching from the third row in the Ag Center. Missing from the group was Helen Maravich. "I know his mother couldn't go to his games because she'd get so worked up," recalled Jackie.

Pete told anyone with a microphone or a notepad not to expect a repeat of the inflated scoring numbers he posted as a sophomore. "Don't look for any 43-point average from this guy," Pete explained to Peter Finney of the *New Orleans States-Item.* "Maybe 30. I'm looking forward to a different kind of year." Pete hoped to increase his assists (he averaged 4 per game), score less, win the SEC, and play in the postseason.

Pete put another 7,000 miles on his car over the summer traveling to basketball camps—where he was now welcomed as a celebrity. One new trick he added to his "Homework" clinic, and couldn't wait to try in a game, was the "wrist-pass." It appeared like a simple two-handed chest past, but instead of traveling forward, the ball shot out at a 90-degree angle to the right or left. When Boston Celtics general manager Red Auerbach witnessed the maneuver, he shook his head in disbelief. "A lot of guys break the laws of gravity. Pete breaks the laws of physics."

The LSU Tigers opened their season on December 2 at Loyola University in New Orleans. For the first time since 1955, when Louisiana native Bill Russell returned home with his dominant University of San Francisco squad, fans filled the Loyola field house to capacity (6,594).

Loyola tried a zone defense, clogging the middle of the court. On LSU's first possession Pete stood 25 feet from the basket with no defenders close by. So he dribbled five feet closer. "Come on gunner, let's see how you shoot from there," taunted a Loyola guard. Pete was confused: *Do they really want me to shoot an uncontested 20-footer?* He shrugged and let it fly. It fell through. On the next possession, Loyola remained in its zone. Pete pumped in another 25-footer. Then another. Loyola's zone wasn't the answer, as Maravich continued his accurate shooting and brazen passing (including a 40-foot, behind-the-back assist).

He finished the game with 52 points (22-34, 8-9, 7 rebounds, 11 assists) in an easy 109-82 victory. "Year two in the reign of Maravich was ushered in with a promise of even better things to come," wrote Will Peneguy of the *Times-Picayune*. "What Maravich did with the ball against Loyola's confused defense bordered on being criminal."

So much for Pete's preseason pronouncement of a "different kind of year."

Five days later the Tigers flew to South Carolina to play Clemson. Before the game Pete led a few teammates on a tour of the sleepy Carolina town where he came of age. The nostalgic journey included stops at the YMCA, the movie theater, the pool hall, the barbershop, and even the drug store where he once won five dollars spinning a ball for an hour.

As tipoff approached, Press witnessed something new: His son's hands were shaking. Pete was nervous in front of the home fans. More than 9,800 were in attendance and many remembered him as a shy, peculiar kid who was never without his basketball. Pete managed to calm down enough to hit eight straight free throws to close out the game, clinching an 86-85 win.

Although Pete finished with 38 points (10-32, 18-22, 4 rebounds, 4 assists), his sub-par shooting (.313) depressed him and he retreated to his room in the Clemson House. Later, there was a knock at the door. Pete ducked under the covers, the signal to turn away all visitors. Jeff Tribbett, who was used to running social interference for Pete, answered.

A man about 6-4 and 220 pounds asked if Pete was available. "So I tell the guy that Pete used to live around here and that he and his father went to visit some old friends and wouldn't be back until real late. And I wasn't nice about it, either," Tribbett recalled. "The guy just stares at me a second and says, 'Okay,' and leaves." Later Pete and Jeff were embarrassed to learn that the "stranger" was Ronnie Maravich.

The Tigers ran their record to 4-1 and, the day after Christmas, headed to Oklahoma for the All-College Tournament. What Maravich achieved over three frigid December nights boggled minds of college basketball fans.

The Tigers first took on the undefeated (7-0) University of Wyoming Cowboys, then ranked 15th in the nation. The Cowboys were led by Harry

Hall, a quick 6-2 guard whose speed and defensive skills had earned him a national reputation. Hall made the youthful mistake of mouthing off to the press that he was going to "jam the Pistol" and hold him to just seven points.

"Over the years when guys made comments like that, we knew subconsciously Pete was going to be ready for the game," said LSU forward, Ralph Jukkola.

On Friday, December 27, a fearsome blizzard hit Oklahoma, making travel treacherous. However, lured by Maravich's name on the marquee, several thousand fans ignored police warnings to stay off the roads and arrived at the State Fair Arena. Future NBA center Alvan Adams was determined to see the Pistol. "The All-City Tournament was always a great tournament and Pete Maravich was big-time," Adams said. "It was the first time I ever saw him. It was amazing."

The Phoenix Suns' general manager Jerry Colangelo also braved the weather. But he was there for a different reason: He hoped to recruit Press Maravich to coach his new NBA team. He later recalled visiting with Press at the Sheraton when Pete sauntered into the room. "Here walked in this kid that I heard so much about and he was just looking for a few bucks to go out with a couple of his teammates," Colangelo said. "Then watching him play in that tournament was a real thrill. He was so very gifted."

Pete immediately went after Hall, pulling up for quick jumpers, or lulling him off balance to force contact. Hall, flustered, picked up four quick fouls. He spent a good portion of the first half on the bench watching Pete compile 29 points. And there were still 20 minutes to play.

Maravich further humiliated Hall by fouling him out of the game midway through the second half. However, Wyoming tore off on a 19-4 run to take the lead, 70-69, with five minutes left in regulation. Pete responded with six straight points to seal an 84-78 LSU victory. Pete's 45 points were supplemented by 17 rebounds from center Dave Ramsden, as the Tigers finally outrebounded an opponent, 44-37.

"Some 5,500 fans braved the driving snow and icy roads to see if Maravich was all they had heard about as a shooter, passer, dribbler and whatever else there is," reported Bob Dellinger of the Oklahoma City *Oklahoman*. "They found out he was."

After the game, Pete addressed Hall's bold proclamation.

"He jammed me all right," said a grinning Maravich. "I went for 45 and fouled him out just after the half. Now that was stupid of him, saying something like that. If I've got to stick the ball through my pants and jump through the hoop myself to win, I'll do it."

Saturday evening's game matched LSU against the host, and defending tournament champion, Oklahoma City University. OCU executed a free-wheeling, fast-breaking offense that averaged 87 points a game. Hot-shooting senior guard Rich Travis led the team with 29.7 points a game. Travis had finished fourth in the national scoring race the previous season so the promise of offensive fireworks attracted another record (8,055) crowd.

Pete was electrifying right from the tipoff. "With one flick, he changed my life," explained sportswriter Skip Bayless of the *Dallas Times Herald*. "The tip went to Maravich, who in one motion caught it in his right hand and whipped it behind his back, three-quarters court, to a teammate for a layup that brought down the house. . . . "

Despite Pete's audacious play, the game was close, with OCU leading 38-37 at half time. But the second half was all LSU, as Pete went 13 of 21 from the field and set up teammates with remarkable skill.

Late in the second half, as LSU pulled away, the Oklahoma fans switched their allegiance to the Pistol. Each time he dribbled up court the crowd screamed in anticipation of the next brilliant shot or assist. "Pete knew more about basketball than anyone in the world. He had discovered another dimension," reported Bayless. "I spent most of that night dancing in my seat."

Pete finished with 40 points (19-36, 2-5, 8 rebounds, 7 assists) and LSU guards Jeff Tribbett and Rich Hickman had season highs of 25 and 24 points. Ralph Jukkola and Dave Ramsden contributed 15 rebounds each, while Tribbett also held the sharpshooting Travis to 18 points. The convincing 101-85 LSU victory was truly a team effort.

"Fantastic . . . fabulous . . . out of this world. The words just aren't strong enough to describe the way Pete Maravich plays basketball," reported Dellinger.

On Sunday morning, the team attended church and was acknowledged from the pulpit. "The LSU basketball team is here, who beat our boys last night," announced the minister. The congregation not only applauded but rose to its feet. "I had never seen a standing ovation in church before," recalled Jukkola.

After a day's rest, the Tigers had a Monday night championship show-down against unbeaten Duquesne University. The 11-0 Dukes were ranked ninth in the nation and first in defense, allowing a measly 53.7 points per game. The team featured 6-10 twin forwards Gary and Barry Nelson, and talented 6-2 shooting guard, Moe Barr. The Dukes' smothering defense had held St. Bonaventure's high-scoring center Bob Lanier to just 10 points in their semifinal game.

Another attendance record was set when 8,336 fans jammed State Fair Arena on December 30. To wear out the taller, slower Duquesne squad, LSU set a quick tempo and led 48-46 at half time. But with 8:24 left in the game, LSU was down 76-66.

Then, with the tournament championship on the line, Maravich went to work. Witnesses say Pete played like a man possessed, reeling off 10 straight points to lift LSU back into the lead, 90-89, with just 52 seconds remaining. His final basket in the spree required more than a bit of luck.

"We were down by one with about a minute left when I drove in the lane," Maravich later recalled in *Sports Illustrated*. "I thought I was open at the time, but here came one of those two big Nelson brothers out of nowhere. I mean those guys are huge and they're tough. Anyway, here he came, so I gave him a pump in the air and thought I was home free for sure. But, oh no. All of a sudden, the other Nelson came flying at me and had me perfectly stuffed. I mean perfect—a pigeon. I thought I was a goner. Well, I didn't yell out, 'It's show time,' or anything, but all I could do was give a couple of more pumps, bring the ball tight into my chest, then flip it as I was going down to the floor. The ball hit the side of the board and banked in. I couldn't believe it."

Neither could the crowd, which went berserk. Gary Nelson quieted the arena when he answered with a quick basket and the Dukes led 91-90 with just seconds left.

Danny Hester, subbing for Dave Ramsden (who took a finger to his eye early in the game), was fouled and hit two pressure free throws to put LSU back up by one. Then, after a Duquesne turnover, Pete was fouled and converted both free throws to complete the thrilling comeback and seal the championship, 94-91.

Maravich was spectacular. He scored 32 of LSU's 46 second-half points and finished with 53 (18-36, 17-21, 2 rebounds, 6 assists). Going into the tournament Duquesne had allowed 53.7 points per game. Pete nearly matched that total by himself.

Complementing Pete's inspired play were clutch performances by Hester, Ramsden, Tribbett, Jukkola, and Hickman. "When we won the All-College Tournament in Oklahoma City in December of 1968, to me, those three games, we played better together on offense and defense than in my whole time at LSU," said reserve Rusty Bergman.

Bob Lanier recalled his first encounter with Maravich during the tourney. "We were riding up in the hotel [Sheraton-Oklahoma] elevator after one of the games and he said, 'Geez, I wear floppy socks and you've got big shoes [then-size 21]. We're [an interesting] combination," recalled Lanier. "Pete did things with the basketball I had never seen before—stuff that you'd do on the playground just goofing around. Pete dared to do it in a game situation and made it work. He was one of the few players in my lifetime that I'd go pay to see."

Maravich and Lanier were named to the All-Tournament team along with Johnny Arthurs of Tulane, Gary Nelson of Duquesne, and Carl Ashley of Wyoming. Pete was the overwhelming choice for MVP. His 138 points over three games (45, 40, and 53) broke Frank Selvy's record of 121 points. His 51 field goals and 36 free throws also set new marks.

"It was the first time I ever saw him play," recalled Bill Bertka, who scouted the games for the Los Angeles Lakers. "Pete was, without a doubt, the most creative player with the ball that I had ever seen."

In a wrap-up story for the *Daily Oklahoman*, Bob Dellinger added, "The All-College Tournament has never seen anyone like him and it may be a long time before it does again."

The Tigers ended 1968 flush with confidence. They were 7-1 and had beaten two nationally ranked teams on the road. Pete was averaging 46.9 points, 7.5 rebounds, and 5.2 assists each game—besting his sophomore numbers. Plus he was shooting an efficient 48.5 percent from the floor. Most importantly, his teammates were all contributing as well. The team was becoming better at recognizing, and reacting to, the defensive schemes thrown at Pete.

The legend of Pistol Pete continued to flourish as media outlets became more fascinated with the mop-topped prodigy. They retold the story of his unorthodox childhood practice routines as well as current family rituals (Press would spin a music box ballerina before every game. Pete would hand wash his famous socks after every game). We learned Pete's favorite home-cooked meal was cabbage rolls and spaghetti and that his dorm room featured the famous poster of President Johnson dressed as a Hell's Angel.

The press also focused on the scoring race between Maravich, Purdue's Rick Mount, and Niagara's Calvin Murphy. They became known as the "Three M's." Reporters compared and contrasted skills, styles, and professional prospects of the hot-shooting threesome. Murphy, just 5-9, started the season strong and set an NCAA single-game record with 68 points in an early season win over Syracuse.

"From the standpoint of pure shooting touch there doesn't seem to be much to choose between," opined an anonymous college coach to Steve Singer in *1968-69 All American* magazine. "But both Pete and Murphy are much better ball handlers, look for the open man better, and are far quicker."

Auburn University's talented forward John Mengelt, who had played high school ball against Mount, had a different perspective. "I'd say Mount's a better shooter than Maravich. His shots are perfect. He has perfect form," explained Mengalt to Pat Zier of the *Atlanta Constitution*. "But Maravich, well, is the best at everything else. I think he's better than anyone in the country. Nobody can pass like Maravich."

In Louisiana, the frenzy around Pete was dizzying. Barely two years after arriving in Baton Rouge, Pete was Louisiana's favorite son. Basketball hoops continued to pop up in front of homes. Small wooden carvings of Pete's likeness were hot sellers at novelty stores. Tribute songs were recorded, the most famous of which was "The Ballad of Pistol Pete" by Bob Tinney and Woody Jenkins. Even Press got into the act by lending his name to a small chain of restaurants called, "Press Maravich's Maryland Fried Chicken."

In January 1969, LSU began play against SEC opponents, and Pete was physically punished in every outing. Defenders pushed, pounded, kicked, tripped, kneed, elbowed, and undercut him in an effort to disrupt his game. "They're attacking him like wolves," Press told reporter Roger Williams.

If you could get Pete mad, the thinking went, perhaps you could throw off his rhythm. Or, better yet, get him ejected. LSU dropped its next five games. Over the first 13 games, father and son were slapped with eight technical fouls.

"The boy's got to learn to settle down. He's a great talent. But sometimes he tends to be a crybaby," said an SEC referee to sportswriter Peter Finney in reference to Maravich's tantrums. "He thinks you can't block a shot or knock the ball out of his hands without committing a foul. He'd better mature before he gets to the pros."

The losses stung but now Pete had Jackie's calming influence.

"Jackie was there to get my mind off the business of basketball and on to other things," Pete wrote in his autobiography. "She saw that basketball made me miserable off and on the court when the team lost, and it didn't make sense to her. So, she purposely directed our conversations away from basketball-related subjects and focused on other things we could both share."

For Jackie, it was difficult to deal with the constant fan and media attention. She disliked the spotlight. She also hated how losing affected the young man she was falling in love with.

"Pete was so down when they lost," Jackie said. "Those big sad eyes said it all."

Pete was wearing down physically as well. He played through terrible pain in his feet. A bulbous bone spur in his right heel became inflamed when he ran, and "walnut size" knots on his big toes caused him to wince with every step. When writer Pete Finney got a close look at Maravich's feet, he described them as "gnarled."

The pounding reached a nadir on January 31 against the University of Pittsburgh. Late in the first half, Pete's legs were cut out from under him and he landed awkwardly on his right thigh. He grimaced, holding his knee.

Trainer Billy Simmons did a quick examination and recommended that Pete sit out the rest of the game. Instead, Pete had Simmons tape him from mid-thigh to mid-calf. Pete hobbled back into the game and, playing on one good leg, still managed 40 points (13-34, 14-18, 8 rebounds, 11 assists) in LSU's 120-79 blowout victory.

The next day Pete learned that he had torn some cartilage in his right knee. The extent was unknown but surgery was recommended. Pete opted, instead, for a pregame wrap from Simmons. The massive tape job on his right leg time-stamped every photograph or game film for the remainder of Pete's junior year.

The injury limited Pete's ability to cut and push off. The night after the fall, on February 1, the Tigers put up a valiant fight in a heartbreaking 84-81 overtime loss to Ole Miss. Pete netted just 31 points (11-33, 9-13, 11 rebounds, 5 assists).

"My knee has been bothering me quite a bit," Pete confessed to reporters after the game. "They tell me I have torn cartilage but no one knows whether an operation will be necessary. In the meantime, it's taped to the ankle and I really can't move to my left that well. So I have to go right most of the time and our opponents know it. That doesn't leave me with much of an alternative, so I simply try and beat them to the right. But I'd have to say that right now I'm playing at 75 percent effectiveness."

Even in his reduced state, Pete managed to overpower Tulane's defense on February 10. Hobbling up and down the court, he made 25 of 51 field-goal attempts and 16 of 20 free throws on his way to a career-high 66 points. He fell two points shy of Calvin Murphy's single game record of 68 set earlier in the season. But LSU still lost, 110-94.

As the season wore on, Pete continued to rack up points and topple records. With 6:30 left in regulation of a sold-out game (11,500) at Kentucky Coliseum, Pete stroked in a soft 15-foot jumper and broke Elvin Hayes' NCAA record for points over two seasons (2,096). Then, in the waning seconds, Pete injured his left arch and limped off the court with 45 points. The Kentucky crowd rewarded Pete's courageous efforts with a standing ovation.

"Anytime we played Kentucky, it was a situation where they were very appreciative of good basketball," said Tribbett. "They enjoyed Pete Maravich as much as any crowd."

As did Kentucky's coach Adolph Rupp. "I would like to have him," Rupp told the *Times-Picayune*. "If we had Pete, we'd give that West Coast [UCLA] bunch a run for their money."

After the Kentucky game (a 103-89 loss), Pete decided to make a significant change. Since playing Biddy ball in Aliquippa, he had always worn the most popular basketball shoe of the day, Converse All Stars. He decided to switch brands, perhaps because the leather construction was easier on his feet (Converse used canvas), or because one of his heroes, Joe Namath, wore white Pumas when he led the Jets to the Super Bowl earlier in the year. In any event, Pete began wearing white Adidas.

Throughout his college and pro careers, Pete always wore low-top basketball shoes, in part to exploit the extreme flexibility of his ankles. Pete's unusual pliability gave him the ability to stop, cut, and pivot at greater speeds than most players. When driving to the basket, it allowed him to keep his body close to the floor (at times it seemed nearly parallel to the ground), making defending him all the more challenging. Many photographs show a streaking Maravich with his foot flat on the floor and his ankle bent beyond 45 degrees.

LSU stood at 12-13 as it prepared for its season finale on March 8, against the University of Georgia in Athens. The team's record had drifted south of .500 after weeks of grueling play against SEC competition. However, Maravich's relentless scoring had continued unabated, and against Georgia he would produce what many consider the most legendary game of his college career.

Through his first 25 games as a junior, Pete amassed 1,090 points (43.6 per game). He needed 49 points in the final game to surpass his sophomore total of 1,138. But, more importantly, an LSU victory would clinch a .500 record for the season.

Pete's return to the University of Georgia had the campus buzzing. "I just spent 40 minutes talking about Maravich on my television show Tuesday night," said Georgia coach Ken Rosemond days before the game. "Even then I couldn't cover everything." The Bulldogs were 13-11 overall and 9-8 in the SEC, compared to LSU's anemic 6-11 conference mark. But everyone knew that with Pete in town, anything was possible. He had set a Georgia Coliseum scoring record as a sophomore with 42 points. Demand for tickets was unprecedented. "The place was packed," said Bulldog guard Herb White. "We sat like 10,500 people and there was probably 13,000 plus that night. How they got 'em all in, I don't know."

The *Atlanta Journal* wrote, "College basketball comes to an end here Saturday night pitting Georgia vs. The Circus." The game attracted so much interest that the paper also posted the betting line: Georgia by six points.

The first half went pretty much as the bookmakers predicted. Georgia took control as 6-4 forward Cauthen Westbrook held Pete to just 16 points. A four-point lead at half time was good enough for Coach Rosemond, but disappointing to the home crowd who booed when the Bulldog offense went into a four-corner stall.

"We were winning the game," remembered Georgia guard Nick Gimpel. "And we felt like we had the better team if the truth be told."

The Bulldogs' dominance continued after half time as they ran their lead to 15 points, 59-44. Then the momentum swung. Pete found his shot and soon Westbrook fouled out. Georgia's lead vanished as Pete scored 29 second-half points, including the final 17. With four seconds left, and LSU leading 72-70, Georgia's Jerry Epling hit a clutch jumper and forced the game into overtime.

The overtime period was a slow, grinding battle. With time running out, Georgia held a two-point lead. "We had the ball and the lead with 15 seconds to go," remembered Herb White. Then Epling, ignoring his frantic coach's pleas to hold the ball, fired up a shot from the top of the key and missed.

"We actually should have won the game," remarked White. "Epling was All-SEC second team a couple years. But he never saw a shot he didn't like and he always wanted to prove to Pete that he could out-shoot him."

Had Georgia simply run out the clock, Pete would have finished the season with 1,090 points, four shy of his sophomore total, and LSU would have fallen to 12-14. "Why he shot I'll never know," shrugged Pete afterward. Epling's jumper certainly could have iced the game, and the season, in dramatic fashion. Instead, Pete gathered the rebound, dribbled the length of the court and scored, sending the contest into another overtime, 78-78.

The second overtime period became the "Pete Maravich show."

"Pete was throwing everything in from everywhere," recalled White. "The place was going nuts. There was no doubt most of the people there were pulling for us but they also wanted to see Pete."

Maravich fired in another nine points as LSU ran its lead to eight. With one minute left, Press called for the "Lucky 7." That meant "freeze." On this night it also meant "Showtime."

Pete began dribbling through and around the increasingly frustrated Georgia defense. *Atlanta Journal* reporter Furman Bisher wrote that the Georgia players "chased after him like fat cooks in a chicken yard."

Amazingly, the fans loved it.

LSU's radio broadcaster Brad Brian was flabbergasted. "It was almost like it was staged. The fans at Georgia were standing on their feet, cheering for Pete!"

Georgia's Tom Brennan was also stunned by the reaction. "The response when he did that was unbelievable. It was like a Globetrotters game," said Brennan. "Nobody had ever seen anything like it before in a real game."

Maravich then placed an outrageous exclamation point on the demonstration. Teammate Rusty Bergman knew what was coming. "I saw him glance up and look at the clock. It might have had five seconds and he started dribbling to the far right side of the court. When I saw that, I said to myself, 'He's gonna throw up that hook shot.'"

LSU's Rich Hickman had the same thought. "He knew what he was going to do. I think he had the shot all planned out. I saw it in his eyes. When he started to dribble out, he looked at me basically saying, 'Get out of the way. I'm coming!'"

Ronnie Maravich was watching both the scoreboard and his little brother. "The clock's clicking down: five, four, three," recalled Ronnie. "Then he hooked it. From half court."

As Pete sent the ball up, he looked at the basket, looked at the clock, turned around, and with his back to the basket, thrust both arms high in the air.

As the ball arched toward the basket, LSU's assistant coach Jay McCreary shouted, "Netsville!"

Netsville indeed. The final buzzer sounded as the ball swished through. Or as Pete liked to say, "Just oxygen."

The Georgia Coliseum erupted with cheers.

"Everybody just went bananas. The Georgia fans were just beside themselves," recalled the Bulldogs' Gimpel. "Cheerleaders came out and rushed Pete. It was like an away game. It was . . . unbelievable."

Brennan remembered the shot had a little extra stardust on it. "Not only did he make it, but it hung the net. Hung the net. A beautifully formed hook shot like [Globetrotter hook shot legend] Meadowlark Lemon, and he splashed it. It was unbelievable."

"That ball hit nothing but the bottom of the net," said Bergman. "The whole place went crazy. It was like we were playing a home game. I was a senior and I was jumping up and down like a little kid."

Tom Brennan, who later became head coach at the University of Vermont, was also caught up in the moment. "As a player, you couldn't help but cheer the guy on," Brennan said. "I wasn't on the floor at the time. I was on the bench. But I was secretly wondering, *Oh, I hope I wasn't carrying on too much.*"

By Maravich's own estimate, the shot traveled 35 to 40 feet. "I was going out of bounds in front of the LSU bench and couldn't have been a few steps from the 10-second line," Maravich said to reporter Steve Ellis.

"It was just the drama of the situation with the show Pete had put on right before," Herb White said. "People just came streaming out of the stands. Picked him up on their shoulders. Dancing around. There were some Georgia cheerleaders in there as well."

Tribbett was overjoyed but wondered what it was like to be in a Bulldogs uniform at that moment. "There was this roar from the crowd and their guys just got beat," Tribbet said. "I wonder what the other team thought."

"It was embarrassing but it was sensational," said Gimpel. "Our guys felt like the Washington Generals [the patsy opponent of the Globetrotters]. The players were [angry] that we lost but we saw something that we had never seen before and probably would never see again. The coaches were very angry. Very angry."

White recalled that a livid Coach Rosemond turned to his players on the bench and screamed an obscenity, and then added, "We didn't deserve that."

Friend and former N.C. State player and coach Les Robinson visited Maravich in the locker room afterward.

"[Great] game, Pete," Robinson said.

"Les, I think that was the greatest game I ever played," Pete said in response.

In the locker room Pete (with the help of two Pistol Pete forgers—LSU booster John Hutchison and radio broadcaster Brad Brian) signed well over 1,000 autographs. Meanwhile Press, in a radio interview, shrugged off Pete's 35-foot hook shot. "He's done that many times in practice."

Atlanta Constitution reporter Michael McCarty, who covered the spectacle, wrote: "Pistol Pete Maravich, provocative to the point of being unbelievable, left all the heads in Bulldog country wagging in awe. An ecstatic crowd of 10,600 hung on every move of the LSU moppet, and he rewarded them with a matchless, devastating 58-point performance."

One footnote to that night in Athens: The LSU film crew ran out of stock as the game extended into its second overtime and, as a result, failed to record Pete's final heroics.

The Georgia film crew captured the overtime, but not for long. "Rosemond was so [angry] that I think he burned it," said Brennan. White agreed, "I think he cut out that hook shot and burned it."

"I don't mind," said Maravich years later. "When I'm 70 years old and telling my grandchildren about that shot, I imagine it will match my age."

In 1999, White discovered a paper bag in his house jammed with unspoiled 16mm film. After a careful telecine transfer to video, it was determined that the film was indeed from the March 8 Georgia vs. LSU game. But, unfortunately, the color footage (which eventually made its way into the CBS documentary, *Pistol Pete: The Life and Times of Pete Maravich*) did not include the legendary heave.

With the regular season concluded, Maravich was, again, the national scoring champion. In 26 games as a junior, he scored 1,148 points, for an average of 44.2 points a game (scoring 50 or more points nine times, or 35 percent of his games). He was a more efficient player, too, shooting less and scoring more. His field-goal percentage improved from .423 to .444, and his preseason goal to set up his teammates was also realized. He totaled 128 assists, raising his average from 4.0 to 4.9 per game. He did most of his damage away from home, averaging 46.5 points in LSU's 15 road games and just 41.0 in the 11 contests at the Agricultural Center.

The "Three M's" scoring race was, ultimately, a blowout. Purdue's Mount finished a distant second with 33.3 points and Niagara's Calvin Murphy took third with 32.4. Pete's 10.9-point margin over Mount remains the largest differential between first and second place in the history of the NCAA.

Maravich was, once more, a unanimous first team All-American selection in polls by UPI, AP, *The Sporting News, Look*, and the rest. Mount, Murphy, Lew Alcindor, and Bob Lanier (or in some polls, Spencer Haywood) rounded out the top five. Alcindor led UCLA to its third consecutive NCAA title and was voted College Player of the Year. He was also the first recipient of the newly created Naismith Award. Pete was runnerup for both awards.

As the accolades poured in for Pete, Press found himself fretting about his son's future. The first armed services draft lottery since World War II was scheduled for December 1969, and Press was worried that Pete, like Ronnie, would end up in Vietnam. In the spring of 1969, Press dropped by the office of Army Reserve Officers Training Corps Colonel James May, a man he'd befriended upon arriving in Baton Rouge three years earlier. May, a fellow Yank, attended all the LSU games. "It was like watching ballet," May said.

"Every time Pete touched the ball, it was a miracle. He was so far ahead of his time." And now Press sought his advice about the draft.

May explained that a national figure like Pete, if commissioned, would most likely land in a sports program playing or coaching basketball. To achieve that status, Pete would have to rejoin the ROTC program (Pete had stopped after two mandatory years).

"Can you do that for Pete?" Press asked.

" . . . I can do that," May assured him. "The first thing we have to do is get Pete a physical."

May arranged an appointment at the Veterans Administration hospital in New Orleans, but Press beat him to the punch.

"I already took him down," Press told his friend.

When the report came back several days later, the colonel was shocked by what he read. "Pete was disqualified. He was 4–F. I couldn't believe it. How could this guy not pass a physical?"

It wasn't his gnarled feet or knee damage that earned Pete the service's lowest physical rating. It was a heart murmur. May was astounded. He had watched Pete tear up and down the court.

May was even more amazed that Press did not order further tests on Pete's condition. The Maraviches decided it was in their best interest not to know any more details. After all, Pete had just scored more points over two years than any player in the history of college basketball. *How bad could his heart be?*

Nineteen years later the sports world would learn, in horrible fashion, the answer to that question. Although he would never know it, Pete Maravich's life was hanging by a thread.

9

The Road Show

"You talk of Jerry West or Oscar Robertson or any of the great ones who scored and passed so well. Maravich is better."
— LOU CARNESECCA, ST. JOHN'S UNIVERSITY COACH

"I always thought of Mr. Maravich as a guy who was putting a concert on, and the place was rocking. That's what it was like to go see Maravich."
— DICK VITALE

Pete Maravich began his senior year at LSU with two goals. The first was to lead the Tigers into a postseason tournament. "If we win the SEC title, it's the NCAA tourney. If not, I hope we do well enough to get invited to the NIT in New York," Pete told Baton Rouge reporters.

To qualify for the NCAA Tournament, LSU would have to vanquish the University of Kentucky juggernaut. Over the summer Pete lifted weights to bulk up for the physical abuse he was sure to encounter. At the time, basketball players, especially guards, were discouraged from lifting due to a belief that it disrupted their shooting motion. But after being manhandled by Kentucky the previous two years, Pete decided to pack on some muscle. Pete hit the football squad's Nautilus equipment and, for the first time, tipped the scales at 200 pounds.

"I don't think it will hurt my quickness or shooting at all," Maravich said. "At 6-5, I can carry that kind of weight, but I'll probably play between 195 and 200. I know I can jump higher now."

Two sophomores, Al "Little Apple" Sanders and Bill "Fig" Newton, would assist the team's effort for a postseason tournament spot. Sanders, a rare Press Maravich recruit from inside Louisiana, stood 6-6 and weighed 225 pounds. He was a local legend, having led Baton Rouge High School to an undefeated season and state title. A two-time all-state selection, he is still regarded among the most gifted athletes to come out of the bayou. Newton arrived from

Rockville, Indiana, thanks to the efforts of assistant coach Jay McCreary, who had recruited several players from the region, including Pete's backcourt running mate Jeff Tribbett. Newton stood 6-9 and weighed 210 pounds. The Hoosier was highly recruited but, after meeting Pete, he was sold on LSU.

"He was the original Showtime," Newton recalled. "I looked up to him. I remember going to watch the Olympic Trials in 1968, with my dad. Rick Mount was set up to be the star of the game, but Pete put on such an amazing exhibition of ball handling and passing that he was given the MVP. Pete personally recruited me on campus. He had a personality—an aura about him—that just drew you to him."

With Newton and Sanders joining 6-8 forward Danny Hester, LSU finally had a formidable front line.

Pete's second goal for his senior year was to become the greatest scorer in major college basketball history.

Maravich had accumulated 2,286 points in his first 52 varsity games and ranked 14th all-time among NCAA scorers. Topping the list was Oscar Robertson, who, in three brilliant campaigns at the University of Cincinnati (1958 to 1960), netted 2,973 points and was thrice named College Player of the Year. He averaged 33.8 points and 15.2 rebounds and led the Bearcats to three straight NCAA Tournament appearances. (Cincinnati won its first NCAA title the year after Robertson graduated.)

In 1969 the Levee Press published the first Maravich biography: *Pistol Pete: The Story of College Basketball's Greatest Star*. It was written by Peter Finney, associate sports editor of the *New Orleans States-Item*, who was a close observer of Pete and Press from the time they arrived in Louisiana. His 95-page book was a fairly comprehensive biography of Pete's life up to that point. Finney had the full cooperation of the Maraviches and the book is stocked with wonderful personal photos from the family album. One of the appendices, entitled "Basketball Tips," was written by Pete. It sold for $1.95 and Pete continually ribbed Finney that he never received a penny of it.

Another book published in time for the season was simply called *Maravich*. Written by John Musemeche (who covered sports for the Baton Rouge *Morning Advocate*) and Steve Ellis, it sold for just one dollar. *Maravich* was a 40-page, oversized photo book filled with great action shots and insightful articles and interviews. Unlike Finney's book, *Maravich* concentrated on Pete's years at LSU.

Maravich was the brainchild of Ellis, branch manager of City National Bank in Baton Rouge and an LSU booster. "I suggested the idea to John and told him that if he would write the stories, I would sell the advertising," recalled Ellis. They sold about 9,000 copies (many at home LSU games) and the remaining 1,000 were dumped off to a book distributor called Claitors. Twenty-five years later, copies of *Maravich* were selling for more than $100 on eBay.

In addition to the two books, and another song "Pistol and his Pop," the December 1, 1969 edition of *Sports Illustrated* featured Pete on its cover once again. The accompanying article was a first-person narrative written by Pete (with an assist from Curry Kirkpatrick) entitled, "I Want to Put on a Show." Pete described how he loved turning on a crowd, the purpose behind many of his ball handling drills (the ricochet, the pretzel, the see-saw), and how he delivered passes on a fast break.

"That is what I really love," wrote Maravich. "Blasting down the middle on a three-on-one or a three-on-two. Sometimes when we start out and I see the play developing, I just want to shout out, 'Hey, here we go. Hey everybody watch this!'"

The intent of the article was to provide readers with an entertaining, inside look at the work ethic and imagination that produced Pistol Pete's startling array of moves and shots. Unfortunately it had the opposite effect for some readers. The idea that showmanship and individual achievement was being emphasized offended basketball purists. That sentiment was exemplified in a letter to the editor of *Sports Illustrated*.

"It was obvious to me, and probably to the vast majority of your readers, that Maravich does not really care about basketball at LSU, winning or any other mundane yardsticks by which greatness is inevitably measured," wrote one reader. "But he cares only about Pete Maravich and what a flashy show he can put on."

A week after the magazine hit the newsstands, Pete was already modifying its message. "Winning, not the showtime stuff, is what it's all about. What I want to do, more than anything else, is to win for my dad," a defensive Pete told the Associated Press. "He's taught me everything I know about this game. Everything. And he's taken such a beating for what he lets me do. I've seen what it's done to him, how it's changed him."

The Maravich tenure at LSU was becoming a double-edged sword for Press and Pete. The desk in Press's office was flooded with fan mail, autograph requests, and love letters for Pete from across the nation. But there was also hate mail.

"We had to change our personal telephone number eight or nine times the last couple of years. Some of the fans are really vicious," Press mentioned to a local reporter.

The strain was building before the season even began. Pete's eyes would glaze over as he answered the same questions again and again. "I almost feel like a wind-up doll," Pete said in 1969. "Turn the key and it says the same thing: 'No, there isn't any friction playing for my dad.' 'He coaches the team and runs the team.' 'Yes, I would do the same if I did it over again.'"

Carl Macmurdo, a freshman player at LSU when Maravich was a senior, witnessed the intrusions. "This father and son drove into Baton Rouge around 11 A.M. on a Saturday," Macmurdo recalled. "They were passing through town because Pistol Pete was this kid's idol and he wanted to get an autograph. Anyway, they came to the dorm, and Pete was in the bathroom inside of Broussard Hall. The student at the front desk said, 'Pete's in the bathroom right now, but he'll be out in a second.' The boy's father said, 'We can't wait. We're in a hurry.' So I followed this father and son into the bathroom. Pete was sitting in the stall and they asked him for his autograph. And Pete obliged them. I wouldn't have believed it if I didn't see it with my own two eyes."

Johnny Carr was a backup forward on the LSU varsity. "Pete was basically a shy, self-conscious guy," Carr said. "After practice we used to go eat pizza, and every time we did, Pete was constantly bothered by everybody. He couldn't go anywhere without being mobbed."

Pete later reflected in his autobiography about the tightening vice. "I found myself slowly becoming a slave to the never-ending pressures placed on me. The demands started coming in all forms and from every direction."

His teammates noticed a sullen demeanor seemed to blanket Pete. He was more withdrawn and became increasingly suspicious of the motives of strangers. He had trouble sleeping. He spent less and less time at the dorm with its constantly ringing hall phone, preferring an off-campus apartment. At times he could still let loose, but the wide-eyed enthusiasm of his freshman year was slowly draining away. Basketball was beginning to own him.

LSU's 1969-70 schedule looked daunting. In addition to the rough SEC, the team was also booked to play Oregon State, USC, and UCLA. Despite the presence of Maravich, no one gave the Tigers much of a chance to be a factor in the conference. When asked about the likelihood of winning the SEC title, Press quipped: "How much chance have you got with Raquel Welch?"

Before the season, the Tigers played an exhibition against Athletes in Action, a Christian outreach organization that fielded teams of talented amateurs. The Tigers won by just three points and Pete was certainly reminded of his rejection of Jesus Christ in California three summers earlier. During this period of his life, Pete routinely ridiculed Christian fans. Their letters that offered to pray for him were immediately tossed in the trash.

The Tigers, sporting a new, robust front line, began the season on a roll. They easily disposed of Oregon State, Loyola of New Orleans, Vanderbilt, and Tulane. Maravich, wearing a small locket that contained a photo of Jackie, averaged 48.8 points over the four-game run. The knee injury that hampered him over the second half of his junior year had healed without surgery.

In the Loyola game, a defender tried a creative way to distract Pete—pinching Maravich on his rear end. In the second half, he kissed Pete on the neck. When Pete whirled around with his fist cocked, the defender smiled and held his hand out for a shake.

"I knew if I punched him I would be out of the game," Pete told John Husarc of the *Chicago Tribune*. "I've played against every type of defense possible but that's the ultimate they can do to shake me up. I was scared to go up for jumpers."

Pete kept his composure and dropped home 45 points (18-36, 9-10, 6 rebounds, 6 assists) in the 100-87 victory.

LSU was off to its best start since Bob Pettit's senior year of 1953-54, but a challenge loomed in the fifth game as USC was coming to Baton Rouge. The Trojans featured a crew of overachieving sophomores and transfers led by Paul Westphal, Mo Layton, and Ron Riley. All three would go on to play multiple years in the NBA. "This game will be a good indicator of how good we really are," Press told *Los Angeles Times* reporter Jeff Prugh.

USC, like LSU, was a high-scoring team. Against their one common opponent, Vanderbilt, both the Trojans and the Tigers had put 109 points on the board. Two weeks before the game USC coach Bob Boyd sent his freshman coach, Jim Hefner, to scout Maravich. Hefner reported: "He's a quicker, faster version of Rick Barry. He mesmerizes everyone in the gym."

Ticket demand outstripped available seating. Several fans broke windows and crawled in through the bathrooms. Fifty fans without tickets rushed a security guard. One enterprising student purchased a block of ice, delivered it to the service entrance, and, once inside, dropped it in the hall and disappeared into the crowd. All 28 sections of the Agricultural Center were packed with fans.

Maravich seemed to disappear in the opening minutes. Shadowed by Layton, Pete missed his first five shots. "I was getting tired out there following him around," said Layton. "When I went up with him and made him force his shots, he'd say to me, 'Good defense. Good defense.'"

Meanwhile, the Trojans were in a groove and led by 23 after just nine minutes. But by half time, LSU had whittled the margin to 13.

With 6:30 remaining in the second half, USC led 92-75. Then the Tigers switched to a zone press and went on a thrilling 21-5 run, as the flustered Trojans committed five turnovers. The jam-packed crowd was ecstatic as it cheered on one of the greatest comebacks in school history.

But it wasn't enough. Despite Pete's 50 points (18-43, 14-16, 6 rebounds, 4 assists), USC handed LSU its first defeat of the year, 101-98. "USC was nationally ranked," said forward Johnny Carr. "It proved to us we could play with a big team from the West Coast."

Maravich's performance that night left a lasting impression on future NBA star Paul Westphal. "The energy Pete used to get around those picks was simply astounding," Westphal said in 2003. "We kept a fresh, aggressive defender on him at all times, yet he would simply not wear down. I never saw anything like it."

Pete's 50 points vaulted him past Seattle's Elgin Baylor (2,500) and Princeton's Bill Bradley (2,503) into fifth place on the NCAA all-time scoring list. "He's the purest, greatest basketball player we've ever seen," Trojan coach Boyd told the *Los Angeles Times* after the game.

It seemed counter-intuitive, with one player averaging 49 points, but the Tigers, at 5-1, were playing great team ball. They were scoring a bit over 101 points a game while allowing 90. The team was shooting over 52 percent. Danny Hester was adding 17.5 points to the bottom line and "Apple" Sanders was pulling down almost 14 rebounds a game.

The day after the grueling USC game, LSU began a two-week road trip. A game scheduled against Clemson was moved to Charlotte Coliseum in North Carolina due to overwhelming ticket demand. Tickets were five dollars for adults, two dollars for students. Press instituted a new "rule" that his son was not allowed to give television interviews before games. In Charlotte, however, the rule was relaxed and Pete agreed to several on game day.

The pregame distraction seemed to relax Pete as he produced the most efficient shooting night of his college career, hitting 22 of 30 shots (.733) and netting 49 points (6 rebounds, 9 assists) in a 111-103 LSU win. "But the figures in the record book will never capture the impression that Pete Maravich made on Clemson's team and the 7,282 fans," wrote Harry Lloyd in the *Charlotte Observer*. "Some of his passing was even more spectacular than his deadly shooting."

The team was scheduled to return to New Orleans after the game, but fog forced the cancellation of its flight. The Tigers stayed in Charlotte and the next morning caught a 5 A.M. flight to Atlanta. There, the team walked across a snowy tarmac to connect to a Dallas flight. From Dallas they flew on to Oregon, landing at 5:30 P.M. Pacific time. The following night, December 22, 1969, against Oregon State University, Pete produced one of the most amazing feats in the history of basketball.

The Tigers were eager to provide a show for the 10,388 fans wedged into the Gill Coliseum. Long gone was LSU's "Globetrotter" circle, but Pete's pregame dribbling and shooting drills drew gasps and applause. One fan who watched with great interest was 10-year-old Danny Ainge, a future NBA star.

"The Pistol was just pure basketball player," recalled Ainge years later. "He did things that nobody else could do. It was because he worked at it. He worked at ball-handling skills. And that's not to say that those other guys didn't work, 'cause I played with Larry Bird and I certainly know he worked. And we all know Michael Jordan worked after getting cut in high school, so I'm not trying to downgrade any of those players. But Pistol still did things that nobody today can do. He was the most exciting player that I ever saw." When Ainge signed with the Boston Celtics, he chose Pete's old NBA No. 44.

Oregon State slowly built a lead and, late in the first half, led by 14. It was a nasty game. "They were a bad bunch—all of them," recalled Tribbett. "I can even remember two old ladies, sitting right up close to the court and cursing at us the whole time. I couldn't believe it." From the LSU bench, the Tiger subs were returning "friendly gestures" to the crowd.

The two sides finally came to blows when Sanders instigated a fight with OSU's Vince Fritz. Both benches emptied as the skirmish escalated. "Guys were swinging out there and grabbing guys around the neck," recalled Oregon State coach Paul Valenti. It took officials five minutes to restore order and Sanders was ejected from the game. Press was livid and earned three technical fouls (there was no automatic ejection in the NCAA at that time). Pete then scored 11 points in a 13-2 Tigers' run as the first half ended with LSU trailing 37-34.

After intermission, OSU used a "controlled" offense to dramatically slow down the pace. They just kept passing the ball to each other. Pete pleaded with future-NBA guard Freddie Boyd, "Shoot the ball, Freddie. Nobody wants to see this." But Boyd wouldn't take the bait. It got so ridiculous that Pete eventually plopped down on the floor, crossed his legs Indian-style, and dared Boyd to dribble by him.

"Can you make a layup now?" Pete taunted.

Soon the Oregon fans began to boo their own team and Coach Valenti abandoned the stall.

OSU's strategy for stopping Pete was simple: foul him. But on this night Pete was in a zone as he stepped to the line and converted 30 of 31 free throws, including 21 in a row. No basketball player in major college or the NBA had ever made 30 free throws in a regulation game. As of 2006, Pete is still the only player to do so.

"Like DiMaggio's 56-straight-game hitting streak, certain records most likely will never be broken," said LSU assistant coach Greg Bernbrock. "OSU kept fouling Pete—which we thought was not very intelligent."

"But do you know the beautiful part?" asked Tribbett with a smile. "We came on to win the . . . game after all that. It was one of the most satisfying wins of the year."

There was little time to celebrate the 86-75 victory, however, as LSU was scheduled to take the floor against UCLA in less than 20 hours. After a two-hour bus ride back to Portland, the Tigers boarded a flight for Los Angeles.

As the team wearily made its way to the plane, Press lamented the back-to-back contests. "I thought that when we lined it up we could use it for a recruiting gimmick. We're stupid for this schedule."

Stupid or not, the Tigers were now heading for a date with UCLA, where Press's unlikely friend John Wooden had assembled the most successful college basketball program of the 1960s and 1970s.

Wooden was a star athlete in high school and at Purdue University. After coaching at Indiana State he took over the UCLA program in 1948. He was a master motivator who stressed discipline, teamwork, and preparation. His quaint homilies still resonate with many of his ex-UCLA players.

"Perfection is an impossibility but striving for perfection is not."

"Failing to prepare is preparing to fail."

"Be quick but don't hurry."

Wooden never had a losing season as a college coach and steered UCLA to an unprecedented 10 national championships. He had a deep appreciation of Pete's catalog of skills. "Pete Maravich could do more things with the basketball than any other player I've ever seen, and that includes those fellas on the Globetrotters," said Wooden.

Wooden was less enamored with his shot selection. "The way Pete could shoot, he should have been shooting 60 percent based on his ability," said Wooden. "In my opinion, if Pete Maravich had taken only the shots he should have taken, he'd have the highest shooting percentage of anybody who ever played in college or the NBA."

Wooden's Bruins were in the middle of a historic run. They had captured five of the previous six NCAA titles, the last three with the help of Lew

Alcindor. The 1969-70 Bruins featured guards Henry Bibby and John Vallely, forwards Sidney Wicks and Curtis Rowe, and center Steve Patterson.

The *Long Beach Press-Telegram* headline read, "UCLA Hosts Pistol Pete's 'Greatest Show on Earth.'"

The Tuesday night game had a rock concert atmosphere. Everyone wanted to see the high-scoring LSU hot-shot take on the best college team in America.

"Among those in the stands at Pauley Pavilion was the mod crowd, with its flashy clothes and wild hair styles," reported Steven Bisheff of the *Los Angeles Herald-Examiner*. Actors Mike Connors and Dustin Hoffman were there. Every seat in Pauley was occupied with hundreds more sitting on the floor behind each basket.

"In my senior year of high school, I knew I was going to UCLA and I attended a lot of games," recalled NBA Hall of Famer Bill Walton. "There was no bigger game than when Pete Maravich traveled to Pauley Pavilion to play UCLA."

Pauley Pavilion was jammed with 12,961 people, the largest crowd at UCLA during Wooden's tenure. Unfortunately the game did not live up to its promise.

The Tigers, who had traveled 5,800 miles in four days, were leg weary. "We felt we could put the pressure on and then really run," said Wooden. The guards doubled Pete and the Bruin fast break was in high gear. UCLA took a 9-0 lead after two minutes. After 11 minutes, the Bruins led 40-20.

"We played so many games in so many days," said Tribbett. "Before you knew it, we were down by 20 points and it just got worse from there. Fatigue was a factor but they were so much better than us."

When it was all over, the balanced and tenacious Bruins had crushed LSU, 133-84.

Pete had a nightmarish outing, he missed 10 of his first 11 shots on his way to 38 points (14-42, 10-12, 4 rebounds, 7 assists). Many of his usually pinpoint passes were way off the mark. A tape of the game shows he turned the ball over 11 times. He analyzed his dreadful evening for Jim Perry of the *Herald Examiner*.

"The other night I hit 22 out of 30 shots. Tonight, it felt like I got 3 out of 90. Maybe I should wash my socks. I haven't cleaned them in a week." Asked about UCLA's performance Pete said, "They are truly something. Every one of those guys is a great player. Were we tired? That's the understatement of the year. But they're just as good as last year. UCLA should join the NBA."

Maravich's declaration was prophetic as Wicks, Bibby, Patterson, Rowe, and Vallely eventually entered the pro ranks.

Still, the game made an impact on one of the UCLA players. "It was a game that was very special for us—which very few games were," recalled Patterson. "We were somewhat jaded, blasé. He electrified things. He brought a sense of humor and a sense of style that probably put gray hair on coaches."

"UCLA Gunners Pistol-Whip LSU" headlined Loel Schrader's article in the *Long Beach Press-Telegram*.

The Tigers couldn't leave Los Angeles fast enough. After setting a personal and national record in the previous two games, Pete had suffered through the most humiliating defeat of his college career. Still, the Tigers had lost only two games and both were to nationally-ranked teams. Plus Pete had now passed Furman's Frank Selvy (2,538) and Wake Forest's Dickie Hemric (2,587) to stand third on the all-time scoring list.

LSU left for Hawaii to play in a relatively new Christmas tournament, the Rainbow Classic, hosted by the University of Hawaii. The field included Drake, Yale, San Francisco, Iowa, St. John's, and the Submarine Forces of the Pacific.

LSU drew the Submarine Forces team in the tourney's first round. Because the Sub team was not an NCAA school, the outcome is not recorded in any official record book. The game occurred on Saturday, December 27, in front of a record 7,433 fans at the Honolulu International Center Arena.

A young Al Michaels was the play-by-play man on local radio and he remembers the excitement Pete generated on the island. "We were all curious to see, in person, what he could actually do on the court," recalled Michaels.

The game against SubPac might be Pete's most interesting of the season because he didn't feel any pressure to maintain his 44-point scoring average. LSU took the contest seriously because losing would mean an embarrassing elimination. The Tigers won, 88–80, with Pete scoring just 26 points. However none of the fans were disappointed because they got to witness Maravich's dazzling dribbling and passing.

"He surpassed our expectations," recalled Michaels. "He was just unbelievable."

Dan McGuire of the *Honolulu Advertiser* wrote, "Pete gave a tremendous show of uncanny passing and floor work that had the SubPac Raiders bewildered throughout most of the game."

Next up was St John's, a team ranked in the nation's top 20 and the tournament favorite. Coached by the fiery Lou Carnesecca, the Redmen had advanced to the NCAA Tournament three years running.

Carnesecca developed an unusual strategy for containing Maravich. He was going to play him straight up, man to man. He outlined his strategy to University of Georgia's Nick Gimpel when the two met over the summer.

Gimpel, who was on the court for Pete's legendary hook shot game, pleaded with him. "Coach, there's no way you can play Maravich man to man. You're not going to be able to do that against this guy."

Carnesecca would not budge. "Listen Nick, we play everybody man to man," he said. "Calvin Murphy we play man to man."

"Coach, you haven't seen anything like this guy Maravich."

It was a tactic not used on Pete all season, and it worked fairly well—in the first half. Maravich had just 13 points and the Redmen, behind the scoring of Billy Paultz and Joe DePre, held a slim 31-29 half-time lead.

"You know what, Pete didn't do much in the first five minutes of the second half either," Carnesecca recalled. "I really thought we had them."

The Pistol, after being held in check for a majority of the game, went on a torrid scoring run. He swished in numerous shots from outside 25 feet, including a long-distance two-hand set shot from nearly 40 feet. Maravich went up, around, and in between the collapsing defenders.

"He was an artist, a dancer, he played with music in his ears," recalled St. John's assistant, John Kreese, years later. "You could not stop him."

LSU sports information director Bud Johnson noted one pass where Pete seemed to defy the laws of momentum. "Against St. John's, one of the LSU players grabbed a rebound, started the fast break and threw the ball to Pete near center court. At about the circle, Pete was in full flight, watching the ball over his shoulder, his left hand outstretched. The first athletic thing he did was to make a complete stop because a defender was positioned at mid-court to take the charge," Johnson said. "Then, in one motion, he took the ball behind his back and passed it between his and the defender's legs— right into the hands of Bill Newton for a layup. It was a half-court assist. I had never seen him do that before."

Jack Lord, star of the popular television series *Hawaii Five-O*, was sitting next to Johnson. He asked, "Does he do that all the time?"

St. John's scored 39 points in the second half but Maravich countered with 40 of his own and finished with 53 points as the Tigers pounded out an 80-70 victory.

"The guy's always entertaining. He's always on," Carnesecca gushed to a roomful of reporters. "He almost hypnotizes you on the court. Here I am trying to coach my club, watching the action all over the court. And what am I doing? Watching him!

"He did some unbelievable things. On one play he faked a dribble, double-pumped and hits this guy with a pass off the wrist. Ever see that? He does it all going at full speed. That's what's so amazing. The more men we put on him, the better he got.

"It was the most electrifying 15 minutes of basketball I've ever seen."

The Pistol's performances created such buzz that tournament officials arranged a statewide telecast of the LSU vs. Yale championship game on KHVH-TV Channel 4. The Ivy League's Yale was the Cinderella team of the tournament, upsetting host Hawaii and San Francisco.

The game started off well for the Tigers, but then Pete was hit with three quick offensive fouls. For veteran NCAA referee Irv Brown, they were easy calls. "Yale got excellent position every time Maravich would drive and Pete picked up three charging fouls. And I was very unpopular." LSU still led 51–42 at the half.

Early in the second half, Brown tagged Maravich with his fourth foul forcing Pete to play conservative ball from that point on. With five minutes remaining, and LSU leading, Yale revved up its five-man shuffle offense and made a successful final push, eventually edging LSU, 97–94.

Yale's 5-11 Jimmy Morgan outscored Pistol Pete, 35-34.

After the game Press lit into the team like never before. "He went absolutely nuts," said Tribbett. "He was just livid. As angry as I have ever seen, and probably had every right to be."

Johnson was impressed by Yale's efforts. "I remember they were all over Pete and almost inviting Rich Hickman to take the shot," Johnson said. "Hick was a streak shooter; he got hot for a while, then cooled off. He blamed himself for the loss and after the game just sat in the locker room and cried."

Even the local press was upset. Jim Becker, a columnist for the *Honolulu Star-Bulletin*, was so incensed by Irv Brown's foul calls on Maravich he wrote a scathing article about the referee. Brown unsuccessfully sued the columnist for libel. "They didn't bring me over there to take care of Pete," recalled Brown. "They brought me over there to be fair."

The team flew home in time to welcome the New Year and the new decade. LSU's schedule lightened up considerably with just three games over the next 25 days, starting with a home game against Alabama.

The Crimson Tide, coached by C. M. Newton, tried to rattle Pete with sarcastic taunts. "Way to go, Pistol Pete." "Keep looking good for everyone." "Take it from us, Pistol Pete, you sure look cute tonight."

The razzing proved ineffective as Maravich rang up 55 points (22-42, 11-18, 7 rebounds, 2 assists) and led LSU to a valuable SEC win, 90-83. There was really no effective defense against Pete. "You just hope he's not on," Alabama's Bobby Lynch explained to the *Tuscaloosa News.*

But LSU dropped its next game to Auburn, 79-70, as Maravich struggled, shooting 18 of 46 from the field. A contingent of national sports reporters, assigned to cover Super Bowl IV at Tulane Stadium in New Orleans, drove in to watch the basketball wunderkid.

"I was tired in the first half, got kicked in the head, and couldn't move laterally," Maravich explained after finishing with 44 points. "I stunk. That's what it amounted to. I had the shots. I was just short."

Pete continued his mini press conference. "[Shooting] from 25, 30 feet— that's not a strain. My percentage out there is as good as it is from 15 feet.

"I'm still hoping to get to New York for the NIT. I've never played in New York at all. There are so many basketball fans in New York and they're so appreciative. They get 19,500 for the Knicks. That's unbelievable. That would jack you up to play ball."

And when asked about closing in on the NCAA scoring record, "I'd much rather win games. Scoring all those points doesn't mean much," Pete replied. "You can have 'em all."

Every arena in the SEC was jam-packed as "Showtime" passed through on its farewell tour. On Saturday, January 24, Maravich made his final trip to Lexington, Kentucky, for a game against the undefeated Wildcats. The official attendance at Memorial Coliseum was announced as 11,500, but, according to the Associated Press, "press table observers estimated the jammed crowd at more than 13,000."

"The students were climbing up the drain pipe trying to get in," said Russell Rice, Kentucky's sports information director. "They were climbing on the television cables. It was an event every time Pete came here." More than 3,000 people were turned away.

Ex-NBA star Paul Seymour, then scouting for the Detroit Pistons, bought his ticket from a scalper for $25. The Pistons were headed for a high draft pick in 1970.

When Pete was introduced at the start of the game, "A terrific roar of applause went up from all over the arena," wrote Roger Stanton in *Basketball Weekly.* "Then the Kentucky student sections started to stand. And everyone else followed their leadership and Maravich had himself a standing ovation in the college basketball capitol of the world. It was deafening." During the demonstration, Pete sheepishly stared at the floor.

Midway through the second half Pete scored his 37th point. The Coliseum announcer informed the crowd that Pete had just passed Elvin Hayes

(2,984) to become the No. 2 all-time scorer in NCAA history. Kentucky coach Adolph Rupp lumbered over to the table and grumbled, "Why . . . did you have to announce that?" The game was temporarily stopped and Pete was presented with the ball.

"Maravich saved the best for the last," reported Dick Fenlon in the *Louisville Courier Journal*. "Pistol Pete drove the ball near the baseline on the right side of the basket with Kentucky's Larry Steele guarding him closely. Pete shifted left and right, transferring the ball from hand to hand, and finally put his left elbow in Steele's face while launching a 15-footer. He landed flat on his back while Steele was whistled for a foul. But the ball went through."

Kentucky, then ranked No. 2 behind UCLA in the national polls, defeated the Tigers 109-96. But Pete had set a Coliseum record of 55 points (21-44, 13-15, 5 rebounds, 4 assists). "I just don't see how you're going to guard a guy like that. He was even better than I thought," Rupp told reporters. "If anyone has any ideas on how to guard Maravich, I'd like to have them."

Another famous Pete, Pete Rose, was courtside in Lexington. "He's the best I've ever seen," said baseball's all-time hit leader.

After the game Pete commented on Kentucky's pregame standing ovation. "They didn't have to do that. They could have just as easily stood up and booed."

Two days later, the Tigers faced the University of Tennessee, the one SEC team that had consistently contained Maravich. This time, however, LSU was wise to Mears' plans (plus defensive specialist Billy Hann had graduated). On one possession Maravich had his back to the basket nearly 10 feet away. He flipped up a two-handed shot, over his head, that banked in.

With six minutes remaining in the game LSU held a sizable lead, so Pete said to his coach, "Dad, let's put this in the deep freeze." LSU held on to the ball for the final minutes as Pete orchestrated a spectacular game of "keep away" with behind-the-back passes and deceptive dribbling. The fans at the Agricultural Center were driven to near hysteria by the demonstration while Mears fumed. LSU finally beat Tennessee, 71-59, with Pete scoring 29 points (12-23, 5-7, 4 rebounds, 9 assists).

"He's one of the greatest players I've ever seen," Mears recalled years later. "You know, we talk about Michael Jordan's moves? No one has the moves Pete had."

Pete was averaging 47.1 points per game and was just 40 points shy of Robertson's record when Ole Miss came to town on January 31, 1970.

"The day of the game, every radio, television and print reporter talked about how tonight would be the night Pete would break Oscar Robertson's record," LSU booster John Hutchison recalled. "He had a millstone around his neck. The pressure must have been unbearable."

Press understood that the game's central drama was more Maravich vs. Robertson than LSU vs. Ole Miss, and addressed the issue head on. "We all want to see him beat Robertson's record," Press told his team before the game. "Once that's done and out of the way, we'll all be a lot more relaxed."

Press was nervous too, gulping down numerous cups of coffee and pacing the locker room. "People and writers have been calling me all week," he explained. "I never felt the pressure like I did for this game."

A crowd of 11,856 packed the Ag Center to cheer on their favorite son and, hopefully, witness sports history. "Sitting and standing, they were jammed into LSU's Cajun Cow Palace, 11,000 of 'em, with a feeling of membership in an exclusive club," wrote Peter Finney for *The Sporting News*. "A feeling shared by folks who watched Roger Maris hit his 61st home run, Bobby Jones hole out for his 1930 grand slam, and Roger Bannister break the four-minute barrier in the mile."

LSU assistant Greg Bernbrock said Maravich was like a prized racehorse, fidgeting in his stall before a big race.

"I think he knew that a monumental record was going to be tumbled that night," said Bernbrock. "Pete could not wait to get out onto the floor. That's what I remember about that night."

From the opening tip, the crowd thundered its approval every time the ball touched Pete's fingertips. However, he didn't get off a shot during the first three minutes and Ole Miss capitalized on turnovers to take an early lead. Pete's first point came on a free throw. Then he tied the game, 11–11, on a three-point play. The packed arena was rocking as the Tigers methodically surged to a 53–40 lead at half time behind Pete's 25 points. As LSU headed to the locker room the big crowd, which included Louisiana Governor John McKeithen, applauded wildly. Pete was just 15 points shy of breaking Robertson's record.

Maravich started the second half on fire. After grabbing Danny Hester's tip, he raced down the court and converted a driving layup for his 27th point. But his momentum caused him to crash into the padded post under the backboard. The crowd quieted as Pete struggled to his feet. He shook off the pain and continued his pursuit of the record. With 8:49 left, he connected on a jumper from the corner for his 37th point. With 7:58 left, he banked in a 25-footer from the left side over the Rebels 2–3 zone, giving him his 39th point and a tie with Robertson. Bedlam broke out in the stands and Maravich mistakenly believed the shot gave him the scoring title.

"I thought I broke it on the basket that tied it," Pete later told a reporter. "But then I heard the roar of the crowd start up again."

The roar Pete heard was the crowd collectively chanting, "One! One! One!"

A battery of photographers lined the Ag Center's baseline, news cameras churned, and the crowd leaned forward. But over the next three minutes Pete could not buy a bucket. First a running jump shot from 23 feet clanked off the front of the rim. Then a 20-footer from the right side hit the back of the iron and bounced over the backboard. Another shot from the top of the key barely grazed metal. A twisting drive up the middle looked good until the ball rimmed out. With each missed shot the tension ratcheted up a notch.

"I was only one shot away, but the next three minutes seemed like forever," Pete remembered in his autobiography.

"One more . . . one more . . . one more . . ." the crowd roared, raising the decibel count in the old arena to rock concert levels.

With just under five minutes remaining, Pete's roommate, Jeff Tribbett, dribbled to the top of the key and passed a few feet to his left to Bob Lang. Lang zipped the ball across the lane to Pete, who found a soft spot in the Rebel defense, 17 feet from the basket. Pete gathered, jumped, and snapped his right wrist. The ball arched over the front of the cylinder and swished through the cotton net.

Pete Maravich was now college basketball's all-time scoring leader. It was his 41st point of the game, giving him 689 points on the season, and 2,977 for his career.

"All [expletive] broke loose the instant that shot went in," recalled assistant coach Jay McCreary. "Pete kept pointing to the scoreboard, pointing out we still had a game to finish."

Looking alternately lost, happy, relieved, and embarrassed, Pete was reluctantly hoisted onto the shoulders of teammates Lang and Al Sanders.

Tribbett, who had shared the wild four-year ride with Maravich, sensed his teammate's uneasiness with the attention. "I think Pete felt uncomfortable with it. I was lucky enough to be on the floor when it happened, and went up and shook his hand and said, 'You finally did it, pal.' And then I walked away because it was his moment. The crowd kept cheering and cheering. He was humble about the whole thing."

The game was delayed for almost 10 minutes while Pete was paraded around the floor and presented with the history-making ball.

An Associated Press wire photographer captured a tender moment at the height of the celebration. In the photo, Pete, on his teammates' shoulders, is smiling at the throng of well-wishers. Press is also in the shot, but off to the side, observing the joyous tableau with a satisfied expression. That photograph was eventually chosen by Pete to grace the cover of his 1987 autobiography, *Heir to a Dream*.

When Pete was finally lowered to the floor he was cornered by television reporter Bob Scearce of WAFB-TV. "Look, we've still got a game to play," Pete said, looking at the scoreboard, which showed LSU leading, 96-76.

Undaunted, Scearce continued his exclusive interview.

"How does it feel?"

"It feels great," Pete said, cracking a cautious smile. "It feels great."

"Pete, what was the shot that did it?"

"The last shot did it," said Pete. "It went through, didn't it?"

"What kind of shot? A jump shot?"

"Jump shot," Pete confirmed.

"Is that your favorite shot?"

Pete smiled. "That's my favorite shot."

After order was restored, the game resumed and Maravich scored 12 of the Tigers final 13 points as LSU won 109-86. Maravich tallied 53 points (21-46, 11-15, 5 rebounds, 12 assists).

In the locker room, father and son breathed a sigh of relief. Press looked at the ground and a twinkle came to his eye. He smiled. "Who would have ever dreamed that that little kid who said, 'Hey dad, give me a shot' would do this?"

Pete felt humbled by the experience and acknowledged the man whose 10-year record he bested. "This is the greatest honor I've ever had," Pete told reporters. "Oscar Robertson is the greatest basketball player ever. I'm fortunate to break his record."

Photographers' flashbulbs, congratulatory handshakes, hugs, and Press's beaming smile filled the locker room from all directions. When asked about the five consecutive misses as he stood on the precipice, Pete said, "Maybe I was worried subconsciously about the record, but I also knew I had 13 more games to do it. My dad said it would be fun to average just three points and 20 assists the rest of the way to keep everyone in suspense."

In the crowd that night was a rare visitor to the Ag Center, Pete's mom, Helen. "I still get nervous when I see him play," she told a local reporter. "But I am very proud of him. This is a wonderful moment in my life, too."

Jackie Elliser quietly watched the postgame frenzy and when she and Pete were finally alone, he presented her with the historic game ball. The inscription read: "To Jackie, the greatest girl in the whole world. I love you, 'Pistol Pete.'"

The game and record sparked another wave of publicity for Pete with a cover story in *The Sporting News* and articles in both *Time* and *Newsweek*. *Basketball Weekly* ran the headline, "Maravich Worth a Million," and *The Tonight Show with Johnny Carson* offered to fly him to New York for a taping, which he politely declined.

A very special congratulatory letter landed in Press's office.

Dear Pete:
You can take great pride in your recent efforts which have established you as the leading scorer in major college basketball history. I just want you to know that the Nixons are among your fans saluting this success.
Congratulations!
>   *With best wishes,*
>   *Sincerely,*
>   *Richard Nixon*

Suddenly Pete's pre-pubescent dreams of a million-dollar contract seemed more than likely. "If the ABA and the NBA are still at war when he graduates, Maravich could command a contract that would make Lew Alcindor's look like cab fare," wrote Dan Kenny of the *New Orleans States-Item*.

Press had been pestered by hordes of would-be agents who descended on Baton Rouge. One agent said that he didn't want "a penny from the first million." But Press couldn't hire a lawyer or agent without Pete forfeiting his NCAA eligibility, so Press sought advice from his friend Art Herskovitz, an attorney in Pittsburgh.

Herskovitz said to Press, "Well, I don't know anything about basketball. Why me?"

"All these weasels are coming down to Baton Rouge and I want to go to someone I know and like," Press explained. "Above all, someone I can trust." Herskovitz agreed (never in writing) to act as Pete's representative "at the appropriate time."

The LSU Tigers won their next two games, crushing Mississippi State at home and the University of Florida in Gainesville. Pete shot 49 percent from the field and added another 102 points to his growing NCAA scoring record.

Pete's greeting from the 7,000 Gator fans was similar to his reception in Lexington, Kentucky. He received a standing ovation and the Gators presented him with a large trophy commemorating Pete's arena scoring record of 50 points, set the previous season. That mark was about to fall.

Most of the Gator fans "wound up pulling for Pete instead of Florida before the game was over," wrote Rick O'Shea in *Sports Shots*. "Every basket he made was cheered enthusiastically. When they announced he had tied the record of 50 in the gym, you'd have thought all the fans were Tiger diehards as they chanted 'Pete! Pete! Pete!' trying to spur him on to a new record." Maravich didn't disappoint and ended with 53 points (20-38, 12-16, 9 rebounds, 7 assists). But the record came at a price. During the game Pete suffered a severe groin pull.

The following Saturday, the Tigers flew into Tuscaloosa, Alabama, on the team's DC-3. Despite the game being televised throughout the South, Maravich drew another record crowd as 15,043 jammed Alabama's Memorial Coliseum. "This was the heart of football country. Bear Bryant," recalled Pete's tutor, Donald Kennard, who accompanied him on the trip. "From the plane we saw a double line of people, a quarter-mile long, waiting for tickets to see Pete."

Maravich netted 22 points in the first half but the game was quite physical and, unlike Florida, Crimson Tide fans relentlessly jeered, yelling "Hot Dog" every time Pete touched the ball.

At one point Pete dribbled deep into the corner with Alabama's David Williams and Jimmy Hollon close behind. Pete jumped, turned, and fired up a shot from the baseline as the two defenders slammed into him. All three tumbled several feet out of bounds. "I'm laying directly on top of Pete Maravich," recalled Williams. "I look back at the basket, and it's perfect—nothing but net."

Pete jumped up and drew back his fist. "But before he could swing at me, a ref got between us and stopped the whole thing," said Williams. "P.S.— he made the free throw."

At a half time ceremony, University of Alabama President Dr. David Matthews presented Pete with a ball and cited his unique contributions to the game of basketball. Pete politely thanked the fans and got ready for a historic second half.

In the final 20 minutes, Pete scored an incredible 47 points for a final total of 69, yet the Tigers lost a heartbreaker, 106-104. As the LSU players left the court, some rowdy fans pelted them with paper cups, triggering a near riot.

"People were always dogging Pete but some fan hooked Coach McCreary with an umbrella on the way out," remembered LSU's Bill Newton. Profanities were exchanged and Pete went after a guy in the stands. Although he was shy and introverted, when provoked, Pete could get quite mean and vicious.

"We came to back him up," said Newton. "Then about 40 members of the Alabama football team, who were sitting on the second row, came out to the floor."

Three or four scuffles broke out, but luckily no one was seriously hurt.

Pete's career-high 69 points set an NCAA record for most points against another Division I opponent, breaking Calvin Murphy's mark of 68. (Pete's single-game scoring record lasted 21 years, until Kevin Bradshaw of U.S. International tallied 72 points against Loyola Marymount in 1991.)

The Tigers tore through their next five opponents, downing Tulane, Florida, Vanderbilt, Auburn, and Georgia with Pete averaging 41.6 points. The victories kept an SEC title and an NCAA Tournament slot theoretically possible as LSU stood 10-3 and within reach of conference leader Kentucky (12-1).

Some members of the media felt the team was destined for the NIT. "Go ahead and assume that come March, Pete Maravich and those other four people they call the LSU basketball team will be playing in the National Invitational Tournament in New York's Madison Square Garden," wrote the *Atlanta Journal*'s assistant sports editor Lewis Grizzard.

To have a shot at winning the SEC, the Tigers had to beat Kentucky in Pete's final home game on February 21.

On the big day, Tiger fans filled the creaky Ag Center as banners lined the arena: "Welcome TVS" and "Pistol Pete Number One." At 1:49 P.M., Pete jogged in and the crowd in the converted rodeo barn exploded into a thunderous standing ovation.

This game took on special significance because it was part of a nationwide television broadcast. In 1970, regular-season college basketball was still being produced and distributed by independent networks. TeleVision Sports (TVS), which held the rights to SEC contests, had been searching for a unique game.

"I wanted to have Pete play outside of the SEC," remembered Eddie Einhorn, who created TVS. "That would have brought interest. When they played UCLA, that was on a day I couldn't use [Tuesday]. At that time, college basketball was regional. The only national games I could sell were teams from one area versus a team from another area. Like UCLA vs. Notre Dame. Nobody outside of the South would give a [expletive] about an SEC game."

Unless that game featured college basketball's all-time points leader.

Affiliates across the nation jumped at the chance to buy the feed for the Kentucky/LSU showdown. "It was seen on more television stations than any college basketball game ever," recalled Kentucky's Dan Issel. "That was a lot of fun getting that kind of recognition." In the end, 206 stations signed on, easily besting the record 150 stations TVS signed up for the epic 1968 UCLA-Houston clash in the Astrodome.

"I remember watching, I was probably 17 years old, charting the game myself in my room," reflected future broadcasting legend Bob Costas, who lived in Long Island at the time. "I drew a court and I charted how many shots he [Pete] took from each place on the court."

At 2:30 P.M., the broadcast kicked off with a short segment on Pete dribbling between his legs, behind his back, and against a wall. Following a short interview, Pistol Pete was shown walking away, casually dribbling a basketball on the grass beneath the landmark oak trees on the LSU campus.

Before the game, play-by-play announcer John Ferguson (Joe Dean handled the color) briefly interviewed each coach, starting with Press Maravich.

"We're going to give the ball to the boy and see what he can do," the coach said. "If he's hot, there's no telling what will happen."

Kentucky coach Rupp was just as adamant about how the Wildcats would handle their strategy. "I know why everybody came to watch television and came out to see the game," said Rupp. "They want to see the show and so do we. So we're going to let him do his thing, but we are going to try and stop the other people."

The game stayed close for the first 30 minutes as Pete played some of his most inspired ball, on both ends of the floor. "In the first half, Pete—not noted for his defense—forced Kentucky into two turnovers himself with adroit guarding," reported Dick Fenlon in the *Louisville Courier Journal*. Offensively he was hitting on all cylinders, but so was Issel. It was a shootout and the fans were eating it up.

With 9:17 remaining, and Kentucky leading 80-78, the Wildcats embarked on a 41-27 run to finish out the game. The final tally was 121-105 and LSU was eliminated from NCAA Tournament consideration.

But it was another night for the record book. Pete's 64 points combined with Issel's 51 to set a new mark for most points by two opponents in a major college game. Still Pete wasn't satisfied. "I missed too many easy shots," he said.

Over his six contests against Kentucky, Pete averaged 52 points. "We played Pistol Pete six times, and we won six times," Rupp reminded Marvin West of the *Knoxville News*. "And we beat Bob Pettit every time we played him, too."

"I used to get a kick out of watching our films after we played, because he [Pete] was always doing something you'd never seen before," remembered

Mike Pratt, Kentucky's tenacious guard. "He could play better than Larry Bird in the open court in transition, and he could pass like nobody before or since."

The Saturday-afternoon telecast etched Maravich into the consciousness of viewers from coast to coast. "It was unbelievable. Nobody played like this guy," said Costas. "He could get his shot from any angle or any place, any time he wanted. And any shot he took he could potentially make. He just didn't have any regrets about the ones he missed. He could get up 35, 40 shots from the guard spot in a 40-minute college game without a shot clock."

The Kentucky game marked Pistol Pete's final appearance in the John M. Parker Agricultural Center. The old rodeo barn, lacking heat and air conditioning, had provided an unlikely center ring for college basketball's most thrilling one-man show. A new assembly center was slated to debut in the fall of 1972.

On March 2, the Tigers were playing the Mississippi State Bulldogs. With 9:54 remaining in the first half, and Mississippi holding a small lead, Pete hit an 18-foot jumper for his 1,215th point of the season, another NCAA record. In 1968, Elvin Hayes scored 1,214 points in 33 games.

Billy Watkins was a high school freshman when he "rented" a student ID for five dollars to watch the game at the sold-out Maroon Gym. "I remember Pete dribbling the ball through State guard Donnie Black's legs, catching it on the other side, and swishing in a 22-footer," said Watkins. "I have since attended two Masters golf tournaments and three Super Bowls. I've seen Reggie Jackson bat at Yankee stadium, Hank Aaron hit a home run, and Muhammad Ali win a championship fight. But watching Pete that night in Starkville is at the top of my list."

LSU led by six points at the half. In the second half, Watkins and the other 5,200 fans watched Pete add 38 points to his first-half total of 17, including a staggering 30 in the final 11 minutes. The Tigers won, 97-87, and Pete finished with 55 (22-44, 11-13, 2 rebounds, 8 assists).

"I saw the Pistol do everything with a basketball except sit down on the court, peel it, and eat it," Kermit Davis Sr., Mississippi State's coach, told reporter Rick Cleveland.

With that victory, LSU tied the University of Georgia for second place in the SEC and had a week to prepare for its final regular-season game in Athens on March 7.

Press had decided that he wanted his old friend, Pittsburgh attorney Art Herskovitz, to handle the upcoming negotiations between Pete and the three professional organizations vying for his services: the NBA, the ABA, and the

Harlem Globetrotters. Herskovitz told Press he wanted to include another Pittsburgh attorney, Les Zittrain, to handle the details.

The lawyers decided to secretly meet with Pete (technically violating NCAA rules) in Athens, the site of his last regular-season game. They flew in from Pittsburgh and drove straight to the Holiday Inn where LSU was staying. Zittrain had spoken to Press over the phone, but never met him. Press was thrilled to see them but Pete, perched on the end of the bed, was skeptical. Zittrain put his hand out and introduced himself.

"Yeah," Pete mumbled. "What do you know about representing basketball players?" Without much thought, Zittrain earnestly told him he didn't know much but he could sure learn.

Zittrain remembered the exchange: "Pete looked at me again, and in that 20 seconds, I can imagine what was going through his mind. Finally he said, 'Look, I have one request of you. I want you to stay one half step ahead of me.' And I knew exactly what he meant. He never wanted to be in a position to say to me, 'Hey, you didn't think of this; you didn't think of that.' Then we shook hands and that was it."

The Georgia game returned Pete to the site of his most spectacular moment, the buzzer-beating, 35-foot hook shot in 1969. Not surprisingly, another sold-out crowd welcomed LSU.

Herb White remembered what it was like trying to cover Pete with LSU's upgraded front line. "It was just basically those three big guys setting brutal blind picks for him all over the floor," recalled White. "Just imagine you're in a pitch dark room full of refrigerators trying to catch a housefly."

This time LSU was able to win without any last-moment theatrics, 99-88.

Zittrain got to watch his future client play for the first time that evening. "Art kept telling me before the game, 'Boy Les, you won't realize how many points Pete will be scoring. It just happens.' And it sure . . . did by the time it was over. I said to myself, '. . . *this is truly exciting.*'"

Zittrain watched Pete drop in 41 points (16-37, 9-13, 3 rebounds, 11 assists). It was the end of his SEC career and, with the win, the Tigers secured second place in the conference and earned an invitation to the NIT in New York City. Their overall record was 20-8, a remarkable turnaround from Press's first year of 3-23. Over the regular season Pete averaged 46.6 points a game while increasing his shooting accuracy to 45 percent. He also upped his assist average to 6 per game and hauled in 5.3 rebounds.

Pete's four years in the SEC left a profound imprint on those lucky enough to witness the spectacle.

"In the history of college basketball there have been other marvelously talented players—Wilt, Russ, Elgin, Big O, West, Bird," wrote Curry Kirk-patrick in *Sports Illustrated* years later. "But at the top of his game, when he was smoking out another outrageous 50-point night, absolutely nobody, no time, nowhere approached Maravich."

Pete was named, for the third consecutive season, First Team All-American. Joining him were Dan Issel, Bob Lanier, Rick Mount, and Calvin Murphy.

On Sunday morning, March 8, Pete and Press flew to Pennsylvania for the finals of the Serbian National Federation Basketball Tournament in Aliquippa. They were welcomed home in a wild and chaotic scene at Aliquippa Junior High, not far from where Pete played his first organized ball.

"More than 3,600 fans greeted their heroes with a standing ovation as they entered while the Serbian tournament game was under way," wrote Ron Boggs in the *Beaver County Times.* "As they made their way to their seats swarms of people poured onto the floor and fought their way to the former Aliquippians. Only by promising more autographs later on could the police persuade the crowd to give Pete a rest."

Pete received a couple of trophies from the Serbs and was proclaimed the greatest basketball player of all time. Pete responded by doing a few of his "Homework" drills—wearing his street clothes and tasseled alligator shoes. The crowd roared its approval after each trick. He attempted a 50-foot hook shot. It clanked off the back of the rim. Pete shrugged and returned to his seat. After signing thousands of autographs, the triumphant father and son left Aliquippa.

"We have to get ready for the NIT," said Press.

"The show must go on," added his son.

10

Nine Days
in Gotham

"We really want to win this for him. My dad's given his life to basketball."
—PETE MARAVICH

"There are those who have it and those who don't. Babe Ruth had it. Joe Namath has it. It's more than great talent. It is indefinable magic that excites people, and such words as 'charisma' and 'showmanship' fall far short of explaining what Pete Maravich did to 19,500 fans in Madison Square Garden."
—GENE WARD, *NEW YORK DAILY NEWS*

The National Invitational Tournament (NIT), begun in 1938, was the brainchild of several sportswriters from the New York City area. The writers were inspired to create the NIT by the example of the Southern Conference, which originated regional postseason play in 1922 and crowned the University of North Carolina as its first champion. The New York writers believed a national elimination tourney could generate tremendous enthusiasm if it included New York area teams, featured Madison Square Garden as the site for its games, and crowned a national collegiate champion.

In the mid-1930s the Garden became a college basketball mecca largely due to the efforts of a sportswriter-turned-promoter named Ned Irish. Irish capitalized on the mushrooming popularity of college basketball by scheduling double headers at the famed arena. Although the country was in the throes of the Depression, Irish's gamble paid off as thousands of fans came to cheer (and openly bet) on local teams like Fordham, New York University, City College, Long Island University, and St. John's. Out-of-town squads included Notre Dame, Stanford, Kentucky, and Purdue.

In 1939, the NCAA began its own postseason championship, but it would take almost two decades before it began to eclipse the NIT in stature and popularity.

Although the NIT had lost some cachet by 1970, the tournament still attracted high-profile schools with nationally prominent players. In addition to LSU and Maravich, the 1970 tournament featured Army, Duke, Duquesne, St. John's, North Carolina, Oklahoma, Georgetown, Cincinnati, Georgia Tech, Louisville, Manhattan, Massachusetts, Miami of Ohio, Utah, and Marquette University. Their rosters included such future pro players as Charlie Scott, Billy Paultz, Julius Erving, Mike Newlin, Garfield Heard, and Dean Meminger.

Before departing for New York, Pete sat for an extensive interview with Bernell Ballard of the *Baton Rouge Advocate*. "Of course I am planning on playing pro basketball," Pete said. "That's how I want to make my bread. As for which league, I don't have any preference. It doesn't matter to me if they play with a green and red ball or a plain one. Right now, I'm just solely concentrating on Georgetown and the NIT."

On Friday, March 13, Delta flight 804 lifted off from New Orleans. The NIT would be the first postseason appearance for an LSU basketball team since 1954. From the aisle of the plane, Press issued a stern warning to his players: "This is not a hick town. Be very careful about what you do. Y'all have never been to New York and I don't want you to end up at the bottom of the Hudson River tomorrow."

The team arrived at the New Yorker Hotel but their rooms were not ready, prompting Pete to joke to a reporter that the delay was due to a shooting. When he finally gained access to his room, Pete was dismayed by its small size. It was so tiny he had to store his luggage in the bathroom. And when he tried to return to the lobby, the elevator malfunctioned.

"Here I was 36 floors up, with this elevator bobbing up and down," Pete recounted. "I kept punching buttons and it kept bobbing between 36 and 37. Then all of a sudden the doors opened and there was nothing but a wall there. Finally it went up to 40 and I got off. I walked down to the lobby."

On Saturday night the team visited Carnegie Hall for a concert by trumpet legend and Louisiana native, Al Hirt, who brought the team on stage for an introduction. Back at the hotel, Pete finally turned off the lights at 2:30 A.M. but, just as he was nodding off, he heard a faint knock at the door.

"Pete, Pete," whispered a female admirer. Maravich lay quiet, hoping she would disappear. She persisted until, just as Pete rose to answer the door, someone shooed her away. Pete, a fitful sleeper, would get only a few hours shut-eye before LSU's opening-round game against the Georgetown Hoyas. And it would cost him.

Georgetown, 18-7, was winding up one of its most successful basketball seasons in 25 years. Naturally the Georgetown players were excited to be in a postseason tournament but were apprehensive about facing the Pistol.

"We were very nervous about Maravich," recalled Paul Favorite, Georgetown's 6-8 center. "His reputation preceded him and he was obviously a fantastic player, shooter, the whole nine yards. Both teams were staying at the same hotel. He got on the elevator with a couple of teammates and he seemed so short to me. I pictured him larger than life. He was just a thin guy."

On March 15, Maravich entered the storied Garden. He looked up and noticed some 3,500 empty seats. "I was scared—I was afraid everybody thought the game was being played somewhere else," Pete confessed to a sportswriter. "The more people there are in the stands, the better I like it."

The empty sections were due to false rumors of a sellout combined with CBS's national broadcast of the contest, using football announcers Pat Summerall and Jack Whitaker to call the game.

Georgetown coach Jack Magee chose senior guard and defensive specialist Mike Laska to handle Maravich.

"I can guarantee you this," Pete told the *Advocate* a week earlier, "he's not going to throw just one man on me. I'm sure he's going to give him help. He might be running a diamond-and-one or a box-and-one. It's not going to be straight man-to-man."

Maravich drew an early offensive foul for plowing into Laska. The foul appeared to set the tone for the contest. "They could have called it either way," Laska told the *Washington Star.* "This told me that I could play my normal game and not worry about fouling."

Later Pete whipped a behind-the-back pass into a crowd of players jockeying for position underneath the board. Miraculously, the pass was right on the money and drew an appreciative gasp from the stands. Unfortunately Maravich's teammate, perhaps suffering a case of Garden jitters, blew the open shot. Georgetown jumped to a 5-1 lead.

Georgetown's defensive scheme, led by the tenacious Laska, proved very effective at stifling Maravich, so he focused on setting up his teammates. "I saw two men on me all the time and I thought, '. . . I'll just throw the ball around and we'll score that way,'" explained Pete. Danny Hester was on the receiving end of many of those passes, connecting on 21 first-half points as LSU went into the locker room leading 47-42. "We knew Hester could shoot," Georgetown's Artie White told the *Washington Post*'s Kenneth Turan, "but that was ridiculous." Pete, meanwhile, had just five points.

A few minutes into the second half, however, Maravich broke free and unleashed a flurry of points and assists. He fired in two long-range jumpers from the corner and then connected with Hickman on a couple of spectacular assists as LSU increased its lead to 73-65. One of those passes caught the eye of Flip Saunders, a 15-year-old Maravich fan watching in his hometown of Minneapolis. "It's still the greatest pass I've ever seen," said Saunders, now an NBA head coach. "A half-court, over the shoulder strike. Right on the money."

Georgetown center Paul Favorite got his Maravich highlight up close. "Pete was dribbling toward the center, and it was at the bottom of the box, so he was in my territory. I was supposed to switch off on him along with Laska. He went for a fade-away jump shot from the deep corner—way deep in the corner. He was still in the air and hadn't shot the ball yet. I took my hand and physically put it on his face. I dropped my hand right on his face so he wouldn't be able to see the basket. I fouled him, but he hit nothing but net. It was the most amazing shot I've ever seen."

The Hoyas hung tough and, with under a minute to play, had narrowed the Tigers lead to 81-80. Maravich was fouled by Laska and, with just nine seconds left, Press called a timeout. "Stop messing around and put the [expletive] ball in the hole," he barked at his son.

As the Georgetown fans jeered, Pete went to the line. He pushed his hair off his forehead with his left hand and then calmly sank both free throws. It proved the difference as LSU won 83-82.

Atypically, though, the story of the game was not Maravich and his scoring but the major contribution provided from LSU's front line of Danny Hester, "Apple" Sanders, and "Fig" Newton. They combined for 56 of the team's 82 points, racked up 43 rebounds, and helped foul out three Georgetown players.

Pete finished with a modest 20 points (6-16, 8-12, 6 rebounds, 5 assists) and, for the second time in his college career, was outscored by a teammate, as Hester hit for 30. "I was pitiful, I was terrible, I stunk," said Pete of his Garden debut. "It was one of my worst, no doubt about it. When I play that bad, I try to forget it."

Maravich's Big Apple debut failed to dazzle the cynical New York press, but it did impress three important Garden spectators: Jim Gardner, owner of the Carolina Cougars of the ABA; Paul Seymour, assistant coach of the NBA's Detroit Pistons; and Pete Newell, general manager of the NBA's San Diego Rockets. The Cougars held Maravich's ABA rights while the Pistons and Rockets were plummeting toward last place in the NBA. The two teams with the worst record would flip a coin to determine first selection in the college draft.

"Pete has made a fan of me," Gardner gushed to a *New York Times* reporter. "He's exciting, he moves, he represents youth and the youth movement. I think he's going to turn out to be the greatest sports personality since Arnold Palmer." Seymour acknowledged that the Pistons had their eyes on St. Bonaventure center Bob Lanier or Michigan forward Rudy Tomjanovich, but he marveled at Pete's floor leadership.

"This Maravich is really something," observed Seymour. "Georgetown is hounding him out there. They leave one or two LSU players open and he's hitting them with passes. Some of his teammates have to be remarkable to know when those passes are coming and to hold onto them."

Newell, who had been watching Pete since his days at youth basketball camps, saw Maravich's marketing potential. "He has electricity that is recognized by fans," he said. "I think he can help any franchise, weak or strong. People just come to be entertained by him, and he does just that."

The next day the observations of Newell, Seymour, and Gardner were validated when it was announced that Pete had received college basketball's greatest individual honor: United Press International's Player of the Year. The award is named after basketball's inventor, James Naismith, and Pete shyly posed with the huge trophy at the popular New York restaurant Mama Leone's. Maravich chalked up an overwhelming 467 votes from writers and broadcasters, while runner-up Bob Lanier garnered a mere 37.

On March 17, LSU faced a formidable University of Oklahoma (18-8) in a quarterfinal matchup. The Sooners, led by Garfield Heard's 34 points and 15 rebounds, had eked out a one-point win over the University of Louisville in the first round. A Garden sellout of 19,500 was the largest crowd to watch Pete during his LSU career. He was determined to please every last one of those spectators.

Both teams started slowly. In the first half, Heard struggled, shooting just 3 for 18. Pete was a bit better, 6 for 16, and had 18 points as the Tigers led 44-38 at half time. In the second half, LSU built a 15-point lead, 85-70, with four minutes remaining. But the Sooners switched to a stifling full-court press and began to chip away at the Tigers' lead. Press Maravich called a time-out and frantically drew out counter strategies in chalk right on the Garden floor. Nothing seemed to work, though, and with 1:29 left the Sooners had closed the gap to six, 92-86. At this point Pete was aggressively fouled and limped noticeably as he hobbled to the free-throw line.

He missed and Oklahoma scored three unanswered baskets to tie the score, 92-92, with 32 seconds remaining.

Pete was brutally fouled again and, before he could shoot, the Sooners called two consecutive timeouts in an attempt to "ice" Maravich. The strategy failed as Pete calmly buried both shots to put the game out of reach. The final was 97-94 and, once again, the key was the control of the boards by LSU's Sanders and Newton. They combined for 33 rebounds as the Tigers dominated Oklahoma in that department, 56-34. LSU, along with Army, Marquette, and St. John's, advanced as the tournament's final four teams.

Pete's stat line showed 37 points (14-33, 9-13, 8 rebounds, 9 assists), but he finished the game with a severely twisted left ankle, a bruised thigh, and a swollen face. "That was a tough, brutal game," recalled teammate Johnny Carr. "They were a physical team and weren't afraid to show it."

Some in the media were mesmerized by Pete's indelible performance. "Pete Maravich is what he is—a vibrant, exciting happening thousands of New York basketball fans will not forget as long as they live," wrote Gene Ward in the *New York Daily News*.

Another scribe, *New York Times* reporter Leonard Koppett, was underwhelmed. "Maravich started out obsessed with 'putting on a show' and some of his spectacular moves, amazing as they were, proved simply unnecessary and led to losing the ball," Koppett reported.

When St. John's coach Lou Carnesecca heard the criticism, he just shook his head. "Some people will criticize a star because it is too bright."

All Press Maravich could see was red. "We played like a bunch of fifth graders," Press told reporters after the game. "These kids have been up till all hours of the night pounding the pavements. Up till 4 A.M. I keep telling them we're in a national tournament now . . . They watch TV 'till all hours and then try to go out and play a [expletive] ballgame. I can tell when they get up in the morning. They look like they've been on a three-day drunk. It's just like when we played in Hawaii.

"I told [them] before they came here, 'Look, this is New York. The NIT. A prestigious tournament. It's not a little Podunk tournament with 30 teams in it. This thing has history behind it.' So what do they do? They watch TV all night. I don't have enough detectives to check all those rooms. And they've got 17,000 channels in this town. Hey, if you radio guys are getting all those, you'd better take out those bad words." Press was articulating what many had observed about the LSU players during their week in New York—they seemed unsupervised. As always, if you hung with Pete, there was no chance of repercussion from the coaching staff.

One evening Pete met face-to-face with one of his sports idols, recalled LSU booster Steve Ellis. "Joe Namath walked into his bar [Bachelors III] that night wearing a suede jacket with fringe. He had two girls on each arm. He recognized Pete, who was standing with me and some team members," said Ellis. "It was about 11 P.M. Joe said, 'Aren't you out a little late there, Pete? Don't you have a game tomorrow?' Pete smiled and answered, 'You're one to talk.'"

The next day, during a practice session at the Garden, a stranger approached a security guard and asked to see Pete. It turned out Pete had dropped his wallet in the cab on the way back from Bachelors III. All the man wanted in exchange was an autograph and a handshake. Maravich, embarrassed and grateful, was happy to oblige.

The wallet incident had a happy ending, but what occurred on March 18 was more controversial. It was the night before LSU's semifinal game with Marquette. Pete had just cancelled an appearance on *The Dick Cavett Show*, opting instead to nurse his injuries from the rough Oklahoma game. He returned to the New Yorker, invited several teammates over, and locked the door. Feeling nostalgic, he leaned back on his pillows and shared memories of the past four years.

"The party continued into the night and I got totally wasted," Pete later penned in his autobiography. "Sitting on the threshold of my very first championship, I drank to feel good and to forget. I had finished a great four years of playing the game, and all I wanted to do was celebrate the end of it all."

"That, in fact, did happen," said Brad Brian, the Tigers radio announcer, who was not personally in the room but made the trip to New York. "I think they all ruined it for themselves by going out drinking the night before."

However, Jeff Tribbett, Pete's closest friend on the team, recalled that evening quite differently. "That's absolutely *not* true. Did we go out *after* the Marquette game? Yes. Did we have a good time? Yes. *But not the night before the game*. We were there to play a game and try to win a championship. After we beat Oklahoma, we were very confident."

Marquette, with a 22-3 record and ranked eighth nationally by the Associated Press, should not have been in the NIT. They were slated to play in the NCAA Tournament, but the selection committee placed Marquette in the Midwest Regional, held in Fort Worth, Texas, instead of the closer-to-home Mideast Regional in Dayton, Ohio. The inconvenient location infuriated coach Al McGuire.

"They wanted to send me to Texas," recalled McGuire. "Notre Dame was using their political power through football. I said no." In a surprise move, McGuire dropped out of the NCAA Tournament and chose to play in the NIT instead.

The colorful McGuire, who once played guard for the New York Knicks, was an infamous recruiter of inner-city players. "I wouldn't recruit a kid if he had grass in front of his house," he often said. "That's not my world. My world was a cracked sidewalk."

McGuire adored Pete's game. "In those days, no one could do what he could. Pistol Pete was the only guy that could really go beyond the Globies and Marques Haynes," recalled McGuire. "It was just like Hank Luisetti when he started it at Stanford—taking the one-hand shot. Now everyone does it—but years ago he was the only guy that really could.

"A lot of people looked on Pete as a 'Hot Dog'—you know, self-centered. He wasn't. This is what put people in the seats. This is what paid the checks and had the concession stands popping.

"Everything he did had his own style. Whether it was the sausage socks or it was the hair flipping, flapping. His style was pre-black. A lot of times when you see that style, you're probably thinking of minorities. But Pistol set a standard. He didn't copy a standard. And I knew them all in those days. I've seen them all. I've had them all. But Pistol was his own. He was like a composer, a [Cole] Porter or something like that. He set a sound in his play that I think the brothers copied. People won't like to hear that. But I think the brothers copied from Pistol."

While the Tigers were out prowling at night, McGuire's Warriors were taking the opportunity seriously and sequestering themselves in a separate hotel. They were the pre-tournament favorites and played like it. Marquette first eliminated the University of Massachusetts and its sensational sophomore, Julius Erving, and then trounced a competitive Utah squad by 20 points.

Press Maravich knew what his team would be up against, and as usual, worried himself into a state of panic. "I was up at six o'clock this morning thinking about it," he told the *New York Times*. "They jump like kangaroos and they're quick as cobras. If we play the same kind of ball we did in our last two games, they'll run us off the court."

LSU trainer Billy Simmons recalled that Walt Frazier of the NBA's Knicks popped into the locker room before the contest.

"I was talking to Pete when in walked Frazier with his signature clothes: brimmed hat, shiny black shoes, full-length fur coat, dressed to the nines," Simmons said. "Frazier turned to Pete and said, 'I got something for you when you come to the pros next year, Pistol Pete. It's a little thing called 'D.' And then he turned and walked away." Pete, nursing his swollen left ankle in the whirlpool, never said a word. Perhaps Pete was still thinking about his activities from the night before.

"When game time rolled around, I began to pay dearly for my foolishness," Pete wrote nearly 20 years later. "Kind reporters blamed the sluggish performance on my last two outings when I ran full tilt as the playmaker. Those who knew saw me still reeling from a poorly timed hangover."

Pete had encountered variations of Marquette's triangle defense during his college career but the Warriors were especially relentless. He was able to dribble and pass effectively during most of the first half, but Marquette's swarming defense dramatically reduced his shot attempts. Pete, shadowed at all times by at least two, and sometimes three, defenders, managed just nine first-half shots (hitting three).

In the second half, Pete's limping was more pronounced. "We should have given him a shot for it," Press later admitted. The game turned into a rout and Pete went almost 19 minutes without a field goal. When he hit a jumper with 1:12 remaining, the Marquette section gave Pete a sarcastic cheer. "It might seem kind of strange to say, but I felt sorry for him at the end of the game," confessed McGuire.

Marquette showed no mercy as it ended LSU's championship bid, 101-79. The LSU front line was out-rebounded 33-25 as Sanders, Newton, and Tribbett all fouled out. Once again Pete shot poorly from the field, hitting for 20 points (4-13, 12-16). His nine assists led all players but his uninspired shooting prompted Marquette's star player Dean Meminger to say that he'd seen better basketball players "that never got to college" on New York City playgrounds and schoolyards.

"I'll play pro ball for cab fare and a hamburger if they just let me play Maravich every night," chimed in Marquette's reserve guard Jack Burke.

Pete was crushed by the loss. He believed he had helped cheat Press out of a championship title and experienced years of guilt about his behavior. "When the realization of what had happened finally sank in, I was totally devastated," Pete eventually confessed. "My stupidity not only contributed to a loss, but humiliated my dad, and that was unbearable. I couldn't even look him in the face."

While Pete's drinking binges had previously resulted in court dates, bar fights, and automobile wrecks, they had never affected his performance on the court.

Two days later, LSU faced Army in the NIT consolation game. Coached by Bobby Knight, Army was an impressive 21-5 and was one of the nation's top defensive programs. For both teams, though, the game was anti-climactic and Press decided it was time for his banged-up son to sit one out. So Pete Maravich, dressed in a suit, concluded his historic college career sitting on a bench in Madison Square Garden.

Despite 21 points from Hester and 20 from Sanders, LSU lost 75-68. It was the Tigers' lowest point total of the season.

Pete's tournament performance was sub-par by his own standards but good enough to earn a spot on the All-Tournament team. In three games he posted 77 points, 23 assists, and 15 rebounds but was overshadowed by Meminger, the tournament MVP.

With his college career officially over, the media became curious about Pete's future. "I haven't even started thinking about the pros yet, but I don't think what happened in the NIT makes a difference," a distraught Pete told a reporter. "You don't base an entire lifetime of basketball on one game or tournament. Nothing has gone right for me here, but it's all over now. I wanted to win the tourney championship for my father. That's all down the drain now."

Despite two season-ending losses, LSU's 1969-70 season had been enormously successful. The Tigers, with a 22-10 record, were college basketball's biggest attraction, as some 356,847 spectators—125,000 at home and 231,847 on the road—turned out to catch the show as they barnstormed America. LSU traveled over 21,800 miles—more than any other college squad.

Pete led the nation in scoring in each of his varsity seasons, with per game averages of 43.8 as a sophomore, 44.2 as a junior, and 44.5 in his senior year.

He also increased his shooting accuracy each year (.423, .444, .447) along with his assists per game (4.0, 4.9, 6.2). The one mark that stuck out above all, though, was his career scoring average: 44.2 points per game.

Maravich's game was more than just outrageous long-range gunning. He drove to the basket with furious determination and almost a quarter of his career points came from the free-throw line. From there he averaged 10.8 points per game. No player in NBA, ABA, or NCAA history has ever averaged that many points from the charity stripe. Not Oscar Robertson, not Jerry West, not Michael Jordan.

Even though his college career was in the rear-view mirror, the scrutiny surrounding the basketball magician was still increasing. "The pressure is just beginning," Pete told reporter William Reed. "I tell you, everybody thinks I got it made but, you know, it's not worth it. There is so much pressure, and people—every day, every day. You know when I had the most fun? When I went to Daytona all by myself and just took it easy. Nobody knew me. Sometimes I wish I could be an accountant or something, man, so I could live right for a change."

Unfortunately, Pete's desire to enjoy a pressure-free, uncomplicated life would have to wait. Two professional basketball leagues were calling. He was already the No. 1 pick in the ABA draft and would learn, on March 23, which NBA team desired his services.

Part 3

NBA

Pete Maravich, NBA rookie.

11

Millionaire

"I don't expect them to resent me because of my contract. Everyone has his own and if any of the players make a zillion dollars, that's their business. Money doesn't have anything to do with the team."

—PETE MARAVICH

"They wanted us to bend to Pete. That's backwards. When I was a rookie, I was treated like one. In Pete's case, they said we should be happy just to play with him."

—LOU HUDSON, HAWK TEAMMATE

When Pete graduated from Needham-Broughton High School in 1965 there were nine teams in the National Basketball Association. By the time he left LSU in 1970, the number of pro basketball franchises had mushroomed to 28, with 17 teams in the NBA and another 11 in the ABA.

The upstart ABA was struggling to survive as its third season ended, but the league hoped to achieve solvency by duplicating the successful business model of the American Football League. Until 1965, the AFL had labored in the long shadow of the NFL, its games sparsely attended and its results relegated to the far reaches of the sports section. But that year the New York Jets signed the nation's top college prospect, Alabama quarterback Joe Namath, to a then-record contract of $427,000 (plus a Lincoln Continental).

The deal caught the attention of the sports world, generating wider interest in the AFL and increasing its television presence. In time, football fans grew curious to see the two leagues competing head to head, which led to the World Championship Game (later renamed the Super Bowl) in 1967. In 1970 the leagues merged and the value of many AFL franchises skyrocketed.

Hoping for a similar fate, the ABA adopted the "Namath model" and attempted each year to sign the top college player. In 1969, Lew Alcindor came tantalizingly close to inking a deal with the ABA's New York Nets before choosing the NBA's Milwaukee Bucks. As the signing season approached in the spring of 1970, Pistol Pete topped the ABA's "most wanted" list.

The effort to sign Maravich was spearheaded by 37-year-old millionaire Jim Gardner, owner of the Carolina Cougars. Gardner made his fortune in the early 1960s when he expanded Wilber Hardee's hamburger stand in Greensboro, North Carolina, into a national restaurant chain.

Gardner and the ABA were convinced that acquiring Maravich would give the league instant credibility and spur CBS to improve its modest television contract with the league. With that in mind, the league hired Jack Dolph, a former CBS sports executive, as its new commissioner, hoping his television background would come in handy during contract negotiations with the Tiffany network. But Gardner's quest to obtain Maravich grew more complicated when the world-famous Harlem Globetrotters joined the fray.

"Maravich is the biggest thing—box-office wise—ever to hit basketball," Globetrotters boss George Gillett said. "Your tall towers, like Alcindor and Chamberlain, don't really excite the public. They have their height and their talent, but Maravich has everything and the fans identify with him to the nth degree. They are mesmerized by his every move."

The Globetrotters reportedly offered Maravich a million dollars to join its roster of entertainers.

During the NIT tournament, the *Boston Herald-Traveler*'s Cliff Sundberg wrote that Pete had accepted and would "start his pro career barnstorming with the Harlem Globetrotters." The column added, "It will mark the first time the Trotters will be integrated."

Both claims were false. The Globetrotters had employed a few white players in the past—most notably Bob Karstens in the 1940s—and Maravich had not agreed to anything. In truth, he had little interest in playing comedy basketball against the hapless Washington Generals. His childhood quest was to win a championship while competing against the best players in the world.

Gardner was also tempting Maravich with serious money and he upped the ante by including Press in the deal. If Pete signed with the Cougars, Gardner promised Press the head-coaching position with the ABA's Pittsburgh Pipers. The job paid $50,000 a year, a substantial bump from his $18,000 LSU salary.

Press was intrigued by the possibility of coaching in the pros so Gardner flew to Pennsylvania to meet with the Maravich family lawyers, Les Zittrain and Art Herskovitz. Unfortunately for Gardner, he made a bad first impression.

"I remember the first thing Gardner said when he came into my office,

'Are we being recorded or bugged?'" recalled Zittrain. "And I said, 'First of all, that's a silly question because if I was bugging you, what am I going to say? Yes?'"

Pete, still an undergraduate, was prohibited by NCAA rules from retaining an agent so Herskovitz and Zittrain were officially representing Press during the negotiations. When Pete was finally eligible to pursue a contract, Zittrain would handle the face-to-face negotiations while Herskovitz would vet the terms.

"Back then there was nothing like the sophisticated sports representation we have today," recalled Zittrain. "There were maybe a handful in the field at the time, but not many more. Professional basketball was in its infancy in big dollars because it didn't enjoy nearly the popularity that it does today. It was just an entirely different picture back then."

Zittrain had no experience negotiating athlete contracts. He pored over *The Sporting News* and the *New York Times* sports section in an effort to educate himself. In late January of 1970, Zittrain attended a three-day seminar in Las Vegas called "Representing Professional Athletes," hosted by the Practicing Law Institute. "Here are all of these people in one room who are representing professional athletes, but they're not allowed to even mention the names," recalled Zittrain. "We were looking at each other and just wondering who represented who." While at the conference Zittrain picked up a local newspaper and saw Pete's photo plastered across the front of the sports section. His future client had just passed Oscar Robertson as the NCAA scoring champion.

Soon another bidder joined the Maravich sweepstakes: 38-year-old Tom Cousins, the principal owner of the Atlanta Hawks. Cousins was a self-made real-estate magnate who brought the NBA and the NHL to Atlanta in an effort to spur development of the city center. "I was concerned with developing 60 acres of downtown Atlanta. A coliseum was the key to the whole thing," he told reporter Furman Bisher.

But to have a shot at Maravich in the NBA draft Cousins needed a high pick. He received some unexpected help midway through the 1969-70 season when Golden State Warriors' rugged center Nate Thurmond went down with a knee injury. Desperate for a quality big man, the Warriors traded their 1970 first-round pick to the Hawks on February 2, 1970, in exchange for the right to "negotiate" with Atlanta's ex-center Zelmo Beaty, who had jumped to the ABA. Beaty didn't sign and the Warriors went into a tailspin, losing 18 of their final 23 games, leaving the team with the third worst record in the NBA. So, at season's end, the Hawks owned the third pick in the annual draft.

"I remembered one of the first things I told [Hawks coach] Richie Guerin was that I'd like for him to get Pete Maravich in Atlanta if it could be done," said Cousins.

Guerin, a former All-Star with the Knicks, had mixed feelings about drafting Maravich. Guerin wanted to build his team around a powerful center, believing, like most NBA coaches, that it was impossible to win a title with a dominant guard. Neither Oscar Robertson nor Jerry West, the premier backcourt men of the 1960s, had led their teams to an NBA championship as of 1970. Still, Guerin could see an upside to picking Maravich. "Why not take a player who will help the franchise? This is, after all, a business," said Guerin. "And drafting Pete Maravich is good business."

As the NBA draft approached, Cousins received more good news. First, the NBA extended its television relationship with ABC, inking a three-year, $16.2-million contract. The money was nearly a five-fold increase over the previous deal. And second, Cousins discovered that Bob Kent, a close friend of Press Maravich, was working as a consultant on Cousins' arena project in downtown Atlanta. In the 1950s, Kent had been the head basketball coach at Beckley College in West Virginia while Press Maravich was a rival coach at Davis & Elkins. The two men forged a close friendship and even roomed together at NCAA conventions. At Cousins' urging, Kent called his old friend in Baton Rouge and arranged a meeting at the New Orleans airport.

"We had a long talk," Press told sportswriter Pete Finney. "Bob told me about the Beaty deal and sounded me out about how Pete would feel playing in Atlanta. I told him Pete had a strong preference for playing in the South and that Atlanta was in the general area where he grew up."

Press also confided in Kent that if Carolina and Atlanta offered similar money, Pete was inclined to choose the NBA, where he could play on the same court as his childhood heroes Oscar Robertson, Jerry West, and Elgin Baylor.

Pete, acting on the sound advice of Zittrain, never publicly revealed that preference, always making sure to mention the possibility of playing in the ABA during interviews. (Zittrain may have been a novice agent but he knew Maravich could profit handsomely from a spirited bidding war.)

The 1970 NBA draft was held on March 23 and the Detroit Pistons and San Diego Rockets flipped a coin to determine which team would pick first. The Pistons won the toss and, predictably, selected St. Bonaventure's massive center Bob Lanier. The 6-11, 260-pound Lanier was the sort of player who could lead a team to a championship.

Now it was San Diego's turn. "We knew Pete would sell a lot of tickets on the road, but that's fool's gold because we wouldn't share in the road receipts," said the Rockets general manager Pete Newell. The team's brass also wondered if the high-scoring Maravich could mesh with their shot-happy superstar, Elvin Hayes. Would one ball be enough for the two gunners? The cash-strapped Rockets selected Michigan's 6-7 forward Rudy Tomjanovich.

The Hawks general manager Marty Blake spoke next. "Atlanta selects Pete Maravich of LSU," he announced over the 17-city telephone hookup, and with that Atlanta owned the NBA rights to negotiate with college basketball's greatest attraction. But could the Hawks outbid the ABA's Cougars?

Gardner began the showdown with a provocative threat. "Tom Cousins will think Quantrill's raiders were a bunch of amateurs if Atlanta lucks out and signs Maravich," he told Hal Hays of the *Atlanta Constitution*. "We're going to take the money and call [Atlanta Hawks stars] Lou Hudson or Walt Hazzard or both of them. And they'll be ready to listen, too."

Maravich was in the catbird seat. Two well-heeled businessmen desired his services and seemed willing to pay any price.

Pete's lawyer, meanwhile, had learned the details of the five-year, $1.4-million contract Lew Alcindor signed as a rookie with the Bucks in 1969. "We were so lucky Alcindor was signed the year earlier because I was able to hone in on that number," explained Zittrain. "In my mind, Pete should have gotten just as much as Alcindor. I knew what we had. Hey, this was Pistol Pete."

Zittrain had four demands: a dollar amount that topped Alcindor's, a signing bonus, a no-cut clause, and a no-trade provision.

The lawyers presented their request to Cousins and Gardner and the negotiating began. Two days later Gardner delivered a staggering final offer.

Zittrain was in Atlanta, haggling with the Hawks, when the phone call came. "It was one of the fellows at my law firm in Pittsburgh," recalled Zittrain. "He said, '. . . there's a six-page telegram for you here from the Carolina Cougars,' and I said, 'Well, read it to me.'"

Recalling this incident years later, Zittrain was reluctant to reveal the exact details of the Cougars' proffer. But according to reporter Smith Barrier, a *Time* stringer based in North Carolina, the Cougars offered Maravich $2.5 million for five years, a $20,000 annuity for life beginning at age 40, a $250,000 life insurance policy, and ownership of several Hardee's hamburger franchises. Plus one final enticement—the head coaching position of the Pittsburgh Pipers for Press Maravich.

The Cougar offer was breathtaking but Zittrain had serious concerns about the long-term solvency of the ABA. What if the league folded in two years? Would Pete still get his money? Were these numbers legitimate? In an earlier, secret meeting with the ABA, Pete and Press got stuck with the hotel bill. Although Zittrain was skeptical about the Cougar offer, he never let on with the Hawks' negotiating team. "Look, whether you believe me or not," Zittrain exclaimed, with his heart pounding, "I just got a very generous offer from the Carolina Cougars. Either you're going to sign this contract or you're not."

After a brief meeting with Cousins, Atlanta agreed. Maravich received a five-year, no-cut, no-trade deal for $1.5 million, plus a signing bonus, the use of a green Plymouth GTX, a country club membership, and an apartment. The complete package totaled nearly $1.9 million and most of the payout was deferred for tax reasons.

"Whether I got enough money for him, I'll never know," Zittrain later confessed. "But I just wanted to be able to tell Pete he had a contract that was a little better than Lew Alcindor." The deal was historic and, for a time, was included in the *Guinness Book of World Records* as the largest contract in pro sports history.

On Thursday afternoon, March 26, 1970, Peter Maravich signed page six of the National Basketball Association Uniform Player Contract. The top of paragraph two read:

> *The Club agrees to pay the Player for rendering services described herein the sum of $1,500,000.00.*

At 23 years of age, Pete Maravich was a millionaire on paper. Thanks to obsessive training, a determined father, and a teenage growth spurt, his goal of making a million dollars playing basketball was coming true. Now he would have the opportunity to chase his biggest childhood dream: an NBA championship.

After he signed, Maravich attended a press conference in Tara Room One of Atlanta's Marriott Motor Hotel. Pete, sporting a gray glen-plaid banker's suit and a vest, sat quietly next to Zittrain, while Press and Herskovitz stood behind them. The small room was filled with reporters, photographers, and well-wishers.

Zittrain did not get far with his statement, "We are most happy to announce that Pete Maravich will play professional basketball for the Atlanta Hawks . . ." before he was drowned out by frenzied cheers.

"They screamed and clapped and then screamed and clapped some more," observed Ron Hudspeth of the *Atlanta Journal*. "It was supposed to be a press conference, but it evolved into a real circus sideshow. Men and women, girls in miniskirts, small kids and little ol' ladies jammed into the small room. Everything from a Brownie Hawkeye to television cameras mounted on tripods snapped and purred while a slightly uncomfortable Maravich stood silently.

"Really, no one said anything, they just took photographs. For a moment, one could almost feel sorry for the young man with the long hair standing there almost like an animal in the zoo. Then, one remembers, this is Pete Maravich and this is just the beginning of what he'll be confronted with."

The room settled down and Zittrain was peppered with questions about the terms of the contract. "Let's just say it's a contract that is fair," Zittrain responded. "One that very handsomely compensates the greatest basketball player in the world."

All eyes shifted to Pete and he playfully responded that he would receive a mere, "$85 a week, a pick, a shovel, and a tractor." When the laughter subsided, Pete acknowledged that he was looking forward to playing in Atlanta. "I'm very pleased," he said. "This is the thing I've been looking forward to. It's like I'm starting out as a freshman again."

A misty-eyed Press was still shaken by the terms of the deal. "It's hard to realize," Press said to the media, "Clemson paid me $3,500 to coach in 1958. Now this little runt is going to make more than that for combing his hair." When the press conference ended, Pete happily signed autographs for all comers, including a young boy who held a sign that read, "Cobb County, Ga. Loves the Maravich Clan."

Following the festivities in Atlanta, Maravich was due back in Baton Rouge to finish the spring semester of his senior year. (Ironically, he was broke and had no travel money so Zittrain passed the hat among his friends and enough funds were raised to buy Pete a plane ticket.) When Maravich returned to LSU, he was greeted with a rude surprise.

A week after signing with the Hawks, LSU's School of Business Administration expelled him. Pete's hectic schedule during the previous two months—SEC games, the NIT, contract negotiations—had prevented him from attending classes. Although he never flunked a course and had amassed 99 of the 128 hours needed for his degree, when his frequent absences came to the attention of a local news crew, the business administration's dean, Dr. William Ross, was forced to take action.

"Due to the pressures and demands made on me during the past two months, I've been unable to put forth my best effort academically," read Pete's press release, authored by Bud Johnson. "I take complete responsibility for my actions and regret that I won't be able to finish my education this year. I plan to return at a later date."

A few weeks after he was booted out of LSU, Maravich won the Jim Corbett Award, an honor accorded to Louisiana's outstanding amateur athlete. Pete, who had won the award in 1969 as well, never showed up for the ceremony.

Maravich began to prepare for the rigors of a grueling 82-game NBA season. "I feel the professional basketball player is the greatest athlete in the world and every rookie has to learn through experience," Pete said. "I'm no different—I'm going to work hard."

Pete embarked on a comprehensive workout routine at Foxy's Health Studio on Rhonda Street in Baton Rouge. Throughout the spring and summer of 1970 he relentlessly pumped iron, hoping to muscle his weight up to 215 pounds.

"The more I mess with the weights, the more I feel the biggest advantage is more mental than physical," Maravich told Pete Finney. "It's as much a mind builder as a body builder."

In Atlanta, the Hawks believed Maravich would bring great benefits to the organization *and* the league. "Pistol Pete was the Great White Hope," explained Hawks teammate Lou Hudson. "Not just for Atlanta, for the NBA."

Hudson was not the only Hawk to perceive Maravich's potential impact on the bottom line. "Let's face it, a white player of his ability is what Atlanta and the NBA needs," Bill Bridges, the Hawks' captain, told Finney. "He may be the greatest gate attraction to come into the league. That could mean a couple-hundred-thousand dollars to all us Hawks. More people, more money."

Guard/forward Joe Caldwell, who had practiced with Pete at two summer camps, was also thrilled to have Maravich in the NBA. "Pete Maravich was a godsend as far as I'm concerned. He changed the whole pay scale for people 6-5 and under. I played in the NBA for six years and Sam Jones, Jerry West, Hal Greer, Oscar Robertson never made any serious money until Pete Maravich came into the league."

Twenty-four hours after Maravich signed, the Hawks' front office had evidence of Pete's drawing power. By 2 P.M. on Friday, March 27, the team had sold 136 season-ticket plans, and when the box office closed for the day, more than 500 season tickets had been scooped up, translating into some

$100,000 in revenue. By June 1, the team surpassed 2,000 season-ticket sales, easily a franchise record. "I've never seen anything like it," Hawks business manager Irv Gack told Atlanta reporter Priit Vesilind.

Pete also contributed to brisk sales around the league. "Maravich created so much interest and fan base at a time when the league really needed it," said Jim Fitzgerald, former owner of the Milwaukee Bucks. Fitzgerald recalled Maravich's impact on attendance at an exhibition game in Madison, Wisconsin.

"We couldn't sell tickets at all until it was confirmed that Maravich was coming," said Fitzgerald. "Then it was a breeze."

Baltimore coach Gene Shue saw a potential gold mine in Maravich. "There are players who come into the league and can make your team an instant winner, like Lew Alcindor and Wes Unseld," Shue observed. "But there aren't many players like Maravich who can consistently fill your arena."

Corporate America was also lining up to ride Pete's fame. He signed national endorsement contracts with Pro-Keds sneakers ($115,000 over three years), the United States Hosiery Corporation (socks), the Seamless Corporation ("Pistol Pete" basketballs), and, most famously, Bristol Myers, the manufacturer of Vitalis "Dry Control" hair products.

Mel Ciociola, a 27-year-old creative director at the advertising firm of Young and Rubicam, pitched Maravich to Bristol Myers. "Maravich was the guy," Ciociola said. "We could never beat him." (Cincinnati Reds outfielder Bernie Carbo was the backup choice.) Bristol Myers agreed with Ciociola and paid Maravich $150,000 for three television spots and a print campaign.

One of the television ads, a spot called "Ice Cream," featured Maravich performing trick shots while a youngster held his ice-cream cone. There was a small role in the commercial for a pretty girl and Bristol Myers offered it to Jackie. (Pete vetoed the idea.) The music and lyrics to the catchy "Dry Control" jingle were penned by songwriter Joe Brooks, who seven years later composed the mega-hit "You Light Up My Life".

The other two Vitalis spots were filmed in a gym on the Lower East Side of Manhattan. In one, directed by Lear Levin, Maravich's mane showed off some silky moves—"His hair fakes left, it looks right, it breaks free"—and in the other, Pete's hair bounced in slow motion as he performed an array of eye-catching drills.

Maravich said the 12-hour shooting days cooled his acting desires. "That commercial killed any feeling I had for making any movies. It wears you out more than a ballgame."

But a grueling workday was not the reason he turned down a starring role in a film directed by Jack Nicholson. Nicholson, trying to maximize the career momentum created by his performance in the cult hit *Easy Rider* (which Pete saw and "didn't understand"), had purchased the film rights to Jeremy Larner's novel *Drive, He Said*. He offered the role of Hector Bloom, the unsavory lead character, to Pete.

"It was going to be the story of a college star who hits the skids. The guy even rapes a girl," Maravich explained to Finney. "That would have been real nice for my image."

On June 15, 1970, Maravich and 15 other newcomers reported to the Hawks rookie camp at the Westminster School in Atlanta. With five openings on the Hawks roster, the players fought hard to impress the coaches. Maravich, wearing No. 6, was a target for his fellow rookies.

"The roughness is good—as it should be," Pete said in an AP story. "It's sort of like the saga of Wyatt Earp. Everybody wants to beat the fastest gun in the West."

As camp progressed, the coaching staff was pleasantly surprised by Maravich's effort on defense. "It's not that I can't play defense," Maravich explained to Frank Hyland of the *Atlanta Journal*. "It's just a matter of gutting it out."

On the final day of rookie camp, a few Hawks veterans joined the scrimmage. Pete matched up against point guard Walt Hazzard, a flashy player who had won an NCAA championship under John Wooden at UCLA. The rookie and the veteran treated the fans to some deft passing, but Hazzard, fearing his days were numbered, felt threatened by Pete.

When the team gathered for publicity pictures, Hazzard grumbled, "What do you got me here for? I'm on my way out."

In August, Pete, Press, Helen, and Diana traveled to Monticello, New York, for the Maurice Stokes Memorial All-Star Game, played in honor of the former Royals star who had passed away the previous April. Stokes was left permanently disabled after a hard fall during the last game of the 1958 season and the charity affair raised money to defray his medical expenses.

"It was serious basketball," said Mark Kutscher, whose family resort hosted the event for more than four decades.

The 1970 Stokes Game, although unofficial, was Maravich's first pro game.

"Pete volunteered. It was very important to him," recalled Zelda Spoelstra, the NBA's director of alumni relations. "Pete seemed to want to be involved and wanted to give back. He was a special young man. He was very gracious."

The game typically drew a few hundred fans but, in 1970, more than 1,500 kids showed up for a clinic conducted by two master dribblers, Pete Maravich and ex-Globetrotter Marques Haynes. "Marques had a game that Pete could pick up, parallel, and then take to another level," recalled NBA coach Phil Jackson.

Pete felt a special connection with youngsters. "Kids are my favorites, especially in the 6-12 age bracket," Maravich said to reporter George Cunningham. "They listen, learn and go back over and do what you tell them. Over that age, they're too interested in the opposite sex, cars, and things like that."

Maravich got a sense of the relaxed atmosphere of the Stokes game when league MVP Willis Reed good-naturedly confronted him before the tipoff. "Don't lay any of that stuff on me tonight, Pete," Reed joked. "I'm not ready. Wait until the season starts."

All eyes were on Maravich as he took the court as part of a Red Auerbach-coached team that included Jo Jo White, Dave Bing, and Dave Cowens. They would face a Dolph Schayes' squad led by Reed, Cazzie Russell, Billy Cunningham, and Kevin Loughery. Maravich made just 4 of 12 field-goal attempts and was pestered by the veteran Loughery who bumped his elbow on every jump shot.

"I'd smile, and he'd smile," Pete recalled. "I'd say, 'Okay, Kevin, I'll get you back.'"

Maravich played point guard and dished out a slew of nifty assists, mainly to game MVP Cowens, who scored 32 points and secured 22 rebounds in an 86-82 win for the Auerbach squad.

"I know I didn't shoot well, but that doesn't bother me. It will come," said Maravich, who finished with 10 points, 12 assists, and 5 steals. "I was very pleased with my defense. You don't get to steal the ball like that from guys like this every day."

Auerbach predicted great things for Maravich. "He's a superstar right from the beginning," Auerbach told the *New York Times*. "I don't know if he'll start, but the starting lineup means nothing to me. It's who's in there at the end who counts."

Back in Atlanta Pete moved into his Hawk-financed lodging, a $280 unit in the Cumberland apartment complex in the Buckhead section of the city. The decor was classic 1970s: thick shag carpeting, a seven-seat bar, fish net hanging from the ceiling, and a pool table. Maravich purchased custom sheets embroidered with the inscription "Pistol."

"It was real nice for back in the day," said Jackie Maravich. "It was very stylish for its time." Others found it less than homey.

Renowned CBS television reporter Heywood Hale Broun visited the apartment for a segment he taped about the young star. "He was so much the instrument of his father's personality that there wasn't much to Pete himself," Broun said in a 2000 documentary. "I once visited his apartment and it looked like a decorator's showroom. It was the most impersonal kind of place. Stainless steel furniture and non-objective paintings. It depressed me just to look at it."

In mid-September the Hawks training camp opened at Bolles Academy in Jacksonville, Florida. Maravich drew some stares when he rolled into town. "Pete's car was really amazing," recalled fellow rookie Herb White. "It was dark green and had an alligator roof on it. It was a hemi 426. I think it was a four speed. It was pretty redneck. And, no doubt, shocked the black guys on our team. They're all driving El Dorados and Mercedes." Even more amazing was the working telephone inside the muscle car.

The veteran players were further shocked when they learned that Atlanta's marketing slogan for the coming season was the "New Hawks." There was also a new insignia, new uniforms (green, blue, and white), cheerleaders, and a mascot.

As far as the veterans were concerned, the "old" Hawks had played quite well and sweeping changes were not in order. Atlanta was coming off two consecutive 48-win seasons and was the defending Western Conference champion. (Fortunately for the Hawks, the Lakers, their conference rival, had played the bulk of the 1969-70 season without the injured Wilt Chamberlain. When he returned to the lineup for the playoffs, L.A. easily swept Atlanta, 4–0.)

Hudson was perturbed when Maravich indirectly expressed interest in wearing No. 23, the same number Sweet Lou had been wearing since entering the league in 1966.

"The first thing the front office did was to call me in and tell me that Pete wanted No. 23 because that was his number in college," Hudson recalled. "I didn't have any allegiance to No. 23, but I told them, 'If Pete comes and asks me like a normal human being for No. 23, I'll give it to him.' Then they got an attitude about my attitude. Therefore I kept No. 23 because he never did ask me for it. It was just about proper respect."

Pete ultimately chose No. 44—his scoring average in college—but the uniform squabble would pale next to the dissension created by his $1.5-million contract.

"It was sort of like management was trying to sabotage the team," Hudson said. "They wouldn't give Lenny Wilkens $50,000 to stay in Atlanta. And they turn around and give Pete $250,000 a year? The resentment toward the money wasn't my deal, but his coming to the Hawks just rearranged the whole team."

The Hawks franchise had a history of stinginess going back to its days in St. Louis. The team's first owner, Ben Kerner, was notorious for signing players to below-market, long-term deals. "Kerner bought the team from a loan he received from his mother, and was known as the cheapest of the NBA's cheapskate owners," said Joe Caldwell, who played for Kerner from 1966 to 1968.

When Tom Cousins bought the team and moved it to Atlanta, the Hawks All-Star guard (and future Hall of Famer) Lenny Wilkens decided to test the new owner by holding out for $60,000. Cousins refused to meet Wilkens' demands. "Lenny was our leader and a great basketball player," explained Hawks coach, Richie Guerin. "But he held out and we had to make a trade. That was the start of our demise." Wilkens was traded for Walt Hazzard and the morale among the veterans deteriorated.

In 1969 the players watched as center Zelmo Beaty, another veteran, was denied big bucks, causing him to jump to the ABA. So, the following year, when the Hawks suddenly had $1.5 million for Maravich, the veterans, quite naturally, felt betrayed.

Caldwell recalled a meeting at the home of Hazzard to discuss the situation. Bill Bridges, Jim Davis, and Lou Hudson also attended. The players wondered how Cousins could afford to pay Maravich $300,000 a year while the rest of the Hawks were earning between $50,000 and $80,000.

"The Atlanta Hawks had used our talent to make the money to pay Pete Maravich," Caldwell said. But for Cousins, it was simple economics. "Joe Caldwell came to my office and said he was a better basketball player than Pete Maravich," said Cousins in 2000. "And I couldn't disagree with that. He probably was."

But Maravich sold tickets. "I tried to explain that to Joe. I used the example that John Barrymore was a better actor than John Wayne," Cousins added. "But John Wayne was paid more because he drew more fans."

Cousins had the facts to back him up. Atlanta was scheduled for five national television appearances in 1970-71 (compared with three the previous year), season-ticket sales were up over 50 percent, an appearance in a preseason double header at Madison Square Garden could net the team $40,000, and a side agreement with ABC's *Wide World of Sports* to televise Maravich's professional debut would bring in another $75,000.

Caldwell was not convinced. The versatile 6-5 guard/forward was a five-year veteran and the most exciting player on the Hawks. Tenacious on defense and explosive on offense, Caldwell's incredible leaping ability had earned him the nickname "Pogo." He was a fan favorite, a two-time All-Star, and coming off a career year with a 21.1-point average. He decided to skip training camp and hold out for a more lucrative contract.

"Joe was the glue that held the team together," said Guerin years later.

The Hawks veterans perceived Maravich's salary as undeserved and it riled them. Team captain Bill Bridges, the 6-6 forward and the team's leading rebounder, was making $50,000 per year. "Who was fourth in the league in rebounds last year? And who had the most playing time on the club? And who's been around here the longest? And who has to be the policeman on the court? I'll tell you who—Bill Bridges. I'm not asking for a million dollars, but I do expect to be compensated for my overall value to the Hawks," Bridges railed to reporter Frank Hyland.

Then there was the matter of the preferential treatment Pete received from the front office.

"We were treated one way and then he was treated another way," said Hudson. "We had been doing things to rookies that most rookies had to go through, and they no longer applied to Pete. Rookies were supposed to carry the clocks in exhibition season, and he didn't have to do that. Pete could do whatever he wanted to do and if we had a problem with that then we were punished or threatened."

Bridges saw it the same way. "We have been programmed to play as a team. I have never played as an individual and I never will. I'm a veteran and he's a rookie. Until he performs with knowledge and consistency, he's still a rookie. No way I'll cater to a rookie until he proves himself."

Maravich and his fellow Hawks struggled to connect off the court as well.

"Pete was desperately trying to make friends," observed Herb White. "Whenever he saw a group of players having a few drinks or something to eat, he'd go over and join them and insist on paying the check. I'm sure Pete didn't realize it, but he was subconsciously rubbing it in, letting them know who had all the money."

Sports Illustrated writer Frank Deford also noticed Pete's overtures were misinterpreted. "It was a well-intentioned effort, but some players resented it, sensing ostentation where Maravich sincerely intended generosity," wrote Deford.

The Hawks began their 12-game exhibition season and Pete, temporarily wearing Richie Guerin's old No. 19, adjusted slowly to the pace of the pro game. His early performances ran the gamut from embarrassing to superior. At his worst he was dribbling into traps, throwing passes into the stands, and forcing bad shots. At his best he showed flashes of his college brilliance.

Hazzard felt that Pete still needed to learn the most important lesson for a point guard: feed the ball inside. "The whole concept he played under LSU was Pete Maravich and the rest of the guys," Hazzard said. "He has to learn to see the big horses. The guards can shoot anytime because they have the ball. If they don't keep the horses happy, they won't get the ball."

After a 119-111 loss to the Celtics in Atlanta, the normally confident Maravich sat confused and dejected at his locker.

"I don't know what the problem is," Maravich confessed to writer George Cunningham. "I don't get it. I just don't seem to be able to get in the groove. I can't seem to get loose."

Wherever the team went, the bulk of the media's attention was focused on Maravich. The other players resented that as well, and Guerin was forced to call several team meetings, excluding Pete.

"I had to tell them that it's not the kid's fault that he got that kind of money," Guerin said. "But I understood how they felt. The first time we came into a city, the papers would say: 'Here comes Pete Maravich. Pete Maravich and the Hawks.' It was like the rest of us were just along for the ride."

The Hawks continued their uneven play during the exhibition season and Maravich struggled to rein in his frantic tempo. During a game against the Celtics in Tampa, Pete dribbled wildly toward the basket, whizzing by Hawks center Walt Bellamy. Bellamy turned to Boston's Dave Cowens and asked, "So how's the game going?"

As his shaky preseason progressed, Maravich started taking flak from the Atlanta beat writers.

"Make no mistake, he is unbridled brilliance, but it is a matter of record that no unharnessed horse ever won the Kentucky Derby," was a "compliment" from George Cunningham of the *Atlanta Constitution*.

Frank Hyland of the *Atlanta Journal* referred to him as, "the Peachtree Popgun."

But his peers could also see Pete's unique skills. "His talent is so far ahead of any other rookie I saw in camp it flabbergasts me," said Bridges. "His quickness is amazing."

"The pros are made for him," Dolph Schayes told columnist Larry Merchant. "He's the greatest ball handler in the history of the game. He hasn't shown half of what he can do."

"The best player I've seen since Marques Haynes," said Caldwell.

The Hawks traveled to Nashville in late October to play Milwaukee in their final exhibition. Whatever resentment Atlanta's veterans felt for Maravich was stoked further as they relaxed in their hotel rooms prior to the game. Watching college football on ABC, the players were dismayed by the network's multiple promos touting its telecast of Atlanta's season opener.

"Come see Pete Maravich take on the Milwaukee Bucks," boomed the ads, relegating the other Hawks players to supporting roles.

ABC was blunt about the fact that it wanted to televise Hawks games solely because of Maravich. "Pistol Pete is the reason," Roone Arledge, then-president of ABC Sports, explained to Dave Anderson in *TV Guide*. "Because of his show-biz style and his college record, his development is of much more national interest than that of the average rookie."

Atlanta closed its exhibition season with a disappointing 4-8 record. Chemistry was horrible, the best player was a hold out, and the veterans were reluctant to share the ball with the team's high-priced rookie.

In this tense atmosphere, Pete Maravich would make his professional debut. Live on national television.

12

Rookie Trials

"All I want to do is simply be a member of a team. I don't want to glow in the dark or have the trumpets sound when I show up. I realize that whatever I do matters not at all unless the Hawks win."

—PETE MARAVICH

"LSU was Tigertown and lots of laughs, then suddenly there was no Tigertown. Pete wasn't a hero anymore . . . he's been shell-shocked ever since."

—RONNIE MARAVICH, PETE'S BROTHER

On October 7, 1970, more than 7,000 fans crammed into Georgia Tech's Alexander Memorial Coliseum to watch the NBA debut of Pete Maravich as the Atlanta Hawks hosted the Milwaukee Bucks. Banks of temporary television lights made the league's smallest arena uncomfortably warm.

Maravich was the sole reason ABC was interested in broadcasting the game, as evidenced by a clause in its contract. If Maravich did not play, ABC had the option to cancel coverage and recover its $75,000 telecast rights fee. Millions tuned in to watch on ABC's *Wide World of Sports*.

The game offered several compelling story lines. In addition to Pete's "coming out" party, Maravich would face two extraordinary Milwaukee players, Lew Alcindor and Oscar Robertson. Alcindor, the Bucks 7-1 center and reigning NBA Rookie of the Year, had been College Player of the Year in 1969, and Robertson, a perennial NBA All-Star, was the man whose NCAA scoring records Pete had shattered.

The Bucks had acquired Robertson that summer from the Cincinnati Royals. Robertson was arguably the most accomplished player of the 1960s (in his second season as a pro he *averaged* a triple-double), but despite a lineup that included future Hall of Famer Jerry Lucas, the Bucks had repeatedly lost in the playoffs to deeper teams like Boston and Philadelphia. The "Big O" hoped that by teaming up with the hugely gifted Alcindor he would finally obtain the championship that had eluded him throughout his college and pro career.

Maravich was not in the starting lineup when the game tipped off at 1:25 P.M. but entered early in the second period with the Hawks leading by six. The media's laser focus on Maravich was already a significant distraction. Over 50 photographers crammed the sidelines. "I've never seen anything like it," Hawks public relations director Tom McCollister told Bill Clark of the *Orlando Sentinel.* "*Newsweek, Sports Illustrated*, the *New York Times*, MGM films, guys from all over. Every time there was a timeout they'd swoop in on our bench, all 50 of 'em, aiming right at Pete."

Maravich started with a bang, breaking up a Milwaukee fast break with a nifty steal and dribbling the length of the court for his first shot, a 20-foot jumper that rattled through. A few minutes later, Pete notched his first assist with a behind-the-back bullet to Walt Hazzard. But that was the end of his highlight reel. Over the rest of the game he was just 2 of 13 from the floor and took a single free throw. Plus, in the second half, a wild cross-court pass was intercepted, resulting in an easy basket. Maravich, the highest paid athlete in professional sports, played less than half the game (22 minutes) and scored seven points in a 107-98 Hawks loss.

Alcindor, beginning the first of six MVP seasons, was dominant, compiling 32 points and 17 rebounds. Robertson, quietly efficient, scored 15 points.

Maravich's pro debut was a bust. "What I played, it's called Bad Ball," a demoralized Maravich told Pete Carry of *Sports Illustrated.* "Physically I was ready. I was playing better. Even the coach said so. But I wasn't ready emotionally. I was totally flushed the minute after I took my first shot. I felt like a ghost was sitting on me."

In the following weeks, the Hawks couldn't get out of second gear. Coach Richie Guerin experimented with various starting lineups, all of which excluded Maravich. "I never sat in my whole life. I never knew that type of frustration," Pete admitted to writer Milton Gross. "I couldn't stand it."

When Pete did get into games his play was hesitant. He seemed more focused on avoiding mistakes than following his natural instincts. One reporter described him as a "spooked horse." He was frequently out of position and his no-look passes often caught unsuspecting teammates on the back of the head or shoulder. He would drive furiously to the basket and spin in midair, desperately looking to dish the ball. But his teammates seemed unwilling to help him out. And once he gave up the ball, the chances of a return pass were slim. The out-of-sync Hawks dropped five of their first six games. To most observers, the obvious solution to the Hawks' problems was to re-sign Joe Caldwell. The Hawks missed his high-flying offense and energetic defense. Caldwell frequently locked down the opposing team's best scorer. "No one defenses me as well as Joe Caldwell," said Knicks guard Walt Frazier in early 1970.

As Maravich stumbled out of the gate and Caldwell kept his distance, Frank Hyland of the *Atlanta Journal* wrote, "The Hawks proved again that a $2-million rookie is not as valuable as a $50,000-seasoned veteran."

Finally, on October 30, Caldwell jumped to the ABA. He signed a five-year, $1.8-million contract with the Carolina Cougars. If Jim Gardner couldn't get Pete Maravich, he was going to get the next best thing. The Hawks lost the heart of their team.

"If anybody was a real fan favorite, it was Joe," said team statistician Hank Kalb. "He was a fantastic athlete. The place would absolutely explode when he would get loose for a dunk. He could jump out of the gym."

The acquisition of Maravich was blamed for Caldwell's departure. "Again, enter the name Pete Maravich," wrote Cunningham in the *Atlanta Constitution*. "Because much of the money that went to Caldwell undoubtedly was ticketed for Maravich, whom Carolina wanted but Atlanta got in the 1970 draft. Had Maravich gone to the Cougars, Caldwell undoubtedly would be playing right now for the Hawks."

Pete was living a nightmare. In one game he was stripped of the ball and made a desperate dive to steal it back. He missed and fell hard, slamming his head on the floor. As he struggled to his feet, fighting to clear his head, he heard a Hawks fan scream, "Give Caldwell his money!"

His struggles grew so desperate that he began talking openly about walking away from basketball—only weeks after his pro debut. In an *Atlanta Constitution* interview on November 5, 1970, Pete told Furman Bisher, "If I could play on the NBA world championship team just one time, I'd be satisfied. I could even quit basketball then."

Pete's adjustment to the pace and athleticism of the pro game was slow but steady. He had played a loose, gambling defense in college because he knew his team depended on him to score. In the NBA, where zone defense was illegal, opponents took advantage of his inexperience by running him into picks.

"He probably never had to play defense in college or high school," Guerin said in 2004. "Every team we played against who defended Pete all said the same thing I said to him, 'Yeah, he's great offensively but he throws the ball away a lot and he's weak on defense.' That was a common refrain. I said to him, 'Look, don't you get embarrassed when you're getting beat by guys? You have to take some pride in this.'"

Oscar Robertson echoed Guerin in an ESPN interview. "He didn't really understand basketball other than dribbling the ball through his legs, behind the back, and passing behind his back," Robertson explained. "He didn't understand the game of basketball. People salivated about getting him in a one-on-one situation."

As his rookie year progressed, the chasm between Pete and his teammates deepened. When Maravich missed practice to film a commercial in Jacksonville, his return was greeted with icy stares from the veterans. The resentment was understandable. The amount Pete received from any one of his major endorsement deals—Keds, Vitalis, and Seamless Basketballs—eclipsed the salary of any of his teammates.

A public television crew was dispatched to film a documentary about Pete's transition to the pro game. The producers asked the Hawks publicity department for on-camera interviews with Hudson, Hazzard, and Bridges. All three declined.

"They were boycotting the interview," said Al Silverman, editor of *SPORT* magazine, who oversaw the project. "The three of them just sat there and wouldn't come out of the office. They'd had enough questions about Pete."

"Every place we go, it's the same old story," Guerin explained in *Super Sports* magazine. "All they want is Maravich. They talk to me about Maravich, they talk to Maravich about Maravich, they talk to the other players about Maravich. The minute we open the locker room door after a game, the reporters pour in and flock to Maravich's locker. One of our guys may have had a hot night. He's standing alone at his locker. Eventually, a few reporters may move over to talk to him, but what's the first question they ask him? 'Say, how's Pete fitting into the scheme of things?'"

The attention was overwhelming. Tom Brennan, a former teammate of Herb White's at the University of Georgia, saw the Hawks play a few times in 1970-71. He met up with Maravich and White after the games. "Obviously his transition wasn't very smooth," Brennan recalled. "It was kind of a catch-22 situation because management wanted him to score and make the fancy moves, but that entailed not including his teammates. It was just a mess. We couldn't go out because Pete was like a rock star; he got mobbed all the time."

Teammate John Vallely said Pete's disdain for celebrity contributed to his anguish. "Pete was a pretty regular guy away from the court," Vallely said. "I remember him specifically telling me, 'I wish I could just go away to an island somewhere where there are no people and nobody could bother me.'"

Hawks assistant coach Gene Tormohlen said that something as simple as a restaurant meal was daunting for the rookie. "I've never had a dinner with Pete where he didn't have to sign 10 autographs. And he was very good about it, too. He was a good guy," recalled Tormohlen.

"If I ask the person to wait until I'm finished for an autograph, he usually goes back over and sits down and stares at me all throughout dinner," Pete told *Atlanta Journal* reporter Ron Hudspeth. "Before long I'm so nervous I can't eat and the whole evening is ruined."

Hawks assistant statistician Hank Kalb, who became a close friend, said Pete preferred the sanctuary of his apartment or the darkness of a movie theater.

"He became very funny about going out in public," Kalb said. "Most of the time we got together we either went somewhere where we were absolutely sure nobody knew who ... he was. Or we would go by his apartment or he would come over to our house. But he was funny about going out in public."

Meanwhile, the losses wrought havoc on Pete's once-supreme confidence. He began losing weight and had difficulty sleeping. "I would lie there on the floor of my room staring at the ceiling until three or four in the morning in pure agony," Pete admitted to a reporter. "I started thinking about how I had decided, when I was still in grade school, that I was going to become a star in the NBA; about how I had devoted my life since then to basketball; about the thousands of hours I had spent learning to pass the ball behind my back; about how loose and good I felt—until I joined the Hawks."

Pete's girlfriend said he internalized much of his frustration. "I could tell he was upset about the situation," said Jackie, who moved to Atlanta to be near him. "We kind of left it there at the gym. But I could tell if somebody had hurt him."

Pete's strained relations with the media added to the pressure. Maravich told a UPI reporter that he had been particularly bugged by "certain sportswriters who don't really care about you as a human being—they just want to get their story out. I'd just as soon tell them to go jump in the lake." Maravich was referring to the Hawks' beat writers, Frank Hyland of the *Atlanta Journal* and George Cunningham of the *Atlanta Constitution*.

"George Cunningham was cutthroat and surly," said Mike McKenzie, who reported for the *Atlanta Journal* in the early 1970s. "Pete hated him."

Kalb confirmed Pete's dislike for Cunningham. "Pete despised Cunningham and thought he was a cheap-shot artist. He felt that Cunningham stabbed him in the back every chance he got."

Two months into the season, the Hawks' record stood 4-12. Only the league's three expansion clubs, Cleveland, Portland, and Buffalo, were worse. Maravich was struggling, averaging just 13.4 points per game, a huge drop from his college average of 44.2, and people began to ask whether he was actually hurting the team.

But despite the losses and dissension, the Hawks were attracting throngs of new fans. A rock star frenzy surrounded Pete as curious spectators, including many young women, came out in droves: 10,460 people in Detroit; 12,005 in Boston; 10,881 in San Diego; 12,965 in Seattle. In 1969-70, the Hawks averaged 5,326 fans on the road, but through the first 16 games of 1970-71, those numbers ballooned to 8,872, an increase of 67 percent. Home attendance jumped 42 percent, from 4,000 to 5,650 per game.

Wherever he went girls would scream "Peeete, Peeete" and shriek if he glanced their way. He was mobbed after every game by autograph seekers. "The team had to build a special door for Pete that went from the dressing room right to his car because he'd be signing autographs for an hour, hour-and-a-half after every game because he couldn't say no to the kids," said Tormohlen. "You can't do that every night. Maybe once a week, but not every night you play."

Pete was becoming an even bigger attraction than in his halcyon days at LSU. He was the subject of numerous magazine stories, Vitalis rolled out its television campaign, and his on-court exploits were showcased in a new, weekly syndicated program entitled, *This Week in the NBA*. Maravich fan clubs popped up across the nation. Pete received 80 percent of the mail—usually 30 to 50 pieces a day—sent to the Atlanta Hawks. He also received an inordinate number of prom invitations from wishful co-eds, along with plenty of marriage proposals.

The media was desperate to know if, and who, he was dating. "I don't like to talk about my private life," Pete said to an AP reporter. "Sure I've a girlfriend, but I like to keep that part of my life to myself." Jackie sat in the stands at home games, often wearing her signature, white knee-high boots, and cheered on her boyfriend. She was usually accompanied by her best friend, Tito, who was dating Hank Kalb.

"Management was trying to please Pete and they didn't care whether or not they were hurting our feelings," Hudson recalled. "For example, they claimed we couldn't catch his passes. They never considered the fact that it could have been that his passes were bad. One time we were playing in Cleveland and we were on a fast break and he rolled the ball on the floor and it just rolled out of bounds. The coach wanted to know why I couldn't get it—when it was clearly a bad pass."

Maravich remembered the play quite differently: "One night at Cleveland, I think it was, I rolled a 60-foot pass on the floor. I went into the game with about eight passes in mind that I knew I wanted to try, but this wasn't one of them. That turns me on. I don't know how to tell you. It was a little bit off, or I would've had 'em tearing the roof off that place."

It was apparent to everyone who followed the Hawks that the team's chemistry was out of whack. Every aspect of Atlanta's game was sub-par, including a league-worst free-throw percentage of 61.2. (For once Pete was blameless: He shot a team-best 80 percent from the foul line for the season.)

While the media pummeled Pete in print, opponents took their shots at him on the court. Chicago Bulls tenacious defender Jerry Sloan had been boasting since the summer about his plans for the high-priced rookie. "Right around the time Pistol Pete had signed his contract, I was at a basketball camp in Springfield, Illinois," recalled ex-high school player Jerry Kurtz. "One of the guest instructors was Jerry Sloan. I can remember it like it was yesterday. Sloan told us that he, 'couldn't wait to get a piece of Maravich.' And that he 'was personally going to welcome Mr. Maravich to the NBA.' I'll never forget the intensity in his voice as he was saying that."

Sloan's strategy was to play Pete rough early in the game. "The tough kid from the oil fields of southern Illinois used to jostle Pete whenever he could get away with it," observed reporter George Vecsey. "It was pure professional hatred—the poor boy against the nouveau riche. The traditional against the innovative." In Pete's first visit to Chicago, Sloan's unrelenting defense held the Pistol to just eight points in a Bulls victory.

Maravich had better luck against the New York Knicks on November 24. Early in the game, as Pete scrambled for a loose ball, the Knicks Dave DeBusschere leveled him with such force that it sent him sailing over a press bench and into the second row. "I was all right except for a bruise in the leg and someone's beer in my face. That bothered me the most because the beer was stinging my eyes," Maravich recalled. As he staggered over to the Hawks bench, Coach Guerin took a whiff and asked, "You been drinking?"

The Knicks were up by 18 points when the Pistol began to catch fire. On one possession Maravich double faked All-Star guard and defensive stalwart Walt Frazier and zipped by him for an easy two points. Pete's next bucket came when he drove right at Frazier, suddenly put on the brakes and arched in a soft jumper from 20 feet. Maravich kept shooting, hitting a jumper from the right side, and then flipping a twisting lay-in over Willis Reed. In the final quarter, a loose ball rolled into Pete's hands and he scooped it off the ground and swished a 10-foot hook shot. The knowledgeable Madison Square Garden fans stood to cheer the exciting rookie who was scoring with great flair against the defending world champions.

Maravich accounted for 18 of Atlanta's final 31 points to finish with his first 40-point night (17-29, 6-6, 6 rebounds, 6 assists). The Hawks lost 128-119, but the game provided a glimmer of hope for Pete and the team.

Frazier, who scored 33 points, had nothing but compliments for the rookie.

"Give him half a season and he's going to be there," assessed Frazier. "Already he's tough, and I don't exactly enjoy thinking about how good he is going to be."

Pete wasn't the only Hawk who shined. Bridges, the 6-6 power forward, played all 48 minutes, scored 21 points, and grabbed 20 rebounds while holding DeBusschere to 12 points and 5 rebounds. When reporters approached Bridges in the Hawks locker room for a comment, the first question he heard was, "What did you think of Maravich's performance?"

From that night on, Maravich developed a new strategy for handling the mandatory postgame interviews—he stayed in the shower an extra 30 to 45 minutes so his teammates could field questions. He turned his back on such well-known columnists as Detroit's Joe Falls and Philadelphia's Jim Barniak, and barely spoke with Atlanta's Hyland and Cunningham.

Although Atlanta had played well against the Knicks, the Hawks were inconsistent and the losses continued to pile up. Heading to Phoenix on December 2, they'd lost five in a row and Pete was in no mood for extra scrutiny. So when a television crew brushed past his teammates to land an interview with him, he shouted, "Not here in front of the guys!"

That night, after the Hawks' losing streak reached six games, Pete had a few too many beers. "I think he got frustrated and upset and went out and tried to relieve those frustrations. I never really saw him drink anything but beer," recalled Guerin. "Gene Tormohlen, my assistant coach, came over and we brought him back to the room from the hotel bar where he got a little emotional. He ended up hitting his head on the table and we had to take him to this hospital in Scottsdale, Arizona, to get stitched up."

After a 125-104 loss in Milwaukee on December 8, Pete snapped at a reporter: "I don't want to talk about the game or myself," he said, almost pleading. "I'm just not up to it." The Hawks won only 7 of 19 games that December.

Soon the team was openly ridiculing Pete. Patricia Jordan Scott, captain of Atlanta's new cheerleading squad, recalled a pregame incident as the team waited to take the court.

"We were all grouped at a door at the tunnel," she said. "That tunnel in the Tech Dome dropped to about six feet. I'm 5-7 and I could scrape it with the top of my hand, so they were hunched over. One night, I'll never forget it, Lou Hudson came down the tunnel singing, 'Here we go a-riding on the Maravich Express.' So the next night I kind of just looked at him and I literally grabbed his shorts and pulled him over to me and said, 'Straighten up. This is a team and you're not going to get anywhere with that mess.' Lou said, 'It's the truth.' I said, 'The money is the truth. You hate the money thing don't you?' They resented the heck out of Pete."

Guerin, however, said Maravich got along fine with his teammates—off the court. "They all liked Pete. He was not an outcast by any stretch of the imagination," said Guerin. "His teammates did not appreciate some of the things he did on the basketball court." On December 31, most of the team, including Pete, brought in the New Year with a raucous party hosted by Hazzard.

Pete believed that much of the blame for Atlanta's poor record was aimed at him. And those feelings of persecution caused his personality to change dramatically as the season progressed. He gave up trying to make friends on the team. He lashed out at the press. "Most guys who write about sports are just little, overweight creeps who never touched a basketball in their lives. These guys couldn't make a foul shot, yet they have the right to write anything about us," he blasted.

"The fact of the matter was, he wasn't at LSU anymore," Hyland told author Phil Berger. "He was not as good as everybody expected. People expected him to set the league on fire. Against the University of Georgia, he'd come in and get his 45 points. But Georgia sucked. Here in the NBA, he wasn't quite as good. And we pointed it out. He became very upset. I'd say to him, 'What's your problem?' He'd say, 'You're crucifying me.' I told him, 'This ain't Baton Rouge.'"

True, Maravich wasn't in Baton Rouge anymore, but his impact on Atlanta was similar to the imprint he left on his college town. In January 1971, Hawks owner Tom Cousins got the news he had dreamed of when city officials approved the construction of his state-of-the-art sports arena. The primary reason for the green light: Pete Maravich. With Pete signed to a five-year contract and attendance on the rise, Atlanta mayor Sam Massell was convinced it was a good investment. On January 18, $17 million in bonds went up for sale. The Omni, also known as "the house that Pete built," was scheduled to open in the fall of 1973.

January 18 was also the day that Maravich's teammates made a significant decision. Prior to a game in Buffalo, the players held a closed-door meeting without Pete. They decided the only hope of salvaging the season was to include Maravich in the offense. His contract might be unfair and management's handling of the "situation" might be frustrating, but it was time to stop freezing Pete out.

"The Hawks finally reasoned if they were to win, they would have to play with Pete—not he with them," wrote Hyland.

The new approach paid off immediately as Maravich scored 41 points (13-25, 15-19) in a 123-113 victory. Pete couldn't help noticing that, when he dribbled into a bind, his teammates now rushed to help out. For his part, Pete reined in the outer edges of his "Showtime" repertoire and concentrated on better shot selection and defense. In the first six weeks of 1971 his shooting improved from 41 to 44 percent while his scoring average rose to 21.9. On defense he insisted on covering the league's most potent guards, such as Earl Monroe, Walt Frazier, and Jerry West.

"It was like somebody threw a switch and Pete said, 'Now I'm gonna go out and play my game,'" said Kalb.

On January 22, the Hawks traveled to Milwaukee to play the league-leading (39-7) Bucks. The Bucks, en route to their first NBA title behind Lew Alcindor, were riding a 10-game win streak overall and a 17-game streak at home. With two minutes remaining, and the Bucks leading 108-104, a boisterous, sell-out crowd of 10,764 sounded confident that Milwaukee's two win streaks would be extended.

"The noise might well have been the final bit of discouragement for the visiting Atlanta Hawks, who have lived with frustration all season," reported Bob Wolf in the *Milwaukee Journal*. "But it worked the other way around for Maravich, who suddenly put on a one-man rally."

With the score 108-105, Maravich sank a 15-foot jumper, followed quickly by a 20-footer and then, after intercepting Oscar Robertson's in-bound pass, he tossed in an uncontested layup. Six straight points in rat-a-tat fashion.

"I watched Oscar throw the ball in three times with sort of a lob pass," Maravich told Wolf. "At the timeout period just before that I made my mind up to try it. I put my head down to make him think I wasn't watching, and when he threw the ball toward Jon McGlocklin, I jumped up and picked it off."

The basket put the Hawks up 111–108. "The noise pumps me up," Pete said. "It's always been like that with me. They're screaming for them [the Bucks], but I feel it for me, too. . . . I know there are 11,000 people in the stands and it jacks me up."

Pete sealed the 117–110 victory with a pair of free throws.

The suddenly improving Hawks began to consider the possibility of making the playoffs. They still had to catch the Cincinnati Royals, who were six and a half games ahead in the Central Division standings. As Atlanta began to slice into Cincinnati's lead, Maravich became more relaxed, a fact noted by the Hawks captain.

"In the beginning, Pete was very much withdrawn," said Bill Bridges. "He was always by himself in the dressing room, on the bus, in the airport. The Hawks are a team. Personally, I was not willing to accept him as an individual, only as a teammate. I think we've relaxed our resistance to him as an individual."

In February the Hawks went 8-7, setting up a March 7 showdown in Atlanta with their division rivals, the Cincinnati Royals. Among the sellout crowd was Georgia governor Jimmy Carter, attending his first NBA game.

"We used to play basketball back in Plains," the future president told Tom Dial of the *Atlanta Constitution.* "But not like this." The Hawks rose to the occasion, winning 122–112, with Pete contributing 30 points and 10 assists.

Pete tweaked his wrist during the game when, uncharacteristically, he dunked the ball. Although reluctant to "stuff" in a game, Pete often practiced dunking with Hawks reserve guard Herb White, colorfully nicknamed "The Elevator from Decatur" because of his extraordinary jumping ability. White forged a league-wide reputation with his spectacular warmup line throwdowns.

"I was teaching Pete all kinds of dunks," recalled White. "I had him doing everything. He was six-five and had long arms. He could even do a 360. But usually when he got wide open in a game, he just laid it in. I would get on him and he would just say, 'Man, I just can't, I'm afraid I'm gonna miss.' I said, '. . . Pistol, you've missed more shots than anyone in basketball history. What do you care?' Pete said, 'I know, but it's different missing a dunk.'"

Three nights later, in one of their best games of the season, the Hawks trounced the Phoenix Suns, 139–98. It was Atlanta's highest point total of the year and its widest margin of victory since the team moved from St. Louis. Maravich had 37 points (13-22, 11-13, 2 rebounds, 9 assists, 5 steals) in 35 minutes. "Pete was dazzling. He made left-handed running hooks, right-handed running hooks, long jump shots, short jump shots. He passed the ball between his legs, behind his back, bowling ball style, football snap style," reported the *Atlanta Journal.* "Once, he even used a conventional two-handed push pass."

Pete still had a hot hand on March 13 as he lit up the gloomy Cincinnati Gardens with a spectacular shooting display, scoring a season-high 44 points (18-27, 8-10). But he was outdone by another rookie sensation, Nate "Tiny" Archibald, a skeeter-bug of a guard who had 47 points (15-22, 17-21) in a thrilling 136-127 Royals win.

Future ESPN sports announcer Dan Patrick and two friends drove over three hours just to watch Maravich in person. "I couldn't take my eyes off of him," Patrick wrote in his book *The Big Show.* "The ball looked like it was on a string every time he dribbled. The ball looked like it was meant to be in his hand every time he shot it. He knew he was a showman; he was paid to be a showman, and he was going to be a showman that night."

Patrick also got a taste of the fan frenzy that surrounded Pete. "Afterwards the three of us waited for Maravich outside the Cincinnati Gardens," Patrick wrote. "We were hoping to get his autograph. There were probably 75 to a 100 people waiting outside with us, hoping to do the same. Maravich finally came out and you would've thought the Beatles had just landed in New York. Men and women were screaming, shoving programs in his face. My friend Zeke Campbell actually reached in and grabbed a lump of Pistol Pete's hair and to this day he's still not sure why he did it. Pete would sign my program. Zeke got his clump of hair."

The chaos continued at the Philadelphia Spectrum where, during the warmups for a game on March 16, five teenage girls lunged at Pete, pulling his hair. "I don't know what they wanted but I ran," Pete told Joe Gross of the *Bucks County Courier Times.* "When people grab your hair, it has a tendency to come out." A couple of Philadelphia cops helped to disengage Pete from the over-zealous teenyboppers.

But other Philly patrons were unimpressed by the high-priced rookie. A large, homemade banner stretched across the balcony of the Spectrum. It read:

HEY, PISTOL PETE, WHY DO HOT DOGS COST TWO
MILLION DOLLARS IN ATLANTA AND ONLY 35 CENTS
IN PHILADELPHIA?

Late in the game Pete answered that question. He went on a tear, scoring 16 fourth-quarter points as the Hawks stormed back from an 18-point deficit to win, 130-125. Maravich finished with 28 points (8-18, 12-15, 7 rebounds, 4 assists) and Hudson poured in 43 as the Hawks closed in on a playoff berth.

Over the final month of the regular season, Pete played with his old confidence. He averaged 29 points (shooting 49 percent) as Atlanta won 13 of its final 17 games. "Without Pete we would not have made it," Bridges told Hyland. "Pete was the reason we made the playoffs."

Pete's turnaround even made an impression on his demanding coach. "No doubt about it now," Guerin said to reporters, "Maravich is the Rookie of the Year. He's the best rookie in this league and I just don't see how anybody could vote otherwise."

Unfortunately for the Hawks, their first-round opponent was the defending world champion New York Knicks. Although the teams had split six regular-season games, Atlanta offered little resistance as the New York juggernaut took the series in five games.

"It's their world championship experience," said Bridges. "I think the Knicks are the finest team I've played against as a pro. They read each other's minds out there."

Maravich led the Hawks with 31 points in the final game, but failed to score in the last 10 minutes, missing a couple of key shots at critical moments. Those misses hit Pete hard. Tears streaked his face as he spoke with reporters.

"I was the one who did it," whispered Maravich, who had shot an anemic 37 percent over the five games. "If it hadn't been for me, we would have won tonight. The points don't mean a thing to me. The one thing I want is to win a championship. I've never done that and I want one so bad I can taste it."

After the season the NBA announced the winners of its two major awards. To no one's surprise Lew Alcindor was the MVP. The other prize was for Rookie of the Year, a wide-open contest involving such budding stars as Maravich, Calvin Murphy, Bob Lanier, Rudy Tomjanovich, Nate Archibald, Dave Cowens, and Geoff Petrie. Ultimately, the Celtics' Cowens and Portland's Petrie shared the honor.

Exactly 192 players participated in the rookie voting but only four voted for Maravich. Maravich was perplexed. "Four votes?" he asked. "I didn't have a good year—okay, they're right about that. But I thought I deserved a little more recognition. Say maybe 10 votes. But four?"

Maravich had to settle for a place on the NBA's All-Rookie Team, along with Petrie, Cowens, Lanier, and Murphy.

Pete lost more games (46) in one year with the Hawks than he had over his four-year college career. Every defeat ate at him. "The general public doesn't understand. When I lose, it tears my heart out," Maravich said. "But I learned what it's like to play 82 games. I learned what it's like to play four games in four nights in four cities. I learned how physical the game is in the pros. I learned that I couldn't do certain things I could do in college."

Maravich scored 1,880 points in 81 games, averaged 23.2 points per game (eighth in the league) and shot 45.8 percent from the floor.

"Pete has the moves, the shots, the quickness, and the agility," Frazier said. "All he really needs is the experience. Sometimes I'm afraid to think what he'll be in a couple of seasons."

Philadelphia's All-Star guard Hal Greer, who once played one-on-one against a 12-year-old Maravich, was even more impressed. "I think Pete will be one of the superstars in this league. In passing and shooting, he already rates with Oscar Robertson and Jerry West."

West, Maravich's boyhood idol, added his analysis. "Considering the things against him, it is a surprise he did as well as he did," West told Cunningham. "The question isn't whether or not he's going to make it. But how big."

Maravich had another ally in Calvin Murphy, the fiery 5-9 Houston Rockets rookie. "Pistol was the new NBA, and he got caught up in a team that didn't want to play with him . . . and anything that went wrong, they placed blame. The old NBA wasn't ready for the new NBA."

Bridges told columnist Larry Merchant, "He proved himself to us. He's going to be much better than Jerry West. He drives better, he handles the ball quicker, he's quicker."

As for Pete, he was just exhausted. "I've never experienced a year like that in my life, and I hope I never have to go through another one like it. In many ways, I feel like I haven't played one year in the NBA; I've played 10."

Maravich's positive impact on the Hawks' finances was undeniable. Average attendance jumped 15 percent and Atlanta had 18 sellouts, compared with just three the previous season. Season-ticket sales more than doubled, gate receipts increased 47 percent (from $632,518 to $930,833), and the team's bottom line was additionally bolstered by more lucrative contracts with local TV and radio outlets.

The entire league also prospered. For the first time in NBA history, season attendance topped five million, a solid 19 percent increase over the previous season. The league's three expansion teams and Pete's drawing power were major factors.

"It's been the most hectic grind of my life," Pete told sports columnist Larry Merchant. "If I write a book about it, it will outsell *The Sensuous Woman*."

13

Avant Guard

"There was probably more pressure on Maravich last season than on any rookie in the history of professional sports."

—JERRY WEST

"If I see an opportunity for a behind-the-back pass. I'll take it. It's still a game for the people up there in the stands. They pay their money to see it. If it wasn't for them there wouldn't be anything. No teams, no league, no anything."

—PETE MARAVICH

P ete Maravich hoped the summer of 1971 would provide an opportunity to relax and recover from the crucible of his rookie season. His vacation got off to a rocky start, though. On April 17, two weeks after the season ended, Pete played a round of golf outside Sarasota, Florida. After winning $5 in a friendly match, he drank a few beers in the clubhouse; then hopped into his car. Minutes later he was pulled over and arrested for driving under the influence. Judge Marvin E. Silverman fined Maravich $150 and gave him a year's probation.

"You have two alternatives," Judge Silverman explained from the bench. "You can forget about alcohol or, if you continue, you will probably end your career around a telephone pole."

Pete spent a good portion of the summer working with Press at a basketball camp they founded. The oddly named California State Teacher's College was located about 35 miles south of Pittsburgh. "In the morning, we did exercises and didn't even touch a basketball," recalled camper Vernon Burt. "After exercises, we did mental exercises. Just sat there with our eyes closed. Pete and Press would try to impress upon us the mental attitude we needed to have about the game. After that, we worked on fundamentals. We went through all the basics of the game before we even practiced or picked up a ball to scrimmage."

It was a family-run camp with Pete, Press, and Ronnie all chipping in. "They slept in the same dorm room. They ate the same food in the cafeteria. At night we'd all watch movies," Burt said.

The campers also glimpsed the dynamic between Pete and his brother. "They could be volatile. Pete and Ronnie actually got into a fight one time at camp where they had to be separated," said Burt.

While Pete advocated a clean lifestyle to his campers, he didn't always practice what he preached. Burt recalled a late night where Pete staggered past the dorm rooms: "Pete came in and he could barely stand up. He was tall, he stood about 6-5 or something, and he leaned up against the wall, which was holding him up. He then started yelling at me, 'Didn't I tell you to be in bed by 11 o'clock?' I'm looking up at him and I'm scared. I thought he might hit me. He was really inebriated."

The next morning, a sheepish Maravich approached Burt. "You didn't see me last night, did you?" he asked. Burt looked him straight in the eye and replied, "I don't know what you're talking about." The two never spoke of the incident again.

"One of the drills Pete performed I'll never forget," Burt said. "He'd line up eight or nine pennies on top of his forearm and held it straight out. Then he would pull his arm back and catch each penny. One at a time. The last one he caught was almost on the ground. Unbelievable hand speed."

When Pete returned to Atlanta, he moved from his one-story apartment into a more upscale complex called The Paces. His $550-a-month, three-level townhouse was a luxury unit that featured a doorman, a polar-bear rug, contemporary furniture, and a stained-glass chandelier. He replaced his monogrammed sheets and shower curtain.

He traded in his Plymouth GTX and had the Hawks lease him a tan and white Cadillac El Dorado. Then he revamped his wardrobe, earning the nickname, "The Wizard of Mod." No outfit seemed too outlandish. "He tried so hard to fit in, and that's why I think he dressed like he did," said Jackie years later. "Because other players dressed the same way."

Former Georgia player Tom Brennan recalled seeing Maravich at a party wearing a floor-length, belted, leather coat.

"It was the first time I had ever seen one," Brennan said. "He was talking to some people in the house, and he hadn't taken it off yet, and I went over to [give him a hard time]. I said, 'Hey Pete, it's 75 degrees in the house. You can take off your coat now.'"

"Oh, that's right," Pete busted right back. "You're going to be a P.E. teacher. You'll be able to afford this coat in about four to five years."

The Hawks' front office had been busy re-working the Hawks roster in the offseason. As expected, Walt Hazzard was traded (to Buffalo). Jim Davis and John Vallely were sent to Houston, and Herb White, Pete's road room-mate, ended his career after one season.

The personnel changes infused Pete with a great deal of confidence. "I don't think there'll be as much pressure. I should be able to concentrate more on basketball," he said. "I know I'll be handling the ball more and that's something I really enjoy." Plus, at 203 pounds, he was near his ideal playing weight.

In its NBA preview issue *Sports Illustrated* predicted the Hawks would beat out the Baltimore Bullets for first place in the Central Division. The magazine cited the maturation of Maravich, the return of Lou Hudson to shooting guard, the acquisition of defensive specialist Herm Gilliam (who came in the Hazzard deal), and the formidable front line of Walt Bellamy and Bill Bridges.

Pete was excited. "This will be my first year," Maravich told *Atlanta Journal*'s new reporter Jim Huber at the start of training camp. "I'll just block that rookie season out altogether."

Maravich told Huber that at times during his first year he felt like buying a pair of gloves to warm his hands, because they got quite cold when his teammates froze him out of plays. Huber asked Maravich if he still needed gloves now that he was the new point guard.

"Nope. Don't need 'em now," he smiled. "I couldn't be more optimistic about this year."

Injuries and illness struck the team during the opening days of training camp in Jacksonville, Florida. Coach Richie Guerin missed two days with a kidney infection. Bellamy spent a week in the hospital battling the flu, and Hudson was out with a strained back.

The day Guerin returned, September 17, Maravich was kicked in the leg and was sidelined for two days. Then, on September 22, Pete arrived for "team picture day" with a towel draped around his neck and sweat pouring from his body. By the end of the photo session he was shaking. He was rushed to a Jacksonville hospital where doctors diagnosed tonsillitis and administered penicillin.

A day later, the diagnosis was amended to strep throat. As Pete's fever hovered at a dangerous 103 degrees, the diagnosis changed once again. Now doctors suspected scarlet fever or mononucleosis. The hospital stay stretched from a few days into a week. As the Hawks prepared to break camp, Pete desperately wanted to leave Florida with the team.

"I was determined to get out of that place, so I arranged for a seat on a flight to Atlanta," Maravich said. But a rash was rapidly spreading onto his face. When the attending nurse got a look, she was stunned.

"She ran out of the room," Pete recalled. "I was weak but got out of the bed and looked in the mirror. My face was swollen. My whole body was covered."

That morning, as he made his rounds, the doctor discovered Pete packing his bags.

"You mean, you won't stay?" the doctor asked.

"No, I'm going," Maravich said firmly.

"I think you have scarlet fever," the doctor countered.

"Well, if I'm going to die, I want to die in Atlanta," Maravich replied.

Before heading to the airport, Pete went to great lengths to conceal his condition. "I put on gloves and then put a stocking on my face," he told sportswriter Ben Olan.

In Atlanta, doctors ordered Pete back to bed and ran more tests, which were still inconclusive. Finally the doctors agreed that Pete had mononucleosis. "They say about 10 percent of the mono cases show up negative," Maravich told Jim Huber. "I'm one of those 10, I guess." The doctor's misdiagnosis and ineffective treatment strengthened Pete's skepticism of the medical profession.

Maravich's illness created some public relations problems for the team. Atlanta had scheduled a number of exhibition games in non-NBA cities and every game was sold out. Upon learning that Pete would not play, more than 400 fans in Huntington, West Virginia, rushed the box office and demanded a refund. In West Palm Beach, Florida, spectators hissed and tossed debris on the court when informed of Maravich's absence.

When the news spread, Maravich's hospital room was flooded with cards and letters from well-wishers. One 11-year-old urged Pete to drink milk and take plenty of "Vitamin G."

Maravich received bushels of flowers but kindly asked fans to refrain from sending more. "I don't mean any disrespect, but flowers remind me of death," Maravich remarked to a reporter. "I feel like I'm in a cold storage when they're around."

Pete had reported to training camp weighing a robust 203 pounds. Three weeks later he had shrunk to 168. The team placed him on the injured reserve list for the first five regular-season games.

Without Maravich the Hawks dropped their first four games. The previous year, the Hawks blamed a poor start on Maravich's presence on the court. Now, his absence was to blame.

"Pete is the team," Bridges told *Newsday*'s Dennis Weintraub. "If I don't have the key to start my car, I can't start it. Pete is our key . . . our leader. We can't go without our key."

All Pete could do was wait it out.

"Man, I want to be out there so bad I can taste it," Maravich told Jim Huber while watching practice from the stands. "I just itch and itch sitting up here. It's agony."

Pete slowly eased back into his basketball routine. In early November he began to work out with the Hawks, participating mainly in half-court scrimmages. One reporter observed that he looked like "a skeleton in sneakers," while another commented that his "big brown eyes bugged out like a squeezed fish."

Maravich, extremely frustrated, told the *Atlanta Journal* that he doubted he would suit up at all. "I love basketball, but it's not worth my life," he said, citing chest pains. "Maybe I should sit it out a year."

When the wire services reprinted Pete's pessimistic prognosis, the Hawks asked him to "clarify" his comments. Ticket sales were sluggish and the front office was loathe to create the impression that Maravich might miss an entire year.

"What I meant was, I don't think I'll be back to where I was last season until I get over this thing," Pete explained the next day.

When Pete's weight climbed to 175 pounds, the Hawks team doctor, Charles Harrison, cleared him for limited playing time. The front office announced that it was "highly possible" Pete would make his season debut at home against Seattle on November 17. The team stood at 4-10 and seemed destined for the cellar of the Central Division.

Before the tipoff, Wayne Smith, the Hawks chaplain, asked the overflow crowd to bow their heads in prayer. "And one other thing, Lord. Isn't it good to see Pete Maravich back in uniform again?" The young minister's "amen" was drowned out by an explosive cheer that rocked the arena. Maravich just stared at the floor, embarrassed.

Not surprisingly, Pete lacked stamina that night. He scored two points in the first half, but was gasping for breath and complained of chest pains. A doctor checked his pulse and gave him the "go-ahead" to finish the game. Pete finished with 18 points in 26 minutes but committed several turnovers.

"The behind-the-back passes were winding up in the hands of the wrong people," one Atlanta reporter observed. "The off-balance shots weren't falling. Some of them weren't even reaching the rim. The dribbling was flashy but it wasn't fooling all of the people all of the time. In short, the young Hawk's return to the court laid an egg."

Seattle, led by Spencer Haywood's 23 points, spoiled Maravich's sophomore debut with a 112-104 win.

After the game Maravich admitted he was not in basketball shape. "My heart, man," he said in the locker room. "I just couldn't take any more. My pulse was way up and I couldn't breathe."

Two days later the Hawks traded team captain Bill Bridges to Philadelphia (for Jim Washington), leaving only Hudson, Bellamy, and Maravich from the 1970-71 team. Hudson was voted the team's new captain.

On December 12, the struggling Hawks (8-19) traveled to Los Angeles to play the Lakers (26-3), the league's hottest team. Two nights earlier the Lakers notched their 20th consecutive victory, tying the record set by the 1970-71 Milwaukee Bucks.

The Hawks put up a good fight in the sold-out Forum, but still, the Lakers ran their win streak to 21 games to set an NBA record. The league's new entertainment division sent a film crew to the Forum to capture what turned out to be a historic game. The cameras also recorded two creative shots from Maravich that made a lasting impression. On one, Pete casually flipped in a high layup that banked in off the top of the backboard, over the outstretched arm of Wilt Chamberlain (who had seven blocks). It was a shot Pete called his "pro layup," designed to neutralize the long reach of seven-foot centers like Chamberlain and Alcindor. Pete said the secret was to shoot it flat footed in order to disrupt the timing of the shot blockers. "Men of color have all the great style," wrote Chamberlain in his 1991 autobiography, *A View from Above.* "The one exception I can come up with is the late great Pistol Pete Maravich. I don't know where he got his flair, but he sure had it."

Pete's flair and creativity combined for another maneuver that would become his most famous NBA shot. The sequence began with a Laker turnover (Chamberlain fumbled a Goodrich pass) and Pete receiving an outlet pass. He took off down court, dribbling hard toward the Laker basket. As he crossed the half-court line, Maravich noticed Hudson heading to the hoop from the left side and the Lakers' Jerry West positioned at the foul line, ready to defend. As Maravich reached West, he cradled the ball in his right arm, faked a behind-the-back-pass to Hudson, pulled the ball back to the front of his body, and banked in a layup. The move, which Pete had done more than a few times at LSU, was based on a deception he had watched the Celtics' K. C. Jones's attempt years earlier on television.

The highlight first played on the syndicated television program *This Week in the NBA*. The 16-millimeter clip was archived by NBA Entertainment and subsequently cut into every montage package of Maravich highlights. As a result, Pete's "now-you-see-it-now-you-don't" move has been replayed and analyzed countless times. "I've seen it a couple times," West chuckled in 2001. "I had a lot of success in making steals and anticipating plays. And sometimes when you anticipate plays, you're certainly not going to be successful."

In 2004, Pete's entertaining maneuver was voted the No. 9 "Ankle Breaker" in the history of the league. (Another, less spectacular, clip of Pete from the same game was edited into the 1978 Walt Disney feature, *The Cat from Outer Space*. In that sequence he dribbled into the corner and had the ball stolen by the Lakers backup guard, Pat Riley.)

Following the loss in L.A., the Hawks played .500 ball over their next 10 games and upped their record to 13-25 by the end of December.

On January 7, 1972, the Hawks faced the Lakers again, this time in Atlanta. The Lakers had stretched their winning streak to an unprecedented 32 games. Before the tipoff Pete went to say hello to West in the visitors locker room and was shocked to find the perennial All-Star sound asleep on a bench. Later, during warmups, he asked West how he could be so relaxed in the middle of a historic run. West replied that a good nap actually helped him escape from the game. West felt that if he was too focused on basketball, too obsessed with his preparation, it actually hurt his performance.

The concept hit Pete like a ton a bricks. "From that point on I did anything possible to avoid thinking about basketball outside of the game situation," Pete wrote in his autobiography. "I started reading everything and anything I could get my hands on to fill my time. I needed to find ways to escape the realities of my circumstances." And thus began his quest for happiness and contentment outside the game.

Pete was still dramatically under weight in mid-January. "I guess I get a little anxiety when 160,000 people a day ask me when I'll be back to normal," Maravich told reporter Jim Huber. "But I can play. As long as I pace myself, I can still play."

On January 17, alone in his townhouse, Pete tuned in to the broadcast of Super Bowl VI. The Dallas Cowboys defeated the Miami Dolphins 24–3, and Pete felt intense pangs of jealousy as he watched the Cowboys celebrate.

That night Pete drilled the Philadelphia 76ers for a career-high 50 points (18-29, 14-16, 3 rebounds, 6 assists) in a 124-116 Hawks victory. Philadelphia's all-star forward Billy Cunningham scored 45 points of his own. "I felt like I was playing at the O.K. Corral," said Pete.

After his scoring outburst Maravich brushed aside parallels to his LSU exploits. "It was expected of me in college. But here it's different. It's my contribution to the team, whether it be 50 or 5. I don't rate this as a good or bad performance. I rate it a victory and that is all that counts."

Atlanta was 17–30 at the All-Star break and hoping to qualify for the playoffs.

Pete flew to California during the five-day layoff for a one-on-one basketball tournament sponsored by Vitalis. The 34-man competition included two players from each NBA team (Pete and Don May represented the Hawks) and the games were played at the University of Southern California. The rules were simple: The first player to get to 20 points, with at least a four-point lead, was the winner. ABC taped the single-elimination tournament and featured the contests throughout the season on its NBA *Game of the Week*.

Pete eventually faced Detroit's center Bob Lanier and the two future Hall of Famers locked horns in a thrilling marathon. Lanier kept backing Pete down while the Pistol kept popping from the outside. The tense contest went back and forth, as the score went into the 40s. Lanier finally prevailed and would go on to defeat Celtic guard Jo Jo White in the championship game, walking away with $15,000 in cash stuffed into a gym bag.

A week later, in Milwaukee, Maravich was spectacular against the defending NBA champion Bucks. He scored 35 points (10-24, 15-15, 8 rebounds, 14 assists), including 14 of the Hawks final 18, in a virtuoso, all-around performance as the Hawks won by 5.

Pete put up those sterling numbers despite still being weak from his bout of mononucleosis. "The Milwaukee Bucks would hate to see him when he is healthy," wrote Bob Wolf of the *Milwaukee Journal*.

On February 5, Maravich had another 50-point game, hitting a remarkable 20 of 27 shots in a 120-117 win over the Cavaliers in Atlanta. Late in the fourth quarter, with the Hawks trailing by 6, Pete pumped in 13 straight points in a span of 3:25. "I'm still not consistent. I can't go hard every game," Maravich said. "I'm down 18 pounds. I was 26 pounds down when I came back."

Despite Pete's scoring, the Hawks stood 25-40 as February neared its end. The team was mediocre but the fans loved Pete. On February 25, a crowd of 8,761 jammed Hershey Arena in Hershey, Pennsylvania, to get a good look at the mop-topped idol. The Hawks took on the 76ers in the same gym where, nine years earlier, Chamberlain had scored 100 points against the New York Knicks. Whenever Maravich touched the ball, throngs of young girls screamed madly. A flurry of camera flashes caused him to miss three consecutive free throws. Five state troopers escorted Pete on and off the court and others stood guard outside the Hawks locker room. They were worried that another wild hair-pulling incident would be repeated.

"We got a call at headquarters to come down here and make sure nothing happened to Maravich," a Pennsylvania state trooper told sportswriter Milton Gross.

In early March, as the team prepared to play the SuperSonics, a Seattle reporter told Guerin that an Atlanta newspaper was about to report that he was being fired.

"Aw, don't pay that any attention," Pete reassured his coach. "Some guy in Baton Rouge wrote the other day that my old man was getting fired, too. So you can't believe everything you read."

The following day, March 6, LSU athletic director Carl Maddox announced the termination of Press Maravich, as well as assistant coaches Jay McCreary and Greg Bernbrock. Maddox said the university would honor Maravich's $17,000-per-year contract, which ran through April 1973.

"It's just one of those things," Press told reporter Danny Young of the *Times-Picayune.* "Naturally, I'm not happy about it, but there is nothing I can do now but start looking for another job."

In reality, the stiff upper lip was a pose. Press was devastated. LSU's assistant trainer Andy Ezell found Maravich and McCreary in tears after the firing.

Maddox was unhappy with Press's indifference to recruiting. "Press's big downfall was that he did not surround himself with big-time, young aggressive basketball recruiters," said his close friend and LSU booster, Jimbo Marchand. "McCreary was an old man by then and all Press would do is say, 'Do you know anybody who might want to come south and play?' He was not up to date on the best players."

Due to his unstable home situation, Press rarely made recruiting trips. One excursion had to be cut short when he got word that Helen was having a dish-breaking meltdown. "Helen was an alcoholic, and Diana would literally get sick every time Press went on a road trip," said LSU sports information director Bud Johnson. "She didn't want to be home alone with her mother. Press adopted that child and raised her as his own, and he did the cooking and the cleaning and the dishwashing and the laundry, and coached a basketball team. Dean Smith wasn't doing that. John Wooden wasn't doing that."

Press's six years at LSU had, on the whole, been a success. Pete's exploits had given the basketball program a national profile but there were other achievements as well: the NIT appearance, a new basketball arena, and, on February 26, 1972, a victory, at last, over Kentucky. Perhaps Press's most significant milestone occurred when he signed Collis Temple in the fall of 1970, the first African-American to play basketball at LSU.

Jackie Maravich believed the university wanted to sever its relationship with Press as soon as Pete left. "I remember when Pete was thinking about becoming a pro, they were already in the process of trying to boot Press out," said Jackie. "Ever since that happened to Press, Pete had a real bitterness toward LSU. For years and years and years."

Press leapt at the first job offer that came his way, a head coaching position at Appalachian State, a small college in Boone, North Carolina. With his home life in disarray and the welfare of a small child to consider, Press felt he couldn't afford the luxury of waiting around for better offers. Pete vehemently disagreed. He thought Press should be coaching at an elite college or in the NBA.

"Here was one of the most creative minds in the basketball world leaving major college basketball for his first job opening that came along," wrote Pete. "I pleaded with him not to be hasty in his decision."

Within weeks of his dismissal Press packed up (including Pete's college game films) and moved his family to the tiny town of Boone. He left with nothing but contempt for LSU.

Press's firing devastated Pete. The subject of his father was taboo with teammates and the media. He dressed quickly after each game and left the locker room before reporters were allowed to enter. He sank into a depression and endured a week-long scoring slump. During a four-game stretch he scored just 24 points and in a home game against Seattle, on March 15, he was completely shut out.

"Pete Maravich, the multi-millionaire second-year pro, played 22 minutes and didn't score a point," reported Frank Hyland. "Nothing. Not a field goal, not a free throw. In fact, the only shot he took all night long was a wild reverse layup."

Hyland's story was headlined: "The Pistol Fires a Blank."

Pete's funk was short lived, though. "Just as suddenly as he went into the dive, he pulled himself out," Jim Huber wrote. "Within a week, he was back to normal."

The Hawks went on a five-game winning streak and faced the Knicks in the season finale, a nationally televised game on March 26. Maravich, still rail-thin at 185 pounds, jump-started the Hawks offense with a no-look, court-length pass that led to an easy bucket. He ended the game with 27 points (9-22, 9-9, 5 rebounds, 5 assists), leading the Hawks to their sixth straight win, 120-106. And once again the Hawks were in the playoffs. Atlanta's record of 36-46 was an exact duplicate of the previous season, but the team's chemistry had vastly improved.

Pete, riding a six-game win streak, was giddy with optimism. He even began to talk seriously about winning a championship. "I remember watching the Super Bowl this year," Pete told Huber. "I know this is only my second year in the pros but it's time for me to bust a few champagne bottles of my own. It's time."

The Hawks drew the Boston Celtics in the opening round. From 1957 to 1969, the Celtics, led by Bill Russell, ruled the NBA, winning 11 championships in 13 years, the most dominant run in modern professional sports history. But Boston had missed the playoffs the previous two seasons and was a franchise in transition. Center Dave Cowens, guard Jo Jo White, defensive specialist Don Chaney, and veterans Don Nelson and John Havlicek led the 1972 team that topped the Eastern Conference with a 56-26 record.

The best-of-seven series began on March 29 in Boston. The Celtics, 4-0 against the Hawks in the regular season, were picked to win easily. The NBA initiated a new format, as teams now alternated home games. The first game in Boston played out as expected as the Celtics won easily, 126-108. Maravich missed 12 of his 19 field-goal attempts and Chaney limited him to 19 points (7-19, 5-6, 4 rebounds, 6 assists).

In the second game, in Atlanta, Hudson dropped in 41 points and the Hawks evened the series with a 113-104 win. Maravich, suffering from a bruised hip, played just 22 minutes and scored 16 points (6-12, 4-5, 2 rebounds, 3 assists).

The Hawks lost Game 3 back in Boston, 136-113, but Pete's outstanding performance caught the attention of many observers. Chaney, the Celtics premier stopper, was assigned the task of shutting him down. "When Pete played against Boston, he played as good as a defensive guard as there was in basketball," recalled Bob Ryan of the *Boston Globe*. "Chaney was an incredible physical specimen, 6-5, long arms, strong, wanted to play defense, had intelligence, smarts, the whole package. He had a [hard] time guarding Pete Maravich."

Maravich took Chaney to the hoop with fierce abandon, drawing a host of fouls. He made 13 of his 14 free throws; no other player on the floor attempted more than 5. By the end of the game Pete had racked up 37 points (12-28, 13-14, 9 rebounds, 6 assists).

More than 25 years later, Ryan was still amazed. "Pete Maravich just completely showed us who he was. The things you learn about people through basketball. He had toughness. He took it to the hoop fearlessly. He was not afraid to get knocked on his rear end and then go to the foul line and sink two free throws. I looked at him differently from that point on. I think he was, by far, the single best reason why the Hawks even had a prayer against the Celtics."

The teams returned to Atlanta for Game 4 and Pete delivered another head-turning performance. Once again he attacked the basket with slashing drives, was fouled repeatedly, and went to the charity stripe 20 times. Overall he netted 36 points (10-15, 16-20, 1 rebound, 2 assists) as the Hawks tied the series with an exciting 112-110 victory.

"It's next to impossible to prevent him from getting to the basket. He's dynamite in that situation," said Chaney.

"Maravich has come up with more moves than a go-go dancer in his drives to the basket," reported the *Atlanta Constitution*'s George Cunningham.

Back in Boston the Celtics dominated Game 5, winning 124-114. White replaced Chaney as Maravich's defender and it proved to be an effective switch. White limited Pete to 21 points (7-24, 7-8, 7 rebounds, 8 assists) and was particularly successful at keeping Pete away from the basket. Maravich took just 8 foul shots, compared to 34 over the previous two games. Pete also committed three crucial turnovers in the fourth quarter.

Back in Atlanta, the Celtics closed out the series, despite a 37-point contribution from Pete (12-23, 13-18, 7 rebounds, 5 assists), and ended Atlanta's season with a 127-118 win. After the game, Pete lingered longer than usual, reviewing the past season. "Nobody wants it to be over," a stunned Pete admitted to Huber.

The series was a remarkable one for Maravich, who torched the Celtics with a per-game stat line of 27.7 points (46 percent shooting), 5.3 rebounds, and 4.7 assists.

"The 1972 playoffs was when I became a big Pete Maravich fan as a pro," said Ryan in 1999. "I had formed the general fan opinion of him as a collegiate and that was he was an incredible phenomenon and he averaged 44 points, which was very special. But you didn't care if they won or lost; you just wanted Pete to get 50. Most people looked at him that way."

Pete's fine season earned him new respect from the league's players, coaches, and sportswriters. "[Celtic head coach] Tommy Heinsohn salivated over Maravich," Ryan observed. "In his mind, if he ever had Pete Maravich running his fast breaks, they'd be 75-7. Heinsohn thought Pete Maravich was put on this earth to run his fast break. I think Pete himself looked at Boston and said, '. . . that's where I belong.' I think whenever Pete played against Boston, he tried to win, but he also tried to show them, 'I belong with you.' Offensively, it would have been the greatest show on earth."

But for Pete, all the praise fell on deaf ears. "Some people worry about statistics, but I worry about winning," he would often repeat. "Statistics are for losers."

Pete's first two years in Atlanta marked the high point of his popularity. He was a mega-personality, arguably pro basketball's first rock star, drawing thousands of new fans into arenas across the NBA. He was profiled in scores of magazine articles and starred in several television commercials. His name and image helped sell calendars, T-shirts, basketball nets, socks, jigsaw puzzles, basketballs, posters, shoes, trading cards, hair products, and training films. The American Cancer Society created a Maravich poster for its "I Don't Smoke Cigarettes" campaign. Bill Gutman wrote a successful biography entitled: *Pistol Pete Maravich: The Making of a Basketball Superstar.*

Pete's 1972 season didn't end with a champagne shower, but the odds of him enjoying one in 1973 improved tremendously on April 9, when Atlanta engineered a stunning personnel move. During a clandestine meeting in Roanoke, Virginia, the Hawks secretly signed a spectacular ABA rookie to a four-year NBA contract. His name was Julius Erving.

Pistol Pete and Dr. J were about to join forces.

14

Omni All-Star

"After the first two years and the things that happened, my chances of being super-optimistic have been killed. All I can pray for is that the illnesses don't come back."
—PETE MARAVICH

"Pete was the most talented player I ever coached. He could go from end line to end line with the basketball, in the heat of battle, quicker and faster than anyone I've ever seen."
—COTTON FITZSIMMONS, HAWKS HEAD COACH

When the Hawks announced on April 11 that they'd signed Julius Erving, Atlanta fans rejoiced and began to entertain fantasies of an NBA championship. With an offense featuring the high-flying Dr. J and the magical Pistol Pete, the Hawks, they figured, would be unstoppable. The team stoked the enthusiasm with a fresh marketing slogan, "It's a Whole New Ballgame in Atlanta." A dark cloud loomed, though, because the validity of Erving's agreement with the Hawks was in doubt.

The issue was not the generous contract—$1.4 million over five years, along with a $250,000 bonus, a new Jaguar, and an apartment—but whether or not Atlanta had the right to sign Erving. The Hawks signed Dr. J two days before the 1972 NBA draft. In that draft Milwaukee picked Erving and immediately filed a complaint with the league's board of governors, claiming they, not Atlanta, held the star's NBA rights.

The dispute remained unresolved when training camp opened in early September in Savannah, Georgia. Erving, fresh from playing summer hoops in Harlem's Rucker League, was jazzed to be Pistol Pete's running mate. "It really was one of the joys of my life to play with Pete and to be in training camp with him," Erving told sportswriter David Friedman. "We used to stay after practice and play one-on-one. We would play for dinner. I did the same thing with George Gervin, once he became my teammate. I pretty much learned that from Pete. If this guy's going to be your teammate, you really need to stay after practice and get to understand his game, and know his likes and his dislikes—where he likes the ball, and that kind of stuff. The best way to do that is to just play."

Mike McKenzie, the new beat reporter for the *Atlanta Journal*, recalled the immediate rapport. "The most memorable part of it was just the raw talent on the court. Everyone just stopped what they were doing to watch. Great veteran players watching Maravich and Erving do their shtick. Together, they were unstoppable."

Ten days into camp, Erving's case was finally adjudicated. The board of governors ruled that Erving's rights belonged to Milwaukee and charged Atlanta with a violation of the league's by-laws. Commissioner Walter Kennedy banned the Hawks from using Erving in practice and exhibition games. Atlanta ignored his edict and even profiled Dr. J in its 1972-73 media guide.

Erving played his first Hawks exhibition game against the ABA's Kentucky Colonels on September 23, 1972, in Frankfort, Kentucky. Wearing No. 54 and high-top Converse All Stars, Erving was stellar, contributing 28 points and 18 rebounds in the 112-109 victory. Maravich pitched in 17 points. It was also the debut of the new Hawks head coach, Lowell "Cotton" Fitzsimmons. (Fitzsimmons stood just 5-8 and Pete used to joke that he could "sleep in a pillow case.")

The next day 4,824 fans crammed into tiny Alexander Memorial Coliseum to see a return match. Erving's Atlanta debut was eagerly anticipated. "The Hawks never drew that many people to an exhibition in their lives at home," observed *Atlanta Journal* sports editor Furman Bisher. Some older Hawks fans, feeling nostalgic, may have showed up because this would be Atlanta's last game in the cozy college arena.

In a nod to the Colonels, the first half was played under ABA rules, with a red, white, and blue ball. A temporary three-point line was painted on the floor with white shoe polish. NBA rules applied in the second half. The Hawks dominated early, at one point leading by 24, but the Colonels fought back and squeaked out a 104-103 win. Erving collected 23 points and 14 rebounds, while Pete added 12 points and nine assists.

NBA Commissioner Walter Kennedy fined the Hawks a record $25,000 for the two games Erving had played and promised to mete out escalating penalties. Even NFL Commissioner Pete Rozelle weighed in. "The action by the Hawks is considered a threat to all professional sports' common player drafts," Rozelle told the *Atlanta Journal*'s Mike McKenzie. The Hawks countered with a $2-million anti-trust suit.

The Hawks defied the league a third time, on September 30, when Erving suited up to play the ABA's Carolina Cougars in Raleigh, North Carolina. Future basketball legend David Thompson, entering his sophomore year at N.C. State, was in the bleachers at Reynolds Coliseum and looked on in amazement. "Man, it was insane. Those two just played like they had been teammates forever," Thompson recalled. "Pete was awesome. He was everything I had read about and more. He was 6-5 but could handle the ball and was quick and could jump. People don't realize how high he could jump. He could shoot anywhere from across the half-court line."

Maravich's deft passing was particularly impressive to Thompson. He remembered Maravich dribbling hard on a fast break, flanked by Erving and Hudson. At the top of the key, Maravich head faked the Carolina defender, locked both elbows as he looked right but threw left—a perfect bounce pass to Erving. Pete's old "wrist-pass" was still effective.

Erving later revealed to David Friedman, "I would just grab a rebound, throw it out to Pete, and get on the wing. Pete would always find you. He got his points, but he loved to pass the ball. He could hit you in full stride in a place where you could do something with the ball. That was a measure of his greatness."

Marty Bell, in his 1975 book *The Legend of Dr. J*, also marveled at the artistry of the duo. "It was like Fred Astaire and Gene Kelly dancing together. Maravich had the most moves of any guard in the league. And Julius had the most moves of any forward."

Erving scored 32 points (14-15) in a 120-106 rout of the Cougars and Maravich had 19 assists, including an array of brilliant passes. Erving and Maravich looked like a sensational fit. Dr. J provided bushels of points and Pete seemed content to feed him passes. Hawks fans couldn't wait for the season to start.

Then their hopes were dashed.

Commissioner Kennedy told the Hawks' new president Bill Putnam that if Erving continued to play the fines would be deducted from Atlanta's cut of its national television revenue. Putnam caved. After just three games, the Dr. J and Pistol Pete show closed.

"Julius was the most creative player that I've ever played with," Pete said in 1987. "It was so easy to play with him. I think during that time my average was about 14 or 15 assists per game. I'd just come down the court and his eyes would see mine—and I knew that he was going to the hoop. I'd just throw a little rainbow up there and it'd be history because nobody could get up like Dr. J."

In 2000, Erving called Maravich "a basketball genius."

Dr. J reluctantly returned to Virginia. He wished it had turned out differently. "I would have been a Hawk for the rest of my career," Erving said in a 2005 radio interview.

Richie Guerin, promoted to general manager, believed the situation was avoidable. "The only time I ever disagreed with [Hawks president] Bill Putnam my entire time in Atlanta was over the handling of the Julius Erving situation," he said in 2003. "Through a series of negotiations and conversations and meetings with Irwin Weiner [Erving's agent], they finally worked out a contract. Now, Irwin Weiner said to Bill Putnam, 'Bill, I have one request from Julius—don't announce this until after his playoffs.' Erving didn't want to let his [Virginia Squires] teammates or the city down during that crucial time. I disagreed with that. My reasoning was that the NBA was going to have their draft in a few weeks. He'd been out of college already and was playing professional basketball. Therefore, he was not eligible for the college draft in our opinion. We should have just announced that we signed Julius Erving, sent his contract into the league office, and if that meant we had to forfeit our No. 1 draft pick for that year, we'd be more than willing to do it."

When Erving retired from the NBA in 1987, Fitzsimmons reminisced to a *Miami Herald* reporter about Dr. J's brief Hawks tenure. "I was the coach, I saw an excitement, even in just those exhibitions, that he was able to bring like no one else. I saw us as one of the great teams." Fitzsimmons added, "I think we could have won a championship."

Guerin was less convinced that Erving and Maravich equaled a championship. "You know what? A championship might have been out of their realm unless they got a little more help up front. But I think we could have been in the running to get a championship. No question about it."

Losing Erving was a big blow and the Hawks had little time to adjust. Soon after his departure, they played an exhibition game against the Houston Rockets on the LSU campus. The game, a charity affair to benefit the Fellowship of Christian Athletes, was slated for Louisiana to capitalize on Maravich's fame. Pete, however, was annoyed about returning to Baton Rouge.

"That's the town that fired my father," he seethed. He was certain that Press's downfall, and the hiring of Dale Brown, was the result of a conspiracy, aided by future LSU athletic director Joe Dean.

Atlanta Journal reporter Mike McKenzie said Maravich was so livid that he didn't want LSU to lay any claim to his legacy. "I remember Pete saying to me before the game: 'They've got my jersey hanging in a trophy case, and it's got a big hole in the back of it . . . right where they stuck the knife.'"

But the local fans were unaware of Pete's feelings and 11,200 of them welcomed him back to LSU with a rousing five-minute standing ovation.

Former LSU student Cheryl Talbot Macaluso, who rarely missed a game when Maravich played for the Tigers, described his return as bittersweet. "I remember how different it was to see him playing in that game," she recalled in a 1988 article for the *State-Times*. "The Assembly Center was packed, but it wasn't the same. Pete didn't belong to us anymore. He wasn't scoring points for LSU."

The Hawks won a thriller, 132-131 in overtime, with Pete contributing 25 points and eight assists. Pete compared his old LSU gym—"the Ag Center was all right for livestock but who wants to fight cows?"—and new facilities that some were saying should bear his name. "The Assembly Center is beautiful. But I don't know why they call it 'Pete's Palace.' I didn't come up with any funds."

Leaving the dressing room after the game, McKenzie heard a young fan yell out: "How long do you intend to play pro ball, Pete?" Maravich shot back: "Until they carry me out in a box."

After two turbulent seasons, many people believed that 1972-73 would be Maravich's breakout year. "Pistol Pete is ready for the role of 'Mr. Wonderful' in his third season in the NBA," predicted basketball scribe Lee Andre. "The Hawks want him for the role the other great guards of the league have played, men like Bob Cousy of the past."

Guerin, who played against Cousy, believed they were both state-of-the-art ball handlers. "Bob was the first guy they called a magician because he did things where people went, 'Wow!' But Pete could do the same things and at a quicker pace," Guerin said. "And Pete was certainly a better shooter than Bob."

In 2000, Bob Cousy added his perspective in Mike Towle's book *I Remember Pete Maravich*. "I think we both were ahead of our times," said the NBA's original showman. "From all the point guards that have played up to now, Pete might have been the most skilled with all the unorthodox things that he could do. There's never been a player, in my judgment, who ever played like Pete . . . Magic Johnson had his own style, and he was imaginative and creative and did it from a 6-9 frame, but in terms of creativity, I don't put him in the same class with Maravich or myself."

Over the summer Pete had abandoned his usual weightlifting routine for martial arts instruction at Tracy's Karate Studio in Atlanta. The school already had a high-profile client in Braves slugger Henry Aaron. Co-owner Jim

Stewart was happy to have Maravich as a customer, even though he generally found that pro athletes and the martial arts were not a good mix. "Most sports superstars find the martial arts frustrating because they can't excel at it right away," Stewart said. "It usually takes two to three years for someone to become proficient to the point where they can handle themselves and become confident. Pete had no problem working toward that goal."

Stewart was impressed by Pete's karate ability. "He was no one to be messed with," Stewart said. "He had these long arms where he could hit you from halfway across the room. He also had a very strong back knuckle strike."

Maravich received karate and kenpo instruction from local black-belt legend Darryl Escalante. Pete spent up to eight hours a day practicing. Escalante used to call his pupil "Rifle Pete," because he had a mean reverse punch. Pete's interest in karate pleased his mother, Helen, who had encouraged him to study the martial arts so he would be better able to protect himself from physical defenders in the NBA. Pete thought the discipline, balance, and leverage would give him an edge over the long basketball season.

Maravich's friend Hank Kalb, on the other hand, gave Pete's new skills a lukewarm review. "I was a fairly strong and a pretty good-sized guy," Kalb recalled. "Pete was showing me all these ridiculous karate moves and finally I just said, 'Well, what would you do about this?' And I just grabbed [him] and threw him to the ground and jumped on top of him and tried to squash him to death. Anyway, we ended up, two grown men, chasing each other around the house in the middle of the night. When I woke up the next morning and go into the living room, there's a . . . hole in my wall where Mr. Karate had chopped my living room wall."

On October 10, the Hawks opened their regular season against the Braves in Buffalo. Gone were their "mod" green, blue, and white uniforms, replaced by a more traditional red and white with a hint of gold. Atlanta slammed Buffalo 120-109, as Pete scored 14 of his 34 points in the fourth quarter. Fans watching the game on channel 17 back in Atlanta got their first glimpse of Maravich's new mustache. It gave him an "ancient mariner" look, or as one reporter described him, "a Serbian arms dealer."

Five days later, Atlanta played the New York Knicks (2-0) in the inaugural game at the Omni. For team owner and real estate mogul, Tom Cousins, the multi-purpose arena was an important first step in his quest to develop a downtown section of Atlanta. The basketball floor was delivered just hours before the game and 13,867 fans filed in for the arena's grand opening. New York's loaded roster featured six future Hall of Famers—Willis Reed, Bill

Bradley, Walt Frazier, Dave DeBusschere, Earl Monroe, and Jerry Lucas—and would capture the NBA title later that season. The Hawks were not intimidated, though, winning 109-101 with the help of 28 points from Maravich. "That was the night Pete made it as a player in the pros," Fitzsimmons said to *Sports Illustrated*. "It was easily his best all-around game and his best defense since he came into the pros."

Maravich was firing on all cylinders until he encountered a minor setback against the Portland Trail Blazers on October 24. He twisted his ankle during a 118-110 victory and was furious about the injury. "See why I told you I'm pessimistic," he said to McKenzie. "I'm snake-bitten, always will be. I'm telling 'ya, I'm jinxed. This is the farthest into a season I've made it."

McKenzie went on to report that after the game a young girl handed Pete four long-stemmed red roses. Maravich mustered a smile, thanked her, and signed her program. Later, in the car, he sniffed the flowers and muttered, "For my grave, I guess."

Fortunately the sprain was not severe and Pete missed just one game but another, more serious, ailment was right around the corner. The trouble began in early November when he took an elbow to the eye during practice. To alleviate searing headaches, Maravich was prescribed medication by team doctor Charles Harrison, but it was ineffective.

Despite "excruciating headaches," Pete scored 31 points against the Houston Rockets, 44 against the Philadelphia 76ers, and 28 against the Baltimore Bullets. The Hawks won all three games.

But on November 9, as the 7-6 Hawks arrived in New York, disaster struck. It was a dank, frigid day and, as Pete stepped off the bus, he was hit in the face with a blast of cold air. Fifteen minutes later in his hotel room, he noticed the right side of his face was numb. He looked in the mirror and saw that his mouth muscles were sagging. He was unable to blink his right eye.

Hawks trainer Joe O'Toole feared Pete might have suffered a stroke. But a neurologist diagnosed Pete with Bell's palsy, a paralysis caused by inflammation of facial nerves. However, the doctor could not determine if the palsy resulted from the elbow to Maravich's eye, or another trigger, such as stress. Nor could the neurologist predict when the palsy would pass. The process might take anywhere from days to years. Pete thanked the doctor, returned to his hotel room and broke down. He feared that another season, and perhaps his career, was in jeopardy.

Maravich was advised to wear a patch and use eye drops. Playing was not recommended. But he ignored the advice and took the floor against the Knicks.

"Even though I decided to play that night, I felt alienated, scared," Maravich said. "I couldn't blink my eye, and if someone stuck a finger in it, I could have had my cornea torn."

Amazingly, Pete scored 25 points (10-23, 5-7, 8 rebounds, 4 assists, 4 steals) in a tough 101-99 loss. (A dazzling color photo from the game, showing Pete flying over a table and into the stands, is included in Bob Ryan's book *The Pro Game*.)

In the locker room, Pete concealed his condition from the media, claiming he was just suffering from an extreme headache. Coach Fitzsimmons didn't appear sympathetic and suggested Pete's ailments were self-created.

"Pete's got it in the back of his mind the fact that something physical seems to have happened to him ever since coming into the pros," Fitzsimmons said to a reporter at the time. "He's the type of dedicated athlete who builds up nervous energy."

Two days later, Maravich took the floor wearing a pair of plastic goggles in a home game against the Milwaukee Bucks. Looking more like a Depression-era stunt pilot than a basketball player, Pete lasted only six minutes (0-1, 1 rebound, 1 assist) before calling it a night. The Hawks, however, flattened the Bucks, 111-102, and moved into first place in the Central Division with an 8-7 record. "I need a witch doctor," Pete mumbled.

Maravich was enduring a private hell and often retreated into deep depressions. Over the next three weeks he would hunch for hours in the corner of the locker room, massaging his face, desperately trying to reverse the palsy.

"My whole head was messed up," Maravich confessed to a reporter. "Every night I had to tape my eye shut in order to get some sleep. Bell's palsy gave me arthritis in the jaw and I had difficulty opening my mouth."

Throughout the ordeal Maravich suited up for every game. His teammates tried to ease some of his stress by gently poking fun at him. "Half Face" was his new nickname. "He looked terrible," recalled Jackie. "His face just drooped to one side. He just didn't know what to do."

As Pete's spirits slumped, so did the Hawks, who went 6-7 for the month of November. But then, as swiftly and mysteriously as it arrived, the Bell's palsy vanished in late November. With Maravich again healthy, the Hawks won 10 of their first 12 games in December. Fitzsimmons, mindful of Pete's stamina, began resting him at the start of each fourth quarter before sending him in to finish the game. The Pistol was scoring almost half of his 26-point average in the final period.

It was a high-risk proposition. "I felt that we were playing Russian

Roulette," Fitzsimmons said of tactic. "The Pistol and Lou Hudson allowed us to win games down the stretch that we could have easily lost. Never the easy win."

In December 1972, a 13-year-old Pistol Pete fan named Randy Brown got an early Christmas present. For months he had been begging his father to take him to a Hawks game. Although the Brown family lived in Iowa, hundreds of miles from the nearest NBA city, Randy's father purchased tickets to an Atlanta Hawks-Kansas City Kings game on December 10. Early that morning the two piled into the family station wagon and headed for snowy Kansas City, 325 miles away. Upon arriving, the two went straight to the Muehlbach Hotel and staked out the lobby, hoping to catch a glimpse of Randy's hero. When Pete exited from an elevator, wearing jeans and a leather jacket, Randy intercepted him and asked for a handshake. He got much more.

Pete was startled when he heard about the Browns' long journey. "You came all this way to see me play?"

Pete then invited the Browns (and several other kids in the lobby) up to his room where he spent over an hour talking basketball with his wide-eyed fans. Randy was amazed that Pete had 10 pairs of basketball shoes and recalled the advice he offered. "Shoot the basketball every day," Pete told the kids. "Because if you do not, there is going to be another kid in Chicago or somewhere who will be shooting that day and if you meet someday, he will beat you."

After the game Pete invited Randy and his father into the locker room where they snapped photos and collected autographs. Randy Brown went on to coach basketball at the University of Arizona, Drake, North Dakota, Marquette, Miami of Ohio, and Stetson. And every December 10, he always sent a note to his father thanking him for his favorite Christmas gift.

On December 27, the Hawks played the 76ers in Pittsburgh's Civic Arena, about 25 miles from Maravich's former hometown of Aliquippa, and the locals gave Pete a hero's welcome. Some 7,400 fans—including Terry Bradshaw, Andy Russell, and Jim Clack of the Pittsburgh Steelers—showed up to see their favorite son. Maravich, feeling especially obligated to "wow" this crowd, fired up what was then a career-high 33 shots, missing his first eight.

A large Serbian contingent cheered his every move. A banner in section B-21 read: "Yea Pete, Local Serbs." At half time, Steven Zernich, Sr. of the St. Elijah Serbian Orthodox Church of Aliquippa presented Maravich with a plaque (and a loaf of Serbian bread). The inscription read: "From his Aliquippa

Friends, to Our Native Son for His Many Achievements in the Sports World and the Honor He Has Brought This Community."

Atlanta, playing without Walt Bellamy, Bob Christian, and George Trapp, trailed 120-119 when Maravich launched a 22-footer from the top of the key with four seconds to play. The shot missed and ricocheted into the hands of Don May, who had just entered the game. May fired up a prayer from the hip. It dropped through for the game-winner. In the locker room after the game, Pete kept repeating, "Donnie May, I love you." Maravich finished with 25 points in the 121-120 victory.

"I took 33 shots," Maravich explained sheepishly, "but 31 of them were wide open."

On his short walk from the Civic Arena to the Chatham Center Hotel, Pete resembled the Pied Piper as hundreds of fans trailed behind him. He let out an appreciative holler, "How about those people from Aliquippa, aren't they nice? These are my people. I just love them."

As December came to a close, the Hawks were playing well and Pete was among the NBA's top ten in both scoring and assists. He was also mastering some veteran tactics. One of his favorite "tricks" was to hook his arm around a defender and take off. "It makes it look like he's hanging on and draws a foul," explained Pete.

The Hawks faced the Chicago Bulls in their first game of 1973. For Pete, the game meant another struggle with the Bulls' brutal defender, Jerry Sloan. "He butchers you to death, actually beats on your hands and wrists," Pete told McKenzie before the game. Pete dealt with Sloan by repeatedly slashing to the basket, hoping to score or draw a foul. The strategy worked. In the second quarter alone he attempted 16 free throws, tying Oscar Robertson's NBA mark for a quarter, a record that stands to this day. Maravich finished the game with 38 points (12-26, 14-20). Unfortunately, Hudson injured his back early in the game and the Hawks lost 100-90.

On January 8, Pete learned he would be in the starting lineup of the 23rd All-Star Game. His selection, the result of voting by sportswriters, marked him as one of the league's elite players. But Pete perceived the honor as a mixed blessing, another individual achievement, and he was careful not to publicly celebrate.

"I don't want to sound ungrateful but I just feel differently about honors than most guys," a subdued Pete explained to McKenzie. "Sure I always wanted to be one of the great players but without all the, what's the right word, recognition and fanfare. I've always been a target and this just means that many more guys will be beating on me. There's no place for my 'thing' in basketball."

Target or not, Pete was virtually unstoppable on the court, especially at crunch time. The night after his All-Star selection he delighted a hometown crowd of 4,612 with a dazzling display of offense in a 120-114 victory over the Rockets. With 5:11 remaining and the score tied at 106, Maravich delivered another package of highlights, scoring eight of his team's final 14 points. He finished with 26 points and 12 assists.

Maravich's brilliance late in games did not go unnoticed by his long-time critic, George Cunningham, of the *Atlanta Journal*. Cunningham, who once wrote that Pete was a spoiled, disruptive, overpaid sideshow, now referred to him as "Mr. Clutch."

"The fourth quarter history of Atlanta's Pistol thus far this season may be without parallel in the history of pro basketball," wrote Cunningham after the Houston game. "It is a story of productive clutch offense that Jerry West in his prime would be proud to claim."

Cunningham then cited some impressive evidence to buttress his bold statement:

- October 10: Atlanta 120, Buffalo 109—Maravich scored 14 points in the fourth quarter.
- October 15: Atlanta 109, New York 101—Maravich entered with 7:26 remaining and his team in the lead, 90-86. He sealed Atlanta's victory by scoring nine of the Hawks last 19 points.
- October 31: Houston 106, Atlanta 105—The Hawks trail, 102-98, with 2:43 left. Maravich scores the team's final seven points in a losing effort.
- November 4: Atlanta 128, Philadelphia 120—Atlanta led 112-107, with 3:53 left, Maravich poured in nine of the Hawks last 16 points.
- November 7: Atlanta 109, Baltimore 107 (overtime)—With the Hawks trailing, 93-84, with 4:16 left in regulation, Maravich turned his game into overdrive by scoring 10 of Atlanta's last 17 points, including four in the final 41 seconds to send the game into overtime. He then scored four of the team's nine points in overtime.
- November 18: Atlanta 126, Phoenix 122—Maravich scored 13 of the Hawks 28 fourth-quarter points, including the last seven.
- December 2: Atlanta 106, Portland 103—Maravich scored nine of the team's 15 fourth-quarter points.
- December 5: Atlanta 122, Portland 121—Maravich quarterbacked the Hawks from behind with 20 fourth-quarter points, including two game-winning free throws with 19 seconds remaining.

- December 7: Atlanta 94, Chicago 89 (overtime)—Maravich scored 10 of Atlanta's last 14 points in regulation, including the final six that sent the game into overtime. Then the high-octane guard scored four more points in overtime, including the buckets that put Atlanta ahead 90-88 and 92-88.
- December 8: Atlanta 134, Baltimore 115—Maravich scored 14 points in the final quarter.
- December 13: Atlanta 121, New York 120—Always up for the Knicks, the Pistol re-entered the game with 7:29 to go and the team trailing 105-101. He fired in six points, including the game-winning 22-foot jumper with seconds left.
- December 16: Atlanta 100, Cleveland 94—Maravich entered the fourth quarter with 5:01 left and the Hawks clinging to a 99-95 lead. Maravich then went on to score eight of the team's final 14 points.
- December 22: Atlanta 110, Buffalo 109—Maravich re-enters in the fourth quarter with the Hawks leading, 99-95, with 2:11 to play and scored six of his team's final 11 points.
- January 6: Atlanta 116, Detroit 111—Maravich scored 30 points, including Atlanta's final eight, after the Hawks led 108-105.

Others observed the flip side of Pete's new role as a closer. "Maravich is obviously a better basketball player than he was three years ago. But not as exciting," wrote Ron Hudspeth of the *Atlanta Journal* that same week. "Making Maravich a patterned NBA player, and the unbelievable amount of pressure heaped on him to produce every game, has killed the old Maravich. It's like destroying the beauty of a wild stallion by taming him.

"Maravich is still the most exciting player in the NBA," Hudspeth continued. "Off the court he has the appeal of a Namath. He is single, a millionaire, mysterious to the point of having a little devil in his eye, and he evokes a curious sort of attraction from females. Maravich cannot win the NBA title by his lonesome. That day awaits the arrival of an Erving. Until then, it would be nice to see a fancy pass now and then. It might fill some empty Omni seats."

Days after Hudspeth expressed his desire for a "fancy pass now and then," Maravich dished out a career-high 18 assists in a thrilling 130-129 overtime win against the Pistons.

At the All-Star practice sessions in Chicago, Pete was in heaven. He played HORSE with Houston's Elvin Hayes and begged Baltimore's Wes

Unseld to throw him an outlet pass. Unseld had a rare ability to fire two-handed overhead passes with laser-like accuracy to almost any spot on the court.

"Come on, Wes. Just once," Pete pleaded.

"All right," replied the center.

As Pete caught the pass in full stride he yelled out like a kid, "Did you see that? Did you see it?"

Pete's first All-Star Game was quietly productive. Wearing No. 45 (No. 44 was worn by veteran Bob Kauffman), Pete had eight points (4-8, 0-0, 3 rebounds, 5 assists) in 22 minutes of play. He completed a between-the-legs pass and a slashing layup but mainly played a conventional non-flashy game. The Knicks' Bill Bradley even offered Pete $100 if he would do something spectacular but he "chickened out." It was Nate "Tiny" Archibald who electrified the crowd with some dazzling passes.

Pete was just happy to be a part of the East's 104–84 victory. "I didn't think of trying to outdo Nate," Pete said quietly after the game. "I'm not supposed to make fancy passes anymore. It seems that I'm supposed to be playing as well as I am because I gave up all that stuff."

Following the All-Star break, Maravich's offensive contributions and leadership sparked Atlanta to its longest win streak of the season. The team won six straight games from February 27 to March 10.

"Two players give me trouble in this league—Maravich and [Tiny] Archibald," said Houston Rockets guard Mike Newlin, considered one of the better defenders at the time. "But Pete is the toughest. His biggest asset is his quickness. He is more of a total player than Nate. I played one of my best games defensively and he still scored 35."

(Tiny Archibald was hardly a slouch, though. He finished the 1972-73 season as the league leader in scoring and assists, making him the only player in NBA history to win both titles in the same year.)

When the regular season concluded, the Hawks had compiled a mark of 46-36, an exact flip of their record from the previous two seasons. It was Pete's first winning season as a pro and his most productive. He finished as the NBA's fifth leading scorer with a 26.1 average (2,063 points) on 44.1 percent shooting. He was also second (behind Archibald) in free throw attempts and free throws made, and sixth in assists, averaging 6.9 per game.

Hudson was the league's fourth leading scorer (27.1 average, 2,029 total points), and he and Maravich became only the second pair of NBA teammates to each score 2,000 or more points in the same season. The Lakers'

Jerry West and Elgin Baylor first accomplished the feat in the 1964–65 season. (Since 1973, only Denver's Kiki Vandeweghe and Alex English, and Boston's Larry Bird and Kevin McHale, have joined the club.)

The Hawks enjoyed a significant jump in attendance as the Omni attracted an average of 7,434 fans per game, up from the previous season's mark of 5,609 in their old building.

Atlanta would face Boston in the first conference semifinals. The Celtics went 68-14 in the regular season, at the time the second best record in NBA history. The Hawks had lost five of their six meetings with the Celtics, including the last one, a 124-108 drubbing on March 23. Sportswriters predicted an easy sweep. "If the Boston Celtics don't beat the Hawks in four straight games," said one Boston newscaster, "They won't be trying." Once again the teams were scheduled to alternate home games.

True to form, the Hawks lost Game 1 at the Boston Garden, 134-109. Veteran forward John Havlicek had a career night, scoring a staggering 54 points (24-36, 6-6), and sportswriters pointedly dubbed the game, "The Boston Massacre." Maravich scored just 16 points (6-17, 4-6, 1 rebound, 5 assists) and committed seven turnovers.

Game 2 at the Omni featured a slightly better effort from Maravich, a game-high 34 points (12-32, 10-13, 7 rebounds, 5 assists), but the Celtics again won easily, 126-113.

Trailing 2-0 and playing in front of a hostile Boston crowd of 15,320, the Hawks, surprisingly, stole a win, 118-105. Pete chipped in 24 points (11-24, 2-2, 5 rebounds, 11 assists) in the unlikely victory. Maravich got plenty of support from Hudson, the game's scoring standout with 37 points, and Herm Gilliam, who added 25.

As the Hawks dressed for Game 4 back in Atlanta, Guerin and Fitzsimmons discovered Pete engaging in a bizarre pregame ritual. "Richie Guerin and I walked into our locker room and found the Pistol, with towels stacked against the shower wall, standing on his head," recalled Fitzsimmons.

"Pistol, what are you doing?" asked his coach.

Pete responded, "I want to get the blood flowing into my head faster so I'll get off to a good start."

"I'll never forget Richie Guerin saying, '. . . I've gotta have a drink,'" said Fitzsimmons.

More than 30 years later, Guerin recalled the incident. "That's the type of thing where you look at one another and go, 'What's the matter with this kid?' It was the first time I ever saw something like that. This was just way out there. But you know what? If it works, it works."

And work it did. In front of 11,675 enthusiastic Hawks fans Maravich led Atlanta to a thrilling 97–94 win, tying the series 2–2. Pete, reprising his regular-season fourth-quarter heroics, hit 13 of Atlanta's final 20 points, to finish with 37 (16-34, 5-5, 7 rebounds, 5 assists).

"This one was for men only—basketball the way cave men planned it as the Hawks would bolt in front and then the Celtics would surge back," reported Cunningham. "The floor mops got triple duty because of the number of bodies that hit the deck."

It was the Hawks' biggest victory since the franchise moved from St. Louis. But it was the final highlight of the season as the Celtics easily overpowered the Hawks in Games 5 and 6. Although he didn't know it at the time, the series would mark Pete's last playoff appearance in Atlanta.

Over his three postseason series, Maravich averaged 25.5 points, 5.1 rebounds, and 5.4 assists per game. His playoff scoring average stood as the Atlanta Hawks' record until it was bested by Dominique Wilkins' career mark of 26.4.

Although the Hawks had improved dramatically in Maravich's third year, he felt the team's early playoff exit negated any regular-season achievements. "As far as I'm concerned, not making it to the championship wipes out everything else," Maravich said to Garth Williams of *Sports Today*. "I want to see that NBA championship ring on my finger at least once before I'm finished."

"The way I look at it," said Pete's father, Press, who watched the hard-fought playoff series from the stands, "is that Oscar Robertson is one of the greatest basketball players in the history of basketball but he never won in the NBA until the team got a guy by the name of Jabbar. And look at Jerry West, Pete's idol. He won when the team got a guy by the name of Wilt Chamberlain. A team is comprised of many pieces and they must all fall into place."

Pete was voted to the All-NBA second team. He joined New York's Walt Frazier, Boston's Dave Cowens, Golden State's Rick Barry, and Baltimore's Elvin Hayes. All would later be inducted into the Basketball Hall of Fame.

The year had begun with Dr. J and the promise of a championship run, and it ended with another early dismissal from the playoffs. In between, Pete had survived a health scare, played in his first All-Star Game, and guided the Hawks to a winning season. He even toned down some of the flashier elements of his repertoire in an effort to please his critics. Pete Maravich was playing his best basketball as a professional, and it still wasn't enough.

15

The Unraveling

"Like Picasso or Joyce, who were also ahead of their time, Maravich has moves that make the normal mind boggle."

—GEORGE VECSEY, SPORTSWRITER

"He was a thrill-a-minute wonder. But I would not call him a man at peace with himself."

—PAT WILLIAMS, HAWKS GENERAL MANAGER

As he stood on the cusp of his fourth year in Atlanta, Maravich had become an NBA All-Star, a marketing icon, and one of the league's greatest attractions. But his basketball achievements left him unsatisfied and he continued to seek fulfillment outside competitive sports. His interest in karate led him to transcendental meditation, which in turn exposed him to UFOs or, as he called it, "UFOlogy." He read whatever he could about the subject and was enthralled with Erich von Daniken's 1971 bestseller, *Chariots of the Gods?*

Some couldn't understand Pete's quest. "He was looking for something in his life. I kept thinking to myself, 'Man, you've already got it. You don't have to be looking any further. You're Pistol Pete!'" said University of Vermont coach turned sportscaster, Tom Brennan.

Pete's eclectic off-court interests might have surprised those who perceived him only as a first-rate partier who sought approval from the "in" crowd. He spent thousands on his wardrobe and sometimes carried $3,000 in cash—in case he needed to suddenly catch a flight or pick up a large bar tab. Jackie warned Pete that carrying so much cash was unwise; it made him a target. "I used to tell him, 'Somebody's going to hit you over the head and steal it,'" said Jackie.

On the road, during what players refer to as the "fifth quarter," Pete would occasionally travel downtown looking for excitement. He began carrying a small knife in his belt. Furman Bisher, columnist for the *Atlanta Constitution*, recalled in 1988, "When he was very young one of his close friends once told me, 'He'll never live to be 30.' He's . . . bent on self-destruction."

But Pete could also be a quiet, fun-loving homebody. He practiced shooting by himself at the YMCA, picked up steaks and Nutrament (a supplement drink) at the local A&P, and happily signed autographs when asked.

Many nights were spent at his condo playing cards, Monopoly, or pool with his girlfriend Jackie (who also brought her poodle, April) and their friends Hank and Tito Kalb. The foursome loved to visit local restaurants or catch movies in Buckhead or Lenox.

One time when they were eating at a neighborhood spot called the Beer Mug, a waitress asked Pete for identification. He told the girl, "I'm Pete Maravich."

She replied, "I really don't give a flying flip who you are, I need you to show me your ID."

Tito Kalb recalled, "We were all dying laughing. And Jackie said, 'Way to go *Pistol!*' Pete was just laughing and said, 'Oh great, I guess I'm not that big of a deal.' He was just fun to be around."

Jackie only used the nickname "Pistol" when she was being playfully sarcastic.

NBA prognosticators expected the 1973-74 Atlanta Hawks to deliver a division title. "Atlanta is burning hot, and the Bullets are all shot," proclaimed *Sports Illustrated* in its annual basketball preview.

When the Hawks assembled at training camp in Savannah, Georgia, the rookie class included future TV sportscaster James Brown, a fourth-round draft pick from Harvard University. Brown arrived believing Pete was overrated. "Those of us in the basketball fraternity thought that maybe he was getting so much publicity because he was every bit the hog. A guy who just threw up everything he touched," recalled Brown. But after observing Maravich up close, Brown changed his tune. "The guy was just phenomenal. Pete could dribble the basketball like no other and was an absolutely sensational passer."

Maravich's basketball skills amazed Brown during a conditioning exercise called the "suicide drill." In the exercise, players ran from the baseline to the closest free-throw line and back, then back and forth between the baseline and center court, then back and forth between the baseline and the opposing team's free-throw line, and, finally back and forth, between the baselines. To increase the difficulty, the players dribbled a ball throughout. Maravich, however, went one step further.

"Pete would use two balls," Brown recalled. "He was dribbling two bas-ketballs and still beat most of us."

Maravich and Brown discovered a mutual interest in the martial arts. "I had been involved about four or five years," Brown recalled, "having studied tae kwon do and then kung fu. Pete and I made it a point to catch Bruce Lee movies. He would pick me up in this big, pretty red Cadillac and take me to the movies, and then take me to get something to eat."

In late September, Brown was summoned to Fitzsimmons' office and told he had been cut. He was devastated but his anguish was eased by the kind treatment he received from Pete. "I was a hungry, passionate rookie who was trying desperately to make the team and to realize my dream," said Brown. "He took me under his wing. He was just a nice, down-to-earth guy."

As the Hawks readied for the season, management unveiled a new mar-keting catchphrase: "To Soar in 1974." The team appeared to have a solid foundation.

"Lou (Hudson), Bells (Walt Bellamy), and myself have been together three years now," a clean-shaven Maravich told an Atlanta reporter. "And Herm Gilliam and Jim Washington have been here two years. Playing together for a while makes a lot of difference for a team."

Atlanta Journal reporter Darrell Simmons illustrated the camaraderie between Maravich and Bellamy when he described a good-natured exchange after a preseason game. Atlanta had defeated the Knicks 97-86 in Princeton University's Jadwin Gym, spoiling Bill Bradley's homecoming. On the bus back to Manhattan, Pete was holding court. Bellamy, according to Simmons, was listening with a bemused expression.

"Fifty-four minutes. Fifty-four minutes," Bellamy finally blurted out. "A new city, state, national, and international record. The Pistol has talked for fifty-four minutes. Solid. Fifty . . . Four . . . Minutes."

Maravich fired back.

"Old record, fifty-three minutes," Maravich said. "Held by Walter Bel-lamy. Numerous times. Nu—mer—ous."

In the early 1970s, NBA teams traveled on commercial flights, and as the huge players ambled through airports, they often drew stares and questions from strangers. Maravich and Bellamy loved to tease these people. Bellamy would proclaim that he was the ambassador of Zimbabwe, and Pete was his translator.

The regular season began with great promise. The Hawks won their first two games, including a 129-102 crushing of the Lakers who were without the retired Wilt Chamberlain. After the game Pete's idol, Jerry West, paid him a compliment. "Maravich, who I think is a great ball player, is starting to put it all together," West told Thomas Rogers of the *New York Times*.

On October 20, the visiting Hawks lost to Phoenix in a nationally televised game on CBS. The Hawks exacted revenge 10 days later, beating the Suns 122-101 as Maravich scored 31 points. The game included a memorable highlight from the Pistol.

Dribbling 22 feet from the basket, and with the Suns' Clem Haskins closing in, Pete bounced the ball further from his body than normal, daring Haskins to lunge for it. When Haskins took the bait, Pete flicked the ball back between his own legs, hopped to his left, and swished home a quick bucket. Haskins, one writer observed, looked as if he "was still groping at the floor like a man trying to pick up loose change."

After 10 games (6-4), the Hawks were the NBA's highest scoring team, averaging 117 points per game, and Pete was averaging 28.7 points with a .486 shooting percentage. At times he was virtually unstoppable, as the Houston Rockets discovered on November 2. Maravich struggled early in the contest, but with three minutes remaining and the Hawks trailing by eight, Pete went on a spectacular spree. Over the next 2:15 he dizzied the Rockets with 15 consecutive points on a variety of baskets—a 29-footer, a layup off a steal, a 21-footer while falling down, a 23-foot shot off an out-of-bounds play, an up-and-under 17-footer, a driving layup plus a foul shot, and another 20-footer. At the end of his outburst the Hawks led 122-121. Gilliam threw in the last three points, giving the Hawks a 125-123 victory that upped Atlanta's record to 7-4. "My game is still explosion," Maravich explained in his postgame press conference. "This was a time when I knew there was no reason to hold back."

Atlanta's impressive start landed Pete back on the cover of *Sports Illustrated*. The cover photograph by Heinz Kluetmeier, taken during Atlanta's win over the Suns, caught Pete mid-air as he flew toward the basket. Inside the magazine, another spectacular shot by Kluetmeier captured Maravich twisting past Houston's Otto Moore for a reverse layup attempt. The near-impossible angle of Pete's left foot illustrated the unusual flexibility of his ankles.

"He does his between-the-legs, behind-the-back, and over-the-shoulder passing and dribbling so fluidly that, along with his phenomenal quickness, they are now taken for granted," wrote Peter Carry for the accompanying article. "Still, in the last year he has proved that there are two things he does superlatively, perhaps better than anyone alive: handle the ball and shoot on the move."

The Hawks closed out November against the Buffalo Braves and their hot-shot rookie, Ernie DiGregorio, whose flashy ball handling and creative passing at Providence College evoked comparisons to Maravich. Pete, nursing a tweaked knee, sat out the first quarter. When he finally entered the game, he hit five of his first seven shots. He dribbled and passed around his back. He even dribbled through "Ernie D's" legs. In the third quarter, Pete attempted 14 free throws and made every one, tying Rick Barry's NBA record for most free throws made in one quarter. Pete finished with a season-high 42 points (12-17, 18-18, 10 assists) in just 32 minutes of playing time. The Hawks won 130-106.

"Oh, he definitely influenced me. No doubt about it," said DiGregorio in 2000. "The things he did with the ball were just amazing. If you compare him to the players of today, it's a joke. He was so much better than anyone out there today."

With Atlanta in first place and Maravich leading the league in scoring, the locker room was a much friendlier place. Gone were efforts to avoid reporters by taking long postgame showers. *The Sporting News* and *Street and Smith's Basketball* magazines ran flattering cover stories. Pete's superb play caught the eye of *New York Times'* columnist Dave Anderson, who wrote a complimentary profile titled: "One for the Show."

"Peter Maravich is basketball's Peter Pan," Anderson wrote of the superstar. "He foresees 6-foot-8 inch players whipping passes behind their backs as often as he does now."

"To me, basketball is almost a form of art. It's improving all the time," Pete explained to the columnist. "Not that my game will revolutionize basketball but my style will influence a gradual evolution."

With life going well on the court, Pete made a pivotal off-court decision. Over Christmas he proposed to his college sweetheart, Jackie Elliser. Pete, she recalled, didn't exactly take the classic "on-bended-knee" position when he asked for her hand.

"He said, 'Here's your engagement ring that you wanted,'" laughed Jackie at the memory. "That was it. We talked about when we were going to get married, but we didn't set a date or anything." As it turned out, the wedding nuptials waited almost two years.

"He was just scared," she said. "Just like everybody else, he was scared to get married."

Maravich's engagement led to another marriage in the Hawks family. While in New York for a New Year's Day game with the Knicks, Pete wanted to buy Jackie a leather coat. Coach Fitzsimmons told Pete of a store owner in the garment district who was a hoops junkie and would sell wholesale. A lunch date was set up for the three men.

"The only problem was, he [the store owner] already had lunch plans—with my future wife," explained Fitzsimmons. "JoAnn was a buyer for Sears. She didn't appreciate him calling her at the last minute to cancel and was not impressed when he told her that we were in his showroom. She had no idea who Pete Maravich or Cotton Fitzsimmons was. So my friend wisely suggested that we all have lunch together. And the rest is history."

Cotton and JoAnn began a long-distance, four-year relationship that ended in marriage.

As the Hawks tipped off against the Knicks on the first day of 1974, the team was two games out of first place in the Central Division, despite their middling record of 19-18. If the Hawks had an Achilles' heel it was their defense, allowing an NBA-worst 114 points a game. Prior to the game Pete learned he had been selected to his second consecutive starting berth in the All-Star Game and was the top vote getter among guards.

"The way I feel, I'd just about say pass on it," he quietly told an AP reporter following the 99-89 loss. "I could use the break to build myself back up." Maravich was underweight and suffering from a dislocated right pinky. The swollen digit had become the widest finger on his hand.

Hudson, the NBA's third highest scorer, was also named to the All-Star team. It would be Hudson's sixth straight appearance and he joined John Havlicek, Dave Cowens, Walt Frazier, and Maravich as starters for the East.

Atlanta dropped its next game and dipped below .500, causing Fitzsimmons to declare, "There will be some changes." Pete's stock was about to tumble. Fitzsimmons shuffled the lineup, removing Maravich, Gilliam, and Bellamy from the starting five. It was the first of several risky moves by Fitzsimmons that, along with injuries to Hudson and Gilliam, would unravel the team.

The Hawks lost four straight but Pete remained quiet about the new lineups.

The struggling Hawks (20-24) faced the league-leading Boston Celtics (31-9) on January 13. The game was the first half of a nationally televised basketball-football double header on CBS. The second half was Super Bowl VIII, between the Miami Dolphins and the Minnesota Vikings. In his 1999 autobiography, *Ahead of the Game*, then Hawks GM Pat Williams recalled a memorable pep talk that Fitzsimmons delivered before the game.

"[Fitzsimmons said] 'I want you to pretend that you're the greatest basketball team in the world,'" recalled Williams. "'And I want you to pretend that this game is for the NBA championship. And I want you to pretend instead of a five-game losing streak, we're on a five-game winning streak. Now go get 'em!'"

The Hawks roared from the locker room but returned with a whimper following a 128-105 pounding. As a disconsolate Fitzsimmons walked off the floor, he felt a light slap on his back.

"Cheer up, Coach," Maravich said. "Just pretend we won!"

Boston's John Havlicek was surprised at how far the Hawks had fallen.

"It's hard to imagine this is really the same team that took us to seven [actually six] games in the playoffs last year," Havlicek told *Atlanta Constitution* reporter Lennox Rawlings. "They don't seem to have the same fluidity."

The next day Maravich and Hudson flew to Seattle for the All-Star Game while their teammates started a three-day vacation. Maravich clocked 22 minutes for the East, contributing 15 points (4-15, 7-9, 3 rebounds, 4 assists) in a losing cause, 134-123.

Meanwhile, off the court, NBA Commissioner Walter Kennedy made an announcement that was to have a profound impact Pete's future. The league was adding a single expansion team before the 1974-75 season. The finalists were San Diego (whose team had moved to Houston), Toronto, Minneapolis, St. Louis, and New Orleans.

When the season resumed on January 17, the front office dreamed up a unique promotion to help fill the Omni: Casanova Night. Any man purchasing a regular-priced ticket for the Trail Blazers game could bring as many women as he wanted for just a dollar each. Whoever brought the most women would win a special prize at half time. A crowd of 8,031, including many Casanovas and their harems, saw the Hawks snap their losing streak with a convincing 126-99 win. Pete scored 34 points with stellar shooting (15-22, 4-6).

But the win was an aberration. Atlanta won just two of its next eight games as the Hawks' playoff hopes were sinking fast. To his credit, Pete never publicly second-guessed Fitzsimmons. But it was getting tougher to hold his tongue.

Some observers believe Fitzsimmons' poky offensive strategy was an albatross because it failed to exploit Pete's fast-break talent and ability to free-lance. "Cotton came in with this Tex Winter offense—the triangle," Gilliam recalled in 2004. "The triangle was an offense that was in its infancy, and you had to run to those spots. Running it to those spots takes away your individuality. I felt it handcuffed a free spirit like Pete."

The situation reached a breaking point on Sunday, February 3. Prior to a game against the Rockets, Pete watched the CBS show *Eye on Sports*. One segment chronicled Atlanta's disappointing season and suggested it was largely Pete's fault. Pete was tense when he arrived at Houston's Hofheinz Pavilion that evening. Near the end of the first half, referee Jim Capers whistled a foul on Maravich. Enraged by the call, Pete protested loudly and received a technical foul. Then he snapped. He charged at the surprised Capers, but was restrained by Hudson, whose nose was bloodied by one of Pete's errant elbows. Surprisingly, he was not ejected.

During half time, Pete sat by himself in the shower. He played just 11 minutes in the second half before Fitzsimmons benched him for the remainder of the game. The Rockets won 123-112, and afterward, Fitzsimmons told reporters that "Pete did not have his head in the game."

That evening, Maravich had a few drinks and caused a disturbance at the hotel. He spent part of the night in Fitzsimmons' room so the coach could keep an eye on his troubled player.

"The main problem was the fact that Pistol couldn't drink," Fitzsimmons said. "Two beers and he'd be off the wall."

On the flight back to Atlanta, the inappropriate behavior continued. *Atlanta Journal* reporter Darrell Simmons quoted a passenger who said Maravich, "ran his mouth for two hours. He never got out of his seat, but he just kept talking. He wasn't slurring his teammates or his coach, but his behavior was embarrassing."

Fitzsimmons realized, "Something had to be done. As a coach and a representative of the NBA, there had to be some disciplinary action."

On Tuesday morning Pete arrived at the Omni, ready for practice. He was summoned to Fitzsimmons' office. In a 45-minute meeting Pete learned that he was being fined and suspended for a minimum of two games. His replacement was Steve Bracey, a second-year guard out of Tulsa.

Then, in Atlanta's first game without Pete, Hudson suffered a back injury that would sideline him for several games. Surprisingly, the Hawks managed two straight wins without their high-scoring duo, downing the Bullets (121-103) and the Lakers (107-103).

The headline in the *Atlanta Journal* read: "Maravich Out, Hudson Hurt, Hawks Win."

"The suspension made things difficult, but what made it worse was that for those two games he was out, we won," Fitzsimmons said. "I'm sure that bothered him a great deal."

On February 7, Fitzsimmons ended Maravich's suspension after a private meeting at Morehouse College, the Hawks practice site. Player and coach put a positive spin on their relationship, telling the media there were no "hard feelings." The reality was quite different. "He never spoke to me for the rest of the season," Fitzsimmons revealed decades later. "He would listen, take direction, but he never would acknowledge me."

According to some observers, Fitzsimmons was partially to blame for the impasse. Trainer Joe O'Toole said the coach did not communicate well with Pete. "Whenever something happened between Pete and [former coach] Richie Guerin, the two of them would just sit down and handle it between themselves."

Teammate Don Adams acknowledged in a 1989 interview with the *Atlanta Journal-Constitution* that Fitzsimmons was also volatile. "If we won, he was always high-fiving and slapping," Adams said. "But if we lost, he wouldn't even speak to you the next day."

When the suspension was lifted, the Hawks had a new strategy. "I want to slow the game down," Fitzsimmons told the *Bucks County Courier Times.* The "slow down" Hawks lost to the worst team in the league, the Philadelphia 76ers (15-39), 104-84. Maravich didn't start, played just 26 minutes, and scored eight points (3-9, 2-3, 3 assists). Before the suspension Pete had been averaging 37 minutes, 28.3 points, and 6.1 assists per game.

"I only took shots that were open," Pete mumbled after the game. "Like I've been told to do."

The loss kicked off another losing streak and the media turned on Pete. Steve Hershey of *The Sporting News* wrote that Maravich was an undisciplined individualist. "There is no game plan when Pete is involved. Patterns are broken, defenses ignored, responsibilities forgotten," Hershey charged.

Furman Bisher blasted Pete in his *Atlanta Journal* column, calling him "a tarnished white hope."

"The NBA simply isn't good enough for his act," Bisher continued. "His is the kind of act that only needs extras, not other stars. It's the kind you find in the center ring of a tent. Or, on a stage where ladies are sawed in half and rabbits are pulled out of hats."

Then Bisher went after Pete's dad. "It was obvious that Press Maravich, his father, created a multi-million basketball commodity when he coached him at LSU. But had not prepared him to play as one-fifth of a pro team."

Even Fitzsimmons got into the act. "I wish he blended in more as a team player," said the coach. "Pete tries hard to win all the time, but he's an individual."

It was all Pete could take. "I will not be a scapegoat. I've been a scapegoat before, and I'm not going to be again," an angry Pete told Simmons of the *Atlanta Journal*. "I've never stepped on anybody's toes in four years here. Mine have been stepped on a lot. I don't have to put up with it. Who needs it? They say the Hawks are losing because of me. I don't believe any of that, but some people do, and it gets publicized. It makes sensational stories."

"I can play any [expletive] style," Maravich said to Pittsburgh's *Beaver County Times* reporter Andy Nuzzo. "Why is it they didn't complain last year when we ended up with a winning season? I was okay then. I was a team man. Now that we're losing I supposedly play an individual style and shoot too much?"

He was still steaming about the *Eye on Sports* segment. "I was misled by the people doing that. I was interviewed by them, and I thought it was a program concerning the entire Atlanta Hawks basketball team," said Maravich. "But when they got through editing and cutting it, it looked more like it was done to show that I can make mistakes on a basketball court."

The program's depiction of Atlanta's dramatic comeback win over Houston the previous November was an example of selective editing, according to Pete. "I scored 32 points, had 15 rebounds, and 7 assists. But the program emphasized me throwing the ball away two times," Maravich explained. "I can make a mistake. I can have a bad game—any player can—but I'm not the Atlanta Hawks. The Atlanta Hawks are 12 players, two coaches, and a trainer. I'm just one of them."

Maravich was so discouraged, he told Simmons that he wanted to quit—not after winning a championship but when his five-year contract expired in 1975. "I'm completely frustrated with basketball. I'm sorry I ever came into this league."

"Money doesn't mean that much. I've been without it," Pete told Nuzzo in the *Beaver County Times*. "I don't want to play 10 years in the NBA and die of a heart attack at 40. I've got other things to do. Who needs basketball?"

Maravich and Fitzsimmons' relationship was beyond repair. One of them had to go. Williams quietly put out feelers hoping to trade Pete, but no team would match his asking price of two elite players.

On March 6, an unconfirmed report said the NBA would place an expansion team in New Orleans. The Hawks were in New York that evening and Walt Frazier had a brief chat with Pete before the second half. "I told him that he should leave Atlanta and go to New Orleans. I told him he could be king there," Frazier explained to the *New York Post* after the 96-94 Knicks victory. Pete replied that he didn't believe the "NBA will go over in New Orleans." On March 7, it became official: New Orleans was the 18th member city of the NBA.

Los Angeles attorney Fred Rosenfeld, who represented several NBA players, including Gail Goodrich and Elgin Baylor, headed up a team of investors that forked over a then-record $6.15 million for the franchise. New Orleans wanted Maravich and one of Rosenfeld's first calls was to the Hawks.

"Any chance of you giving up Pete?" Rosenfeld asked Williams.

"You don't have enough money to acquire Pete Maravich," Williams informed Rosenfeld. "Plus you don't have any players."

But Williams left the door ajar. "Create something, Fred," Williams coaxed. "Put something together for me that's creative."

On March 10, the Hawks lost to the Pistons and were mathematically eliminated from the playoffs. It was the first time the team missed the post-season since 1962, when the franchise was still in St. Louis. Injuries hurt the team's chances as Gilliam and Hudson were sidelined for a combined 37 games. The loss of Gilliam, in particular, was devastating. "We were on a pretty good roll until Gilliam injured his knee," recalled Fitzsimmons. "He was our best defensive guard and without a replacement for him, we just fell apart."

Atlanta split its last eight games to finish with a 35-47 record. For Fitzsimmons, the losing season was the first in his coaching career. Pete led the team in scoring with a 27.7 average, and finished second in the NBA behind Buffalo's Bob McAdoo.

Meanwhile, the secret negotiations for a Maravich trade to New Orleans continued. The interested parties went back and forth, exploring seven different options. Finally, an offer was made that seemed so lopsided in Atlanta's favor that Tom Cousins urged Williams to seek no further concessions.

"Tom Cousins said, and I'll never forget this line, 'Don't ask for anything more,'" recalled Williams. "'They may not have enough to field a team and then we won't get anything.'"

The proposed deal was, on paper, extremely one sided. In exchange for Maravich, the Hawks would receive:

- Two players (a forward and guard) from the expansion draft.
- New Orleans' first-round pick in 1974.
- New Orleans' first-round pick in 1975.
- New Orleans' second-round pick in 1975.
- New Orleans' second-round pick in 1976.
- An option to swap first-round draft positions in 1976.

- An option to swap first-round draft positions in 1977.
- An "understanding" that New Orleans would select Walt Bellamy in the expansion draft.

On Monday, April 15, Maravich and his attorney, Les Zittrain, met with Atlanta's general manager and president to "clear the air" about the disappointing season. The negotiations with New Orleans were still a secret so Maravich and Zittrain had no idea the team was trying to unload Pete. The four-hour meeting was cordial and Maravich left with the impression that his concerns had received a fair hearing. He made it clear that he hoped to remain in Atlanta for the final year of his contract but did not want to play for Fitzsimmons.

Hudson remembered a happy phone call from Maravich later that day.

"Pete called me and said excitedly on the phone, 'I'm getting rid of Cotton,'" recalled Hudson. "Then a half-hour later, Cotton called me and said he had some bad news. He said, 'We're getting rid of Pete.'"

On April 16, Williams asked Pete to meet him at his apartment to "go over a few technical things." Pete thought the GM was about to trade a teammate and wanted, as a courtesy, to notify him in advance.

"We sat down and I got right to the point," Williams said. "I said, 'Pete, we've made a trade. We're sending you to New Orleans. This is hard for me to do, but that's about it.'"

Pete was stunned. Less than 24 hours earlier the Hawks president had led him to believe the team wanted him to stay.

"How much did you get for me?" a shaken Maravich inquired. Williams recited the terms of the unprecedented deal: Six (possibly eight) players for one.

Pete quietly asked, "Is that all?"

"I could tell that he was not impressed," Williams said. "Tom Cousins said, 'Don't ask for any more.' And Pete said, 'Is that all?'"

Williams had another surprise. Waiting outside in a car, he told Pete, was New Orleans president Fred Rosenfeld, along with VP of Basketball Operations, Bill Bertka. Pete felt ambushed and was livid. Williams tried to explain why the negotiations were held in secret, but Pete was in no mood to hear it.

"I dealt honestly with these people. I can't tolerate any more deceit and deception on the part of the coach and present administration," Pete told the *Times-Picayune*. "Pat Williams and Cotton Fitzsimmons have lied to me."

Maravich's contract contained a "no-trade" clause so he had the power to nix the deal. He decided to meet with the New Orleans brain trust. "Pete really didn't want to be traded. He liked Atlanta," recalled Bertka. "He wanted to play on a team that could compete. He told me he would just rather retire." For New Orleans, this would be a disaster. So Bertka took Pete for a stroll outside and presented his best case. Pete would be in New Orleans where his name was "magic," the team would play in the massive, soon-to-be-completed Superdome, and most importantly, as an established star, his high salary would not evoke jealousy from his new teammates.

Pete's lawyer then laid out the options. "Legally they don't have the right to do this. I can stop it. You can end up playing out your contract in your current happiness or unhappiness here in Atlanta," Zittrain told Maravich. "Or you can go back to your home state in Louisiana, where I have some leverage."

Pete reluctantly agreed to the trade.

"Some people might wonder why I just didn't say no, since I did have that contractual right; but the realities of the game were different in the early seventies because players didn't have the options they have today," Maravich recollected in his autobiography. "If I refused the trade, I probably would have sat on the bench, collecting splinters. Facing the hard facts, I knew it was over for me in Atlanta."

Atlanta Journal reporter Ron Hudspeth wrote in an April 30 editorial that it was ridiculous to blame Maravich for the Hawks' underachieving season:

> *The truth of the matter is:*
>
> *The trading of Maravich isn't likely to give Atlanta a winner. The keeping of Maravich isn't likely to give Atlanta a winner.*
>
> *Maravich isn't the reason the Hawks are losers. They lost because of the absence of big men who can dominate play.*
>
> *They came close to being winners once when they almost landed Julius Erving, but when that deal fizzled, so did the Hawks' real chances of being anything but an also-ran.*

On May 3, 1974, the trade became official. For its part, the New Orleans management felt its acquisition of Maravich was a shrewd move and sound business. "We were happy with the deal," recalled Bertka. "Our goal was to bring instant credibility to an expansion franchise."

Most Atlanta fans, many drawn to the team because of Pete, were crestfallen.

"I had never been to a professional basketball game until he came to

Atlanta, but after seeing him play, it became my favorite sport," Atlanta resident Betty Glennon wrote to the *Atlanta Journal*. "I won't be buying any more tickets to your games."

Riding the bus home from school, eight-year-old Michael Gearon, Jr. heard the news about his favorite player and broke down. "I was bawling," said Gearon. Almost 30 years later Gearon led a group of investors who bought the Hawks.

The deal was dubbed the "The Louisiana Purchase," but unlike the purchase of 1803, it was not perceived as a good deal for Louisiana. "I still have a mask and a gun in my room," Fitzsimmons chuckled afterward. General managers across the league thought the trade was one-sided and borderline illegal. It appeared that the Hawks had swindled the new franchise. But that's not the way it turned out.

When Maravich left town, Hawks attendance plummeted 34 percent, at a time when overall league attendance increased 10 percent. And Atlanta failed to improve on the court.

"All good plans of mice and men can go astray," admitted Fitzsimmons years later. "It turned out the worst trade and most unpopular thing I ever did in my entire career."

Stung by the trade, Pete moved on with an increasingly negative view of pro basketball. "To that point in my career, I had witnessed other mishandled trades, but for the first time, I realized what a cold, flesh-peddling business basketball could be."

At least one person in Pete's orbit liked the move. Jackie was happy to be living much closer to her parents and sister in Baton Rouge.

Maravich was deeply scarred by his four years in Atlanta. He overcame a slew of challenges, including the pressure of being sport's highest paid athlete, unwelcoming teammates, mononucleosis, Bell's palsy, and a hostile media. He had persevered and proved he could excel in the world's premier basketball league. Forty points against Mississippi State may not have impressed the doubters, but the same amount against the world champion New York Knicks turned a lot of heads. But after four seasons, he was no closer to a championship.

"I just don't think he was able to overcome his initial entrée to the team," observed *Atlanta Journal* reporter Mike McKenzie. "And then when they didn't win, it made things worse. People loved writing that, too. Same old Pete—he'd gun it, flash it, but didn't win it."

Clockwise from top left:
1. Pete's parents, Helen and Press
   Maravich, on their wedding day in 1946.
2. Baby Pete with his mother, Helen.
3. Pete's first basketball circa 1948.
4. Pete with Press in the pool.
5. A young Pete Maravich.

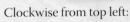

Clockwise from top left:
1. Pete with older brother, Ronnie.
2. Pete Maravich school photo circa 1954.
3. Pete as a Broughton High gym rat.
4. Pete at Broughton High, 1965.
5. Pete as the youngest member of the Daniel High varsity team.

Clockwise from top left:
1. Pete receives tournament MVP award while at Southwood College, 1965.
2. Press Maravich became Pete's coach at LSU.
3. College Basketball's all-time shooting leader in action.
4. The only player to ever score more than 1,000 points as a sophomore, 1968.
5. Pete in action at LSU.

Clockwise from top left:
1. Razzle-dazzle against Pittsburgh, 1969.
2. Pete drives the ball against Florida State, 1967.
3. Another sold-out arena watches the hot-shooting Maravich at Hinkle Fieldhouse, 1968.
4. Pete and Press (holding Diana Maravich) accept a family portrait at the Tip-Off Club with Pete Duncan (left), and the artist, Alice Grima Ellis, 1970.

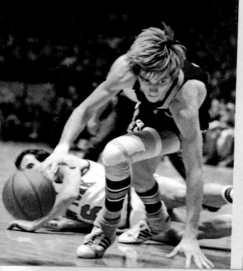

Clockwise from top left:
1. Rookie Maravich at Madison Square Garden, 1971.
2. "Pistol" tries to cover "Clyde" Frazier.
3. Rookie Maravich receives instructions from Hawks coach Richie Guerin, 1970.
4. Pistol Pete with another textbook jumper in the first Jazz game, 1974.
5. A stylish Maravich and New Orleans Jazz President Fred Rosenfeld hold press conference, 1974.

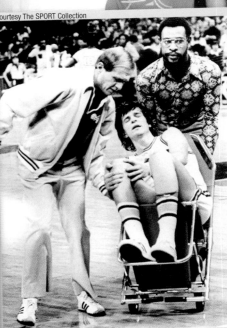

Clockwise from top left:
1. Pete and Jackie enjoy a moment together.
2. Wedding day for Pete and Jackie, 1976.
3. A half-court through-the-legs pass resulted in a severe knee injury, 1978.
4. Maravich finishes out his career with the Celtics, 1980.

Clockwise from top left:
1. Joshua and Jaeson pose for the Maravich Family Christmas Card.
2. Pete and his father, Press, at Clearwater Christian College, 1985.
3. Pete's boys, Joshua and Jaeson, flank their mother, Jackie, 2005.

Gilliam, Pete's closest teammate, said his friend carried a heavy burden during his time in Atlanta. "Pete was never his own person because he was so torn in many different ways," Gilliam said. "The thing he resented the most was being a 'Great White Hope' and he fought that. He felt like he wasn't accepted by the black players. That hurt him a lot. All he wanted to do was just play basketball."

Even Fitzsimmons recognized the unfair expectations heaped on Maravich. "They thought he was going to be the savior. It's not fair to tell a guard he's got to bring them a championship," said his coach. "He never really recovered from that first year."

On June 22, 1974, his 27th birthday, Pete signed a three-year contract with New Orleans. His yearly salary was increased from $300,000 to $375,000, plus he was given use of a Porsche and a gas card. He was uncertain about his new situation but the New Orleans management was thrilled to have him back in the bayou. His name alone—Maravich—gave the franchise what it most desired: instant credibility.

As he left for Louisiana, Pete realized his contrasting reputations—selfish gunner vs. basketball genius—had crystallized during his years in Atlanta. To his detractors, he was a spoiled showboat who seemed unable, and unwilling, to improve his team's fortunes. To his legion of fans, he was a fierce competitor who possessed the most mind-boggling arsenal of basketball skills ever witnessed.

Pete, acutely aware of this ongoing debate, yearned to convert his critics but suspected it was an impossible task. He often used the analogy of cutting open a pillow at the top of the Empire State Building and then trying to recover all the feathers after they had flown off.

But Pete Maravich would keep trying. This time in New Orleans.

16

The Louisiana
Purchase

"You know I like the name Jazz. There's a certain catch to it. It's smooth."
—PETE MARAVICH

"Pound for pound, ounce for ounce, I've always felt that Pete was the most talented basketball player around. Pete can run, pass, shoot, drive, jump. He can do it all."
—BILL BERTKA, JAZZ VP OF BASKETBALL OPERATIONS

When Pete Maravich agreed to be traded to New Orleans, the team didn't even have a name. "Jazz" was the easy winner of a naming contest and the team would wear the Mardi Gras colors of purple (justice), green (faith), and gold (power).

Pete was still skeptical when he arrived in the Crescent City. "I knew it would be a long time before the Jazz were a contender and my dream for a championship seemed to be slipping away," he wrote in his autobiography.

Pete plunked down $300,000 for a two-story, five-bedroom home on Cleveland Place in the New Orleans suburb of Metairie. The 3,500-square-foot home included a swimming pool, a whirlpool, a sauna, and a 25-inch TV. "It was at the end of a street and was very private," Jackie, then his fiancée, recalled. "Pete loved lying on the raft in the backyard pool and getting sun."

The first Jazz practices were anything but relaxing. "We had two veterans from every team. We might have had 40 guys, four or five rookies, and it was just chaos," recalled Aaron James, the Jazz's first draft pick. "It created a lot of problems."

To generate local interest, six of the Jazz's seven exhibition games were held in Louisiana. Beginning with a loss to the Houston Rockets at the Rapides Coliseum in Alexandria, the team dropped their first three games. But on October 6, at the Monroe Civic Center, the Jazz earned its first preseason victory over the Washington Bullets. New Orleans ran their winning streak to two when they beat the Bullets in front of 1,300 fans at the tiny Hirsch Youth Center in Shreveport, Louisiana.

Then, on October 9, while at practice at Tulane's gym, Pete received an urgent phone call. He learned that his mother, Helen, had shot herself in an apparent suicide attempt. Jackie booked him on a flight to Charlotte, North Carolina, and en route, Pete prayed, pleaded, and even bargained with God to spare his mother's life.

Pete had to change planes in Atlanta. "He was going to call me from Atlanta to see if I heard any updates about his mom," remembered Jackie. "While he was still in the air, they called me and told me she didn't make it. I had to tell him to call Ronnie because there was no way I could tell him."

On a pay phone at Atlanta's Candler Field Airport, Pete learned from his older brother that his prayers went unanswered.

"Pete, Mom didn't make it," Ronnie said. "She's dead."

Helen had fired a single shot into her head with a .22 caliber handgun. Ronnie was speaking on the phone with her at the time. "She told me she was going to do it and did it," Ronnie said years later. "Talk about the most helpless feeling in my life. That was it. There was nothing I could do about it."

Compounding the tragedy, eight-year-old Diana Maravich was in the house and had to summon the police. Helen, barely alive, was rushed to Catawaba Memorial Hospital. But she never regained consciousness and died a few hours later on October 10. She was 49 years old.

It wasn't the first time the officers were called to the Maravich home. "I remember going to the Maravich house once or twice before on a suicide threat," recalled officer William Watford in 1999. "The first time she was found behind the couch in the living room. Like she was hiding or something. We talked to her and she was fine and then we left."

Rusty Bergman, assistant coach at Appalachian State, observed Helen's struggle first hand. "I'd been over to their house many times," Bergman said. "When she was totally sober and when she had something to drink. Press kept trying to get Helen dried out."

Helen's battle with alcohol and depression had consumed her. Pete wrote in his memoirs: "I believe with all of my heart that my Mom was past the point of controlling her own actions. Her will had finally been broken."

Pete, along with Press, Ronnie, Diana, and Jackie, flew to Pennsylvania for the funeral. Helen, the prettiest cheerleader at Aliquippa High, was laid to rest beside her mother's grave in Aliquippa's Serbian Orthodox Cemetery. "Pete didn't say anything during Helen's funeral," recalled Maravich's attorney, Les

Zittrain. "He was there in body. [Only] God knows where he was elsewhere."

Press's former N.C. State player and friend Les Robinson attended as well and said the heaviness lifted a bit after the burial. "It was a very sad funeral, primarily Aliquippa people," Robinson said. "But the get-together after, at the lodge, was good because we celebrated her life. We had a great big meal, told funny stories. I left there feeling better."

"She was a sweet person, just loved Pete, Ronnie and Diana," remembered Jackie.

Pete, however, took years to get over his mother's death and always carried a burden of guilt and regret. "I think he felt bad because he never got enough time to spend with his mom," said Jackie. "He didn't think he had done enough for her—to help her. He felt like he could have done more."

"I think she died of loneliness," remembered Jackie. "I really do because Press traveled so much."

Although emotionally wrung out, Pete returned to New Orleans for the Jazz's inaugural season. He had missed the final two exhibition games (both losses, one of which was played at LSU) but arrived in time to join the Jazz on a season-opening four-game road trip, beginning in New York City against the Knicks.

Outwardly he tried to project confidence, but the emotional trauma was apparent. "The tragedy was in Pistol," observed Jazz teammate Stu Lantz. "You could see it in his eyes almost all the time. As a team, you try to go on. But every time we looked in Pistol's eyes, you knew."

Coach Scotty Robertson named his starting five. Stu Lantz joined Pete in the backcourt. The forwards were E. C. Coleman and Bud Stallworth, with veteran Walt Bellamy at center. Maravich was voted team captain.

For the record, the first points scored in a New Orleans Jazz game came 39 seconds into the contest when Knicks forward Phil Jackson cut behind his defender, received a bounce pass, and scored an uncontested layup (Bill Bradley, well-versed in executing the "backdoor," provided the assist). The Jazz dogged the Knicks into the second half, trailing 58-56 with 5:02 left in the third quarter. But the Knicks tightened their defense to win 89-74. Pete got into foul trouble and had just 15 points (4-16, 7-9, 3 rebounds, 4 assists).

Curiously, the game would be Bellamy's final NBA appearance. It was a peculiar ending for a superb yet inconsistent player, who once scored 45 points against Bill Russell, played in four All-Star Games, and was a member of the legendary 1960 Olympic basketball team. In 1993, he was enshrined into the Basketball Hall of Fame.

"We thought we had a center and then he was just gone," said Lantz.

Bellamy was never part of the Jazz's plans—management was hoping to trade him but no team was interested.

While the Knicks game was the end of the Jazz's brief association with Bellamy, it marked the start of a relationship with play-by-play broadcaster "Hot" Rod Hundley—an association that continues into the 2006-07 season.

The local television rights to Jazz games were held by WDUS-TV, channel 6, in New Orleans. "That opening game with the Knicks, I'll never forget it. They could not sell one commercial minute," said Bud Johnson, the Jazz's public relations director. "This is the Knicks at Madison Square Garden, an elite game. I was brought down to earth rather rudely because I knew that we had such an uphill climb."

Losing was the theme of the Jazz's first road trip. They dropped all four contests and Pete was having a tough go of it professionally and emotionally. A game in Washington on October 19 was typical. The *Washington Post* headline read: "With Maravich, Jazz Looked Blue."

"Things are not going well for Maravich," reported David DuPree. "His mother committed suicide two weeks ago and Maravich has not been his flashy self since. The flair is gone. He played only 19 minutes last night, scoring 13 points. Going into the game, he was shooting a dismal 7 for 33 from the field and had a 15 points per game average."

Bullets guard Kevin Porter also noticed Maravich's play wasn't up to par. "It gives me a little extra incentive to play against a ballplayer like Pete Maravich," said Porter. "But I do think he is still down after his tragedy."

The Maravich family's grief was revealed in an October 24, 1974, letter that Press sent to his good friend Jimbo Marchand:

> *Hi Jimbo & Family,*
>
> *I appreciated your sympathy card and your sincere friendship. It happened and I don't know why. I don't question God's ways, but I hope he will somehow tell my why.*
>
> *It is tough to take and tough to adjust, especially living with one woman for 29 years. I guess I can look back and enjoy some of my memories.*
>
> *Diana and I are keeping busy. She comes to my office everyday at 2:40 P.M. Then she goes swimming in the university pool for about 1 1/2 hours, and finally she comes to the gym to see the last hour of practice. I am trying to get her in a karate class on Tuesday and Thursday. We just have to keep busy or it will destroy us both.*
>
> *Pete and Ronnie both took the death real bad. I lived on 3 and 4 tranquilizers per day. An earthquake could have happened and I wouldn't have felt*

a thing. I couldn't have taken Helen's death without those T's. I know Pete right now doesn't care whether he plays or not. I did talk to him last night and told him to snap out of it and start leading the club. I said you have to lead the club regardless whether you win or lose you have to be the leader. He was deeply fond of his mother, Jimbo. Maybe Pete never showed it, but underneath his skin he is like a jellyfish. He is just like me. Ronnie is another one. We are all like that.

I have received over 300 letters and cards this past week and I am trying to answer them one at a time, but with Diana, coaching, teaching, washing and ironing clothes, etc., it leaves little time for me and I have to start going to bed earlier since I have to get up at 6:30 A.M. every morning with Diana. That's the part that kills me is trying to go to bed early and get up early.

Thanks again Jimbo. I'll probably see you around Xmas.
Your friend,
Press

The Jazz returned for their home opener against the Philadelphia 76ers on October 24. The Superdome would not be ready for another year, so the game was held at the antiquated 7,853-seat Municipal Auditorium. Besides NBA basketball, ticket holders were treated to a concert featuring New Orleans trumpeter Al Hirt. And before the opening tip, Revered Arthur T. Screen led the arena in prayer.

The fans were pumped, cheering wildly at the spectacle. "The Jazz could do no wrong," recalled local sports television and radio broadcaster, Buddy Diliberto. "They cheered for everything."

One highlight that pulled the fans from their seats was a creative maneuver executed by Pete. Dribbling hard down the middle of the court, flanked by teammates Ollie Johnson and Jim Barnett, Pete reached the top of the key and slapped at the ball with his right hand—intentionally missing it as his hand whiffed underneath. He then reloaded and slapped at the ball again, this time connecting and delivering a perfect tap pass to Johnson, who converted the layup.

Pete's baffling sleight of hand threw off the timing of Philadelphia defenders Doug Collins and Clyde Lee. Lee, twisted around, lost his footing and wound up on his back. It was one of seven assists from Pete that evening and was fortunately caught on film for the television series *This Week in the NBA*. The "slap pass," along with the "fake behind-the-back" layup from 1971, remain the two most recognizable deceptions from Maravich's bag of tricks.

"When you see him coming down the lane and then slap pass blind to somebody, it was just amazing," marveled broadcaster Bob Costas. "Maravich obviously was a great player by any reckoning. But he was an even greater stylist—somebody who helped you enjoy the game and who also unleashed a kind of creativity."

Despite Pete's "creativity," the Jazz dropped their fifth straight game, 102-89.

By November 10, when they hosted the Portland Trail Blazers, the losing streak had reached 11. It was the first meeting between Pete and three-time College Player of the Year, rookie Bill Walton. "His first step was unstoppable," recalled Walton. "Pete was the quickest and fastest player I had ever seen, and those are two totally different skills. And he always did it with a deadpan expression. Generally when you're competing with someone who's really great, you have to study their eyes to figure out what they're thinking, what it is they're seeing. With Pete you could never figure it out because those eyes were completely deadpan."

The Trail Blazers led 73-50 with 6:20 left in the third quarter. It looked like loss No. 12 for the hapless Jazz. Coach Robertson called timeout and told the players that if they had any pride left, they would dig deep and at least make it respectable. Pete, along with backup center Mel Counts, took up the challenge. With Counts slowing down Walton (who still finished with 25 points and 16 rebounds), Pete went on a scoring tear. He fired in 20 second-half points, saving the best for last. With seconds remaining, Portland's 23-point lead had dwindled to just one.

"With the game on the line, he had the ball at the top of the circle and drives away from the basket into the corner," recalled Walton. "He jumps and turns away from the basket to the point where he's falling out of bounds."

Jazz center Neal Walk watched the ball arc toward the basket. "Walton was right on my shoulder under the basket," Walk said. "I was looking up at Pete's shot and I said to myself, 'This one's going through.'"

Walton also recalled the moment. "I'm watching this high-arcing ball back-spinning in slow motion as it sailed downward and through the net. That was Pete Maravich in a nutshell."

With that basket the Jazz, by the slimmest of margins, 102-101, had their first win. Many in the crowd of 5,465 swarmed the court. "You would have thought we won the world championship," said Maravich to the *Times-Picayune*. "I was just trying to go somewhere that was open. I went baseline and saw somebody tall on me. All I could do was shoot a fade-away." Maravich finished with 30 points (11-26, 8-8, 11 rebounds, 12 assists, 4 steals). It was his first of five triple-doubles that season.

But the celebration was short lived as the Jazz dropped their next three games. The patience of the Jazz management had run dry. On November 17, with a record of 1-15, Robertson was fired. His tenure was the briefest ever by a coach of an expansion team.

"He worked as hard as any man I've ever seen," said Jazz player Jim Barnett. "He tore his heart out to get us together."

Maravich was also sympathetic. "The way the circumstances were with us—the injuries, a lot of personal things, and the way we did not play as a team—Jesus [himself] could have coached us and been fired."

But several players thought Robertson was in over his head. "I think Scotty was more of a college coach because he came from the college ranks," said forward Aaron James. "It was difficult for him to deal with pro players when he was so used to college kids."

Robertson took the firing quite hard. "They gave me no warning," said a distraught Robertson after cleaning out his desk at the Jazz's Braniff Place office. "I have been a coach all my life. I really have nowhere to go." Actually Robertson continued to secure a series of assistant and head-coaching positions in the league for the next 30 years. "He was fired in 1974 and has been a part of the NBA ever since," said *Times-Picayune* writer Marty Mule after seeing Robertson at the Jazz's 20th reunion in 1994. "He told me that Pete Maravich could have started and starred on any team in the NBA in the last quarter of a century, including the Chicago Bulls."

The Jazz's new coach was Willem "Butch" van Breda Kolff. He had successfully coached college sensation Bill Bradley at Princeton, as well as high-scoring NBA guards Jerry West and Dave Bing. Jazz management believed those experiences made van Breda Kolff a good fit with Maravich's game.

There was an immediate contrast in styles to the meticulous Robertson. Bud Johnson, the Jazz public relations director, remembered van Breda Kolff's first practice. "Butch shows up at the Tulane gym. No whistle, no socks, no clipboard, no practice plan. He didn't have anything to write with. I introduced myself and he asked, 'May I borrow your pen?' He took out a matchbook cover and started drawing up notes and I asked, 'What are you doing?' He said, 'I'm making up my practice plan.' I really thought it was a good publicity gimmick but as soon as practice was over, I was shocked that he covered so much. They worked on a bunch of stuff. So much was accomplished by such little preparation other than the matchbook cover. When practice was finished, I asked, 'Butch, can I have that matchbook cover?' And then he looked at it and said, 'Huh, hey I didn't get any out of bounds plays in.' He stuffed the matchbook back in his pocket and walked off."

But van Breda Kolff's tenure began like Robertson's ended—with a loss.

Next up was a "home" game at the LSU Assembly Center against Pete's old team, the Atlanta Hawks.

November 22 marked a convergence of Pete's previous eight years. As a member of the New Orleans Jazz he would face the Atlanta Hawks on the court of Louisiana State University. "My plan was to beat Atlanta into the ground every time we played them," wrote Pete in his autobiography.

The task seemed implausible, given the Jazz were a pitiful 1-16 and struggling to play cohesive team ball. "It is difficult for me, or any of our players, to be patient. We want to be competitive right away," said Pete before the game. "But executing a pass requires timing and coordination with other players and I'm working with an entirely new group of people."

Pete attempted only one shot in the first 19 minutes on the LSU court. With less than nine minutes to go, Pete had just eight points. Then, as if turning on a switch, he came alive and embarked on another fourth-quarter scoring barrage.

"Pete took charge," said his old Atlanta coach, Cotton Fitzsimmons. "[He] started looking toward the basket and doing the things he does best."

Pete scored 13 of the Jazz's final 16 points. To show he retained his flair for the dramatic—after twisting through the Hawks defenders for four consecutive layups—he calmly flipped in a 25-footer to seal the game. The Jazz had their second victory, 96-90, and Pete finished with 21 points (10-17, 1-4, 5 rebounds, 3 assists, 3 steals).

Maravich had his revenge and van Breda Kolff had his victory. "When I got the job we were 1-15 and the second game I coached we won," van Breda Kolff later said. "I thought, *I'm 1-1. We're doing a . . . lot better than before.* Next thing I knew, we had to play on the road forever."

"Forever" was a grueling 40-day, 17-game road trip. The Jazz left New Orleans on November 23, and criss-crossed the country several times, playing straight through the holidays. Only two home games broke up the trip in early December. "Never have I seen a schedule like this one," nine-year veteran Jim Barnett told the *Times-Picayune.* "Two home games in six weeks? It's twice as bad as anything I've been involved with."

Compounding matters, the Jazz couldn't buy a victory. In Los Angeles, where van Breda Kolff had been dismissed by the Lakers in 1970, the Jazz lost 127-122. Pat Riley scorched Pete with a career-high 38 points. In Portland, the Jazz scored only 85 points—the lowest output of any Portland opponent in the franchise's five-year history.

Not only was the team losing on the court, but the franchise was hemorrhaging money at an extraordinary rate. Initial projections of a $750,000 first-year loss were being upgraded to perhaps double that amount. And the extended road trip had created a cash-flow problem. At the time, home teams received 100 percent of the gate receipts. "We have no money coming in except the national television package revenue," said Jazz Vice President of Operations, Barry Mendelson.

A news item claimed the Jazz was unable to meet its expansion-fee payments to the other franchises. (The $6,150,000 purchase price was payable over five years at two payments per year.) "After reading today that New Orleans is delinquent in its payments to other clubs," said NBA commissioner Walter Kennedy, "I want to correct the report. New Orleans is up to date with everyone."

The Jazz ship was taking on water and the fall guy was team President Fred Rosenfeld. The owners had a meeting and leaned on Rosenfeld to make a move. He resigned. The man who was instrumental in bringing an NBA franchise into New Orleans and had engineered the trade for Maravich, was forced out.

Sam Battistone, a 34-year-old millionaire, replaced Rosenfeld as president. Battistone, whose father founded the Sambo's restaurant chain, was an unlikely choice because he lived in Santa Barbara, California (one of the complaints with Rosenfeld was that he spent too much time commuting) and was busy running the Hawaiians, a World Football League franchise.

Battistone faced some formidable financial challenges. "One reason the losses will be higher than expected is the fact we are unable to get into The Dome," he explained. "But considering our record, the response has been fantastic. And the same goes for the enthusiasm. I think we have a nucleus. You just have to stay with it." The Jazz started a booster club and began offering limited partnerships to the public.

Maravich tried to keep himself, and the team, focused. The team record was a dismal 2-23. "We have a job to do and that's to get ready for battle," Pete said. "Anything that happens to management is management's business, not ours."

The Jazz then lost 121-108 to Seattle and lost Walk and Pete to injuries. Walk chipped a bone in a finger and was out for at least three games. Pete strained ligaments in his left ankle and was out for two games.

The one Jazz player to catch a break that evening was Stu Lantz. "Pistol and I were at the movies together the night I got traded," said Lantz, who went to the Lakers in exchange for a future draft consideration and some much-needed cash. "I had fun playing in the backcourt with Pistol. He enjoyed playing the game so much. The things that he did, he did so easily. When he threw a pass, it was on the money. The best passer I've ever seen.

"But I also remember the terrible time of losing. Just the atmosphere around the team when you're losing those numbers of games. Nobody should have to go through that."

On December 13, the Jazz were in Chicago for a game against the Bulls and Pete was under severe pressure. His team was playing horribly and the franchise was bleeding money. Plus his ankle had not yet fully recovered, denying him access to his favorite refuge, the basketball court.

Pete played only seven minutes that evening and was forced to witness a crushing 109–76 defeat. At times it seemed as if his decision to allow the trade with New Orleans was a colossal mistake. Afterward, Pete headed out in the Windy City.

"We had to go looking for him and we found him in a bar and he was pretty well lit," remembered Walk. "I got him back to the hotel and we got him cleaned up and put him to bed. I got him up in the morning and made him take a cold shower. He was pretty unhappy with me."

As the 40-day odyssey wound down, the Jazz had won just one game. They saved their worst for last. On January 7, the final day of the trip, the Warriors humiliated the Jazz, 134–92. Pete had six points.

The Jazz stood at a pitiful 3-34.

Pete and his band of rookies and veterans were closing in on the worst season in NBA history (the 1972-73 76ers won nine games). "It was so bad that for the first time in a nine-year career, I was getting very depressed playing basketball," recalled Jazz guard Jim Barnett.

Every loss bolstered the view that Pete was a one-man show. That criticism, however, wasn't accurate this time. In fact, Pete was reluctant to shoot—perhaps as a form of self-preservation. That way, if the Jazz lost, at least he could not be blamed for gunning up the ball. He was passing up many shots and averaging a paltry 16 points while delivering more than seven assists per game. He concentrated on being a playmaker.

Still, the criticism persisted. "I can't understand why everything is negative, negative, negative," Pete told the *Times-Picayune*. "I shoot 30 times a game and I'm a gunner. Now I shoot eight times a game and I'm over the hill."

Returning to New Orleans, the team was forced into yet another temporary arena. The Municipal Auditorium was booked for Mardi Gras events, so the team scheduled 15 games at the Field House at Loyola University. The arena had been home years earlier to the short-lived New Orleans Buccaneers of the American Basketball Association. It was a peculiar venue for basketball. There was no heat or air conditioning, no seating behind the baskets, little parking, and, most odd, a basketball court elevated three feet off the floor.

"It was really bizarre," said Walk. "At practice time it was so humid that guys would slip on the court, which was dangerous. Everybody's played on a floor that was over-waxed or had wet spots, but with the wax, humidity, and sweat, it was silly at times."

Silly and dangerous. "The floor was raised off the ground probably because the city is below sea level," said Johnson, the PR director. "The front row seats were about chin level with the floor. You were looking up at the floor the first few rows."

Fearing a player would fall into the stands from the raised floor, the league intervened and instructed the Jazz to rectify the problem. They adopted an old solution—hanging nets from the rafters to the floor that would run the length of the court. In professional basketball's early years, the entire court was surrounded by wire, then cloth, netting (hence the term "cagers"). The nets and rigging cost the cash-strapped Jazz $5,000—plus any chance of selling unobstructed-view seats.

To test the netting, Players Association President Bob Lanier made a special trip to New Orleans. "He was 350 pounds and nearly seven feet, with a size 23 shoe," recalled Barry Mendelson. "He got out of the cab and found out where the net was. Then he took off running and just jumped in. The net held, and he said, 'If it's good enough for me, it's good enough for the players.' He got back in his taxi cab and left New Orleans."

Pete entered the games at Loyola feeling frustrated. He loved playing up-tempo, fast-break basketball. But, under van Breda Kolff, he felt harnessed. "The coaches want me to slow things down," Pete told the *New York Times*. "They want me to run the so-called offense."

The Jazz coach responded in *Sports Illustrated*: "I want everyone on my team sound and to be involved," he said. "I want flair, that's part of the game. But it has to be at the right time. You can't go wild with four guys waiting for the ball. That's where intelligence comes in."

Pete decided to change tactics. "As a playmaker, I wasn't going to be doing that much scoring," he told *Times-Picayune* reporter Peter Finney. "But, being realistic, I felt I had to do some scoring to help us win. My bag is speed and quickness. So why not get more flamboyant? We weren't going anywhere."

Playing behind the mesh screens, Pete was unleashed. On January 10, against the Rockets, he led the team in points (38), rebounds (11), and assists (8) in a 111-108 victory. Then the Seattle SuperSonics were the victim of one of the NBA's most outrageous triple-doubles as Pete delivered 42 points (16-34, 10-12, 10 rebounds, 17 assists) in a 113-109 victory. The Jazz had their first winning streak.

Next up were the Buffalo Braves, who were treated to a 40-point (17-37, 6-7, 14 rebounds, 13 assists) night from Pete. "Maravich is playing exceptionally well," said Braves coach Jack Ramsay. "He seems to have taken control of the team."

Over three home games at Loyola, Maravich averaged 40 points, 12 rebounds, and 13 assists, while shooting 47 percent from the field. "We don't have a home, but I'd rather play here," said Pete. "It has more of a basketball atmosphere. You can hear the noise and feel the fans' enthusiasm. It's like a snake pit."

Just as things were looking up, Pete received some more disappointing news. Press, still distraught over Helen's suicide, had resigned from Appalachian State University. For the first time in over 25 years, Press Maravich was not coaching during basketball season. He turned the team over to his assistant, Rusty Bergman. "Press was totally, mentally blown away," Bergman said. "Not for two or three weeks, but for about nine months. He could not concentrate on his job. And he was also raising Diana. He just seemed as if he could not overcome it all."

Meanwhile the Jazz made a few significant personnel moves. First they signed free agent center Otto Moore (who Bertka spotted in the stands in Detroit). Then the team sent Walk and Barnett to New York in exchange for Henry Bibby, $100,000, plus the Pistons' No. 1 draft choice in 1975.

Walk didn't want to leave New Orleans despite being subject to some Cajun-style abuse. "I was a vegetarian and they thought that was weird," he said. "I could take the people tossing carrots at me, I think someone had even chunked a piece of raw meat at me. Fortunately, the nets caught them."

The Jazz also acquired shooting guard Nate Williams and free agent Bernie Fryer (the future NBA referee was working for his father as an insurance salesman when he signed on). The Jazz had just 10 players on their roster. Louie Nelson and Pete were the guards, E. C. Coleman and Bud Stallworth the forwards, and Otto Moore was at center. The bench consisted of Aaron James, Mel Counts, Bibby, Williams, and Fryer. Incredibly, this unlikely gang of 10 started to pile up victories.

The players' spirits were bolstered when they sold out the Municipal Auditorium (700 were turned away) on February 2, 1975. The Jazz cruised to a 118-114 win over the Knicks as Pete bucketed 33 points (14-31, 5-6, 6 rebounds, 12 assists, 4 steals).

Several days later the Jazz secured their first road win (after 28 losses) against the Atlanta Hawks. In front of 13,653 patrons, the largest gate at the

Omni all season, Pete dropped in a season-high 47 points (18-37, 11-12, 8 rebounds, 5 assists) in a 106-102 victory. "Pete was out of sight; he played spectacularly," said Fitzsimmons. "And I thought he got after it on defense."

Hawks radio and television announcer Skip Carey said in his postgame wrap-up: "I hope all the people who still write me about how unfair I am to Pete Maravich listened to this game because it would be impossible to broadcast it without pointing out that he was absolutely sensational—as he was so often as a member of the Hawks. The Pistol shot us down tonight. He buried us."

"I'm playing better defense," an upbeat Maravich said after the game. "We take pride in playing team defense. The attitude on this team is fantastic. I'm enjoying playing basketball."

Leading the team's defense was sophomore forward E. C. Coleman. He was fast becoming one of the NBA's premier defenders. "It's a real trip to take on the league's big scorers," said Coleman.

The Jazz downed the Hawks again two days later, 96-89, in New Orleans to secure a winning record (5-3) over Pete's old franchise. Playing care-free, up-tempo ball, the Jazz won 18 of their final 34 games, including a six-game winning streak.

"Give Pete Maravich credit for our looseness," Nelson told the *Times-Picayune.* "He has a lot of fun playing the game and his attitude has kind of spread throughout the team."

After a 3-34 start, the Jazz finished at 23-59. "Really, we weren't that bad. At least we didn't set any records for losing streaks or most losses in a season," recalled teammate Bud Stallworth. "Pete made it exciting. While Stu Lantz, Otto Moore, Aaron James, and I were pretty much average, Pete would light it up. Life in the NBA was fun."

Of the league's 18 expansion franchises, from the 1961 Chicago Packers to the 2004 Charlotte Bobcats, the Jazz's .280 inaugural season winning percentage ranks fourth best.

Winning games seemed to inspire and hearten Pete. Between his mother's suicide, his father's resignation from coaching, and his team's nightmare start, he had survived yet another tumultuous year of pro basketball. Although he averaged just 21.5 points, he finished fifth in the NBA with 6.2 assists per game.

One year earlier, the frustration of pro ball was so severe that Maravich had talked about retirement. Now it was just the opposite—he had rediscovered his passion for the game and wanted to continue, perhaps another 10 years. "I figure if I can escape injury, I can play until I'm at least 35."

At a postseason awards banquet thrown by local Jazz owner Andrew Martin, Pete seemed gracious, content, and mature. His behavior was a revelation to *Times-Picayune* sports editor Bob Roesler, who had observed Pete since his days at LSU. Roesler thought Pete was a spoiled brat in college and a sulking, moody introvert as a pro. That night Roesler observed Pete as he laughed heartily at host "Hot" Rod Hundley's barbs, performed his impressions of Sammy Davis Jr. and Groucho Marx, and gave a heartfelt speech.

"This has been a fantastic year," Pete said. "It's great to come from Atlanta to a fantastic place like New Orleans. The players here are real close and have great attitude and character. We will bring to this community a championship."

After the banquet Roesler sent a note to Jazz statistician Bob Remy, who had asked Roesler to soften his negative perception of Pete:

> *Dear Bob,*
>
> *Just a note to thank you for the kind words. You're absolutely right: better late than never. I'm delighted with Pete Maravich's attitude. He is a new person. And so refreshing.*

Press, still reeling from Helen's suicide, planned a special trip for Pete and himself. Using his connections from his days as a Navy flier, Press arranged a series of basketball clinics on, and near, military bases across Europe.

Before leaving, Pete participated in an ABC made-for-television event in Florida. *The Superstars* was a series of athletic competitions between premiere athletes from various sports. Despite winning the bowling (against John Havlicek) competition and placing in tennis, Pete was eliminated in the second round.

Pete shaved his unkempt moustache and goatee before departing on May 20 for Torrejon Air Force Base in Madrid. Pete and Press held basketball clinics in tiny gyms, large air bases, and even on the narrow sidewalks of Europe. One afternoon, *Pistola Pedro* and Press were taking photos in the mountain-top town of Arcos when a boy handed Pete a soccer ball. Pete adroitly spun it on his finger, rolled it down his arms, across his back, and then kicked it off his leg. Soon a large crowd formed and Pete's spontaneous clinic lasted almost an hour.

The Maraviches traveled by military jet and their pilot, Lt. Edward Beck, took extra time to impress Press, the ex-fighter pilot, by flying over the top of Pompeii, Mount Vesuvius, and three live volcanoes.

The tour ran through Naples, Sigonella, Sardinia, Sicily, and ended in West Germany. Special Services Director Bryan Fleming said it was the "best received of any tour show or entertainment ever to hit the Mediterranean."

More than 10,000 people saw the demonstrations.

Press's June 10 return to the States was brief. After spending two weeks at Campbell College, he and Diana flew to Sweden. Press had accepted a coaching position with the Swedish Basketball Federation through longtime friend and former LSU player Nelson Isley. Press thought the change of scenery would do wonders for his emotional state.

Back in New Orleans, Pete mapped out his mission for the rest of the summer: to get in the best shape of his life. Along with NFL players Jim Taylor and Archie Manning, he embarked on an intense regimen to increase strength, coordination, and stamina.

"Pete worked the light bag at the Saints camp," said Bud Johnson. "His hand speed just mesmerized Manning. He couldn't believe anybody had that kind of hand speed or control."

But Pete had more on his mind than just a physical transformation. "Over the summer, he called me and said, 'I want No. 7,'" remembered Jazz trainer Don Sparks. "I asked him two or three times if he was serious because I knew how much he loved that No. 44. I even called Jackie to make sure he was serious."

"The number 7 keeps popping up in my life," explained Pete, who now studied numerology. "My address in Florida is 700, Apt. 707, I have a ring with seven diamonds, and everywhere I go the number keeps following me. Maybe it's an omen."

Jazz management was furious. The team had invested a great deal promoting No. 44 (*Sports Illustrated* had run a life-sized poster) and now, because of an eccentric whim, a sizable expense was needed to placate their star. But Pete was undeterred and ultimately got his way.

Pete had one more change in mind. He called a meeting with van Breda Kolff, and they spoke at length about Maravich's dedication to team play. The conversation kept returning to Pete's idol, Jerry West, who had retired in the spring of 1974. They decided that for Maravich to become the new West, he would have to play a more efficient, well-rounded game. To demonstrate his commitment to that goal, Pete decided to eliminate his most celebrated trademark: the floppy socks.

For nine seasons, Pete had worn a pair of heavy gray socks. Lacking elasticity, they bunched at his ankles. From Pete's perspective, they made his (size 14½) feet look smaller and thus he felt faster and more nimble. From the world's perspective, the socks represented a wonderful individualism.

But Pete was no longer the skinny whiz kid with the bunchy socks. It was time to unveil a stronger, more mature model.

17

Under the Dome

"The whole franchise had formed itself around him. Every marketing piece, every article, every decision filtered back through Pete. It was all on him."

—RICH KELLEY, JAZZ TEAMMATE

"No one man wins or loses a basketball game. When the Jazz wins, praise us as a team; when we lose, we lose together."

—PETE MARAVICH

Thanks to the taxpayers of Louisiana, Pistol Pete Maravich and the New Orleans Jazz would be playing in the league's newest facility: the colossal Superdome.

Construction began in 1971, and when it opened for business on August 4, 1975, the Superdome was the largest steel-enclosed room in the world. In fact, Houston's 50,000-seat Astrodome could fit comfortably inside the massive structure. The 52-acre stadium was built on reclaimed swampland and soon hosted such diverse events as baseball, track, soccer, motorcross, boxing, parades, auto and boat shows, rodeos, and rock concerts.

The primary tenants were, of course, the NFL's Saints, who finally had a permanent home after eight losing seasons in Tulane's venerable stadium. True to form, the hapless Saints began their residency in the Dome with a 21-0 loss to the Cincinnati Bengals on September 28, 1975.

The Dome would also be home for the Jazz and, to bring fans closer to the action, an entire section of bleachers (3,289 seats) was rolled across the artificial turf (MardiGrass) to corner in the basketball court. "My first game, I sat several rows back near mid-court. My seats were on the football field," recalled one fan. "The people on the other side of the court were sitting in permanent football stadium seats. It was just a weird place to watch a game."

Maravich seemed inspired by the new stadium. "This is a very large snake pit," he said. "We wore those people down in those places (Loyola and Municipal Auditorium) with the heat. I guess here we'll freeze 'em to death." To avoid becoming lost in the myriad tunnels and hallways, Pete would always arrive and leave through the same doors.

Everything about the Superdome was oversized, including the rent. Vice President of Business Operations, Barry Mendelson, negotiated a five-year lease. The 11 percent city and state tax on tickets cut into revenue (another eight percent went to the league office). Mendelson calculated the Jazz needed 8,200 fans per game just to break even. Reserved tickets ranged from $3.50 to $7.50. No revenue from parking, programs, souvenirs, or food concessions went to the team.

As the preseason approached, the Jazz's rookie class worked out at the Jewish Community Center on St. Charles Avenue. Just two would make the team: Rich Kelley, a 7-0 center from Stanford, and Jim McElroy, a 6-3 guard from Eastern Michigan.

Pete was decidedly upbeat about the upcoming season. The Jazz's VP of Basketball Operations, Bill Bertka, noticed a stark difference. "Pete came in clean shaven, full of vim, vigor, and ready to play," said Bertka. "It was like a different person. The first year he had a beard. He was scruffy. He was moody."

Pete was confident that a summer-long training regimen would extend his career. "I've been lifting weights and doing situps. It's not fun, though. Doing 300 situps in a seven- or eight-minute period isn't easy. I'm hardly at my peak—that will come between the ages of 30 and 35."

New Orleans began its exhibition season with two games in North Carolina against the ABA's Denver Nuggets. The games marked not only a return to North Carolina for Pete but a "coming out" party for David Thompson, the Nuggets' exciting rookie. Thompson, with his remarkable 42-inch vertical leap, had led N.C. State to a national championship in 1974 and was instrumental in ushering in a new high-flying brand of basketball.

The Atlanta Hawks drafted Thompson with the first selection in the NBA draft, a pick they had acquired in the "Louisiana Purchase" trade. But Thompson chose the ABA, as did the Hawks' other first-round pick, Providence grad Marvin Webster. The Hawks' double failure delighted Pete, who remained bitter about his departure from Atlanta. "They already lost Webster. They needed to sign David Thompson to save the organization," gloated Pete. "I wish them luck. They're going to need it."

The Charlotte Coliseum was sold out for the first game of the inter-league matchup, won easily by the Nuggets, 94-79. Pete, in midseason form, scored 33 points on 15 of 20 shooting, while Thompson had a respectable pro debut with 19 points and six rebounds. The next night, with 12,400 fans looking on at Reynolds Coliseum, New Orleans won 115-101 in what became a costly victory. Pete injured his right knee in the fourth quarter while planting his foot on the court's Tartan-covered surface. "Instead of slid-ing, as it would on wood, the floor didn't give," Pete told reporters. "So my foot was stationary."

After the game a disgusted Maravich spoke to reporter Ron Brocato. "Maybe I was never meant to play this game. This is my sixth season and I'm six for six with injuries of some sort. I'd like to go to one of those religious people who can heal you by touching you. It certainly couldn't hurt anything."

Maravich missed three games, but with his knee wrapped from thigh to mid-calf, he returned in San Antonio to face the ABA's Spurs. Pete thought that second-year guard George Karl's defense was too aggressive. "I told Karl to get his hands off of me," recalled Maravich. "He kept it up so I had enough. I had to let him have it."

Pete threw a vicious elbow that crashed solidly into Karl's jaw. Karl retal-iated with his own punch to the face. Pete tried to hit him back but missed and fell. Karl jumped on top of him, swinging wildly with both fists. In his book *This Game's the Best!* Karl recalled the incident.

"He [Pete] just blatantly jabbed me. It was very late in the game and I said, 'You're not going to get away with this.' This is when you were allowed to throw a punch and not get suspended for many games," wrote Karl.

Pete finished with 15 points and a bruised ego. Karl had 13 points and became one of few players ever to fight with Maravich. The Jazz won in a squeaker, 105-104.

A few days later, New Orleans opened its regular season with a loss to the Hawks in Atlanta. Pete, still nursing his knee, sat out.

On Friday, October 24, the Superdome held its first NBA game. The five-piece Magnolia Jazz Band, with Grand Marshal Ellyna Tatum presiding, led the team onto the floor. Tatum, wearing her signature top hat, danced and spun her parasol while an appreciative crowd egged her on.

As a gesture of appreciation, the team gave away Jazz Frisbees to each of the 9,348 fans attending the inaugural game. Unfortunately, at half time sev-eral thousand spectators "returned" the gift, flinging the plastic discs out onto the hardwood floor.

The Jazz continued the festive mood by whipping the Pistons, 114-106.

Pete played without the blessing of his doctor and racked up 31 points (13-19, 5-6, 7 rebounds, 4 assists). "When the doctors told me I'd be in pain for six or seven weeks, even if I didn't play, I said the [expletive] with it," Pete told reporter Nat Belloni. "I couldn't cut at all and when I stopped I got kind of a shock through my legs. Fans later told me I looked like I was wincing with every step."

Two days later, more than 13,000 people turned out when the powerful New York Knicks came to town. Many bought tickets for the Superdome's upper deck, where 15,000 seats were available in the "high terrace" sections, nine to 13 floors above the court. The *New York Times* described the view as, "Equivalent to watching a chess match from the balcony of a movie theater." Tickets for the high terrace cost just $1.50—available only on game day.

"Going the $1.50 route, you had to arrive at the Dome before 5:30 P.M. when the gates opened so that you could buy your ticket which gave you carte blanche to any seat in the upper section," recalled longtime Jazz fan Steve Crane. "Then there was a mad rush up the long, long ramp to the top of the Dome. The prize was gaining a courtside front-row seat, which offered an unobstructed view to the court—almost straight down beneath us. If you got there a little late and could not get the first row, you had to go up to about nine rows to avoid having to look through the railing."

At the opposite end of the ticket scale, Mendelson came up with the idea of courtside VIP seats. Sandwiched between the scorer's table and the players' bench, these seats cost a then-unprecedented $15 (giving the Jazz the most—and least—expensive tickets in the NBA). Not everyone loved the idea. When visiting Knicks' coach Red Holzman realized a fan was sitting right next to him, he went ballistic. The volatile coach lobbed a torrent of expletives at the refs, Jazz management, and everyone at the scorer's table. But the customer remained and premium VIP seating was born.

The game itself became a classic shootout between Pistol Pete, who had his right leg wrapped from thigh to ankle, and another flamboyant showman, Earl "The Pearl" Monroe. "One of the things I learned early in my career was to play to the crowd," said Monroe, who had a unique, jerky, syncopated style. Filmmaker Woody Allen wrote of Monroe in *SPORT* magazine: "I ranked him with Willie Mays and Sugar Ray Robinson as athletes who went beyond the level of sports as sport to the realm of sports as art."

Monroe's most notorious move was his ability to spin around a defender in either direction with lightning speed. The maneuver was so popular and identifiable it actually became known as "pearling." Maravich remembered the futility of trying to stop it. "The best one-on-one player I ever played against was Earl Monroe," said Pete. "It was ridiculous to even try and guard him. He would just keep spinning and spinning and spinning. It would drive you nuts."

The Knick–Jazz game was close as the lead changed eight times. New York held a three–point edge when Phil Jackson fouled E. C. Coleman with 29 seconds remaining. Coleman sank both free throws to close the margin to one. Next, Maravich intercepted Bill Bradley's inbound pass at mid–court and streaked down for an easy layup to put the Jazz up by one. As the stadium reverberated with cheers, Walt Frazier coolly knocked down a 12-foot jumper over Maravich to restore New York's lead. Six seconds remained.

Maravich took the inbound pass and noticed Monroe sneaking in for a steal. So, as Pete recalled, "I put one of his own patented moves on him. Spinning around as I got the ball and stopping short. Earl climbed up my back and the whistle blew." Maravich went to the line for his 17th and 18th free throws of the game. He missed the first but made the second to force overtime.

With a minute to go in the first overtime, and the Jazz down by four, Pete hit a 25-foot jumper, followed by a layup off a perfectly executed out-of-bounds, backdoor play. "The play came from where we expected," explained Frazier. "He just beat me." As the Superdome rocked with excitement, the game went into a second overtime.

Pete scored another 10 points in the period and fouled Monroe out of the game with 37 seconds left. Frazier and Jackson also fouled out trying to contain the Pistol. Pete went to the foul line 26 times and made 23 (both career highs). He finished with 45 points (11-21, 23-26, 11 rebounds, 8 assists) in a thrilling 125-114 victory. Monroe knocked down 36 for the Knicks.

Pete was so pumped up by the win he didn't fall asleep until after 5 A.M. "In my career I've played hundreds of basketball games, more than 500 as a pro alone, and in most cases as soon as one night's over, I forget about it and start thinking about the next one. That's the way the game is," recalled Pete later that year. "If there's one I'll remember for a long time, it would be against the New York Knicks early in this season when they came to the Louisiana Superdome for the first time."

Three games into its sophomore season, the Jazz had two wins and were over .500 for the first time ever. It had taken 25 games to get three wins during the inaugural season. When the Jazz won its next three games to go to 5-1, the idea of a legitimate basketball contender in New Orleans suddenly seemed reasonable. "There's a thin line between winning and losing," said Maravich. "Winning breeds winning." Next up, the Lakers, led by Kareem

Abdul-Jabbar, were coming to town and more than 11,000 tickets were sold in advance as pro basketball fever swept the Big Easy.

Jabbar, winner of the league MVP award three times in his first six seasons, had been traded to Los Angeles from Milwaukee. New Orleans was excited to see this legendary giant but eight inches of rain on game day caused severe flooding throughout the metropolitan area. Pete's home in Metairie was one of many hit hard by the storm. He spent over three hours wringing out dozens of towels trying to stay ahead of the seeping waters. As game time approached, a neighbor offered to take Pete to the Superdome—in a boat. "No thanks, Milton," said Pete. "I don't think we can get downtown in that thing."

When Pete finally arrived at 6:45 P.M. (with a police escort), he was shocked by what he saw. The water around the Dome was beyond ankle deep and, yet, thousands of people were still trying to get in. The game was delayed 30 minutes and when the turnstiles finally stopped clicking, a staggering 26,511 customers sat inside. It was the largest single-game crowd in the NBA's 29-year history.

Pete seemed worn out from battling the storm as he missed several easy shots early in the game. The Lakers built a 13-point lead, but as the minutes ticked away, the massive crowd seemed to invigorate the fatigued Maravich. With the chant of "Go Jazz Go" echoing through the Dome, Pete led all scorers with 30 points (13-28, 4-5, 5 rebounds, 7 assists) to help rally the Jazz to an improbable 113-110 victory. Abdul-Jabbar had 25 points.

Backup Jazz center Mel Counts gushed about the huge turnout. "When you think of all the great Laker teams, the great Knick teams, the great Celtic teams, and realize they never pulled 26,000," said Counts. "It makes you stop and think what happened here."

"It might have been 30,000 if we hadn't had the greatest rain since Noah's Ark," quipped Pete in the locker room while sipping a Michelob. "If this keeps up, we're going to get 70,000 people in here." At 6-1, the club was 48 games ahead of its expansion-year pace.

Two weeks later, in a practice at Tulane, Pete dove for a loose ball and suffered a second-degree shoulder separation that would sideline him for a month. "I just started to get my strength back in my legs on moves to the goal and then this had to happen," Pete said quietly. "It seems like this has been the history of my career."

While Pete was rehabbing his shoulder injury by himself at the Metairie YMCA, New Orleans dropped eight of its next 10 games. The headline in the local papers read: "Pete We Miss You."

After sitting out 17 games, Pete returned to the struggling Jazz (11–18) for a Christmas Day contest against the Houston Rockets. "You can't just run three or four miles a day and expect to get in good basketball shape," Maravich commented before the game. "You have to play yourself into shape." Although he was in for just 30 minutes, Pete contributed 19 points (8–16, 3–6, 8 rebounds, 4 assists, 4 steals) as the Jazz squeaked by Houston, 101–99.

After a loss at New York, the Jazz went on a five-game winning streak—the final three on the road. When the team's Delta flight returned from Detroit on January 10, more than 500 fans, along with the Magnolia Band, welcomed the team home. It was a wild scene as the 17–19 Jazz were greeted like returning heroes. The chaotic tableau reminded Coach van Breda Kolff of the homecoming reception his Princeton team enjoyed after reaching the Final Four in 1965. As for Pete: "Nothing like this ever happened in Atlanta. I hope they don't greet us with a lynch mob if we lose the next three."

The next day, January 11, 1976—seven years and four months after first seeing her at the Southdowns bar in Baton Rouge—Pete married Jackie Elliser. It was a small service witnessed by family members, including Jackie's grandparents, who flew in from France. Ronnie served as the best man. Pete was 28 and Jackie was 29. The day was not without incident. "We were waiting for the preacher to come and my dad was waiting outside," recalled Jackie. "The preacher accidentally passed up the house and my daddy went down the street running after him trying to get him to come back."

The couple had little time to celebrate (they would later honeymoon in San Francisco) as Pete headed back to the road—and back to an increasingly troublesome relationship with his coach.

Van Breda Kolff was pulling Pete out of games in order to rest him. Pete preferred to play more minutes but stayed quiet, hoping to avoid a repeat of his rocky relationship with Cotton Fitzsimmons. But it was blatantly clear that there was a growing disconnect between van Breda Kolff's basketball philosophy and Maravich's. "It wasn't just about minutes. Butch was an eastern coach—cutting, moving without the ball, hit the open man type," explained Bertka. "Pete would dominate the ball and create off the dribble. Running, wide-open, fast-break basketball—that was his game."

Although Maravich was a superstar in New Orleans, few fans knew him well. After games he would graciously sign autographs but he was generally wary of strangers and their motives. His guard was constantly up and he suspected most people were friendly only out of a desire to exploit him. Just a few teammates, family, and close friends were privy to the wise-cracking, happy-go-lucky side of his personality.

Van Breda Kolff, on the other hand, was a garrulous, back-slapping barfly who plunged gleefully into the New Orleans lifestyle. He was a postgame fixture at local watering holes, like Pat O'Brien's, where he enjoyed hoisting cold beers with friendly strangers. His outgoing personality made him extremely popular around town and his colorful sideline theatrics helped draw fans into the Dome.

The veteran coach loved to jaw with the referees and was proud of his league-leading status in ejections. One night in the Dome, Pistons center Bob Lanier got into an altercation with Jazz center Rich Kelley and slapped him across the face. Van Breda Kolff raced onto the court and squared up against the 6-11, 265-pound Lanier. The crowd ate it up.

Despite friction with the coach, Maravich was playing some of the best ball of his career. Many were starting to notice, but not in time for the All-Star Game.

"Pete Maravich not being selected for the NBA All-Star team typifies why the whole thing is a joke," said Cleveland coach Bill Fitch after the Jazz edged his Cavaliers, 96-95, on February 1. "You saw it tonight. We talked about what he's [Pete's] going to do in the timeout. And yet he still did it." Pete, saddled with five fouls, made four consecutive layups in the final two minutes.

"I've played in the All-Star Game so it's no big thing," said Pete. "It's like traveling around the world or seeing *Deep Throat*—once you've done it, why do it again? The All-Star Game is political, just like the Olympics, when I was on the plane for the tryouts and I was told I wouldn't make the team."

The Jazz's hot play continued after the All-Star break with an impressive win at Houston. Led by Pete's 35 points (15-24, 5-9, 6 rebounds, 6 assists), the Jazz overcame a 21-point deficit to beat the Rockets.

The team's winning streak reached five games with a home victory over the Kansas City Kings. Pete scored 31 points (14-24, 3-5, 3 rebounds, 9 assists). "How Pete didn't make the All-Star Game is beyond me," said Kings coach Phil Johnson. "Maravich is playing super basketball and he is the reason New Orleans wins."

Over the five-game win streak (Knicks, Hawks, Cavaliers, Rockets, and Kings), Pete averaged 33.4 points while shooting over 57 percent from the floor. The team was 24-24 but trouble between Pete and van Breda Kolff continued to brew.

The coach continued to rest his star player during games. "I don't feel 40 minutes would hurt me," Pete explained. "I've always been the type of player who loses his rhythm sitting on the bench." It was becoming a battle of wills and van Breda Kolff was notoriously stubborn. In Los Angeles, he famously refused to put Wilt Chamberlain back into Game 7 of the 1969 NBA finals.

The Jazz ended their win streak with a loss to the Bulls before heading west on a four-game swing.

First up was a matchup with the defending NBA champion Golden State Warriors, who were 24-3 at home. Some 11,000 fans in the Oakland Coliseum were treated to a high-scoring thriller that stretched into overtime. In the extra period Maravich scored the final five points as the Jazz notched an impressive road win, 130-124. Pete finished with a season-high 49 points (18-36, 13-18, 3 rebounds, 4 assists, 3 steals), and E. C. Coleman put on a defensive clinic, limiting the Warriors high-scoring Rick Barry to 18 points on 5 of 23 shooting.

Maravich was leading the Jazz to a respectable record but he rejected the notion that he had changed as a player. "I am no better than I have ever been. If you are on a winner, then they say you are great. If you are on a loser, they accuse you of not being a team player." The Golden State win was New Orleans' 13th road victory of the season compared to just three the previous year.

"As an opposing coach, we just couldn't do very much to stop him," Warriors coach Al Attles later explained. "Pete was an innovator. He did things with the basketball that nobody had done before."

But van Breda Kolff was displeased with Pete's performance against the Warriors. Maravich, he felt, was not playing within the offense. So the following evening, in Seattle, Pete was benched for much of the game. Less than 24 hours after scoring nearly 50 points in a road win over the defending NBA champs, Pete played 18 minutes and took a mere three shots against the Sonics. The Jazz lost 93-90.

For Pete, this confirmed his suspicions about van Breda Kolff. The stubborn coach was punishing Pete for playing his "style" of basketball. It was a battle of egos and neither player nor coach appeared willing to back down.

In New Orleans, the newspapers were buzzing about the Maravich/van Breda Kolff feud. One headline blared: "Is Pete Mad at Butch? Butch Mad at Pete?"

Van Breda Kolff's battles were not limited to sparring with Maravich. He also had his differences with front-office executive, Barry Mendelson. The feisty coach didn't respect Mendelson. He thought the myriad promotions—Gym Bag Night, Poster Night, Frisbee Night, Tote Night—were silly and distracted fans from the action on the court. Several sponsors (Shoe Town, Rolex, a Ford dealership) were featured during the games and the shilling infuriated van Breda Kolff.

Nothing angered him more than a Burger King promotion. If the Jazz scored 110 points at home, ticket stubs could be redeemed for a free order of fries. Van Breda Kolff was disgusted every time he heard thousands of fans screaming, "Free Fries. Free Fries. Free Fries."

On February 25, against the Washington Bullets at the Superdome, Pete reached a milestone. With 2:06 remaining in the second quarter, he drove past Dave Bing and dropped in a layup, giving him 10,000 career points. The game was stopped and approximately 9,000 fans applauded for two minutes while Pete was presented with the game ball. He went on to score 39 points (17-32, 5-7, 8 rebounds, 6 assists) in a 105-104 Jazz win.

"I really wasn't concerned about scoring 10,000," he told reporter Bill Rainey afterward. "This is a business. You can take all the personal records and ship them to the moon. I'd much rather have my name associated with the title world champion and have that ring on my finger. Then I'd have something to talk about when I retire. No one listens to a loser."

"I've enjoyed winning before, but not since I've been in the pros," he explained to Mark Engel in *Basketball Weekly*. "Any player would rather be on a winner than a loser. It's obvious, but it can't be that way for everybody." Pete liked to use the example of Steve Bracey, a backup guard who was Maravich's teammate for two seasons in Atlanta. Both were traded in 1974. "I went to New Orleans and he went to Golden State. He got a world championship ring the next year. Some of us are fortunate, some are not."

As the season lurched to a conclusion, Maravich played his heart out, trying to elevate the Jazz into the playoffs, but the hill was too high. With the weight of the franchise on his shoulders, he took each loss personally, and as the team's playoff chances faded, his mood darkened.

There were still occasional highlights. One night in March he promised the first Jazz win over the (eventual NBA champion) Celtics and delivered. Pete recorded a triple-double: 39 points, 11 rebounds, and 10 assists. He shot 54 percent from the floor (13-24, 11-11) as New Orleans crushed Boston, 117-99, in a game played in Hartford. The win was particularly sweet for Pete because Tommy Heinsohn, the Celtics coach, had excluded Pete from the All-Star roster that year, instead picking Boston's Jo Jo White.

After the game, van Breda Kolff commented, "Pete played a [great] game but he couldn't do it by himself. And he knows that."

The Jazz ended the season with a record of 38-44, still the third best mark ever for a second-year NBA expansion team. "I was very proud of that," said team GM Bill Bertka in 2006. During the season, New Orleans lost three key players—Ron Behagen, Coleman, and Maravich—to injuries for a combined 49 games. The team was 6-14 without Maravich and 32-30 with him in the lineup, and undefeated in games where Maravich tallied 40 points or more.

When the postseason honors were announced, Maravich was selected, along with Rick Barry, Kareem Abdul-Jabbar, Nate Archibald, and George McGinnis, for the All-NBA first team. The five players received a $500 bonus from the league while members of the second team pocketed $250.

The Jazz franchise had rebounded nicely from a near disastrous first season. Financial stability remained a distant goal, but with a unique arena in the Dome and a star attraction in Pistol Pete, a solid foundation had been laid. New Orleans was a significant draw on the road, but curiously, none of its games had been televised nationally by CBS.

Maravich's second year in New Orleans was undoubtedly his most productive to that point in his pro career. Playing with an improved attitude, a new number, and without his trademark socks, the Pistol shot a career-high .459 from the floor and was, once again, the NBA's highest scoring guard at 25.9 points per game.

As the bicentennial summer of 1976 approached, Pete looked forward to several months of wedded bliss with Jackie. Little did he know that the coming season would provide even greater exhibitions of his basketball wizardry, and his most legendary night on the hardwood.

18

Scoring
Champion

"Robertson was the best guard I ever played against. Jerry West was the best I ever played with. And Pete is the best I've ever seen."

—ELGIN BAYLOR, JAZZ COACH

"We tried everything we could do to stop him. His performance was the best by a guard I've ever seen."

—RED HOLZMAN, N.Y. KNICKS COACH ON PETE'S 68-POINT GAME

In the spring of 1976, after nine colorful seasons and an estimated $50 million in losses, the American Basketball Association folded. Only six franchises were operating at the end, and four of those—the New York Nets, the San Antonio Spurs, the Indiana Pacers, and the Denver Nuggets—paid $3.2 million each to join the NBA. The two remaining franchises were paid off by the other four: Kentucky with straight cash and St. Louis with a combination of cash and a percentage of future television revenue.

The NBA owners also ushered in an era of modified free agency when they settled the six-year-old "Oscar Robertson Suit." Unfortunately for the Jazz, that meant relinquishing their draft rights to St. Louis Spirits' center, Moses Malone.

Although Maravich never played in the ABA, the upstart league had a profound influence on his professional basketball experience. The Atlanta Hawks were able to draft Pete only because Zelmo Beaty decided to jump leagues. A spirited interleague bidding war resulted in Maravich's historic contract. And Joe Caldwell's departure from the Hawks to the ABA had major repercussions. All these events combined to make Pete's early NBA years difficult to navigate—yet extremely lucrative.

Some people believed Pete's flashy style of play would have been better suited for the ABA, with its three-point shot and its vibrant multi-colored ball. Pete, however, had no regrets about signing with the Hawks instead of the Cougars. "All I'd have [in Carolina] is a string of Hardee's hamburger franchises," he quipped.

According to Denver's David Thompson, the incoming ABA players were anxious to make an impression in their new league. "Every single ABA alumnus played with one thought in mind that season," Thompson said. "To show they belonged in the NBA and that the ABA had not been a refuge for the lame, the halt, and the blind."

The NBA also appropriated the defunct league's dunking contest, spreading the competition over the season. The Nuggets' Darnell Hillman eventually copped the NBA's inaugural Slam-Dunk crown.

Maravich was in the third and final year of his 1974 Jazz contract and, although the Jazz were improving, they were not yet an elite team. "I want to play on a championship team just once. Can you imagine me on the Celtics or the Lakers?" Pete asked *SPORT* magazine's Robert Ward. "But I love New Orleans. My roots are here and my friends. I love the food in this city and the style of living . . . the only way I'd leave the Jazz is if I didn't think there was any chance we could really improve."

Pete was still desperate to play for a winner, convinced that a championship ring would negate all the criticism he had endured through the years.

Pete entered the new season in prime shape, having worked out (along with teammates Rich Kelley and Bud Stallworth) with the New Orleans Saints strength and conditioning coach, Alvin Roy. "He took to weightlifting like he took to dribbling," Roy told Mackey Shilstone of *Gridweek* magazine. "The little devil worked really hard. He would spend two hours a day, four days a week, weightlifting and running cross-country. Pete's doing what Bob (Pettit) did years ago. If you work out properly, you'll get strong and not hinder your shot." Many local residents recall Pete and Jim Taylor running along the levees of Lake Pontchartrain in the hot summer mornings.

The third Jazz season saw a major change in the front office. A power struggle of sorts had developed between Barry Mendelson and Bill Bertka, and when the dust settled, Mendelson, the promotions expert, was now running the team. He was given the title of executive vice president and was charged with overseeing the day-to-day operations. Bertka, who ironically hired Mendelson in 1974, was shifted to director of scouting and director of player personnel.

"Needless to say, the first two years of commuting back and forth between my home in California and New Orleans wasn't the easiest thing in the world," Bertka told the *Times-Picayune*. "From a management standpoint, it's very difficult to be a GM if you're not in the office every day."

The ambitious 33-year-old Mendelson lived full time in Louisiana and was promoted partly because of his enormous success in bolstering ticket sales. The Jazz finished fifth in attendance in 1975-76 as attendance more than doubled to 513,282, an increase of 7,680 spectators per game. The gate set a record for a second-year expansion team. The ascension of Mendelson was not welcome news for van Breda Kolff, who openly ridiculed the team's huckstering. "Just look at our office. Everything here is geared toward sales promotions," van Breda Kolff complained to the *Times-Picayune*. ". . . we're a basketball team. If we win, people will come. If we don't, they won't. How many people do you think really come to get a free bag?"

Mendelson made an immediate splash when he signed the NBA's first free agent, the Lakers' five-time All-Star guard Gail Goodrich. Although the Jazz needed help on the front line, everyone seemed to agree that the savvy, steady-shooting, 6-1 Goodrich would be a worthwhile addition to the Jazz backcourt. He certainly had an excellent résumé, leading his team in scoring during championship seasons at both UCLA and the Lakers.

The 33-year-old Goodrich signed a $400,000, no-cut, two-year contract and was excited to be playing in New Orleans with Maravich. "Some people are saying we'll need two basketballs, but I don't think so," Goodrich explained. "Pete and I are going to score a lot of points. Basketball is still a five-man game. Always was and always will be."

Pete was equally confident he could play harmoniously with Goodrich. "I don't care if it's Godzilla, I can complement anybody on the court," Pete told *Sports Illustrated*'s Jerry Kirshenbaum. "With an intelligent, experienced player like Gail, there's no problem at all. He's a great shooter and I'm going to get the ball to him. He's also going to make me better."

One unresolved issue of the Goodrich transaction was the compensation the Jazz would provide to the Lakers. "Compensation" was an added wrinkle for NBA owners and players in the new free-agent era. Because Goodrich was *signed* and not *traded*, the Lakers were minus a player and New Orleans was required to reimburse Los Angeles with an equivalent player, draft pick, or cash to make the Lakers "whole" again. The compensation the Lakers eventually received from New Orleans would have historic implications for both franchises.

Goodrich reported to camp early and got off to a shaky start. Ron Brocato of the *States-Item* reported that, "Goodrich's tendon was aggravated" while participating in a rookie workout at the Jewish Community Center. It was an injury he had developed eight months earlier. He sat out the first two preseason games.

Mendelson then signed another free agent, Portland's power forward, Sidney Wicks. "Gail and Sidney are both All-Stars and they can help our club," said Pete when he heard about the acquisition. But the deal unraveled despite a handshake agreement between the parties.

Ultimately the league ruled in Wicks' favor (he eventually signed with the Celtics) and the decision reinforced Maravich's paranoia about the NBA office in New York. "They don't particularly care about balance," Pete fumed to Robert Ward in *SPORT* magazine. "Just the TV markets. Everyone says we got Sidney Wicks but I don't see him here . . . the reason all those teams like Chicago, New York, and Boston get the good players is because they are in the major TV markets."

Pete went into his third year in New Orleans frustrated with the front office's inability to obtain a power forward but happy that his father, Press, and sister, Diana, were back in town from Sweden. Pete arranged a scouting job for his dad with the Jazz. Press and Diana were now seen at most home games, sitting at the end of the court near the Jazz bench—a few rows up so "Papa Press" could see patterns develop and, on occasion, send over "special situation" plays to the coaches.

It must have made the old basketball coach proud to see his family name adorning the back of his son's jersey. The league banned nicknames on uniforms so "Pistol" was replaced by "Maravich."

The Jazz opened the 1976-77 season with a 111-98 home win over the Suns. Next up, the league's hottest road show: Julius Erving and the Philadelphia 76ers. Following his short stint with the Hawks in the 1972 preseason, Dr. J had blossomed into the ABA's biggest star and NBA fans were eager to see his legendary sky-scraping exploits. A record 27,383 patrons streamed into the Superdome on October 26 to catch Erving and his talented supporting cast (George McGinnis, Doug Collins, World B. Free, Joe Bryant, and Darryl Dawkins). Before the contest, *States-Item* reporter Ron Brocato asked the Jazz players how they would defend Dr. J if he went up for a dunk.

"After he's in the air, there's really not much you can do except watch," replied defensive specialist E. C. Coleman. "I've asked other players what he likes to do. They tell me he does everything. Man, I don't know what I'm going to do with a guy who can do everything."

Pete just smiled and said, "I'd get in my Porsche and drive home. The way I look at it is, whether he hits the 40-foot jumper, a layup, or a stuff, it's only two points. So why try to commit suicide?"

Although Philadelphia won the game, it was McGinnis who led the way, scoring 37 points, while Erving was held to 10 by Coleman. Pete chipped in 28 points (10-27, 8-9, 2 rebounds, 3 assists) and Goodrich, still hobbled by a tender Achilles, added 16.

The Jazz rebounded three nights later with a 111-93 win over the Washington Bullets. Pete had a respectable night with 25 points. "I know I missed a lot of shots tonight [8-27]. But in a week or two, those shots are going to fall and I'm going to have a 70-point game," Pete predicted in the locker room.

The following evening Pete netted 39 (17-36, 5-7, 5 rebounds, 10 assists) in a 115-112 win over the Knicks in New York. It was the first Jazz victory at Madison Square Garden. Pete always got "turned on" playing in New York, competing against Walt "Clyde" Frazier. "Clyde is one of the great guards in the game and it's a challenge to cover him one-on-one. If I have a good night, hold him down while I'm playing a good game myself . . . It gives me an awful lot of satisfaction," Pete told Nat Belloni.

Spike Lee, the influential director and rabid hoops fan who had attended Knicks games since the early 1970s, recalled Pete's exploits on the Garden floor. "Nobody could stop him. Pete could make you look bad," wrote Lee in his 1998 basketball memoir, *The Best Seat in the House*. "Pete used to kill Clyde, lay waste to him. Nothing predictable for Clyde to pick up and exploit on defense. Pete never had to use the same move twice."

Frazier shared Spike's insight, "He dribbles the ball so well. If you think you can steal it from him, that's just when he'll go right by you."

After a loss in Cleveland, the Jazz hosted the defending world champion Boston Celtics (4-0) at the Superdome. It was a hard-fought contest and van Breda Kolff (who split his pants much to crowd's delight) was ejected in the third quarter after receiving his second technical. Assistant coach Elgin Baylor took over and implemented a simple strategy: let Maravich fire away. Pete was happy to oblige and ended the night with 43 points (17-40, 9-11, 10 rebounds, 5 assists) in a surprising 115-97 victory. His stellar performance included a 65-foot, behind-the-back pass to Paul Griffin, who slammed it home. "It was a thrill to be out there," said the giddy rookie afterward.

New Orleans was off to a 4-2 start and Maravich believed he had found a formula for staying healthy: He eliminated red meat from his diet, cut out sugars and salts, and ate only fresh fruit, vegetables, fish, and chicken. For a man who once loved steaks, burgers, pancakes, and French fries, this was a dramatic turnaround. This adjustment sparked an interest in nutrition and vitamins that would continue for the remainder of his life.

Maravich initially kept his diet secret from the media, remembering how NBA players like Bill Walton and former teammate Neal Walk were ridiculed for their vegetarianism.

Through the first seven outings, Goodrich, still suffering from his tendon injury, averaged just 24 minutes per game. A deal to bring high-scoring forward Bob McAdoo to the Jazz fell through and the former league MVP signed with the Knicks. The near miss left Pete feeling dispirited.

"Put any guard on a team with big studs who can get the rebounds and score on the inside and that guard can play for 20 years. He doesn't have to work as hard for his shots," Pete explained. "And he's going to get better shots because the defense is sloughing back on the big men."

Even though the team was 10-7, Pete found himself struggling to stay motivated and even contemplated taking a midseason break. Boston's Dave Cowens had the same idea and temporarily walked away from the Celtics. "Cowens did what I've been thinking about doing for some time now. It's funny in a way because Dave beat me to the punch. Now I can't do what he did," Pete told the *Times-Picayune*. "Also, the difference is Dave has been a winner. He's got a world championship."

Van Breda Kolff, though, had no sympathy for Pete's psychological struggle. "I don't know what's wrong with him," the coach snapped. "He gets something in his head and he won't play. . . . If you're paid a ton, you ought to play a ton."

In a 121-105 win against the Hawks on December 3, van Breda Kolff benched Maravich in the fourth quarter. Maravich had been lighting up the Hawks, and the unhappy crowd greeted the coach's decision with a hearty round of boos. "We have to think about tomorrow night and Sunday and not just think about his [Maravich's] point scoring," explained van Breda Kolff.

In the next game, at Chicago, Pete played 36 minutes and scored 34 points in a 107-99 loss. Motivation problems aside, he still bristled and pouted when benched for long stretches. Van Breda Kolff must have found it telling that Pete was sporting a gold pendant that read: "Me First." The chasm between coach and player widened.

Maravich further enraged van Breda Kolff after a loss in San Antonio on December 11. Following the game, Maravich and Paul Griffin spent the night bar hopping and stumbled into the hotel lobby at 6:15 A.M., just as the team was checking out. On the bus to the airport, Maravich maintained a steady stream of loud chatter. "Just shut up, I don't want to hear another word," blared van Breda Kolff. At the airport coffee shop, Maravich offered to buy breakfast for everyone in the restaurant. There were close to 100 diners and the bill came to about $400, recalled center Rich Kelley.

The next day, the tension between van Breda Kolff and Mendelson, which had been heightening all season, reached a peak. Andy Walker, New Orleans seventh-round draft pick, was placed on waivers at Mendelson's request and without the coach's knowledge. According to the *Times-Picayune*'s Marty Mule, when van Breda Kolff heard the news he screamed, "Then . . . let him coach them."

It would be his last tirade as the Jazz coach. He was fired the next day, replaced by Elgin Baylor on an interim basis. New Orleans was 14-12 at the time.

"Basic philosophical differences," explained Larry G. Hatfield of the Jazz's executive committee to reporter Will Peneguy. "We were unable to feel comfortable with Butch's view of the head coaching job."

Jazz announcer Rod Hundley believed van Breda Kolff did not fit the profile of a typical NBA coach. "Butch was a big drinker, so I don't know if he had the respect of the players," Hundley said. "This was a drinking and partying town and Butch was right there with the best of them every night. He was a showman just like Pete. Butch had a lot of fans in New Orleans."

The fans were irate when the news broke. Signs lined the Superdome reading "Bring Butch Back." Mendelson was jeered whenever he was spotted at games. "First Bill Bertka, one of the best minds and judges of talent, was gone. Then we lost Sidney Wicks and Bob McAdoo. Now Butch. There's one person responsible," said Jazz season-ticket holder Mark Schneider.

Maravich's reaction to the firing was curt and flippant. "The last time I was surprised is when I found out that ice cream cones were hollow."

"It's like having your best friend die," Elgin Baylor told Ron Brocato of the *States-Item*. "Butch and I were very close. It's hard for me to think about taking his place."

Jazz management hoped Baylor's All-Star pedigree would enable him to relate to Maravich. In Baylor's first game he gave Pete free rein, playing him for 47 minutes (Pete averaged 38 minutes under van Breda Kolff). Pete took full advantage and pumped in a career-high 51 points (18-38, 15-18, 7 rebounds, 6 assists) in a narrow 120-117 victory over Kansas City. Despite the win, chants of "We want Butch" echoed through the arena.

After two games, Baylor was hired for the remainder of the season and all of 1977-78. Bertka was promoted to assistant coach.

The day after Christmas, Maravich dropped 50 points (23-39, 4-5, 3 rebounds, 5 assists) on the Washington Bullets, spearheading a 109-100 comeback victory. The Bullets were out gunned despite boasting three future Hall of Famers in Elvin Hayes, Wes Unseld, and Dave Bing. "I couldn't believe Pete tonight. I had two men on him and it didn't do much good," said Bullets coach Dick Motta.

Bullets guard Phil Chenier echoed his coach. "There are just so many things he can do offensively that it's almost impossible to stop him," Chenier told David DuPree of the *Washington Post.* "We were hoping he'd get tired."

Maravich played all 48 minutes and showed no signs of fatigue. "I actually get stronger in the second, third and fourth quarters," Pete told the *Post.* He scored four points in the first quarter, 16 in the second, 15 in the third, and 15 in the fourth. One shot, in particular, electrified the crowd. Maravich stole a pass from rookie Mitch Kupchak, drove past Chenier, and threw up a wild no-look, left-handed spin shot. The ball kissed the glass and fell through as Maravich tumbled off the court and slammed into the support bracket. The crowd of 17,613 stood and cheered for 30 seconds.

"The only reason I didn't give him a standing ovation after some of his moves was because I wasn't a spectator," marveled Chenier.

Chenier believed that Maravich and David Thompson were the best guards in the NBA. "The thing I admire about Pete is that he gets the job done every night. He can get a shot any time he wants to," Chenier told the *Post.* "Just like Oscar Robertson could or Jerry West or Earl Monroe. The great ones are like that. They can not only shoot, but can handle the ball and get it to other people. They make the others play better."

Maravich was tearing through opponents. Against Atlanta he collected 38 points (14-34, 10-11, 6 rebounds, 7 assists) in a 93-88 win. "We don't have to apologize for Pete getting 38 points tonight," Hawks coach Hubie Brown told the *Times-Picayune.* "Be happy he didn't get 40."

Off court, the news was less sunny. Goodrich's tendon injury had worsened and would require season-ending surgery. Goodrich was looking like damaged goods, while the three who signed elsewhere—Sidney Wicks, Moses Malone, and Bob McAdoo—were all making substantial contributions to their new teams.

In a February 6 game against Houston, Pete scored 43 points (17-33, 9-10, 6 rebounds, 5 assists) and Coleman provided a defensive masterpiece, holding the Rockets top scorer, Rudy Tomjanovich, to a single point. The Jazz chalked up another victory, 99-90. After the game Houston coach Tom

Nissalke raved about Maravich. "Anything that Pete does, does not surprise me. He is, by far, the best guard in the NBA."

Pete wrote about that Houston victory in his autobiography 10 years later:

> *Between the demands I placed on myself and the external demands placed on me to perform every night, the pressure was unbelievable. One game against the Houston Rockets I went into the locker room with 35 points at the half and I thought of quitting the game. From the age of 7 I had thought that basketball could do it all for me. But with the pressure to produce eating away at me, I questioned why I was even playing the game.*

Maravich was leading the league in scoring, and players, coaches, writers, and fans recognized his singular talents. When the All-Star Game was played in midseason, Pete made his third appearance and his third start. His 235,544 votes were far and away the most for any guard in the NBA.

Pete had a few creative ideas about how to improve the All-Star contest. He suggested it would be wise to stop awarding an MVP. "That might eliminate all of the 'It's my turn shooting,'" Pete explained to Jim O'Brien of *The Sporting News*. "In the past, they've given cars for the most valuable player . . . some guys couldn't shoot the ball fast enough."

Another, more radical, idea was to have the 10 best players in the NBA go at it the entire game—without substitutions. Five-on-five, just like the playground. "All out for 48 minutes! Now there's something I can get my head into. Under those conditions, you'd see the greatest game," Pete exclaimed.

The 1977 game was, in many respects, the first modern All-Star Game. In addition to featuring NBA and ABA stars, the contest was moved from Tuesday night to Sunday afternoon, a prime slot for television sports. The NBA was setting attendance records and CBS was itching to ride the league's growing popularity. The Sunday broadcast was the beginning of what morphed into "All-Star Weekend."

The game was loaded with former ABA players, including five of the 10 starters. It was a thrilling cross pollination of talent and styles. Basketball fans could finally see the likes of Julius Erving, George Gervin, and David Thompson competing against John Havlicek, Walt Frazier, and Elvin Hayes.

The *Washington Post's* David DuPree recalled the excitement of seeing Pistol Pete in action. "I remember sitting in my seat just waiting for Maravich to do something spectacular and I remember the goose bumps I got when I saw it coming. He was dribbling down on the break with Erving on his right and, in the middle of his dribble, he deliberately missed the ball with his right hand, looked to the left, and then swatted the ball with his left hand to Erving for a dunk."

Although Pete shot poorly (5-13) in the West's 125-124 victory, he chipped in four spectacular assists. Besides the slap pass, he also hit Dr. J with a between-the-legs pass and an over-the-shoulder variety that resulted in easy layups. Pete also frustrated Bob Lanier with one of his patented "pro layups," sailing the ball just over the big man's fingertips to the highest part of the backboard where it banked off the glass and dropped into the basket.

However, the game ended with Maravich wearing the "goat" tag. Down by a point with 16 seconds remaining, the East coaches designed a pick-and-roll play for Maravich and Bob McAdoo. As Pete dribbled toward McAdoo, Paul Westphal, playing in his first All-Star Game, stripped the ball and cleared it down court, securing the West victory.

"I felt I could slap it away. I was very fortunate to get a piece of it," said Westphal afterward.

McAdoo was certain Maravich had been fouled. "You could hear the contact," the big man said.

"I probably got a little of his arm," admitted Westphal in a 2003 interview. "But I give Pete credit. He didn't whine about it. They asked him if I fouled him. And he just said, 'No.'"

But the biggest Jazz-related news that Sunday was not Pete's missed opportunity or Elgin Baylor's acceptance into the Basketball Hall of Fame. It was an explosive story by local reporter Brocato concerning the deal that brought Goodrich to the Jazz. Brocato had learned that the "compensation" for Goodrich was much more than expected. He reported that the Lakers would receive New Orleans' first draft pick in both 1977 and 1979, and also had the option of swapping first-round picks in 1978 if it was to the Lakers' advantage. And, Brocato's story alleged, Mendelson misled the Jazz over the details of the compensation.

The Goodrich deal now appeared to be a major disaster. The team had exchanged two first-round draft picks for a gimpy 33-year-old guard on the down side of his career. Milwaukee coach Don Nelson simply stated, "It would not have been a good deal even if Gail was in his prime."

Because of an ongoing litigation between the players union and the league, Mendelson was under strict orders from David Stern, then the NBA's attorney, not to discuss any details of the deal. "The conversation was that they should not discuss it. Period," said Stern. "Things in dispute are better off not tried or litigated in the newspapers." It was the beginning of the end for Mendelson.

"It wasn't the deal, it was the compensation," Mendelson later acknowledged. Although Jazz president, Sam Battistone, signed off on the agreement, Mendelson was dismissed at the end of the season.

Twelve days after the All-Star break, with the Goodrich controversy still simmering, the Jazz readied for a home game against the New York Knicks. Seven years earlier, on January 10, 1970, Pete had sat in the LSU locker room, dejected after a close loss to Auburn. He felt his poor shooting (18-46) had cost the Tigers a victory. Head in hands, Maravich shared a recurring dream with several national sports reporters in town for the Super Bowl. "One of these nights, everything is going to go in. If I take 40 or 45 shots, I'm going to hit 40. I just know it is coming."

On February 25, 1977, seven years and 50 days after his locker-room prediction, Pete's dream of near-perfect shooting was realized. His performance that night would add another chapter to the legend of Pistol Pete.

A crowd of 11,033 was in the Dome and many more were watching the Knicks' WOR-TV telecast. Pete was energized by crowds, even one 1,500 miles away. "The game was being sent back to New York on television. That meant more than a million people were watching. If there is one thing that really turns me on, it's playing in front of a lot of people. The more people who come to a game, or see it on the tube, the more intense about the game I get. It makes me play harder and, I hope, better," Pete explained.

On hand in the Superdome were Pete's attorneys, Les Zittrain and Arthur Herskovitz. They had traveled from Pittsburgh to begin contract negotiations with Mendelson. "We just want to give Pete a long-term contract to play out his career here in New Orleans," the embattled VP explained to reporters before the contest. Heading into the game Pete was leading the league in scoring with 28.9 points per game.

New York's starters were Walt Frazier, Earl Monroe, Bob McAdoo, Jim McMillian, and Tom McMillen. Baylor countered with Maravich, Bud Stallworth, Paul Griffin, Otto Moore, and Jim McElroy. As was often the case in his pro career, Pete's team was vastly over matched. The Knick lineup featured four future Hall of Famers in Monroe, McAdoo, Frazier, and Bill Bradley, while the Jazz had Maravich and a cast of journeymen. On paper, the game looked to be an easy win for New York. But Pete was one of those rare players who could dominate a game.

"When he had everything going, he could beat you by himself," explained future Hall of Fame coach Jack Ramsay. "You were never quite sure what he was going to do with the ball in the open court. He had a thousand moves to either shoot it or pass it."

As the players took the court, Knick color commentator Cal Ramsey observed that Frazier had drawn the unenviable assignment of covering Pete. Overhearing the comment as he walked past the scorer's table, Monroe laughed and said, "That's nice."

The Knicks were leading 4-0 when Pete started to heat up. He hit four of his first five shots along with three free throws as the Jazz built a 17-12 advantage. Knicks coach Red Holzman substituted Butch Beard for Frazier. On the very next possession, Maravich greeted Beard with a stutter fake, a quick dribble, and then drained a 20-foot jumper. "Tom McMillen came over to help Butch Beard out and they were both all over him and he still got that shot in," announcer Cal Ramsey marveled. "Boy, he is an offensive machine." Pete scored 13 of the Jazz's first 19 points.

Pete hit another long jumper and, later, drew a foul from Beard with a convincing ball fake. "Pistol Pete really played Butch like a fiddle that time," observed announcer Andy Muesser. Maravich sank both free throws and then Baylor removed him for the rest of the first quarter. He had 17 points, missing just two of his shots. But he also had two fouls.

Marty Mule of the *Times-Picayune* was watching from his regular seat on press row. "I was with Will Peneguy who was the assistant sports editor. And Wayne Mack, he was a television and radio sportscaster. We were sitting together, telling cynical jokes, laughing and so on and so forth. You know how press people are—they develop a cynical sense of humor." But Mule and his colleagues sensed something was different about this night. "For the first time that season, about midway through the first quarter, we all three fell silent."

Pete endured a brief cold streak in the second quarter, missing four consecutive shots, but he began to heat up again just as Frazier re-entered the game. Pete welcomed the Knicks guard by nailing a fade-away jumper from the key. "What move doesn't this guy have?" Muesser asked incredulously.

Nate Williams and Mo Howard hit outside jumpers for the Jazz and then, after an inbound steal, Pete fired in a 23-footer. Holzman called time-out and replaced Frazier again, this time with Dean Meminger, Pete's nemesis from the 1970 NIT tournament.

Pete did not miss a beat. He ran Meminger into a Williams screen and tossed in a 20-foot jumper. Several possessions later he arced in a 10-foot hook shot from the right baseline. Holzman had seen enough. Meminger was out and Beard returned. But Maravich, playing with three fouls, was unstoppable. He dribbled down court with Beard on his hip, stopped, and fired in a 15-foot jumper.

Maravich was also making big contributions on the defensive end of the court. He blocked a Beard jump shot from behind and thwarted a breakaway by McMillian, slapping his layup attempt against the backboard. The wheels were falling off for the Knicks and Holzman was unable to find an effective combination of players. He shuttled in Phil Jackson, Bill Bradley, "Ticky" Burden, and Lonnie Shelton. But nobody caught fire.

Over on press row, Mule and his crew sat in amazement. "We knew we were watching something extraordinary."

The Jazz led 65-43 at the half. Pete had 31 points (12-18, 7-7, 5 assists, 3 rebounds, 2 steals, 2 blocks).

The second half began with yet another Knick guard, this time Burden, assigned to Maravich. Burden quickly discovered that intermission had done nothing to cool off the Pistol. He opened the third quarter by nailing three consecutive 20-footers. The third one gave him nine baskets in his last nine attempts. The Knick announcers were awed by the offensive display.

Cal Ramsey: "I don't know how you stop him. He is too much."

Andy Muesser: "I am running out of things to say about Maravich."

After missing a couple shots, Maravich drove to the hoop and converted a left-handed lay-in, despite a hard push from McMillian. Pete sank the free throw to complete the three-point play and run his total to 40 points. It was the most points by a player against the Knicks that year, besting Pete's own 39-point game in October.

Then Pete, looking tired, clanked four shots in a row. Worse, he picked up his fourth foul attempting to rebound one of his missed shots. On the following inbound play he broke the full-court press, dribbled the length of the floor, and made another layup. "It's awfully tough to press a man with his dribbling ability," gushed Ramsey.

Pete's 47th and 48th points were set up by a between-the-leg dribble drive that froze Beard. After blowing by the Knick guard, Pete raced to the hoop and banked in a shot over the outstretched arms of Monroe and McAdoo. With 1:30 remaining in the third period, Pete sat down for a rest, just four points shy of his NBA career high of 51.

During Pete's visit to the bench, Holzman was assessed a technical foul for arguing a call against Jackson. Had Pete been in the game, he surely would have attempted the penalty shot that McElroy converted.

The final period began with Pete hitting one of his first two attempts.

Then, several possessions later, Pete began an electrifying shooting sequence. It began with Pete standing on the left side of the court about 23 feet from the hoop. He held the Wilson basketball in his right hand—not by his side, but out in front of his body, palming it like a grapefruit. Quick as a flash he took two dribbles, floated up, and stroked a jump shot that flashed through the net. The basket gave Maravich 52 points, a career high. There were still nine minutes left.

Seconds later Pete returned to almost the same exact spot and swished another 22-footer over Beard. Holzman brought in Frazier but he was helpless as Maravich dropped in yet another jump shot from his new favorite spot. When he returned a fourth time, Frazier had had enough. He fouled Maravich hard. Pete walked to the line and drained points 57 and 58. Holzman called a timeout with 6:59 remaining.

Mule remembered Maravich's confusion in the ensuing Jazz huddle. "When he came to the sidelines on a timeout E. C. Coleman came out with a towel for Pete. And all of the guys on the team were congratulating him and Pete had this real perplexed look on his face."

Pete remembered listening in disbelief to his teammates, "I honestly didn't know I had that many points until E. C. Coleman told me during a timeout that I needed only three more points. I thought he meant my personal scoring high of 51."

Coleman was referring to Jerry West's NBA record for points in a game by a guard. West had knocked down 63 (22-36, 19-22) in an overtime win against the Knicks on January 17, 1962, in front of just 2,766 fans at the Los Angeles Sports Arena. "My big game was played virtually in private," West would later write.

As play resumed Maravich needed five points to tie the record. He dribbled slowly over half court holding his index finger in the air, indicating a high-post play. He lobbed the ball in to Griffin and cut around him. Pete caught Griffin's bounce pass in full stride and twisted in a reverse layup for his 60th point.

Jazz announcer Bob Longmire bellowed "Pistolllllll Pete" over the Superdome sound system as the crowd roared.

The celebration came to an abrupt halt 50 seconds later when Maravich was accidentally tripped from behind by Burden. Pete crumpled to the floor and skidded to a stop. Jazz trainer Don Sparks raced onto the court and ministered to Pete's ankle as Andy Muesser asked: "Wouldn't it be something if this fine player got hurt in a game when he came up with a performance like this?"

Fortunately, Maravich's flexible ankles proved sufficiently pliable and, after rising slowly, he meandered to the free-throw line and converted his 61st point.

On his next trip down the court, Pete saw an open lane to the basket. He drove hard and spun in a bank shot just as McMillen slid down to front him. Incredibly, second-year referee Dick Bavetta called a foul—on Pete. This not only saddled Maravich with his fifth infraction (one more meant automatic ejection) but the basket was waved off, as well as a trip to the free-throw line.

Pete's next attempt was a shot more suited to a game of HORSE. He received an inbounds pass from Aaron James about five feet from the basket. With his back to the backboard, and Meminger guarding him tightly, Pete jumped and flipped up a no-look, over-the-shoulder shot. The ball careened off the backboard and spun into the net as he and Meminger crashed to the floor. "Look at that move! What a basket! He put the right spin on that ball," blurted a startled Muesser.

The circus shot gave Maravich 63 points, tying him with Jerry West. He passed his boyhood idol with his next attempt, draining a jumper and causing teammates Coleman and Howard to leap with joy. Seconds later Meminger fouled Pete away from the ball and Pete swished the free throw, upping his total to 66. With the crowd on its feet chanting, "Pete, Pete, Pete, Pete," Aaron James and Ron Behagen scored the next four points for New Orleans.

With 1:58 to play Maravich came up with another steal and took the ball to the hoop for an easy layup. The count was 68. The Knicks inbounded the ball and, with the frenzied crowd on its feet, Maravich slapped the ball away, chased it down, dribbled between his legs, and flipped a left-handed pass to Behagen. It looked like an easy two points but the surprised Behagen traveled before he could get to the hoop.

With 1:18 remaining in the game Pete drove to the basket and was called for an offensive foul when he collided with McMillen. It was his sixth foul and he was out of the game with 68 points. As a result, Pete holds the distinction of scoring the most points in an NBA game while also fouling out.

Many people still believe that Pete scored all of his 68 points against the defensive wizard, Frazier. Not true. Although the game started with Frazier guarding Maravich, Holzman shuttled his star guard in and out of the game frequently. "Clyde" only played 18 minutes that night. Monroe, Beard, Burden, Meminger, and Frazier all had taken turns guarding Maravich. None were able to stop him. In the end, only the referees were able to put the clamps on Pistol Pete.

Final score: Jazz 124, Knicks 107.

Frazier was so upset after the game he refused to talk to the media. Monroe just shook his head: "There was no way we could stop him."

McAdoo added: "The man beat us by himself."

Coach Baylor was amazed: "I mean, what can you say about a performance like that? Not only did Pete score all those points but he also did a great defensive job on Walt Frazier, holding him to just six points. We played here as a team."

Pete's lawyer Les Zittrain would never forget that game. "Pete really laid it on the Knicks that night. And, of course, that didn't hurt our negotiations a bit."

It was later revealed that Pete almost didn't suit up that night. Jazz team doctor Charles Brown explained that, before the historic game, Pete was complaining of severe chest pains. "It turned out to be just muscle strain from lifting weights," said Brown. "Maybe Pete should worry like that before every game."

Afterward, Maravich downplayed his achievement. He deflected attention toward the team. "The shots just fell tonight. It's nice to have a game like that and win. Hey, a lot of times I did this in college and we didn't win," explained Pete whose top three scoring outbursts at LSU (69, 66, and 64 points) came in losing efforts. "We should have a shot at the playoffs if we keep playing like we did tonight." Maravich's final stat line read: 68 points (26-43, 16-19), 6 rebounds, 6 assists, 2 blocks, 3 steals.

Pete's demeanor throughout his record-breaking game was noteworthy. Playing with a quiet intensity, he never celebrated his exploits. After sinking shot after shot, he would simply lower his head and run back down the court. His modest affect stands in stark contrast to some of today's athletes who punctuate even modest achievements with dances, screams, chest punches, and "stare downs." Later he explained why he was hesitant to celebrate. "The accomplishment was too personal," Pete said in 1984. "I think if I had let myself enjoy it too much I would have been crucified."

Saturday's newspaper headlines trumpeted Pete's achievement: "Pete Pistol Whips Knicks," "Pistol Riddles Record Book," "Pistol Power," and "68 in Rout of Knicks." For Maravich the landmark game left him feeling troubled. In his autobiography, he wrote:

> The next day I wanted nothing more than to stay in bed and hope the world would somehow disappear. All I could think of was the expectations of the New Orleans fans, the club owners, the coach, the players, my dad, and worst of all, me. I figured the only way I could be accepted by the public would be to score 68 points again and again.

Almost 30 years later, Maravich's performance still stands as a remarkable achievement. At the time, only two players had scored more points in an NBA game, Wilt Chamberlain (on several occasions) and Elgin Baylor.

Since that February night in 1977, among guards, Pete's total has only been bested three times. Denver's David Thompson did it first when he notched 73 points on April 9, 1978. But the circumstances were quite different. Thompson was gunning for the scoring title in the last game of the regular season (he eventually lost to George Gervin) and his Nuggets teammates were feeding him the ball at every opportunity. Thompson converted an amazing 28 of his 38 shots but Denver still lost to the Pistons.

On March 12, 1990, Chicago's Michael Jordan lit up the Cleveland Cavaliers with 69 points (his career high) in an overtime victory. Unlike Thompson, Jordan was playing in a regular-season game with playoff implications. But Jordan benefited from the three-point rule, which wasn't in place for Pete's night in 1977, as well as from five minutes of overtime. At the end of regulation, Jordan had 61 points.

Phil Jackson was coaching the Bulls when Jordan torched the Cavaliers and it triggered his memories of the Superdome. "Remember, I saw Pete Maravich get 68 one time, and he was terrific. But Michael was equal to that tonight."

On January 22, 2006, Kobe Bryant topped them all, except Chamberlain, with a spectacular 81 points in a comeback win against the Toronto Raptors.

Pete's 68-point outburst was remarkable, but what occurred in Phoenix three weeks later was, in its own way, just as stunning. On March 18, following an afternoon shoot-around, five Jazz players hopped into a Checker cab. James McElroy and Nate Williams crammed into the front with the driver, Jesse Abbott. Bud Stallworth, Otto Moore, and Aaron James scrunched together in the back. The players were headed for a pregame meal at Mother's Soul Food Kitchen.

As Abbott made his way to the restaurant one, of the players felt he was driving too fast and asked him to slow down. According to James, Abbott turned to the back seat and bragged, ". . . I drove for 20 years in New York and never had an accident." By the time Abbott turned back, he had run a red light and slammed into a car.

All the players were rushed to the Good Samaritan Hospital where the doctors advised them to sit out that evening's game. They returned to the Caravan Hotel.

That left the Jazz with just seven players, one under the NBA minimum.

A forfeit was avoided when Baylor received a special waiver from the commissioner. The 10,285 fans in the Veterans Memorial Coliseum were buzzing in anticipation of what they imagined would be a comically lopsided game. Suns trainer Joe Proski recalled the atmosphere. "We had 12 men against seven. The feeling was, 'We're going to kill these guys.'"

Maravich, Coleman, Behagen, Kelley, Griffin, and the recently acquired Mo Howard held a mini pep rally before the game. "We can save a horrendous season if we play and play hard," Pete told them.

Before the national anthem, the arena announcer asked for a moment of silence for the five injured players. Al McCoy, the longtime voice of the Suns, recalled, "The Suns at that time had a tough team: Paul Westphal, Ricky Sobers, Alvan Adams, Keith Erickson, and Dick Van Arsdale. The Suns felt they were going to have a very easy evening. They felt they could run the Jazz into the ground."

They were badly mistaken. Maravich carved up Phoenix with a stunning shooting exhibition, dropping long bombs from all angles, a display so impressive it caused large sections of the Phoenix crowd to openly root for him. "He was on fire and pretty much unstoppable," recalled Westphal years later.

When it was over Maravich had 51 points (21-34, 9-10, 6 rebounds, 1 assist) and the undermanned Jazz had eked out a remarkable comeback victory, 104-100. Pete set a Veterans Coliseum scoring mark, besting Abdul-Jabbar's 48.

Behagen, who contributed 15 points and nine rebounds, said afterward, "We all wanted to prove we could do it. I haven't seen a bench this empty since I played summer street ball." Center Rich Kelley dished out a career-high 12 assists.

"That was the most amazing game I have ever seen," said a giddy Baylor. "If I thought it would work every time, I'd take seven players everywhere."

But the elation turned somber when the team later learned that Stallworth's injuries were much worse than initially believed. "I had a herniated disk out of that accident," explained Stallworth, who had been a charter member of the Jazz. He never played another game in the NBA.

Next, the Jazz headed to Los Angeles to take on the Lakers. More than 14,000 fans at the Forum were treated to another entertaining effort by the under-staffed Jazz. Maravich smoked the nets with 46 points to keep New Orleans close, but the Lakers prevailed, 100-95. After the game, Oscar-winning actor and Lakers fan Jack Nicholson approached Maravich and said, "Past, present, or future, no one will be able to carry your jock." Pete quickly replied, "Jack, we needed the chief tonight," a reference to the burly Native American character in Nicholson's Academy-Award winning film *One Flew Over the Cuckoo's Nest.*

Jim Murray of the *Los Angeles Times* wrote a column that captured the despair of watching Maravich play for the Jazz. It was entitled: "How About Expedition to Rescue Maravich?"

> *I never saw anything sadder than Pistol Pete Maravich pouring the most glittering of statistics of National Basketball Association history through the basket for the New Orleans Jazz. It's painful to watch.*
>
> *He can do more with the basketball than Houdini can do with a rabbit. He can score over his shoulder, behind his back, under his arm, jumping, standing, lying, sitting. But it all falls in the category of an exhibition, as meaningless as a Globetrotter routine as long as he does it for the New Orleans Jazz. It's like watching Babe Ruth take batting practice.*
>
> *It pains basketball purists to see Pistol Pete, night after night, give a dazzling recital in a cellar. You'd think they would mount an expedition to rescue him. It's like getting a great scientist out from behind the Iron Curtain or MacArthur out of Corregidor. It's almost un-American to leave him there, like abandoning a guy in a train wreck.*
>
> *Poor devil. He's a bird in a rusty cage.*
>
> *"All my life I've played to get one thing—a (championship) ring. I'm destined to be one of those persons who never gets that ring. I would be a 17-point scorer if I could play on a good team."*
>
> *He admits he fantasizes about playing with Kareem Abdul-Jabbar. But wouldn't he find it frustrating to be Abdul-Jabbar's caddy?*
>
> *"Caddy, I'd be his caddy, his chauffeur, his valet. I'd take his clothes to the cleaner and brush him off if that gets me a ring. He's the best center in basketball. Look at the guys he keeps around and in this league. Look what he did for Oscar. You'd have something to tell your grandchildren instead of the stigma, 'OK you scored a lot, but you were a loser.'"*

New Orleans finished the year out of the playoffs with a 35-47 record, slightly worse than the previous season's 38-44. On the last day of the season the Jazz defeated the Nuggets, 134-125, in an ABA-style shootout. For the only time in NBA history, three players (Maravich, Nate Williams, and Denver's David Thompson) scored at least 40 points in a non-overtime game. Pete added 11 rebounds and 10 assists to close the year with another triple-double.

"The intensity of that game was phenomenal," said Pete later. "We blew those [guys] right out of there."

Maravich's 45 points (13-34, 19-22) gave him a season total of 2,273 in 73 games, an average of 31.1 per game. He was the NBA's scoring champion (Indiana's Billy Knight finished second at 26.6). Plus Pete became only the third player, joining Paul Arizin and Rick Barry, to lead both the NCAA and NBA in scoring. No one has done it since.

Maravich also became the fourth guard in league history to average more than 30 points for a season, joining Oscar Robertson, Jerry West, and Nate Archibald. He also led the league in free throws made (501) and minutes per game (41.7).

After the Denver game, Pete delivered several $100 bottles of 1969 Dom Perignon champagne to players, staff, and even the media. One local television reporter, however, did not receive a custom "thank you" bottle of bubbly. Maravich had not forgotten that Buddy Diliberto accused him, on the air, of orchestrating van Breda Kolff's departure the previous December.

"It was a very good season for me, but I don't look for personal achievement," Maravich told Marty Mule of the *Times-Picayune*. "I do think, however, we gave the fans some exciting moments."

When the NBA playoffs began, Maravich found himself behind a microphone providing color commentary for CBS during the early-round games. The offseason employment prompted Maravich to reflect on a post-basketball career.

"I'd like to get into the movies, into acting," Pete told *The Sporting News*. "I'd like to be in comedies, or even a Clint Eastwood-type role. You know, 'Dirty Pete,' or something like that."

When the postseason honors were doled out Pete was again voted to the All-NBA first team. His ballot totals reflected his rising stock among writers and broadcasters.

Kareem Abdul-Jabbar (107)
Pete Maravich (104)
Elvin Hayes (82)
David Thompson (62)
Paul Westphal (55)

Maravich and Abdul-Jabbar were the only repeaters from the previous season's first team.

"To tell you the truth, before I played with Pete, I didn't think too much of him," said Henry Bibby. "You think of him only as a scorer. But you know something? He's the best passer I have ever played with. I played with Doug Collins and Lloyd Free. I have played with Walt Frazier and Earl Monroe. I think I should know a top-notch guard.

"When Pete is doing his thing in the way only he can, there is absolutely no other player in the league who can pour in the baskets the way he can. I firmly believe he is as good as two players," added Bibby.

Maravich appreciated the respect of his peers and the prestigious awards, but as another long summer began, he was still without a championship trophy. He was 30 years old, not a young man by NBA standards, and time was running out. His contract with the Jazz had expired and he was now a free agent. He had a crucial decision to make.

Should he re-sign with the struggling Jazz and hope its fortunes improve? Or should he seek an NBA title with another team in another town?

19

Wounded Knee

"There's nothing I want to do more than go down Bourbon Street with the confetti falling over me, buying drinks and crawfish for everyone. I'd like nothing more than to win a championship for this city because I plan to make it my home forever."
— PETE MARAVICH

"Pistol Pete Maravich. In my opinion, the greatest playmaker playing today."
— RED AUERBACH, CELTICS GM

Pete Maravich understood that the New Orleans Jazz was unlikely to win an NBA title without a dominant center. He had long dreamed of playing along side a big man with the talent of Kareem Abdul-Jabbar. "They called Oscar Robertson 'Numero Uno,' but he was a loser most of his career until he had Kareem to throw the ball to," Pete explained.

Jabbar, of course, was happily ensconced in Los Angeles so Maravich urged the front office to pursue three other quality players on the market: Bob Lanier, Jamaal Wilkes, and Leonard "Truck" Robinson.

Lanier admitted he was tempted. "I thought about going to New Orleans with Pistol [Maravich] and Truck [Robinson]. That would have given the Jazz what I call the three crucial spokes in the wheel: Strong center, power forward, and heady guard to run the club," Lanier told the *Los Angeles Times*. "But my wife has a business here [Detroit]. My family is settled here."

To help navigate the free-agent waters, Jazz principal owner Sam Battistone hired Lewis Schaffel as the new general manager. Schaffel was a former player agent whose company had represented Nate Archibald, Phil Chenier, and Austin Carr. Schaffel also had close ties to Robinson, a free agent near the top of Pete's short list.

Robinson was unhappy in Atlanta. Since joining the Hawks, the 6-7, 235-pound Robinson had averaged an impressive 22 points and 12 boards a game, leading his team in both categories. But the Hawks were reluctant to meet his salary demands and put him on the market. And if the Jazz wanted Robinson, the Hawks wanted Maravich in return.

"The caveat under which everyone is operating is that the team is to be made whole for the loss of the player," Hawks GM Mike Storen told the *Times-Picayune*. "If the team is to be made whole, that means we need a starting forward who is 24 years of age who can average 24 points and 12 rebounds a game. If you look at the New Orleans roster, the only player that an impartial third person could say could make up for that would be Maravich."

"Well, they can't have me," Maravich pronounced when he heard Storen's analysis.

On June 28, 1977, Robinson signed with New Orleans, and three months later, Atlanta received Jazz forward Ron Behagen and $175,000 in return. With the high-scoring Robinson on board, Maravich was much more inclined to re-sign with the Jazz. Over the summer, Pete and his attorneys hammered out a new deal.

On August 10, 30-year-old Pete Maravich signed a five-year, $3-million, no-cut, no-trade deal. At $600,000 per year it was exactly double the salary of his historic Hawks contract from seven years earlier. However, the agreement eliminated a perk Pete had enjoyed since arriving in the NBA: the use of a car.

The $3-million-dollar man celebrated his signing with a party and press conference at Moran's Riverside Restaurant in New Orleans. "I busted my butt to get to where I am," he told *Times-Picayune* reporter Peter Finney. "Sure I'm making big money, but look around. Ali gets $5 million for leaning on ropes; Elton John does a lot of screaming, makes a lot of faces, and he makes better than $10 million. There's no difference in me playing ball and LeVar Burton playing Kunta Kinte in *Roots*. It's all entertainment. It's all one big conglomerate. None of these guys worked harder than me."

Pete still had a championship on his mind. "The money is great. Make no mistake about that. But what I want, money can't buy."

Before the season began, Pete agreed to participate in a HORSE competition against some of the NBA's best players: Rick Barry, George Gervin, Bob McAdoo, Rudy Tomjanovich, Paul Westphal, and Jo Jo White were among the 32-man pool. Taped in September, the rounds would be shown throughout the season during half time of the CBS *Game of the Week*.

Pete beat the Nets' Robert "Bubbles" Hawkins in the first round and then defeated McAdoo, a former league MVP and three-time scoring champion, in the second. "He was like a magician," marveled McAdoo.

In the quarterfinals, Maravich met Gervin. The gangly 6-8 sharpshooter

took it right to Pete, firing in a series of long-range jumpers and announcing "all day" as shot after shot ripped through the net. Maravich was up to
the challenge, however, and sent the "Iceman" home with a $2,000 check.

In the semifinals Pete faced Kevin Grevey. "The Bullets needed a representative to face the Pistol," Grevey recalled. "Elvin Hayes and Wes Unseld had
been asked, but they didn't want to look foolish. [Washington Bullets GM] Bob
Ferry called me one morning and told me there'd be $500 in it for me."

After Grevey dispatched his first three opponents (Bingo Smith, Tomjanovich, and White) he found himself sharing an elevator ride with an
attractive young woman. "I had just beat Jo Jo and there was this really good
looking lady that got on the elevator with me," Grevey said. "I'm wearing my
uniform. I just won and I'm feeling pretty good. I wanted to make some time
with her so I asked her out on a date." The woman was Jackie Maravich.

"When I went down to play Maravich, he pretended he was angry and
said, 'Hey Grevey, what's the deal coming on to my wife?' I was shocked
because this guy was my idol growing up. I said, 'Pistol, I didn't know.' Then
Pete wrapped his arm around me and laughed. 'Don't worry about it, Grevey.
I'm gonna take it out on your hide in HORSE.'"

After falling behind by two letters, Pete stormed back and easily beat the
former Kentucky Wildcat. "He was probably the best HORSE player in the
world," said Grevey.

To celebrate, Pete spun the ball on his finger, pushed it into the air, and
banked it into the basket. Grevey received a check for $5,000 while Pete won
the right to face Westphal for the title. The live showdown was scheduled for
half time of Game 2 of the 1978 NBA finals.

Throughout the HORSE tournament, Pete displayed his full arsenal of
imaginative shots. He tossed in an around-the-back, through-the-legs reverse
layup. He threw a one-handed pass over his shoulder, caught it with the same
hand, and completed another reverse layup. He jumped in from out of
bounds under the basket and banked in a shot off the glass. And, again starting from out of bounds, he jumped in, tapped the ball on the bottom of the
backboard and flipped it through the net with his back to the basket.

Surprisingly, two of Pete's most effective weapons were a simple underhand scoop and a bank shot while seated on the floor. In an interview with
CBS's Don Criqui, Pete explained that his creative shots were the result of a
childhood dedicated to practice. "You don't get here by wishing it," said Pete.

The Jazz had many reasons for optimism when the team reported to
training camp in the fall of 1977. The starting lineup included the powerful

Robinson, plus Goodrich, apparently fully recovered from his tendon injury. Maravich, now considered the best guard in the game, was healthy and looking forward to the season. "I've yet to have my greatest year, and I will. You can book that," Pete declared in the Jazz's media guide. The front office unveiled a new catch phrase: Jazzmatazz. The only sour note was the loss of free agent E. C. Coleman, first team all-defense, to the Warriors.

New Orleans played eight preseason games on a wild barnstorming tour through Alabama, Texas, Arkansas, Kentucky, Louisiana, and Florida. (In Florida the Jazz beat the Bullets in a converted airplane hangar called the Sportatorium.) Goodrich was pain free in all eight contests and the Jazz compiled an encouraging 6-2 record.

After dropping its first regular-season game, New Orleans ripped off five straight wins, including impressive road victories over New Jersey and Philadelphia. The latter game featured a classic Maravich moment. "Pete got a pass in the corner near the baseline," teammate Tommy Green recalled to reporter Joe Macaluso. "As he went up for the shot, a guy from the 76ers brushed his eye. Pete grabbed his eye and turned, and as he kind of walked off the court, I'll be [expletive] if the shot didn't go in. Took five minutes to shut the crowd up."

New Orleans found itself in unfamiliar territory—first place in the Central Division. Robinson was delivering, averaging 25 points and 18 rebounds. "Leonard Robinson is the best addition the Jazz have ever made," Pete told the press. "He's improved the club dramatically."

But Maravich was also on fire, averaging 31 points and six assists. Bob Logan of the *Basketball Times* lauded the Jazz backcourt, writing that Maravich and Goodrich were "the best shooting combination since Annie Oakley and Buffalo Bill." In the broadcast booth, "Hot" Rod Hundley referred to Maravich as the "Magic Man" and dubbed Robinson the "Chairman of the Boards."

Then New Orleans hit a rough patch, losing several games in a row in early November. After the fifth loss, a 117-83 defeat in Seattle, Robinson made a pointed observation to a reporter. "Some people are going to have to start giving up the ball." Maravich got the message.

In the next two games, a petulant Maravich passed up many open shots. Against New York he dished out nine assists and made four shots in a 108-104 loss. "There were other guys open in better position than me so I passed the ball—that's fundamental basketball. I get paid the same whether I score 1 or 100," Maravich explained to the *Times-Picayune*. Robinson and Rich Kelley led the team with 20 points apiece.

In a 127-116 home victory over Seattle, Pete attempted only five shots and doled out 15 assists. Robinson tallied 33 points. Despite the win, Jazz fans booed Maravich for his lack of intensity. "Some people have to make sacrifices," Pete said after the game. "We lost six in a row. I think I played a very good defensive game. I didn't pass up any open shots."

Baylor cornered his star player. "What do you think you're doing out there?" Baylor asked. Maravich explained he was just playing "winning basketball." "Then you need to be shooting the ball," Baylor countered.

Two days later, on November 19, Maravich fired in 39 points (19-33, 1-1) and hit the game-winning jump shot in a thrilling 103-101 road win over Houston.

Afterward Maravich launched into a revealing monologue. "It's difficult to be happy in this business," he admitted. "When you win, you're the happiest guy in the world. When you lose, you're in the coldest business you can imagine. If you lose a game, it's your fault. You're making the most money so it's your fault."

Over the next several games the Jazz were wildly inconsistent, winning big one night and losing badly the next. Maravich's mood swings were a contributing factor.

One day he was a happy-go-lucky guy but 24 hours later he could be sullen and aloof. "He was a difficult guy psychologically speaking. When he was feeling great, he was wonderful to be around. But he was prone to dark periods and moods," recalled Rich Kelley.

When he was sociable Pete enjoyed playing video games or backgammon. One of his favorite activities was car racing. Teammates called him "Speed Racer" because he loved to see how far he could push the pedal. Guard Fred Boyd would challenge Maravich on Interstate 10 after practice. "He had a Porsche, I had a Jensen-Healey. He was fascinated by speed," recalled Boyd.

Former teammate Bud Stallworth described Maravich as a player with an artistic disposition. "He was a very funny guy and we got along better off the court as friends," remembered Stallworth. "But if things didn't go his way, he was a tough guy to be around. That's not a knock on him as a person, but that's just the way he was. Most artists and musicians have temperaments that are a little to the left."

Through all his temperamental swings, Pete was posting impressive numbers and continuing to gain the respect of his peers.

"Pete's the best offensive scorer in the league," Celtics' great John Havlicek told a national sports magazine at the time. "He's extremely quick for a guy 6-5, and although he prefers the jump shot, he can penetrate and that's what makes him so dangerous. His biggest improvement has been on defense. He didn't know how to play it when he first came up."

Cleveland coach Bill Fitch was equally effusive. "He can do anything humanly possible with the basketball," he said. "It almost seems to be a part of his body. I think he's the biggest attraction in the NBA. We would probably win the whole thing with him in the lineup."

Washington Bullets forward Elvin Hayes: "There's nobody in the league with more talent. Too many people think of Pete only in relation to hot-dog plays. That's a bad rap. In this game you have to have the big guys."

Detroit Pistons center Bob Lanier: "Pete is smooth and uncommonly good. The only one I'd pay money to see night after night. This is a team game and Pete's a team player. Give him a center and a forward, and he'd be all-everything."

Milwaukee Bucks guard Junior Bridgeman: "The best ball handler I've ever seen. No player can do more things with the ball, and I had the honor of working with Leon Hilliard of the Harlem Globetrotters in a couple of basketball camps. Leon was a wizard with the ball, but Pete was better."

Houston Rockets coach Tom Nissalke: "New Orleans can't win unless Pete has a great night every night. He's not selfish. Some players can hide in the game and have a bad night. Any time Pete has a weak performance, everybody knows about it. That's pressure."

Warriors announcer Bill King: "You also get the feeling there are two Maraviches. The one whose ability to shoot and pass the ball looks like great fun. And the Maravich who still seems to be conforming to a father's demand for perfection, a kid who doesn't smile, or allow himself to be open or friendly. I was told that in Atlanta he had trouble sleeping."

Insomnia or not, Maravich could light it up on the court. On December 13, 1977, in front of more than 31,000 ragin' Cajuns in the Superdome, he scored 40 points (19-35, 2-2, 4 rebounds, 6 assists) as the Jazz downed Abdul-Jabbar and the Lakers, 117-94. It was a well-balanced team effort. Robinson contributed 22 points and 26 rebounds; Goodrich 16 points and seven assists; Aaron James 17 points and 10 rebounds; James McElroy six assists; and Joe Meriweather and Rich Kelley nine rebounds each.

Ron Brocato of the *States-Item* analyzed Abdul-Jabbar's one-man attack (33 points, 16 rebounds, 5 blocks) with an observation that might have applied to Maravich as well. "No matter how great the individual, no one player is greater than the team."

Three nights later, during a 126-113 home loss to Phoenix, Maravich had an altercation with a Jazz season-ticket holder named Henry Rosenblatt. In the third quarter, as Goodrich came into the game to replace Maravich, Rosenblatt began jawing at Pete and an angry Maravich walked over and screamed at him, "I want everyone to know that you are not a fan!" After the game Maravich told a reporter that he had ". . . never gone after a fan before. This guy has been on my case for years."

A week and a half later Maravich squared off in Cleveland against Frazier, who had been traded from the Knicks to the Cavaliers. A capacity crowd of 19,548 jammed the Coliseum for what looked like a mismatch on paper. New Orleans was 3-13 on the road while Cleveland was 11-3 at home.

The game was close until the fourth quarter when "Maravich put on some sort of barrage," according to the Cavaliers' radio announcer Joe Tait. Pete scored 18 points in the final 12 minutes, hitting shots from all angles and distances in a 113-102 Jazz victory. "I could sit here and talk to you about Pete Maravich until three o'clock tomorrow morning and still not be able to adequately describe some of the baskets he hit in this fourth quarter," Tait exclaimed on WWWE radio.

Maravich's final basket was a dunk off a steal and gave him a season-high 42 points (17-29, 8-9). Frazier racked up 29, his best output with the Cavaliers. Bill Fitch, Cleveland's head coach and GM, said he would gladly trade all of the Cavaliers' draft picks for the next five years in exchange for Maravich.

The win featured New Orleans at its best (Robinson had 20 points and 25 rebounds) but the team could not shake its wild inconsistency, and as 1977 drew to a close, the Jazz were a disappointing 14-20.

Pete's personal difficulties reached beyond the team's win-loss record. He continued to struggle with the demands of his fame and was still wary of strangers in hotel lobbies and airports. If he was in his car and another vehicle stopped in front of him, he stayed back an extra few feet in order to provide an escape route. On December 31, he made a poignant entry in his diary:

> I pray that before I'm through with this entire life of mine, I will be happy, peaceful, and my mind at ease about life and God. How can I be unhappy? It is very simple. There are millions of people who have not found a deep sense of purpose and meaning. I am one of them. . . . With all the trophies, awards, money, and fame, I am not at peace with myself.

The calendar turned to 1978, and finally, the Jazz began to click. Beginning on January 14 in Oakland, Maravich dropped in 35 points (13-27, 9-10,

5 rebounds, 8 assists) as New Orleans bashed the Warriors 118-111. The Pistol added to his highlight portfolio when a film crew captured his running, lefthanded scoop-hook over Rick Barry.

Three days later in New Orleans, the Jazz bumped off the Houston Rockets, 99-95, in a game that featured two entertaining matchups. Pete and his old college rival, Calvin Murphy, got into a shootout while the league's top two rebounders, Robinson and Moses Malone, battled it out under the boards. Malone out-boarded Robinson 21 to 15 and Pete edged out Murphy 30 to 29.

The next night, Maravich scored four clutch points in the final 22 seconds to seal a 108-106 win over Atlanta in Charlotte. He finished with 34 points and ten assists, earning a glowing review from the Hawks coach. "This is the best I've seen Maravich play since I've been around the NBA," remarked Hubie Brown to the *Times-Picayune*.

The three-game winning streak improved the Jazz record to 19-24. Next up was Portland, the defending NBA champions, who had a league-best record of 35-6 and were undefeated at home. The methodical Trail Blazers, anchored by center Bill Walton (who would be named league MVP months later), were a well-tuned basketball machine outscoring opponents by an impressive 9.9 points a game.

Peter Finney of the *Times-Picayune* noted the contrasting styles of the two clubs when he wrote, "Watching may be like listening to a musical duel between Spike Jones and the Boston Symphony." But New Orleans squeaked by Portland, 101-100, and the win streak reached four.

Then a controversy flared when Finney reported that Schaffel was considering the possibility of trading Maravich. For Pete, it confirmed suspicions that people in the front office were conspiring to undermine him. According to Finney, Pete was "hounded by a persecution complex, something he has been unable to shake."

Maravich lashed out at Schaffel in the press. "I know for a fact he tried to trade me. But he can forget it. I'll never leave this city. Who does he think he is? If the Jazz trades someone, it should be him," Pete told the *State-Times*. "He should take a long vacation in Iraq."

As the dust-up played out in the media, the Jazz faced the Detroit Pistons. Ex-Jazz guard Stu Lantz was courtside making his debut for CBS as a color analyst. His play-by-play partner was Bob Costas. As the game progressed they discussed the Maravich trade situation. "You couldn't convince too many people in New Orleans," Costas said, "that Pete Maravich needed to be traded." To which Lantz replied, "You couldn't convince many people anywhere that he should be traded."

On the floor Maravich scored 30 points (12-29, 6-6, 4 rebounds, 7 assists) and the Jazz ran their win streak to five with a 100-97 victory.

The Jazz then defeated the Celtics, with Maravich scoring 31 points (11-27, 9-10, 8 rebounds, 7 assists, 3 steals). Afterward Pete was unable to account for the team's turnaround. "Honestly, we haven't done that much different from the first game of the year," he told Austin Wilson of the Associated Press.

Writing in his diary, Maravich analyzed the team's playoff odds:

Fantastic win! Our sixth straight. If the Lord could just let us keep winning, it would solve everything. But we have a nine-game road trip in February. We would have to win four of the nine to have a chance at the playoffs.

The streak reached seven with a win over Kansas City. Four players had at least 20 points, with Pete scoring a team-high 31 (14-31, 3-3, 3 rebounds, 7 assists).

When asked to reveal the secret to his team's success, Baylor just shook his head, "If I knew the answer to that—if any coach knew the answer to that—we'd make a fortune. I don't know what's in a player's head. I know I'm not doing anything different."

As Pete noted in his diary, however, to make the playoffs the team had to play well on the road. The Jazz went into Indianapolis's Market Square Arena in late January and downed the Pacers, 107-91, to even its season record at 24-24. Maravich's diary entry for January 29, 1978 read:

Unbelievable! We won our eighth straight game. We have really snowballed. I had a great game—35 points, 11 assists and 5 steals. Boy, does this feel great.

Pete was having the best basketball year of his life and ranked among the league's top 10 in four categories. He was first in scoring (28.2 points per game), sixth in assists (6.7), eighth in steals (2.02), and fifth in free-throw percentage (.875). Truck Robinson was the NBA's top rebounder at 16.3 per game.

"For that three-month period, Peter finally figured out what it meant to be a great pro. He was our second-leading rebounder, averaging seven or eight assists, maybe turning the ball over twice. He was shooting less, but scoring the same," recalled Rich Kelley. "But there was always this frantic edge to Pete that made him unstable as a teammate. There are times when you are in awe of the artistry, but plenty of other times when you wish the artist would come to work and do the job and not be so . . . artistic."

Maravich and the Jazz hosted the struggling Buffalo Braves (16–28) on January 31. It was eight years to the day since Maravich had bested Oscar Robertson's NCAA scoring record. Late in the game, with New Orleans leading by 21 points, Maravich, encouraged by the crowd, decided it was time for a little razzle-dazzle.

He set the scene in his autobiography:

The reality of winning nine straight hit the whole team, but no one on the squad was more elated than I. Knowing we had more than a good chance to get in the playoffs and start our run for championship rings was an incredible feeling. With time ticking away, I rode the crest of the crowd's enthusiasm. They were with me.

With 4:20 left Maravich snared his fifth rebound, faked an outlet pass, and began dribbling up the sidelines. He saw Aaron James wide open and streaking down the court ahead of him. Buffalo's Marvin Barnes stepped in front of Maravich at mid-court so Pete faked left, jumped in the air, and fired a 40-foot, between-the-legs strike to James, who slammed it through. A rousing ovation accompanied Pete's 15th assist of the night.

But, as he made the pass, Pete's throwing arm clipped the back of his right leg, causing him to tumble awkwardly. "We were close to the floor and on the side where he was," recalled his sister, Diana Maravich-May. "So we could see him coming down the floor and throw the basketball between his legs. I was following the basketball. But I heard the pop. And I heard the scream. I turned back and he was on the floor."

Times-Picayune writer Marty Mule heard the same, stomach-churning noise. "You could hear it on the press bench," Mule said. "The snap—it sounded sickening."

While Maravich writhed on the floor, clutching his knee and moaning in pain, Barnes kept repeating to anyone who would listen, "I didn't touch him. I didn't touch him." The Dome fell silent. Trainer Don Sparks helped Pete onto a chair and rolled him off the court as the crowd began chanting, "Pistol, Pistol, Pistol."

The injury was initially diagnosed as a "twisted knee" that would sideline Maravich for at least a week. That meant he'd miss a home game against Chicago and the All-Star Game in Atlanta, where, for the fourth time, Pete had been voted a starter (the top three vote getters were Julius Erving, David Thompson, and Maravich). Robinson also was selected, marking the first time the Jazz had two All-Stars.

Maravich had strained the cartilage in his right knee once before, during his junior year at LSU. That time he wrapped his leg from mid-thigh to mid-calf and played through the injury. Pete mistakenly believed he could do so again. He also thought he could overcome his injury with a combination of massage, vitamins, and a high-protein diet. No one really knew the extent of the injury because Maravich shunned X-rays, fearing the machines caused cancer. Team doctor Kenneth Saer recommended an arthroscopic exam. Pete refused. He did not want a medical instrument poking around inside his knee.

Within days the swelling subsided and Pete was able to climb stairs without a cane. After 10 days he was at the Metairie YMCA shooting baskets and working out on a stationary bike and leg extension machine. But the swelling returned, and Maravich finally allowed his knee to be drained on February 13. A bloody fluid was extracted, indicating a rupture of some type, but barring a closer examination a precise diagnosis was impossible. Later that day, in his diary, Maravich contemplated the worst-case scenario.

For the first time, I feel my career may be over. I drove across the bridge to think things out. I spent about two hours over there watching the waves break against the wall. One thing I do not want is to play on a bum leg the rest of my career. It would hurt me too much. My insides would turn knowing I could not do the things on the court I've always done.

Pete finally agreed to the arthroscopic probe. The exam revealed a torn lateral meniscus with a stretched, but not torn, cruciate ligament. Surgery might not be required after all. The doctor prescribed a rehabilitation regimen of bicycle riding and lightweight training. Maravich began his workouts and aimed for a March 1 return.

Without Maravich, the Jazz went into a free fall. The team dropped eight of its next nine games and, as February dwindled away, was barely in contention for the last playoff spot.

Cindy Marshall, a friend of the Maravich family, learned that Pete was depressed by his injury. She and her brother, Chet, tried to boost Pete's spirits by sending him a series of funny letters.

"His favorite was our fake letter to the NBA commissioner, asking for workers' compensation for wives of injured 'so-called-professional' athletes," said Cindy. "We outlined all the benefits due these women for their having to put up with [everything] these guys—especially Pete—were capable of dishing out when laid up. Pete thought it was a riot and even carried it with him for a while. Jackie thought it right on target, and was ready to file her claim!"

Maravich missed his return date of March 1, but New Orleans began to play well and had pushed its record back near .500 (35-37) by the time Pete rejoined the team on March 21. His knee was still not 100 percent, however. "I'm like a car with no brakes," Pete told a UPI reporter. "It takes me two or three steps to stop. I can no longer stop on a dime and explode up for my jump shot, which is my forte."

Before his return against the New Jersey Nets, Pete received a cortisone shot to numb the pain. He played 12 minutes and did not score but had three assists in a 117-114 victory. Maravich assessed his play for Brocato of the *States-Item*: "Psychologically, I was fearful tonight. My timing was off tonight and I found it hard to coordinate my brain with my body. I couldn't make certain moves I used to. Offense is timing and having your legs under you. Right now I don't have my legs."

The next evening Maravich played 25 minutes against the Bullets with his knee tightly wrapped, scoring 12 points (6-9, 0-0, 0 rebounds, 5 assists) in a losing effort. His knee ballooned after the game and was drained once again.

On March 24, the Jazz played the Hawks. Both teams were fighting for the sixth and final playoff spot in the East. Maravich took another cortisone shot and scored 17 points (8-17, 1-2, 3 rebounds, 3 assists) over 36 minutes in a tough overtime game. The Hawks prevailed 94-92 as their rookie guard, Eddie Johnson, threw down 29 points, including the game-winning free throws.

After the game Pete's knee swelled again and more bloody fluid was drained. Surgery now seemed inevitable. But Maravich wanted to wait until New Orleans' playoff fate was determined. Bad knee or not, if the team made its first ever postseason appearance he wanted to play. But the Jazz, without Pete, went into a late-season funk, lost four in a row, and relinquished the final playoff spot to the Atlanta Hawks.

The Jazz closed the season with a memorable game against San Antonio at the Superdome. Earlier that day Denver's David Thompson had scored 73 points in a loss at Detroit that put him ahead of San Antonio's George Gervin in the NBA scoring race. Gervin, napping at his New Orleans hotel, woke up to the news that he needed 58 points to surpass Thompson's final average of 27.15.

When Gervin opened the game by missing his first five shots he asked his teammates to stop feeding him. They refused and the "Iceman" soon got hot. With Maravich watching in street clothes, the graceful Gervin went on a scoring barrage, hitting 20 points in the first quarter. He added 33 more in the second quarter (breaking Thompson's eight-hour-old mark of most points in a quarter) and ended the game with 63 points (23-49, 17-20) to win the scoring title. The Jazz, however, won the game, 153-132.

New Orleans finished with a record of 39-43, its best mark ever, and Robinson, the league leader in rebounding, was selected to the All-NBA first team. Maravich, despite playing just 50 games, was named Second Team All-NBA. New Orleans was 26-24 with Maravich in the lineup and 13-19 without him.

During the postseason Pete joined the CBS team and provided color commentary for some early-round playoff games. Maravich's injury prevented him from participating in the HORSE final so Paul Westphal was awarded the $15,000 first prize.

Maravich's accomplishments over his first four seasons in New Orleans placed him among the NBA's elite guards and, eventually, among the greatest of all time. But New Orleans' success, and Pete's lightning-in-a-bottle performances, did not completely erase his reputation, born in LSU and nurtured in Atlanta, of being a "me first" gunner.

Pete's midseason injury cost him another scoring title and, perhaps, the Jazz's first playoff appearance. Rich Kelley, who once colorfully described Pete as "an American phenomenon. A stepchild of the human imagination," believes the January 31, 1978, game against the Braves was a turning point for both Maravich and pro basketball in New Orleans.

"We were on that 10-game winning streak and up by a sizable amount of points with three minutes left to play and he ended up brutally tearing up his knee by throwing a half-court, behind-the-back, underneath-the-legs, bounce pass for a layup," Kelley said.

"In a lot of ways, that sums up the joy and the sadness of his career. The whole franchise was never the same after that. And neither was he."

20

Lenox Hill

"The five years in New Orleans were like one big year. If anything changed, it changed for the worse."

—ROD HUNDLEY, JAZZ ANNOUNCER

"If some kid comes up to me and asks for advice, I'd tell them to take up an individual sport like tennis or golf. Then, if you lose, it really is your fault."

—PETE MARAVICH

On May 19, 1978, nearly three months after injuring his right knee, Maravich finally underwent surgery. He had resisted to the last moment, hoping a regimen of vitamins, massage, and exercise would result in a "natural" recovery. After making a four-inch incision, Dr. Kenneth Saer trimmed and repaired Maravich's shredded lateral meniscus.

"The operation was successful—he is in good condition," reported Dr. Saer. Pete remained hospitalized for a week, and Jackie smuggled in fresh fruits and vegetables.

Maravich had been tinkering with his diet since turning pro in 1970. He was inspired by teammates like Neal Walk and Henry Bibby, who introduced him to vegetarianism and vitamins. By mid-1976, he had all but eliminated red meat, coffee, sugar, white bread, and salt from his meals.

As a nutrition expert, Pete was eager to proselytize his sometimes-radical views. He told George White of the *Houston Chronicle* that, with a proper diet, human beings could live 150 years. He was convinced eating fast food as a teenager prevented him from reaching a height of 6-8. He also believed a healthy diet could keep cancer at bay.

According to Pete, the food, advertising, medical, and insurance industries actively conspired to keep the population unhealthy. "It's going to continually get worse because America is built on one basic principle: Greed," Pete explained to White. "But if you put anything good in your body today you're exposed as a health-food nut. Pete Maravich is paranoid. Why am I paranoid to put something good in my body? I don't put trash in it. That's all. The other people are weirdoes, not me. I used to be a weirdo, but not anymore."

During his hospital stay he listed his daily intake for *Times-Picayune* reporter Peter Finney:

- Breakfast: Two (fertile) eggs, any style. Two slices whole wheat bread. Fresh fruit (never canned).
- Lunch: A large blended glass of vegetable juice containing carrots, celery, beets, and cabbage. A grilled cheese (no calcium chloride) on whole wheat.
- Dinner: One-half organically-fed chicken, baked fresh vegetables, and raw milk straight from the cow. Or mineral water.

Maravich acknowledged that it was difficult to adhere to his diet while on the road. He admitted eating red meat a few times even though he knew it could lead to "heart disease, colon cancer, and colitis." He also nursed the occasional beer despite its sugar content. After he retired from the NBA, Maravich planned on becoming a strict vegetarian, but while playing he stuck to organic chicken, turkey, and rabbit.

Pete had no idea how long his rehabilitation would last. The initial trauma of any major knee injury is exacerbated by the surgery so, depending on the individual and the extent of the damage, recovery can range from three months to several years. In Pete's case, the injury was aggravated by the three games he played after the initial tear.

Still, he tried to remain positive. One afternoon, with his leg still in a cast, Pete watched his father and family friend Chet Marshall casually shoot baskets in the driveway.

"Pete looks at us, and says, in typical Pete fashion, '. . . I can hardly even walk and I can kick your [expletive] in a game of HORSE,'" remembered Marshall. "Press gives a chuckle and he's got his tobacco chaw and says, 'How much?' And Pete says, 'I'll kick all your [expletive] and loser has to buy dinner.' So Press is just rolling with laughter. He loves it. So we start out. We're shooting pretty straight shots. Then 'bounce this, spin this' and Press is the first one out.

"Now its just Pete and me. H-H, O-O, R-R. I'm thinking . . . I might actually beat Pistol. Of course his leg is still in a cast. But what the [expletive]? We get down to S-S and it's my shot. I miss.

"Pete says, 'You know what? I'm tired of [messing] around. This shot's gonna end the game and that's the way it's gonna be.' So he turns his back to the basket—he's about two, three feet in front of the basket. 'I'm throwing this ball straight up in the air. It bounces once and it's in.'

"Well Press just starts howling. 'Oh, that'll be the greatest [expletive] shot I've ever seen.' Pete throws it up with a kind of backspin—it hasn't even reached the apex—and he starts limping off toward his car. Doesn't even turn around. He just sticks his hand up and says, 'See you, sucker. You owe me dinner.' Sure enough, ball bounces, nothing but net."

Pete convalesced at his condominium in Clearwater, Florida. "It was quiet there and he loved that place," Jackie said. "To get into the condo, you had to pass through security and know the proper codes. Pete liked it there because nobody bothered him."

Late in the summer Maravich spent five days in Iowa acting in a movie entitled *Dribble*. The low-budget sports comedy, written and directed by Michael DeGaetano, told the story of a U.S. Army basketball team that played an all-girl squad. Pete was cast as a member of the Army team.

Maravich arrived at the Cedar Rapids airport on August 26, sporting mirrored sunglasses, a visor, a rakish moustache, and a Rolls-Royce insignia stitched on his blue jeans. He rode into town in a Rolls-Royce with license plates that read: A FLASH. At a mini press conference, the first questions concerned Pete's knee.

"I don't think there will be any problem when the season starts," Pete told Mark Dukes of the *Cedar Rapids Gazette*. "I tried to come back last year but it didn't work. I've been on a strenuous rehabilitation program about seven months. If my knee stabilizes, I feel I can play as long as I want."

Pete also revealed that his trademark floppy socks actually fell apart during the famous "flood" game with the L.A. Lakers on November 5, 1975. He had promised to forgo the socks earlier that season and the storm sealed the deal.

"We still had 35,000 people despite the rain. But the roof was leaking. There were about seven or eight minutes left in the game and I was at the free-throw line. My socks were wet and dropping. When I went to pull them up, they came all the way up to my thighs. That was the end of those."

Filming began the next day at the Regis High School gymnasium. At one point, as technical problems halted production, Maravich could not resist entertaining a captive audience of about 500 idle extras. First, he threw a looping, two-handed set shot that hit the metal support high above the basket and dropped through. "Don't you ever doubt me!" he kidded the thrilled crowd. Then he bet a local resident $50 that he could make a half-court shot—on a bounce. He was allowed three chances. The first attempt went long and the second was a bit short. "He stood at mid-court," wrote Bob Herson in the *Gazette*. "Lofted a shot that almost hit the ceiling, then bounced on the court and up into the basket."

That night, Pete hosted a small party in his room at the Ramada Inn. The get-together was a golden opportunity for 16-year-old Maravich fan Joe Huruska. "A friend of mine worked at the Ramada. One Sunday night he called me at home and told me that Pete Maravich was in town for the movie *Dribble* and was staying at his hotel. He also said that a phone call from Pete's room indicated that they would pay $100 for a 12-pack of beer. In Iowa at this time the bars closed at 10:00 P.M. on Sundays, so he asked if I could get a 12-pack. And if I did, he would let me take it up to his room and meet Pistol Pete. But it had to be there by 11:30. So I went downstairs in my family's home and raided the refrigerator.

"My friend [the night manager] then called Pete's room and told him that we had the beer. I went up and knocked on the door. The door opened and I could tell there was a party going on. They handed me the money and I gave them the beer. But still no Pistol Pete. I was devastated, so I camped out in the lobby all night. In the morning Pete finally came down. Since I adored everything that he did, I was stunned to see Pete wearing a pair of jeans that had flowery embroidery from top to bottom. I could just never see me wearing them."

Over the next three days Maravich filmed several scenes, and he even managed to insert some nutritional advice into the film's dialogue. In his final sequence, shown under the closing credits, Pete danced in a disco line. Unfortunately for writer/director DeGaetano, *Dribble* was an uneven, forgettable comedy. The movie was eventually re-cut and released to the home video market under the title *Scoring*.

When training camp opened, the Jazz unveiled a new slogan that acknowledged Truck Robinson's increased prestige: "The Pistol and the Power." Unfortunately, the "Power" was a no-show at camp. Robinson wanted to renegotiate his contract. Along with his agent Don Cronson, he claimed the Jazz were operating under a double standard.

"The Jazz has two sets of rules," Cronson told reporters. "One for Pete and one for the rest of the players," implying that the Jazz had renegotiated Maravich's contract the previous year. But Cronson was mistaken. Maravich had been a free agent when he re-signed in the summer of 1977, doing so, ironically, only after the Jazz picked up Robinson.

Robinson felt underpaid and under-appreciated. He had just led the league in rebounding and minutes played, while posting career highs in points, rebounds, and free throws. He was first team All-NBA and the Jazz recorded a franchise-high 39 wins. After Pete went down with his knee, he was the team's main threat.

"It was all frustration," Robinson told John Papanek in *Sports Illustrated*. "I'd come in, put on my clothes, play 45 minutes and we'd get our tails kicked. . . ."

The two sides were deadlocked. After 17 tense days Robinson backed down and returned to training camp, but remained disgruntled, demanding a higher percentage of his contract be paid upfront. He publicly demanded to be traded.

An unhappy, high-profile teammate, however, was only part of Pete's problems. His knee had not sufficiently stabilized over the summer, so Pete agreed to wear the Lenox-Hill Derotation knee brace, a medieval-looking contraption designed to keep the knee aligned while limiting its motion. The two-pound brace, consisting of an array of hinges, canvas, buckles, and elastic straps, was invented in the early 1970s to help Joe Namath cope with his chronic knee failure.

Midway through the preseason Pete assessed his injury for Phil Scheuer of *Super Sports* magazine. "My leg is about 20 percent weaker and it will probably stay that way throughout the year," Pete explained. "[The brace] affects my mobility a little bit but it does stabilize my knee. I know that I'll experience pain, especially when we play three or four nights straight. But I can put that out of my mind . . . I don't expect to put myself to the ultimate test until October 13."

That date marked the opening of the regular season, Maravich's ninth in the NBA. He was now part of an older generation. The 11-man Jazz roster had just two players born in the 1940s, Maravich and Gail Goodrich. And at age 35, Goodrich was the league's oldest player that season. The team's youth movement continued by adding two promising rookies to the roster, 6-8 forward James Hardy and 6-1 guard Tommy Green.

With a weakened knee and a discontented power forward, Pete was facing another uphill NBA season. But the Maravich family received some good news when it learned that Jackie was pregnant with her first child. The baby was due in early April.

The season began ominously for Pete and the Jazz. In the first two games (losses to Washington and Milwaukee) he converted a meager 9 of 40 shots from the floor. Plus his bulky brace had an unintended consequence. Although it stabilized his knee, the heavy device stressed Pete's lower back, triggering debilitating muscle spasms.

Pete received several vigorous massages and by the third game his back had loosened up. He pulled out of his shooting slump and scored 36 points (16-27, 4-5) in a 114-109 win over Detroit on October 17.

On November 10, Pete reached the 40-point plateau for the final time as a pro when he dropped in 41 points (16-28, 9-9) in a 113-109 win over the San Antonio Spurs. When Maravich put a lot of points on the board his teams did astonishingly well. The Hawks and Jazz won 82 percent (28 of 34) of their games when Pete scored 40 or more.

But on November 23, after a 106-98 comeback victory over the Golden State Warriors, Pete developed tendonitis in his knee. This created a catch-22. He needed to strengthen his knee with exercise, but the treatment for tendonitis was rest. Pete tried to cater to both needs. When the tendons flared up, he would simply sit out a game or two. The situation created some tension with Coach Baylor because Pete, the team captain, began missing practices.

Baylor wasn't the only one who was unhappy with Pete. According to Troy Spatafora, the "Shoe Town" ball boy, there was bad blood between the Pistol and the "Power."

"All the ball boys loved Pete. He was real nice to us," recalled Spatafora. "But Truck hated playing with Pete. There would almost be fights during timeouts."

An article in *Sports Illustrated* by long-time Maravich chronicler Curry Kirkpatrick triggered more team friction. The in-depth story, "No One Can Cap the Pistol," featured some wild quotes from Pete about, among other subjects, international financial conspiracies. He said he wished he could be "invisible so I could kill the heads of all the rich banking families, redistribute the wealth and make the world a better place." He also weighed in on extra-terrestrials, saying he would paint a target on the roof of his house that read, "Come Take Me."

Times-Picayune writer Marty Mule was in the Jazz locker room when Pete made the infamous space ship claim. "You have to put it into context with his sense of humor. I remember a guy who was coming from *Sports Illustrated*, it might have been Curry Kirkpatrick," recalled Mule. "I remember being in the locker room when Pete said to him about aliens coming to take us all away, and the reporter started writing all of this down and Pete goes, 'No, no. Don't use that. I'm just kidding.' The guy still put it down, and sure enough, it appeared in the story."

The public thought it was true. "That never happened," said Jackie years later. "If he were that cuckoo I wouldn't have stayed with him."

But it was Pete's statements about his own teammates that caused the most consternation in the locker room.

"Maybe I would be happier somewhere else," Pete told Kirkpatrick. "In Philly, I could knock in 20 a game off my nose and be happy. Those guys are so great. I'd never be double-teamed there."

Robinson fired back. "Sometimes it's tough to play for a guy who gets on us for not having any talent. . . . "

The next day, practice was halted and the entire team and coaching staff sat on the floor at mid-court for a "rap session." The players vented their frustrations and Pete attempted to clarify his remarks.

With the air cleared, the Jazz readied for a three-game home stand. Before the first game, against the 76ers, PBS talk show host Dick Cavett interviewed Pete and Julius Erving from the floor of the Superdome for his program. In a wide-ranging conversation Pete and Dr. J spoke of knee injuries, sex before games, bad fans, hot-dogging, dunking, compensation, and acting. Erving brought a film clip from *The Fish Who Saved Pittsburgh*. Pete, fortunately, had nothing to show from *Dribble*. One question that caught Pete off guard concerned his many injuries.

"I really don't think I'm injury prone more than anybody else," Pete said earnestly. "I think it's the type of game I play out on the basketball court that may lead me to be injury prone because I take a lot of chances on the court. I'm best when I have my speed up."

After the interview Pete demonstrated his wrist-pass, bullet ricochet, and some other "Homework" drills, while Dr. J slammed home a few dunks and played keep-away with the Pistol.

An NBA record crowd of 35,139 watched Maravich throw down 32 points as the Jazz trumped Dr. J and the 76ers. Two nights later, Pete scored 28 points as New Orleans downed David Thompson and the Denver Nuggets. In the third game of the home stand, on December 1, the Jazz lost a barnburner, 117-115, to the streaking (eight straight) defending NBA champion Washington Bullets. Pete scored 19 of his 37 points in the fourth quarter.

"Maravich, who is learning to play better with a still-ailing knee, wouldn't let his team falter," reported Paul Attner in the *Washington Post*. "He got into one of his incredible shooting streaks, in which he turns 25-footers into layups."

"Wasn't he something?" asked Bullets guard Greg Ballard afterward. "He was uncanny out there . . . With that brace, he's probably lucky he can play. One thing for sure, even with one leg, he's worth the price of admission."

As the season progressed the Jazz were competitive at home and dismal outside the Superdome. Pete's moodiness was exacerbated by the loneliness of the road. He rarely ventured from his hotel room and didn't request many "comp" tickets for friends and family. "Basketball used to be so much fun," Pete told Kirkpatrick. "Now I don't sleep for a week at a time. There's a reason I never smile out there anymore."

At the end of one horrific road trip, New Orleans pulled out a most unlikely victory. On December 26, the Jazz staggered into Los Angeles riding a five-game losing streak and holding the league's worst road record, 1-16. The Lakers, on the other hand, owned the NBA's best home mark, 15-3.

The game see-sawed back and forth in front of 12,212 at the Forum until Abdul-Jabbar's 18-point third quarter seemed to seal the Laker victory. But with 1:33 remaining in the game and New Orleans down by eight, the Jazz embarked on an unlikely 10-0 run and won, 125-123. It was the franchise's first victory in Los Angeles. Pete scored a modest 19 points but dished out a season-high 11 assists. Robinson led the Jazz with 31 points, including the game-winning basket. Abdul-Jabbar finished with 35.

Thanks to a Canadian Maravich fan named David Miller, a copy of that telecast still exists. Miller had been shooting Super 8mm home movies of Maravich whenever the Jazz visited Buffalo to play the Braves. In late November 1978, he traveled to New Orleans to catch several games in the Superdome. Before returning home, Miller went to WGNO-TV seeking copies of Jazz telecasts. He was astonished to learn that the station didn't maintain any archive so he paid a technician several hundred dollars to record two Jazz road games and mail them. One video contained the Jazz victory in Los Angeles, one of only four road wins during the entire season. The tape captures a struggling team on the brink of a major overhaul.

On January 5, the Jazz swapped their backup center Joe C. Meriweather to New York for 6-8 forward Spencer Haywood. For a star like Haywood, it was a shock to be traded straight up for a journeyman like Meriweather. But Haywood had not panned out as a "savior" in New York and had a growing reputation for being difficult. His arrival, however, did nothing to ease the tension between Robinson and Maravich. The two were still trading barbs in the media when Pete made a shocking statement.

"Probably the best thing for me would be to let them trade me," said Pete on January 11, 1979, in a national Associated Press story. "I don't really want to go. My roots are here, everything is here. I said when I signed that my relationship with New Orleans was like red beans and rice. I guess the pot has been burnt."

The Jazz were looking to end the feud. "We have not kept it a secret that we are trying to better ourselves," said Bill Bertka, the Jazz's director of player personal, in the same article. "We're not talking about fringe players. We're talking about the premiere power forward in basketball, and one of the great guards in the game, even with an injured knee."

The younger, healthier Robinson seemed to be more attractive trade bait than Maravich, who still had several years left on a monster contract. But at least one general manager was interested in Pete.

"Auerbach Beaming at Bird, Dreaming about Maravich" blared the headline of the *Washington Post* on January 5, 1979. Boston's Red Auerbach, taking advantage of a loophole, had already drafted Larry Bird as a junior at Indiana State. But now a dream combo was possible. "Picture the Boston Celtics with Pete Maravich at guard and Larry Bird at forward," wrote Bryon Rosen. "Picture the Celts rising from the ashes." However Celtics owner John Y. Brown also pictured writing the check. "I'm aware that Red has always been fond of him, but I'm also aware of Maravich's contract."

Auerbach was extremely impressed with Maravich's skills. "He could do things with that ball that nobody else could," Auerbach explained in 2000. "He was a great point guard. Magic, Cousy, Isiah, Stockton . . . he's in that group." Auerbach frequently used Pete on his "Red on Roundball" instructional series that was broadcast during half time of NBA games (CBS) in the mid-1970s. On one episode Pete demonstrated his "wrist-pass." Pete's arms went straight out but the ball made a hard left. Red turned to the camera and pleaded with the kids watching at home, "Don't try it! Don't try it! It's ridiculous."

Maravich ultimately stayed in New Orleans and, on January 12, Robinson was traded to the Phoenix Suns. The Jazz received Ron Lee and Marty Byrnes, two No.1 draft picks (1979 and 1980), and $500,000. "The Pistol and the Power" era was over.

For Rich Kelley, an incident in the aftermath of the trade illustrated the cold nature of pro basketball. The team was warming up for a game when the trade became official. The addition of Lee and Byrnes to the roster swelled the team to 13 players, one over the limit. Somebody had to go immediately. Less than an hour before tipoff Baylor made a harsh decision.

"He's talking to everyone in the locker room," remembered Kelley. "Then he turns around and says, 'Ira, would you come into my office?' He cut Ira Terrell. Right in front of everyone. He was in his uniform. . . . It was ugly." Terrell played just 19 more NBA games.

In early February, Pete was voted into his fifth All-Star Game. He is one of a just a few players to start in each of his All-Star appearances. Washington's Elvin Hayes had fond memories of hanging out with Pete at those games. "We would play HORSE every year, and he would just amaze me and show me so many different shots and moves," said Hayes. "That's what I looked forward to the most. He would come with a bag of tricks, things I couldn't even imagine or dream a player could do."

Although Maravich's tender knee limited him to 14 minutes, he hit for 10 points (5-8, 0-0, 2 rebounds, 2 assists) in what would be his final All-Star Game.

The Jazz were slipping out of contention, but Spencer Haywood was enjoying playing alongside Maravich. In his autobiography, *The Rise, The Fall, The Recovery*, he wrote:

> The team's leader was "Pistol" Pete Maravich, my pick as the most talented guard and the most misunderstood soul ever to play the game.
>
> The rap on Peter was that he was selfish, wasn't a team player. Completely untrue. He had unbelievable skills; he could score on anyone. But he loved to pass the ball, too, to involve his teammates in the offense. He never played on a great team, however, so the scoring burden always fell on him—along with the reputation of being a gunner.
>
> Believe me, if you got open, Peter got you the ball and loved doing it, and amazed you every night with the ways he found to do it. If ever there was a genius jazz musician in a basketball uniform, it was the Pistol, taking riffs up to the rafter of that Superdome, bending notes around the corner, playing from the soul . . .

After a 115-112 loss in Denver on February 18, the team decided it was time for Pete to end his season. He contributed 29 points (7-22, 3-4, 3 rebounds, 7 assists) in 39 minutes, but his knee was deteriorating.

"My right knee has atrophied some more, another half-inch," Pete told reporter Jimmy Smith of the *Times-Picayune*. "I lack the muscle structure to support the knee and there's a great degree of possibility something else could go wrong." The team was 19-42. "If we were 42-19 and in the midst of the playoffs, I'd chance the odds," Pete added.

In retrospect he regretted his premature comeback the previous season. "I shouldn't have come back at all to play those three games," Pete said. "It was idiotic. I don't know what goes through an athlete's mind—facing the lions no matter what the circumstances are."

With Maravich sidelined, attendance in New Orleans dropped by more than 4,000 customers per game. On the final day of the season 4,006 fans rattled around in the cavernous Superdome while the Jazz fell to the Bucks, 140-131. The loss dropped the team to 26-56. After four years of steady improvement, New Orleans was headed in the wrong direction.

The Jazz had the league's worst record and normally would have participated in a coin toss to determine first selection in the college draft, but New Orleans had traded away its top pick to Los Angeles when they signed Gail Goodrich in 1977. So, in 1979, the Lakers and the Chicago Bulls were the coin flip participants. Rod Thorn, then representing the Bulls, shouted "heads" as the quarter fell to the floor. It landed "tails." The Lakers selected Earvin "Magic" Johnson from Michigan State University.

The franchise's balance sheet was also headed south, hemorrhaging close to $1 million per year. Several factors contributed to the red ink: high local taxes (11 percent), no significant corporate sponsor, and low season-ticket sales. Because of the Dome's size, fans had no incentive to buy tickets in advance. Good seats were always available. As a result, the Jazz sold a mere 2,565 season tickets in 1978-79.

On the corporate front, the best New Orleans could do was a local retailer, Shoe Town. Of course, Shoe Town did not have pockets as deep as other NBA sponsors, companies like Delta Airlines in Atlanta or Chevron Oil in Houston.

The team's principal owners, Sam Battistone and Larry Hatfield, were both from California and wanted the Jazz in a more profitable location, preferably near the West Coast. During the spring of 1979, Ted Wilson, the mayor of Salt Lake City, and Wendell Ashton, the publisher of the *Deseret News*, Utah's biggest paper, relentlessly courted the Jazz owners. In late April 1979, Battistone and Hatfield agreed to move the Jazz to Salt Lake.

The news came as a shock to Rod Hundley. "They snuck out of town and shipped everything to Salt Lake City." Then he added, "If we had selected Magic Johnson, we would have never left New Orleans."

All that remained were the memories.

NBA guard and Dallas Mavericks coach Avery Johnson grew up in New Orleans. "I used to go and sneak into the games anyway I could," he told the *Dallas Morning News*. "Just seeing Pistol Pete and watching him do all the things that made him one of a kind on the court. Then the next morning, I'd be out there working on all the things I saw The Pistol do the night before."

Jazz fan Steve Crane recalled the magnificent view from the upper deck of the Superdome. "Watching from up there, the passes that the Pistol made were just awe inspiring," Crane said. "You could actually see the plays develop and get an early warning where Pete's next no-look pass might be headed."

Teammate Rich Kelley recalled the joy of running the court. "He was so fast and so creative that it was just an overpowering feeling when he was coming at you on the break. I remember that so distinctly from my rookie year on, how much fun it was, running down the lane, playing fast-break basketball with Pete Maravich."

Bob Dylan, in his 2004 book *Chronicles Vol. 1*, remembered Maravich. "He was something to see—mop of brown hair, floppy socks—the holy terror of the basketball world—high flyin'—magician of the court," wrote Dylan. "The night I saw him he dribbled the ball with his head, scored a behind-the-back, no-look basket—dribbled the length of the court, threw the ball off the glass and caught his own pass. He was fantastic. Scored something like 38 points. He could have played blind."

After a five-year run the show closed in New Orleans. In the center ring stood Pete Maravich. A born showman whose imagination and improvisation elevated his sport into art—a dream player for a team named the Jazz. A moody, confused virtuoso who hoped his next magical shot, pass, or victory would lead him back to happiness. His stage was a polished wooden floor in the same rollicking city where, years earlier, Scott Joplin, Jelly Roll Morton, Louis Armstrong, and Sidney Bechet reinvented the language of music.

Admission: $1.50.

Now, with infant son Jaeson in tow, the Maraviches prepared to move from the boisterous Crescent City to the lush valley of Salt Lake.

21

The Mormon
Trail

"Pete was The Man. I used to love to watch him play. I'd just sit there and shake my head and say, 'How'd he do that?' Then sometimes I'd go out and try some of the things he did. And I couldn't do it."

—EARVIN "MAGIC" JOHNSON, LOS ANGELES LAKERS

"When injuries occur, you are like a wounded tiger. You can look at the faces around you, at the faces of the management of different clubs and you can see the flesh-peddling that goes on."

—PETE MARAVICH

An NBA franchise in Utah became a reality on June 8, 1979, at the Sheraton O'Hare Hotel in Chicago, where team owners unanimously approved the transfer of the five-year-old New Orleans Jazz to Salt Lake City.

Sam Battistone and his fellow owners were taking a gamble by moving to Salt Lake. The town had no major corporate presence and, with a population of less than one million, it was by far the smallest market in the NBA. But chamber of commerce president Wendell Ashton convinced Battistone, whose wife was a Mormon, that the NBA could thrive in Utah.

Among Ashton's selling points was the success of the ABA's Utah Stars. In 1970, the Los Angeles Stars, a struggling ABA franchise, relocated to Utah. In its first year in Salt Lake, the Stars won the ABA championship. Over the next three seasons Utah easily won the ABA's Western Division title and, in 1974, the team returned to the finals, losing to the Julius Erving-led New York Nets. But in the fall of 1975, just 16 games into what was to be the final ABA season, the franchise folded and missed out on the possibility of joining the NBA.

Now that the team would make its home in Utah, the Jazz management flirted with the idea of a name change. No one seemed to think that pairing "Utah" and "Jazz" was a good idea. A contest was organized and "Saints" (for *Church of Jesus Christ of Latter-day Saints*) was the overwhelming winner. But Battistone overruled the voting and retained the name Jazz. He wanted to honor the team's Louisiana roots while not further angering the city of New Orleans, whose NFL team was called the Saints. Also, it saved the unwanted expense of new uniforms.

"I think [the Jazz's] first mistake was not changing the name," said *Salt Lake Tribune* sports editor John Mooney in 1979. "The Utah Jazz doesn't mean anything. It's a joke. If they are here three years from now, I'll buy anybody a steak dinner."

Battistone kept the Mardi Gras uniform colors of purple, green, and gold, but he released most of his coaching staff, including Elgin Baylor.

Frank Layden, assistant coach of the Atlanta Hawks, was offered one of two positions: general manager or head coach. He selected the GM job, thinking, perhaps, that the position guaranteed more long-term security than the coaching slot.

"We're going to win here," he said to longtime employee Dave Fredman. "Let's just hope we're still employed here when it happens."

Fredman, who ascended in the New Orleans organization from "gofer" to director of public relations, was one of the few employees who made the move to Utah. The new location provided a bit of culture shock. "I'm Jewish and I recall that my mom called me on the phone when I arrived," said Fredman. "She wanted to know whether there were any temples. I looked out the window at the Salt Lake Temple, and said, 'Mom, don't worry about it. There are temples here.'"

Pete and Jackie Maravich moved to Utah with trepidation. Jackie, especially, was concerned about starting over in a new city with a five-month-old child. Her fears were allayed after the family moved into a condo in the friendly community of Bountiful, Utah. "You couldn't find nicer people," recalled Jackie. "They did everything for us. Neighbors offered us their 4 x 4. They had lots of kids, so I never had to worry about a babysitter. Super nice families."

The Maraviches would use the neighbor's truck to chase down goat's milk for son Jaeson, who was allergic to regular milk. "We'd drive 45 minutes through the snow and stand in line with other families at 4 A.M. just so that Jaeson could have goat's milk," recalled Jackie.

The only sour note was a wretched perm Pete received from a well-meaning neighbor. He was left with unruly curls tumbling wildly all over his head. "I couldn't even get that right," Pete sighed to Rod Hundley.

The Jazz's new home was the 12,000-seat Salt Palace, the smallest arena in the NBA. The decade-old venue was hardly state of the art. According to trainer Don Sparks, the training room was "a closet" that barely accommodated two players. The arena's lighting was so poor that Milwaukee Bucks broadcaster Eddie Doucette said it was "like playing basketball in a cocktail lounge."

On the plus side, Utah would start the season with 3,000-plus season-ticket holders, more than the team's highest total in New Orleans.

Three dozen players, a mix of veterans, free agents, walk-ons, and rookies, showed up for tryouts and training camp at Salt Lake's Highland High School gymnasium. There had been dramatic roster changes. Gail Goodrich retired and Aaron James, who played more games for the Jazz than any other player, jumped to a pro league in Italy. Rich Kelley was then traded to the New Jersey Nets for Jim Boylan, John Gianelli, Bernard King, and cash. Spencer Haywood was sent to Los Angeles for Adrian Dantley.

Only Maravich and second-year forward James Hardy remained from the New Orleans roster. It was very much a team of strangers.

Pete befriended 10th-round draft pick Paul Dawkins. "Pete was kinda happy-go-lucky at the beginning and he took a liking to me," recalled Dawkins. "He used to call me 'rook.' He once showed me those 'railroad tracks' from the surgery on his knee. He said, 'It looks worse than it feels.'"

Maravich's fixation with nutrition continued in Utah. "Pete would come into the locker room with these concoctions in a clear plastic bottle," said Dawkins. "It had a weird green and orange color. He'd be shaking it up and say, 'It's celery and carrot juice, grape juice, and it's good for your liver.' He would drink all kinds of concoctions I couldn't keep up with it. I said, 'Hey I'll just stick to the Gatorade.'"

When he wasn't preaching about the benefits of goat's milk or railing about the soda manufacturers' conspiracy, Maravich experimented with transcendental meditation and immersion tanks.

The Jazz played four preseason games (2-2) in such basketball "hot spots" as Ogden and Logan. As the preseason progressed, new head coach Tom Nissalke felt pessimistic about the upcoming season. "I remember a reporter saying to me in training camp, 'They look pretty good,'" Nissalke said. "I told him, 'We're going to be horrible.'"

Still, the opening-day lineup appeared to be a formidable offensive team.

It featured Bernard King and Adrian Dantley at forward, Maravich and Don Williams at the guard spots, and 6-8 James Hardy at center. On Friday, October 12, 1979, in Portland, the Utah Jazz played its first regular-season game and lost badly to the Portland Trail Blazers, 101-85, as Maravich scored just four points. Jazz backup forward Alan Bristow lost his wedding ring that night. "Maybe I knew right then it was going to be a bad season," he said.

Three nights later the Jazz played their first home game, facing the Milwaukee Bucks in front of about 6,000 fans in the Salt Palace. Shortly before tipoff, Layden flung open the doors and stopped charging admission. He wanted to goose attendance to make a favorable impression on NBA commissioner Larry O'Brien, on hand for the opening game.

Before the game, the players climbed into the stands, shaking hands and thanking fans for their support. O'Brien threw up the ball for the ceremonial opening tap. "There are no miracles; this will take time," he cautioned the crowd. "I'm . . . confident this team is here to stay, so give them a good look." Milwaukee crushed the Jazz 131-107 despite Pete's game high 29 points.

Utah dropped its next two games to fall to 0-4. On October 22, the Jazz faced the San Diego Clippers in a matchup that included five of the greatest gunners in NBA history: Dantley, King, and Maravich for the Jazz, and Freeman Williams and World B. Free for the Clippers.

The Utah Jazz eked out its first victory, 110-109, as Maravich led the way with 28 points (11-22, 6-6, 6 rebounds, 6 assists) in 42 minutes. King banked in a jump shot with 12 seconds left to seal the win.

Maravich played without his Lenox-Hill brace and his game, although graceful, was less explosive than years past. "The first time I saw him play in a game from the bench, I was just watching how smooth and effortless he was," recalled Dawkins. "He was like a gazelle. His shot was soft and ripped the net. It was one thing to watch him on television but to actually witness all these incredible things he did with the basketball, especially if you've played the game. I saw him pull up, for some threes without any effort. I saw him stop on a dime, pull up and bank off glass with no effort, dribble around the back, no-looks, between the legs. I still saw flashes of brilliance every night. . . . I could only imagine what he was like 10 years earlier."

Three days later, in a win over the Chicago Bulls, Pete scored 31 points, hitting seven straight shots to open the third quarter. Among his baskets were consecutive three-pointers and an astounding 12-footer flipped in over his head. He scored 15 of his points in a 2:59 span. The headline in Chicago's *Daily Herald* read, "Smoking 'Pistol' stops Bulls."

On a November 3 trip to San Diego, Bristow got a glimpse of Pete's star power. "I've played with some great players in my career—George Gervin, Mark Aguirre, Alex English—and I've been around star players, but none, ever, has been as well known as Pete was," Bristow said. "Cab drivers, people on planes, elderly ladies of 65 and 70, women who wouldn't have any other clue about pro basketball players, knew Pete Maravich. He'd walk into a lounge and it was like the parting of the Red Sea."

After the game, a 126–109 loss, Dr. Jack Kleid, a volunteer physician for the Clippers, was casually checking on the Jazz players. (At that time the home team doctor treated both teams.) Kleid noticed Maravich in the corner with a pained expression. Pete explained that he had experienced some chest discomfort and shortness of breath.

Kleid, a cardiologist, insisted on having a listen and was greatly disturbed by what he heard. "It was a murmur," Kleid said in 2000. "I was astounded. I said, 'Look, Pete, I want to see you in my office.'"

Pete mumbled "thanks" and took his card but never called. Kleid was concerned enough to speak to one of the Utah coaches who, according to Kleid, replied, "Don't worry. It's okay."

As the season wore on, Maravich's game was increasingly spotty, and Dantley supplanted him as the team's first scoring option. The 6-4 forward was averaging over 29 points per game and shooting 58 percent from the floor. If Pistol Pete represented the Jazz past, "A.D." was its future.

"Pete couldn't do what he was used to being able to do. He wasn't at his full potential and that bothered him," recalled backup center Ben Pouquette. "He could dish the ball and shoot, but when it came time to be able to stop somebody on defense, he was leery of hurting himself. Once your opponent knows that, especially the good players, they will exploit it."

"Offensively, he was not a problem. Defensively, he had no lateral movement," said Jazz assistant coach Gene Littles. "Guys who had no business blowing by him, did."

On November 21, 1979, Maravich contributed just eight points in a 98–93 road loss to the Detroit Pistons. It was the last time Pete played in a Jazz game.

The team returned to Salt Lake with a 2-18 record and a six-day gap in its schedule. Maravich had played in 17 of the 20 games, averaging 17.1 points with a career-low 42.1 shooting percentage. Major changes were on the horizon.

During the week off Layden added guards Mack Calvin and Terry Furlow and Maravich began to skip the afternoon practice sessions.

"I remember Pete couldn't take part in two-a-days," recalled Jazz trainer Don Sparks. "He'd sit out with ice on his knee."

"That didn't help matters any," said Pouquette. "Nissalke had his rule that if you didn't practice, you didn't play."

On November 27, with the Lakers in town, the Jazz planned a special promotion at the Salt Palace. The game would pit the two "Magic Men"— Earvin Johnson and Pete Maravich—against each other for the first time. (Johnson, injured, missed the first meeting between the teams in Los Angeles.) "Pistol and Magic" posters were given away at the turnstiles and the largest crowd of the young season—11,649—packed the Palace.

For Johnson, a 6-8 point guard, the game was a chance to face one of his basketball idols. Johnson's game was an amalgam of several players he had studied over the years: Dave Bing, George Gervin, Earl Monroe, and Maravich. But the "magic" component of Johnson's game was pure Pistol Pete— the no-look passes, up-tempo, fast-breaking, shuttle passes, and deft ball handling. Like Maravich, Johnson was a charismatic showman who loved entertaining. "On the court I can express myself," explained Earvin. "The crowd is going crazy and there's all that energy. And if you look down into your popcorn you might just miss something."

But when Nissalke announced his starting five for "Pistol and Magic" night, Pete's name was missing from the lineup. Veteran guard Ron Boone started in his place. Dantley continued his hot streak, scoring a then-career-high 50 points against his old team, but the Jazz lost 122-118. A humiliated Maravich never made it into the game. His stat line read: "DNP." Did not play.

"I really wanted to be on the same court with him," Johnson said years later. "I got to play against Dr. J and George Gervin but Pete was on the bench that night. Yeah, that was really disappointing."

Utah's coach had stuck to his rule. "I just don't play guys who don't practice well," Nissalke explained to Los Angeles Times reporter Scott Ostler.

"I thought he deserved a little more respect," Dawkins said. "Come on. He was a seasoned pro. A former All-Star. Why beat him up? You could see his knees were hurting him."

Some believed the slight was personal. Years earlier, while at LSU, Maravich torched a Nissalke-coached Tulane team for 58 points. Perhaps the DNP was payback. But Nissalke defended his actions in 2001. "It was a decision I get blamed for, but it was a joint decision. We were going to go another direction. He just wasn't getting it done in practice."

Bristow agreed with his coach. "He just couldn't do the same things he was once able to do. He wasn't putting in practice time and his timing was off."

To Fredman, failing to exploit Maravich's drawing power was a major blunder. "To me, it was one of the worst decisions in the history of basketball not to play Pete Maravich. We were like an expansion franchise starting all over again. Pete Maravich was still a name. Pete Maravich still had some basketball ability. The knee was not totally shot because he wasn't even wearing a knee brace when he came back. I thought it was very unfair that he was being sat down."

Just 10 months after starting in the NBA All-Star Game, Maravich was relegated to the end of the bench.

Dawkins said the situation was heartbreaking. "Pete became pretty solemn and everybody could feel the tension," said Dawkins. "Bernard [King] and I used to talk about it. 'Why isn't he putting in Pete? What is the purpose? He's healthy enough. He just scored 28. The fans are chanting for him.'"

King replied, "Man, who knows? Always remember this is business. For all we know, they're trying to trade Pete."

King's hunch was exactly right. Peter Vecsey's November 28 column in the *New York Post* broke the story: Utah was trying to unload the Pistol. "Maravich does a lot of good things," said an anonymous Jazz source. "Unfortunately, they are not the things that will win ball games. He's a crowd pleaser . . . the fact remains though he's more of a liability than an asset."

On December 3, the Jazz played the Milwaukee Bucks in Salt Lake and fans spent the bulk of the second half chanting for Maravich. After the game Nissalke confirmed the trade rumor to a UPI reporter. "We are looking to make a deal that will benefit both the team and Pete."

One week after the poster-night debacle, the Jazz faced the world champion Sonics in Seattle. Again, Maravich sat out as the Sonics mauled Utah, 115-96. After the game, a sullen Maravich tried to drown his despair with beer. He returned to the Washington Plaza Hotel and made a loud ruckus outside of what he thought was his hotel room. The room, however, was occupied by a Mormon bishop and Maravich had to be escorted by hotel security to his own room one floor below.

Maravich was, understandably, hurt and angered by his playing status. His sanctuary—the basketball court—was no longer accessible.

Ernie DiGregorio recalled that Maravich once offered him some important advice.

"One time I was playing in Buffalo and I got benched," DiGregorio recalled. "We saw each other in the hallway before the game. He said, 'Hey, Ernie D. Remember, don't ever let them get your confidence. Once they do, it's *One Flew Over the Cuckoo's Nest*.'"

Over the next 24 games, Pete put on his Jazz uniform but never played. "We got booed every place we went," recalled Bill Bertka. "It was a nightmare." Fans carried placards at games that read, "Pete, We Love You!" and "Release the Hostage," a topical reference to the 66 Americans being held by Iranian extremists.

"I remember Pete after those games would just put on his jacket and leave," said Dawkins. "He wouldn't even shower."

Lon Levin, son of former San Diego Clippers owner Irv Levin, recalled a December game in San Diego.

"The Jazz were fools not to play him," Levin said.

Levin snapped a poignant photo of Pete, still in his warmup outfit, standing on the outskirts of the Jazz huddle looking uninvolved and uninterested.

"That shot said it all to me," Levin said.

One night former Jazz statistician Bob Remy witnessed an angry locker-room rant by Maravich. "Their dressing room in Utah wasn't very big," Remy recalled. "It was like high school all over again. So I see Pete and we're catching up, and Nissalke's right there—three feet away. And Pete starts in on him. 'That . . . coach doesn't play me. I don't know what's wrong with him. [He] doesn't know what he's doing.' He's going on and on, knocking Nissalke really bad. Obviously, he wanted the coach to hear him. And I'm the only person standing between these two guys."

Pete endured many sleepless nights fretting about the downturn in his career. He had long talks with Press, who counseled him to hang tough, reminding him that if he broke his contract and walked away, Utah would owe him nothing.

Jazz assistant coach Gene Littles recalled that Maravich began to entertain thoughts of coaching. "Pete knew I was from High Point, North Carolina, and he wanted to go back to Raleigh where he was from," Littles said. "He said one time on the bench, 'Shoot, we just ought to go back there and coach' because he was getting so frustrated from not playing."

General manager Frank Layden let Maravich know that there was a future coaching opportunity with the Jazz. "I offered Pete a coaching position here when he was done," Layden said. "I said, 'Why don't you come with us and be the heir apparent? Be the assistant coach for a while and then I'll turn it over to you.'"

But Pete was convinced he could still contribute. "My basketball death is very premature," he told *States-Item* reporter Ron Brocato. "I know I can play this game four or five more years."

Maravich vented his frustrations to Dave Blackwell of the *Deseret News*. "It's like being in an airplane. You don't have any control," Pete explained. "Maybe I've overstayed my welcome. I doubt whether I'll finish the season here. Yet I really don't believe another team would pick me up. My salary is just too large. I guess you could say I am a victim of my own circumstances."

Meanwhile his attorney, Les Zittrain, was searching desperately for a solution and reached out to Sam Battistone. "I said, 'Sam, this is a ridiculous situation. You've got this superstar and you're paying him all of this money and he's sitting on the bench. He's very unhappy. The coach is unhappy. The fans are unhappy.'

"He said, 'You're right.' So I invited Sam to come to Pittsburgh, and he did, and we sat and talked. He's a nice guy, and we worked out some details. If two people want to work something out, that's what will happen."

Utah owed Maravich $1.8 million for the final two-and-a-half years of his contract. Battistone agreed to honor that commitment, although the payments were stretched out over a longer period of time, with the last checks coming in 1988 instead of 1983. On January 17, 1980, the Jazz placed Pete Maravich on waivers. The press release read:

> We are pleased that we have been able to reach a settlement that will be good
> for both the team and Pete. Pete Maravich has been a big part of the Jazz
> since the team's inception nearly six years ago in New Orleans.

During the next 48 hours any NBA team could assume Maravich's Jazz contract. If no team chose to do so Maravich would become a free agent, eligible to negotiate on the open market. (The NBA had a minimum salary of $30,000.)

The jockeying to acquire Maravich began almost immediately after the 48-hour window closed. His first choice, Los Angeles, was not interested. But several teams were, notably the Philadelphia 76ers and the Boston Celtics. The interest of those powerhouses was wonderful news for Maravich because he yearned to play for a title contender. At the time, Philadelphia topped the Eastern conference (35-11) and Boston was close on its heels (34-12).

Initially, Philadelphia looked like the front runner because it needed to replace Doug Collins, who had suffered a severe foot injury. Maravich was excited by the prospect of playing again with Julius Erving. He well remembered their electric collaboration in the fall of 1972.

Before committing to Maravich, the 76ers wanted to look closely at his surgically repaired knee. On January 21, Pete underwent an extremely detailed and thorough examination supervised by Dr. Michael Clancey at Temple University Hospital in Philadelphia.

Many news outlets began to report that the 76ers would sign Maravich if he passed his physical. The Sixers even made up a No. 44 jersey with "MARAVICH" embroidered on the back.

When Dr. Clancey declared that Maravich's knee was 100 percent, Philadelphia offered a contract. But Pete demurred, telling the Sixers he wanted to study offers from Houston and Boston. In reality, Pete was only interested in Boston's overture, so the next day he flew to Logan Airport.

At 5:55 P.M. Pete walked into Boston Garden to meet with Celtics President and GM Red Auerbach. An hour later Pete's attorneys, Zittrain and Art Herskovitz, arrived from Pittsburgh. At 7:25 P.M., Auerbach and Maravich left to watch the Celtics play the Rockets while Zittrain and Herskovitz began negotiating with Celtics' business manager Jan Volk. At half time, John Havlicek escorted Pete back to Auerbach's office where Celtics Vice President Jeff Cohen announced there would be a press conference following the game. At 10:50 P.M. on January 22, 1980, Auerbach, with his trademark cigar in hand, proudly announced that Pete Maravich was the newest member of the Boston Celtics.

Pete, wearing a leather jacket over an open-collared plaid shirt, smiled broadly and said, "I've been trying to get here for 10 years."

Ultimately, the Utah Jazz won just 24 games in its maiden season in Salt Lake. On New Year's Day 1980, Bernard King was arrested on five felony sex charges and was later admitted to a rehab center for substance abusers. King's legal troubles presaged a litany of tragedies for Jazz players. Terry Furlow, the young guard who replaced Maravich, died in a car accident. Forward Bill Robinzine committed suicide in 1982. John Drew was also admitted into rehab.

"Coaching back then was like lion taming," said Nissalke. "You were just trying to keep everything under control."

For several years after Maravich's departure the Utah Jazz teetered on the brink of collapse. The team played several "home" games in Las Vegas and seriously considered a merger with the Denver Nuggets. But, with a nucleus of Dantley, Darrell Griffith, Rickey Green, and Mark Eaton, the team gradually clawed its way to respectability.

Then, with the 16th pick of the 1984 draft and the 13th pick of the 1985 draft, Utah acquired John Stockton and Karl Malone. That same year a local auto dealer named Larry Miller bought out Sam Battistone and became the principal owner of the team. The stellar play of Stockton and Malone, and the steady guidance of Miller, eventually helped the Jazz blossom into one of the NBA's premier franchises.

"Poor Sam Battistone lost $2 million a year for about 10 years, and then he sold the team right when it turned around," Rod Hundley said. "His timing was like the *Titanic*."

A quarter century after the Jazz came to Salt Lake City, few remembered its humble start. But not Frank Layden.

"The thing about the Jazz, when they think about them, they immediately think of Stockton and Malone, and the great teams we've had in the last decade," Layden said in 2000. "When you mention the Utah Jazz to me, I tell them, 'Pete Maravich was the heart of the Jazz.'"

22

Celtic Farewell

"I lost my basketball ego a long time ago. I don't have one, and I don't care to have one."

—PETE MARAVICH

"I could never, ever get over the fact that I was on the floor while Pistol Pete was on the bench. I couldn't even imagine it was happening."

—M. L. CARR, BOSTON CELTICS

By the end of 1979 Pete Maravich's incomparable basketball career had skittered to a halt. He was 32 and his once-dominant skills were partially diminished by injury. But he still burned to win a championship and, to that end, signed with the most successful franchise in NBA history, the Boston Celtics.

"A lot of people say nice things about the Celtics, but I think it's justified because they have 13 flags here," said Maravich, flanked at his first Celtic press conference by Red Auerbach and head coach Bill Fitch. "All I have in my house is one little United States flag."

Maravich arrived as the Celtics were making an impressive turnaround from a horrible 29-53 season in 1978-79, their worst mark in 29 years. The transformation was due, in large part, to the glittering play of 6-9 rookie Larry Bird. The 1979 College Player of the Year at Indiana State, Bird entered the NBA, like Maravich nine years earlier, amid oversized expectations. He had averaged 30.3 points and 13.3 rebounds in college, joining Maravich and Oscar Robertson as the only NCAA players to score 900 or more points in each of three college seasons. In 1978, during Bird's junior year, Boston took advantage of a loophole and made the so-called "Hick from French Lick" the sixth pick in the NBA draft. Bird finished out his college career and signed for $3.28 million over five years, becoming the highest paid rookie in sports.

Boston hoped Maravich, playing about 24 minutes a game, would provide instant offense off the bench. The NBA had added the three-point shot before the 1979–80 season and the Celtics believed Maravich would convert a slew of the bonus shots. Coach Fitch was a longtime admirer of Pete. "He's multi-talented. He can do some things Tiny [Archibald] can do, some things M. L. [Carr] can do, and some things Larry [Bird] can do," he gushed after the signing.

The team offered Pete a two-year deal, but he wanted to prove himself first and signed for just the season at $80,000. He had gone from being the highest paid athlete in professional sports to his team's lowest-salaried player. "He's the only player on the team who makes less than I do," joked Fitch. (Maravich, of course, was still receiving hefty paychecks from the Jazz.)

Some skeptics doubted Maravich could mesh with Boston's legendary selfless play. No Celtic had ever led the league in scoring. But for Auerbach, the decision was easy. "He [Pete] was one of the great passers, shooters, and ball handlers who ever played," he told *Boston Globe* reporter Dan Shaughnessy in 1984.

And Auerbach knew that so-called "showy" players could also produce wins. His Celtics had enjoyed great success in the late 1950s and early 1960s with flashy guard Bob Cousy running the point. "Flamboyancy has nothing to do with fundamentals," explained Auerbach. "You can be flamboyant and still be basically sound. And Pete was basically sound. He knew how to run that fast break. He knew how to be the focal point of that break down the middle and he could hit the open guy."

On Maravich's first official day as a Celtic he was introduced to Mike Cole, a young man working in Boston's promotions department. "When he signed the contract, Red, Bill Fitch, Pete, and myself went out to have dinner," recalled Cole. "We went to this famous fish place in Boston called the No Name Restaurant, which is right on the water. Pete asks the waiter, 'How far is the fish caught off the shore?' He believed that if the fish was caught 200 feet within the shore, it might have pollutants. The further out, the healthier the fish."

Maravich, who had not played for seven weeks, was placed on injured reserve. Eager to improve his conditioning, he was surprised to discover he would be training separately from the team. Maravich was not pleased; he believed competing with fellow pros was the only way to get into peak game shape. Fitch arranged for him to work out with Steve Riley, a front office worker and former Division III player. Pete was able to mingle with the team, however, when he lifted weights at Boston's practice site at Hellenic College in Brookline, Massachusetts.

"I want to be with a winner," Maravich told *Boston Globe* reporter Leigh Montville. "I've wondered, all of my career, how it would have been if I had gone with a winner in the first place. I've always thought the picture would be different about me. My life would have been different. I've always wondered . . . and now I'm here."

With Cole's help, Pete rented an apartment in Longfellow Place, a high-rise near the Garden. The harsh Boston winter did not agree with Jackie Maravich.

"It was cold, damp, and miserable," recalled Jackie. "I didn't know anyone and I had to take a taxi everywhere or walk with the baby." Plus, finding goat's milk in Boston for nine-month-old Jaeson proved problematic. Pete attempted to track down a distributor by running an ad in the local papers.

In early February Pete started to practice with the team. Trainer Ray Melchiorre had heard stories about Maravich's gloomy personality but he saw no trace of it. He observed a devoted husband and father, a humble man who spread the gospel of vegetarianism and never failed to pick up a check.

"Most pro players have an agenda," Melchiorre said. "I found him to be very generous to people around him and the people who worked for him."

One Celtic happy to see Pete was center Dave Cowens. Their connection dated back to college and included several wild summers together barnstorming the basketball camp circuit.

"He was going through a transition in his life and he was trying to figure out what his place was. He was like the Pied Piper of basketball," Cowens said. "He didn't want to be the show and all of that. He came to work everyday and worked hard. He just wanted to win."

Maravich's relationship with Larry Bird proved more complex. "Larry's a funny guy," said Cole. "He's tough to get to know. At that time, Larry was eating a lot of junk food and Pete wasn't, so there was a little conflict there. They kidded each other. Larry did some McDonald's ads and Pete was saying, 'You're eating cows' noses,' and had some good-natured fun, but there was never that real bonding between them."

M. L. Carr recalled classic HORSE contests between the two before practice. "He and Larry just went at it. I can recall Pete spinning the ball on his finger, then off his head, and into the basket."

Fitch, dismayed at Pete's poor conditioning, announced that Maravich would not get a free pass into the starting lineup. In an article titled "Pistol Pete's Last Shot" for the inaugural issue of *Inside Sports*, David Halberstam reported the following exchange between Fitch and Maravich.

"You're disappointed in me, aren't you?" Maravich said to his coach.

"Yes," Fitch replied. "I am. I can't believe what kind of shape you're in. I just don't understand it."

"Don't give up on me," Maravich pleaded. "I'm coming around, I'm coming around. I know I am. I know I can do it."

"I hope so," Fitch said.

In another practice, Pete drew Fitch's ire when he threw a behind-the-back-pass and missed an open man.

"Hold it, hold it, hold it!" Fitch screamed as the gym fell quiet. "Pete, you've gotta stop that [expletive]. We don't need it."

On February 8, 1980, Maravich finally made his debut for the Boston Celtics. He stayed on the bench for the first half, but early in the third quarter, a chant began to build, "We want Pete, we want Pete." By the fourth quarter they were yelling and as Pete checked in, with 7:04 left in the game, the Boston Garden faithful rose to their feet.

"I thought I'd be real tight when I first went in," Maravich told Larry Whiteside of the *Boston Globe* afterward. "But the moment I got in there, I was loose. I heard the crowd calling for me and I appreciated it very much. It came as quite a surprise and made me feel great."

Immediately, he rewarded the sold-out arena with a fancy pass to Eric Fernsten that resulted in an easy basket. Maravich took three shots, hitting one, before Fitch pulled him with under two minutes left. The Celtics rolled over the Indiana Pacers 130-108.

Two nights later against the Pistons, Maravich entered in the second quarter and scored 10 quick points in four minutes, finishing off the half with a twisting, off-balance layup at the buzzer. His spree ignited another standing ovation from the sellout crowd in the Garden. Pete finished with 14 points and dished out four assists in 14 minutes of play. Larry Bird anchored the team with 24 points, 11 rebounds, and 7 assists. The win was Boston's seventh straight and extended its lead over Philadelphia in the Atlantic Division to three games.

The *Boston Globe* headline read: "Pistol, Bird Blast Pistons, 128-111."

"This is the first time I've played with a team that plays the way I like to play," Maravich said after the game. "Today it was easy for me to score."

Still, Maravich was cautious. "I've got a long way to go with this team," Pete told Whiteside. "I'm just happy to be with a team like this. I've been on the outside looking in for a long time."

Pete was finally, as he liked to say, on the "flip side." His role was to provide instant offense. Fitch brought Maravich along slowly, playing him an average of 11 minutes instead of the promised 24.

Maravich said his diminished playing time made him feel like "a donkey among thoroughbreds."

Still, Maravich was making a significant impact. In four key games he made the following contributions:

- February 23: 14 points, including 10 points on 4-of-4 shooting in the second quarter, in a 124-105 road win over the Denver Nuggets.
- March 7: 13 points, including a 35-foot three-pointer at the buzzer in a 111-92 victory over Philadelphia.
- March 9: 20 points (8-16) in 14 minutes in an OT loss to the Bullets. He shared the game MVP award with Cedric Maxwell.
- March 17: 12 points (6-10) in 17 minutes, including five consecutive baskets in the third quarter, in a 117-92 win at New Jersey.

Off the court Maravich was getting to know his new teammates. Several were struck by his unusual eating habits. Chris Ford remembered that Pete used to carry his own supply of fruit juice.

Pete preached sound nutrition everywhere, even 30,000 feet in the air. "It was unimaginable to him that anyone would put a morsel of airline food in their mouth," the *Globe*'s Bob Ryan recalled. "I remember him giving me some line about breakfast on the airlines. He said, 'Those scrambled eggs had your name on it three days ago.'"

Peculiar dining habits aside, Carr said it was a dream to play alongside Maravich. "Pete was something very special to me," Carr said. "I'm sure he had a big impact on a lot of lives, but there's not another athlete who went on to play professional sports that felt closer to Pete than I did. He meant so much to me because he really sparked my interest in the game."

On March 18, with Ford out and Cedric Maxwell hurt, Pete was inserted into the starting lineup against the Indiana Pacers at the Hartford Civic Center. He made the most of the opportunity, draining 10 points in the first quarter as Boston took a 29-19 lead. In the second quarter, as Bird and Cowens rode the bench with foul trouble, Pete popped in another 11 points.

"Included in his second-period performance was a one-minute burst that would have been very recognizable to the folks in Raleigh, Baton Rouge, and New Orleans," wrote Ryan. "He nailed a long turn-around jumper, a banked-in runner [plus a foul shot], and a pull up jumper." Seven points in 1:05.

In a 114-102 victory, Maravich led all scorers with 31 points (12-18, 7-7, 3 rebounds, 3 assists) in 42 minutes. The headline in the *Boston Globe* read: "Pistol Riddles Pacers."

"I didn't know I was going to start until just before the game," Pete told reporter George Smith. "It doesn't matter to me whether I start or not. I'm here to contribute. That's the only thing I ever wanted to do in basketball."

The win put the 57-18 Celtics two-and-a-half games ahead of Philadelphia.

Two nights later Maravich got another start, this time in Detroit where five months earlier, he played his last game with the Jazz. He scored a team-high 20 points (8-15) in 28 minutes in a 124-106 win.

Maravich was serving notice that he still ranked among the NBA's sharpest shooters.

"I remember Pete saying that he was so amazed at how easy it was for him to have scored 60 points on those nights," remarked Mike Cole. "But he was always afraid to stand out too much because of this feeling he had that the players might not like him as well. He was very humble; he went out of his way not to cause problems."

Pete's most dramatic performance as a Celtic occurred on March 25 against the Washington Bullets at a sold-out Capital Centre. With Ford back in the starting lineup, Maravich provided electrifying offense off the bench in the fourth quarter, hitting seven of eight shots as the Celtics drew to within two. He then fired a running 12-footer that skipped off the rim. The ball was batted around until Bullets center Wes Unseld knocked it away—and right into Pete's hands. The Pistol fired up a three-pointer that swished through with 51 seconds remaining. The shot ultimately gave the Celtics a 96-95 win.

"Maravich Rescues Celtics," read the *Boston Globe* headline.

"What you saw tonight was the best of Maravich for 15 minutes and that's what we got him for," Fitch explained to *Washington Post* reporter David DuPree. "The one ingredient we were lacking before we got him was a jump shooter down the stretch. Now we have it."

Washington's Kevin Grevey kept the game close by hitting three three-pointers. "The combination of things Pete could do was deadly," Grevey said years later. "He was well before his time. I've played against Michael Jordan, Magic Johnson, Larry Bird. And Pistol was by far the best player. He had it all."

Pete finished with 19 points, including 17 in the fourth quarter, and was awarded the game ball.

The next night, at home against the Knicks, Boston trailed by four after three quarters when Maravich got into a late-game shooting duel with Earl Monroe. In the fourth quarter Pete scored 12 points, to Monroe's 14, in a 129-121 Celtics win.

Now, for the first time in his numerous games against the Knicks, Maravich had the stronger roster. His running mates included three future Hall of Famers in Bird, Archibald, and Cowens; while Monroe was teamed with journeymen like Bill Cartwright, Ray Williams, and Marvin Webster. It was the last meeting between Maravich and Monroe, two of the NBA's most innovative and influential players.

Taking the floor against the Cavaliers on March 28, the Celtics needed one win to clinch the Atlantic Division crown and home-court advantage throughout the playoffs. A late comeback gave them a 130–122 victory. As the final seconds ticked away, Maravich dribbled out the clock in Globetrotter fashion and then, in a rare emotional outburst, spiked the ball when the buzzer sounded.

By winning 32 games more than the previous year, the 1979–80 Celtics set a record for the largest turnaround in NBA history, besting Milwaukee's mark of 29 games set in 1969-70. Ryan, in the *Globe*, listed the five major reasons for the historic improvement.

1. *The signing of Bird.*
2. *The signing of M. L. Carr as a free agent.*
3. *The simultaneous personal comebacks of Cowens and Archibald.*
4. *The signing of Fitch as coach.*
5. *The signing of Pete Maravich, who ultimately made the difference between finishing first and second in the Atlantic Division.*

Bird was voted Rookie of the Year and first team All-NBA, while Fitch was named Coach of the Year.

Pete averaged 11.5 points a game, his lowest scoring average since making the Daniel High varsity while in eighth grade in 1960. But he shot a career-high 49 percent, a clear indication that individual statistics can be greatly influenced by teammates. Sharing the court with exemplary players, he shot with greater accuracy than Boston starters Bird, Archibald, Cowens, and Ford. Pete made 91 percent of his free throws, another career high, and easily the best on the team. From three-point territory, Pete converted 10 of 15 shots on the season. Although his three-point sample is small, Pete's .667 shooting percentage indicates he would have thrived at that distance.

For the first time since 1973, Maravich was in the playoffs.

Boston took two days off after the season ended before embarking on an eight-day, pre-playoff training camp. (Boston's division title earned the team a first-round bye.) Pete worked out with a fierce determination. "A championship would culminate my whole basketball life," Pete told John Papanek of

Sports Illustrated. "The other stuff—the trophies, plaques, scoring championships—you can throw it in the Mississippi River for all I care."

A new sign went up in the rafters of the Boston Garden, right next to the ones that read: "Ford, A Winning Idea" and "Welcome to Bird Land." This banner read: "For Pete's Sake."

Boston's first opponent was the Houston Rockets, featuring Moses Malone, Calvin Murphy, Rudy Tomjanovich, and off the bench, Rick Barry. Before Game 1, Pete confided in Barry that he was still only about 60 percent. To Barry's eye, that seemed about right. In many ways, the Celtics Maravich was no longer *Pete Maravich*. Of course, he could still score in bundles but he showed little of his explosive athleticism. There was crafty passing and fluid ball handling but nothing too spectacular. Plus, as a result of an early-season perm, his hair was still crazily puffed out and Pete, superstitiously, didn't want to cut it while the Celts were winning.

Pete was used sparingly as the Celtics took four straight from the Rockets. It was Maravich's first victory in a playoff series and he watched it mainly from the bench. He hit four straight baskets in the second quarter of Game 2, but on the whole, was not a factor in the series. Game 4 marked Rick Barry's final appearance in the NBA.

"Pete Maravich professes not to be upset or concerned over his limited playing time in this series," wrote Ryan. "He only played 25 minutes in the first three games. Chris Ford has been playing so well that there hasn't been a need for a Maravich, or anybody else. The Pistol knows his time will come."

The Celtics faced the Philadelphia 76ers in the conference final. Maravich's decision to sign with Boston instead of Philadelphia seemed wise as the series began. But the Sixers were loaded with talent and playoff experience. Although fans anticipated a seven-game shootout between Bird and Erving, it was not to be. After the teams split the first two games, the 76ers won three straight to eliminate the Celtics. Pete made a nice contribution in Game 2 when he scored eight points (4-5, 0-0, 1 rebound, 1 assist) in Boston's 96-90 victory. He scored 31 points over the other four games. Many observers said Philadelphia was helped by the steady guard play of Lionel Hollins. The 76ers signed Hollins only after being spurned by Maravich.

As Boston's season wound down in the closing minutes of Game 5, Maravich snapped a no-look pass to Jeff Judkins, who buried a three-pointer from the left wing. It was Pete's sixth assist of the playoffs and, as it turned out, the last time he would touch a basketball in an NBA game.

The team voted Pete a half share of the playoff bonus money but it was small consolation. Another season had ended without a championship.

Before heading home to Louisiana, Maravich presented a $500 check to Cole. "This is for all of the things you've done for me, my wife, and my son," Pete told him.

Cole took the check with the caveat that he would use the money to visit Maravich in Louisiana over the summer.

Back in Metairie, Pete watched the Lakers face Philadelphia in a memorable final. The sixth and final game featured a masterful performance by rookie Magic Johnson as he poured in 42 points (14-23, 14-14, 15 rebounds, 7 assists, 3 steals) to lead the Lakers to a championship. The crowd-pleasing Lakers of the 1980s would adopt Maravich's old LSU nickname, "Showtime."

Watching the finals, Maravich wondered whether, given his limited playing time (16 minutes per game), he would have been satisfied even if Boston had won the NBA crown. Would a championship ring still be meaningful if his contribution had been minimal? The question gnawed at him.

Cole made good on his promise and visited the Maravich family during the summer. Pete took his guest into New Orleans for a taste of the Big Easy.

"We went to the French Quarter," Cole said. "His older brother Ronnie worked in a bar there. Ronnie said to me, 'Mike Cole, I don't know who . . . you are, but you must be one heck of a friend to my brother because he would never come out and do this normally.' Every place we went into, we never waited in line. At Pat O'Brien's, there must have been 200 people in line. When they spotted Pete, they brought us right in. Every bar had his jersey hanging up. Either it was an LSU jersey or a Jazz jersey. The reception we got from people was amazing. It was like visiting the Pope at the Vatican. Pete and his brother really didn't have a warm relationship but he came out with us and we hit the town that night. It was the only time I ever saw Pete drink."

Maravich spent the summer lifting weights and running wind sprints along the levee. He had decided to give pro basketball one last shot but only if he could provide a larger contribution.

"Pete told them he wasn't coming back unless he started," said friend and former University of Florida basketball coach John Lotz. "So they said, 'Okay, we'll give you a shot.'"

Boston agreed to bump Maravich's salary to $200,000. Pete had a strong ally in Auerbach. "If I was coaching, there's no doubt I would've used him a lot more minutes. But Fitch didn't see it that way," said Auerbach in 1999. "I was the president, but I don't interfere with the coach. If you go second guessing every time the coach makes a substitution and stuff like that, it's terrible. I've never done that."

Cracking Boston's starting lineup at age 33 would not be easy. "That year's camp had a lot of guys hungry for spots, you had McHale and Parish coming in," said Cole. "By no means did Pete not have a position on the team, but it was tough on him physically with the two-a-days."

Maravich asked to be excused from the second practice. But Fitch said he would not accord special treatment to any player.

"It pained me to see Bill treat Pete that way because Pete busted his [butt] on both offense and defense," recalled Celtics assistant coach K. C. Jones. "I just felt bad for him because he was a great player and I appreciated the way he was playing. He just had an issue with the coach."

Fitch also had a short fuse. "One time in training camp I got so frustrated that I just kicked the ball," M. L. Carr recalled. "The ball whizzed by the coach's head."

"Fitch didn't see who did it," said Kevin McHale who recalled the incident in Jack McCallum's book *Unfinished Business*. "But he whirled around and screamed, 'Maravich [expletive]!' Just like that. And I'm thinking to myself, '... [H]e talks to Pete Maravich like that, what's he going to say to me?'"

Pete stayed silent. "I was ready to jump in and tell Fitch it was me, but Pete told me to be quiet," recalled Carr. "He took the blame because at that stage of his career it didn't really matter and he didn't want me to get into trouble."

Boston capped off a grueling, 10-day training camp with its traditional Green and White game on September 19.

"The White team was always the starters and the Green team was always the support players," recalled Carr. "There was always incredible competition between those two teams. There were incredible wars. Some of the best games we ever played in."

Maravich suited up with the Green Team. His teammates were Carr, McHale, Gerald Henderson, Don Chaney, Eric Fernsten, and Rick Robey. They would face Bird, Ford, Archibald, Cowens, Parish, and Cedric Maxwell. The Greens looked decidedly overmatched. But, again, Pete rose to the occasion. Facing four future Hall of Famers, Maravich scored 38 points to lead the bench warmers to a stunning upset.

"He was on fire," Carr said. "We were going crazy. We just gave him the ball."

Maravich hoped his brilliant performance would convince a skeptical Fitch that he deserved to start. It did not. Ford remained the starter.

"I couldn't stop thinking about what might happen if we made it all the way to the playoffs and I had spent the year on the bench in disgrace," Maravich wrote in his memoirs.

Years later Carr analyzed Fitch's decision. "I think if you asked who was a better player, clearly Pete was," said Carr in 2004. "But if you asked who was the better player for *that team*, Chris Ford was the right one. He was a very cerebral player. He knew what his role was and didn't try to go beyond that. Chris liked the ball, but didn't need the ball to be effective. Pete, on the other hand, needed the ball and that was going to take a little away from the front line. We won two world championships with Chris Ford in the lineup."

Maravich decided he could not stomach another year on the bench. He told friend Chet Marshall, "I left my sneakers hanging in the locker room and walked away."

It was over. Pete Maravich was done playing basketball.

He phoned Auerbach and then Fitch. "I think I've shot one basket too many," he explained.

Attorney Les Zittrain was the recipient of another call, "Les, I'm retired. It's over, and it's a done deal and I'm happy about it." But that avowal was not necessarily the truth.

Cowens, also considering retirement, had a long talk with Maravich. "I think mainly that he lost his competitive edge," Cowens observed. "And the fact that he didn't hit it off with the coach sort of solidified it."

Johnny Most, the Celtics' broadcaster, also received a call the day after Pete's departure. Maravich told him he felt a bit betrayed by Fitch and Auerbach, both of whom had led him to believe he would play a significant role with the Celtics.

"I wanted to play for a contender, but I also felt I had to be in the regular rotation," Maravich explained to Most. "It was important to me that I would be able to make a legitimate contribution every night. If I was only going to get five minutes here and there, then it wasn't going to be worth it."

Globe reporter Bob Ryan was convinced Pete could still play. "I never understood why Bill was so hard on him. I think Pete might have come back for another year if somebody else were coaching."

Ryan, who had grown fond of Maravich, knew he would miss the quirky veteran.

"At that point in his life, Pete Maravich was a completely engaging individual, a team guy, a friendly person," Ryan said. "I was really looking forward to getting to know him for the next year."

Maravich's quiet exit from the NBA stood in stark contrast to his celebrated entrance in 1970. There was no press conference, no good-bye tour, no retirement ceremony.

At the time he left, Pete's NBA career scoring average of 24.2 points per game ranked him eighth in league history behind Chamberlain, Abdul-Jabbar, Baylor, West, McAdoo, Pettit, and Robertson.

His 10-year pro career was a mixture of searing frustration and staggering accomplishment. He scored more points in the 1970s than any other NBA guard, but the numbers tell just a fraction of the story. It was how he scored and how he played that forged his legend.

"There simply wasn't anything he couldn't do with a basketball," wrote *Washington Post* reporter David DuPree. "He played with a unique flair, pizzazz, and showmanship that made it look like he was put on earth to play basketball."

Now, Pete wondered, what on earth would he do next?

Part 4

Reborn

Speaking at a 1987 Billy Graham Crusade.

23

Withdrawal

"The only thing that ever mattered to me was basketball. I sold my soul to the game."

—PETE MARAVICH

"Raw-talent wise, he's the greatest who ever played the game. But always, no matter what he does, he will be a loser. That's his legacy."

—LOU HUDSON

Maravich left Boston and went into seclusion at his five-bedroom home in Metairie, Louisiana. His childhood quest for an NBA title ended without a championship ring. Sad and embittered, Maravich piled his many trophies and awards into boxes and gave them away to friends and Goodwill. His pal Randy Drude received dozens of items, including posters, warmups, programs, and jerseys.

"He just didn't want the stuff anymore," Drude said. "I still have those items to this very day."

Adjusting to life without basketball was a brutal process. "One day I was playing—I scored 38 points—and the next day I quit basketball," Maravich explained. "That was it. I was like a drug addict coming off heroin. I had gone cold turkey."

In November, Dave Cowens visited Pete. Just days after Pete walked away from the Celtics, Cowens also retired. Teammate Larry Bird recalled his reaction to the departure of his teammates. "I couldn't believe they quit. We had a good team. I was like, 'Why would you do something like that?'"

While dining at the Chart House restaurant in New Orleans, Cowens suggested the pair rejoin the team. Go back to Boston for one final shot at glory. But Pete wasn't interested and he retreated further into isolation, eventually changing his phone number so old friends couldn't reach him.

"I never saw him after he immediately retired," said former LSU trainer

Billy Simmons. "He didn't do anything socially with people. He stayed around the house. He didn't have anything going. Didn't even want to coach, got completely out of basketball. All he ever wanted to do was play basketball."

Maravich had long pined for days when he could just relax by his swimming pool.

"Ever since I was seven years old, people had been telling me the way of the world was success," Maravich said in 1985. "Get as much as you can. Get, get, get, get. Once you get all the money, once you get all the power and sit back in your backyard by your pool, you will twinkle your toes in the water with your drink in your hand and say, 'What a life!' I did that. But I was miserable."

He turned down requests for interviews as well as offers to appear in television commercials, most notably the Miller Lite "Tastes Great, Less Filling" campaign. Maravich had no desire to endorse alcoholic beverages.

"When I retired in 1980, I was asked to do those types of commercials and I'm sure I would have made a few hundred thousand dollars," Maravich explained to Larry King in 1986. "But I didn't want young people to look at that TV screen and think, 'Boy, after I become real successful, I drink beer all day.' That's just a lie."

As Jackie watched, Pete's moods swung between confusion, resignation, and despair.

"It was heartbreaking," said Jackie. "I knew he was probably searching for something and trying to fill the void. Basketball was his life since he was six or seven, and here he is at home with nothing to do."

During the initial months of retirement Maravich focused on 18-month-old Jaeson, spending hours teaching the toddler to solve puzzles meant for children three times his age.

"The reason I did that was because I don't have a degree," Maravich explained to Phoenix radio talk show host John Moynahan in 1985. "I don't have a B.A., a master's, or a Ph.D., or a 4.0, or degrees of certification hanging on my wall or this or that. But I wanted it for my son. I felt like I could get him intellectually started and get his thinking patterns going. I was reading all types of books on how if you educate your kids early, you could make him a genius."

In January, three months after leaving the Celtics, Pete participated in ABC's *Superstars* competition in Key Biscayne, Florida. Maravich's first experience on the show, in 1975, had been disappointing—he won only the bowling. This time around he was much improved, winning the golf and tennis events, and placing third in the half-mile bike race, the half-mile run, bowling, and the 50-yard swim. He finished ahead of the NFL's Preston Pearson, Mercury Morris, Carl Eller, and Fred Biletnikoff, as well as Olympic skier Jean-Claude Killy, boxer Joe Frazier, and long jumper Bob Beamon. Only Bob Seagran, a two-time Olympic medalist in the pole vault, finished in front of Maravich (who pocketed $8,600 for second place).

Pete's vegan lifestyle continued unabated. He planted his own vegetable garden and was soon harvesting robust tomatoes, zucchinis, cucumbers, squash, and bell peppers.

"Pete toiled away in that garden every day. I guess it was a kind of therapy for him," Jackie said. "He was so proud of the large vegetables that he could grow."

In addition to home-grown vegetables, Maravich's diet included soy burgers, soybean paste, kombu, sprouted wheat bread, plain spaghetti, beans, rice, salads, bottled spring water, and bananas. Lots of bananas.

"I used to go to the grocery store by the house in Metairie," recalled Jackie. "I'll never forget one time a cashier asked me, 'Do you have a monkey?' I answered, 'Yeah, a 6-5 monkey.' He'd make those drinks [smoothies] probably seven or eight times a day. He got a blender and would use carrots and celery. That was real time consuming."

Maravich experimented with the "Elimination Diet," a strict regimen explained in the best-selling book *Tracking Down Hidden Food Allergy* by pediatrician William G. Crook. He even tried fasting, once existing solely on water and fresh-squeezed juices for 25 days.

"On the 22nd day, hard particles were still coming out of my pores," Maravich claimed to *Knight-Ridder* reporter Stan Hochman. "Meat that I had eaten months before that had never digested." Friends and family worried as his weight dipped to 170 pounds, almost 30 pounds below his playing weight.

"I was just testing myself," Maravich remarked to *Sports Illustrated*'s Lisa Twyman.

Pete's willpower amazed Jackie.

"While he was fasting, he was still cooking our food," Jackie recalled. "I said to him, 'How can you cook our food and not be tempted to eat?'"

"Discipline, discipline, discipline," he smiled.

Weeks would pass when Pete rarely left the house. "My wife came to me one day and said, 'Pete, you need to go see someone because you're really flipping out,'" Maravich recalled. "I said, 'What do you mean?' She said, 'You haven't left the house in two weeks.' I said, 'Yeah, I have. I go out to the garage and stuff.' I was really lost."

As Maravich searched to find meaning in his life, more compulsive behavior emerged. Jackie recalled that Pete became a "neat freak," scrubbing pots and pans with a fervor, meticulously raking leaves, or vacuuming the entire house several times a week. He threw himself into old interests like UFOs, yoga, astral-projection, hypnosis, reincarnation, radical nutrition, Hinduism, meditation, plus two new obsessions: survivalism and investing.

"UFOs, vitamins, health foods—everything was pursued with a vengeance," said friend Cindy Marshall. "Pete could speak with great authority about any of the topics that interested him, and he could quote author, book, page, and paragraph if necessary to back up his argument. He would follow me around the house, or call me at home, challenging me, pestering me, teasing me, cajoling me into coming around to his way of thinking."

On May 14, 1981, Pete, Jackie, and Randy Drude sat down in the den of the Maravich home to watch Game 6 of the NBA finals. Seven months earlier Maravich had been a Celtic. Now Boston led the Houston Rockets 3-2 and was on the verge of winning its 14th championship.

"I can remember there was about two minutes left in the game, and it was obvious they were going to win," Drude recalled.

Pete stood up and smiled, "Well, it just goes along with everything else in my life."

"Pete walked out of the house and went onto the levee in his backyard and walked around," recalled Drude. "I ended up leaving. It was something he strove for all of his life, and he missed it by quitting that one season. I remember I felt very bad for him."

Jackie turned off their 25-inch Zenith set. "Well, that's it," Jackie said. "We're snake-bit."

The term "snake-bit" was heard often in the Maravich household. "It's a pattern of bad breaks," Jackie explained. "Not earth-shattering breaks, but enough to really bug you."

Pete continued his hermit-like existence through the spring of 1981. Press, who lived nearby in the Beau Chene subdivision, occasionally enticed Pete out of the house for a round of golf, and Jackie could persuade him to join her for an afternoon of "antiquing." They scoured small towns north of New Orleans, searching for "treasures" for their Metairie home. On one trip, they first entertained the notion of moving to a smaller city.

Compounding Pete's inner turmoil was a recurrence of Bell's palsy, the condition that had paralyzed his facial muscles in 1972. "I remember meeting him at the condo in Clearwater, and he wouldn't be seen," said attorney

Les Zittrain. "He'd sit in the shadows. That was another bad thing that came about from his seclusion."

In July 1981, Pete called Jim Krivacs, a sports agent and former basketball star at the University of Texas. Krivacs operated several basketball camps in Clearwater and had contacted Maravich in the past about starting up a new camp. The two men agreed to a meeting.

About this time Pete discovered the world of personal investing. The Jazz still owed him well over $1 million and he was determined to invest the money wisely. Each morning he turned to the business section of the newspaper to monitor the performance of his stocks. If his portfolio showed a gain, his mood temporarily improved.

But Maravich's investments were not limited to stocks. He put significant money into orange groves, a local bank, and a strip mall. Unfortunately they provided little return. He stockpiled gold Krugerrands and silver bars in an Arkansas bank, convinced that precious metal would be the only safe asset after the imminent "crash of the world economy." He bought property, including 30 acres in Folsom, Louisiana, where he planned to build a new home and a bomb shelter.

Pete also continued to invest in his own physical health, ordering hundreds of dollars worth of special vitamins from overseas, believing they would help extend his life past 100.

On March 25, 1982, Pete and Jackie welcomed their second son, Joshua Simon, into the family. But the joy created by the arrival of a new child quickly wore off and Pete sank back into his ever-deepening funk. He began to think about suicide.

One night, as he drove his Porsche along the 23-mile Pontchartrain Causeway, he had an ominous thought. "All I had to do was turn the wheel just 10 degrees and I would be history," Maravich recalled in 1987. "Everybody would say, 'What an accident. Isn't it terrible what happened to Pistol Pete?'"

Even those closest to Pete were surprised when they learned of the depth of his despair.

"You could have knocked me over with a feather when I heard that," his wife, Jackie, said. "I had never heard him say anything or act like he was that despondent. I read it many times and it was a surprise to me. I never saw him at a point where he was that down."

On a November night in 1982, while Jackie and the boys slept upstairs, Maravich sat in his den staring at the television. Around midnight he turned off the set and quietly slipped into bed.

As Maravich struggled to fall asleep, uncomfortable scenes from his past played in his head. He remembered his first sip of beer at age 14 on the steps of the Methodist Church in Clemson, South Carolina. He recalled the night at LSU when, drunk on beer, he rammed his car into a parked vehicle at 55 mph. The police had to knock out the shattered windshield in order to extricate Pete. Although his car was totaled, Pete barely had a scratch. A police officer at the scene shook his head and said, "Pete, you're the luckiest man I've ever seen." Maravich dismissively replied, "You don't understand, I've gotta play pro ball."

Lying next to Jackie, Pete pondered the impact of alcohol on his life and family. It had driven his mother to suicide. It had nearly destroyed his chance at a basketball career. And now Ronnie was caught in its addictive grip.

He reflected on enemies he'd made and ugly things he had said or done to people. "It was almost as if toothpicks were in my eyes," Maravich recalled. "Things that I had done to myself. The abuses I'd made toward people and myself. Everything kept coming. It was never like this before. I couldn't get it out of my mind. It was driving me nuts."

The clock next to his bed read 2 A.M.

He recalled that long-ago weekend at Lake Arrowhead in California when he was supposed to put on a basketball clinic for the Campus Crusade for Christ. For three days Maravich heard the gospel of Jesus Christ, but it had no impact.

"I don't have time for you, Christ. My goals are set," Pete had said. "I've got my scholarship, and from here on, I'm going to the pros. I'm going to make my million dollars and I'm going to get my ring. I don't have time for you."

Maravich remembered the many letters from fans praying for his salvation. Pete believed that those people were weak and threw their letters in the trash.

For hours and hours Pete lay awake, tortured by his memories. Then, as he wrote in his autobiography, he had a revelation. There was an overriding theme to his painful recollections, a through-line he could no longer ignore: sin. Pete, drenched in sweat, peered at the clock. It was 5:40 A.M.

He sank to his knees at the foot of the bed.

With tears streaming down his face, he prayed, "God, I've punched you. I've kicked you. I've cursed you. I've used your name in vain. I've mocked you. I've embarrassed you. I've done all those things. Will you really forgive the things I've done?"

He then heard a voice.

"Be strong. Lift thine own heart."

The words were delivered as "loud as thunder," Maravich often said. Shocked, he opened his eyes and looked around. He shook his wife awake.

"Jackie, Jackie, did you hear that? Did you hear what the Lord said? Did you hear?" Pete asked.

Jackie squinted at her husband with bleary eyes, "Pete, you've really gone nuts, haven't you? I didn't hear a thing." Then she went back to sleep.

Having experienced a transcendental moment, Pete returned to the foot of the bed and prayed for salvation.

"Jesus, I know you're real because I've tried everything else," Pete said through his tears. "I've got nowhere to go. If you don't save me, I won't last two more days."

Then, a calm feeling flooded through his body, washing his tension away. Pete's immense burden was lifted.

"From that moment on," Maravich recalled, "my life was never to be the same again. When I took God into my heart, it was the first true happiness I ever had."

24

Reborn

"I once was lost but now am found. Was blind but now I see."
—AMAZING GRACE, TRADITIONAL HYMN

"I'm not into religion. I'm into Christianity. Christianity is a relationship, a fellowship."
—PETE MARAVICH

The morning after his startling revelation, Pete described it to Jackie. "He told me the next day that God had told him, 'Be strong and lift thine own heart,' and I went, 'Huh?'" Jackie recalled. "Pete went through so many other things. I thought it was just another phase. But it wasn't. It was for real."

Pete was eager to tell others about his experience. "I remember going over to his house on a Saturday and Pete told me, 'I heard a voice,'" recalled friend Randy Drude. "I was at the kitchen table, and Jackie was there. I didn't know what to think because he came right out of the blue with it. There was no beating around the bush. I said, 'Well, that's good,' and just kind of left it at that. He said, 'Randy, I'm telling ya, it was this very loud and clear voice.' He said he couldn't believe it didn't wake Jackie up, but it was just as clear as a bell."

Pete focused his voracious reading habits on the Bible, reading scriptures three times a day. He also started attending different church services around Metairie. (Jackie remained a Catholic.)

There was a noticeable transformation in his demeanor. "He was just so at peace," Jackie said.

He let go of old resentments, most notably his bitterness toward LSU. He accepted an offer from former LSU player Collis Temple to conduct a basketball clinic on campus. It was Pete's first visit to his alma mater in nearly a decade.

"It was a free camp and no one was making any money off it," said David

"Bo" Bahnsen, LSU basketball-team manager at the time. "He was still pretty reserved."

For Bahnsen, later an associate athletic director at the university, getting Maravich back at LSU was an important first step. "It was like a long-lost brother coming back into the fold and being part of the family again. Being able to forgive and forget," Bahnsen said. "It was tough when Pete left and his dad was fired."

The idea of creating his own basketball camp excited Pete. He, of course, had years of experience as a guest coach and even operated a camp in the 1970s in California, Pennsylvania. But Pete envisioned a camp unlike any other. It would combine three disciplines: religion, basketball, and nutrition.

"He [Pete] was very enthusiastic when he spoke about the camp," recalled friend Chet Marshall. "He said, 'It will be a holistic, vegetarian, Christian place where kids can go.' Basketball was about the third or fourth rung on the ladder."

To get the camp operating, Pete reached out to Jim Krivacs in Clearwater, Florida. Krivacs became the camp's first administrator, along with Del Wubbena.

The effervescent Wubbena, head coach of the Clearwater Christian College basketball team, recalled the day he joined the venture. "Pete asked me if I'd be interested in running basketball camps with him, his dad, and Jim Krivacs. I told him I'd have to think about it," said Wubbena. "I thought about it for a tenth of a second and said 'Yes.' That's how we got started back in 1983." (In 1993, Wubbena was named the National Christian College Athletic Association Division II Coach of the Year. He was later inducted into the association's Hall of Fame.)

The Pistol Pete All-Star Basketball Camp opened in August 1983. Located at Clearwater Christian College, it accepted boys from ages 8-17 (a year later it added a week for girls). The opening two weeks completely sold out. But if campers thought Maravich intended to treat them to a fun-filled week of "Showtime" basketball, they were in for a rude surprise. Before the kids arrived, Pete taped up all the water faucets in the gym and unplugged all the soda and vending machines in the dormitories.

"If you can't last four days without a soft drink or candy, you have a discipline problem," Maravich told the boys. "If you can't say 'No' for four days, you may not be able to say 'No' to more harmful things in your life down the road."

Carl Von DemBusche, Jr. was among the first 140 attendees. "Plus it was the first time I was away from home," said Von DemBusche, Jr., then just eight years old. "I was homesick and Pete could tell, and he just took me under his wing. He really took care of me throughout the week and would often carry me on his back from the gym to the cafeteria."

Maravich's food selections were not popular with the young campers. He offered them a 22-item salad bar, a fruit bar, fresh fish, organic-fed chicken, and bottled water. No sugar, no salt, no red meat, no caffeine.

"Everyone complained about how bad the food was," Von DemBusche, Jr. remembered. "Everything we ate was healthy—lots of fruits, lots of vegetables. They served this veggie pizza that was just terrible. Pete had some kind of punch that was tasteless. We called it 'Pistol Pete's Puky Punch.' It was just so terrible but we kept on drinking it because we were so thirsty."

Some kids couldn't take it and snuck junk food and sodas into the dorm. Maravich told reporter Rick Stroud of the *St. Petersburg Times* how he shamed the young smugglers.

"They had Cokes, potato chips, candy—you name it," Maravich said. "I just put everything in a bag and said, 'You disappointed me' and walked out of the room. That's the best thing I could have done."

On another occasion, Pete utilized a more military punishment after a camper brazenly ordered a pizza delivered to the dorm. When caught, he was forced to run around the track while Pete and Press ate the contraband. "They kept him out there running until they finished the entire pizza," recalled Jaeson Maravich. "In all honesty, the food at the camp at that time was nasty and I couldn't blame the kid."

Even Jackie urged Pete to reconsider his zero-tolerance policy for junk food.

"We wasted so much food there, and health food is expensive," said Jackie. "The kids wouldn't eat the homemade pizza [whole wheat pita bread topped with all-natural cheese and thinly sliced vegetables]. It just didn't go over well. I had to pull Pete aside and say, 'You're not going to change their eating habits in a week.' Poor Pete."

Food aside, the campers received first-rate basketball instruction for nearly nine hours a day. The program, designed by Press, rotated the youngsters through a series of ball handling, shooting, passing, and defending drills at various "stations." Full-court scrimmages were held after dinner.

Along with basketball and nutrition, religion received special focus.

"The spiritual emphasis was real critical. It was just as important to Pete as the basketball," Krivacs told a television reporter in 2000. "Pete would always have people come in and give their testimonies about what Jesus did in their life and how Jesus Christ changed their life, and with really touching moments in the process."

Tonya Crevier, a former star at the University of South Dakota and then with the Iowa Comets of the short-lived Women's Basketball League, met Pete while making the movie *Dribble*. The 5-1 dynamo dazzled campers with a display of dribbling and ball spinning that concluded with seven balls twirling simultaneously. After her jaw-dropping demonstration, Crevier shared her Christian faith with the campers.

"Pete had a strong conviction for the Lord because he was so changed— because of his belief in Jesus Christ," Crevier said. "He just had such a fun, energetic, caring attitude toward the kids after he became a Christian. All he wanted to talk about was the Lord. He now had a purpose."

Maravich oversaw every aspect of his business. He had observed many camps and concluded most were rip-offs. "They rolled a ball out at mid-court and let the youngsters have at it," Pete used to say.

"Most all-star camps have the athlete there one hour a week," Maravich explained to *Shreveport Times* reporter Jim McClain. "They get the kids to come to the camp through false advertising. Then the stars don't put any money back into their camps. They put it in their back pockets."

Pete steered away from that kind of greed. More than a third of the budget went for food. He also purchased more than 400 certificates, plaques, and trophies to dispense at the end of each camp. The awards, one reporter noted, "would rival those handed out in the NBA."

Maravich was determined to make his camp a positive influence on his young campers, and he led by example. "Pete would read his Bible two or three hours a day," recalled Wubbena. "He knew the Scriptures, and he studied. He would read his Bible an hour after camp even though we'd be done at 11:30 or 12:00. Then he'd get up at 5 A.M. and read his Bible again before camp started at 6:30."

Pistol Pete's All-Star Basketball Camp was an immediate success and word-of-mouth praise led to a yearly overflow of applicants. Maravich was so encouraged by the response that he planned to open others across the country.

In the fall of 1983, Press Maravich was hired by long-time friend Fred McCall to be assistant men's coach at Campbell College in Buies Creek, North Carolina. It was a homecoming of sorts; the Campbell campus was the site of the long-running summer basketball camp. The job also allowed Press to be near Diana, a pre-med student at Campbell.

During this period Pete befriended John Lotz, then the assistant athletic director at the University of North Carolina.

"We just hit it off right away. We probably spoke every day or every other day after that," recalled Lotz in 2000. "What amazed me about Pete was that someone of his stature would commit his life to the Lord and was real in his faith. He lived the high life, he had the cars, the house, the worldwide travel, the whole deal, and it never did anything for him. He used to say, 'There ain't nothing on the next rung of the ladder without Christ.'"

There were a few times when Pete's faith was tested. Late in 1983, he drank a few bottles of beer. Donny Liles, his pastor in Clearwater, was with him that day. "My relationship with Pete was that we were friends and we still did things together. We had fun," said Liles. "He had a one-time relapse after he became a Christian."

On December 13, 1983, Pete, mortified by his lack of discipline, uncorked every bottle in his extensive wine collection and, as Liles watched, poured the contents down the sink.

Jackie believed that Pete purposely exaggerated the extent of his drinking to make his testimony more compelling. "When I met him at LSU, he was crazy. We both were, and I drank too. But I didn't see where it affected school or basketball," Jackie said. "I don't think he was an alcoholic. He certainly wasn't a closet drinker. And he didn't drink every other day. I think it might have been overly emphasized to prove a point. Pete was trying to get people to turn their lives around through shock value."

Brother Ronnie, a long-time bartender, agreed. "Pete mostly drank beer. He didn't have a problem with alcohol," he said. "I've seen people with alcohol problems. I've been a bartender for more than 30 years and it doesn't matter who you are—young or old—there's nothing pleasant about being a drunk."

As 1983 came to a close, Pete reluctantly accepted an invitation to participate in the NBA old-timers game scheduled for January 28, 1984. The game, along with a slam-dunk contest, would provide the Saturday programming for the inaugural "All-Star Weekend." ESPN would broadcast both competitions. The league had not held an old-timers game since 1964, when George Mikan, Bob Davies, Ed McCauley, Bill Sharman, Bob Cousy, Vern Mikkelsen, Nat Clifton, Harry Gallatin, and 15 others participated in a brief contest prior to the All-Star contest in Boston. Mike Cole, Pete's friend in the Celtic organization, was instrumental in getting Maravich included on the roster. Maravich, though, was lukewarm about participating. "The world has changed," he told Shelby Strother of the *Denver Post*. "Nobody remembers Pistol Pete anymore. I went into a dark closet and that's fine with me."

"Most of the guys in this game had a big sendoff when they retired, but I just kind of faded away," Pete explained to David Remnick of the *Washington Post*. "I had my spot. I had my minute of time. We come. We go. That's the way it is."

But memories of Pistol Pete were still strong, especially among fans. When Pete checked into his Denver hotel, reporter George Shirk recorded the scene for *Knight-Ridder News Service*:

The spacious lobby of the aging Brown Palace Hotel already was crowded and in a state of near-chaos Friday when he walked in, his razor-cut black hair tousled by the warm wind outside and a lost sort of grin creasing his face.

Pete Maravich scanned the crowd in front of the check-in desk and then, turning his attention to the business at hand, put down his luggage. It took maybe two seconds for the crowd to quiet and just as little time for the people to begin their friendly assault on him.

When Maravich looked up from his bags, everyone, it seemed, was looking at him, welcoming him. There was sporadic applause.

"Hey, Pistol, man, where you been?"

Pistol Pete Maravich smiled broadly and yelled back, his Southern drawl softening the sound of his voice. "You know," he said, "just minding business, man, bein' a recluse. You know how it is."

"That Pistol?" It was another voice, this time from behind him.

"Hey, Pistol, you still got the showtime?"

There was laughter, and there were low-fives.

"Yeah, man," Maravich said. "Still got the showtime."

He made a motion with his hands, pretending they held a basketball and that he was about to do some of his magic. He dribbled the imaginary ball behind his back, then between his legs. His eyes focused on it as he dribbled it high into the air, caught it, then flicked one of his famous broken-wrist passes.

"Aww-riiiight," the man said.

Another voice: "Knee all right, Pete?"

"The knee's history," Maravich said. "Feels fine."

For basketball junkies, the 1984 NBA old-timers game provided a dazzling trip down memory lane. The 40-minute contest featured such legends as Jerry West, Oscar Robertson, John Havlicek, Earl Monroe, Bill Sharman, Dick McGuire, Bob Pettit, Connie Hawkins, Rick Barry, Sam Jones, Hal

Greer, Wes Unseld, Dolph Schayes, Nate Thurmond, Dave Bing, and Tommy Heinsohn. Oxygen tanks and masks stood at the ready in Denver's McNichols Sports Arena.

Maravich, 36 and a trim 190 pounds, looked as though he could still play in the league. The thought was not a stretch; two members of his 1970 rookie class, Bob Lanier and Dan Issel, were, in fact, still active. Only five years prior to his old-timers appearance Maravich had been the East's starting guard in the actual All-Star Game. Much had changed since then.

"In five years not only have the names of the players changed, but the style has, too," observed Charlie Vincent of the *Detroit Free Press*. "Where Isiah Thomas and Magic Johnson—starters in Sunday's game—are expected to display a flair for showmanship, Maravich, one of the originators of that style of play, was discouraged from flamboyance. He was ridiculed as a showboat, a man who cared only about himself."

Pete noticed the new respect for players with flair. "Magic and Isiah talk about putting on a show. If I had ever stated that I was going to put on a show, I'd have been stoned," Maravich told Vincent. "Other players thought you were showing them up and they'd bring guys off the bench to get you."

Thomas, the youngest All-Star and eventual MVP, appreciated the path that Maravich and others had blazed. "The guy who changed basketball for me was Pistol," Thomas said. "He changed the way we all played the game."

"Maravich and Earl Monroe definitely brought a style to the game," Thomas explained to the *Detroit Free Press*. "Opened it up where you are much more able to be creative without being labeled hot-doggish."

The NBA now openly encouraged and promoted crowd-pleasing passing, dribbling, and shot making. TV ratings were rising and attendance spiked as fans flocked to see charismatic players like Thomas, Magic Johnson, Larry Bird, and Dominique Wilkins. "Pistol Pete Maravich sang a different song when nobody wanted to listen. Today the music belongs to someone else and everybody knows the words," wrote the *Chicago Tribune*'s Bernie Lincicome. "Showtime sells the National Basketball Association while Maravich [at his vegetarian basketball camp] is munching celery with someone else's children in Clearwater, Florida."

The game presented the delightful sight of Maravich and Robertson playing guard alongside each other. Maravich, the youngest of the 21 old-timers, was the game's top scorer with 18 points (8-13, 2-2, 1 rebound, 1 assist, 2 steals) in 18 minutes. The Pistol was still a point-a-minute man. He produced one "Showtime" moment. After stripping the ball from Barry, he slid to his knees and pounded the basketball in rat-a-tat-tat fashion until he restored his dribble. The crowd roared its approval but then, just as quickly, Pete passed it off to Dave DeBusschere. Pete's East squad lost in a squeaker, 65-63.

The weekend in Denver also gave Pete an opportunity to share his religious transformation. "Money didn't change me," Maravich told a television reporter. "Or power, or fame, or All-Star games, or being Pistol Pete. Those were only brief interludes of ego gratification. The only thing that ever changed me was Jesus Christ."

"Of all the old-timers, Maravich was the one who had changed the most," noted *Philadelphia Daily News* reporter Stan Hochman. "Christianity had changed him from the eyebrows up, vegetarianism changed him from the eyebrows down."

He signed hundreds of autographs that weekend, still as "Pistol Pete," but now with a biblical chapter and verse under his signature. Among his favorites were:

- 1 John 3:16 (This is how we know what love is: Jesus Christ laid down his life for us.)
- Mathew 16:26 (What good will it be for a man if he gains the whole world yet forfeits his soul?)
- Galatians 2:20 (The life I live in the body, I live by faith in the Son of God, who loved me and gave himself for me.)
- Ephesians 2: 8, 9 (For it is by grace you have been saved, through faith—and this not from yourselves, it is the gift of God—not by works, so that no one can boast.)
- Romans 1:16 (I am not ashamed of the gospel, because it is the power of God for the salvation of everyone who believes.)

When Maravich returned to Louisiana he continued to simplify his life. He jettisoned more reminders of his "selfish" life, replacing his vast album collection (including Marvin Gaye, Stevie Wonder, comedian Steve Martin, Average White Band, Wilson Pickett, the Temptations, Santana, Little Anthony, Alan Parsons, Al Green, and Earth, Wind and Fire) with inspirational Christian music. He purchased a modest Chevrolet Caprice and added a biblical verse to the bottom of his personal stationery.

The steps of a good man are ordered by the Lord: and he delighteth in his way. (Psalm 37:23, KJV)

Maravich wanted to share his testimony far and wide, but first, his pastor Donny Liles advised Pete to change his presentation. "I said, 'Look Pete, you don't know enough about the Bible, you don't know the doctrine, you don't know theology, so don't go out there trying to relate everything to Christianity,'" Liles counseled. "'Just give them your testimony because no one can refute what Jesus Christ has done in your life.'"

Soon after, Liles accompanied Maravich to a national pastors' conference where Pete shared his story of redemption with more than 120 clergymen. Heeding Liles' advice, Maravich presented his life's journey in a heartfelt, personal way. Everyone in attendance was moved by the riveting tale of the tortured basketball genius.

"That just launched him out there, and churches everywhere in the country invited him to come and give his testimony," Liles said.

Armed with a Bible and a compelling story, Pete Maravich felt a new sense of purpose.

He was reborn.

25

Purpose
Driven Life

"I want to be remembered as a Christian, a person that serves Him to the utmost. Not as a basketball player."

—PETE MARAVICH

"I am not trying to make anyone a Christian anymore than I could make someone a Corvette."

—PETE MARAVICH

Pete Maravich was in high demand from organizations eager to hear his inspiring testimony. His calendar became filled with speaking engagements at churches, service organizations, high schools, revivals, youth groups, colleges, basketball camps, prayer breakfasts, hospitals, and even prisons.

Through a mutual friend, Maravich was introduced to Bill Glass, a former pro football player who started a prison ministry in 1972. Over the years Glass has worked with such athletes as Reggie White, Roger Staubach, Tom Landry, Earnie Shavers, and Michael Jordan.

"Pete was invited to our 'Weekend of Champions,' where we bring in about 25 guests and talk to prisoners over the course of a long weekend," Glass said. "People think you have a captive audience and nothing could be further from the truth. Inmates will call other inmates wimps if they went to a Christian program. But Pete Maravich was always a great draw."

Even more memorable than his testimony was a shooting performance by Pete at a Florida prison.

"They had a real outdoor basketball court with a grandstand," Glass recalled. "He started behind the three-point line in the corner and hit it. Then he moved five feet to the left, shot it, and made it. Then he went all the way around and all the way back again three or four times and never missed a shot! It was just unconscious. He did not miss. It was unreal. It was like the ball was guided into the hole. He hit it from every conceivable angle and over and over again. I went back to that prison five years later and the inmates were still talking about Maravich."

After witnessing the remarkable transformation of her husband, Jackie decided to dedicate her life to God and was baptized at First Baptist Church in Kenner, Louisiana. Pete cried throughout the ceremony.

"The way I looked at it was, everybody's trying to get to the same place," explained Jackie. "My parents and sister still go to Catholic church. They were glad for me." Pete soon purchased two $1,000 lifetime memberships to Jim and Tammy Bakker's PTL Club.

Jackie and Pete finally found their ideal house in Covington, Louisiana, about 40 miles north of Metairie. "I've always dreamed of raising the kids in a Victorian, gingerbread-type house in the country," Pete told Lisa Twyman of *Sports Illustrated*. The 100-year-old home, which required major renovations, was still located within walking distance of the city's quaint sidewalk cafes, art galleries, boutiques, and antique shops where Jackie could indulge her passion for collecting.

The two often spoke of raising their boys in a rustic, rural environment and the sparsely populated Covington, accented by large pine and moss-draped oak trees, seemed the perfect place. Pete coordinated the $450,000 home renovation. "Pete oversaw almost every bit of construction," Jackie said. "He was at the house almost every day checking up on its progress."

In mid-1984, Pete joined 10 retired NBA players on a six-game, 26-day exhibition tour of China, Taiwan, Hong Kong, and the Philippines. Captain Earl Monroe led a roster that included Calvin Murphy, Nate Thurmond, Dennis Awtry, Rick Barry, Bobby Dandridge, Cazzie Russell, Connie Hawkins, and player/coach Phil Jackson.

"People used to say, 'You're going to go on this tour with Pete? You're not going to have enough basketballs,'" recalled Barry. "Well, that was ridiculous because I could play without the ball. So when we played on that tour, we played really well together. If I played with Pistol Pete Maravich [in the pros], I would have scored a ton of points because I know that if I got open, he was going to get me the ball."

What their international opponents lacked in skill, they more than made up for with physicality. "It was like rugby," Maravich commented to Don Worthington of the *Alexandria-Pineville Town Talk*. "I was just out there trying to dodge people."

Despite Pete's long absence from the game, his shots were still falling.

After a game in Taiwan, during which he scored 30 points in 19 minutes, making 14 of his 16 shots, he half seriously announced a return to the NBA. At half time throughout the tour, Pete would demonstrate his array of ball handling and spinning drills, always concluding by bouncing a shot into the basket—off his head. The NBA veterans won every game and their tour helped to increase the popularity of basketball throughout the Far East.

A few days after returning to Louisiana, Pete and Jackie took the boys to Covington to check up on their dream home. "We were reminded of all the trips of the past few years to the little community in the country," Pete wrote. "We often had stopped for picnics or looked at potential homes for purchase. On this day we were all excited to see the progress on our new home."

A couple that lived on the block came by to welcome the Maraviches to the neighborhood. Pete took them on a tour of the 5,200 square-foot house, enthusiastically explaining his vision for each room. The two-inch thick front door had the words "COMMIT THY WORKS UNTO THE LORD" carved into its dark mahogany. Pete purchased the ceiling from an abandoned warehouse in New Orleans. All the doors were oversized and had to be custom designed.

Approaching the staircase, the Maraviches noticed the banisters (Pete found them in Atlanta) had not been attached. Pete and Jackie gripped their sons' hands tightly and led them up to the second floor. Pete explained that the three-inch pine wooden soundboards were installed to muffle the sounds of a dribbling basketball. He planned to mount a seven-foot-high basketball goal on a support.

Meanwhile Jaeson and Joshua wandered into the upstairs guest room and discovered a small closet. Curious, they went inside. On the floor was an air conditioning duct covered by a layer of yellow insulation. As Pete and Jackie spoke to the neighbors, three-year-old Joshua stepped onto the insulation and, when it gave away, he plunged 17 feet to the hardwood floor of the master bedroom.

"All of a sudden I heard a 'thump,'" recalled Jackie. "I went to the closet and I saw Jaeson looking down at this hole and I screamed. Pete literally took three steps to get down to the bottom of the stairs. Joshua's head missed steel rods that were inches from him. I thought he was dead."

So did Pete. Joshua was unconscious and lying in an ever-widening pool of blood. The upper right side of his face had absorbed the impact, and his cheek, eye, and forehead were grossly misshapen. Joshua's right eye was already swollen shut and he barely had a pulse. Pete scooped his son's limp body into his arms and ran to his car.

"I didn't want Jackie and Jaeson to see how Joshua looked, just in case he was dying or if he were already gone," Maravich explained in his memoirs. "That horrible sight could linger in their minds for the rest of their lives."

While Pete fumbled for his car keys, his neighbor held Joshua. The two men sped off as Jackie watched in horror from the second-floor window.

At St. Tammany Hospital, doctors diagnosed severe head trauma and what looked like torn muscles behind Joshua's eye. They advised Pete that extensive eye surgery would probably be necessary and warned that this type of injury usually resulted in brain damage.

"I chose to believe with all of my heart that the will of God could be done," Pete wrote in his autobiography. "My faith was being tested."

Jackie soon joined Pete and they watched a team of doctors and nurses tend to their motionless child. Suddenly, Joshua's tiny voice cried out and Pete and Jackie embraced, thankful he was still alive. Pete climbed into bed and lay with his son for the next 36 hours. Joshua's wound began healing without surgery. When he left the hospital he had full use of his eye. Six months later there was no trace of the injury.

"The doctors said it was a miracle that Joshua didn't lose his eye," Maravich told Lisa Twyman of *Sports Illustrated*.

If Pete had any doubts about his faith, they were laid to rest that afternoon.

On June 23, 1984, Pete was scheduled to be inducted into the Louisiana Sports Hall of Fame in Natchitoches. The incoming class that year included basketball standouts Bo Lamar and the late Jackie Moreland; jockey Eric Guerin; football heroes Max McGee and Johnny Robinson; and the late Southern University coach "Ace" Mumford.

Donald Ray Kennard, Pete's former academic counselor, and Bud Johnson, LSU's one-time sports information director, recalled encountering Maravich in the Holiday Inn restaurant the day before the ceremony. When Pete saw the men approaching, he tossed a napkin over his plate.

The three exchanged pleasantries and then Kennard pointed to the plate and asked, "What are you doing?" Maravich sheepishly lifted the napkin to reveal a thick steak. Pete confessed he was about to eat red meat, something he had avoided for close to five years.

"I'm up here where nobody would know me in this little town, and I just wanted to see what a steak would taste like," Maravich laughed. "And now you walk in and catch me violating my own personal code. So it means I'm not supposed to eat this steak." Interpreting the chance meeting as an omen, Maravich paid the bill and walked off with the two men, leaving his steak untouched.

Jerry Pierce, the director of the Hall of Fame, planned a morning golf tournament and a late afternoon reception. Maravich participated in the golf outing but was absent as the banquet began. He had befriended some locals on the golf course and had accompanied them home, where he spent the afternoon playing basketball with their children. Pete sped to the banquet and arrived just in time to see a short film chronicling his career. After the lights came up, Maravich, according to Pierce, "delivered a speech that just floored us all."

Pete paid tribute to both his parents. Press looked on proudly along with the other 350 guests.

"When we came to LSU, football was king," Maravich said. "Basketball was a second-rate citizen. We sparked an amount of enthusiasm that brought people back into the arena. We lifted LSU out of the doldrums."

After his induction, Pete asked Pierce for a quick tour of the Hall.

"It was 10:30 or 11:00 at night," Pierce recollected. "Prather Coliseum was dark. So I had the lights turned on, and just the two of us walked along the showcases. Pete was like a kid himself: 'Hey, Willis Reed is in here!' He'd yell, 'Look, Bob Pettit! There's Billy Cannon.'"

As the two strolled along, admiring the artifacts, Pete asked if the Hall desired a piece of Maravich memorabilia. Pierce said that the Hall had already made a request by letter. Two days later Pierce received Maravich's 1970 NIT wristwatch.

Frank Schroeder, an LSU alumnus, was a big admirer of Maravich and interviewed him for ESPN's *Dr. J's Sports Focus*. The short segment profiled Maravich's roller-coaster basketball career and his new-found happiness in retirement. The two men hit it off and Schroeder left with the feeling that Maravich's life story might make a compelling movie.

"You couldn't do my life," Maravich told him. "We couldn't get it all in two hours. Do me at 13. That's really when it began—and there isn't anything I did at LSU or in the NBA I couldn't do at 13." With that conversation, the seed for *The Pistol: The Birth of a Legend* was planted.

Schroeder contacted Darrel Campbell, a staff writer for the NBC soap opera *Days of Our Lives*, and arranged for him to meet Maravich at Los Caballeros, a resort in Fountain Valley, California. Keeping to Pete's original vision for the project, then entitled, *The Pistol: How the Legend Began*, Campbell went to work, focusing the screenplay on Maravich's eighth grade year during his "happy days" in Clemson.

At a later meeting, Maravich handed Campbell a diary he had kept sporadically during his pro years. Campbell read the entries and became convinced that Pete's story would also make a great book.

"Pete was very insightful and a deep thinker," Campbell said. "He could talk about a specific moment in a specific quarter in a specific game, how much time was on the clock, who had the ball, what was about to happen, and what should have been done about it."

In addition to the book, Schroeder came up with the idea to tape a fresh version of the "Homework Basketball" film and use the proceeds to defray the production cost of the movie.

"It all turned into four or five big projects at one time," Campbell said. "The screenplay turned into a book, which turned into a four-part videotape series, which would raise money for a film on Pete's life."

Maravich agreed to join Meadowlark Lemon's Shooting Stars, a Christian version of the Harlem Globetrotters. According to the tour manager, Joe Albanese, Pete's presence "meant that instead of playing smaller high schools, we could play in big arenas."

As the team prepared to shoot publicity photos, Pete decided to test his basketball skills. "He didn't even bring any gear with him. So Joe, the tour manager, got him a jersey, shorts, and shoes," recalled the Stars "referee" Mark Shannon. "So he went out there, took 10 or 15 shots, and hit about 80 percent of them. He came back to where I was and said, 'I've still got it. It's like riding a bike.'"

Maravich then announced that he could make 100 shots from beyond 25 feet and not miss two in a row. The dubious Shooting Star players took him up on the challenge.

"So three guys maybe got eight or nine out of 20. Pete hit his first 10 in a row," said Shannon. "Then Pete continued shooting and maybe missed five or six shots out of 60 attempts. *But he wouldn't miss two in a row.* He proceeded to nail 99 shots. Then he intentionally missed a shot so that if he missed the next one, he would have to start all over. He went two feet out of bounds, put his feet at a 90-degree angle, and launched this high-arching shot from behind the backboard and hit nothing but the bottom of the net. When it went in, all of the fellows looked at each other and said, 'Whoa, he's just messing with us.'"

Haskell Cohen, the former publicity director of the NBA, asked Pete and Press if they would like to conduct a series of clinics in Israel for the Federation of Basketball Coaches in May of 1985. The idea of a pilgrimage to the land where Jesus had once walked greatly appealed to Pete. So, over five days, Pete and Press held clinics attended by more than 225 Israeli coaches. Unfortunately, Press fell ill on the last night of the tour and was rushed to the hospital.

The two hurried back to Louisiana for more tests. The prognosis was horrid. Darrel Campbell, who was interviewing Maravich for the autobiography, remembered the awful day.

"Press was still looking good and was a nice aging gentleman with silver hair," Campbell recalled. "So I met Press and within a matter of minutes I see him talking privately to Pete. I could tell it was a pretty serious deal. Later, Pete confided in me Press was diagnosed with cancer that very day. Pete said the cancer was in the bone marrow." The cancer, which began in his prostate, was spreading.

Press began attending church regularly in Indian Rocks, Florida. At the end of one of the services, Press answered an altar call to dedicate his life to God. His decision to become a Christian pleased Pete, who now counseled his father in spiritual matters.

Carl Von DemBusche, Jr. remembered that Press retained his feisty personality despite his increasing pain. "Every time we got together on Sunday nights, he would always captivate everybody with his war stories about flying in World War II," Von DemBusche, Jr. said. "The great stories he told. He was also a great man of God."

Press left his fate in the hands of his Creator according to a July 1, 1985, letter to Del Wubbena:

> I still haven't decided what I'm going to do. Like you, I still want to coach. I am not looking for a head coaching job because I had my run with that for 25 years. I just want to teach youngsters how to play the game. I believe He will tell me what to do. I leave it all in His hands.

Pete was busy reading Scripture, raising his children, attending church, and working on his book, video, and movie projects. He also continued to speak to groups across the United States about his relationship with Jesus. He opened a special checking account called "JIL" (Jesus Is Lord). Any income earned from speaking engagements was deposited into that account and, at year's end, donated to charity.

In October 1985, Maravich made an appearance in Phoenix at the behest of an estate and business planner named Jimmy Walker.

"Among all the athletes that I know, there are very few legends," Walker said. "Pete was a legend. Pete stood out with enormous charisma without seeking it. If you visited Pete in the last five years of his life, he wasn't talking about the NBA—he was talking about the Lord. More than anything, Pete wanted people to find Christ."

Walker invited Maravich to speak at an outreach party for inner-city kids on October 9. Singer Glen Campbell kicked off the event with a five-song set, and then NBA standout Paul Westphal introduced Maravich to the hundreds of people crammed into Walker's backyard. Westphal, who respected Maravich's artistry as a player, had not seen him since his retirement and was amazed by the transformation.

"It was a fantastic thing to witness," Westphal said in 2003. "Pete went from this guy who was chasing everything to having an inner calm. You looked at him and he had a different look in his eye. Once he became a Christian, he developed a focus that was real. It was as if he just started living."

Maravich related the story of his life in brutally stark terms. He then issued an ominous prediction:

> I don't have much time left, and the time I have left, I'm giving to the
> Lord Jesus Christ. I'm giving it to him because that's what I'm called
> to do.

His testimony shot through the crowd like a thunderbolt.

"Everybody was spellbound," Westphal said. "It was brilliant. There were very few dry eyes. It was told with such clarity and wisdom. You had to be moved by it because here was a guy who had all the success in the world and he realized in the blink of an eye it's over, and in the ultimate picture, it doesn't mean anything." (A videotape of this speech is included in "The Inspirational Edition" of *The Pistol: The Birth of a Legend*.)

Shortly before Thanksgiving, Maravich approached Alfred Young, a pastor at the Christ Temple in Covington, and asked how he could help during the holiday season.

"It was Pete's idea to help the needy," Young said. "He would say, 'Anybody can write a check, but you need to be involved in people's lives.' What he did was he bought 100 turkeys, and we loaded them down in his car. He wouldn't let us get a truck or station wagon. We put them in his car—dripping, running, frozen turkeys—and we went all over our neighborhood passing out turkeys to the elderly and the needy, carrying them in. He enjoyed it so much he said, 'Alfred, you and I are going to make this an annual event and we'll call it the Turkey Train.'"

On December 14, 1985, Pete and his family watched as the Utah Jazz raised Maravich's jersey to the rafters at the sold-out Salt Palace. No. 7 was the first Jazz number retired. "I'm kind of thrown back by it," an over-whelmed Maravich told Rick Barry on TBS after the half-time ceremony. "I don't know if I can speak. It's a great honor and one I didn't expect." He then managed a few words about his camp and his 68-point night against the Knicks.

The event also provided a sweet reunion for Pete and some of his New Orleans Jazz family, including Dave Fredman, Don Sparks, Rod Hundley, and Sam Battistone.

Pete's former Celtics coach, Bill Fitch, coaching the visiting Houston Rockets, reminded Maravich of his last game in a Celtics uniform.

"He said, 'Do you remember the last game you ever played?'" Maravich told Larry King two months later. "I said, 'No, I don't. I can't remember.' 'Well, it was the Green and White Game.' He said, 'You know how many points you had?' 'No, Bill, I had a few.' He said, 'Pete, you had 38.'"

Maravich approached his former Atlanta coach Cotton Fitzsimmons, who was also in attendance. Their relationship had been ice cold since Pete's suspension in February 1974 and Fitzsimmons' participation in the trade that sent Pete to New Orleans.

"I was never mad at Pete," said Fitzsimmons in 1998. "I was never bitter. It was not a personal thing. I made the trade to make the team better. Even though he refused to speak to me, I never stopped speaking to him. I would always say, 'Hi, how are you?' and he would never respond. Then one night, I walked into the Salt Palace in Salt Lake City, and out of the blue, Pete speaks to me. This is after years of silence. And he spoke to me as if nothing had ever happened. As though we had spoken the day before."

Pete returned from Utah and his busy schedule continued. He had cut his teeth as a college color commentator for the University of South Florida on WTOG-TV during the 1984-85 season. In early 1986, NBC brought him up to broadcast several national games. His first assignment was on February 22, at the University of Georgia, site of his famous "hook shot" some 17 years earlier. Maravich worked alongside Bob Costas who, at 33, had just become the youngest person ever named Sportscaster of the Year. "Pete was substan-tially mellowed out and was into Christianity. He wasn't proselytizing but he would let you know in a gentle way that that's where he was at," recalled Costas in 2000. "He was definitely recognized. People called out to him from the stands."

Five days later, in Washington, D.C., Maravich was interviewed on radio by Larry King, who introduced Pete as, "An incredible member of the world of the hardwood. There was no other like him."

Then Pete and a few members of the Shooting Stars met President Reagan and the First Lady at the White House. The team donated a portion of their profits from their tour to the Nancy Reagan Campaign Against Drug Abuse in Schools. Pete presented the First Lady with the obligatory team jersey, along with a basketball and a kiss.

"It's not really just a job. Athletes are really hero-worshipped in this land and sports are supposed to be a character builder," Pete told reporters on the White House lawn afterward. "I think it's the responsibility of the athlete to realize that."

That night he flew to Los Angeles to prepare for the NBC broadcast of the UCLA-DePaul game the next afternoon. "I'm involved in so many things," he told reporter Kim Brazzel. "I just really don't have time to do any more. And it's important to me to spend a lot of time with my family."

Later on that month, Maravich joined the Shooting Stars for its "Commitment with a Purpose" tour. Meadowlark Lemon's squad provided an entertaining mix of basketball and slapstick comedy while spreading its message of clean Christian living. Surprisingly, Wilt Chamberlain also agreed to join the team.

"The team came out as a Christian organization that was going to witness to people while out on the road," recalled Mark Shannon. "There was a vow of no drugs, no tobacco, or alcohol. We held a press conference when someone asked, 'Let me see if I have this straight: no drugs, tobacco or alcohol, right? Well, how come your player, Wilt Chamberlain, is the spokesperson for Canadian Whiskey?'

"Management just froze. Shooting Stars vice president Marc Whitmore pulled Wilt aside and asked him to not be a spokesman for the whiskey company. Wilt said, 'I'll happily step aside as their spokesperson if you match my pay.'" That marked the end of Chamberlain's involvement with the Stars.

Meadowlark Lemon was impressed by how quickly Maravich learned the Stars' intricate choreography based on the old Globetrotter shows.

"I find that it takes about three years for the players to really get into the flow," Lemon said. "It took Pete about 10 minutes. I mean, it was like Pete would throw it into me and he would move. It was like he was dancing."

Sherwin "Shake" Durham, a Stars player, recalled his futile efforts to guard Maravich during practice.

"I'm like, 'OK, I want Pete Maravich tonight,'" remembered Durham. "I'm a cocky kid, I take my defensive stance at the top of the key and he pulls up from 25 or 30 feet and hits the bottom of the net. I was playing him like everyone else, like I'm not going to let him get to the basket. He wasn't interested in going to the basket." Maravich racked up 16 points in three minutes.

Off the court, Maravich was always generous with his Stars teammates.

"Pete wasn't making that much money with the Shooting Stars, but he picked up every single check in the time that I knew him," said referee Mark Shannon. "Our per diem back then was only $15 a day. Pete would go in there and see all the guys going through their sweats, looking for money. He would go right to the front of the counter and tell the order taker he was buying. One time the guys said, 'Pete, you're always buying. Please, let us buy.' He told them, 'You know what? You know how you guys can repay me? When you're on this team five years from now and you're the star. You can take the rookies to breakfast and lunch and pick up the check.'"

Maravich was similarly charitable with fans. "I remember up in Iowa, we were in a gym signing autographs," Lemon recalled to a television reporter. "We signed for about an hour and the custodian asked us to leave because he was putting the lights out. It was around maybe 10 or 20 degrees above zero and ice was all over the place and they put us out. And I said, 'Pete, I'm going to catch the bus.' Pete stayed there with those kids. Not only did he sign autographs, but also he talked about basketball. And he talked to them about life."

According to Les "Pee Wee" Harrison, the Stars' 5-9 guard, Maravich avoided situations he deemed un-Christian.

"I remember one time he told me he didn't want to go to the beach because there were a bunch of half-naked women out there," Harrison said. "Another time, we were in Sarasota, Florida, when the restaurant Hooters had just opened up. They had us come by after the game for a promotional appearance. Because the place was new, no one knew what it was about. When we got there, it was obvious what the place was about. Pete just stayed on the bus."

Maravich's presence on the tour was perplexing to Meadowlark's son, George.

"At times, I was somewhat annoyed at him to be perfectly honest with you," George Lemon recalled. "One night I said, 'Pete, why on earth are you doing this? You've got enough money to live on forever; you're so popular you could be the governor of Louisiana. You're going to be in the basketball Hall of Fame. You've got life made. Why are you out here? I know why we're all out here, but why are you out here?'"

Pete's answer was simple.

"'When I'm out here playing basketball, because of this ball in my hand, we could have a press conference and anywhere from five to 25 reporters will show up. And you know what? They'll listen to what I've got to say. If I want to talk about Jesus, I can. If I want to talk about a program, I can do that, too. You take the ball and you use it—as a tool to help people. So that's why I'm doing this,'" Lemon recalled.

On October 14, 1986, the Shooting Stars rolled into Baton Rouge and played in front of about 800 people at the LSU Assembly Center. In the hours before the game Maravich stood outside the arena with Mark Shannon and reminisced about his college days.

"He was talking about how he'd never come back to LSU because of how they treated his father," Shannon recalled. "I remember standing there in front of the building that would eventually be named after him. It was still light outside and the football stadium loomed in the background. Pete finally spoke and said, 'This place really hasn't changed, but I have.'"

Jackie Maravich was one of the faithful inside the arena that night but found the contrived comedy basketball show difficult to witness.

"It hurt my heart to watch him," Jackie said. "It was mostly comic stuff on the court, not playing. That wasn't Pete because he was such a competitor. It just gave me a funny feeling. I don't want to berate that team, but it wasn't the essence of Pete. And I think Pete realized that too, and stopped."

As Jaeson and Josh grew, Maravich tried to create a nurturing atmosphere at home. "The first five years of a child's life are the most important," Pete told George Vecsey of the *New York Times*. "I have to be there to make sure their behavior and nutritional patterns are established."

But when Jaeson entered first grade, he learned of his father's past. "My dad never talked about basketball or who he was when I was a kid," recalled Jaeson. "I was at St. Peter's in the first grade, and my teacher, Mrs. McGee, was calling roll on the first day. When she got to me she said, 'Maravich? Are you any kin to Pistol Pete Maravich?' When I told her I was, she got excited and said, 'I was a huge fan of your dad.'"

When Jaeson got home from school, he asked his father, "Are you Pistol Pete?"

Maravich acknowledged that he was and eventually showed Jaeson some NBA footage of the old man in action. At first Jaeson was indifferent. But when Pete took him to a court and threw in several half-court shots, the young Maravich's eyes widened and he began his own basketball journey.

In the fall of 1986, the NCAA followed the lead of the NBA and added a three-point shot. (In 1945, the NCAA had first experimented with a three-point shot during a game between Columbia and Fordham.) The rule change was not welcome news to most coaches.

Coach Billy Tubbs of Oklahoma said, "We've got a great game, but we're going to screw it up the way we're going."

"A step backward," complained Louisville coach Denny Crum.

"A Mickey Mouse shot," said St. John's head man Lou Carnesecca.

"If I were coaching, I'd be against it too," added TV commentator Dick Vitale. "It's another gimmick to haunt you."

College sharpshooters, however, were thrilled. Indiana's Steve Alford exclaimed, "You've got to love it," and UCLA's Reggie Miller simply said, "Thank you!"

Several former NCAA greats commented on how close (19-feet, 9-inches) the three-point line was to the rim. "That's where I took most of my shots from," exclaimed Rick Mount. "It probably would have added another 15 or 16 points to my average."

Austin Carr, who averaged over 38 points a game for Notre Dame between 1969 and 1971, said, "The three-point line that they have in college, to me, is a joke. There's no challenge there for a good shooter. I had a call from an alumnus of Notre Dame who told me I would have at least had 70. Between 70 and 75."

And thus began the quest to estimate how many extra points Pete Maravich would have scored if the three-point shot existed during his college years. Long-time Maravich observer Sam King of the *Baton Rouge State-Times*, examined old LSU shot charts and concluded that Pete would have added 7.8 points to his 44.2 point varsity average.

Broadcaster Bryant Gumbel said in 2000, "Conservatively you'd have to give him 10, 12 points a game more, which gets him up in the 55, 56 points a game."

Billy Packer said, "He would have been a 50-point-a-game scorer without question."

Certainly Pete Maravich hit hundreds of shots during his LSU career from beyond 19-feet, 9-inches (many well beyond). If those baskets had counted for three points, his career point totals and scoring averages would have been higher. But opponents, most likely, would have adjusted their defenses to force him to drive to the basket, perhaps cutting down his long-distance attempts. Ultimately, any speculation about what Maravich would have, or could have, achieved with a three-point shot is just that—speculation.

However, it is clear that the three-point shot (and the shot clock in 1985) was introduced to increase scoring opportunities. Basketball changed in the fall of 1986 and every college shooter since then has enjoyed an advantage over those who came before them.

Pete, of course, loved the idea of a three-point shot. "Pete and I were shooting baskets in Van Nuys," recalled Darrel Campbell. "He went out to the three-point line and asked me to rebound. Pete had a funny way of expressing himself. He said, 'Darrel, the college three-point line is a duck shot. Can you imagine how much fun I would've had if I had this?'

"I said, 'What do you mean by *duck shot*?' He shot the ball and when it ripped through the net, he went 'quack.' He moved around the three-point line and tore off about 40 straight shots and then missed one. He looked over to my wife, Pam, and said, 'That won't happen again.' He then proceeded to quack some more and ripped off another 20 in a row."

Campbell remembered a similar shooting exhibition prior to a college game Pete was covering for the USA Network.

"He went out before the game, took his broadcasting jacket off, and started pumping them in," Campbell recalled. "He started doing the same thing—quacking every time he made a shot. He just kept swishing and quacking. The USA Network rolled tape and later showed Pete shooting before the game. How many times before a game do you see the announcer taking shots?"

In October 1986, Maravich and 10 others were nominated as candidates for election to the Naismith Memorial Basketball Hall of Fame. Lee Williams, the recently retired executive director of the Hall, submitted Maravich's application. Celtics legend Bob Cousy headed a 24-person committee charged with reviewing all the nominees. Enshrinement required a minimum of 18 "yea" votes.

The mere possibility of Pete's enshrinement delighted Press. Unfortunately his strength was deteriorating and he was undergoing painful radiation treatments. In November, a dangerous blood clot sent Press back into the hospital. He spent the holidays in Covington with Pete, Jackie, and his grandsons. There he developed pneumonia and spent another two weeks in the hospital.

Upon his release, he returned to the Maravich home where Pete and Jackie cared for him. "I'd go and check on him from time to time and catch him sleeping with a Bible on his chest," Jackie said. "It was just heartbreaking."

In late January 1987, Maravich received the thrilling news that he had been selected for enshrinement into the Basketball Hall of Fame—on the first ballot. Pete climbed the stairs to his father's room and whispered the news in his ear. "Through the pain of the cancer his eyes had lit up, and for a few moments the happiness relieved him of his suffering," Pete recalled in his memoir. He prayed his father would be healthy enough to accompany him to the May induction ceremony in Springfield, Massachusetts.

Pete flew to Seattle to play in the Legends ("Legends" replaced "Old Timers" in 1985) contest during the NBA's All-Star weekend. It was his fourth consecutive appearance and he made a solid showing, moving well and scoring 9 points (3-7, 2-2) as his East squad lost to the West, 54-43, in the 24-minute mini game. Afterward Maravich, drenched in sweat, repeated one of his long-held convictions to a television reporter. "The game is entertainment for the fans. It's for the fans. It's not for the coaches. It's not for the players. It's for the fans," said Pistol. "If you don't have that product that's marketed right, that's out there, that's entertaining—nobody will show up."

As if to make Pete's point, that evening's Slam Dunk and the three-point shooting contests were thrilling fan-friendly exhibitions. Michael Jordan sealed the former with two dunks for the ages: a pumping Dr. J-style, take-off-from-the-foul-line jam, and a slashing, leaning (almost 90 degrees) gravity-defying slam. Larry Bird walked away with his second consecutive three-point shooting crown.

The trip to Seattle was a family affair as Pete brought Jaeson along with him. The seven-year-old enjoyed meeting all the players but not the "corporal punishment" delivered after he wandered away from his seat during a half-time presentation. It was the only time in his life that Pete spanked his son.

During the festive weekend, Maravich was officially announced as a member of the Hall of Fame's induction class of 1987. He was joined by Walt Frazier, Rick Barry, Bob Houbregs, and Bobby Wanzer. Maravich told reporters that the honor represented "the Oscar of basketball achievement."

Maravich returned from Seattle to find his father declining rapidly. Pete arranged for Press to be treated by Dr. Hans Napier, a renowned German physician who was experimenting with aggressive cancer treatments. Before the two departed for Hanover, Germany, Pete wrote a letter to his sons:

Dear Jaeson and Joshua,

I have to go out of town today. Jaeson, please say a prayer for Papa. Josh, you can say one, too.

Listen boys, please behave and listen to your mother while I am gone.

She loves you so much. Jaeson, please try and help mama while I am gone. You, too, Josh, help mama because she does so much for us and we don't really help her. Pick up your toys and clothes that are on the floor.

Jaeson, you eat right. Mama cooks great meals to make both of you strong.

Jaeson, I'm real proud of you making a 100 on your subtraction test. Do the best you can son. Remember, Jesus is always there for you and Josh. Whenever you feel down, you can just talk to Jesus. He will always comfort you.

I am really going to miss you both. And you, Jackie. I love you so much and will constantly keep you in my prayers. I love all of you.

Dad

Press and Pete flew to Germany on February 11, 1987. Dr. Napier hoped to strengthen Press's immune system with daily injections. Two days later Press's cough disappeared and he was able to crack a smile for his son. It was false hope, though. The cancer had spread to his lungs.

On February 20, father and son headed home. Pete stood for the entire flight so Press could lie across two seats. Their suitcases were stocked with medicines, including a six-month supply of liquid morphine. Upon landing Pete carried his father to the car and then to his bed. So many years ago in Clemson, Press had done the same for Pete, carrying the sleeping youngster to his room after a long practice or a road game.

Press wrote a relative on February 27:

Since I have this affliction I should be joyful and rejoice because God is testing me. If Jesus heals me then I will go around to the various churches, clubs, schools, and give my testimony to the unbelievers. I'll entitle it, 'From Life to Death and Death to Life.' Pete has given me strong spiritual strength and the Holy Spirit has been working through him. My attitude is more positive and my heart is slowly filling up with joy. If the Lord takes me, fine, and if He heals me, I will praise God—east, west, north, and south.

By late March, Press could no longer eat or drink and was admitted into Highland Park Hospital in Covington. On April 15, 1987, with Pete holding his hand, Press slipped away. Jackie overheard Pete whisper to his father, "I'll be with you soon."

Press was flown to Pennsylvania and buried (with a basketball) next to Helen at the St. Elijah Serbian Orthodox Church Cemetery in Aliquippa. Not far from his final resting place stood a lamppost where, some 65 years earlier, Press Maravich and the "Daniel Boys" first hung an apple basket.

26

Springfield

"If people just see a basketball player when they look at me, forget it, my life is nothing. The old Pete Maravich is dead and buried."

—PETE MARAVICH

"Seek pleasure and happiness and you'll never, never find it. Have the wisdom to seek obedience in Christ and happiness will find you."

—PETE MARAVICH

On April 28, 1987, less than two weeks after the death of his father, Pete Maravich stood in front of 35,000 people and a television crew at Williams-Brice Stadium in Columbia, South Carolina. Pete, a featured speaker during the eight-day Billy Graham Crusade, delivered a 10-minute version of his testimony. "I wouldn't trade my position with Christ for a thousand NBA championships," he told the crowd.

The following week Pete and his family traveled to Springfield, Massachusetts, for the Naismith Memorial Basketball Hall of Fame induction ceremony on May 5. Press was very much on Pete's mind as he prepared to accept the game's biggest honor.

Dozens of Maravich fans made the pilgrimage to Springfield, including 27-year-old businessman Sean Stormes. "It was the way Pete played the game that got me hooked," Stormes said.

The day-long festivities began with a 9:15 A.M. press conference. "The dreams that I had as a child didn't reach the Basketball Hall of Fame," Pete told the reporters. "My goals were a lot lower. My goals were basically to be on that championship team and get that ring. And yet here I am today to receive an even greater ring."

As Maravich was whisked from the press conference, Stormes and others enjoyed one of the Hall's most popular diversions—firing baskets into hoops with balls supplied by a conveyor belt. Suddenly Stormes noticed flash-bulbs popping and turned to find Maravich standing next to him.

"Balls, balls, I need balls," Maravich playfully clapped to Stormes. Taking the cue, Stormes began tossing basketballs to his childhood idol.

"I remember thinking, *I'm feeding Pete Maravich!*" said Stormes. "He was a good 18 to 20 feet from the basket. He had his jacket off, but he's got on a long-sleeve shirt, a tie, and slacks, and he nails three in a row. When I started feeding him the ball, he nailed another 15 in a row. Finally, he just threw up his hands and said, 'Okay, that's it folks.' I turned to look at my wife and my buddy, John, who were both in tears because they knew how I felt about Pete and what he meant to me growing up."

Stormes' magical day was not yet finished. He mustered the courage to say, "Pete, you will never know how much you've meant to me. I grew up without a whole lot. I've had a little success in my life. I just want you to know how much you've meant to me."

Maravich was genuinely moved. "I just never realized what kind of effect I've had on people who grew up watching me play," Pete replied. "But I realize it now and I appreciate your words very much."

Many noticed that Pete had aged considerably. Jackie recalled a comment by a former New York Knick before the ceremony.

"Phil Jackson said that Pete looked old, and Pete heard him and just smiled," remembered Jackie. "And I have to say that Pete didn't look so good in the end, either."

Pete was enshrined with Walt Frazier, Rick Barry, Bob Houbregs, and Bobby Wanzer.

Billy Packer, in his introductory remarks, spoke glowingly of Press Maravich's coaching achievements. "He was a brilliant strategist," said Packer, the former Wake Forest star who met the Maravich family back in Clemson. "As far as an understanding of the game and an understanding of how to teach the game, he was one of the best of all time. I'm sure your dad is with us tonight."

Pete's escort was "Easy" Ed McCauley, a former College Player of the Year and member of the 1958 NBA champion St. Louis Hawks. McCauley was the youngest player (32) ever enshrined by the Hall. He read the following evocation: "Pete, by virtue of your election by the authority vested in me by the trustees of the Naismith Basketball Hall of Fame, I have the distinguished honor to enshrine you as a player in the Basketball Hall of Fame with all the rights and privileges. Congratulations."

And with that Pete became the Hall's second youngest inductee. "When

I was a kid of seven years old, my dreams never really reached the clouds of the Hall of Fame," Pete said. "I felt like the Hall of Fame was something that was too far out, so I never thought about it. It never entered my mind."

Pete thanked his fellow honorees, the fans, coaches, GMs, owners, his wife and children, opponents (noting his battles with Frazier in particular), his mother, Helen, and then Press. "We had such a unique relationship. Not only as a coach and player, but also as a father and son. He meant so much to me, his influence. He was really the hero of my life. God was so special to both of us, especially over the last five-and-a-half months. It was really a dream that was fulfilled in his life to see his son make it to the Hall of Fame."

Pete concluded: "Lastly, I would just like to thank from the deepest part of my being, from the heart of hearts in my soul, my Savior and Lord Jesus Christ. Four-and-a-half years ago He came into my life and literally transformed me. It was such a transformation that took place, that I'd just like to thank Him for being able to be here tonight to receive this tremendous award and honor. Thank you all very much."

Custom-made rings were presented to the inductees. For some, the Hall of Fame ring was even more desirable than an NBA championship. But for Maravich, rings, trophies, and plaques were just symbols that glorified human achievement, and he now lived with different priorities. The ring was appreciated but not coveted.

After the presentation Pete confided in a friend, "You know what verse came to me when I received this ring? Matthew 16:26, 'For what will a man profit if he gains the whole world but loses his soul? What will a man give in exchange for his soul?'"

Later Pete chuckled when he learned that the entrée at the banquet was filet mignon.

When Pete returned home he put the finishing touches on his autobiography, *Heir to a Dream*, and began pre-production on the four-part video series, *Homework Basketball*. In late May, he spent six grueling 12-hour days videotaping the many basketball drills he and his father had developed. The shoot, directed by Frank Campbell, took place in the Albany High School gymnasium, about 35 miles from Covington.

The exhausting week produced four instructional tapes that covered shooting, dribbling, passing, and ball handling. All who watched were amazed at how easily the 39-year-old Maravich executed the drills, even those that required speed and flexibility. Pete would stand at the free-throw line and casually whip around-the-back passes off the backboard with either hand. He methodically swished a series of jumpers and "pro-layups." He demonstrated a bizarre exercise called "scrambled eggs," which combined "between-the-leg dribbling while walking" with "syncopated hand pats against your thigh, stomach, chest, and head." After each extraordinary demonstration, Pete would turn to the camera and exclaim, "Do it!" He seemed genuinely oblivious to the fact that a mere handful of humans shared his talent.

"He is a preacher, selling hoop excellence," wrote *Los Angeles Times* reporter Scott Ostler after watching the tapes. "But beyond that, they are a showcase of Pistol Pete's magic. In a way, they are his legacy. Most of the drills look simple, but none are. Some are difficult. Others are impossible. All, executed full speed by the Pistol, are incredible. On the film, I'm watching the product of zillions of hours of work, of an entire youth spent in gyms and the privacy of his bedroom, driving himself toward perfection."

Before he died, Press asked Pete to price the tapes as inexpensively as possible. "I want every kid who wants to know anything about basketball to know how to do 'Homework Basketball,'" said Press. He hoped each video would sell for less than $10.

ESPN eventually aired *Homework Basketball* and sold the complete set for $89.99. Purchasers also received a bonus video entitled, *Maravich Memories: The LSU Years*, a treasure trove of game footage culled from films Press took with him when he left LSU. Since 1987, tens of thousands of copies of *Homework Basketball* have been sold. Coaches on every level, including Duke's Mike Krzyzewski, still recommend the series to players who need to improve their ball-handling skills. The series was reformatted to DVD and it continues to introduce players of all ages to Pete and Press's "creative fundamentals."

As the summer of 1987 approached, Pete was still coping with the sorrow of his father's death. "The pain is always there for me. I still have aftershocks. I'd be driving down the highway and I'll bust out crying for 10 minutes," Maravich told reporter Kevin Thomas. "I try to think of Christ, of heavenly things, of where he is . . . and that one day I'll be with him."

Friend Randy Drude recalled detailed conversations with Maravich regarding the afterlife. "It's really strange how much Pete harped about the end and how it could all end in the snap of a finger," Drude recalled. "He said, 'Randy, you could go in a split second. It's going to be *bam!* and you could be done. It's going to be over. Be prepared.' The one thing that really blew me away was one time we were in his study in Covington and just out of the clear blue he said, 'You know what Randy? You know what really blows me away? I'm going to meet Jesus Christ face to face.'"

In June, Pete returned to his camp in Clearwater. It would be his first summer without Press. Maravich was grateful when his friend John Lotz agreed to help with the day-to-day operations. One new camper was Rick Barry's eldest son, 20-year-old Scooter, who'd met Pete during the recent Hall of Fame weekend.

Scooter was a struggling member of the University of Kansas basketball team. He shot an anemic 31 percent and played scattered minutes over his first two seasons. He always enjoyed Pete's outrageous game. "When I was a kid playing with friends, we'd all pick a pro player to imitate. They always told me to be Rick Barry," he told Linda Robertson of the *Miami Herald*. "But I always wanted to be Pistol Pete."

Barry arrived at camp hoping for some pointers from his idol, but he got much more. "It completely changed my basketball career," Barry explained to David Kiefer of the *Peninsula Times Tribune*. "Pete convinced me that I could be a player. It was incredible. We'd be in a little gym in Clearwater, Florida, while all the kids had gone to sleep, and he would be teaching me his ball-handling exercises. I didn't like my shot, but he did. He said all I needed to do was shoot and know the ball was going in, not hope it would go in."

When Rick Barry came for his son at the end of camp, Pete ran out to greet him. "The way he was running at me when I first saw him, I thought something happened to Scooter," recalled Barry. "I was really nervous. '. . . don't tell me something has happened to Scooter.' And Pete said, 'Man, Scooter can play.' So I was relieved a little bit, 'Well, yeah, I know he can play.' 'No, he really can play. I mean he's really a good player.'

"So I felt really good to hear that. But it was so good for my son to hear it coming from Pete, because coming from me it doesn't mean anything, 'cause I'm his father. But coming from Pete it meant so much. It just bolstered his confidence. He really learned a lot from those drills. I think it helped turn his basketball career around."

A confident Scooter Barry returned to Kansas and became the pivotal sixth man on the Jayhawks 1988 Cinderella NCAA championship team. As a senior, he was starting point guard and voted co-captain.

"Those two weeks with Pete were intense. We really got close. He was so compassionate," recalled Scooter. "I would just absorb everything he had to say. He will always be an inspiration to me." (Scooter's younger brother Brent, who was a member of the San Antonio Spurs 2005 championship team, is another Maravich devotee.)

In the fall of 1987, a 40-year-old Maravich appeared on several television shows, including *The Today Show*, *The 700 Club*, and ESPN's *Sports Look*, promoting his book and video series. He also gave numerous newspaper interviews to a new generation of writers.

"He was a marvel, a phenomenon, a dazzling ball handler and shot creator," wrote Ostler in the *Los Angeles Times*. "His vision saw the basketball court as a spawning ground for physical excitement and originality. That was a weird concept two decades ago, unless you were a Harlem Globetrotter. In 1966, when Pistol Pete came out whirling and passing and shooting at LSU, most coaches would bench you if you dribbled through your legs, let alone through someone else's legs. Even when his remarkable scoring and playmaking continued in the NBA, Pete remained a misunderstood genius, a Vincent van Gogh of the hardwood."

On October 13, 1987, before flying to a prayer breakfast in Peoria, Illinois, Maravich wrote the following note to his wife:

Dear Jackie,

As I go on this trip to Peoria, I just want to write a short note to you. I could never ever thank you enough for the love you give to Jaeson, Joshua, and me. Day after day, you cook, clean, run errands, pick up, wash, dry. Well, I just want you to know that my love for you grows with every tick of the clock. I appreciate you so much, and I know that I often do not express that appreciation. But, nonetheless, it is there, deep within my heart. You remind me so much of my mother. She too possessed a great love for her family and was fierce in protecting them.

God has gifted you, Jackie, with a love that remains humble. Just to hold you brings a great joy to my life. You, through the grace of God, are the glue which cements our family. You mean so much to me and the kids. I shutter to think that I could ever hurt you in any way. I love you so much.

Please try to understand, that I want more than anything, to share what Christ has done in my life. I will be allright. "Be strong and courageous, do not tremble or be dismayed, for the Lord Your God is with you wherever you go." I love you, Jackie, and I see everyday how God has used you to strengthen me. Thank you for always being there with me, you have always been there.

Please kiss the boys for me. I love them so much, also. Oh, how I love them. They are both going to be super athletes, but with a Christly heart. I love all of you. Lord willing, I will see you tomorrow.

All my love,

Peter

John 14:27

(Peace I leave you with; my peace I give you.

Do not let your hearts be troubled and do not be afraid.)

At the prayer breakfast Pete began his remarks with these words: "Thank you for having me here in Peoria. Of course, I did not fly all the way here to talk about a jump shot, or to talk about a behind-the-back dribble. I came here to bear witness to Jesus Christ, who is my personal Savior and Lord. And who has literally transformed my life in such a dramatic way that I will never be the same. Each day that passes, it only becomes greater.

"I can bear witness to what Paul said, not a lot, just a little bit, when he told the Corinthians, 'We are afflicted in every way, but not crushed. Perplexed but not despairing. Persecuted but not forsaken. Struck down, but not destroyed.'"

The audience was rapt as Maravich weaved his story of redemption and rebirth. His speech was, by now, well rehearsed but his father's death had inspired a new ending. "I remember, after my dad had passed away that night, he passed away at 6:30 P.M. I was there for his last breath. I was shocked. I couldn't believe the last breath my father took. He died of respiratory depression. He drowned. He took that last breath. It was like he took every last bit of oxygen in the room he was trying to grab. The human body was trying to stay alive. Then it first came to me—Psalms: Man is like a mere breath, his day like a passing shadow" (Psalm 144:4).

Pete loved being at home with his sons. The youngest, Joshua, recalled the time he convinced his father, the most skilled ball handler in history, to dunk. Another fond memory involved a nightly ritual of hide and seek. "I used to hide in the den under the furniture. I'd see him walk down the hallway toward me, and he always knew where I was," recalled Joshua. "It was like our little game we had with each other."

Jaeson, three years older than Joshua, was even closer to his father. He often pleaded with Maravich to join him to watch basketball on television, and every so often Pete would plop down to take in an NBA game. Philadelphia's Charles Barkley was a particular favorite among 1980s players, along with Isiah Thomas, Magic Johnson, Michael Jordan, and Larry Bird.

Maravich's bitterness toward LSU had softened and when coach Dale Brown invited him to be honored on campus, he accepted. On December 5, 1987, at half time of an LSU game, Maravich was presented with a large oil portrait of himself and Press. He delivered a teary tribute to his father and donated the painting to the university. The hatchet was finally buried.

Later that month Maravich began open tryouts in the New Orleans area to find a young actor to portray him in the movie *The Pistol: Birth of a Legend*. The auditions were the first of 20 scheduled in major cities across the country. Pete tested kids in groups of six, asking them to dribble and spin the ball on their fingers. A Shreveport boy named Adam Guier caught his eye. The ambidextrous Guier possessed fairly impressive basketball skills and bore a striking resemblance to Maravich, circa 1959.

Ultimately, Guier was cast as the young Pete.

At the end of the year Pete decided to sell his Clearwater condominium. He enjoyed the ocean-front view and the privacy, but he was only using it about a month each year. Maravich enlisted a few friends from the Clearwater Church to help with the move.

"When we were carrying furniture down the elevator, at one point I saw Pete reach over and grab his arm while rubbing it," recalled Guy Priest. "I asked, 'Are you alright?' He said, 'I'm fine. I'm fine. Let's get back to work.' He made some sort of comment about neuritis in his shoulder, so I didn't think anything of it. A little while later, when we were riding in the elevator, he looked down at his knees and they were shaking. I said, 'Look at that,' and he got real disgusted about it, even mad. He said, 'Man, I am so out of shape.' His knees were visibly shaky. It really bothered him because he was a professional athlete and in such great shape before."

Clearwater pastor Donny Liles also remembered Maravich commenting about his health.

"Pete knew something was wrong with him—that's not even a question in my mind," Liles said. "He said to me, 'Something is wrong with me physically and I don't know what it is. I've had my cholesterol checked, but I know something is wrong with me.'"

Neuritis, an inflammation of the nerves, afflicted Pete's neck and right shoulder. Jackie and Pete believed it was caused by his efforts to care for his father. Toward the end of his life, Press was unable to walk, and Pete often carried him around. Jackie believed the strain triggered the painful condition.

"One night he was in such pain, they [the doctors] prescribed him morphine," Jackie said. "Every once in a while, I'd go to his office and catch him sleeping and he'd say, 'Oh, you caught me catnapping.' He was always so physically fit, but he was the type that didn't like to go to doctors." One evening Pete sat in the shower for 30 minutes while hot water streamed onto his right shoulder.

Some blamed Pete's strict vegetarian diet for his weakened condition.

"Looking back, you started to understand what the problem was," said Jim Krivacs. "I used to give him a hard time and say, 'You know, you go out and you talk so hard about nutrition.' I said, 'Who wants to look like you?'"

Friends in North Carolina noticed his unhealthy pallor when a gaunt Maravich returned to Raleigh in late December for the retirement of his Broughton High School jersey.

"I'm glad they're doing it now while I can enjoy it," Maravich joked with a reporter when learning of the honor. "Usually they wait until you are dead."

The ceremony was held December 29, between semifinal games of the Raleigh Times High School Basketball Festival.

Pete spent three nights at the home of his good friend Bob Sanford. "He was happy with what he was doing—in spreading the Word to young people and living for Christ," said Sanford.

That message resonated with former Broughton teammate Billy Trott, who had not seen Maravich in more than two decades. Trott remembered Pete as "fidgety and egotistical," but was surprised to find a calm, humble man. Pete spoke about his mother's suicide, his father's struggles, and his own journey.

"Pete said Press was down to 100 pounds and he had to pick up him up and carry him into the living room to sit and watch TV. He'd also have to pick him up to take him to bed and give him his pain medication. The child had become the father," remembered Trott. "He said he and his father gained this incredible, intense, close relationship as a result of this. It led him to become a better Christian. He said, 'If I die tomorrow, I will be at peace with the earth and peace with the Lord.' *Happy* isn't the word for it. He was at peace as anybody you'd ever seen."

Ed McLean, Pete's former Broughton coach, was also on hand. "It was great because I got to spend some time with him," McLean said. "It was strange, though, because he told me that his shoulder was killing him. I said to him, 'You really need to get that thing checked.' He said, 'Well, I did get it checked out and it was neuritis.' Other than that, I had never seen him happier. He was really feeling good about everything in his life, especially his ministry and his new book. He was a man on the go and loving every minute of it."

On December 30, Maravich flew from Raleigh to Oklahoma. The All-College Basketball Tournament was inducting Maravich into its Hall of Fame. LSU had romped through the tournament in the winter of 1968 as Pete averaged 46 points over three games to cop the MVP trophy.

"He was the best I ever saw," said former Oklahoma City coach Abe Lemons. "He was the most exciting player I ever knew." Lemons said that

Maravich's style of play was so mesmerizing that even his wife secretly cheered for him.

Maravich returned to Covington for a quiet New Year's Eve with Jackie and the boys. He expected 1988 to be a prosperous year. He had a book in the stores, four instructional tapes for sale, and a feature film in the early stages of development. He was solidly booked for speaking engagements, basketball clinics, and color commentary work. He felt blessed.

His first order of business in 1988 was a trip to California. He was scheduled to appear on Dr. James Dobson's syndicated radio show, *Focus on the Family*, and then meet with screenwriter Darrel Campbell.

On Sunday, January 3, Pete was in his office at home studying Scripture. "The last time I saw him was the day before he left for California," recalled Jaeson. "I saw him in his study with his Bible and he was praying. That was probably 7 P.M. He left the next morning and I never saw him again."

Maravich packed for his trip and phoned various friends. His last call was to John Lotz, who noticed that Pete seemed uneasy.

"I don't think he had any inclination to die," said Lotz. "At the end of the conversation, he said, 'I don't know what anybody else wants to do, but all I want to do is share the gospel with young people across the country.' Those were the last words I heard out of his mouth."

On Monday, January 4, Maravich drove to the airport and flew with Frank Schroeder to Los Angeles. They rented a car and checked into the San Dimas Inn, a motel near Pomona. That night in Utah, the Jazz were hosting the Celtics at the Salt Palace. Boston announcer Johnny Most was calling the game on radio and Pete was scheduled for a short telephone interview. Maravich never called in.

He did phone Jackie. She detected fatigue in his voice, but nothing about their conversation gave her cause for alarm.

"As usual, we said 'I love you,'" shrugged Jackie. "But when we hung up, I certainly didn't think it was going to be the last time I was going to talk to him."

27

Broken Heart

"I'd like to play in the game when I'm 100. I'd like to be oldest human being still playing the game. Still filling the lanes."

—PETE MARAVICH

"An American original died today."

—DAN RATHER, *CBS EVENING NEWS*

In the early morning hours of January 5, 1988, Gary Lydic, the director of ministry services for Focus on the Family, was minutes away from realizing a dream—he was about to meet and play basketball with Pete Maravich. His church group, which normally held pick-up games on Monday, Wednesday, and Friday mornings, had changed its schedule to accommodate Maravich's Tuesday appearance.

"For a bunch of 'duffers' like us to invite a superstar like Pete to play with us took some gall," Dr. James Dobson wrote in his 1995 book *Life on the Edge*. "He was the Michael Jordan or the Magic Johnson of his day."

Lydic arrived at the San Dimas Inn about 6:20 A.M. and, moments later, Maravich and Frank Schroeder piled into his car for the 20-mile trek to the First Church of the Nazarene in Pasadena.

"Pete started sharing Jesus Christ with me immediately," Lydic recalled. "He shared about his relationship with his dad, Press, and how difficult that was. Then he shared about his dear wife, Jackie, and his two sons. I can remember halfway to Pasadena we definitely got into a traffic jam on the freeway. I decided to take a shortcut because we were going to be late. Just as I made a decision to do that, I pulled out into another lane and a car came from nowhere and just about clipped us. I remember swerving back into my lane and thinking, *Lord, not today. Any other day, but not with Pistol Pete in the car.* We ended up taking a few back roads and got to the Church of the Nazarene."

They arrived a little after 7:00 A.M. and began warming up at a free basket. Pete continued to share the story of his last days with Press: "Many times I took my dad off the airplane, carrying him as we were seeking a cure for cancer. I didn't know whether my father was alive or not as I took him off the plane."

Then Lydic mentioned that his own father was dying of bone cancer. "I remember Pete coming over and putting his arm around me, 'Gary, I've been there, and I want to walk you through this,'" recalled Lydic. "Then Dr. Dobson called for us and we went over and met the rest of the guys. I'm not a very bright guy, but I was allowed to choose teams. I think you can guess who I picked first."

The nine players included Ralph Drollinger, a 7-2 center who won two NCAA titles at UCLA and played briefly with the Dallas Mavericks.

They split into teams of four and played a few half-court games. Norm Moline, the ninth man, stood on the sidelines videotaping the action with his VHS camcorder.

Maravich seemed to be enjoying the friendly, slow-paced games. "He certainly didn't have to play hard against us. He was hardly perspiring," recalled Lydic. "He was outclassing us without even trying." After Pete's team lost a couple of games, Dobson offered to trade some players.

"No, we're going to get you guys," Maravich teased.

After playing three games to 11 points, the men stopped for water. Dobson estimated it was between 7:45 and 8:00 A.M. During the break, Maravich and Dobson—who were meeting for the first time—chatted. Maravich told Dobson that his father's ordeal and his own painful neuritis had kept him from even thinking about touching a basketball.

"You can't give up this game, Pete," Dobson said. "It has meant too much to you through the years."

"You know, I've loved playing this morning," replied Pete. "I really want to get back to this kind of recreational basketball. But it wouldn't have been possible in the last few months. The pain in my shoulder has been so intense that I couldn't have lifted a two-pound ball over my head."

"How do you feel now?" Dobson asked.

"I feel great," Maravich replied.

As Dobson turned to walk away Maravich suddenly fell. Dobson thought he was horsing around and expected him to jump up with a smile on his face. But Maravich stayed down. He was pale and his eyes had rolled up into his head. "He never took another breath on his own," said Dobson. Drollinger and Dobson started performing CPR while another player called 911.

Dobson noticed that Pete's T-shirt read: "Looking unto Jesus."

"It was the kind of situation where you think time is just dragging and dragging. The paramedics finally came in and pulled out the paddles," said Lydic. "Everybody started working on his heart. All of us who were playing basketball all knelt and literally cried out in prayer, 'Lord, why now?'"

Maravich was rushed to the emergency room at St. Luke's Medical Center in Pasadena where, at 9:24 A.M. on January 5, 1988, he was pronounced dead by Dr. Vincent Bufalino.

All indications pointed to massive cardiac failure.

Before Maravich's body was removed to the L.A. County Coroner's Office, the men formed a circle around the gurney and began to pray.

"I can remember us holding hands as Pete's body just lay there," recalled Lydic. "I've never before or after seen a more peaceful face in my entire life. Pete's body was there—the shell was there—but he had already gone home to be with the Lord."

Just eight-and-a-half months after his father's death, Pete was also gone. He was 40 years old.

Darrel Campbell recalled getting a phone call from Frank Schroeder moments later. "We were going to play some basketball and then go over the first draft of the screenplay," recalled Campbell. "Finally, the phone rang and it was Frank. He said, 'It's Pete . . .' He said his name in a certain tone that was weird, and I could tell something was wrong. He was searching for the words, but couldn't find them. So in the pause, I spoke up, 'Don't tell me he blew his knee out.' I was thinking about the knee problem Pete had in the pros. Frank said, 'I'm at St. Luke's.' I said, 'Is it his knee?' He paused and said, 'Pete's dead.' I felt hollow and the walls started spinning. He said, 'You need to get over here because the media is going to want someone to talk to. I can't do it.'"

Schroeder's next phone call was much tougher. He called Jackie in Covington. A housekeeper answered and put Jackie on the line. Schroeder delivered the devastating news.

"Not my Pete!" cried Jackie. She dropped the phone and ran out of the house. Five-year-old Josh heard his mother's anguished cries as she ran across the street.

"That was the weirdest day," Josh recalled. "Our maid answered the phone, and then Mom just started screaming. I walked into the bathroom and just stared at myself in the mirror and said, 'Dad's dead.' I had no idea, but I just kind of guessed it. Then I started to hear my mother scream, and then she got the maid's kids to come over here. It was really weird, I swear to you.

And I really didn't know what death was at that point. I had a dream that he would be back tomorrow. For two weeks, I kept counting down the time when he'd be back. I kept saying, 'Dad's coming back tomorrow.'"

Jaeson, then eight, was at school. "I was eating and the principal came over to me and said, 'I just got a call from your mother. You need to go home.' I remember having a strange feeling because I never got called home from school. I knew something was up, but nothing like that. When I got home, a bunch of people were sitting around the house and my mother was crying. I knew then that something very serious had happened. I just remember my mama crying and putting her arms around me and saying, 'Dad just passed away.' I was kind of shocked and started crying. Then Josh started crying. It was a sad day."

Ronnie Maravich was tending bar in the French Quarter when a friend called around lunchtime. "My friend said, 'Turn on the channel 6 news. They've got a story about your brother,' and he wouldn't tell me," said Ronnie. "So it was around noon our time and they announced it—Pete Maravich died of a heart attack. That just wiped me out. I was out of it for about six months. I think I was in another dimension. All I really had was Pete. You know, I'm not married or nothing, so that's all I had."

News of Maravich's death spread quickly. ESPN devoted 24-hour coverage, while the three major networks reported the death on the evening news. CNN's Nick Charles aptly summed up Maravich's star-crossed basketball life, "So talented he made you gasp, so tortured at times, he made you wince."

The news rocked the basketball community. How could Pete Maravich—the health food junkie, the man with boundless energy who ran up and down the court night after night—have died so suddenly?

Kareem Abdul-Jabbar, just two months older than Pete, was uncharacteristically available for comment. "It comes as complete shock. I have a hard time believing somebody his age and in his condition could pass like that."

Elgin Baylor: "When they said it was a heart attack, it was hard to believe. Pete was such a health enthusiast."

Bob Lanier: "To hear this today is devastating, because he's a young guy. I mean we graduated from school in 1970 together. It's unbelievable. I've been down since I heard about it two hours ago. The last time I talked to Pete was at the NBA All-Star Game two years ago. He played in the Legends game and was telling me about all the stuff he was doing with his son. He worked with him all the time and had a basketball hoop just the right height for a kid to learn the right way to shoot the ball. It makes you think. Life don't promise you anything."

Maravich's basketball idol Jerry West called it, "A great tragedy. Someone at that time of life, you just don't think things like that are possible. My fondest memory of him was the great anticipation that came with him when he came into the NBA, the wonderful excitement he brought to every game he played. He brought thrills and entertainment to the league when the league needed it."

NBA Commissioner David Stern issued a press statement: "Pete Maravich will long be remembered as one of the greatest players in basketball history. His unique flair for showmanship made a great contribution to the NBA's quality and fan popularity in the seventies. He also had a tremendous love for the game. He will be sorely missed by anyone who knew him or enjoyed the thrill of seeing him take his picture-perfect jump shot or deliver the bounce-pass on the fast break."

Richie Guerin, who coached Pete in Atlanta and in his last Legends game, said, "He would want to be remembered as a good father, a good husband, and a good Christian."

Rick Barry: "He was the greatest ball handler I've ever seen in my life. He could do things with the basketball that were unbelievable. There was nobody close to him. It's really such a tragic thing because Pete was such a wonderful person. Forget the basketball part of it, Pete was just a very giving human being. I'm going to miss him a great deal."

Larry Bird: "He was one of the truly great players that could fill an arena. He was an excellent player. He could dribble with both hands, shoot with both hands, and see the whole court. I enjoyed playing with Pete. His biggest influence to my mind was his ability to pass. When he stepped on the court, it was like a warning sign: 'Watch out. I know how to play this game.'"

Elvin Hayes: "Pete found Christ in his life. He began to do wonderful things with different ministries across the country. And he really just became a totally different person. He had a purpose and a new direction in life. I think that out of all Pete did in basketball, out of all he accomplished in basketball— and I think he would say it—his last part of his life was the best for him."

Magic Johnson: "Through following basketball and enjoying his flair for the game, I feel as though I knew him. He was a great scorer and a great passer at the same time. The passes he made were unbelievable. He was so ahead of his time."

Isiah Thomas: "Pistol was a big influence on me. I've often tried his moves on the basketball court. What he did on the court are things that players today still can't do."

Dave Cowens: "One of the most exciting players to watch ever in the history of college and professional basketball. When he had the ball, anything could happen. He was born to play basketball."

Dan Issel: "Things Pete started to do and was thought of as a hot-dog for doing—the behind-the-back dribble, behind-the-back pass, between-the-legs dribble—now all guards do it today and nobody even thinks about it. But nobody had ever done it in the game before Pete did it. He certainly had more impact from the backcourt standpoint than any player who ever played."

Pete's old Hawks coach Cotton Fitzsimmons: "I don't know if we'll have another one. It takes a lot of courage to play the way he played. Everybody who came through the turnstiles to see the Pistol, they never got cheated. Pete gave them a show—every night."

LSU coach Dale Brown: "Pete's death is a great tragedy, but in a way it's also a victory. Because he had at long last found God, he had also found himself. He joins his father, whom he loved most dearly. He died doing what he did better than anyone else ever did or will do, putting the ball through the hoop."

The Lakers longtime announcer Chick Hearn: "He was a startling player. One of a half dozen I've ever seen who I'd buy a ticket to see play. He was as dazzling a passer and as great a ball handler as I've ever seen. He was like a great singer with a style all his own, a pacing that was different, a flair for the unusual."

Lakers coach Pat Riley (who once told *Sports Illustrated* that Maravich was an "overrated superstar"): "He was the original. When you talk about 'Showtime,' you talk about creativity and bringing a whole different concept to the game of basketball. Pete was the original. He opened the minds of a lot of players as to how the game should be played. What he could do with the basketball at full speed was incredible. He was the best ball handler I ever saw. Ever."

Paul Westphal: "The way Pete played transcended the game. He was an artist. His canvas was the floor and his brush was the basketball. Only one guy got to be Elvis. And only one guy got to be Pistol Pete."

Columnists, reporters, and broadcasters around the country eventually added their perspectives.

Scott Ostler, *Los Angeles Times*: "There was a magic about the guy, an aura. He was a brooding, mysterious character, with as many critics as fans.

And he could do stuff with a basketball that boggled everyone's mind but his own."

Author Mike DeCourey: "He was more than a showman, but as a showman, he had no peer."

Sports columnist Jay Mariotti: "He holds a special place in the game's history, that of a loose-limbed free spirit who brought creativity and fun to the hardwood. Rarely has sport produced a more complex and unhappy hero. As much as he loved playing the game, he hated to fail. Long before he fell to the floor of a church gymnasium yesterday, faint of heart, basketball killed Pete Maravich."

Curry Kirkpatrick, *Sports Illustrated*: "He personified why I love basketball; why I enjoy watching it; writing about it; why sports itself is such an important part of human existence."

Bob Ryan, *Boston Globe*: "The man was a true virtuoso. There were no Pete Maraviches before he came along, and there never has been since. This Mozart of the Hardwood never should have played for his father in college, never should have entered the NBA billed as a 'Great White Hope,' and never should have gone to New Orleans as a franchise savior. The truth is that Pete Maravich was a brilliant, fearsome professional . . . a true American original."

Author Alex Sachere: "He was the most creative offensive talent in history, an innovator who bridged the gap from playground to the pros . . . He could score from anywhere on the court, using a variety of shots ranging from twisting, improvisational layups to textbook jumpers. And his passing was brilliant, combining the precision of the craftsman with the creativity of the artisan."

Mike Lupica, *New York Daily News*: "Maravich, who was 40 when his heart gave out, will be remembered as Pistol Pete, who could put the ball behind his back, between his legs, and finally through a hoop. And he ought to be remembered for a distinctive flair, a genius only he possessed."

Bob McEwen, *Rochester Times Union*: "He was to basketball what the *Sgt. Pepper* album was to pop music: revolutionary and liberating."

One reporter, Andy Nuzzo, a sportswriter for the *Beaver County Times*, found a copy of a story he'd filed back in 1974. Written just after Maravich's suspension from the Atlanta Hawks, Pete spoke of an early retirement from the NBA. The quote was remarkable for its prescience.

"I don't want to play 10 years in the NBA and die of a heart attack at age 40," said Maravich.

"I just took it and wrote it and didn't think anything of it until he died," Nuzzo said. "I happened to be working that day and I was supposed to do a local reaction to Maravich's story, and when I got to the office, there it was on my desk. I sat down and looked at it. It was pretty eerie."

Talk show host and columnist Larry King was also especially shocked. One day earlier, on January 4, while recovering from bypass surgery, he received a package containing a leather Bible with his name embossed on the cover. Accompanying the Bible was a letter dated December 31, 1987:

> *Dear Larry,*
>
> *I'm so glad to hear that everything went well with your surgery. I want you to know that God was watching over you every minute and even though I know you question that, I also know that one day it will be revealed to you. My prayer is that you remain open and God will touch your life as He has mine. Once I was a disbeliever. When I could not fill my life with basketball, I would simply substitute sex, liquid drugs or material things to feed my internal shell-like appearance. I was never satisfied. I have finally realized after 40 years that Jesus Christ is in me. He will reveal this truth to you, Larry, because He lives.*
>
> *Pete Maravich, 'Pistol Pete'*

Days after his death, the *Los Angeles Times* interviewed Pete's personal physician in Covington, Dr. Henry Mitchell. Mitchell said Maravich had last undergone a full physical about a year prior to his death. The examination included an electrocardiogram and standard tests for high blood pressure and cholesterol levels. Mitchell saw nothing alarming in Maravich's EKG, and his blood pressure and cholesterol levels were within the normal range. Additionally, Mitchell tested Maravich for symptoms of Marfan syndrome, an inherited, connective tissue disorder common to tall people, which puts them at risk for heart failure. He said Maravich exhibited no signs of Marfan.

On January 6, Bob Dambacher, a spokesman for the L.A. County Coroner's Office, announced that a preliminary autopsy indicated Pete's collapse was caused by heart failure. However, Dambacher said, "Additional microscopic analysis will be conducted to determine the exact cause of death."

Back in Louisiana, Jackie was overcome with grief and had to be medicated. She was unable to cope with the details of Pete's funeral so her father coordinated the entire event. He also retrieved Maravich's car, still parked at the New Orleans airport.

Sadly, on the day of the burial, a foul-up at the funeral home prevented Jackie from saying a final good-bye. "Everything is still a blur. I don't remember who I saw at the church, who came or what," said Jackie. "The only thing

I remember is the day I had to bury him. My mom, dad, and I went to the funeral home and there was some old man in the room in a casket where Pete had been. I mean, I went nuts. I didn't know where Pete was. They had already taken him to the church. I wanted to say my own good-byes to Pete. There were 50 people around his casket all the time and that's the only thing I ever regret—not being able to be alone with Pete to say my good-byes."

Nearly 700 people braved icy winds to attend the funeral on Sunday, January 10. The service was held in the 1,600-seat First Baptist Church in Baton Rouge, not far from the LSU campus where Pete and Press's version of "Showtime" first gained national attention.

Pete's sister, Diana, and brother, Ronnie, led the procession. Jaeson and Josh were left at home as Jackie felt the funeral would be too painful for them to endure.

Rich Hickman and other LSU teammates were in the church, as well as a group of Pete's friends from Clearwater, who had driven 12 hours to pay their final respects. Donald Ray Kennard, Jay McCreary, Elgin Baylor, Bucky Waters, Jim Taylor, Sam King, Collis Temple, Don Redden, Carl Von Dem-Busche, Jr., Del Wubbena, and Colonel Jim May were also among the mourners. Pallbearers included Ronnie Maravich, Darrel Campbell, Jimmy Walker, Randy Drude, and Frank Schroeder.

For to me, to live is Christ and to die is gain. (Philippians 1:21)

The above scripture graced the funeral program. Pastor Rodney Wood of the Trinity Evangelical Free Church began the service, followed by Alfred Young of the Christ Temple Church. John Lotz and Dr. James Dobson eulogized Pete, focusing mainly on his religious faith and love for humanity rather than his athletic prowess. None of the speakers referred to him as "Pistol Pete."

Alfred Young, who met Maravich after his retirement from basketball, told the mourners, "I did not know Pete Maravich, the basketball player. I did not know Pete Maravich, the superstar. God gave me the privilege of knowing Pete Maravich, the man."

Dobson added, "His last 45 minutes on earth was at a church playing basketball, which seemed somehow fitting. Basketball might have been his greatest love at one time. But his greatest passion was the love of the Lord he served."

After the service, the funeral procession traveled to the Resthaven Gardens of Memory on Jefferson Highway in East Baton Rouge. Many of the onlookers recall 11-year-old Carl Von DemBusche, Jr. clad in a purple and gold LSU jacket, gently laying a rose on Pete's casket.

On an overcast January afternoon, as the strains of "Amazing Grace" pierced the damp air, Pete Maravich's coffin was lowered into the ground.

Two days after the funeral, on January 12, the L.A. County Coroner's Office released the findings of Maravich's autopsy. The report concluded that Pete's fatal heart arrhythmia was due to an undiagnosed "congenital anomaly."

The exact details of that *anomaly* would stun the medical community and recast Pete's life and athletic career.

Dr. Joseph H. Choi, chief examiner of the Los Angeles Forensic Medical Division, was amazed to discover that Pete had been born with a dangerously malformed heart. A normal heart consists of two coronary arteries, left and right, providing oxygen-rich blood.

Maravich's right artery was present but the left artery never developed.

"The news of his death stunned everyone," said Dr. Choi who, along with Dr. Ronald Kornbluth, authored a study entitled, *Pete Maravich's Incredible Heart*, published in the *Journal of Forensic Science*. "Even more astonishing was the condition of his heart, specifically the single coronary artery."

Dr. Barry Maron, a cardiologist with the National Heart, Lung, and Blood Institute in Bethesda, Maryland, told *USA Today*, "This is so unusual, it would be impossible to put any kind of meaningful number on its occurrence."

Earl Ubell, a science reporter for CBS in New York, added, "All those years his life hung by a thread."

Typically the rare condition triggers a fatal heart attack before adulthood.

"In general, when someone dies from congenital heart disease, they don't die at 40. They drop dead at 16," explained Dr. Paul Thompson, a sudden death expert at Brown University. "To me, the most surprising thing is that this guy played basketball all that time with a single coronary artery. How could a guy like that run up and down the court for 20 years?"

Dr. Thompson hit on just one of several vexing questions. How had a congenital heart defect gone undiagnosed for all these years? And how did Pete survive his teens and become such a dominant force in a demanding, anaerobic sport like basketball?

Unfortunately Pete's condition was virtually undetectable using normal procedures: a stethoscope, X-rays, EKG, or a stress test. "You're dealing here with the rarest of the rare," explained Frank Litvack, associate director of heart testing at Cedars-Sinai Medical Center. "Until people die, nobody will know that they have this."

However, if any NBA team had provided advanced testing like an ultra-sound or angiogram (injecting dye into the blood), the condition probably would have been revealed.

"When you think about what he was able to accomplish with that heart," marveled basketball writer Peter Vecsey. "It just raises his stature to a degree that's unbelievable."

Exercise helped tremendously. "It's strictly conditioning that allowed him [Pete] to do the things he had done," opined Dr. Ken Dooley, director of pediatric cardiology at Emery University. "In his later years, emphasizing diet and exercise were probably right—more than he knew."

Exercise and nutrition might have prolonged Pete's adult life, but how did he survive childhood?

The answer reads like science fiction. Pete's right coronary artery managed to grow around the heart and provide some blood to the left chamber.

The L.A. County Coroner's Office was astonished. "Doctors have seen lots of combinations but no one has ever seen anything like this," said spokesman Bob Dambacher.

Pete's heart had temporarily saved itself.

"Rather than having two coronary arteries, his wrapped around the right side of the aorta," explained Dr. Thompson. "Saying that it was a medical miracle is not an unfair description."

After years of living on borrowed time, Pete Maravich's miraculous heart finally stopped beating on a basketball court inside a church gymnasium.

"I look at it today as a blessing and a curse. It was a blessing because he was not supposed to live past the age of 20," said his son Jaeson in 2005. "But then I look at it as a curse. Because if somehow it could have been detected, maybe he would still be here with us."

28

Heirs to
a Dream

"Sometimes, when I'm playing, I wish I could look up and see him in the stands. Then telling me what I did right or wrong."

—JAESON MARAVICH

"Pistol Pete is a legend to all who understand the history of basketball."

—JASON KIDD

At midnight on the evening of Pete's death, his former LSU academic advisor, Donald Ray Kennard, called Dale Brown, Press Maravich's coaching successor at the school, to discuss how best to honor Maravich. The two men decided it would be fitting to add Pete's name to LSU's basketball arena.

Kennard had his fellow state legislator, Francis Thompson, introduce a bill to rename the arena and on April 27, 1988, after aggressive campaigning by Brown, the bill passed and was signed by Governor Buddy Roemer. The "Pete Maravich Assembly Center" was born.

Ironically, the university's athletic council still barred Pete from entering the LSU Hall of Fame because he never graduated. That rule was overturned in 1994, and non-grad legends like Maravich, Shaquille O'Neal, and Billy Cannon were finally inducted. (O'Neal received his diploma in December 2000.)

For the remainder of the 1988 season, Utah Jazz players wore a No. 7 patch on their jerseys, and Louisiana native Karl Malone, going a step further, wore a No. 7 jersey at the 1988 All-Star Game. "Wearing this number meant a lot to me because of what Pete did for the game of basketball," Malone said in his press conference. "I also did it for all the kids in Louisiana who may not have gotten a chance to see Pete play."

While the basketball world was coming to grips with Pete's death, Jackie, the love of his life, was having trouble coping with her loss.

"I was in a daze the first week or two," said Jackie. "Then six or seven months later, it really hit me. Everybody had gone on with their lives and I was alone. The boys had gone back to school, while I stayed on the sofa a long time. I wouldn't go anywhere, just didn't want to do anything for two or three months. That's when I was grieving. Then I got to thinking about it—here's Press, he died right before Pete, and I never really got to grieve for Press because then Pete died. It was hard. My dad and Alfred (her pastor) kind of took care of things. You know, in the Bible, it says you're supposed to take care of the widow. I try and do things right by Pete, but you never know if people will do right by you."

Despite her grief, Jackie took Jaeson and Josh to a specialist for comprehensive heart exams. She was relieved to learn both boys had healthy, properly functioning hearts.

A 1988 letter written to Clearwater basketball coach Del Wubbena and his wife, Connie, reveals Jackie's struggle as a new widow:

> *Thanks for the memorial contribution and all your love and support. It was good talking to you, Connie.*
>
> *The kids and I are doing okay. They have had a couple of crying spells and oh how my heart still aches. I just pray to God everyday for strength to raise my boys and to help me in making major decisions. He will not fail me. I look forward to seeing you this summer. Please pray for me and the boys.*

Pete's immediate family members were special guests at the Superdome on October 17, 1988, for the "Pistol Pete Shootout." At half time of the Bullets-Jazz exhibition contest, Pete's No. 7 jersey was retired. It joined Archie Manning's New Orleans Saints' jersey on the stadium's Wall of Fame.

It soon became clear that the profits from *Homework Basketball* videotapes would be insufficient to finance a motion picture about Pete's childhood. The producers even tried a bit of stunt casting by offering former president Ronald Reagan the role of Pete's high school coach. Reagan, who starred in more than 50 films, politely declined.

So the production company privately raised $650,000 and commenced a six-week filming schedule on February 5, 1989, in and around Hammond, Louisiana. Adam Guier played the 13-year-old Maravich and, as part of his preparation, diligently studied the *Homework* tapes.

The Pistol: Birth of a Legend was a wholesome family film depicting a single year of Pete's boyhood in Clemson, South Carolina. Although the story took some dramatic license (Daniel High didn't participate in the district championship game nor did they play an all-black team), it accurately dramatized Pete's dedication to basketball and his close relationship with his father. But no Hollywood studio, major or minor, would release it. "With the cost of marketing today, we didn't feel we'd see a return on our investment," explained Warner Distribution chief Barry Reardon at the time. "[Pete's] NBA career would be a lot more interesting."

The G-rated movie seemed fated for a limited release in a few small theaters until producer Rodney Stone got a clever idea. Why not sell "ad space" to a sponsor and insert a commercial prior to the start of the movie? The ad revenue could cover the distribution, advertising, and print costs. One potential sponsor was the Atlanta-based chicken sandwich chain, Chick-Fil-A. Stone flew to Georgia to pitch his idea to the company's founder and CEO, Truett Cathy.

After a private screening, Cathy was delighted. "I want every kid in America to see this film. What's it going to cost?" he asked.

"$650,000," replied Stone. Cathy wrote the check against his personal account.

Even with the backing of Chick-Fil-A, the movie had a very limited domestic run. Eventually it aired on cable's Family Channel and, later, enjoyed a rebirth in the home video market.

To the adult eye, Pistol comes off a bit old fashioned but children generally find the movie captivating and inspirational. Many college hoopsters and more than a few NBA players (like Seattle's Luke Ridnour) say they were first motivated to play—and practice—basketball after watching *The Pistol: Birth of a Legend*.

In 2005, the film was released on DVD, and a Christian version, "The Inspirational Edition" (including Pete's testimony) came out in 2006.

In the 1980s the intense rivalry of Larry Bird's Celtics, Magic Johnson's Lakers, and Isiah Thomas' Pistons re-energized the NBA and ushered in what many believe was a golden age of basketball excellence. Toward the middle of the decade a legion of fans were drawn to an emerging star from the Chicago Bulls, Michael Jordan. The heir apparent to Dr. J, Jordan dazzled spectators with high scoring and spectacular "above-the-rim" play. And, like Maravich years earlier, Jordan's exploits transcended the game and captured the imagination.

Also, like Pete, Jordan had trouble advancing in the postseason. In fact, until he teamed with Scottie Pippen, Jordan's Bulls never had a winning season and were eliminated in the first round of the playoffs for three consecutive years, winning just one of 10 postseason games. Despite Jordan's early playoff exits, the NBA decided to capitalize on his popularity via the burgeoning home video market.

The NBA joined the home video revolution in 1981 when it began producing a yearly review of the championship run. But with Jordan's growing popularity, the league decided to also focus on a single player's highlights. The gamble paid off handsomely, and 1989's *Michael Jordan: Come Fly with Me* became the biggest-selling sports video of all time.

One year later, NBA Entertainment released another highlight video entitled *NBA Showmen—The Spectacular Guards*, featuring Jordan along with archival footage of Bob Davies, Dick McGuire, Bob Cousy, Earl Monroe, Nate Archibald, Isiah Thomas, Magic Johnson, and Maravich. The video contained the first significant film-clip package of Pete's pro career. The highlights included the fake behind-the-back pass from 1971, the slap pass from 1974, the left-handed running scoop-hook in 1978, as well as a potpourri of shuttle passes, hesitations shots, behind-the-back dribbling, and looping layups.

The video captured the imagination of then 12-year-old Kobe Bryant who was living in Italy where his father, Joe, was finishing his pro career. Bryant received the video from his grandparents, who routinely sent him basketball tapes from America. Although he loved Jordan's *Come Fly with Me*, it was *NBA Showmen* that became Bryant's favorite. He told *ESPN* magazine's Tom Friend that he watched the tape over and over, learning spin moves from Earl Monroe and "all my tricks" from Pete Maravich.

"I was the type of kid that, if I saw something on TV, I would go out in the backyard and try to do it," said Bryant. "I wanted to have every move possible."

Kobe's study of vintage film clips did not end in childhood.

"Kobe is unique in his pursuit of learning about the game," explained Lakers assistant coach Bill Bertka years later. "It's not unusual for him to come to my room and request Maravich tapes to see how he played."

In the early 1990s, Jordan finally shed his "one-man show" image and led the Bulls to a string of six titles, and is now generally accepted as the greatest basketball player of all time. As Jordan's exploits were branded onto the national psyche, Maravich's career became a distant memory. Although traces of his style were evident in the games of mid-1990s players like Mark Jackson and Tim Hardaway, most young fans were unaware of Pete and his impact on the game.

However, beginning in 1995, three events helped introduce Pistol Pete to a new generation. Over a two-year period the NBA named its 50 greatest players, the Classic Sports Network debuted on cable, and Jason Williams, an exciting Maravich-like guard, was drafted by the Sacramento Kings.

NBA Commissioner David Stern decided the league would devote the first half of the 1996-97 season to celebrating its 50th anniversary. Basketball historians were quick to point out that the NBA had not technically existed until the summer of 1949—when the Basketball Association of America absorbed what was left of the National Basketball League—but the NBA had used the summer of 1946 as its birth date for years, so 50 it was, and the "NBA at 50" became a marketing bonanza for Stern.

To mark the milestone the league assembled a panel of ex-players, front office personnel, coaches, and writers to select the top 50 players from NBA history. They were given just two guidelines: Players could not vote for themselves and the list had to be compiled without regard to position.

On Tuesday morning, October 29, 1996, the media gathered at New York's Grand Hyatt Hotel for the roll call of basketball kings. Alphabetically sandwiched between Moses Malone and Kevin McHale was the name Pete Maravich.

But there was some controversy.

Many people did not find the list to be representative of the NBA's best. Still others complained that trying to compare and contrast athletes from different eras was impossible. It's just too subjective a task, they argued. (This debate accompanied baseball's Hall of Fame selections for decades.) Some panelists will put a premium on statistics while others favor championships. Others prize defense while others value longevity and consistency. And some are just nostalgic and select players from their youth.

"I am prejudiced toward people who moved the game along," wrote Tony Kornheiser in the *Washington Post* the day after the list was announced. "People who thrilled me with their flash. That's why my top 50 absolutely, positively has to have Connie Hawkins and David Thompson."

Hawkins and Thompson were not on the NBA's list and neither were such impact players as Bob McAdoo (the only league MVP not named), Dominique Wilkins, Joe Fulks, Bob Lanier, Bernard King, Dan Issel, Adrian Dantley, and Alex English.

The lively debate motivated others to publish their own lists. *SLAM Magazine's* cover read, *The Real Top 50*. Names were added and subtracted to the roster depending on the whims of the various authors. And, after all the additional lists had been assembled and published, every single one included "Pistol" Pete Maravich.

SPORT magazine on Pete: "Most entertaining player of all-time. Scored at will while embarrassing opponents and mesmerizing fans. Had the whole package: Floppy socks, floppy hair, disco dribbling routine and length-of-the-floor, around-the-back passes. Ten years from now, he'll still be way ahead of his time."

The Sporting News: "Whatever he could imagine, he could do."

Athlon Sports: "Hair flopping, eyes dancing, arms flailing, legs churning and socks drooping. Maravich was the guy who showed us how to slip a basketball through a straw—and how to do it after taking the basketball between the legs and tossing it behind the back. To see the narrow 6-foot-5 Maravich leading the fast break was to see a basketball player as determined to thrill the crowd as he was to befuddle the defenders. He usually did both."

USA Today: "One of the often-overlooked creative geniuses of the game."

SLAM Magazine: "Nobody did the stuff Maravich was doing. He did things in game situations that you only do in the sandlot. If Maravich was playing today, he'd be a god."

Pete's sensational decade in the NBA, long overshadowed by his "Ruthian" collegiate career, was finally being recognized.

"The NBA at 50" celebration concluded with a historic presentation at half time of the 1997 All-Star Game in Cleveland's Gund Arena. Forty-seven of the 49 living honorees were on hand (Shaquille O'Neal and Jerry West were absent) as the NBA officially presented the honor roll to thousands of adoring fans in the arena and millions more watching on television.

The dramatic roll call began with the guards. Michael Jordan . . . John Stockton . . . Clyde Drexler . . . Isiah Thomas . . . Magic Johnson . . . George Gervin.

As their names were announced, each player stepped onto a modest wood platform. When the name "Pete Maravich" was called, his surviving sons, Jaeson and Joshua, joined the NBA greats on the simple dais. It was an emotional moment as the teenagers, just 14 and 17 at the time, stood proudly alongside grown men.

"I was honored to do that," remembered Joshua. "It was kind of weird to see 49 of them living and my dad not there. I thought about him at that moment."

As the young Maravich boys stood in for their dad, Pete's wife and sister, Jackie and Diana, watched from the sidelines. "I think it was hard on them," said Jackie. "But they loved getting to meet all the players."

"I was talking that day to Isiah, and Magic Johnson, and Jordan. Being around them was exciting," recalled Jaeson. "I had never met [Charles] Barkley before and I didn't know what he was like. People perceive him one way, but he was one of the nicest guys there. I remember sitting in the stands and he was waving to us. They all had such great things to say about how they incorporated some of his stuff into their games, watching tapes of my dad. It was one of the best days of my life."

In an interview with reporter Bud Shaw of the *Cleveland Plain Dealer* Jackie added, "I'm happy that this is happening. But it's kind of bittersweet. He left an unbelievable legacy for the children and everybody else. It's still hard, though."

Pete's inclusion on the NBA's All-Time Top 50 Team was, perhaps, his greatest basketball honor, even more impressive than his induction into the Basketball Hall of Fame. The Hall considers basketball achievements outside the NBA and has more than 200 inductees. In 1996, the NBA created a more exclusive sub-set of professional basketball stars, and Maravich made the cut.

"If he was playing today, he'd be the most popular player in the league," Walt Frazier told reporter Bud Shaw.

"Like a master chess player, Pete Maravich saw things that nobody else did," explained Bill Walton. "We talk often in basketball about being so good that the ball becomes an extension of your mind. Well, that was Pete. I don't think anyone ever came even remotely close to Pete in that whatever he could dream up, he could execute."

"Pete was ahead of his time in so many ways," said Magic Johnson. "He was a great player whose style made many fans for the game of basketball."

When the NBA opened for business in the fall of 1946, one of its charter players was a hustling, scrappy guard for the Pittsburgh Ironmen named Press Maravich. Fifty years, and more than 2,000 players later, the league bestowed an honor unimaginable to the Serbian basketball lifer. The name "Maravich" was placed in the basketball pantheon.

The selection of the NBA's 50th anniversary team coincided with the launch of a new cable network named Classic Sports. It began airing sporting events from yesteryear, a dicey proposition because no one knew if fans would be willing to watch events where the outcome was already known.

Surprisingly, it was an instant success as sports junkies embraced their own nostalgia channel. Viewers got a kick out of hearing old announcers or seeing the vintage uniforms, TV graphics, and arenas. But the real thrill of Classic Sports was watching long-retired athletes competing once again. For older viewers it offered a chance to relive the glories of their childhood heroes. For many young fans, Classic Sports provided their first glimpse of athletes they'd only read or heard about. The network's motto was: "Where the Legends Play."

In late 1996 the network's new program *Fan Mail* invited viewers to request a "classic" athlete or game. Shockingly, Classic Sports received more requests for Pete Maravich than any other athlete: more than Namath or Ali, Mantle or Chamberlain. The network responded with a 1978 CBS telecast of a contest between the Jazz and the Pistons. Classic Sports, now known as ESPN Classic, has since aired several Maravich retrospectives.

In 1998, a 6-1 University of Florida dropout named Jason Williams was hoping to join the NBA. Growing up in West Virginia, Williams practiced his ball-handling skills obsessively. He sometimes wore gloves, as Pete had done, to help develop fingertip control. Over time, he became extraordinarily skilled. The Sacramento Kings selected him with the seventh pick in the draft.

Although he didn't debut until February 1999 (because of a labor dispute), Williams hit the NBA in full stride. Every night, it seemed, ESPN's *SportsCenter* featured another highlight of the player nicknamed "White Chocolate." In the post-Jordan NBA (it would be another two years before MJ's second comeback), Williams' fearless, flamboyant style provided a shot of adrenaline. "Nobody thinks a skinny, white kid can play," he said. "I try to make each game a highlight. A behind-the-back pass is as easy for me as a chest pass." His No. 55 jersey became the league's top seller and Sacramento games were added to the national television schedule.

The similarity to Pete was obvious. "He doesn't have Maravich's size or his scoring ability, but he sure can handle the ball like Maravich did," observed David DuPree in *USA Today*. "And he has that Maravich thing where it looks like he's going three directions at once, and the only person you can be sure he isn't going to pass the ball to is the one he's looking at."

Kings assistant coach Pete Carrill, architect of Princeton University's patient, methodical offense, was disturbed by Williams' style. Every time Jason whipped off a flamboyant pass Carrill said he felt, "a little pain in my chest." The statement was an echo of Richie Guerin's reaction to Pete's antics years earlier.

Williams finished second in the Rookie of the Year voting behind Vince Carter, but his thrilling passing and dribbling, according to *SLAM Magazine*'s Robert "Scoop" Jackson, had "reawakened the ghost of Pistol Pete."

Pete's basketball camp at Clearwater Christian College still thrives. Despite no advertising, the camp attracts kids from across the country. In 2005, more than 200 applicants were turned away. "It's amazing when you think about it because the camp is strictly word of mouth," remarked Jackie.

Every June, camp director Del Wubbena declares, "Sportsmanship is in at the Pistol Pete Camp!" The campers watch coach Mike Gold demonstrate how large the rim is by stepping through it. They learn how to wear two pairs of socks and the "BEEF" shooting technique: Balance, Elbow, Eyes, Follow-Through.

Although there have been changes—burgers, candy, and soda dispensers are allowed—the emphasis on faith and hoops remains constant. The far wall of the gymnasium reads: "Built to the Glory of God."

One night in the summer of 2000, before the evening's full-court scrimmages, a 15-year-old boy tried to explain how the three beings in the Holy Trinity were still all part of the same entity. "Like a single egg has the white, the yolk, and the shell," he explained to the several boys gathered around. The youngster was a perfect example of what Pete hoped to achieve at Clearwater—a supportive environment where youngsters could learn the fundamentals of basketball while developing a deeper relationship with Christ.

Every summer Jackie and her boys visit Florida to continue Pete's work of basketball and religious instruction. "I'll keep putting this camp on as long as Del runs it," said Jackie. She still greets each camper personally and signs old action photos of Pete while Jaeson and Josh help run the drills they learned as children.

In 1999, the sports production company Black Canyon (best known for HBO's *When It Was a Game* series) began work on a documentary for CBS Sports entitled, *Pistol Pete: The Life and Times of Pete Maravich*. Produced under the supervision of stylish editor George Roy, and gracefully written by Steven Stern, it would feature never-before-broadcast game footage, plus a host of rare interviews, including the camera-shy Jackie. It became the most comprehensive documentary about Maravich ever produced. It was first broadcast on CBS during the Final Four Tournament on April 1, 2001. It notched an impressive 6.8 rating and a 12 share, along with a host of wonderful reviews.

"The saga of Pete Maravich is as absorbing as the legend of James Dean, of Steve Prefontaine, of John Lennon, of every generation's icon who died young," gushed the *Fort Worth Star Telegram*. "The fruits of Press Maravich's love for his son, and of Pete's intense desire to please his father, could be seen in the grainy films from the Pistol's college days. His story is timeless."

Raleigh News Observer: "Buy, rent, or borrow a VCR. Program it for today's showing of *Pistol Pete: The Life and Times of Pete Maravich*. The 90-minute special on CBS is that good. The action sequences are good enough that you'll want to pull it out again and use the freeze frame to make sure that you actually saw what you thought you saw."

New York Post: "The editing and story-telling throughout *Pistol Pete* is so superb that one is able to pay attention to yards and yards of footage of Maravich doing remarkable, incredible things with a basketball while never losing sight of the human price tag attached to his achievements. The blend of marvel and sorrow is inescapable."

Around the same time, ESPN aired a retrospect on Pete as part of its *Sports Century* series. Although it was not as detailed as the CBS program, the documentaries helped to further spread the compelling story of Pistol Pete.

Pete Maravich's transcendent game still resonates deep into the NBA. Brent Barry, Kobe Bryant, Jason Kidd, Steve Nash, Gilbert Arenas, Rafer Alston, Jason Terry, Dan Dickau, Luke Ridnour, and Shaun Livingston were all inspired and influenced by the Pistol.

"The stuff that Pistol did with the ball was the breaking ground for what we can do today," said Jason Kidd in 2003.

"I've got a lot of Pistol Pete in my game," said Phoenix Suns guard Steve Nash.

When asked, of all the players who ever played in the NBA, who he would most like to meet on the court, the Pistons' Chauncey Billups didn't hesitate. "Pistol Pete Maravich. He just has so many tricks. He was unbelievable."

In fact, players from every level of basketball, most of whom were born well after Pete's career ended, are also devotees. Ryan Appleby, Jacki Gemelos, Laurie Koehn, Jonathan Loe, Kaili McLaren, Percy Miller, Sheana Mosch, Kristin Popovics, and Lindsay Whalen all cite Maravich as their major influence.

But Pete's legacy isn't limited to the hardwood. It can also be found on the blacktop. *Streetball*, an entertaining mix of remarkable (and often illegal) ball handling, passing, and dunking, gained a national following with the release of a 1998 promotional tape from a then-fledgling apparel company, AND1.

The breakout star of the very first tape was Rafer Alston, aka "Skip-To-My-Lou."

"I grew up with a lot of Pistol Pete tapes," said Alston, who now plays in the NBA. "He was so deceptive with the ball and that's what I wanted to be: the guy who could fool you with the basketball. I still watch his tapes."

While AND1 was marketing *Streetball*, another company was capitalizing on a demand for "authentic" copies of Maravich uniforms. In the 1990s, Mitchell and Ness, a small mom-and-pop sporting good store, started to manufacture replicas of vintage baseball jerseys. The old-time jerseys were faithfully duplicated, matching the fabric, color, weight, and logo of the originals. "I figured my market was 35- to 75-year-old, conservative, college-educated, suburban, white men—'fuddy-duddies' like me," explained Peter Capolino, who worked for his father in the store. But when Capolino began to offer baseball uniforms from the 1970s and 1980s, a new market emerged. It was far from fuddy-duddy.

In 1998, Antwan Patton (aka "Big Boi" of the rap duo OutKast) appeared in an MTV video with a Mitchell and Ness-manufactured Nolan Ryan jersey. The garish, rainbow-striped jersey got noticed in a big way and, suddenly, prominent rappers had to have a wardrobe full of what are now called "throwbacks."

By 1999, Mitchell and Ness had acquired the rights to vintage NBA apparel. The league directed its share of royalties to the retired-players association. The jerseys quickly became a hot fashion item, easily out-distancing football and baseball sales.

Musicians, athletes, actors, journalists, fans, and teens coveted jerseys of retired hoopsters. In music videos, at award shows, in postgame press conferences, the throwbacks were a common sight. Allen Iverson, Ja Rule, Keyshawn Johnson, LeBron James, Jason Kidd, Jay-Z, Shaquille O'Neal, Fat Joe, Kobe Bryant, Jason Terry, Sean Combs, and Master P were all seen in the handiwork of Mitchell and Ness.

For some, the old-school apparel was more than just pricey fashion. "I have respect for the players that paved the way before us," explained Iverson. "Respect for the people that made me want to play the game, people that I idolized. People that enabled us to have our own images."

So far, to keep up with escalating demand, Mitchell and Ness have manufactured eight different Maravich throwbacks. Every team in Pete's NBA journey is represented in the collection. Collectors and fans can choose from Pete's 1971-72 Hawks green or blue (both incorrectly using quotes around the name PISTOL); the 1973-74 Hawks red or white; the 1976-77 Jazz white; the 1979 All-Star Game white; and the 1980 Celtics green or white. Michael Jordan was shocked when his sons wanted multiple Maravich throw-backs. (The *Washington Post's* Michael Wilbon sported his "Pistol" jersey on ESPN's *Pardon the Interruption*.)

Other companies have joined the fray. Replicas of Pete's Daniel High School (Taylor & Madison) and LSU (Vintage Sportswear) jerseys are now available.

It seems that Maravich as an endorsement name still has cache in the new century. Electronic Arts created a "virtual" version of the Pistol for their NBA Live video game series. In 2005, McFarlane Toys introduced a new set of basketball legends figures using Pete. In 2006, Adidas created a new Pistol Pete basketball sneaker and a clothing line. The reselling of Pete's old basket-ball cards, magazines, DVDs, posters, photos, and promotional items (flip books, soda cans, bobble heads, etc.) are a cottage industry on eBay and other online auction sites.

When photographer Greg Foster visited Jackie to compose a shot for the *NBA at 50* coffee-table book, he was shown a few items of memorabilia she kept in plastic garbage bags. (Pete had given away most of his keepsakes after retirement.) Foster was dazzled by the treasure trove and six years later Jackie decided to auction off—for a local charity—several items that were just gath-ering dust beneath a bed.

"I have a real hard time letting go of it. I know it's just stuff because that's what Pete called it all the time," said Jackie. "He'd say, 'Don't put your happi-ness into material things.'"

Many items were one of a kind: the basketball Pete gave Jackie after set-ting the NCAA scoring record in 1970, the 1979 NBA All-Star Game jersey (size 42), the Basketball Hall of Fame ring (size 10), the basketball from the 68-point game vs. the Knicks, an LSU game ball inscribed to Press, the 10,000-point NBA ball, a hat, other balls, photos, assorted shoes, equipment bags, endorsement contracts, All-Star rings, and even cancelled checks.

But it was the sale of a white home jersey from Pete's sophomore season at LSU that caught the attention of the sports memorabilia world. The final sale price of $103,500 easily set a record for the highest amount paid for a basketball jersey. "We were just hoping to surpass the $63,394 Bill Russell jersey," said Howard Rosenkrantz, the CEO of the auction house.

In 2002 (22 years after the Jazz left for Utah), New Orleans landed another pro-basketball franchise. The Hornets arrived from Charlotte and announced they would retire Pete's number. "We think, with the NBA returning to New Orleans, it's a respectable and honorable thing to do," explained Hornets spokesman Harold Kaufman. "It's one NBA team paying tribute to a player that has meant so much to the league." Maravich's No. 7 was retired on October 30, 2002, with Jackie, Jaeson, Josh, and several former Jazz players in attendance.

That night Pete joined Jackie Robinson, Johnny Unitas, Michael Jordan, and Wayne Gretzky as the only athletes to have their numbers retired by professional teams for which they never played.

In the years following Pete's death, Jackie had her hands full raising two boys with a famous surname. She decided to remain in the renovated house in Covington.

"My kids were in school and they had their friends," Jackie explained. "I didn't want to add another big trauma to their life. As it turned out, it was the best thing I have ever done. My kids just love it here and the town has embraced us."

Jaeson, the eldest, was eight when his father died. He recalled traveling with his dad when Pete was calling games for the USA Network. "I remember him telling me when I was little, 'I don't care if you ever pick up a ball in your life as long as you live your life for Christ. That's my one goal for you. I want you to be committed to Christ,'" recalled Jaeson. "I was extremely tight with him. I did everything with him. I didn't look at him as a legend. I just looked at him as my dad."

Basketball came fairly easy to Jaeson. He was featured in one of the *Homework* tapes demonstrating the "figure eight" and won a national "Biddy" championship. But, as he got older, the pressure of playing as a "Maravich" proved daunting. In the eighth grade he averaged close to 30 points a game, but he felt uneasy around people and the world started closing in on him. With each shot attempt a flurry of light bulbs popped. It burned his eyes. "Sometimes I wish my last name was Smith," he once admitted.

Strangers demanded autographs. National television commentators (like CBS's Billy Packer) angled for interviews. His exploits were reported in the New Orleans paper. It got so uncomfortable that Jaeson enlisted teammate Donald Peltier to switch jerseys after a game and have him sign the autographs while Jaeson hid below the bleachers. After playing one season for the St. Paul High School team, the attention became too overwhelming and he quit, burned out in ninth grade.

"I was too young and everything was happening at once. People started comparing me to my dad and at that young age I couldn't handle it," said Jaeson. He didn't play for the next two years.

"He was a hermit crab. He just stayed in the house constantly," recalled his brother, Josh. "The Maravich name definitely did get to him. He was a lot closer to my dad than I was. I think his death hit Jaeson 10 times harder than it hit me."

"I'm still not over it. I just wish I could see him one more time," Jaeson admitted in 2003. "I think about him every day. The most painful thing is coming to a game and knowing he's not there. I'll have dreams and see him up there in the stands."

Jaeson returned for his senior season at St. Paul's and averaged 17 points and six rebounds. Taking the advice of then-Iowa State coach and long-time Pete Maravich fan, Tim Floyd, Jaeson enrolled at New Hampton Prep in New Hampshire. Unfortunately, he tore a ligament in his back while lifting weights during the summer and missed the entire season.

The following year he was enrolled at the University of Alabama and made the team as a "walk-on," or non-scholarship player. But Jaeson felt uncomfortable in the Alabama program and transferred to Mississippi Gulf Coast Community College in Perkinston. Jaeson's game finally came together in the 1999-2000 season when he averaged 27.3 points, third in the nation for junior college players. He had games of 45 and 49 points. He was then recruited by Tubby Smith of Kentucky but instead chose McNeese State, a small Division I university in Lake Charles, Louisiana. But he reinjured his back and never played for McNeese.

Jaeson's next stop was William Carey College, a private Southern Baptist school in Hattiesburg, Mississippi. Under the guidance of coach Steve Knight, Jaeson thrived and had two successful seasons for the Crusaders. He was a back-to-back NAIA (small college) All-American. One highlight came on January 5, 2003, against Athens State University in Alabama. The date marked the 15th anniversary of Pete's death and Jaeson decided to dedicate the game to his father. "I wanted to have a good game for him," he said. He scored 34 points.

"When players say they're feeling real good on the floor, they say everything is in slow motion," Jaeson said. "Everything was in slow motion."

In his final season, *The Sporting News* named Jaeson to its NAIA All-American First Team. He was invited to the Portsmouth Invitational Basketball Camp, an annual opportunity for college seniors to showcase their talents for NBA scouts. Jaeson was the only NAIA player among the 60 prospects. In the opening game of the tournament he scored 16 points (hitting four NBA-distance three-pointers) and ultimately received the camp's Sportsmanship Award. He was not selected in the subsequent NBA draft but remains a prospect in the NBA's developmental league.

Amazingly, Jaeson has continued to heed his dad's advice and, to this day, he has never smoked, drank alcohol (or Coca-Cola), or eaten a Big Mac. He has, though, acquired three tattoos. On his left arm, in Old English–style lettering, is the word "Pistol." A second tattoo features two praying hands and an emblem of his father's monument in the cemetery. The third one, on his chest, is a large basketball bearing his dad's college and NBA uniform numbers: 44, 7, and 23. One quadrant of the ball is empty. "I left a spot here for my number in case I make it in the pros," he said.

"I said three tattoos are enough," explained Jackie Maravich.

"A lot of people ask me why I'm quiet," Jaeson told USA Today's Tom Weir. "I just miss my dad."

Josh, only five when his father died, took a different track than Jaeson. He seemed to inherit the more wild and playful aspects of Pete's personality and, most times, enjoyed attention. "My boys represent both parts of Pete's personality," observed Jackie. "Jaeson is the older version while Josh is the younger version."

Josh is no stranger to soda and fast food. "We always kid each other when we eat something bad like chocolate chip cookies," Jackie said with a laugh. "We say, 'Pete's probably pitching a fit right now.'"

Josh also loved basketball and never seemed to mind the Maravich name on his jersey. He played throughout high school and enjoyed an excellent senior season at St. Paul's, leading the Wolves in scoring (15.5 points per game) and rebounding (4.8). He was voted co-MVP in his district and was picked for the conference All-Star Game. The following year he turned a lot of heads when he decided to attend LSU.

"When he said he was going, I was kinda shocked at first," said older brother Jaeson. "But I know if anyone could handle it, he could. He's a strong person." For Josh, the old man's alma mater seemed the perfect choice. He did not receive an athletic scholarship, however, so he made the team as a walk-on. He didn't mind practicing and playing in an arena emblazoned with his last name. "I've always wanted to come here since I was a kid, regardless of my last name," said the 6-3 Josh. "It feels like home."

On December 17, 2003, in a home game against Prairie View A&M, Josh converted a layup with 8.1 seconds remaining. It was the first LSU basket by a Maravich in more than 33 years. And it was the first basket by someone named "Maravich" in the Maravich Assembly Center. "Everybody went crazy," Josh said. "They gave me a standing ovation. But you know 90 percent of my fan base is old people. Many times, they tell me the same stories over and over about my dad. But I never get aggravated.

"It's not that I always wanted my dad to see me play. I just wanted a dad. I just missed him. I didn't see him as Pistol Pete. I saw him as my father, like anybody else would. That's all I miss now—growing up without a father.

"I know that he'd be proud of me," said Josh. "Sometimes, I hear him whispering in my ear: 'You can do it. Keep trying.' That's what motivates me to keep going."

Jackie was in the stands of the Assembly Center when Josh scored his first NCAA basket. "It was pretty emotional," she said after the game. "I was very happy for him. Josh has worked so hard for two years now. And his dad would've been so proud."

In February of 2003, Curry Kirkpatrick, the former *Sports Illustrated* writer whose prose 35 years earlier helped popularize the legend of Pistol Pete, returned to Louisiana to tape a segment for ESPN's *SportsCenter*. It focused on the contrasting college careers of his offspring and was entitled: "Sons of a Gun." In his introduction, Kirkpatrick showed he had lost none of his narrative flair.

"Pistol Pete Maravich was Showtime before the game was turned showy," Kirkpatrick intoned. "Magic before Magic. A mystical icon of entertainment who redefined both dribbling and passing while shooting his way to his own very special place in the game."

More than 25 years after his retirement, professional basketball has yet to see another player like Pete Maravich.

Philadelphia's Allen Iverson is arguably the closest match. "The Answer" is a thrilling, unique, electric player, and all eyes are drawn to him when he's on the court. There are differences. Pete was a more accurate shooter and Iverson is a more tenacious defender. But Allen, like Pete, can take over a game, create his own shot, and bears responsibility for his team's success or failure.

Outside the basketball court, one might have to go back to Gayle Sayers, the daring running back for the Chicago Bears in the 1960s, to find a similar athlete. He was also something to see. Sayers amazed spectators with an array of mind-bending moves and, unfortunately, never came close to a championship. Both Sayers and Maravich thrilled spectators within the context of the game—not in contrived, self-glorifying posturing.

Ultimately, Maravich remains beyond compare. "The Pistol was inimitable," wrote John Feinstein in the *Washington Post*. "He was a transcendent player in that there was never anyone like him before and there has never been anyone like him since."

Although it is said that "records are made to be broken," some marks actually seem beyond the reach of the modern athlete: Joe DiMaggio's 56-game hitting streak, Wilt Chamberlain's 100-point game, and Wayne Gretzky's 92-goal season are often cited as "unbreakable." Pete's college scoring average of 44.2 belongs on that list, despite what his father predicted years ago.

"Someday, I don't know how soon, some young kid will come along and score the points," said Press in 1970. "Somebody will break it. But Pete's name will be in the record books for the next 30 to 40 years." It's been more than 35 years and counting, and not one player has come close. In fact, the gap is widening.

So the question remains, will his record ever be broken? It's certainly possible, especially with the addition of the three-point shot, but any player with that kind of ability would probably leave college to sign a pro contract at age 19.

Although Pete is best known for his prolific scoring, it could be argued that his most enduring legacy is revolutionizing the art of ball handling. Honed by obsessive practice and fueled by a startling imagination, Pete's audacious and complex skills continue to inspire young and old.

It's unfortunate that Pete did not live to see his impact on the modern game. Like an artist whose work goes unappreciated until after his death, the sports world was slow to embrace Pistol Pete's contribution. Jackie, who does not actively promote his basketball legacy, is astounded by the renewed interest in her husband's life.

"I remember Pete making the comment before he died, 'People forget so soon after you're gone,'" Jackie said. "I always remembered that and I figured people would forget, but I'm so happy they haven't. What a tribute to know that so many people love him. He's always in our hearts and our minds. I think about him every day. He was the love of my life."

Pete had an unshakable belief that basketball was played for the fans. "They paid the freight," he would often say. The game had room for entertaining, artistic self-expression, not just in exhibitions by the Globetrotters or AND1 tours, but on the floor of great arenas during competition at the highest level. Pete left behind thousands of what historian Nelson George called, "Those moments. Those moments when one player does something so amazing, so unexpected."

Ultimately, though, Pete wished to impact lives well beyond the basketball court. He grew tired of being the Pistol and spent the last five years of his life explaining and demonstrating his faith. He gave his life over to Christ and, with that surrender, found the peace, happiness, and understanding he so desperately craved.

Pete Maravich died on January 5, 1988, when his unusual heart finally gave out. He was on a basketball court in a church.

"Even though his life was shortened, when you look back and examine those 40 years, there's something for everyone to benefit from," said NBA great Julius Erving.

Jackie Maravich, now remarried, still lives in the home she and Pete renovated in Covington, Louisiana, although the house is much quieter now. The basketball hoops on the pillar upstairs were removed after one too many windows were broken.

The two boys who grew up there, now young men, are still drawn to the game mastered with uncommon flair by their father.

And hopefully, Pete and Press are together again, without pain, playing basketball for the glory of God.

Part 5

Appendix

Courtesy Joe Heidcamp

Eating with the campers at the first basketball camp
in Clearwater, Florida, 1983.

Acknowledgments

This project would not exist without the generous participation of Jackie, Jaeson, and Joshua Maravich. They graciously shared their memories of Pete Maravich—the husband and father. They also provided access to Pete's archive of letters, videos, notebooks, calendars, diaries, clippings, posters, awards, and photographs. They invited us into their home. We hope this book justifies the trust they placed in us.

We are also indebted to:

James McLachlan III.

Joe Bolster for his many contributions as an editor and shaper of this book.

Our team of freelance editors who helped craft our tone and style: Steve Gonzalez, Neil Greenberger, Rich Hale, Cheryl Hosmer, Greg Korn, Carolyn Terrill, and Mike Terrill.

New Orleans Jazz historian Bob Remy and Pete Maravich archivist Joe Heidkamp provided a treasure trove of detailed clippings, photographs, and statistics.

Zelda Spoelstra, David Stern, Todd Caso, John Hareas, and Joe Amati of the NBA.

Del Wubbena, Shaun Brown, Dave Drury, Mike Gold, staff, and campers from Clearwater Christian College, where the Pistol Pete Basketball Camp is still in operation.

Hank Hersch, Jack McCullum, and the erudite Alexander Wolff at *Sports Illustrated*.

Herb Vincent, Joe Dean, Dale Brown, and David "Bo" Bahnsen at Louisiana State University.

Robert Bradley and the feisty, knowledgeable crew at the Association of Professional Basketball Research (www.apbr.org).

The staff at the following public libraries: Aliquippa (Mary Elizabeth Columbo), Beverly Hills, Fulton County, Indianapolis, Jefferson Parish, Lexington (KY), New York City, and Oklahoma City.

The massive Paul Ziffren Sports Resource Center at the Amateur Athletic Foundation in L.A. (formerly the Helms Sports Library).

Matt Zeysing and Michael W. Brooslin, curators of the Hickox Library at the Naismith Basketball Hall of Fame (also Teresa Collins).

Linda B. DiSante, librarian, *Beaver County Times*.

There are a number of valuable research sites on the Internet. We found Justin Kubatko's statistical database (www.basketball-reference.com) extremely helpful.

Also Jon Scott's amazing University of Kentucky historical archive (http://www.ukfans.net/jps/uk/wildcats.html).

Aaron Mintz has an incredible collection of broadcast audio and video (http://www-unix.oit.umass.edu/~ahmintz/).

George Roy, Steven Stern, Erik Kesten, Lauren McDonald, and Marc Kinderman, for their documentary work, research, and support.

Basketball historian Sean Stormes prepared detailed chapter outlines.

Jason Thomas provided graphics, scans, and artwork.

Benita Federman provided film-to-tape transfer.

Jeff Abraham, Kathy Busby, Julie Bush, Heather Church, Joe Devanon, Stephanie Gutierrez, Kevin Hench, Matthew McGough, Marijane Miller, Andrew Mondshein, Dave Rath, Rebecca Shulman, Billy Simmons, Joy Tom, and Kara Welker helped in preparing the manuscript.

Authors Peter Finney, Bill Gutman, Tom Saladino, Darrel Campbell, Phil Berger, and Mike Towle, whose books on Pete Maravich continue to inspire and inform.

And our diverse interview subjects: classmates, teammates, owners, opponents, critics, fans, broadcasters, campers, journalists, trainers, relatives, preachers, friends, coaches, and acquaintances. Most were more than happy to speak openly—a tribute to the kind of life Pete Maravich led.

They include: Billy Abrams, Alvin Adams, Joe Albanese, Chip Alexander, Red Auerbach, Al Attles, Larry Bagley, John Bach, David "Bo" Bahnsen, Greg Ballard, Jim Barnett, Earl Barrios, Rick Barry, Sam Battistone, Elgin Baylor, Judy Beam, Dean Bentley, Walter Berglind, Rusty Bergman, Greg Bernbrock, Mark Bernbrock, Bill Bertka, Eddie Biedenbach, Dave Bing, Furman Bisher, Susan Lindsay Bishop, John Block, Alan Blumquest, Senator Bill Bradley, Bob Bradley, Dave Branon, Johnny Brantley, Tom Brennan, Brad Brian, Junior Bridgeman, Allan Bristow, Robert Bricune, Olin Broadway, Ted Broer, Leon Brock, Dale Brown, Irv Brown, James Brown, Randy Brown, Bob Bruner, Hook Bruner, Richard Bruner, Charlie Bryant, Vernon Burt, Joe Caldwell, Darrel Campbell, Pete Carlisle, Johnny Carr, M. L. Carr, Wendell Carr, Tommy Casanova, J. Patrick Carter, Don Carver, Mary Carver, Todd Caso, Dick Cavett, Len Chappell, Mel Ciociola, Archie Clark, Bill Clark, Franklin "Rusty" Clark, Ed Coakley, Pete Coker, Jerry Colangelo, Mike Cole, Mary Elizabeth Colombo, Bill Combs, Ann Milford Cooper, Bob Costas, Gunther

Coulby, Mel Counts, Dave Cowens, Crossie McDowell Cox, Frank Cox, Walter Cox, Steve Crane, Tonya Crevier, David Crosier, James Cunningham, Paul Dawkins, Joe Dean, Ernie DiGregorio, Buddy Diliberto, Eddie Doucette, Dave Drury, Randy Drude, Sherwin Durham, Eddie Einhorn, Steve Ellis, Jim Epps, Andy Ezell, Robert Farr, Paul Favorite, Jack Federline, Ralph Ferrante, Jim Fitzgerald, Lowell "Cotton" Fitzsimmons, Bryan Flanagan, Jim Fox, Ron Fox, Dave Fredman, David Friedman, Irv Gack, Tim Gallagher, Jody Gardner, Jerry Gargus, "Boots" Garland, Alvin Gentry, Herm Gilliam, Joe Gilmartin, Nick Gimpel, Bill Glass, Mike Gold, Mike Gorman, Jim Gray, Gary Gregor, Brent Gregory, Lamar Green, Roger Greene, Kevin Grevey, Paul Griffin, Richie Guerin, Coulby Gunther, Jim Hamilton, Dave Hanna, Patrick Hannon, Billy Harper, Les "Pee Wee" Harrison, Phil Hart, John Havlicek, Lola Hawkins, Marques Haynes, Jim Healey, Rich Hickman, Wes Hicks, Betty Higby, Craig Hill, Bruce Hoefer, Jr., Jim Howard, Joe Hruska, Danny Hubbs, Lou Hudson, Kim Hundley, Rod Hundley, David Hudson, John Hutchison, Nelson Isley, Aaron James, Jim Jeffreys, Bud Johnson, K. C. Jones, James F. Jones, Mike Jordan, Patricia Jordan-Scott, Ralph Jukkola, Ron Juth, Herb Kane, Marvin Kahl, Hank Kalb, Tito Kalb, Craig Kalb, Herb Kane, Michael Keller, Rich Kelley, Donald Ray Kennard, Ben Kinchlow, Sam King, Barry Kivel, Dr. Jack Kleid, Mildred Kosanovich, Sam Kosanovich, Jerry Kurtz, Mark Kutscher, Randy Lamont, John Lange, Bob Lanier, Stu Lantz, Dave Lattin, Kent Lawrence, Frank Layden, George Lemmon, Jimmy Lever, Lear Levin, Lon Levin, Grady Lewis, Joe Lewis, Richard Lewis, Bob Light, Gene Littles, John Lotz, Robert Lowther, Sr., Robert Lowther, Jr., Gary Lydic, Joanne Mogavero, Carl Macmuro, Archie Manning, Jackie Maravich, Jaeson Maravich, John Maravich, Joshua Maravich, Lawrence Maravich, Chet Marshall, Sr., Chet Marshall, Jr., Cindy Marshall, Brian Martin, Jimbo Marchand, Colonel James May, Dan Mayock, Joe Maughan, Julius McCants, Ed McLain, David McCollough, Mike McCormack, Al McCoy, David McDuff, Jon McGlocklin, Al McGuire, Mike McKenzie, Ed McLean, McCoy McLemore, Ray Mears, Ray Melchiorre, Peter Mehlman, Barry Mendelson, Paul Milanovich, Al Michaels, David Miller, Vera Mitchell, Art Montini, Marty Mule, Bill Newton, Tom Nissalke, Andy Nuzzo, Georgeanne Olive, Joe O'Toole, Bill Panzer, Larry Parker, Joe Pawlowski, Mike Pedneau, Carol Percy, Gene Peterson, Geoff Petrie, Bob Pettit, Paul Phillips, Jerry Pierce, Alex Popovics, Tom Poppino, Linda Durham Price, Ben Pouquette, Lou Pucillo, Guy Priest, Joe Proski, Joe Pukach, Jack Ramsay, Bob Remy, Paul Rich, Bob Richey, Dan Richey, Tommy Risher, Larry "Gator" Rivers, David Rivlin, Jules Rivlin, Dubby Robinson, Les

Robinson, Bob Ryan, Ernie Salvatore, Eileen Sabshon, Bob Sanford, Flip Saunders, Charlie Scott, Larry Seitz, David Senn, Tommy Senn, Mark Shannon, Lee Shelton, Jere Shockey, Steve Shumaker, Jeff Simon, Billy Simmons, Ed Singler, Jerry Smith, Don Sparks, Troy Spatafora, Zelda Spoelstra, Dick Snyder, Bud Stallworth, Doug Stark, Sandi Stevens, Jim Stewart, Rodney Stone, Sean Stormes, Hank Stram, Charles Stuart, Jr., Jim Sutherland, David Tate, Jack Thomas, Jim Thompson, David Thompson, Dr. Paul Thompson, Glen "Boomer" Titan, Wayne Tipton, Gene Tormohlen, Jeff Tribbett, Jeff Trim, Dan Trogdon, Billy Trott, Jeff Twiss, John Vallely, Dick Van Arsdale, Tom Van Arsdale, Butch van Breda Kolff, Eddie Vaughn, Herb Vincent, Carl Von dem Bussche, Sr., Carl Von dem Bussche, Jr., Dale Voss, Bill Waid, Neal Walk, Dickie Walker, Jimmy Walker, Bill Walton, Kermit Washington, Ed Watkins, William Watson, Scott Wedman, Frank Weedon, Jerry West, Paul Westphal, John Wetzel, Charlie White, Herb White, Harold Wiegel, Jr., Casey Williams, David Williams, Pat Williams, Dag Wilson, George Wilson, Kim Wise, Greg Wittman, Howard Wizenberg, Rodney Wood, Jane Cobb Wolfe, John Wooden, and Les Zittrain.

We would also like to thank the team at SPORTClassic Books—Jim O'Leary, Wayne Parrish, Greg Oliver, and the indexer, Elaine Melnick. And, of course, our agent, Tony Seidl of TD Media.

Finally, we'd like to thank those closest to us who supported us through seven years of research and rewrites: Carolyn Feruzzi and Zoe Terrill.

WAYNE FEDERMAN
MARSHALL TERRILL
www.MaravichBook.com

Career Statistics:
NCAA and NBA

LOUISIANA STATE

YEAR	G	PTS	PPG	FGM	FGA	FG%
1967-68	26	1,138	43.8	432	1,022	.423
1968-69	26	1,148	44.2	433	976	.444
1969-70	31	1,381	44.5	522	1,168	.447
TOTALS	83	3,667	44.2	1,387	3,166	.438

YEAR	FTM	FTA	FT%	AST	APG	RB	RBG
1967-68	274	338	.811	105	4.0	195	7.5
1968-69	282	378	.746	128	4.9	169	6.5
1969-70	337	436	.773	192	6.2	164	5.3
TOTALS	893	1,152	.775	425	5.1	528	6.4

NCAA DIVISION I BASKETBALL RECORDS

- Highest scoring average, career: 44.2
- Highest scoring average, season: 44.5
- Most points career: 3,667
- Points season: 1,381
- Games scoring 50 or more, career: 28
- Games scoring 50 or more, season: 10
- Consecutive games scoring 50 or more: 3
- Games scoring 40 or more, career: 56
- Field goals made, career: 1,387
- Field goals made, season: 522
- Field goals attempted, career: 3,166
- Field goals attempted, season: 1,168
- Free throws made, 3-year career: 893
- Free throws attempted, 3-year career: 1,152
- Free throws made, game: 30 (of 31, 12/22/69)
- Combined points, two players from opposing teams: 115 (Maravich 64, Issel 51; and 2/21/70)

All single season marks were set during Maravich's senior year, 1969-70. The three consecutive 50-plus games occurred in Maravich's junior year on February 10, 12, and 15, 1969.

NBA REGULAR SEASON

YEAR	TEAM	G	MIN	PTS	PPG	FGM	FG%	3PM	3P%
1970-71	Atlanta	81	2,926	1,880	23.2	738	.458	—	—
1971-72	Atlanta	66	2,302	1,275	19.3	460	.427	—	—
1972-73	Atlanta	79	3,089	2,063	26.1	789	.441	—	—
1973-74	Atlanta	76	2,903	2,107	27.7	819	.457	—	—
1974-75	New Orleans	79	2,853	1,700	21.5	655	.419	—	—
1975-76	New Orleans	62	2,373	1,604	25.9	604	.459	—	—
1976-77	New Orleans	73	3,041	2,273	31.1	886	.433	—	—
1977-78	New Orleans	50	2,041	1,352	27.0	556	.444	—	—
1978-79	New Orleans	49	1,824	1,105	22.6	436	.421	—	—
1979-80	Utah	17	522	290	17.1	121	.412	7	.636
	Boston	26	442	299	11.5	123	.494	3	.750
TOTALS		658	24,316	15,948	24.2	6,187	.441	10	.667

NBA PLAYOFFS

YEAR		G	MIN	PTS	PPG	FGM	FG%	3PM	3P%
1970-71	Atlanta	5	199	110	22	46	.377	—	—
1971-72	Atlanta	6	219	166	27.7	54	.446	—	—
1972-73	Atlanta	6	234	157	26.2	65	.419	—	—
1979-80	Boston	9	104	54	6	25	.49	2	.333
TOTALS		26	756	487	18.7	190	.423	2	.333

NBA QUICK FACTS

- Selected third overall by Atlanta Hawks,1970 NBA draft
- NBA All-Rookie team, 1971
- Traded to New Orleans for Dean Meminger, Bob Kauffman, and four (possibly six) draft picks, 3/3/74
- First Team All-NBA, 1976, 1977
- Second Team All-NBA, 1973, 1978
- Selected All-Star Game starting guard, 1973, 1974, 1977, 1978, 1979
- NBA leading scorer, 1976-77 (31.1 ppg)
- Career single-game high 68 points vs N.Y. Knicks, 2/25/77
- Signed by Boston Celtics, 1/22/80
- Average Pete Maravich NBA game: 21.3 FG attempted, 9.4 FG made, 6.6 FT attempted, 5.4 FT made, 4.2 rebounds, 5.4 assists, 24.2 points
- Inducted into Basketball Hall of Fame (first ballot), 1987
- Selected to NBA Top 50 All-Time Team, 1996

FTM	FT%	RB	RPG	AST	APG	STL	BLK	TO	PF
404	.8	298	3.7	355	4.4	—	—	—	238
355	.811	256	3.9	393	6	—	—	—	207
485	.8	346	4.4	546	6.9	—	—	—	245
469	.826	374	4.9	396	5.2	111	13	—	261
390	.811	422	5.3	488	6.2	120	18	—	227
396	.811	300	4.8	332	5.4	87	23	—	197
501	.835	374	5.1	392	5.4	84	22	—	191
240	.87	178	3.6	335	6.7	101	8	248	116
233	.841	121	2.5	243	5	60	18	200	104
41	.82	40	2.4	54	3.2	15	4	45	30
50	.909	38	1.5	29	1.1	9	2	37	49
3,564	.82	2,747	4.2	3,563	5.4	587	108	530	1,865

FTM	FT%	RB	RBG	AST	APG	STL	BLK	TO	PF
18	.692	26	5.2	24	4.8	—	—	—	14
58	.817	32	5.3	28	4.7	—	—	—	24
27	.794	29	4.8	40	6.7	—	—	—	24
2	.667	8	.9	6	.7	3	0	9	12
105	.784	95	3.7	98	3.8	3	0	9	74

TOP SIX NBA GUARDS POINTS PER GAME:

1. Michael Jordan — 30.1
2. Allen Iverson * — 28.0
3. Jerry West — 27.7
4. George Gervin — 26.2
5. Oscar Robertson — 25.7
6. Pete Maravich — 24.2

TEAM WINNING PERCENTAGE IN NBA GAMES WHEN PLAYER SCORED 40+ POINTS:

1. Pete Maravich — 82%
2. Michael Jordan — 69%
3. Allen Iverson * — 68%
4. George Gervin — 63%
5. Jerry West — 61%
6. Oscar Robertson — 57%

* (through 2006)

STATISTICAL ODDS AND ENDS

- Most free throws made in a regulation NCAA or NBA game: 30 vs. Oregon State 12/22/69 (31 attempts)
- Averaged 10.76 points per game from the free-throw line at LSU. Highest career average in NCAA, NBA, and ABA history
- Most points scored by any NBA guard in the 1970s
- Most points scored by an NBA player while also fouling out: 68 vs. Knicks 2/25/77
- Most points by an NBA player on Super Bowl Sunday: 50, Hawks vs. 76ers 1/16/72
- Highest NBA and ABA career regular season 3-point goal percentage: 67% (minimum 10 attempts)
- One of two players to lead NCAA in scoring for three consecutive years (Oscar Robertson 1957-60, Maravich 1967-70)
- One of three NCAA players to score at least 900 points in each of three seasons (Oscar Robertson 1957-60, Maravich 1967-70, Larry Bird 1976-79)
- One of three players (Paul Arizin, Rick Barry) to lead both the NBA and NCAA in scoring
- One of six players to score at least 65 points in a NBA game in a winning effort (Wilt Chamberlain, Elgin Baylor, David Robinson, Michael Jordan, Kobe Bryant)
- One of seven NBA players to make more than 25 field goals in a single game (Joe Fulks, Wilt Chamberlain, David Thompson, Elgin Baylor, Rick Barry, Michael Jordan, Kobe Bryant)

Game-by-Game
Scoring at LSU

Pete Maravich's career scoring average of 44.2 points per game is considered one of sport's untouchable records. The next highest career average is nearly 10 points behind him (Austin Carr's 34.6).

The mark is even more amazing when one considers it was set before the introduction of the three-point line or the shot clock. Game charts reveal that Maravich hit nearly eight (7.8) shots per game from behind the three-point distance of 19 feet, 9 inches while at LSU.

Average Pete Maravich college game: 38.1 FG attempted, 16.7 FG made, 13.9 FT attempted, 10.8 FT made, 6.4 rebounds, 5.1 assists, 44.2 points.

- Led nation in scoring, 1968, 1969, 1970
- Unanimous selection First Team All-American, 1968, 1969, 1970
- College Player of the Year, 1970
- Naismith Award, 1970

Sophomore (1967-68) Record: 14-12; 8-10 in SEC

Date	Opponent	FG-A	FG%	FT-A	REB	AST	PTS	LSU-OPP
12/2	Tampa	20-50	.400	8-9	16	4	48	97-81
12/4	at Texas	15-34	.441	12-16	5	5	42	87-74
12/9	Loyola (New Orleans)	22-43	.512	7-11	9	4	51	90-56
12/15	at Wisconsin*	16-40	.400	10-13	9	6	42	94-96
12/16	Florida State*	17-41	.415	8-10	5	9	42	100-130
12/19	Mississippi	17-34	.500	12-13	11	3	46	81-68
12/22	Mississippi State	22-40	.550	14-16	8	3	58	111-87
12/30	Alabama	10-30	.333	10-11	6	5	30	81-70
1/3	Auburn	20-38	.526	15-17	9	1	55	76-72
1/6	at Florida	9-22	.409	14-17	10	8	32	90-97
1/8	at Georgia	14-37	.378	14-17	11	5	42	79-76
1/11	at Tulane	20-42	.476	12-15	5	8	52	100-91
1/24	Clemson	14-29	.483	5-6	6	2	33	104-81
1/27	Kentucky	19-51	.373	14-17	11	2	52	95-121
1/29	Vanderbilt	22-57	.386	10-15	6	3	54	91-99
2/3	at Kentucky	16-38	.421	12-15	8	3	44	96-109
2/7	Tennessee	9-34	.265	3-3	6	0	21	67-87
2/7	at Auburn	18-47	.383	13-13	6	1	49	69-74
2/10	Florida (OT)	17-48	.354	13-15	7	3	47	93-92

Sophomore (1967-68) Record: 14-12; 8-10 in SEC (continued)

Date	Opponent	FG-A	FG%	FT-A	REB	AST	PTS	LSU-OPP
2/12	Georgia	20-47	.426	11-18	4	2	51	73-78
2/17	at Alabama	24-52	.462	11-13	12	3	59	99-89
2/19	at Mississippi State	13-38	.342	8-12	7	7	34	94-83
2/21	Tulane	21-47	.447	13-15	5	0	55	99-92
2/24	at Mississippi	13-26	.500	14-16	4	8	40	85-87
3/2	at Tennessee	7-18	.389	3-4	3	1	17	71-74
3/4	at Vanderbilt	17-39	.436	8-11	6	9	42	86-115

*Milwaukee Classic.

Junior (1968-69) Record: 13-13; 7-11 in SEC

Date	Opponent	FG-A	FG%	FT-A	REB	AST	PTS	LSU-OPP
12/2	at Loyola (New Orleans)	22-34	.647	8-9	7	11	52	109-82
12/7	at Clemson	10-32	.313	18-22	4	4	38	86-85
12/14	Tulane (2 OT)	20-48	.417	15-20	7	2	55	99-101
12/18	Florida (OT)	17-32	.531	11-15	8	5	45	93-89
12/21	Georgia	18-33	.545	11-16	10	5	47	98-89
12/26	Wyoming**	14-34	.412	17-24	6	2	45	84-78
12/28	at Oklahoma City**	19-36	.528	2-5	8	7	40	101-85
12/30	Duquesne**	18-36	.500	17-21	2	6	53	94-91
1/4	at Alabama	19-49	.388	4-4	10	5	42	82-85
1/9	at Vanderbilt	15-30	.500	8-13	4	3	38	92-94
1/11	at Auburn	16-41	.390	14-18	5	5	46	71-90
1/25	Kentucky	20-48	.417	12-14	11	2	52	96-108
1/27	Tennessee	8-18	.444	5-8	4	2	21	68-81
1/31	Pittsburgh	13-34	.382	14-18	8	11	40	120-79
2/1	Mississippi (OT)	11-33	.333	9-13	11	5	31	81-84
2/3	Mississippi State	14-32	.438	5-6	11	10	33	95-71
2/8	Alabama	15-30	.500	8-12	5	6	38	81-75
2/10	at Tulane	25-51	.490	16-20	10	1	66	94-110
2/12	at Florida	14-41	.341	22-27	6	2	50	79-95
2/15	Auburn	20-44	.455	14-15	3	5	54	93-81
2/17	Vanderbilt	14-33	.424	7-8	8	8	35	83-85
2/22	at Kentucky	21-53	.396	3-7	5	2	45	89-103
2/24	at Tennessee	8-18	.444	4-8	3	7	20	63-87
3/1	at Mississippi	21-39	.538	7-11	3	1	49	76-78
3/3	at Mississippi State	20-49	.408	15-19	4	5	55	99-89
3/8	at Georgia (2 OT)	21-48	.438	16-25	6	4	58	90-80

**All-College Tournament at Oklahoma City

Senior (1969-70) **Record: 22-10; 13-5 in SEC**

Date	Opponent	FG-A	FG%	FT-A	REB	AST	PTS	LSU-OPP
12/4	Oregon State	14-32	.438	15-19	5	7	43	94-72
12/9	Loyola (New Orleans)	17-36	.500	9-10	6	6	43	100-87
12/11	Vanderbilt	26-54	.481	9-10	10	5	61	109-86
12/13	at Tulane	17-42	.405	12-19	4	5	46	97-91
12/18	Southern California	18-43	.419	14-16	6	4	50	98-101
12/20	at Clemson	22-30	.733	5-8	6	9	49	111-103
12/22	at Oregon State	9-23	.349	30-31	1	8	48	76-68
12/23	at UCLA	14-42	.333	10-12	4	7	38	84-133
12/29	St. John's***	20-44	.455	13-16	8	1	53	80-70
12/30	Yale***	13-28	.464	8-11	5	8	34	94-97
1/3	Alabama	22-42	.524	11-18	7	2	55	90-83
1/10	Auburn	18-46	.391	8-11	6	2	44	70-79
1/24	at Kentucky	21-44	.477	13-15	5	4	55	96-109
1/26	Tennessee	12-23	.522	5-7	4	9	29	71-59
1/31	Mississippi	21-46	.526	11-15	5	12	53	109-86
2/2	Mississippi State	21-40	.525	7-9	3	6	49	109-91
2/4	at Florida	20-38	.526	12-16	9	7	52	97-75
2/7	at Alabama	26-57	.456	17-21	5	4	69	104-106
2/9	Tulane	18-45	.400	13-15	4	6	49	127-114
2/11	Florida	16-35	.457	6-10	3	8	38	94-85
2/14	at Vanderbilt	14-46	.304	10-13	5	3	38	99-89
2/16	at Auburn	18-46	.391	10-15	8	4	46	70-64
2/18	Georgia	17-34	.500	3-6	2	6	37	88-86
2/21	Kentucky	23-42	.548	18-22	4	7	64	105-121
2/23	at Tennessee	10-24	.417	10-13	7	6	30	87-88
2/28	at Mississippi	13-43	.302	9-14	9	4	35	103-90
3/2	at Mississippi State	22-44	.500	11-13	5	8	55	97-87
3/7	at Georgia	16-37	.432	9-10	3	11	41	99-88
3/15	Georgetown (NIT)	6-16	.375	8-12	6	6	20	83-80
3/17	Oklahoma (NIT)	14-33	.424	9-13	8	9	37	97-94
3/19	Marquette (NIT)	4-13	.308	12-16	1	9	20	79-101
3/21	Army (NIT)	DNP/ankle & hip injuries						

***Rainbow Classic at Honolulu

The Pistol's
25 Greatest Games

Pete Maravich competed in 688 NBA games (including playoff and All-Star appearances) and 83 varsity NCAA games. The authors believe he was at his best as a pro, as evidenced by this Top 25 list.

1. February 25, 1977, New York at New Orleans
In front of 11,033 in the Superdome and a massive television audience in New York, Pete bedazzled the Knicks by dropping 68 points (along with 6 assists) before fouling out with 1:18 remaining. The Jazz racked up an easy victory and Pete produced one of the NBA's legendary performances.

2. March 18, 1977, New Orleans at Phoenix
Before the game, five Jazz players were injured in a car accident. With just seven players in uniform, Pete put on an LSU-style show. Playing all 48 minutes, he compiled 51 points, 4 assists, 6 rebounds, 5 steals, and 2 blocks in an improbable 104-100 victory.

3. April 8, 1973, Boston at Atlanta
Pete's career-playoff-high 37 points led all scorers in Atlanta's 97-94 win over the Boston Celtics (who held the NBA's best record). Pete also recorded 7 rebounds, 5 assists, 3 steals, and 1 turnover.

4. March 8, 1969, LSU at Georgia
In a legendary double-overtime win in a jam-packed gymnasium in Athens, Pete scored 58 points but none more dramatic than his final two. After avoiding Bulldog defenders with a Globetrotter-esque dribbling exhibition, the Pistol flipped up a 35-foot hook shot that swished through the net as time expired.

5. October 26, 1975, New York at New Orleans
The "Pistol" and the "Pearl" battle it out in the brand new Superdome. When the smoke cleared, Pete had 45, Earl 36, and the Jazz won by 11. New York hacked Pete all night (Walt Frazier, Phil Jackson, and Earl Monroe fouled out), and Pete converted 23 of 26 free throws (both career highs in the pros) along with 8 assists and 11 rebounds.

6. *February 21, 1970, Kentucky at LSU*

This Saturday afternoon, coast-to-coast telecast rocketed the floppy-socked Pete into the national consciousness. His entire arsenal was on display in this shootout: the no-look passes, behind-the-back dribbling, and wild shooting. In his final home game at LSU the Pistol shot 55 percent and piled up 64 points. But Dan Issel pumped in 51 in a 121-105 Kentucky win.

7. *January 23, 1972, Atlanta at Milwaukee*

Eighteen pounds underweight and recovering from mononucleosis, Pete and the Hawks met the defending NBA champion Bucks, led by league MVP Kareem Abdul-Jabbar. Pete dropped 35 points and 14 assists on Oscar Robertson and led the Hawks to a thrilling 118-113 victory.

8. *December 30, 1968, Duquesne vs. LSU*

The final game of the Oklahoma All-College Tournament showcased an undefeated Duquesne (then ranked 15th in the nation) against high-scoring LSU. Despite an ice-storm that blanketed Oklahoma City, a record 8,336 fans jammed the State Fair Arena, lured by the magical Maravich. Pete delivered, bucketing 53 points as LSU came from behind to win, 94-91.

9. *January 17, 1975, Seattle at New Orleans*

Before the Superdome was completed, the Jazz played home games in a few locations but none more bizarre than the Loyola Field House. Because of its dangerous elevated floor, the league was required (by the player's union) to hang safety nets that ran the length of the court to keep players from falling into the crowd. Playing in this "cage" atmosphere inspired Pete, who netted one of pro basketball's greatest triple-doubles: 42 points, 17 assists, 10 rebounds (and 4 steals). The Jazz won this thriller, 113-109.

10. *December 22, 1969, LSU at Oregon State*

A wild night in Corvallis as Oregon State fans packed Gill Coliseum and witnessed a flurry of technical fouls (three on Pete alone) and more than a few fights. The Beavers decided to foul Pete hard each time he attempted a shot. The strategy backfired. Pete attempted 31 free throws and made 30 of them—an NCAA record that stands to this day. In fact no player in the NBA has ever made 30 free throws in a regulation game. Pete finished with 46 points in LSU's 76-68 road victory.

11. *December 17, 1977, New Orleans at Cleveland*

Pete faced Walt Frazier for the final time in their careers on a Saturday afternoon

CBS broadcast. It was the biggest road crowd of the year as 19,548 fans filled every seat in the Richfield Coliseum. The Pistol didn't disappoint as he dropped in 42 (18 in the fourth quarter). Pete's last shot was a dunk. Frazier had his Cavalier game high with 29 as the Jazz won 113-102. Walt and Pete met up 10 years later when they entered the Basketball Hall of Fame together.

12. April 11, 1977, Denver at New Orleans
The final game of the 1976-77 regular season. Pete scored 45 points, his teammate Nate Williams got 41, and the Nugget's David Thompson hit for 40. That was the first, and only, time that three players scored 40 or more points in a non-overtime NBA game. Pete also gathered 11 rebounds and 10 assists to lead the Jazz to a 139-125 win. Pete's triple-double capped his scoring title season (31.1 ppg).

13. August 3, 1965, N.C. East-West High School All-Star Game
Pete finished his All-American high school career with a record-setting performance. In front of the largest crowd ever at Greensboro Coliseum, Pete started out ice cold. He missed his first nine shots and the fans began to voice their displeasure. Unrattled, Pete kept shooting and hit 17 of his next 25 attempts (plus 8 for 8 from the line). By the time the final buzzer sounded, the skinny senior totaled 42 points—a North Carolina All-Star record that stands to this day. With 50 seconds remaining, coach Leon Brock pulled Pete and the hot-shot ended his high school career with an easy win . . . and a standing ovation.

14. March 18, 1980, Indiana at Boston (Hartford)
Pete realized a dream when, at age 32, he became a starting guard for the famed Boston Celtics, replacing Chris Ford (who was attending his mother's funeral). Early in the game Boston's Larry Bird and Dave Cowens went to the bench with foul trouble but Pete ran the show masterfully. He played 43 minutes and scored 31 points (12-18, 7-7) in the 114-102 victory over the Pacers.

15. January 31, 1970, Mississippi at LSU
Entering the contest Pete needed 40 points to pass Oscar Robertson's NCAA career scoring record. With 7:58 remaining, Pete banked in a 25-footer, giving him 39 points. The overflow crowd began booming in unison "one, one, one, one . . ." As the news cameras turned and the photographers' flash bulbs popped on his every field-goal attempt, Pete missed five consecutive shots. Finally, with 4:43 on the clock, he swished in a 17-foot jump shot. Maravich finished with 53 points and 12 assists in a 109-86 LSU victory. He has been college basketball's

most prolific scorer since that night. In 2003, the inscribed basketball from the game was sold at auction for $42,093.

16. February 10, 1976, New Orleans at Golden State
Playing in the hostile confines of the Oakland-Alameda Coliseum, it was near impossible to beat the defending world champion Golden State Warriors. But Pete's 49 points, 4 assists, and 3 steals helped propel the Jazz to a stunning overtime upset, 130-124.

17. February 5, 1972, Cleveland at Atlanta
The Hawks were down by six points with 3:30 to play in the game when Pete went on a tear. He poured in the Hawks' final 13 points on three jumpers (from 15, 14, and 20 feet), a layup, and five free throws, and Atlanta overtook Cleveland to win a barn burner, 120-117. For the game, the Pistol put up 27 shots and made 20 en route to another 50-point night.

18. February 8, 1975, New Orleans at Atlanta
The first road victory for the Jazz organization came at the expense of the Atlanta Hawks, the team that traded Pete. In front of the largest gate of the season at the Omni (13,653), the Pistol dropped in 18 of 37 shots and 11 of 12 free throws—netting 47 points along with 8 rebounds and 5 assists. It was sweet revenge as the Jazz nipped the Hawks, 106-102.

19. November 28, 1973, Buffalo at Atlanta
Pete gave Rookie-of-the-Year candidate Ernie DiGregorio a lesson in Showtime. Although the Pistol didn't even enter the game until the second quarter, he shot 12 for 17 from the field and 18 for 18 from the line. Braves announcer Van Miller exclaimed "Someone's gotta lay that Pistol down!" during the local (channel 4) TV broadcast. In just three quarters Pete totaled 42 points and brought the crowd to its feet with behind-the-back dribbles, no-look passes, and, late in the game, a pin-point bounce pass between Ernie D's legs. The Hawks cruised over the Braves 130-106.

20. November 2, 1973, Atlanta at Houston
The Hawks were trailing the home-town Rockets with three minutes remaining when Pete took over and hit seven consecutive baskets (from 29, 21, 23, 20, and 17 feet, plus two layups) and added a free throw. Fifteen points in 2:15. The Hawks stunned the Rockets 125-123.

21. December 29, 1969, LSU vs. St. John's (Hawaii Classic)
Facing top-20-ranked St. John's University in a Christmas tournament, Pete helped cement his legend with a spectacular finish. After intermission Pete outscored the entire Redmen team with 40 second-half points (total of 53) as he steered the Tigers to an 80-70 victory. Pete's final exclamation point was a half-court pass off the backboard for an assist. "He almost hypnotizes you on the court. Here I am trying to coach my club, watching the action all over the court. And what am I doing? Watching him," gushed St. John's coach Lou Carnesecca afterward. "It was the most electrifying 15 minutes of basketball I've ever seen."

22. January 16, 1973, Detroit at Atlanta
Pete was cold this evening, missing his first six shots, so he reverted to running the team. He dished out a career-high 18 assists and then made the final two free throws to ice a 130-129 overtime victory against the Pistons.

23. January 16, 1972, Philadelphia at Atlanta
Super Bowl Shootout. A scrawny, under-weight Pete dueled Billy Cunningham and when the smoke cleared, the Kangaroo Kid had 45 and the Pistol had a then-career-high 50. The Hawks beat the 76ers 124-116.

24. November 10, 1978, San Antonio at New Orleans
Wearing a two-pound Lenox Hill knee brace, Pete recorded his final 40+ game. Battling the man who would lead the league in scoring, the Spurs' George Gervin (who finished with 33), Pete bucketed 27 second-half points for a total of 41 in a 113-102 comeback victory for the Jazz.

25. November 2, 1976, Boston at New Orleans
Facing the undefeated, defending NBA champion Celtics, Pete put on a clinic and scored 43 points, 10 rebounds, and 5 assists in a 115-97 comeback victory. Late in the game Pete fired a three-quarter-court, behind-the-back pass to rookie Paul Griffin who slammed it home, sending 17,104 Superdome fans into a frenzy.

Selected References

BOOKS

Armstrong, Robert. *Pete Maravich*. Creative Education, Inc., 1978.

Arneson, D.J. *Basketball's Awesome Guards*. Western Publishing, Inc., 1991.

Axthelm, Pete. *The City Game*. Harper's Magazine Press, 1970.

Benagh, Jim. *Incredible Basketball Feats*. Grosset & Dunlap, Inc., 1974.

Benson, Marty (editor). *Official NCAA Men's Basketball Records*. Triumph Books, 2003.

Beers, Paul. *Profiles in Pennsylvania Sports*. Stackpole Books, 1975.

Berger, Phil. *Forever Showtime: The Checkered Life of Pistol Pete Maravich*. Taylor Publishing, 1999.

Bird, Larry with Bischoff, John. *Bird on Basketball*. Addison-Wesley, 1983

Bjarkman, Peter C. *The Biographical History of Basketball*. Masters Press, 2000.

Bjarkman, Peter C. *The Encyclopedia of Pro Basketball Team Histories*. Carroll & Graf Publishers, Inc., 1994.

Bradley, Robert. *Compendium of Professional Basketball*. Xaler Press, 1999.

Branon, Dave. *Slam Dunk*. Moody Press, 1994.

Brown, Dale. *Tiger in a Lion's Den*. Hyperion, 1994.

Bukata, Jim. *One on One: The Great Matchups, Highlighting over Fifty Great NBA and ABA Cage Stars*. Stadia Sports Publishing, 1973.

Mike Carey and Jamie Most. *High Above Courtside: The Lost Memoirs of Johnny Most*. Sports Publishing L.L.C., 2003.

Chamberlain, Wilt. *A View from Above*. Villard Books, 1991.

Clary, Jack. *Basketball's Great Dynasties: The Celtics*. Smithmark, 1992.

Clary, Jack. *Basketball's Great Moments*. McGraw-Hill Book Company, 1988.

Cole, Lewis. *A Loose Game: The Sport and Business of Basketball*. The Bobbs-Merrill Company, 1978.

Conner, Floyd. *Basketball's Most Wanted*. Brassey's, Inc., 2001.

DeCourcy, Mike. *Sporting News Selects the Legends of College Basketball*. Sporting News, 2003.

Denberg, Lazenby, & Stinson. *From Sweet Lou to 'Nique*. Longstreet Press, 1992.

Devaney, John. *The Story of Basketball*. G.P. Putnam's Sons, 1965.

Dobson, James. *Life on the Edge*. Word Publishing, 1995.

Douchant, Mike. *Inside Sports Magazine College Basketball*. Visable Ink, 1995.

Dolin, Nick, Chris Dolin and David Check. *Basketball Stars*. Black Dog & Leventhal Publishers Inc., 1997.

Dylan, Bob. *Chronicles. Vol. 1*. Simon and Schuster, 2004.

Feinstein, John. *The Punch*. Back Bay Books, 2002.

Finney, Peter. *Pistol Pete: The Story of College Basketball's Greatest Star*. The Levee Press, 1969.

Firestone, Roy. *Up Close*. Hyperion, 1993.

Garber, Gene. *Basketball Legends*. Friedman & Fairfax Publishers, 1993.

Garfunkel, Bernard. *Champions*. Platt & Munk, 1973.

George, Nelson. *Elevating the Game*. Harper Collins, 1992.

Goldaper, Sam. *Great Moments in Pro Basketball*. Grosset & Dunlap, 1977.

Gutman, Bill. *Pistol Pete Maravich: The Making of a Basketball Superstar*. Grosset & Dunlap, 1972.

Halberstam, David. *The Breaks of the Game*. Alfred A. Knopf, 1981.

Hareen, Dave. *The Basketball Abstract*. Prentice-Hall, 1988.

Harris, Merv. *On Court with the Superstars of the NBA*. The Viking Press, 1973.

Haywood, Spencer. *The Rise, The Fall, The Recovery*. Amistad, 1992.

Hobson, Howard. *Scientific Basketball*. Prentice-Hall, 1949.

Hoffman, Ann Byrne and George Kalinsky. *Echoes from the Schoolyard*. Hawthorn Books, Inc., 1977.

Hollander, Zander. *The Pro Basketball Encyclopedia*. Corwin Books, 1977.

Hubbard, Jan. *The Official NBA Encyclopedia*. Doubleday, 2003.

Hundley, Rod and Tom McEachin. *Hot Rod Hundley: You Gotta Love It, Baby*. Sports Publishing, L.L.C., 1998.

James, Joe. *Basketball, the American Game*. Follet Publishing Company, 1971.

Kalb, Elliot. *Who's Better, Who's Best in Basketball?* McGraw-Hill, 2003

Katz, Fred. *Sports Heroes of Today 1970*. Random House, 1970.

Kirkpatrick, Mac C. and Thomas K. Perry. *The Southern Textile Basketball Tournament: A History, 1921-1997*. McFarland & Company, Inc. Publishers, 1997.

Klein, David. *Rookie: The World of the NBA*. Tempo Books, 1970.

Koppett, Leonard. *24 Seconds to Shoot*. The Macmillan Company, 1968.

Lewis, Michael C. *To the Brink*. Simon & Schuester, 1998.

Liss, Howard. *Basketball Talk*. Pocket Book, 1970.

Maravich, Pete. *Keds, Pass, Shoot & Rebound, a Benco Booklet*, 1972.

Maravich, Pete with Darrel Campbell. *Heir to a Dream*. Thomas Nelson, 1987.

Meschery, Tom. *Caught in the Pivot.* Dell Publishing, 1973.

Menzer, Joe. *Four Corners.* Simon & Schuster, 1999.

McCallum, Jack. *Unfinished Business—On and Off the Court with the 1990-91 Boston Celtics.* Summit Books, 1992.

McCreary, Jay. *Winning High School Basketball,* Prentice-Hall, 1956.

Musemeche, John and Ellis, Steve. *MARAVICH.* Franklin Press, 1969.

NBA Register 1996, 2004. Sporting News.

NBA Guides 1968, 1969, 1977, 1979, 1986, 2004. Sporting News.

New York Times Scrapbook History. *The Complete Book of Basketball.* Arno Press, 1979.

Patterson, Wayne, and Lisa Fisher. *100 Greatest Basketball Players.* Crescent Books, 1989.

Pluto, Terry. *Loose Balls.* Simon & Schuster, 1990.

Rappoport, Ken. *The Classic—History of the NCAA Basketball Championship.* The Lowell Press, 1979.

Robertson, Oscar. *The Big O: My Life, My Times, My Game.* Rodale, 2003.

Rosen, Charles. *God, Man and Basketball Jones.* Holt, Rinehart and Winston, 1979.

Ryan, Bob. *The Pro Game.* McGraw-Hill Book Company, 1975.

Sabin, Lou. *Basketball Stars of 1972.* Pyramid Books, 1972.

Sabin, Lou. *Pete Maravich Basketball Magician.* Scholastic Books, 1973.

Sabin, Lou. *Hot Shots of Pro Basketball.* Random House, 1974.

Sachare, Alex. *100 Greatest Basketball Players of All Time.* Pocket Books, 1997.

Saladino, Tom. *Pistol Pete Maravich: The Louisiana Purchase.* The Strode Publishers, 1974.

Schouler, Ryan, Smith, Koppett, Bellotti. *Total Basketball.* SPORTClassic Books, 2003.

Schuyler, Pamela. *Through the Hoop: A Season with the Celtics.* Houghton Mifflin Company, 1974.

Towle, Mike. *I Remember Pete Maravich.* Cumberland House Publishing, 2000.

Thompson, David, Sean Stormes and Marshall Terrill. *Skywalker.* Sports Publishing L.L.C., 2003.

Vancil, Mark. *NBA at Fifty.* Park Lane Press, 1996.

West, Jerry with Libby, Bill. *Mr. Clutch: The Jerry West Story.* Grosset & Dunlap, 1969.

Wolff, Alexander. *Big Game Small World.* Warner Books, 2002.

MAGAZINES

1968-1969 All Americans; 1978 Pro Basketball Guidebook (Action) 1970-71, 1971-72; *Annual Basketball; Athlon Sports Pro Basketball Annual, 1988; Basketball All-Pro Annual* 1971; *Basketball's Best* 1971-72; *Basketball Annual* 1968-69, 1971-72; *Basketball Digest* 1/76, 4/76/, 1/77, 6/77, 2/79,1/80, 4/86; *Basketball News Yearbook* 1974, 1978; *Basketball (Pro) Special,* 1970; *Basketball Sports Stars* 1969, 1971, 1973; *Basketball Weekly; Boys Life* 2/1990; *Christianity Today, Coaches Digest* 1971; *College, High School, Basketball Extra* 1969-70; *College Hoops Illustrated* 1994; *College Pro High School Basketball Yearbook* 1969; *Coronet* 3/1971; *Countrywide Sport* 12/ 1970; *Decision* 1/1989. *Entrée,* 10/1972, *Family Weekly* 2/1969, *Game Plan, Pro Basketball* 1977-1978 (Annual Preview); *Hoop Magazine* 1986, 1988; *Inside Basketball 1970; Inside Sports* 1/ 30/1980; *Life* 2/7/1969; *Look 1/27/1969; Nation-Wide Basketball* 10/1968; *New Orleans Magazine* 11/2004; *Newsweek* 1/22/ 1973, 1988; *Police Gazette.* 12/1970; *Popular Sports All-Pro Basketball,* 1973, 1975; *Pro Basketball,* 1971, 1973, 1998; *Pro Basketball Almanac,* 1971; *Pro Basketball Guide, 1974; Pro Basketball Illustrated* 1972, 1977, 1979; *Pro Basketball Special* 1970-1971, 1971-1972; *Pro Basketball Sports Stars* 1974, 1975; *Pro Basketball Sports All Stars,* Winter 1971; *Pro Basketball Today,* 1977; *Pro Basketball Yearbook,* 1977; *Pro Sports* 1971, 1973; *The Salvation Army War Cry* 2/13/1988; *Serb World* 5/1997; *Slam* 5/1995, 9/1997; *Slam Classic,* 2003; *Sport* (1969-1996); *Sport Folio Southwest* 1968; *The Sporting News* (1968-1987); *Sports All Stars* 1971; *Sports Scene* 1970, 3/1972; *Sports Scene Basketball* 1971. *Sports Illustrated* (1962-1988); *Sports Quarterly Basketball Special* 1970-1971; *Sports Stars of 1972; Sports Today* 2/ 1973, 2/1974; *Street And Smith's College & Pro Basketball* Yearbook 1973, 1974, 1975, 1976, 1977, 1978, 1980; *Street And Smith's Greatest College Basketball Players* 2004; *Super Sports* 4/1971, 12/1972, 4/1979; *Time* 1/19/1968, 2/16/1970; 4/21/1980, 1/18/1988; *Trailer Boats* 2/1981; *T.V. Guide* 10/10/1970; *Vegetarian Times,* 1/1984.

NEWSPAPERS

Alexandria Town Talk; Aliquippa South News; Arizona Republic; Associated Press; Atlanta Journal and Constitution; Baton Rouge Morning Advocate; Baton Rouge States-Times; Beaver Valley Times; Binghamton Press & Sun-Bulletin, Birmingham News; Boston Globe; Boston Herald American; Charlotte Observer; Charlotte News; Chicago Tribune, Chicago Sun-Times, Colorado Springs Gazette Telegraph; Daily Reflector; Dallas Morning News; Denver Post; Detroit Free Press; Fayetteville Observer-Times; Gazette Telegraph; Greenville News; Greensboro Record; Greensboro Daily News; Honolulu Star Bulletin; Houston Post; The Independent (Anderson, S.C.); *Indianapolis Star; Jackson Daily News; Jackson Sun; Kentucky Courier-Journal; Knoxville News-Sentinel; Las Vegas Review-Journal; Lexington Herald-Leader; Long Beach Press-Telegram; Los Angeles Daily News; Los Angeles Times; The Messenger; Miami-Herald; Milwaukee Journal Sentinel; The Morning Union,* (Springfield, Mass); *New York Daily News; New York Post; New York Times; The News and Observer,* (Raleigh, N.C.); *Newsday; The Oklahoman; Pasadena Star-News; Philadelphia Daily News; Pittsburgh Post Gazette; Plain Dealer* (Cleveland); *Raleigh Times; Rochester Times-Union; San Diego Union-Tribune; San Francisco Chronicle; Sampson Independent, Shreveport Journal; Shreveport Times; Springfield Republican; Springfield Union; The States-Item* (New Orleans); *Sunday Herald Traveler; The Tampa Tribune; The Tiger Rag; Tulsa World; The Times-Picayune; The Tuscaloosa News; United Press International; USA Today; The Washington Post.*

MEDIA GUIDES

Louisiana State University 1967, 1968, 1969, 1970, NIT (1970), 2001, 2004; *Atlanta Hawks* 1970, 1971, 1972, 1973, 1974, 1975; *New Orleans Jazz* 1975, 1976, 1977, 1978, 1979; *Utah Jazz* 1980, 2004; *Boston Celtics* 1980; *Philadelphia 76ers* 2004; *Sacramento Kings,* 2004; *San Antonio Spurs,* 2004.

AUDIO

Games: 1968 LSU vs Auburn; 1969 LSU at Kentucky; 1970 LSU vs Georgia; 1972 Hawks at Knicks; 1974 Jazz at Knicks; 1975 Jazz at Hawks; 1975 Jazz at Bulls; 1977 Jazz at Cavs; 1977 Jazz vs San Antonio
Maravich half-time interview w/ Skip Caray January 1973
Maravich interview, *John Moynahan Radio Show,* 1985
Testimony, Southwestern University, 1985
Testimony, Phoenix, Arizona, October 9, 1985
Maravich interview, *Larry King Mutual Radio,* February 27, 1986
Testimony, Peoria, Illinois Prayer Breakfast, 1987
Church Covington, Louisiana, January 1988
Focus on the Family, 1989.

VIDEO

Games: 1967 LSU at Tennessee; 1968 LSU at Georgia; 1969 LSU vs Tennessee; 1969 LSU at UCLA; 1970 LSU vs Georgia; 1970 LSU at Kentucky; 1970 LSU at Ole Miss; 1970 Hawks at Suns; 1973 NBA All Star Game; 1977 Jazz vs Knicks; 1977 NBA All-Star Game; 1978 HORSE; 1978 Jazz vs Pistons; 1978 Jazz at Lakers; 1978 Jazz at Celtics; 1979 NBA All-Star

Game; 1980 Celtics vs. Hawks; 1980 Celtics at 76ers; 1980 Celtics at Rockets Game 4; 1980 Celtics vs. 76ers Game 1; 1980 Celtics vs. 76ers Game 2; 1980 Celtics vs. 76ers Game 3; 1980 Celtics vs. 76ers Game 4; 1980 Celtics vs. 76ers Game 5; NBA Legends (1984, 1985, 1986, 1987)
Other: Vitalis Dry Control TV Commercial, 1971
Individual Offensive Techniques, Instructional film (Pro-Keds) with Lou Hudson and Ed McCauley, 1972
The Dick Cavett Show, PBS, 1978
Lakers at Warriors (commentary) 1977
Superstars, ABC, 1978
The Cat from Outer Space, 1978
Dribble, 1979
Outdoor Life, 1980
Red on Roundball, 1983 (VHS)
ESPN *Now and Then* with Dr. J, 1984
Utah Jazz #7 Retirement Ceremony, 1985 TBS
Great Moments in College Basketball, 1985
Jimmy Walker Benefit, Phoenix, Testimony October 1985
Duke University, Testimony, 1986
Kentucky at Georgia (commentary) with Bob Costas, 1986
Kentucky at Mississippi USA (commentary) with Bob Carpenter, 1987
NBA Entertainment Interview (with Todd Caso), 1987
Billy Graham Crusade, Columbia, South Carolina, 1987
Basketball Hall of Fame Enshrinement, May 1987
The 700 Club with Ben Kinchlow, 1987
Homework Basketball (Vol. 1 thru 4), 1987
The Today Show, 1987
ESPN's *Mazda's Sports Look* with Roy Firestone 1987
Obituaries (NBC, ABC, CBS, CNN, ESPN, various local) 1988
"A Shooting Star" 1988 local New Orleans television
NBA Showmen, 1989
Maravich Memories: The LSU Years, 1990
Pistol: Birth of a Legend, 1990 (DVD 2005)
Inside the NBA 1991—Court Vision segment
NBA At 50, 1996
NBA's 100 Greatest Plays, 1998
Inside the NBA, 1998—Career Retrospect
NBA Showmen, 2000
Vintage NBA, 2000

ESPN *Classic Sports Century: Top 50 and Beyond*, March 2001
CBS *Pistol Pete: The Life and Times of Pete Maravich*, April 2001
ESPN SportsCenter— "Sons of a Gun," March 7, 2003
Ankle Breakers Vol. 1, 2004
ESPN Classic *Who's Number One? Greatest Performances*, 2004
Fox Sports List – Top College Players, 2004
S.I./Spike TV *Top College Basketball Players*, 2004
ESPN-U *10 Greatest College Basketball Players*, 2005

Index

About the Authors

WAYNE FEDERMAN is an actor, writer, and stand-up comedian. Federman has contributed to the official Ronald Reagan biography, *Dutch,* and to articles published in *Sports Illustrated* and the *Wall Street Journal*. He has provided commentary on NPR and also served as a senior consultant on CBS's award winning documentary "Pistol Pete: The Life and Times of Pete Maravich." Federman resides in West Hollywood, California.

MARSHALL TERRILL is the author of a dozen books, including best-selling biographies of Steve McQueen and Elvis Presley. He recently finished *Palm Springs a la Carte* with businessman Mel Haber, which will be published in 2008. Terrill is also a reporter for the *Ocotillo Tribune* in Chandler, Arizona, where he resides with his wife, Zoe.

FOCUS ON THE FAMILY®

Welcome to the family!

Whether you purchased this book, borrowed it, or received it as a gift, we're glad you're reading it. It's just one of the many helpful, encouraging, and biblically based resources produced by Focus on the Family for people in all stages of life.

Focus began in 1977 with the vision of one man, Dr. James Dobson, a licensed psychologist and author of numerous best-selling books on marriage, parenting, and family. Alarmed by the societal, political, and economic pressures that were threatening the existence of the American family, Dr. Dobson founded Focus on the Family with one employee and a once-a-week radio broadcast aired on 36 stations.

Now an international organization reaching millions of people daily, Focus on the Family is dedicated to preserving values and strengthening and encouraging families through the life-changing message of Jesus Christ.

Focus on the Family Magazines

These faith-building, character-developing publications address the interests, issues, concerns, and challenges faced by every member of your family from preschool through the senior years.

| Focus on the Family **Citizen®** U.S. news issues | Focus on the Family **Clubhouse Jr.™** Ages 4 to 8 | Focus on the Family **Clubhouse™** Ages 8 to 12 | **Breakaway®** Teen guys | **Brio®** Teen girls 12 to 16 | **Brio & Beyond®** Teen girls 16 to 19 | **Plugged In®** Reviews movies, music, TV |

FOR MORE INFORMATION

 Online:
Log on to www.family.org
In Canada, log on to www.focusonthefamily.ca

 Phone:
Call toll free: (800) A-FAMILY (232-6459)
In Canada, call toll free: (800) 661-9800

More Great Resources
from Focus on the Family®

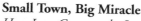

Small Town, Big Miracle
How Love Came to the Least of These
by Bishop W.C. Martin with John Fornof
Possum Trot, an East Texas town so small it's not on most maps, hardly sets the stage for big miracles. But when a local pastor and his wife adopt two children, something amazing happens . . . their church follows in their footsteps! Who would have thought that God would inspire this small-town church community to take in 72 of the foster system's most troubled kids? You'll be moved and inspired by this heartwarming tale of modern-day miracles.

Castaway Kid
One Man's Search for Hope and Home
by R.B. Mitchell
Castaway Kid is the real-life story of a child abandoned in an orphanage, one of the last in America. As a young man, he was on an emotional roller coaster of bitterness . . . until finding his home and hope in knowing God.

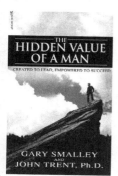

The Hidden Value of a Man
Created to Lead, Empowered to Succeed
by Gary Smalley and John Trent, Ph.D.
Often men are ridiculed for being men. The media portray them as sitcom buffoons, money-hungry corporate raiders, or angry criminals. The truth is that a man has great value and incredible influence on his family—and his world. In *The Hidden Value of a Man*, Gary Smalley and John Trent show men how to use their God-given power to build strength, love, and unity in their families and the world.

FOR MORE INFORMATION

Online:
Log on to www.family.org
In Canada, log on to www.focusonthefamily.ca.

Phone:
Call toll free: (800) A-FAMILY
In Canada, call toll free: (800) 661-9800.

BP06XP1